# WESTERN SOCIETIES

## A DOCUMENTARY HISTORY

### VOLUME II

# WESTERN SOCIETIES

## A DOCUMENTARY HISTORY

### VOLUME II

---

**BRIAN TIERNEY**

*Cornell University*

**JOAN SCOTT**

*Brown University*

ALFRED A. KNOPF  NEW YORK

THIS IS A BORZOI BOOK

PUBLISHED BY ALFRED A. KNOPF, INC.

---

First Edition
98765
Copyright © 1984 by Alfred A. Knopf, Inc.

**Library of Congress Cataloging in Publication Data**
Main entry under title:

Western societies, a documentary history.

    1. Civilization, Occidental—Sources.  2. Europe—
Civilization—Sources.  I. Tierney, Brian.  II. Scott,
Joan.
CB245.W4847  1984        909′.09821        83–19929
ISBN 0–394–32691–1 (v. 1)
ISBN 0–394–32692–X (v. 2)

Manufactured in the United States of America

# PREFACE

HISTORIANS are always asking new questions of the past; that is why we need new collections of sources from time to time. This one includes readings drawn from many different types of material—poems, plays, chronicles, government records, letters, diaries, treatises of various kinds. In studying these sources we can enter into the life of past generations on their own terms, so to speak. Such study enhances our own personalities by making us more aware of the whole range of human thought and feeling. Historical study can also help us to understand our present-day society better by learning how its various characteristics—ideas and institutions, achievements and dilemmas—grew out of the life of the past.

Some of the new questions that historians ask arise out of contemporary concerns. Many students nowadays want to know more about women's roles and patterns of family structure in earlier times. Modern interest in ecological problems has led us to ask how people in other ages viewed their relationship to the natural environment. Concern over a possible future era of "diminishing expectations" may stimulate questions about earlier theories of human progress (or regression or cyclical recurrence). Experience of social change in the modern world encourages new forms of writing on social history and especially on the sources of social conflict. The difficulties that many "less developed countries" encounter in seeking to "modernize" their economies redirect our attention to the processes of industrialization, urbanization, and demographic expansion that first created a modern society in the Western world. In making the present collection we have tried to bear in mind all these interests of recent historians.

The most evident change in the teaching of history at American colleges during the past decade has been the great growth of courses in the history of women and the family. This is proving to be more than a mere passing fashion (if it ever seemed to be that). Scholars in the field have explored new ranges of source material and raised significant new problems for research. It seems important that such work should not remain isolated in courses on Women's History but should be drawn into the mainstream of teaching on the evolution of Western society. One purpose of the present book is to make this task easier. Many readings dealing with women's roles and family relationships are included, and every chapter contains material by or about women.

A major problem for makers of anthologies is that new interests do not supplant old ones, but rather supplement them. Historians deal with the whole life of people in society. And to understand the life of any people adequately we need to ask about their religion, their economy, their forms of government, their whole world picture. These are subjects of traditional historical disciplines—"history of religions," "economic history," "political history," "history of ideas." Most teachers of Western Civilization courses will not want to neglect such topics. We have aimed therefore to provide a framework of readings illustrating the traditional themes of Western history, but also to include within the framework many readings related to the newer interests of historians.

The authors wish to thank Saphira Baker for research assistance and Ellen Furlough for her contribution to the organization of materials in Volume II.

# CONTENTS

## XV POSTWAR POLITICS—COLD WAR AND THIRD WORLD    518

# WESTERN SOCIETIES

## A DOCUMENTARY HISTORY

### VOLUME II

# I

# THE SEARCH FOR ORDER—ABSOLUTISM AND ARISTOCRACY

*THE SEVENTEENTH CENTURY was a time of great intellectual vitality but also of much political instability. Historians often refer to the age as one of "general crisis." Frequent wars caused widespread devastation. A perceptible worsening of climatic conditions, marked by colder and wetter summers, led to a series of bad harvests and recurring famines. The economic expansion of the sixteenth century came to a halt. In many countries peasant uprisings or aristocratic rebellions occurred.*

*In these circumstances there was a widely felt need for stability and order. One consequence was that theories of royal absolutism became popular among political thinkers. They ranged from the severely rationalist arguments of Thomas Hobbes to various religious doctrines of divine right and patriarchal authority. (Modern political philosophers are usually most impressed by the rationalist arguments, but seventeenth-century people usually found the religious ones more simple and satisfying.)*

*During the reign of Louis XIV (1643–1715), France became the model of a centralized, absolute monarchy. Royal authority was supported by a large army, a loyal church, and a network of local government officials who were closely supervised by the central government. Louis coped with the problem of an unruly aristocracy by inducing many French nobles to take up residence in the great palace he built at Versailles and to pass their days in the intricate ritual of court life that grew up there. The king's great finance minister, Jean Colbert—following the common "mercantilist" doctrine of the seventeenth century—aimed to enhance France's wealth and power by increasing the country's manufactures and reducing dependence on imports from abroad. For a time it seemed that France might dominate all western Europe.*

*Meanwhile, in eastern Europe, two other absolutist states experienced changing fortunes. The Turks, who throughout the seventeenth century had threatened to invade the Christian lands of the west, were finally defeated at Vienna in 1683. And Russia took the first major steps toward westernization under Peter the Great. These events helped to shape the course of European history in the modern world.*

# SOCIAL CONDITIONS

## Germany

*Jacob von Grimmelshausen, who served as a soldier in the Thirty Years' War, wrote a picaresque novel about the adventures of a "Simpleton" in those grim times.*

## From Jacob von Grimmelshausen, *Simplicissimus (1669)*

### The Fate of a Farm

When these horsemen took over my father's smoky house, the first thing they did was to bring in their horses; then each one started to destroy everything and tear everything to pieces. Some were killing the cattle, and broiling or roasting the carcasses; others were going through the house, determined not to miss any thing good there might be for them to find; even the privy was not safe from their investigations, as if we had hidden there Jason's Golden Fleece. Others were making great bundles of linen and clothes and all sorts of stuff, as if they were going to open a flea market someplace, and what they weren't going to carry away with them they pulled to pieces. Some shoved their swords through the piles of straw or hay as if they hadn't had enough pigs to kill; others shook the feathers out of the mattresses and filled them with bacon and salt meat and other things as if they expected to sleep on them better that way. Others were breaking down the stoves and the window panes, as if they thought that summer was going to last forever. They were smashing the tableware and carrying away with them these useless pieces of copper or pottery or pewter. They burnt beds, and the tables, and the chairs, and the benches, when they could have found plenty of dry fire-wood in the yard. Of pots and of pans they shattered the lot; either because they didn't want to eat anything but roast meat any more, or because they only planned to stay with us for one single meal. Our maid underwent such treatment

From Jacob von Grimmelshausen, *Simplicissimus* (1669), in Eugen Weber, *The Western Tradition*, 2nd ed., Vol. II, pp. 392–393, trans. Eugen Weber. Copyright © 1965 by D. C. Heath and Company. Reprinted by permission of the publisher.

in the stables that she could hardly walk coming out. Is it not shameful to have such things happening? As for the groom, they laid him on the ground, they put a funnel into his mouth, and they poured in a whole tubful of foul matter. They called this "a little drink in the Swedish manner"; but he didn't find it at all to his taste. They also forced him to guide them on another raid, where they captured both people and cattle whom they brought into our yard. Among them they got my father, and my mother, and my sister Ursula.

Then they started to take the flints out of the cocks of the pistols in order to use them as thumbscrews, and to torture the poor beggars as if they were sorcerers who needed to be punished before being burnt. As a matter of fact, the soldiers had already shoved one of the captured peasants into the oven and they were trying to keep him warm in there (so he would tell them the hiding place of his little hoard). They had tied a cord around the head of another, and they were tightening the cord with a garrot, so that with every turn they gave it, the blood gushed out of his mouth, his nose and his ears. In short, each man was busy working out some new kind of torture for the peasants and so each victim had his own particular kind of torment.

However it seemed to me at the time that my father was the luckiest of them all, because he admitted with roars of laughter what the others were forced to reveal in the midst of sufferings and fearful plaints.

This kind of honor was his, no doubt, because he was the head of the family. The soldiers put him before a great fire, they tied him so that he couldn't move his arms or his legs, and they rubbed the soles of his feet with damp salt; then they had our old goat lick it off. He was so tickled by this that he nearly died of laughter. It all seemed to me so pleasant and so silly—I had never seen nor heard my father laugh so long—that, either because his laughter was contagious, or else because I couldn't understand what was going on, I had to laugh too. That is how my father told the raiders what they wanted to know, and revealed the hiding place of his treasure which consisted of gold and pearls and jewels; a much richer hoard than one would have expected a peasant to own.

I cannot say anything about the treatment of the women, the maids, and the young girls who had been captured, because the soldiers didn't let me see what they were doing to them. I know only that one heard sighs and groans in various corners, and I thought that my mother and my sister Ursula were probably no better off than the others.

# Spain

*This letter written by an anonymous official in mid-seventeenth century survives in the Spanish Archivo Histórico Nacional.*

## From Letter to the Queen of Spain

Señora, every day the occupation of my office brings me to many places in which I see and recognize necessities and miseries that until these times were never seen or heard of; towns that only a few years ago had one thousand *vecinos* [heads of families] do not have five hundred today, and in those that had five hundred there are scarcely signs of one hundred. In all these places there are innumerable persons and families that pass one or two days without eating, and others who merely eat herbs that they have gathered in the countryside as well as other types of sustenance never heard of or used before; and this, Señora, is not rumor or wild fancy, but something that Your Majesty can easily recognize and see.... And therefore, it is certain, Señora, that there have been many deaths and illnesses everywhere this year, and everyone has assured me that these have been caused by mere want. La Mancha, Señora, has been depopulated and many families have emigrated to Madrid, where there have now gathered more poor people than have ever been seen. La Alcarria is deserted, prostrate, and poor; parents cannot help their children, nor brothers their brothers, even though they are watching them die. And in places where poor people were never seen, today they roam about in great gangs. The rest of the province of Toledo is in the same condition, and if it was not for that pastor and prelate (the Cardinal Pascual de Aragon) who gives so many lavish and repeated alms and helps with so many necessities, it is certain that one would see misfortunes never imagined, but since it is not possible to help everyone, many are experiencing these misfortunes already.

And consequently, Señora, today most of the kingdom is in the same state of affairs, and I only wish that it were possible for Your Majesty to visit your kingdom so that you could see these conditions first hand and feel sympathy for them....

From O. and P. Ranum, eds., *The Century of Louis XIV* (New York: Walker and Company, 1972), pp. 200–201, trans. R. Kagan. Reprinted by pemission of the publisher.

# France

## From Report of the Estates of Normandy (1651)

*Saint-Quentin.* Of the 450 sick persons whom the inhabitants were unable to relieve, 200 were turned out, and these we saw die one by one

From the translations in Cecile Augon, *Social France in the XVII Century* (London: Methuen and Co. Ltd., 1911), pp. 171–172, 189.

as they lay on the roadside. A large number still remain, and to each of them it is only possible to dole out the least scrap of bread. We only give bread to those who would otherwise die. The staple dish here consists of mice, which the inhabitants hunt, so desperate are they from hunger. They devour roots which the animals cannot eat; one can, in fact, not put into words the things one sees. . . . This narrative, far from exaggerating, rather understates the horror of the case, for it does not record the hundredth part of the misery in this district. Those who have not witnessed it with their own eyes cannot imagine how great it is. Not a day passes but at least 200 people die of famine in the two provinces. We certify to having ourselves seen herds, not of cattle, but of men and women, wandering about the fields between Rheims and Rhétel, turning up the earth like pigs to find a few roots; and as they can only find rotten ones, and not half enough of them, they become so weak that they have not strength left to seek food. The parish priest at Boult, whose letter we enclose, tells us he has buried three of his parishioners who died of hunger. The rest subsisted on chopped straw mixed with earth, of which they composed a food which cannot be called bread. Other persons in the same place lived on the bodies of animals which had died of disease, and which the curé, otherwise unable to help his people, allowed them to roast at the presbytery fire.

## From *Letters of the Abbess of Port-Royal*

*(1649)* This poor country is a horrible sight; it is stripped of everything. The soldiers take possession of the farms and have the corn threshed, but will not give a single grain to the owners who beg it as an alms. It is impossible to plough. There are no more horses—all have been carried off. The peasants are reduced to sleeping in the woods and are thankful to have them as a refuge from murderers. And if they only had enough bread to half satisfy their hunger, they would indeed count themselves happy.

*(1652)* People massacre each other daily with every sort of cruelty. . . . The soldiers steal from one another when they have denuded every one else, and as they spoil more property than they carry off, they are themselves often reduced to starvation, and can find no more to annex. All the armies are equally undisciplined and vie with one another in lawlessness. The authorities in Paris are trying to send back the peasants to gather in the corn; but as soon as it is reaped the marauders come to slay and steal, and disperse all in a general rout.

# FOUNDATIONS OF ABSOLUTISM

## Rationalism

### From Thomas Hobbes. *Leviathan*

In the first place, I put for a general inclination of all mankind, a perpetual and restless desire of power after power, that ceaseth only in death. And the cause of this, is not always that a man hopes for a more intensive delight, than he has already attained to; or that he cannot be content with a moderate power: but because he cannot assure the power and means to live well, which he hath present, without the acquisition of more.

Hereby it is manifest, that during the time men live without a common power to keep them all in awe, they are in that condition which is called war; and such a war, as is of every man, against every man.

Whatsoever therefore is consequent to a time of war, where every man is enemy to every man; the same is consequent to the time, wherein men live without other security, than what their own strength, and their own invention shall furnish them withal. In such condition, there is no place for industry; because the fruit thereof is uncertain: and consequently no culture of the earth; no navigation, nor use of the commodities that may be imported by sea; no commodious building; no instruments of moving, and removing, such things as require much force; no knowledge of the face of the earth; no account of time; no arts; no letters; no society; and which is worst of all, continual fear, and danger of violent death; and the life of man, solitary, poor, nasty, brutish, and short.

The final cause, end, or design of men, who naturally love liberty, and dominion over others, in the introduction of that restraint upon themselves, in which we see them live in commonwealths, is the foresight of their own preservation, and of a more contented life thereby;

From Thomas Hobbes, *Leviathan* (London: Andrew Crook, 1651), Chs. 11, 13, 17, 18.

that is to say, of getting themselves out from that miserable condition of war, which is necessarily consequent, as hath been shown, to the natural passions of men, when there is no visible power to keep them in awe, and tie them by fear of punishment to the performance of their covenants.

The only way to erect such a common power, as may be able to defend them from the invasion of foreigners, and the injuries of one another, and thereby to secure them in such sort, as that by their own industry, and by the fruits of the earth, they may nourish themselves and live contentedly; is, to confer all their power and strength upon one man, or upon one assembly of men, that may reduce all their wills, by plurality of voices, unto one will: which is as much as to say, to appoint one man, or assembly of men, to bear their person; and every one to own, and acknowledge himself to be author of whatsoever he that so beareth their person, shall act, or cause to be acted, in those things which concern the common peace and safety; and therein to submit their wills, every one to his will, and their judgments, to his judgment. This is more than consent, or concord; it is a real unity of them all, in one and the same person, made by convenant of every man with every man, in such manner, as if every man should say to every man, *I authorize and give up my right of governing myself, to this man, or to this assembly of men, on this condition, that thou give up thy right to him, and authorize all his actions in like manner.* This done, the multitude so united in one person, is called a COMMONWEALTH, in Latin CIVITAS. This is the generation of that great LEVIATHAN, or rather, to speak more reverently, of that *mortal god,* to which we owe under the *immortal God,* our peace and defence. For by this authority, given him by every particular man in the commonwealth, he hath the use of so much power and strength conferred on him, that by terror thereof, he is enabled to form the wills of them all, to peace at home, and mutual aid against their enemies abroad. And in him consisteth the essence of the commonwealth; which, to define it, is *one person, of whose acts a great multitude, by mutual covenants one with another, have made themselves every one the author, to the end he may use the strength and means of them all, as he shall think expedient, for their peace and common defence.*

And he that carrieth this person, is called SOVEREIGN, and said to have *sovereign power;* and every one besides, his SUBJECT.

A *commonwealth* is said to be *instituted,* when a *multitude* of men do agree, and *convenant, every one, with every one,* that to whatsoever *man,* or *assembly of men,* shall be given by the major part, the *right* to *present* the person of them all, that is to say, to be their *representative;* every one, as well he that *voted for it,* as he that *voted against it,* shall *authorize* all the actions and judgments, of that man, or assembly of men, in the same manner, as if they were his own, to the end, to live peaceably amongst themselves, and be protected against other men.

From this institution of a commonwealth are derived all the *rights*, and *faculties* of him, or them, on whom the sovereign power is conferred by the consent of the people assembled.

First, because they covenant . . . they that have already instituted a commonwealth, being thereby bound by covenant, to own the actions, and judgments of one, cannot lawfully make a new covenant, amongst themselves, to be obedient to any other, in any thing whatsoever, without his permission. And therefore, they that are subjects to a monarch, cannot without his leave cast off monarchy, and return to the confusion of a disunited multitude; nor transfer their person from him that beareth it, to another man, or other assembly of men: for they are bound, every man to every man, to own, and be reputed author of all, that he that already is their sovereign, shall do, and judge fit to be done.

Secondly, because the right of bearing the person of them all, is given to him they make sovereign, by covenant only of one to another, and not of him to any of them; there can happen no breach of covenant on the part of the sovereign; and consequently none of his subjects, by any pretence of forfeiture, can be freed from his subjection.

Thirdly, because the major part hath by consenting voices declared a sovereign; he that dissented must now consent with the rest; that is, be contented to avow all the actions he shall do, or else justly be destroyed by the rest. For if he voluntarily entered into the congregation of them that were assembled, he sufficiently declared thereby his will, and therefore tacitly covenanted, to stand to what the major part should ordain.

Fourthly, because every subject is by this institution author of all the actions, and judgments of the sovereign instituted; it follows, that whatsoever he doth, it can be no injury to any of his subjects; nor ought he to be by any of them accused of injustice. For he that doth anything by authority from another, doth therein no injury to him by whose authority he acteth: but by this institution of a commonwealth, every particular man is author of all the sovereign doth: and consequently he that complaineth of injury from his sovereign, complaineth of that whereof he himself is author; and therefore ought not to accuse any man but himself; no nor himself of injury; because to do injury to one's self, is impossible. It is true that they that have sovereign power may commit iniquity; but not injustice, or injury in the proper signification.

Fifthly, and consequently to that which was said last, no man that hath sovereign power can justly be put to death, or otherwise in any manner by his subjects punished. For seeing every subject is author of the actions of his sovereign; he punisheth another for the actions committed by himself.

# Divine Right

From Bossuet. *Politics Drawn from the Very Words of Holy Scripture*

There are four characters or qualities essential to royal authority: First, royal authority is sacred; second, it is paternal; third, it is absolute; fourth, it is ruled by reason. . . .

## Royal Authority Is Sacred.

*God established kings as his ministers and rules peoples by them.*

We have already seen that all power comes from God. "The prince," St. Paul adds, "is the minister of God to thee for good. But if thou do that which is evil, be afraid; for he beareth not the sword in vain; for he is the minister of God, a revenger to execute wrath upon him that doeth evil." [Rom. 13:4]

Thus princes act as ministers of God, and as his lieutenants on earth. It is by them that he exercises his rule. . . .

Thus we have seen that the royal throne is not the throne of a man, but the throne of God himself. . . .

*The person of kings is sacred.*

It thus appears that the person of kings is sacred and that to make an attempt on their lives is a sacrilege.

God has had them anointed by his prophets with a sacred unction as he has his pontiffs and his altars anointed.

But without the external application of this unction, they are sacred by their office, as being the representatives of the divine majesty, deputized by his providence to the execution of his designs. . . .

The title of Christ is given to kings; and they are everywhere called christs, or the anointed of the lord.

## Royal Authority Is Paternal and Its Proper Character is Goodness.

After what has been said, this truth has no need of proof.

We have seen that kings take the place of God, who is the true father of the human species. We have also seen that the first idea of power which exists among men is that of the paternal power; and that kings are modeled on fathers.

From J. B. Bossuet, *Politics Drawn from the Very Words of Holy Scripture* (1709), in Brian Tierney, Donald Kagan, and L. Pearce Williams, eds., *Great Issues in Western Civilization*, 3rd. ed., Vol II, pp. 613–615 (adapted), trans. L. Pearce Williams. Copyright © 1967, 1972, 1976 by Random House, Inc. Reprinted by pemission of the publisher.

Everybody is also in accord, that the obedience which is owed to the public power can be found in the ten commandments only in the precept which obliges him to honor his parents.

Thus it follows from this that the name of king is a name for father and that goodness is the most natural character of kings. . . .

It is a royal right to provide for the needs of the people. He who undertakes it at the expense of the prince undertakes royalty: this is why it has been established. The obligation to care for the people is the foundation of all the rights that sovereigns have over their subjects.

## Royal Authority Is Absolute.

Without this absolute authority, he cannot do good nor can he repress evil: it is necessary that his power be such that no one can hope to escape him; and finally the only defense of individuals against the public power ought to be their innocence. . . .

Princes, then, must be obeyed in the same way as justice itself; otherwise there can be no order and no finality in men's affairs.

They are gods, and participate in some sense in the divine independence. "I have said, You are gods, and you are all children of the Most High." [Ps. 81:6.]

There is no one save God alone who may judge their decisions and their lives. . . . The prince may himself redress his own errors when he sees that he has committed a wrong; but against his authority there can exist no remedy save in his authority itself.

## There Can Be No Coactive Power Opposing the Prince.

A "coactive power" is a power to compel and execute that which is legitimately commanded. Legitimate command belongs to the prince alone; to him alone, therefore, belongs the "coactive power."

It is for this reason that St. Paul gives the sword to him only. "If you do not act rightly, be afraid; for it is not for nothing that he has the sword." [Rom. 13:4.] . . .

Thus it is that for the good of the state, all its force has been united in a single person. Let force exist elsewhere, and you divide the state and destroy the public peace; you set up two masters, contrary to this maxim of the Gospel: "No man can serve two masters." [Matt. 6:24.]

The prince is by his office the father of his people; he is placed by his grandeur above all petty interests; even more: all his grandeur and his natural interests are that the people shall be conserved, for once the people fail him he is no longer prince. There is thus nothing better than to give all the power of the state to him who has the greatest interest in the conservation and greatness of the state itself.

### Kings Are Not by This Above the Laws.

". . . And it shall be, when he sitteth upon the throne of his kingdom, that he shall write him a copy of this law in a book out of that which is before the priest the Levite: and it shall be with him and he shall read therein all the days of his life: that he may learn to fear the Lord his god, to keep all the words of this law and these statutes to do them: that his heart be not lifted up above his brethren and that he turn not aside from the commandment to the right hand, or to the left: to the end that he may prolong his days in his kingdom, he, and his children." [Deut. 17. 18–20]

It should be noticed that this law does not include only religion, but the law of the realm as well to which the prince was subject as much as any other, or even more than others by the justness of his will.

This is something princes find difficult to understand. "What prince can you find me," asks St. Ambrose, "who believes that what is not good is not permitted, who considers himself bound by his own laws. . . ."

Kings therefore are subject like any others to the equity of the laws both because they must be just and because they owe to the people the example of protecting justice; but they are not subject to the penalties of the laws: or, as theology puts it, they are subject to the laws, not in terms of its coactive power but in terms of its directive power.

# Patriarchy

*Bossuet observed that royal power was "paternal." Sir Robert Filmer built a whole political theory around this idea.*

## From Robert Filmer. *Patriarcha*

As Adam was lord of his children, so his children under him had a command and power over their own children, but still with subordination to the first parent, who is lord-paramount over his children's children to all generations, as being the grandfather of his people.

I see not then how the children of Adam, or of any man else, can be free from subjection to their parents. And this subjection of children being the fountain of all regal authority, by the ordination of God himself; it follows that civil power not only in general is by divine institution, but even the assignment of it specifically to the eldest parents, which quite takes away that new and common distinction which refers

From Robert Filmer, *Patriarcha* (London: Richard Chiswell, 1680), Ch. 1.

only power universal and absolute to God, but power respective in regard of the special form of government to the choice of the people.

This lordship which Adam by command had over the whole world, and by right descending from him the patriarchs did enjoy, was as large and ample as the absolutest dominion of any monarch which hath been since the creation.

It may seem absurd to maintain that kings now are the fathers of their people, since experience shows the contrary. It is true, all kings be not the natural parents of their subjects, yet they all either are, or are to be reputed, the next heirs to those first progenitors who were at first the natural parents of the whole people, and in their right succeed to the exercise of supreme jurisdiction; and such heirs are not only lords of their own children, but also of their brethren, and all others that were subject to their fathers. And therefore we find that God told Cain of his brother Abel, "His desires shall be subject unto thee, and thou shalt rule over him."

If we compare the natural rights of a father with those of a king, we find them all one, without any difference at all but only in the latitude or extent of them: as the father over one family, so the king, as father over many families, extends his care to preserve, feed, clothe, instruct, and defend the whole commonwealth. His war, his peace, his courts of justice, and all his acts of sovereignty, tend only to preserve and distribute to every subordinate and inferior father, and to their children, their rights and privileges, so that all the duties of a king are summed up in an universal fatherly care of his people.

*Because many seventeenth-century authors insisted that a king was like the father of a family, some modern historians have suggested that a study of actual family relationships might help us to a better understanding of seventeenth-century society and government.*

## From David Hunt. *Parents and Children in History*

Why did adults find it necessary to insist so emphatically on the obedience of children? Eriksonian theory suggests the beginnings of an answer. In his most thorough attempt to relate the second phase of childhood to the quality of social life, Erikson writes:

> We have related basic trust to the institution of religion. The basic need of the individual for a delineation of his *autonomy* in the adult order of things seems, in turn, to be taken care of by the *principle of "law and order,"* which in daily life as well as in the high courts of law apportions to each his privileges and his limitations, his obligations and his rights. The sense of autonomy which

From David Hunt, *Parents and Children in History* (New York: Basic Books, 1970), pp. 134–135. Copyright © 1970 by Basic Books, Inc. Reprinted by permission of the publisher.

arises, or should arise, in the second stage of childhood, is fostered by a handling of the small individual which expresses a sense of rightful dignity and lawful independence on the part of the parents. . . .

In short, parents need certain specific cultural and political supports if they are to accept with equanimity the first manifestations of infantile will. If we look for a moment at the kinds of reinforcements available to parents of the old regime, I think we can understand why they reacted as they did to the second stage of childhood.

In the seventeenth century, childrearing took place in a hierarchical society characterized by a very uneven distribution of wealth and dominated by forces of political and religious authoritarianism. It was not a social order in which most individuals found it possible to maintain "a sense of rightful dignity and lawful independence." For the vast majority of French subjects in this period, the concept of "law and order" could hardly have had much relation to their own very precarious existence. Such a social order naturally influences styles of childrearing. The adult who in his own life had little experience of genuine self-determination and only limited opportunity to observe it in the conduct of others, was not able to tolerate his child's efforts to be self-determining. The difficulty parents experienced in dealing with infantile will grew out of the inequitable character of their experience "in marriage, in work, and in citizenship."

Admittedly, these are sweeping statements. One might well object that I am arguing almost tautologically: if the society is authoritarian, methods of childrearing (and probably every social relationship) will also be authoritarian. All known societies contain some element of hierarchy. For generations, historians have been debating about the nature of the social system whose character I seem to be taking for granted. Many have argued that individuals of the old regime were used to the graded ranks into which they were born and did not feel differences in status and power as hindrances to close personal ties or to living a satisfying and happy life. These historians claim that modern criticisms of the old regime are anachronistic. With our legalistic and bureaucratic notion of the way a society works, we lack the means to understand a world held together by mutual loyalties, a shared tradition, the "existential bond" between master and servant.

Paternalism is implicit in these defenses of the old regime. To its champions, this system worked like a large family. Rulers were similar to benevolent parents, often autocratic, but at the same time attentive to the welfare of their "children." A study of childrearing, and particularly of the stage of autonomy, can give us an especially informative slant on the problem. If the concept of paternalism has been called into question, then presumably the best setting in which it might be evaluated would be within the family itself. Here the human consequences of old regime hierarchy should be most characteristically demonstrated.

*It happens that we have a detailed account of the infancy of Louis XIII of France, recorded in the diary of the court doctor, Jean Héroard. (Louis was born in 1601.)*

## From *Journal of Jean Héroard*

*9 Oct. 1603*    Awake at 8.00. He is obstinate, is whipped for the first time.

*5 Sept. 1604*    At 8.15 the king arrives and wants to make him give a kiss. He flies into such a bad temper that he is whipped for it by His Majesty. Mme de Montglat also whipped him five or six times. The king asked him, "What was that for?" He answered angrily, "For you . . ." The king left. "I want papa," he said. The king came back and kissed him. At 10.00 the king and queen took him to Mass.

*13 Oct. 1604*    At 3.30 he is taken through the great gallery to the garden of pines. . . . The king wants to take his hand, he does not want to. The king takes his hat off his head and throws it on the ground, really angry. The king goes away and leaves him. He calms down, goes to find the king, and without a word takes his hand.

*23 Oct. 1604*    (Louis wanted to play with his drum, "one of his great pleasures.") So he goes to the king unwillingly, by compulsion. The king says to him, "Take off your hat." . . . He is reluctant to remove it. The king takes it off and he is irritated. Then the king takes from him his drum and drumsticks, which is still worse. "My hat, my drum, my drumsticks." The king to spite him puts the hat on his own head. "I want my hat." The king hits him with it on the head; he is really angry with the king and the king with him. The king takes him by the wrists and lifts him in the air stretching out his little arms. "Hey, you're hurting me, Hey, my drum, Hey, my hat." The Queen gives him back his hat and drumsticks; it was quite a little tragedy. He is taken away by Mme de Montglat bursting with rage . . . will not kiss or hug Mme de Montglat . . . finally is whipped. . . . His nurse takes him aside alone and says, "Monsieur, you have been obstinate, it won't do, you must obey papa." He answers, gasping, "Kill Mamanga (his governess) she is bad. I will kill everybody. I will kill God."

*7 Dec. 1604*    He goes to the king and is very well behaved. The king and queen go hunting. Mlle de Ventelet says to him, "Monsieur who is the master of papa?" He answers, "God is." "And who is your

From *Journal de Jean Héroard sur l'enfance et la jeunesse de Louis XIII* (Paris: Firmin, Dido Frères, 1868), Vol. I, pp. 55, 74, 85, 93, 95, 106, 194, 251, trans. B. Tierney master?" "I don't want to say." It was never possible to make him acknowledge a master. The day before, the King made him very angry when he said, "I am the master and you are my servant." He was extremely irritated by that word.

*26 July 1606*    The king, pointing to Monsieur the first president and other deputies of Normandy, says to him, "See those people, you will command them after me." He answers coldly, "Good, papa." He is very subdued with the king, whom he fears.

*12 Feb. 1607*    At 8.45 undressed and put to bed, says his prayers, "God give a good life to father, my good friend, and mother, my good friend." Mme de Montglat asks him, "Do you love your father?" "I love him more than Pataut" (his nurse's dog). "Monsieur, you shouldn't speak so. You should say you love him more than yourself." "More than myself! Hey. One ought not to love himself. One should love other people but not himself."

# THE COURT OF LOUIS XIV

## Portrait of a Monarch

*The Duke of Saint-Simon lived for many years at the court of Louis XIV and left a detailed account of day-to-day life there.*

### From *Memoirs of the Duke of Saint-Simon*

His natural talents were below mediocrity; but he had a mind capable of improvement, of receiving polish, of assimilating what was best in the minds of others without slavish imitation; and he profited greatly throughout his life from having associated with the ablest and wittiest persons, of both sexes, and of various stations. He entered the world (if I may use such an expression in speaking of a King who had already completed his twenty-third year), at a fortunate moment, for men of distinction abounded. His Ministers and Generals at this time, with their successors trained in their schools, are universally acknowledged to have been the ablest in Europe; for the domestic troubles and foreign wars under which France had suffered ever since the death of Louis XIII had brought to the front a number of brilliant names, and the Court was made up of capable and illustrious personages.... Glory was his passion, but he also liked order and regularity in all things; he was naturally prudent, moderate, and reserved; always master of his tongue and his emotions. Will it be believed? he was also naturally kind-hearted and just. God had given him all that was necessary for him to be a good King, perhaps also to be a fairly great one. All his faults were produced by his surroundings. In his childhood he was so much neglected that no one dared go near his rooms. He was often heard to speak of those times with great bitterness; he used to relate how, through the carelessness of his attendants, he was found one evening in the basin of a fountain in the Palais-Royal gardens....

His Ministers, generals, mistresses, and courtiers soon found out his weak point, namely, his love of hearing his own praises. There was nothing he liked so much as flattery, or, to put it more plainly, adulation; the coarser and clumsier it was, the more he relished it. That was

From *The Memoirs of the Duke de Saint-Simon*, ed. F. Arkwright (New York: Brentano's, n.d.), Vol. V, pp. 254, 259–263.

the only way to approach him; if he ever took a liking to a man it was invariably due to some lucky stroke of flattery in the first instance, and to indefatigable preserverance in the same line afterwards. His Ministers owed much of their influence to their frequent opportunities for burning incense before him. . . .

It was this love of praise which made it easy for Louvois to engage him in serious wars, for he persuaded him that he had greater talents for war than any of his Generals, greater both in design and in execution, and the Generals themselves encouraged him in this notion, to keep in favour with him. I mean such Generals as Condé and Turenne; much more, of course, those who came after them. He took to himself the credit of their successes with admirable complacency, and honestly believed that he was all his flatterers told him. Hence arose his fondness for reviews, which he carried so far that his enemies called him, in derision, "the King of reviews"; hence also his liking for sieges, where he could make a cheap parade of bravery, and exhibit his vigilance, forethought, and endurance of fatigue; for his robust constitution enabled him to bear fatigue marvellously; he cared nothing for hunger, heat, cold, or bad weather. He liked also, as he rode through the lines, to hear people praising his dignified bearing and fine appearance on horseback. His campaigns were his favourite topic when talking to his mistresses. He talked well, expressed himself clearly in well-chosen language; and no man could tell a story better. His conversation, even on the most ordinary subjects, was always marked by a certain natural dignity.

His mind was occupied with small things rather than with great, and he delighted in all sorts of petty details, such as the dress and drill of his soldiers; and it was just the same with regard to his building operations, his household, and even his cookery. He always thought he could teach something of their own craft even to the most skilful professional men; and they, for their part, used to listen gratefully to lessons which they had long ago learnt by heart. He imagined that all this showed his indefatigable industry; in reality, it was a great waste of time, and his Ministers turned it to good account for their own purposes, as soon as they had learnt the art of managing him; they kept his attention engaged with a mass of details, while they contrived to get their own way in more important matters.

His vanity, which was perpetually nourished—for even preachers used to praise him to his face from the pulpit—was the cause of the aggrandisement of his Ministers. He imagined that they were great only through him, mere mouthpieces through which he expressed his will; consequently he made no objection when they gradually encroached on the privileges of the greatest noblemen. He felt that he could at any moment reduce them to their original obscurity; whereas, in the case of a nobleman, though he could make him feel the weight of his displeasure, he could not deprive him or his family of the advantages due to his birth. For this reason he made it a rule never to admit a *seigneur* to his Councils, to which the Duke de Beauvilliers was the only exception. . . .

But for the fear of the devil, which, by God's grace, never forsook him even in his wildest excesses, he would have caused himself to be worshipped as a deity. He would not have lacked worshippers. . . .

# Life at Versailles

## From *Memoirs of the Duke of Saint-Simon*

Very early in the reign of Louis XIV the Court was removed from Paris, never to return. The troubles of the minority had given him a dislike to that city; his enforced and surreptitious flight from it still rankled in his memory; he did not consider himself safe there, and thought cabals would be more easily detected if the Court was in the country, where the movements and temporary absences of any of its members would be more easily noticed. . . . No doubt that he was also influenced by the feeling that he would be regarded with greater awe and veneration when no longer exposed every day to the gaze of the multitude.

His love-affair with Mademoiselle de la Vallière, which at first was covered as far as possible with a veil of mystery, was the cause of frequent excursions to Versailles. This was at that time a small country house, built by Louis XIII to avoid the unpleasant necessity, which had sometimes befallen him, of sleeping at a wretched wayside tavern or in a windmill, when benighted out hunting in the forest of St. Leger. . . . The visits of Louis XIV becoming more frequent, he enlarged the *château* by degrees till its immense buildings afforded better accommodation for the Court than was to be found at St. Germain, where most of the courtiers had to put up with uncomfortable lodgings in the town. The Court was therefore removed to Versailles in 1682, not long before the Queen's death. The new building contained an infinite number of rooms for courtiers, and the King liked the grant of these rooms to be regarded as a coveted privilege.

Ie availed himself of the frequent festivities at Versailles, and his excursions to other places, as a means of making the courtiers assiduous in their attendance and anxious to please him; for he nominated beforehand those who were to take part in them, and could thus gratify some and inflict a snub on others. He was conscious that the substantial favours he had to bestow were not nearly sufficient to produce

From *The Memoirs of the Duke de Saint-Simon*, ed. F. Arkwright (New York: Brentano's, n.d.), Vol. V, pp. 271–274, 276–278.

a continual effect; he had therefore to invent imaginary ones, and no one was so clever in devising petty distinctions and preferences which aroused jealousy and emulation. The visits to Marly later on were very useful to him in this way; also those to Trianon, where certain ladies, chosen beforehand, were admitted to his table. It was another distinction to hold his candlestick at his *coucher;* as soon as he had finished his prayers he used to name the courtier to whom it was to be handed, always choosing one of the highest rank among those present. . . .

Not only did he expect all persons of distinction to be in continual attendance at Court, but he was quick to notice the absence of those of inferior degree; at his *lever,* his *coucher,* his meals, in the gardens of Versailles (the only place where the courtiers in general were allowed to follow him), he used to cast his eyes to right and left; nothing escaped him, he saw everybody. If any one habitually living at Court absented himself he insisted on knowing the reason; those who came there only for flying visits had also to give a satisfactory explanation; any one who seldom or never appeared there was certain to incur his displeasure. If asked to bestow a favour on such persons he would reply haughtily: "I do not know him"; of such as rarely presented themselves he would say, "He is a man I never see"; and from these judgements there was no appeal.

He always took great pains to find out what was going on in public places, in society, in private houses, even family secrets, and maintained an immense number of spies and tale-bearers. These were of all sorts; some did not know that their reports were carried to him; others did know it; there were others, again, who used to write to him directly, through channels which he prescribed; others who were admitted by the backstairs and saw him in his private room. Many a man in all ranks of life was ruined by these methods, often very unjustly, without ever being able to discover the reason; and when the King had once taken a prejudice against a man, he hardly ever got over it. . . .

No one understood better than Louis XIV the art of enhancing the value of a favour by his manner of bestowing it; he knew how to make the most of a word, a smile, even of a glance. If he addressed any one, were it but to ask a trifling question or make some commonplace remark, all eyes were turned on the person so honored; it was a mark of favour which always gave rise to comment. . . .

He loved splendour, magnificence, and profusion in all things, and encouraged similar tastes in his Court; to spend money freely on equipages and buildings, on feasting and at cards, was a sure way to gain his favour, perhaps to obtain the honour of a word from him. Motives of policy had something to do with this; by making expensive habits the fashion, and, for people in a certain position, a necessity, he compelled his courtiers to live beyond their income, and gradually reduced them to depend on his bounty for the means of subsistence. This was a plague which, once introduced, became a scourge to the whole country, for it did not take long to spread to Paris, and thence to the armies and the provinces; so that a man of any position is now estimated entirely according to his expenditure on his table and other luxuries. This folly, sustained by pride and ostentation, has already produced widespread confusion; it threatens to end in nothing short of ruin and a general overthrow.

*The obsession with status and precedence at Louis XIV's court appears in the following letter. (The Duchess of Orleans was married to the king's brother, the much younger Duchess of Burgundy to the king's grandson.)*

## From *Letter of the Duchess of Orleans*

4th January, 1704, Versailles.

To the DUCHESS OF HANOVER.

I must really tell you how just the King is. The Duchesse de Bourgogne's ladies, who are called Ladies of the Palace, tried to arrogate the rank and take the place of my ladies everywhere. Such a thing was never done either in the time of the Queen or of the Dauphiness. They got the King's Guards to keep their places and push back the chairs belonging to my ladies. I complained first of all to the Duc de Noailles, who replied that it was the King's order. Then I went immediately to the King and said to him, "May I ask your Majesty if it is by your orders that my ladies have now no place or rank as they used to have? If it is your desire, I have nothing more to say, because I only wish to obey you, but your Majesty knows that formerly when the Queen and the Dauphiness were alive the Ladies of the Palace had no rank, and my Maids of Honour, Gentlemen of Honour, and Ladies of the Robe had their places like those of the Queen and the Dauphiness. I do not know why the Ladies of the Palace should pretend to anything else." The King became quite red, and replied, "I have given no such order, who said that I had?" "The Maréchal de Noailles," I replied. The King asked him why he had said such a thing, and he denied it entirely. "I am willing to believe, since you say so," I replied, "that my lackey misunderstood you, but as the King has given no such orders, see that your Guards don't keep places for those ladies and hinder my servants from carrying chairs for my service," as we say here. Although these ladies are high in favour, the King, nevertheless, sent the majordomo to find out how things should be done. I told him, and it will not happen again. These women are becoming far too insolent now that they are in favour, and they imagined that I would not have the courage to report the matter to the King. But I shall not lose my rank nor prerogatives on account of the favour they enjoy. The King is too just for that.

From G. S. Stevenson, ed., *The Letters of Madame,* (New York: D. Appleton and Co., 1924), pp. 232–233.

*In the next reading a modern author comments on the ritual of court
etiquette.*

## From W. H. Lewis. *The Splendid Century*

Court etiquette was a life study. Who for instance could guess that at
Versailles it was the height of bad manners to knock at a door? You
must scratch it with the little finger of the left hand, growing the finger
nail long for that purpose. Or could we know that you must not *tutoyer*
an intimate friend in any place where the King was present? That if
the lackey of a social superior brought you a message, you had to receive him standing, and bareheaded? You have mastered the fact that
you must not knock on a door, so when you go to make your first
round of calls in the great houses in the town, you scratch: wrong
again, you should have knocked. Next time you rattle the knocker, and
a passing exquisite asks you contemptuously if you are so ignorant as
not to know that you give one blow of the knocker on the door of a
lady of quality? Who could guess that if you encounter the royal dinner on its way from the kitchens to the table, you must bow as to the
King himself, sweep the ground with the plume of your hat, and say
in a low, reverent, but distinct voice, *La viande du Roi?* Many times
must the apprentice courtier have echoed the psalmist's lament, "Who
can tell how oft he offendeth?" And it behoved you not to offend, for
the King had an eye like a hawk or shall we say, like a school prefect,
for any breach of etiquette, and not even the most exalted were safe
from his reproof. One night at supper his chatterbox of a brother put
his hand in a dish before Louis had helped himself: "I perceive," said
the King icily, "that you are no better able to control you hands than
your tongue." Once at Marly, Mme. de Torcy, wife of a minister, took
a seat above a duchess at supper. Louis, to her extreme discomfort, regarded her steadfastly throughout the meal, and when he reached
Mme. de Maintenon's room, the storm broke; he had, he said, witnessed a piece of insolence so intolerable that the sight of it had prevented him from eating: a piece of presumption which would have
been unendurable in a woman of quality. It took the combined efforts
of Mme. de Maintenon and the Duchess of Burgundy the rest of the
evening to pacify him. Decidedly not a king with whom to take liberties, or even make mistakes. . . .

From W. H. Lewis, *The Splendid Century* (New York: Morrow, 1954), pp. 39–
40. Copyright © 1954 by W. H. Lewis. Reprinted by permission of William
Morrow & Company and Methuen London.

# ABSOLUTISM IN PRACTICE

## Religion

*The Edict of Nantes (1598) had granted a measure of toleration to French Protestants. Its revocation was followed by renewed persecutions.*

### From *Revocation of the Edict of Nantes (1685)*

1. Be it known that of our certain knowledge, full power, and royal authority, we have, by this present perpetual and irrevocable edict, suppressed and revoked, and do suppress and revoke, the edict of our said grandfather, given at Nantes in April 1598, in its whole extent. . . .

2. We forbid our subjects of the R.P.R.[1] to meet any more for the exercise of the said religion in any place or private house, under any pretext whatever. . . .

3. We likewise forbid all noblemen, of what condition soever, to hold such religious exercises in their houses or fiefs, under penalty to be inflicted upon all our said subjects who shall engage in the said exercises, of imprisonment and confiscation.

4. We enjoin all ministers of the said R.P.R., who do not choose to become converts and to embrace the Catholic, apostolic, and Roman religion, to leave our kingdom and the territories subject to us within a fortnight of the publication of our present edict, without leave to reside therein beyond that period, or, during the said fortnight, to engage in any preaching, exhortation, or any other function, on pain of being sent to the galleys. . . .

7. We forbid private schools for the instruction of children of the said R.P.R., and in general all things whatever which can be regarded as a concession of any kind in favor of the said religion.

[1]"Religion prétendue réformée," i.e., "the so-called reformed religion "

From F. A. Isambert, *Recueil général des anciennes lois français* (Paris, 1821–23), trans. in J. H. Robinson, *Readings in European History* (Boston: Ginn and Co., 1906), Vol. II, pp. 289–291.

## From *Memoirs of the Duke of Saint-Simon*

The first-fruits of this dreadful plot were the wanton revocation of the Edict of Nantes, without a shadow of a pretext, and the proscriptions which followed it; its ultimate results were the depopulation of a fourth part of the kingdom and the ruin of our commerce. For a long time the country was given over to the authorised ravages of dragoons, which caused the deaths of, literally, thousands of innocent people of all ages and both sexes. Families were torn asunder; men of all classes, often old and infirm, highly respected for their piety and learning, were sent to toil in the galleys under the lash of the overseer; multitudes were driven penniless from their homes to seek refuge in foreign countries, to which they carried our arts and manufactures, enriching them and causing their cities to flourish at the expense of France.

*After Louis XIV's death it was proposed that the Huguenot exiles be recalled. Saint-Simon then took a very different line.*

I reminded [the Regent] of the disturbances and civil wars caused by the Huguenots from the reign of Henry II to that of Louis XIII; pointing out that even when they were comparatively quiet they had formed a body apart within the State, having their own chiefs, courts of justice specially appointed to deal with their affairs, even when they concerned Catholics, with strong places and garrisons at their disposal; corresponding with foreign Powers; always complaining and ready to take up arms: subjects, in short, merely in name, and yielding just as much or as little allegiance to their Sovereign as they thought fit. I recapitulated the heroic struggles by which his grandfather, Louis XIII, had at last beaten down this Hydra; thereby enabling his successor to get rid of it once for all by the mere expression of his will, without the slightest opposition.

I begged the Regent to reflect that he was now reaping the benefit of these struggles in a profound domestic tranquility; and to consider whether it was worth while, in time of peace when no foreign Power was thinking about the question, to make a concession which the late King had rejected with indignation when reduced to the utmost extremities by a long and disastrous war. I said, in conclusion, that if Louis XIV had made a mistake in revoking the Edict of Nantes it was not so much in the act itself as in the mode of carrying it out.

*Throughout his reign Louis XIV commanded the support of the established Catholic church (which, in the past, had often been hostile to the claims of absolute monarchy).*

From *The Memoirs of the Duke de Saint-Simon*, ed. F. Arkwright (New York: Brentano's, n.d.), Vol. V, pp. 296, 437.

## From *Declaration of the Gallican Church*

We, the archbishops and bishops assembled at Paris by order of the King, with other ecclesiastical deputies who represent the Gallican Church, have judged it necessary to make the regulations and the declaration which follows:

That St. Peter and his successors, Vicars of Jesus Christ, and the whole Church herself, have received power of God only in things spiritual, and pertaining to eternal salvation, not in things civil or temporal, the Lord Himself having said, "My kingdom is not of this world," and also "Render unto Caesar the things that be Caesar's, and unto God the things that are God's"; as also firmly declareth the Apostle, "Let every soul be subject unto the higher powers; for there is no power but of God; the powers that be are ordained of God; whosoever therefore resisteth the power, resisteth the ordinance of God."

Therefore kings and princes are in no wise subjected by God's appointment to any ecclesiastical power in temporal things; neither can the authority of the Keys of the Church directly or indirectly depose them, or their subjects be dispensed from the obedience and fidelity of their oaths to the same; and this doctrine we affirm to be necessary for the maintenance of public peace, no less profitable to the Church than to the State, and to be everywhere and every way observed as agreeable to the Word of God, to the tradition of the Fathers and the example of the Saints. . . .

From F. A. Isambert, *Recueil général des anciennes lois française* (Paris, 1821–23), trans. in T. C. Mendenhall, B. D. Henning and A. S. Foord, *Ideas and Institutions in European History* (New York: Holt, Rinehart and Winston, 1948), Vol. I, p. 318.

*Under Louis XIV the church became virtually a department of government*

## From Louis XIV. *Letter to His Heir*

I have never failed, when an occasion has presented itself, to impress upon you the great respect we should have for religion, and the deference we should show to its ministers in matters specially connected with their mission, that is to say, with the celebration of the Sacred Mysteries and the preaching of the doctrine of the Gospels. But because people connected with the Church are liable to presume a little too much on the advantages attaching to their profession, and are willing sometimes to make use of them in order to whittle down their most rightful duties, I feel obliged to explain to you certain points on this question which may be of importance.

From J. Longnon, ed., *A King's Lessons in Statecraft*, H. Wilson, trans. (New York: Albert and Charles Boni, 1925), p. 149.

The first is that Kings are absolute *seigneurs,* and from their nature have full and free disposal of all property both secular and ecclesiastical, to use it ˙ wise dispensers, that is to say, in accordance with the requirements of their State.

The second is that those mysterious names, the Franchises and Liberties of the Church, with which perhaps people will endeavour to dazzle you, have equal reference to all the faithful whether they be laymen or tonsured, who are all equally sons of this common Mother; but that they exempt neither the one nor the other from subjection to Sovereigns, to whom the Gospel itself precisely enjoins that they should submit themselves.

# Military Organization

*Voltaire, writing in the mid-eighteenth century, looked back on the reign of Louis XIV as a time of order and grandeur.*

## From Voltaire. *The Age of Louis XIV*

He was the legislator of his armies as well as of his people as a whole It is surprising that, before his time, there was no uniform dress among the troops. It was he who, in the first year of his administration, ordered that each regiment should be distinguished by the color of its dress or by different badges; this regulation was soon adopted by all other nations. It was he who instituted brigadiers and who put the household troops on their present footing. He turned Cardinal Mazarin's guards into a company of musketeers and fixed the number of men in the companies at five hundred; moreover, he gave them the uniform which they still wear today.

Under him there were no longer constables, and after the death of the Duke of Epernon, no more colonel generals of infantry; they had become too powerful, and he quite rightly wanted to be sole master. Marshal Grammont, who was only colonel of horse of the French Guards under the Duke of Epernon and who took his orders from this colonel general, now took them only from the King, and was the first to be given the title of Colonel of the Guards. The King himself installed his colonels at the head of the regiments, giving them with his own hand a gilt gorget with a pike, and afterward, when the use of pikes was abolished, a spontoon, or kind of half-pike. In the King's Regiment, which he created himself, he instituted grenadiers, on the scale of four to a company in the first place; then he formed a company of grenadiers in each regiment of infantry. He gave two to the French Guards. Nowadays there is one for each battalion throughout the whole infantry. He greatly enlarged the Corps of Dragoons, and ga 'e them a colonel general. The establishment of studs for breeding horses, in 1667, must not be forgotten, for they had been completely abandoned beforehand and they were of great value in providing mounts for the cavalry, an important resource which has since been too much neglected.

It was he who instituted the use of the bayonet affixed to the end of the musket. Before his time, it was used occasionally, but only a few companies fought with this weapon. There was no uniform practice and no drill; everything was left to the general's discretion. Pikes were then thought of as the most redoubtable weapon. The first regiment to have bayonets and to be trained to use them was that of the Fusiliers, established in 1671.

The manner in which artillery is used today is due entirely to him. He founded artillery schools, first at Douai, then at Metz and Strasbourg; and the Regiment of Artillery was finally staffed with officers who were almost all capable of successfully conducting a siege. All the magazines in the kingdom were well stocked, and they were supplied annually with eight hundred thousand pounds of powder. He created a regiment of bombardiers and one of hussars; before this only his enemies had had hussars.

In 1688 he established thirty regiments of militia, which were provided and equipped by the communes. These militia trained for war but without abandoning the cultivation of their fields.

Companies of cadets were maintained in the majority of frontier towns; there they learned mathematics, drawing and all the drills, and carried out the duties of soldiers. This institution lasted for ten years, but the government finally tired of trying to discipline these difficult young people. The Corp of Engineers, on the other hand, which the King created and to which he gave its present regulations, is an institution which will last forever. During his reign the art of fortifying strongholds was brought to perfection by Marshal Vauban and his pupils, who surpassed Count Pagan. He built or repaired a hundred and fifty fortresses.

To maintain military discipline, the King created inspectors general and later directors, who reported on the state of the troops; from their reports it could be seen whether the war commissioners had carried out their duties.

He instituted the Order of Saint-Louis, an honorable distinction which was often more sought after than wealth. The Hôtel des Invalides put the seal on his efforts to merit loyal service.

It was owing to measures such as these that he had, by 1672, a hundred and eighty thousand regular troops, and that, increasing his forces as the number and strength of his enemies increased, he finished with four hundred and fifty thousand men under arms, including the troops of the navy.

Before his time such powerful armies were unknown. His enemies could scarcely muster comparable forces, and to do so they had to be united. He showed what France, on her own, was capable of, and he always had either great successes or great resources to fall back on.

# Economy and Local Administration

*Louis XIV's finance minister, Colbert, strove to build up French commerce and manufactures.*

## From *Colbert's Memoranda*

### A Memorandum, 1669

The commerce of all Europe is carried on by ships of every size to the number of 20,000, and it is perfectly clear that this number cannot be increased, since the number of people in all the states remains the same and consumption likewise remains the same. . . .

Commerce is a perpetual and peaceable war of wit and energy among all nations. Each nation works incessantly to have its legitimate share of commerce or to gain an advantage over another nation. The Dutch fight at present, in this war, with 15,000 to 16,000 ships, a government of merchants, all of whose maxims and power are directed solely toward the preservation and increase of their commerce, and much more care, energy, and thrift than any other nation.

The English with 3,000 to 4,000 ships, less energy and care, and more expenditures than the Dutch.

The French with 500 to 600.

Those two last cannot improve their commerce save by increasing the number of their vessels, and cannot increase this number save from the 20,000 which carry all the commerce and consequently by making inroads on the 15,000 to 16,000 of the Dutch.

"A Memorandum, 1669": From Charles W. Cole, *Colbert and a Century of French Mercantilism* (New York: Columbia University Press, 1939), p. 320. Copyright 1939 by Columbia University Press. Reprinted by permission.

## A Memorandum, 1670

[Formerly] the Dutch, English, Hamburgers, and other nations bringing into the realm a much greater quantity of merchandise than that which they carried away, withdrew the surplus in circulating money, which produced both their abundance and the poverty of the realm, and indisputably resulted in their power and our weakness.

We must next examine the means which were employed to change this destiny.

Firstly, in 1662 Your Majesty maintained his right to 50 sols per ton of freight from foreign vessels, which produced such great results that we have seen the number of French vessels increase yearly; and in seven or eight years the Dutch have been practically excluded from port-to-port commerce, which is carried on by the French. The advantages received by the state through the increase in the number of sailors and seamen, through the money which has remained in the realm by this means and an infinity of others, would be too long to enumerate.

At the same time, Your Majesty ordered work done to abolish all the tolls which had long been established on all the rivers of the kingdom, and he began from then on to have an examination made of the rivers which could be rendered navigable in order to facilitate the descent of commodities and merchandise from inside the realm toward the sea to be transported into foreign lands. Although everything that invites the universal admiration of men was still in disorder in these first years and although the recovery work was a sort of abyss, Your Majesty did not delay in beginning the examination of the tariffs of the *cinq grosses fermes* and scrutinized the fact that the regulation and levying of these sorts of duties concerning commerce had always been done with a great deal of ignorance on the basis of memoranda by tax farmers, who, being solely concerned with their own interests and the increase in the profits from their tax farms while they possessed them, had always overvalued the commodities, merchandise, and manufactured items of the realm which they saw leaving in abundance, and favored the entrance of foreign merchandise and manufactured items, in order to have a greater quantity of them enter, without being concerned about whether money was as a result leaving the realm, for they were indifferent to this as long as their tax farms produced gain for them during the period of their possession.

Finally, after having thoroughly studied this matter, Your Majesty ordered the tariff of 1664, in which the duties are regulated on a completely different principle, that is to say, that all merchandise and man-

"A Memorandum, 1670": From P. Clement, *Lettres, instructions et mémoires de Colbert* (Paris, Imprimerie Nationale, 1870). Translated excerpts in O. and P. Ranum, *The Century of Louis XIV* (New York: Walker, 1972), pp. 120–123. Reprinted by permission of Walker and Company, Inc.

ufactured items of the realm were markedly favored and the foreign ones priced out of the market, though not completely; [for] having as yet no established manufacturers in the realm, this increase in duties, had it been excessive, would have been a great burden for the *peuple*, because of their need for the aforesaid foreign merchandise and manufactured items; but this change began to provide some means of establishing the same manufactures in the realm; and to this end:

The fabric manufacture of Sedan has been reestablished, and enlarged to 62 from the 12 looms there were then.

The new establishments of Abbeville, Dieppe, Fécamp, and Rouen have been built, in which there are presently more than 200 looms.

The factory for barracan was next established at La Ferré-sous-Jouarre, which is made up of 120 looms;

That of little damasks from Flanders, at Meaux, consisting of 80 looms;

That for carpeting, in the same city, made up of 20 looms . . .

That for tin, in Nivernois;

That for French lace, in 52 cities and towns, in which more than 20,000 workers toil;

The manufacture of brass, or yellow copper, set up in Champagne;

That for camlet of Brussels, in Paris, which will become large and extensive;

Brass wire, in Burgundy;

Gold thread of Milan, at Lyons . . .


[*Many other new enterprises were listed.*]

And since Your Majesty has wanted to work diligently at reestablishing his naval forces, and since for that it has been necessary to make very great expenditures, since all merchandise, munitions and manufactured items formerly came from Holland and the countries of the North, it has been absolutely necessary to be especially concerned with finding within the realm, or with establishing in it, everything which might be necessary for this great plan.

To this end, the manufacture of tar was established in Médoc, Auvergne, Dauphiné, and Provence;

Iron cannons, in Burgundy, Nivernois, Saintonge, and Périgord;

Large anchors, in Dauphiné, Nivernois, Brittany, and Rochefort;

Sailcloth for the Levant, in Dauphiné;

Coarse muslin, in Auvergne;

All the implements for pilots and others, at Dieppe and La Rochelle;

The cutting of wood suitable for vessels, in Burgundy, Dauphiné, Brittany, Normandy, Poitou, Saintonge, Provence, Guyenne, and the Pyrenees;

Masts, of a sort once unknown in this realm, have been found in Provence, Languedoc, Auvergne, Dauphiné, and in the Pyrenees.

Iron, which was obtained from Sweden and Biscay, is currently manufactured in the realm.

Fine hemp for ropes, which came from Prussia and from Piedmont, is currently obtained in Burgundy, Mâconnais, Bresse, Dauphiné; and markets for it have since been established in Berry and in Auvergne, which always provides money in these provinces and keeps it within the realm.

In a word, everything serving for the construction of vessels is currently established in the realm, so that Your Majesty can get along without foreigners for the navy and will even, in a short time, be able to supply them and gain their money in this fashion. And it is with this same objective of having everything necessary to provide abundantly for his navy and that of his subjects that he is working at the general reform of all the forests in his realm, which, being as carefully preserved as they are at present, will abundantly produce all the wood necessary for this.

## A Memorandum, 1672

ꟻ the King conquers all the provinces subject to and forming part of the States of the United Provinces of the Netherlands, their commerce becoming commerce of the subjects of the King, there would be nothing more to desire; and if afterwards His Majesty, examining what would be most advantageous to do for the commerce of his old and new subjects, thought it for the good of his service to divide the advantages of this commerce by cutting down a part of that of the Dutch so as to transfer it into the hands of the French, it would be easy to find the necessary expedients to which the new subjects would be obliged to submit.

*Much of Colbert's voluminous correspondence was concerned with the supervision of local government officials.*

## From *Colbert's Correspondence*

To the Count de Grignan, Lieutenant-General of Provence, Paris, 25 December, 1671

I have informed the King of the disorderly conduct in which the Assembly of the Towns of Provence has persisted; and, as His Majesty is not disposed to countenance it longer, he has given the orders necessary to prorogue it and, at the same time, has dispatched ten *lettres-*

"A Memorandum, 1672": From Charles W. Cole, *Colbert and a Century of French Mercantilism* (New York: Columbia University Press, 1939), p. 320. Copyright 1939 by Oxford University Press. Reprinted by permission.

*de-cachet,* to commit the ten most discontented deputies to Granville, Cherbourg, Saint-Malo, Morlaix and Concarneau.

### To the Same, Versailles, 31 December, 1671

I have made a complete report to the King of all which has transpired in the Assembly of the Towns of Provence since the 20th of the month. You will see, through the orders which His Majesty sends, how little pleased he is with the conduct of those who have served as deputies this year. And, as soon as His Majesty has accepted their offer of 450,000 livres, his desire is that, following the orders which you will receive, you send to the provinces of Normandy and Brittany ten of those deputies who have displayed the most ill-will toward the good of his service. All of Provence will see the troublous extremities in which the obstinacy of these deputies has placed them. I very much doubt whether His Majesty will see fit to call them together for a long time, and in any case, he will give them sufficient leisure to repent the bad conduct to which they held. However, with your own conduct, His Majesty is very satisfied.

### To M. de Creil, Intendant of Rouen, Saint-Germain, 3 February 1673

Of all the abuses which come before us from the *généralités*[1], there is none at present which seems more important to the Council than that [practised] by the assistants to the Receivers of the *Tailles*[2], who, under the name of the Receivers, make assessments, in conjunction with the magistrates, to defray the court costs and fees and which they apply to their own profit. As was provided by the order of the Council of 4 July 1664, concerning the regulation of this disorder, pray inform me if it is known or practised in the *généralité* of Rouen, and particularly apply yourself to finding out if any of the Receivers of *Tailles* or Commissioners of Revenue are guilty of this, in order that you may either apply the necessary remedy through your authority or advise me about it.

### To M. de Bezons, Intendant of Limoges, 16 November 1680

The King having been advised by M. de Marillac, intendant in the *généralité* de Poitiers, that a man named Baudoin has been guilty of a

---

[1]Administrative districts.
[2]Land taxes.

Colbert's Correspondence: From P. Clement, *Lettres, instructions et mémoires de Colbert* (Paris, Imprimerie Nationale, 1870), translated in T. C. Mendenhall, B. D. Henning and A. S. Foord, *Ideas and Institutions in European History* (New York: Holt, Rinehart and Winston, 1948), pp. 315–316, 321.

great many frauds in several parishes of the province of Saintonge, under the pretext of collecting for the *corvées* to repair roads, and on the strength of a commission of the tribunal of the King's lands at Paris giving him permission, His Majesty gave *Sieur* de Marillac verbal powers to institute proceedings against Baudoin; and, this having been done, he has been condemned to the galleys for life and forced to make restitution to those whom he had swindled.

As *Sieur* de Marillac has informed me that in the process of trying Baudoin, he learned that, in the *généralité* of Limoges, there are several other people who have similar commissions and who, under the same pretext, are plaguing the people, I feel free to request that you hunt them down, throughout the entirety of the *généralité* of Limoges, in order to halt their depredations. If you have the facilities there to try them and to make examples of them, the King will, upon your request, send you the authority to try them and to impress the maximum penalties. . . .

## To M. d'Herbigny, Intendant of Grenoble, Versailles, 16 November, 1680

I was surprised to learn, by your letter of the 28th last, that you had levied on the *élection* of Vienne an assessment of 4,700 livres, for the construction, subject to my approval, of a bridge to facilitate the transportation of the harvest to Grenoble.

You know as well as I that it is not permissible to make such an assessment on the people without a writ of the King affixed with the Great Seal, and you must take care to do nothing contrary to that general usage of the realm, and never to give so bad an example to the authorities of that province, who are only too much inclined to go beyond the bounds, and to those who will succeed to your position.

## To M. Morant, Intendant of Aix, Sceaux, 1 July, 1682

I shall report at the next meeting of the Council on the suggestion which you have sent concerning the public works and the tolls; I am certain that His Majesty will agree with them. You ought afterwards to apply yourself to repairing the roads and to forcing the *seigneurs* to repair and maintain those roads on which they levy the tolls.

As you fully appreciate the importance of these public works to the good of the province, I am sure that you will give them your complete attention. . . .

# EASTERN EUROPE

## The Turkish Menace

*An anonymous seventeenth-century observer reflected rather cynically on the probable reaction of Louis XIV to a Turkish invasion of Germany.*

### From *The Present State of the German and Turkish Empires*

Some perhaps will ... retort that though Vienna had been taken by the Turk, there was no great fear of his further progress into Germany: Because Louis the King of France surnamed the Great for the things he has done already, would oppose him in such a case with a puissant army, and force him back again to the great loss of the Turks and his own immortal glory.

This indeed would be great in Louis the Great; and in truth in such a conjuncture of affairs he would be the only prince of Europe in a capacity to stop the progress of such a potent enemy. But first, we may justly question whether he would in such a case be willing, or not, till such time as he were forced to it, for his own defence. For every one knows that knows anything, that clipping the wings of the Austrian eagle (or House of Austria) will extremely add to the splendour of the French monarchy. Whilst then the Turks were invading Germany on the one side, would not both self-preservation, honour and interest invite the French King to be busy on the other? And divide perhaps Germany with the Turks, since in all likelihood he could do no better.

All Europe knows into what extreme distress the States of Holland were brought by the French King's first and second campaign against the Hollanders: And had Germany been invaded by the Turks, the lillies [emblem of the French monarchy] perhaps had ere now taken such deep roots in Holland, that it had not been easy (to say no more) to pull them out again. But as Germany was then in peace with the Turks, the Emperor united all the German princes together, for their common interest, and set on foot in the beginning of winter, an army of near 40,000 horse and foot.... The good success whereof occa-

From *The Present State of the German and Turkish Empires* (London, 1684), pp. 38–44.

sioned a great change in the affairs of Holland. For then the French thought it no longer secure for them to remain there, and deserted on a sudden the cities they had taken in it partly by force; partly by a free surrender, so that after having caused the citizens to redeem their liberties with great sums of money the French retreated from their new conquests, which they had never done, if the forces of Germany had been diverted by a Turkish invasion.

Out of all this discourse, we may gather that although the French King were able alone to beat the Turks out of Germany, in case they had succeeded in their designs; it's not certain whether he would have been willing to do it, at least till he had been himself possest of the best part of Germany, of Flanders, and Holland likewise. . . .

# Peter the Great

*Peter the Great combined westernizing reforms with savage repression in his rule of Russia (1682–1725). Bishop Burnett met the emperor on his visit to England in 1698.*

## From *Gilbert Burnett's History*

He is a man of a very hot temper, soon inflamed and very brutal in his passion. He raises his natural heat by drinking much brandy, which he rectifies [i.e., distills] himself with great application. He is subject to convulsive motions all over his body, and his head seems to be affected with these. He wants not capacity, and has a larger measure of knowledge than might be expected from his education, which was very indifferent. A want of judgment, with an instability of temper, appear in him too often and too evidently.

He is mechanically turned, and seems designed by nature rather to be a ship carpenter than a great prince. This was his chief study and exercise while he stayed here. He wrought much with his own hands and made all about him work at the models of ships. He told me he designed a great fleet at Azuph [i.e. Azov] and with it to attack the Turkish empire. But he did not seem capable of conducting so great a design, though his conduct in his wars since this has discovered a greater genius in him than appeared at this time.

. . . He was, indeed, resolved to encourage learning and to polish his people by sending some of them to travel in other countries and to draw strangers to come and live among them. He seemed apprehensive still [i.e. ever] of his sister's [i.e. the Princess Sophia's] intrigues.

From J. H. Robinson, *Readings in European History* (Boston: Ginn and Co., 1906), Vol. II, pp. 303–306, 310–312.

There was a mixture both of passion and severity in his temper. He is resolute, but understands little of war, and seemed not at all inquisitive that way.

After I had seen him often, and had conversed much with him, I could not but adore the depth of the providence of God that had raised up such a furious man to so absolute an authority over so great a part of the world. David, considering the great things God had made for the use of man, broke out into the meditation, "What is man, that thou art so mindful of him?" But here there is an occasion for reversing these words, since man seems a very contemptible thing in the sight of God, while such a person as the tsar has such multitudes put, as it were, under his feet, exposed to his restless jealousy and savage temper.

*While Peter was traveling abroad, his sister, Sophia, was involved in a rebellion of the Moscow guard, the* Streltsi. *(Von Korb was an Austrian diplomat stationed in Moscow.)*

## From *Von Korb's Diary*

How sharp was the pain, how great the indignation, to which the tsar's Majesty was mightily moved, when he knew of the rebellion of the Streltsi, betraying openly a mind panting for vengeance! He was still tarrying at Vienna, quite full of the desire of setting out for Italy; but, fervid as was his curiosity of rambling abroad, it was, nevertheless, speedily extinguished on the announcement of the troubles that had broken out in the bowels of his realm. . . . Nor did he long delay the plan for his justly excited wrath; he took the quick post, as his ambassador suggested, and in four weeks' time he had got over about three hundred miles[1] without accident, and arrived the 4th of September, 1698,—a monarch for the well disposed, but an avenger for the wicked.

His first anxiety after his arrival was about the rebellion,—in what it consisted, what the insurgents meant, who dared to instigate such a crime. And as nobody could answer accurately upon all points, and some pleaded their own ignorance, others the obstinacy of the Streltsi, he began to have suspicions of everybody's loyalty. . . . No day, holy or profane, were the inquisitors idle; every day was deemed fit and lawful for torturing. There were as many scourges as there were accused, and every inquisitor was a butcher. . . . The whole month of October was spent in lacerating the backs of culprits with the knout and with flames; no day were those that were left alive exempt from scourging or scorching; or else they were broken upon the wheel, or driven to the gibbet, or slain with the ax. . . .

To prove to all people how holy and inviolable are those walls of the

[1]German miles, each equivalent to about five English.

city which the Streltsi rashly meditated scaling in a sudden assault, beams were run out from all the embrasures in the walls near the gates, in each of which two rebels were hanged. This day beheld about two hundred and fifty die that death. There are few cities fortified with as many palisades as Moscow has given gibbets to her guardian Streltsi.

[In front of the nunnery where Sophia was confined] there were thirty gibbets erected in a quadrangle shape, from which there hung two hundred and thirty Streltsi; the three principal ringleaders, who tendered a petition to Sophia touching the administration of the realm, were hanged close to the windows of that princess, presenting, as it were, the petitions that were placed in their hands, so near that Sophia might with ease touch them.

## From *De Missy's Life of Peter*

The tsar labored at the reform of fashions, or, more properly speaking, of dress. Until that time the Russians had always worn long beards, which they cherished and preserved with much care, allowing them to hang down on their bosoms, without even cutting the moustache. With these long beards they wore the hair very short, except the ecclesiastics, who, to distinguish themselves, wore it very long. The tsar, in order to reform that custom, ordered that gentlemen, merchants, and other subjects, except priests and peasants, should each pay a tax of one hundred rubles a year if they wished to keep their beard; the commoners had to pay one kopeck each. Officials were stationed at the gates of the towns to collect that tax, which the Russians regarded as an enormous sin on the part of the tsar and as a thing which tended to the abolition of their religion.

These insinuations, which came from the priests, occasioned the publication of many pamphlets in Moscow, where for that reason alone the tsar was regarded as a tyrant and a pagan; and there were many old Russians who, after having their beards shaved off, saved them preciously, in order to have them placed in their coffins, fearing that they would not be allowed to enter heaven without their beards. As for the young men, they followed the new customs with the more readiness as it made them appear more agreeable to the fair sex.

From the reform in beards we may pass to that of clothes. Their garments, like those of the Orientals, were very long, reaching to the heel. The tsar issued an ordinance abolishing that costume, commanding all the boyars (nobles) and all those who had positions at the court to dress after the French fashion, and likewise to adorn their clothes with gold or silver according to their means.

The dress of the women was changed, too. English hairdressing was substituted for the caps and bonnets hitherto worn; bodices, stays, and skirts, for the former undergarment. . . .

The same ordinance also provided that in the future women, as well as men, should be invited to entertainments, such as weddings, banquets, and the like, where both sexes should mingle in the same hall, as in Holland and England. It was likewise added that these entertainments should conclude with concerts and dances, but that only those should be admitted who were dressed in English costumes. His Majesty set the example in all these changes.

# II

---

# THE SEARCH FOR ORDER—
## CONSTITUTIONALISM
## AND OLIGARCHY

WHILE MANY COUNTRIES of Europe turned to absolutist governments in the seventeenth century, the English reshaped their medieval institutions into a new kind of constitutional regime.

England inherited from the late Middle Ages a system of government based on cooperation between king and parliament. The king conducted affairs of state; parliament levied taxes and enacted laws. The relative powers of crown and parliament were not clearly defined, but the system worked well enough so long as no serious policy differences arose between the king's government and the wealthy, powerful classes represented in the House of Lords and the House of Commons.

Signs of strain began to appear under James I (1603–1625). Under Charles I (1625–1649) the religious and financial policies of the crown came under attack in the House of Commons from the first years of the reign. When parliament refused grants of taxes to support policies of which it disapproved, Charles turned to extra-parliamentary expedients. But this only embittered the situation still more. By 1642 the two sides had become so estranged that England drifted into a civil war.

Charles's adversaries entered the conflict with the declared purpose of defending the ancient rights and institutions of England. But, during the war, ideas much more radical than those of the parliamentary leaders emerged and found support. The leaders of parliament soon quarreled with the generals of the army that they had created. The war ended with the execution of the king, the dissolution of parliament, and the establishment of a military dictatorship under Oliver Cromwell.

When Cromwell died, Charles II (1660–1685) was welcomed back to England with almost universal support. However, the "Restoration" of 1660 was a restoration of parliament as well as of monarchy, and tensions between crown and parliament persisted under Charles II.

The final resolution of the situation came in the next reign. James II (1685–1688) converted to Catholicism and married a Catholic wife. The unwelcome prospect that a permanent Catholic line of succession to the throne would be established united royalist and parliamentary supporters in a common cause. They offered the throne to Prince William of Holland and his wife Mary (a daughter of James II). When William took power he promised to rule in cooperation with parliament and a Bill of Rights was enacted to define the future pattern of English government.

# CROWN AND PARLIAMENT

## Earlier Views

*Sir John Fortescue used the phrase "political and regal dominion" to describe the English system of limited monarchy as it had developed by the fifteenth century.*

### From Fortescue. *The Governance of England (1471)*

There are two kinds of kingdom, of which one is a lordship, called in Latin *dominium regale,* and the other is called *dominium politicum et regale.* And they differ in that the first king may rule his people by such laws as he makes himself. And therefore he may set upon them tallages and other impositions such as he wills himself without their assent. The second king may not rule his people by other laws than those that they assent to. And therefore he may set upon them no impositions without their own assent. . . .

But, blessed be God, this land is ruled under [the] better law; and therefore the people thereof are not in such penury nor thereby hurt in their persons but are wealthy and have all things necessary to the sustenance of nature. Wherefore they are mighty and able to resist the adversaries of this realm and to beat other realms that do or would do them wrong. Lo, this is the fruit of the *ius politicum et regale* under which we live.

From Sir John Fortescue, *The Governance of England,* ed. C. Plummer (Oxford: Clarendon Press, 1885), pp. 109–114.

*Queen Elizabeth I's last parliament was much aggrieved by royal grants of commercial monopolies. The queen won over the members with a gracious speech.*

### From *Elizabeth's "Golden Speech" (1601)*

Mr. Speaker,

You give me thanks; but I doubt me, that I have more cause to thank you all, than you me. And I charge you, to thank them of the

From H. Townshend, *Historical Collections* (London, 1680), pp. 264–266.

lower house from me: for had I not received a knowledge from you, I might have fallen into the lapse of an error, only for lack of true information.

Since I was queen, yet did I never put my pen unto any grant, but that, upon pretext and semblance made unto me, it was both good and beneficial to the subject in general; though a private profit to some of my ancient servants, who had deserved well at my hands. But the contrary being found by experience, I am exceedingly beholding to such subjects as would move the same at the first. . . . And I take it exceedingly gratefully from them; because it gives us to know that no respects or interests had moved them other than the minds they bear to suffer no diminution of our honour and our subjects' loves unto us. The zeal of which affection, tending to ease my people, and knit their hearts unto me, I embrace with a princely care; for (above all earthly treasure) I esteem my people's love, more than which I desire not to merit.

That my grants should be grievous to my people and oppressions privileged under colour of our patents, our kingly dignity shall not suffer it: yea, when I heard it, I could give no rest unto my thoughts until I had reformed it. . . .

To be a king and wear a crown is a thing more glorious to them that see it than it is pleasing to them that bear it: for myself, I was never so much enticed with the glorious name of a king, or royal authority of a queen, as delighted that God had made me his instrument to maintain his truth and glory and to defend this kingdom (as I said) from peril, dishonour, tyranny, and oppression.

There will never queen sit in my seat with more zeal to my country, care for my subjects, and that sooner with willingness will venture her life for your good and safety, than myself. For it is not my desire to live nor reign longer than my life and reign shall be for your good. And though you have had, and may have many princes, more mighty and wise, sitting in this state; yet you never had, or shall have any that will be more careful and loving.

*James I (1603–1625) liked to lecture his parliaments about the immensity of royal power. In 1610 he emphasized his role as "father" of the country.*

## From James I. *Speech to Parliament (1610)*

The state of Monarchy is the supremest thing upon earth; for kings are not only God's lieutenants upon earth and sit upon God's throne, but even by God himself they are called gods. There be three principal similitudes that illustrate the state of Monarchy: one taken out of the Word of God and the two other out of the grounds of policy and phi-

From *The Works of the Most High and Mighty Prince James* (London: James Montague, 1616), pp. 529–531.

losophy. In the Scriptures kings are called gods, and so their power after a certain relation compared to the Divine power. Kings are also compared to the fathers of families, for a king is truly *parens patriae* [father of his country], the politic father of his people. And lastly, kings are compared to the head of this microcosm of the body of man.

Kings are justly called gods for that they exercise a manner or resemblance of Divine power upon earth. . . .

As for the father of a family, they had of old under the Law of Nature *patriam potestatem* [paternal power], which was *potestatem vitae et necis* [power of life and death], over their children or family. . . . Now a father may dispose of his inheritance to his children at his pleasure, yea, even disinherit the eldest upon just occasions and prefer the youngest, according to his liking; make them beggars or rich at his pleasure; restrain or banish out of his presence, as he finds them give cause of offence, or restore them in favour again with the penitent sinner. So may the King deal with his subjects.

And lastly, as for the head of the natural body, the head hath the power of directing all the members of the body to that use which the judgment in the head thinks most convenient. . . . It is sedition in subjects to dispute what a king may do in the height of his power; but just kings will ever be willing to declare what they will do, if they will not incur the curse of God. I will not be content that my power be disputed upon, but I shall ever be willing to make the reason appear of all my doings, and rule my actions according to my laws.

*The House of Commons responded with complaints about extra-parliamentary taxation and legislation.*

## From *Petition of Grievances (1610)*

The policy and constitution of this your kingdom appropriates unto the Kings of this realm, with the assent of the Parliament, as well the sovereign power of making laws as that of taxing or imposing upon the subjects' goods or merchandises, wherein they have justly such a propriety as may not without their consent be altered or changed. . . .

We therefore, your Majesty's most humble Commons assembled in Parliament, following the example of this worthy care of our ancestors and out of a duty to those for whom we serve, finding that your Majesty, without advice or consent of Parliament, hath lately in time of peace set both greater impositions and far more in number than any your noble ancestors did ever in time of war, have with all humility presumed to present this most just and necessary petition unto your Majesty, That all impositions set without the assent of Parliament may be quite abolished and taken away. . . .

[Also] it is apparent both that proclamations have been of late years much more frequent than heretofore, and that they are extended not only to the liberty but also to the goods, inheritances, and livelihood of men: some of them tending to alter some points of the law and make them new. . . .

By reason whereof there is a general fear conceived and spread amongst your Majesty's people that proclamations will by degrees grow up and increase to the strength and nature of laws; whereby not only that ancient happiness, freedom, will be as much blemished (if not quite taken away) which their ancestors have so long enjoyed, but the same may also (in process of time) bring a new form of arbitrary government upon the realm.

We therefore, your Majesty's humble subjects the Commons in this Parliament assembled . . . have thought it to appertain to our duties, as well towards your Majesty as to those that have trusted and sent us to their service, to present unto your Majesty's view these fears and griefs of your people, and to become humble suitors unto your Majesty that thenceforth no fine or forfeiture of goods or other pecuniary or corporal punishment may be inflicted upon your subjects . . . unless they shall offend against some law or statute of this realm in force at the time of their offence committed.

# CIVIL WAR

## Two Modern Views

*Some historians think the English civil war was caused mainly by social and economic problems; others emphasize religious and constitutional issues.*

### From C. H. George. *Revolution*

At this point of analysis the Marxian hypothesis proves useful in explaining the division in the nature of English rulership, as it does later for the same split in French power. For if one looks very closely into the economic self-interest of the leading oligarchies of power, their conflicts help explain the loss of the medieval sense of alliance between the wellborn, the priests, and the rich. The increasing opportunities for wealth and power in business, farming, and the State, induced an increasing competition which placed great strain on the social structure and political mechanisms of old England. The traditional ruling barons used their status to grab trading and industrial "monopolies" from the Court; they were hated by excluded entrepreneurs from the towns, and in turn were themselves divided into peers who made out at Court and those "Country" aristocrats who did not. The lesser country aristocracy were also increasingly divided in their relations to one another and the government by the new economics of estate management and its relation to the cloth industry. Finally, the masses of the economically undistinguished in town and village found almost nothing they liked in the emerging order of things—the "drones" at Court, monopolists, enclosing landlords, rack-renters, price-riggers, usurers, and the like, meant unemployment, depopulation, dislocation, pauperism, and a generally terrifying rise in insecurities about the most basic needs of life. Bread and shelter and dignity of person were harder to come by in Stuart England than they had been in the England of the Plantagenets.

There were also religious issues which divided the ruling classes, though they were not of great importance. This was not a "Puritan" revolution. . . .

From Charles H. George, *Revolution: European Radicals from Hus to Lenin* (New York: Scott, Foresman, 1971), pp. 71–72.

## From J. H. Hexter. *Storm Over the Gentry*

And now one final word before we emerge at last from the storm over the gentry. The two scholars whose combined but clashing efforts raised that storm have at least one thing in common. It is the main purpose of both Professor Tawney and Professor Trevor-Roper to show that the seventeenth-century revolution in Britain was closely related to prior shifts in the personnel of the landowning classes and shifts in the dimensions of their estates, their incomes, and their economic prospects. That a revolution prepared by conflicts over Parliamentary privilege, royal prerogative, judicial independence, arbitrary arrest, power of taxation, and the rule of law in England, triggered by a religious upheaval in Scotland, and traversed by the complex lines of fission that separated Anglican from Puritan, courtier from country man, was indeed closely related to the matters that have especially engaged their attention, neither Tawney nor Trevor-Roper has proved. And what such masters of the materials of seventeenth-century history and of historical forensics cannot prove when they set their minds to it, is not likely ever to be proved. Yet the destruction left in the wake of the storm over the gentry need not enduringly depress us. At least one amateur of seventeenth-century history observes the havoc with a sense of relief, even of emancipation. He takes faith and freedom rather seriously himself; and he has not felt that in so doing he is necessarily eccentric. He is inclined to think that a good many men in the mid-seventeenth century took them seriously too. For such a one it is something of a relief to feel that the outcome of the storm over the gentry licenses him to turn part of his attention from rent rolls, estates accounts, and recognizances of debt to what a very great scholar [William Haller] calls *Liberty and Reformation in the Puritan Revolution.*

# Charles I. The Break with Parliament

*The House of Commons attacked the policies of Charles I (1625–1649) from the beginning of the reign.*

## From *Petition of Right (1628)*

To the King's Most Excellent Majesty

Humbly show unto our Sovereign Lord the King the Lords Spiritual and Temporal and Commons in Parliament assembled, that whereas it is declared and enacted by a statute made in the time of the reign of King Edward the First commonly called Statutum de Tallagio non Concedendo that no tallage or aid should be laid or levied by the King or his heirs in this realm without the good will and assent of the archbishops, bishops, earls, barons, knights, burgesses and other the freemen of the commonalty of this realm; and by authority of Parliament holden in the five and twentieth year of the reign of King Edward the Third it is declared and enacted, that from henceforth no person should be compelled to make any loans to the King against his will because such loans were against reason and the franchise of the land. . . .

Yet, nevertheless of late divers commissions directed to sundry commissioners in several counties with instructions have issued, by means whereof your people have been in divers places assembled and required to lend certain sums of money unto your Majesty. . . .

And where also by the statute called the Great Charter of the Liberties of England it is declared and enacted, that no freeman may be taken or imprisoned or be disseised of his freehold or liberties or his free customs or be outlawed or exiled or in any manner destroyed, but by the lawful judgement of his peers or by the law of the land.

And in the eight and twentieth year of the reign of King Edward the Third it was declared and enacted by authority of Parliament, that no man, of what estate or condition that he be, should be put out of his land or tenement, nor taken, nor imprisoned, nor disherited, nor put to death without being brought to answer by due process of law.

Nevertheless against the tenor of the said statutes and other the good laws and statutes of your realm to that end provided, divers of your subjects have of late been imprisoned without any cause shown. . . .

They do therefore humbly pray your most excellent Majesty that no man hereafter be compelled to make or yield any gift, loan, benevolence, tax or such like charge without common consent by Act of Parliament, and that none be called to make answer or take such oath or to give attendance or be confined or otherwise molested or disquieted concerning the same or for refusal thereof. And that no freeman in any such manner as is before mentioned be imprisoned or detained.

*Members of the House of Commons accused Charles's ministers of "popery" during a turbulent session in 1629.*

## Commons Protestation (1629)

This day, being the last day of the Assembly, as soon as prayers were ended the Speaker went into the Chair, and delivered the Kings com-

From W. Notestein and F. H. Relf, eds., *Commons Debates for 1629* (Minneapolis: University of Minnesota Press, 1921), pp. 101–106.

mand for the adjournment of the House until Tuesday sevennight following.

The House returned him answer, that it was not the office of the Speaker to deliver any such command unto them, but for the adjournment of the House it did properly belong unto themselves; and after they had settled some things they thought fit and convenient to be spoken of they would satisfy the King.

The Speaker told them that he had an express command from the King as soon as he had delivered his message to rise; and upon that he left the Chair, but was by force drawn to it again by Mr. Denzil Holles, son of the Earl of Clare, Mr. Valentine, and others. And Mr. Holles, notwithstanding the endeavour of Sir Thomas Edmondes, Sir Humphrey May, and other Privy Councellors to free the Speaker from the Chair, swore, Gods wounds, he should sit still until they pleased to rise. . . .

Sir John Eliot. God knows I now speak with all duty to the King. It is true the misfortunes we suffer are many, we know what discoveries have been made; how Arminianism creeps in and undermines us, and how Popery comes in upon us; they mask not in strange disguises, but expose themselves to the view of the world. In search whereof we have fixed our eyes not simply on the actors (the Jesuits and priests), but on their masters, they that are in authority, hence it comes we suffer. The fear of them makes these interruptions. You have seen prelates that are their abettors. That great Bishop of Winchester, we know what he hath done to favour them; this fear extends to some others that contract a fear of being discovered, and they draw from hence this jealousy. This is the Lord Treasurer, in whose person all evil is contracted. I find him acting and building on those grounds laid by his Master, the late great Duke of Buckingham, and his spirit is moving for these interruptions. And from this fear they break Parliaments lest Parliaments should break them. I find him the head of all that great party the Papists, and all Jesuits and priests derive from him their shelter and protection.

In this great question of Tonnage and Poundage, the instruments moved at his command and pleasure; he dismays our merchants, and invites strangers to come in to drive our trade, and to serve their own ends.

The Remonstrance was put to the question, but the Speaker refused to do it; and said he was otherwise commanded from the King.

Whereupon Mr. Selden spake as followeth:

"You, Mr. Speaker, say you dare not put the question which we command you; if you will not put it we must sit still, and thus we shall never be able to do any thing; they that come after you may say they have the Kings command not to do it. We sit here by commandment of the King, under the great Seal of England; and for you, you are by his Majesty (sitting in his royal chair before both Houses) appointed our Speaker, and yet now you refuse to do us the office and service of a Speaker."

Then they required Mr. Holles to read certain Articles as the Protestations of the House, which were jointly, as they were read, allowed with a loud *Yea* by the House. The effect of which Articles are as followeth:

First, Whosoever shall bring in innovation in Religion, or by favour or countenance, seek to extend or introduce Popery or Arminianism or other opinions disagreeing from the true and orthodox Church shall be reputed a capital enemy to this Kingdom and Commonwealth.

Secondly, Whosoever shall counsel or advise the taking and levying of the Subsidies of Tonnage and Poundage, not being granted by Parliament, or shall be an actor or instrument therein, shall be likewise reputed an innovator in the government, and a capital enemy to this Kingdom and Commonwealth.

Thirdly, If any merchant or person whatsoever shall voluntarily yield or pay the said subsidies of Tonnage and Poundage, not being granted by Parliament, he shall likewise be reputed a betrayer of the liberties of England and an enemy to the same.

These being read and allowed of, the House rose up after they had sitten down two hours.

The King hearing that the House continued to sit (notwithstanding his command for the adjourning thereof) sent a messenger for the serjeant with the mace, which being taken from the table there can be no further proceeding; but the serjeant was by the House stayed, and the key of the door taken from him, and given to a gentleman of the House to keep.

After this the King sent Maxwell with the black rod for the dissolution of Parliament, but being informed that neither he nor his message would be received by the House, the King grew into much rage and passion, and sent for the Captain of the Pensioners and Guard to force the door, but the rising of the House prevented the bloodshed that might have been spilt.

*After this episode Charles ruled without parliament for eleven years. Then a rebellion in Scotland forced him to summon a new parliament and to accept statutes guaranteeing a substantial role for parliament in future English government.*

## Acts of Parliament (1641)

### Act Against Dissolving the Long Parliament

Whereas great sums of money must of necessity be speedily advanced and provided for the relief of His Majesty's army and people in the northern parts of this realm . . . which credit cannot be obtained until such obstacles be first removed as are occasioned by fears, jealousies and apprehensions of divers His Majesty's loyal subjects, that this present Parliament may be adjourned, prorogued, or dissolved, before justice shall be duly executed upon delinquents, public grievances redressed, a firm peace between the two nations of England and Scotland concluded, and before sufficient provision be made for the re-payment of the said monies so to be raised . . . be it declared and enacted by the King, our Sovereign Lord, with the assent of the Lords and Commons in this present Parliament assembled, and by the authority of the same, that this present Parliament now assembled shall not be dissolved unless it be by Act of Parliament to be passed for that purpose. . . .

## Triennial Act

Whereas by the laws and statutes of this realm the Parliament ought to be holden at least once every year for the redress of grievances, but the appointment of the time and place for the holding thereof hath always belonged, as it ought, to His Majesty and his royal progenitors: and whereas it is by experience found that the not holding of Parliaments accordingly hath produced sundry and great mischiefs and inconveniences to the King's Majesty, the Church and Commonwealth; for the prevention of the like mischiefs and inconveniences in time to come:

Be it enacted by the King's Most Excellent Majesty, with the consent of the Lord's spiritual and temporal, and the Commons in this present Parliament assembled . . . that in case there be not a Parliament summoned by writ under the Great Seal of England, and assembled and held before the 10th of September, which shall be in the third year next after the last day of the last meeting and sitting in this present Parliament . . . and so from time to time, and in all times hereafter, if there shall not be a Parliament assembled and held before the 10th day of September, which shall be in the third year next after the last day of the last meeting and sitting in Parliament before the time assembled and held . . . that then in every such case as aforesaid, the Parliament shall assemble and be held in the usual place at Westminster. . . .

*Extra-parliamentary taxes that the king had levied were declared illegal. One of the most unpopular was "Ship Money."*

From S. R. Gardiner, ed., *The Constitutional Documents of the Puritan Revolution*, 2nd ed. (Oxford: Oxford University Press, 1899), pp. 144–145, 158–159.

## Abolition of Ship Money

Be it therefore declared and enacted by the King's Most Excellent Majesty and the Lords and the Commons in this present Parliament assembled, and by the authority of the same, that the said charge imposed upon the subject for the providing and furnishing of ships commonly called Ship-money ... and the said judgment given against the said John Hampden, were and are contrary to and against the laws and statutes of this realm, the right of property, the liberty of the subjects, former resolutions in Parliament, and the Petition of Right made in the third year of the reign of His Majesty that now is.

From S. R. Gardiner, ed., *The Constitutional Documents of the Puritan Revolution,* 2nd ed. (Oxford: Oxford University Press, 1899), p. 191.

*The Acts of 1641 did not settle the issue of ultimate sovereignty. Rather, the crisis worsened. A Scottish Presbyterian army was encamped in the northern counties of England. A Catholic rebellion broke out in Ireland. When parliament continued to attack royal policies and claimed a right to appoint the king's ministers, Charles tried to arrest five leading members of the House of Commons on charges of treason.*

## Case of the Five Members

And as his Majesty came through Westminster Hall, the Commanders, etc., that attended him made a lane on both sides the Hall (through which his Majesty passed and came up the stairs to the House of Commons) and stood before the guard of Pensioners and Halbedeers (who also attended the king's person) and, the door of the House of Commons being thrown open, his Majesty entered the House, and as he passed up towards the Chair he cast his eye on the right hand near the Bar of the House, where Mr. Pym used to sit; but his Majesty not seeing him there (knowing him well) went up to the Chair, and said, "By your leave, Mr. Speaker, I must borrow your chair a little." Whereupon the Speaker came out of the Chair and his Majesty stepped up into it; after he had stood in the Chair a while, casting his eye upon the members as they stood up uncovered, but could not discern any of the five members to be there, nor indeed were they easy to be discerned (had they been there) among so many bare faces all standing up together. Then his Majesty made this speech.

"Gentlemen, I am sorry for this occasion of coming unto you. Yesterday I sent a Serjeant at Arms upon a very important occasion, to apprehend some that by my command were accused of high treason; whereunto I did expect obedience and not a message. And I must declare unto you here that, albeit no king that ever was in England shall be more careful of your privileges, to maintain them to the uttermost

From John Rushworth, *Historical Collections* (London, 1721), Vol. 4, pp. 477–478.

of his power, than I shall be; yet you must know that in cases of treason no person hath a privilege. And therefore I am come to know if any of these persons that were accused are here. For I must tell you, Gentlemen, that so long as these persons that I have accused (for no light crime, but for treason) are here, I cannot expect that this House will be in the right way that I do heartily wish it. Therefore I am come to tell you that I must have them wheresoever I find them. Well, since I see all the birds are flown, I do expect from you that you shall send them unto me as soon as they return hither. But I assure you, on the word of a king, I never did intend any force, but shall proceed against them in a legal and fair way, for I never did intend any other.

"And now, since I cannot do what I came for, I think this no unfit occasion to repeat what I have said formerly, that whatsoever I have done in favor and to the good of my subjects, I do mean to maintain it.

"I will trouble you no more, but tell you I do expect as soon as they come to the House you will send them to me; otherwise I must take my own course to find them."

*After this abortive attempt the houses of parliament raised an army on their own authority, without royal consent, and civil war broke out.*

## Militia Ordinance

Whereas there hath been of late a most dangerous and desperate design upon the House of Commons, which we have just cause to believe to be an effect of the bloody counsels of Papists and other ill-affected persons, who have already raised a rebellion in the kingdom of Ireland; and by reason of many discoveries we cannot but fear they will proceed not only to stir up the like rebellion and insurrections in this kingdom of England, but also to back them with forces from abroad.

For the safety therefore of His Majesty's person, the Parliament and kingdom in this time of imminent danger.

It is ordained by the Lords and Commons now in Parliament assembled, that Henry Earl of Holland shall be Lieutenant of the County of Berks, Oliver Earl of Bolingbroke shall be Lieutenant of the County of Bedford, &c.

And shall severally and respectively have power to assemble and call together all and singular His Majesty's subjects, within the said several and respective counties and places, as well within liberties as without, that are meet and fit for the wars, and them to train and exercise and put in readiness, and them after their abilities and faculties well and sufficiently from time to time to cause to be arrayed and weaponed, and to take the muster of them in places most fit for that purpose.

From S. R. Gardiner, ed., *The Constitutional Documents of the Puritan Revolution*, 2nd ed. (Oxford: Oxford University Press, 1899), pp. 245–246.

# A "Royal Martyr"?

*By 1648 Charles was defeated. A majority of parliament intended to retain him as king, though with limited powers. But the army generals were determined to put Charles on trial and execute him. In December 1648, the generals "purged" parliament of all its more moderate members. The surviving remnant or "rump" then enacted these decrees.*

## Declaration of Sovereignty

(Resolved) That the commons of England, in parliament assembled, do declare that the people are, under God, the original of all just power. And do also declare, that the commons of England, in parliament assembled, being chosen by and representing the people have the supreme power in this nation. And do also declare, that whatsoever is enacted, or declared for law, by the commons in parliament assembled, hath the force of a law; and all the people of this nation are concluded thereby, although the consent of king, or house of peers, be not had thereunto.

From W. Cobbett, *Parliamentary History of England* (London, 1868), Vol. 3, col. 1257.

## Act Establishing a Court to Try the King

Whereas it is notorious that Charles Stuart, the now King of England, not content with the many encroachments which his predecessors had made upon the people in their rights and freedom, hath had a wicked design totally to subvert the ancient and fundamental laws and liberties of this nation, and in their place to introduce an arbitrary and tyrannical government, and that besides all other evil ways and means to bring his design to pass, he hath prosecuted it with fire and sword, . . . be it enacted and ordained by the [Lords] and Commons in Parliament assembled, and it is hereby enacted and ordained by the authority thereof, that the Earls of Kent, Nottingham, Pembroke, Denbigh and Mulgrave, the Lord Grey of Wark, Lord Chief Justice Rolle of the King's Bench, Lord Chief Justice St. John of the Common Pleas, and Lord Chief Baron Wylde, the Lord Fairfax, Lieutenant-General Cromwell. &c. [in all about 150], shall be and are hereby appointed and required to be Commissioners and Judges for the hearing, trying and judging of the said Charles Stuart.

From S. R. Gardiner, ed., *The Constitutional Documents of the Puritan Revolution*, 2nd ed. (Oxford: Oxford University Press, 1899), pp. 357–358.

*Charles prepared a speech in his own defense but was not allowed to deliver it at the trial.*

## Charles's Defense

Having already made my protestations, not only against the illegality of this pretended Court, but also, that no earthly power can justly call me (who am your King) in question as a delinquent, I would not any more open my mouth upon this occasion, more than to refer myself to what I have spoken, were I in this case alone concerned: but the duty I owe to God in the preservation of the true liberty of my people will not suffer me at this time to be silent: for, how can any free-born subject of England call life or anything he possesseth his own, if power without right daily make new, and abrogate the old fundamental laws of the land which I now take to be the present case? . . .

And admitting, but not granting, that the people of England's commission could grant your pretended power, I see nothing you can show for that; for certainly you never asked the question of the tenth man in the kingdom, and in this way you manifestly wrong even the poorest ploughman, if you demand not his free consent; nor can you pretend any colour for this your pretended commission, without the consent at least of the major part of every man in England of whatsoever quality or condition, which I am sure you never went about to seek, so far are you from having it. Thus you see that I speak not for my own right alone, as I am your King, but also for the true liberty of all my subjects, which consists, not in the power of government, but in living under such laws, such a government, as may give themselves the best assurance of their lives, and property of their goods; nor in this must or do I forget the privileges of both Houses of Parliament, which this day's proceedings do not only violate, but likewise occasion the greatest breach of their public faith that (I believe) ever was heard of. . . .

This I intended to speak in Westminster Hall on Monday, January 22, but against reason was hindered to show my reasons.

From John Rushworth, *Historical Collections* (London, 1721), Vol. 7, pp. 1403–1404.

## The Sentence

[He is author of the] unnatural, cruel, and bloody wars, and therein guilty of high treason, and of the murders, rapines, burnings, spoils, desolations, damage, and mischief to this nation acted and committed in the said war, and occasioned thereby. For all which treasons and crimes this Court doth adjudge that he, the said Charles Stuart, as a

From John Rushworth, *Historical Collections* (London, 1721), Vol. 7, p. 1425.

tyrant, traitor, murderer, and public enemy to the good people of this nation, shall be put to death by the severing of his head from his body.

[After the sentence was read], His Majesty then said, Will you hear me a word, Sir?

PRESIDENT OF THE COURT. Sir, you are not to be heard after the sentence.

HIS MAJESTY. No, Sir?

PRESIDENT. No, Sir, by your favour, Sir. Guards, withdraw your prisoner.

HIS MAJESTY. I may speak after sentence, by your favour, Sir, I may speak after sentence, ever. By your favour, hold—I am not suffered to speak, expect what justice other people may have. . . .

*On the scaffold Charles was finally allowed to speak.*

## Last Words

[As] for the people—truly I desire their liberty and freedom as much as anybody whosoever. But I must tell you that their liberty and freedom consists in having of government those laws by which their lives and goods may be most their own. It is not for having share in government. That is nothing pertaining to them. A subject and a sovereign are clean different things, and therefore, until they do that—I mean that you do put the people in that liberty as I say—certainly they will never enjoy themselves.

Sirs, it was for this that now I am come here. If I would have given way to an arbitrary way, for to have all laws changed according to the power of the sword, I needed not to have come here. And therefore I tell you (and I pray God it be not laid to your charge) that I am the martyr of the people.

From *England's Black Tribunal* (London, 1720).

# OLIVER CROMWELL

## War and Religion

### From *Letters and Speeches*

[*On army officers, 1645*]

I had rather have a plain russet-coated captain that knows what he fights for, and loves what he knows, than that which you call a gentleman and is nothing else. I honour a gentleman that is so indeed.

[*On the battle of Naseby, 1645*]

Sir, this is none other but the hand of God; and to Him alone belongs the glory, wherein none are to share with Him. The General [Fairfax] served you with all faithfulness and honour: and the best commendations I can give him is, that I dare say he attributes all to God, and would rather perish than assume to himself. Which is an honest and a thriving way, and yet as much for bravery may be given to him, in this action, as to a man.

[*On tolerance, 1645*]

Presbyterians, Independents, all had here the same spirit of faith and prayer; the same pretence and answer; they agree here, know no names of difference: pity it is it should be otherwise anywhere. All that believe, have the real unity, which is most glorious, because inward and spiritual, in the Body, and to the Head. As for being united in forms, commonly called Uniformity, every Christian will for peace-sake study and do, as far as conscience will permit; and from brethren, in things of the mind we look for no compulsion, but that of light and reason.

[*On Catholics, 1650*]

For that which you mention concerning liberty of conscience, I meddle not with any man's conscience. But if by liberty of conscience, you mean a liberty to exercise the Mass, I judge it best to use plain dealing, and to let you know, Where the Parliament of England have power, that will not be allowed of.

From Thomas Carlyle, ed., *The Letters and Speeches of Oliver Cromwell,* 3 vols. (New York: G. P. Putnam's Sons, 1904), Vol. 1, pp. 154, 204, 218, 468–469, Vol. 2, p. 15.

[*On the massacre at Drogheda (Ireland), 1649*]

... The enemy retreated, divers of them, into the Mill-Mount: a place very strong and of difficult access, being exceedingly high, having a good graft, and strongly palisadoed. The Governor, Sir Arthur Ashton, and divers considerable Officers being there, our men getting up to them, were ordered by me to put them all to the sword. And indeed, being in the heat of action, I forbade them to spare any that were in arms in the town, and, I think, that night they put to the sword about 2,000 men, divers of the officers and soldiers being fled over the Bridge into the other part of the Town, where about one hundred of them possessed St. Peter's church-steeple, some the west gate, and others a strong round tower next the gate called St. Sunday's. These being summoned to yield to mercy, refused, whereupon I ordered the steeple of St. Peter's Church to be fired, where one of them was heard to say in the midst of the flames: "God damn me, God confound me; I burn, I burn."

The next day, the other two towers were summoned, in one of which was about six or seven score; but they refused to yield themselves, and we knowing that hunger must compel them, set only good guards to secure them from running away until their stomachs were come down. From one of the said towers, notwithstanding their condition, they killled and wounded some of our men. When they submitted, their officers were knocked on the head, and every tenth man of the soldiers killed, and the rest shipped for the Barbadoes. The soldiers in the other tower were all spared, as to their lives only, and shipped likewise for the Barbadoes.

I am persuaded that this is a righteous judgment of God upon these barbarous wretches, who have imbrued their hands in so much innocent blood; and that it will tend to prevent the effusion of blood for the future, which are the satisfactory grounds to such actions, which otherwise cannot but work remorse and regret.

# Authority and Consent

*In 1653 Cromwell dismissed the remnant or "rump" of parliament and became, in effect, a military dictator. Although he experimented with several types of assemblies, he never created a representative body that could legitimize his power.*

## Dismissal of the Rump Parliament

Calling to Major-General Harrison, who was on the other side of the House, to come to him, he told him, that he judged the Parliament

From C. H. Firth, *The Memoirs of Edmund Ludlow* (Oxford: Oxford University Press, 1894), Vol. 1, pp. 352–354.

ripe for a dissolution, and this to be the time of doing it. The Major-General answered, as he since told me, "Sir, the work is very great and dangerous, therefore I desire you seriously to consider of it before you engage in it." "You say well," replied the General, and thereupon sat still for about a quarter of an hour; and then the question for passing the Bill being to be put, he said again to Major-General Harrison, "this is the time I must do it"; and suddenly standing up, made a speech, wherein he loaded the Parliament with the vilest reproaches, charging them not to have a heart to do any thing for the publick good, to have espoused the corrupt interest of Presbytery and the lawyers, who were the supporters of tyranny and oppression, accusing them of an intention to perpetuate themselves in power, had they not been forced to the passing of this Act, which he affirmed they designed never to observe, and thereupon told them, that the Lord had done with them, and had chosen other instruments for the carrying on his work that were more worthy. This he spoke with so much passion and discomposure of mind, as if he had been distracted. Sir Peter Wentworth stood up to answer him, and said, that this was the first time that ever he had heard such unbecoming language given to the Parliament, and that it was the more horrid in that it came from their servant, and their servant whom they had so highly trusted and obliged: but as he was going on, the General stept into the midst of the House, where continuing his distracted language, he said, "Come, come, I will put an end to your prating"; then walking up and down the House like a madman, and kicking the ground with his feet, he cried out, "You are no Parliament, I say you are no Parliament; I will put an end to your sitting; call them in, call them in": whereupon the serjeant attending the Parliament opened the doors, and Lieutenant-Colonel Worsley with two files of musqueteers entered the House; which Sir Henry Vane observing from his place, said aloud, "This is not honest, yea it is against morality and common honesty." Then Cromwell fell a railing at him, crying out with a loud voice, "O Sir Henry Vane, Sir Henry Vane, the lord deliver me from Sir Henry Vane." Then looking upon one of the members, he said, "There sits a drunkard"; and giving much reviling language to others, he commanded the mace to be taken away, saying, "What shall we do with this bauble? here, take it away." Having brought all into this disorder, Major-General Harrison went to the Speaker as he sat in the chair, and told him, that seeing things were reduced to this pass, it would not be convenient for him to remain there. The Speaker answered, that he would not come down unless he were forced. "Sir," said Harrison, "I will lend you my hand"; and thereupon putting his hand within his, the Speaker came down. Then Cromwell applied himself to the members of the House, who were in number between 80 and 100, and said to them, "It's you that have forced me to this, for I have sought the Lord night and day, that he would rather slay me than put me upon the doing of this work."

*The following account concerns a man who refused to pay a tax levied by Cromwell without parliament's consent.*

## From *Clarendon's History*

Maynard, who was of counsel with the prisoner, demanded his liberty with great confidence, both upon the illegality of the commitment, and the illegality of the imposition, as being laid without any lawful authority. The judges could not maintain or defend either, but enough declared what their sentence would be; and therefore the Protector's Attorney required a farther day to answer what had been urged. Before that day, Maynard was committed to the Tower, for presuming to question or make doubt of his authority; and the judges were sent for, and severely reprehended for suffering that license; and when they with all humility mentioned the law and *Magna Charta*, Cromwell told them, their *magna farta* should not control his actions, which he knew were for the safety of the commonwealth. He asked them who made them judges; [whether] they had any authority to sit there but what he gave them; and that if his authority were at an end, they knew well enough what would become of themselves; and therefore advised them to be more tender of that which could only preserve them; and so dismissed them with caution, that they should not suffer the lawyers to prate what it would not become them to hear.

From Lord Clarendon, *The History of the Rebellion and Civil Wars in England* (Oxford: Oxford University Press, 1839), Vol. 6, pp. 351–352.

*Ludlow was a parliamentary general who regarded Cromwell as a usurper.*

## From *Ludlow's Memoirs*

Then I drew near to the council-table, where Cromwell charged me with dispersing treasonable books in Ireland, and with endeavouring to render the officers of the army disaffected, by discoursing to them concerning new models of Government. I acknowledged that I had caused some papers to be dispersed in Ireland, but denied that they justly could be called treasonable. . . .

'You do well,' said he, 'to reflect on our fears . . . I now require you to give assurance not to act against the Government.' I desired to be excused in that particular, reminding him of the reasons I had formerly given him for my refusal, adding, that I was in his power, and that he might use me as he thought fit. 'Pray then,' said he, 'what is it

From C. H. Firth, *The Memoirs of Edmund Ludlow* (Oxford: Oxford University Press, 1894), Vol. 2, pp. 10–11.

that you would have? May not every man be as good as he will? What can you desire more than you have?' 'It were easy,' said I, 'to tell what we would have.' 'What is that, I pray?' said he. 'That which we fought for,' said I, 'that the nation might be governed by its own consent.' 'I am,' said he, 'as much for a government by consent as any man; but where shall we find that consent? Amongst the Prelatical, Presbyterian, Independent, Anabaptist, or Leveling Parties?' I answered, 'Amongst those of all sorts who had acted with fidelity and affection to the publick.'

## Cromwell's Deathbed Prayer

Lord, though I am a miserable and wretched creature, I am in Covenant with Thee through grace. And I may, I will, come to Thee for Thy People. Thou hast made me, though very unworthy, a mean instrument to do them some good, and Thee service; and many of them have set too high a value upon me, though others wish and would be glad of my death. Lord, however Thou do dispose of me, continue and go on to do good for them. Give them consistency of judgment, one heart, and mutual love. And go on to deliver them, and with the work of reformation; and make the Name of Christ glorious in the world. Teach those who look too much on Thy instruments to depend more upon Thyself. Pardon such as desire to trample upon the dust of a poor worm, for they are Thy people too. And pardon the folly of this short Prayer: Even for Jesus Christ's sake. And give us a good night, if it be Thy pleasure. Amen.

From Thomas Carlyle, ed., *The Letters and Speeches of Oliver Cromwell*, 3 vols. (New York: G. P. Putnam's Sons, 1904), Vol. 3, p. 217.

# A Royalist View

## From *Clarendon's History*

He was one of those men, *quos vituperare ne inimici quidem possunt, nisi ut simul laudent;* [whom his very enemies could not condemn without commending him at the same time:] for he could never have done half that mischief without great parts of courage, industry, and judgment. He must have had a wonderful understanding in the natures and humours of men, and as great a dexterity in applying them; who, from a private and obscure birth, (though of a good family,) without interest or estate, alliance or friendship, could raise himself to such a height, and compound and knead such opposite and contradictory tempers,

From Lord Clarendon, *The History of the Rebellion and Civil Wars in England* (Oxford: Oxford University Press, 1839), Vol. 6, pp. 349–350.

humours, and interests into a consistence, that contributed to his designs, and to their own destruction; whilst himself grew insensibly powerful enough to cut off those by whom he had climbed, in the instant that they projected to demolish their own building. What Velleius Paterculus said of Cinna may very justly be said of him, *ausum eum, quæ nemo auderet bonus; perfecisse, quæ a nullo, nisi fortissimo, perfici possent:* [he attempted those things which no good man durst have ventured on; and achieved those in which none but a valiant and great man could have succeeded.] Without doubt, no man with more wickedness ever attempted any thing, or brought to pass what he desired more wickedly, more in the face and contempt of religion, and moral honesty; yet wickedness as great as his could never have accomplished those trophies, without the assistance of a great spirit, an admirable circumspection and sagacity, and a most magnanimous resolution.

# SOCIETY AND RELIGION

## Social Legislation

*Many people came to resent the harsh enforcement of Puritan legislation by Cromwell's military government.*

### From *Acts and Ordinances*

Whereas the Acts of Stage-Playes, Interludes, and common Playes, condemned by ancient Heathens, and much less to be tolerated amongst Professors of the Christian Religion is the occasion of many and sundry great vices and disorders, tending to the high provocation of Gods wrath and displeasure . . . It is ordered and ordained . . . That all Stage-players and Players of Interludes and common Playes, are hereby declared to be, and are, and shall be taken to be Rogues, and punishable, within the Statutes of the thirty ninth year of the Reign of Queen Elizabeth, and the seventh year of the Reign of King James.

And because the prophanation of the Lords-day hath been heretofore greatly occasioned by May-Poles, (a Heathenish vanity, generally abused to superstition and wickedness.) The Lords and Commons do further Order and Ordain, That all and singular May-Poles, that are, or shall be erected, shall be taken down and removed. . . .

And be it further Enacted by the authority aforesaid, That if any man shall from and after the Four and twentieth day of June aforesaid, have the carnal knowledge of the body of any Virgin, unmaried Woman or Widow, every such man so offending . . . as also every such woman so offending . . . shall for every such offence be committed to the common Gaol, without Bail or Mainprize, there to continue for the space of three Months. . . .

And it is further Enacted and Declared, That every person and persons which upon the said Lords Day, days of Humiliation or Thanksgiving, shall be in any Tavern, Inn, Alehouse, Tobacco-house or Shop,

From C. H. Firth and R. S. Rait, eds., *Acts and Ordinances of the Interregnum* (London: His Majesty's Stationery Office, 1911), Vol. 1, p. 421, Vol. 2, pp. 385, 388, 861.

or Victualling-house (unless he lodge there, or be there upon some lawful or necessary occasion) ... and every person or persons which upon the said days shall be dancing, prophanely singing, drinking, or tipling in any Tavern, Inn, Alehouse, Victualling-house, or Tobacco-house or Shop, or shall harbor or entertain any person or persons so offending; or which shall grinde or cause to be ground in any Mill, any Corn or Grain upon any the said days, except in case of necessity, to be allowed by a Justice of the Peace, every such Offender shall forfeit and pay the sum of ten shillings for every such offence, to be levied as aforesaid.

Whereas the Publique Meetings and Assemblies of People together in divers parts of this Nation, under pretence of Matches for Cock-Fighting, are by experience found to tend many times to the disturbance of the Publique Peace, and are commonly accompanied with Gaming, Drinking, Swearing, Quarreling, and other dissolute Practices, to the Dishonor of God, and do often produce the ruine of Persons and their Families; For prevention thereof, Be it ordained by His Highness the Lord Protector, by and with the Advice and Consent of His Council, That from henceforth there shall be no Publique or Set-meetings or Assemblies of any persons within England or Wales, upon Matches made for Cock-Fighting. . . .

# Radical Dissent

*During the civil war period many new religious sects appeared. Sometimes they combined religious dissent with political radicalism. The "levellers" argued for egalitarian democracy.*

## From *The Free-Man's Freedom Vindicated*

Adam ... and ... Eve ... are the earthly original fountain of all and every particular and individual man and woman in the world since, who are, and were, by nature all equal and alike in power, dignity, authority, and majesty, none of them having by nature, dominion or magisterial power one over or above another; neither have they, or can they exercise any, but merely by institution or donation, or assumed by mutual consent and agreement. . . . And unnatural, irrational, sinful, wicked, unjust, devilish, and tyrannical, it is for any man whatsoever, spiritual or temporal, clergyman or layman, to appropriate and assume unto himself a power, authority, and jurisiction to rule, govern or reign over any sort of man in the world without their free consent, and

From John Lilbourne, *The Free-Mans Freedom Vindicated* (London, 1646).

whosover doth it . . . do thereby, as much as in them lies, endeavour to appropriate and assume unto themselves the office and sovereignty of God (who alone doth, and is to, rule by his will and pleasure) and to be like the Creator, which was the sin of the devils, not being content with their first station, would be like God, for which sin they were thrown down into Hell. . . .

## From *A Fiery Flying Roll*

Thus saith the Lord: Be wise now therefore, O ye Rulers, &c. Be instructed, &c. . . . Yea, kisse Beggers, Prisoners, warme them, feed them, cloathe them, money them, relieve them, release them, take them into your houses, don't serve them as dogs without doore, &c.

Owne them, they are flesh of your flesh, your owne brethren, your owne Sisters, every whit as good (and if I should stand in competition with you) in some degrees better than your selves.

Once more, I say, owne them; they are your self, make them one with you, or else go howling into hell; howle for the miseries that are coming upon you, howle.

The very shadow of levelling, sword-levelling, man-levelling, frighted you, (and who, like your selves, can blame you, because it shook your Kingdome?) but now the substantiality of levelling is coming.

The Eternall God, the mightly Leveller is comming, yea come, even at the door; and what will you do in that day. . . .

From Abiezer Coppe, *A Fiery Flying Roll* (London, 1649).

*The "Diggers" advocated a communistic utopia and began to dig up common lands to put their ideas into practice.*

## From Winstanley. *Letter to Lord Fairfax*

Our digging and ploughing upon George-hill in Surrey is not unknown to you, since you have seen some of our persons, and heard us speak in defence thereof: and we did receive mildness and moderation from you and your council of war both when some of us were at Whitehall before you and when you came in person to George-hill to view our works: we endeavour to lay open the bottom and intent of our business as much as can be, that none may be troubled with doubtful imaginations about us, but may be satisfied in the sincerity and universal righteousness of the work.

We understand that our digging upon that common is the talk of the whole land; some approving, some disowning, some are friends filled with love, and sees the work intends good to the nation, the

From *A Letter to the Lord Fairfax* (London: Giles Calvert, 1649).

peace whereof is that which we seek after; others are enemies filled with fury, and falsely report of us that we have intent to fortify ourselves, and afterwards to fight against others and take away their goods from them, which is a thing we abhor: and many other slanders we rejoice over, because we know ourselves clear, our endeavour being no otherwise but to improve the commons, and to cast off that oppression and outward bondage which the creation groans under, as much as in us lies, and to lift up and preserve the purity thereof.

And the truth is, experience shows us that in this work of community in the earth, and in the fruits of the earth, is seen plainly a pitched battle between the lamb and the dragon, between the spirit of love, humility, and righteousness, which is the lamb appearing in flesh; and the power of envy, pride, and unrighteousness, which is the dragon appearing in flesh, the latter power striving to hold the creation under slavery, and to lock and hide the glory thereof from man: the former power labouring to deliver the creation from slavery, to unfold the secrets of it to the sons of men, and so to manifest himself to be the great restorer of all things.

And these two powers strive in the heart of every single man, and make single men to strive in opposition one against the other, and these strivings will be till the dragon be cast out, and his judgment and downfall hastens apace, therefore let the righteous hearts wait with patience upon the Lord, to see what end he makes of all the confused hurley-burleys of the world. . . .

## A Digger Song (1649)

> You noble Diggers all, stand up now, stand up now,
> You noble Diggers all, stand up now,
>     The waste land to maintain, seeing Cavaliers by name
>     Your digging do disdain and persons all defame.
> Stand up now, stand up now.
>
> Your houses they pull down, stand up now, stand up now,
> Your houses they pull down, stand up now;
>     Your houses they pull down to fright poor men in town
>     But the gentry must come down, and the poor shall
>         wear the crown.
> Stand up now, Diggers all! . . .
>
> To conquer them by love, come in now, come in now,
> To conquer them by love, come in now;
>     To conquer them by love, as it does you behove,
>     For He is King above, no power is like to love.
> Glory *here*, Diggers all.

From C. H. Firth, *Clarke Papers* (London: Camden Society, 1891–1901), Vol. 2, p. 221.

*Parliamentary leaders and army generals had no sympathy with such extreme views. The Leveller and Digger movements were both suppressed.*

## Women's Roles

*This view of family structure comes from 1634.*

### From *Domesticall Duties*

But what if a man of lewd and beastly conditions, as a drunkard, a glutton, a profane swaggerer, an impious swearer and blasphemer, be married to a wise, sober, religious matron, must she account him her superior and worthy of an husband's honor?

Surely she must. For the evil quality and disposition of his heart and life doth not deprive a man of that civil honor which God hath given unto him. Though an husband in regard of evil qualities may carry the image of the devil, yet in regard of his place and office, he beareth the Image of God: so do Magistrates in the Commonwealth, Ministers in the Church, Parents and Masters in the Family. Note for our present purpose, the exhortation of St Peter to Christian wives which have infidel husbands, 'Be in subjection to them: let your conversation be in fear'. If Infidels carry not the devil's image and are not, so long as they are Infidels, vassals of Satan, who are? Yet wives must be subject to them.

From William Goudge, *Of Domesticall Duties* (London, 1634), p. 274.

*During the civil war some women were drawn into political activities. The following lines were written in a satirical vein by a Royalist.*

### From *Hudibras*

> Women, that were our first apostles,
> Without whose aid we'd all been lost else;
> Women, that left no stone unturned
> In which the Cause might be concerned;
> Brought in their children's spoons and whistles,
> To purchase swords, carbines and pistols. . . .
> What have they done, or what left undone,
> That might advance the Cause at London?
> Marched rank and file, with drum and ensign,
> T' entrench the City for defence in;
> Raised ramparts with their own soft hands,

From Samuel Butler, *Hudibras*, ed. T. R. Nash (New York: D. Appleton and Company, 1847), pp. 245–247.

To put the enemy to stands;
From ladies down to oyster-wenches
Laboured like pioneers in trenches,
Fell to their pickaxes and tools
And helped the men to dig like moles.
Have not the handmaids of the City
Chosen of their members a committee
For raising of a common purse
Out of their wages, to raise horse? . . .

*In 1649 John Lilbourne, the Leveller, and three companions were arrested. A large group of London women petitioned for their release.*

## Women's Petition (1649)

The Humble Petition of divers well-affected women of the Cities of London and Westminster, etc. Sheweth, that since we are assured of our creation in the image of God, and of an interest in Christ equal unto men, as also of a proportional share in the freedoms of this Commonwealth, we cannot but wonder and grieve that we should appear so despicable in your eyes, as to be thought unworthy to petition or represent our grievances to this honorable House.

Have we not an equal interest with the men of this Nation, in those liberties and securities contained in the Petition of Right, and the other good laws of the land? Are any of our lives, limbs, liberties or goods to be taken from us more than from men, but by due process of law and conviction of twelve sworn men of the neighborhood?

And can you imagine us to be so sottish or stupid, as not to perceive, or not to be sensible when daily those strong defenses of our peace and welfare are broken down, and trod under foot by force and arbitrary power?

Would you have us keep at home in our houses, when men of such faithfulness and integrity as the FOUR PRISONERS our friends in the Tower are fetched out of their beds, and forced from their houses by soldiers, to the affrighting and undoing of themselves, their wives, children and families? Are not our husbands, ourselves, our children and families by the same rule as liable to the like unjust cruelties as they? . . . Doth not the Petition of Right declare that no person ought to be judged by Law Martial (except in time of war) . . . ? And are we Christians and shall we sit still and keep at home, while such men as have borne continual testimony against the unjustice of all times, and unrighteousness of men, be picked out and delivered up to the slaughter . . . ?

No. . . . Let it be accounted folly, presumption . . . or whatsoever in

From J. O'Faolain and L. Martines, *Not in God's Image* (New York: Harper and Row, 1973), pp. 266–267.

us . . . we will never forsake them, nor ever cease to importune you . . . for justice . . . that we, our husbands, children, friends and servants may not be liable to be thus abused, violated and butchered at men's wills and pleasures. . . .

*Some radical religious groups held that women could be preachers and ministers. Mary Cary was associated with the "Fifth Monarchy" sect. George Fox was the founder of the Quakers.*

## From Mary Cary. *The New Jerusalem's Glory*

And if there be very few men that are thus furnished with the gift of the Spirit; how few are the women! Not but that there are many godly women, many who have indeed received the Spirit: but in how small a measure is it? how weak are they? and how unable to prophesie? for it is that that I am speaking of, which this text says they shall do; which yet we see not fulfilled. . . . But the time is coming when this promise shall be fulfilled, and the Saints shall be abundantly filled with the spirit; and not only men, but women shall prophesie; not only aged men, but young men; not only superiours, but inferiours; not only those that have University learning, but those that have it not; even servants and handmaids.

From M. Cary, *The New Jerusalem's Glory* (London, 1656), p. 238.

## From George Fox. *A Collection of . . . Epistles*

And there are Elder Women in the Truth, as well as Elder Men in the Truth; and these Women are to be teachers of good things; so they have an Office as well as the Men, for they have a Stewardship, and must give account of their Stewardship to the Lord, as well as the Men. Deborah was a judge; Miriam and Huldah were prophetesses; old Anna was a prophetess. . . . Mary Magdalene and the other Mary were the first preachers of Christ's Resurrection to the Disciples . . . they received the Command, and being sent, preached it: So is every Woman and Man to do, that sees him risen, and have the Command and Message. . . . And if the Unbelieving Husband is sanctified by the Believing Wife, then who is the Speaker, and who is the Hearer? Surely such a Woman is permitted to speak and to work the Works of God, and to make a Member in the Church; and then as an Elder, to oversee that they walk according to the Order of the Gospel.

What, are Women Priests? Yes, Women Priests. And can Men and Women offer Sacrifice without they wear the holy Garments? No:

From J. O'Faolain and L. Martines, *Not in God's Image* (New York: Harper and Row, 1973), pp. 265–266.

What are the holy Garments Men and Women must wear? ... the Priest's Surplice? Nay. ... It is the Righteousness of Christ ... this is the Royal Garment of the Royal Priesthood, which everyone must put on, Men and Women.

*The claim of women to play traditionally male roles in church affairs seemed to many people subversive of all established order and to deserve harsh punishment.*

## From *The Sufferings of the People Called Quakers*

The earliest account of the Sufferings of this People in Cambridge-shire bears Date in the same Month wherein Oliver Cromwell had assumed the Title of Protector, viz. in December, 1653, when Elizabeth Williams and Mary Fisher, the one about fifty and the other about thirty Years of Age, came from the North of England to Cambridge ... Complaint was forthwith made to William Pickering, then Mayor, that two Women were preaching: He sent a Constable for them and examined them ... He asked their Names: They replied, their Names were written in the Book of Life. He demanded their Husbands Names: They told him, they had no husband but Jesus Christ, and he sent them. Upon this the Mayor grew angry, called them Whores, and issued his Warrant to the Constable to whip them at the Market-Cross until the Blood ran down their Bodies ... The Executioner commanded them to put off their Clothes, which they refused. Then he stript them naked to the Waste, put their Arms into the Whipping-post, and executed the Mayor's Warrant far more cruelly than is usually done to the worst of malefactors, so that their Flesh was miserably cut and torn ... and in the midst of their Punishment they sang and rejoiced, saying, "The Lord be blessed, the Lord be praised, who hath thus honoured us, and strengthened us thus to suffer for his Name's sake."

From J. Besse, *A Collection of Sufferings of the People Called Quakers* (London, 1753), Vol. 1, pp. 84–85.

*Even in such troubled times many people lived tranquil lives; most females continued to carry out traditional roles; some young women made happy marriages. The letters of Dorothy Osborne, written from her father's country house, to William Temple, the young man she would eventually marry, remind us of this side of life.*

## From *Dorothy Osborne's Letters*

You ask me how I pass my time here. ... I rise in the morning reasonably early, and before I am ready I go round the house till I am weary

From E. A. Parry, ed., *Letters from Dorothy Osborne to Sir William Temple 1652–1654*, 3rd ed. (London: Griffith, Farren, Okeden and Welsh, 1888), pp. 37, 61, 80, 91, 100, 170, 290.

of that, and then into the garden till it grows too hot for me. About ten o'clock I think of making me ready, and when that's done I go into my father's chamber, from whence to dinner, where my cousin Molle and I sit in great state in a room, and at a table that would hold a great many more. . . . The heat of the day is spent in reading or working, and about six or seven o'clock I walk out into a common that lies hard by the house, where a great many young wenches keep sheep and cows, and sit in the shade singing of ballads. I go to them and compare their voices and beauties to some ancient shepherdesses that I have read of, and find a vast difference there; but, trust me, I think these are as innocent as those could be. I talk to them, and find they want nothing to make them the happiest people in the world but the knowledge that they are so. Most commonly when we are in the midst of our discourse, one looks about her, and spies her cows going into the corn, and then away they all run as if they had wings at their heels. . . . When I have supped, I go into the garden, and so to the side of a small river that runs by it, when I sit down and wish you were with me. . . .

I can assure you we are seldom without news, such as it is; and at this present we do abound with stories of my Lady Sunderland[1] and Mr. Smith; with what reverence he approaches her, and how like a gracious princess she receives him, that they say 'tis worth one's going twenty miles to see it. All our ladies are mightily pleased with the example, but I do not find that the men intend to follow it. . . .

Nothing can alter the resolution I have taken of settling my whole stock of happiness upon the affection of a person that is dear to me, whose kindness I shall infinitely prefer before any other consideration whatsoever, and I shall not blush to tell you that you have made the whole world besides so indifferent to me that, if I cannot be yours, they may dispose of me how they please. Henry Cromwell[2] will be as acceptable to me as any one else. . . .

*[The next letter refers to Oliver Cromwell's seizure of power in 1653.]*

But, bless me, what will become of us all now? Is not this a strange turn? . . . Tell me what I must think on't; whether it be better or worse, or whether you are at all concern'd in't? For if you are not I am not, only if I had been so wise as to have taken hold of the offer was made me by Henry Cromwell, I might have been in a fair way of preferment, for, sure, they will be greater now than ever. Is it true that Algernon

---

[1]Lady Sunderland was the sister of Algernon Sidney, a radical parliamentary leader.

[2]Dorothy's father had been a royalist commander, but this did not discourage Henry Cromwell, the second son of Oliver Cromwell, from becoming one of her suitors.

Sydney was so unwilling to leave the House, that the General was fain to take the pains to turn him out himself? Well, 'tis a pleasant world this. If Mr. Pim were alive again, I wonder what he would think of these proceedings, and whether this would appear so great a breach of the Privilege of Parliament as the demanding the 5 members? But I shall talk treason by and by if I do not look to myself. 'Tis safer talking of the orange-flower water you sent me. . . .

The less one knows of State affairs I find it is the better. My poor Lady Vavasour is carried to the Tower, and her great belly could not excuse her, because she was acquainted by somebody that there was a plot against the Protector, and did not discover it. She has told now all that was told her, but vows she will never say from whence she had it. . . .

I have sent you my picture because you wished for it; but, pray, let it not presume to disturb my Lady Sunderland's. Put it in some corner where no eyes may find it out but yours, to whom it is only intended. 'Tis not a very good one, but the best I shall ever have drawn of me; for, as my Lady says, my time for pictures is past, and therefore I have always refused to part with this, because I was sure the next would be a worse. There is a beauty in youth that every one has once in their lives; and I remember my mother used to say there was never anybody (that was not deformed) but were handsome, to some reasonable degree, once between fourteen and twenty. It must hang with the light on the left hand of it; and you may keep it if you please till I bring you the original.

[*Dorothy lived contentedly with her husband for forty years. But she experienced two misfortunes typical of the hazards of seventeenth-century life. Just before her marriage she suffered a severe attack of smallpox which left her face permanently disfigured. Later she had six children, but only one of them lived to maturity.*]

# FROM RESTORATION TO REVOLUTION: ENGLAND AND HOLLAND

## Restoration

### From *John Evelyn's Diary*

*May 29, 1666*  This day, his Majesty, Charles the Second came to London, after a sad and long exile and calamitous suffering both of the King and Church, being seventeen years. This was also his birthday, and with a triumph of above 20,000 horse and foot, brandishing their swords, and shouting with inexpressible joy; the ways strewed with flowers, the bells ringing, the streets hung with tapestry, fountains running with wine; the Mayor, Aldermen, and all the Companies, in their liveries, chains of gold, and banners; Lords and Nobles, clad in cloth of silver, gold, and velvet; the windows and balconies, all set with ladies; trumpets, music, and myriads of people flocking, even so far as from Rochester, so as they were seven hours in passing the city, even from two in the afternoon till nine at night.

## The "Glorious Revolution"

### From *John Evelyn's Diary*

*June 25, 1686*  Now his Majesty, beginning with Dr. Sharp and Tully, proceeded to silence and suspend divers excellent divines for preaching against Popery.

*November 29, 1686*  I went to hear the music of the Italians in the new chapel, now first opened publicly at Whitehall for the Popish Service.... The throne where the King and Queen sit is very glorious, in a closet above, just opposite to the altar. Here we saw the Bishop in his

From *Diary of John Evelyn*, ed. W. Bray, 4 vols. (London: Henry G. Bohn, 1862), Vol. 1, p. 365, Vol. 2, pp. 265, 273, 286, 291, 295–297.

mitre and rich copes, with six or seven Jesuits and others in rich copes, sumptuously habited, often taking off and putting on the Bishop's mitre, who sat in a chair with arms pontifically, was adored and censed by three Jesuits in their copes. . . . I could not have believed I should ever have seen such things in the King of England's palace, after it had pleased God to enlighten this nation; but our great sin has, for the present, eclipsed the blessing, which I hope He will in mercy and His good time restore to its purity.

*February 3, 1687*   Most of the great officers, both in the court and country, Lords and others, were dismissed, as they would not promise his Majesty their consent to the repeal of the test and penal statutes against Popish Recusants.

*June 10, 1688*   A young Prince born, which will cause disputes.
About two o'clock, we heard the Tower-ordnance discharged, and the bells ring for the birth of a Prince of Wales. This was very surprising, it having been universally given out that her Majesty did not look till the next month.

*September 30, 1688*   The Court in so extraordinary a consternation, on assurance of the Prince of Orange's intention to land, that the writs sent forth for a Parliament were recalled.

*October 7, 1688*   In the mean time, [the king] called over 5,000 Irish, and 4,000 Scots, and continued to remove Protestants and put in Papists at Portsmouth and other places of trust, and retained the Jesuits about him, increasing the universal discontent. It brought people to so desperate a pass, that they seemed passionately to long for and desire the landing of that Prince, whom they looked on to be their deliverer from Popish tyranny, praying incessantly for an east wind, which was said to be the only hindrance of his expedition with a numerous army ready to make a descent. To such a strange temper, and unheard-of in former times, was this poor nation reduced, and of which I was an eye-witness.

*November 5, 1688*   I went to London; heard the news of the Prince having landed at Torbay, coming with a fleet of near 700 sail, passing through the Channel with so favourable a wind, that our navy could not intercept, or molest them. . . .
These are the beginnings of sorrow, unless God in His mercy prevent it by some happy reconciliation of all dissensions among us. This, in all likelihood, nothing can effect except a free Parliament; but this we cannot hope to see, whilst there are any forces on either side. I pray God to protect and direct the King for the best and truest interest of his people!

*December 18, 1688*   I saw the King take barge to Gravesend at twelve o'clock—a sad sight! The Prince comes to St. James's and fills Whitehall with Dutch guards. A Council of Peers meet about an expedient to call a Parliament; adjourn to the House of Lords. The Chancellor, Earl of Peterborough, and divers others taken. . . .

All the world go to see the Prince at St. James's, where there is a great Court. There I saw him, and several of my acquaintance who came over with him. He is very stately, serious, and reserved.

# Patterns of Government

*Sir William Temple (Dorothy Osborne's husband) became ambassador to Holland and wrote this account of Dutch government.*

## From *Observations upon the United Provinces of the Netherlands*

In the first constitution of this government, after the revolt from Spain, all the power and rights of Prince William of Orange, as Governor of the Provinces, seem to have been carefully reserved. But those which remained inherent in the Sovereign, were devolved upon the assembly of the States-General, so as in them remained the power of making peace and war, and all foreign alliances, and of raising and coining of monies: in the Prince, the command of all land and sea forces, as Captain-general and Admiral, and thereby the disposition of all military commands, the power of pardoning the penalty of crimes, the chusing of magistrates upon the nomination of the towns; for they presented three to the Prince, who elected one out of that number. Originally the States-General were convoked by the council of State, where the Prince had the greatest influence: nor, since that change, have the States used to resolve any important matter without his advice. Besides all this, as the States-General represented the sovereignty, so did the Prince of Orange the dignity, of this State, by public guards, and the attendance of all military officers; by the application of all foreign ministers, and all pretenders at home; by the splendor of his court and magnificence of his expence; supported not only by the pensions and rights of his several charges and commands, but by a mighty patrimonial revenue in lands and sovereign principalities and lordships, as well in France, Germany, and Burgundy, as in thy several parts of the Seventeen Provinces; so as Prince Henry was used to answer some that would have flattered him into the designs of a more arbitrary power, that he had as much as any wise Prince would desire in that

State; since he wanted none indeed, besides that of punishing men, and raising money; whereas he had rather the envy of the first should lie upon the forms of the government, and he knew the other could never be supported, without the consent of the people, to that degree which was necessary for the defence of so small a State against so mighty Princes as their neighbours.

## From *The Bill of Rights (1689)*

Whereas the said late King James II having abdicated the government, and the throne being thereby vacant, his Highness the prince of Orange (whom it hath pleased Almighty God to make the glorious instrument of delivering this kingdom from popery and arbitrary power) did (by the advice of the lords spiritual and temporal, and diverse principal persons of the Commons) cause letters to be written to the lords spiritual and temporal, being Protestants, and other letters to the several counties, cities, universities, boroughs, and Cinque Ports, for the choosing of such persons to represent them, as were of right to be sent to parliament, to meet and sit at Westminster upon the two and twentieth day of January, in this year 1689, in order to such an establishment as that their religion, laws, and liberties might not again be in danger of being subverted; upon which letters elections have been accordingly made.

And thereupon the said lords spiritual and temporal and Commons, pursuant to their respective letters and elections, being now assembled in a full and free representation of this nation, taking into their most serious consideration the best means for attaining the ends aforesaid, do in the first place (as their ancestors in like case have usually done), for the vindication and assertion of their ancient rights and liberties, declare:

1. That the pretended power of suspending laws, or the execution of laws, by regal authority, without consent of parliament is illegal.

2. That the pretended power of dispensing with the laws, or the execution of law by regal authority, as it hath been assumed and exercised of late, is illegal.

3. That the commission for erecting the late court of commissioners for ecclesiastical causes, and all other commissions and courts of like nature, are illegal and pernicious.

4. That levying money for or to the use of the crown by pretense of prerogative, without grant of parliament, for longer time or in other manner than the same is or shall be granted, is illegal.

5. That it is the right of the subjects to petition the king, and all commitments and prosecutions for such petitioning are illegal.

From *The Statutes: Revised Edition* (London: Eyre and Spottiswoode, 1871), Vol. 2, pp. 10–12.

6. That the raising or keeping a standing army within the kingdom in time of peace, unless it be with consent of parliament, is against law.

7. That the subjects which are Protestants may have arms for their defense suitable to their conditions, and as allowed by law.

8. That election of members of parliament ought to be free.

9. That the freedom of speech, and debates or proceedings in parliament, ought not to be impeached or questioned in any court or place out of parliament.

10. That excessive bail ought not to be required, nor excessive fines imposed, nor cruel and unusual punishments inflicted.

11. That jurors ought to be duly impaneled and returned, and jurors which pass upon men in trials for high treason ought to be freeholders.

12. That all grants and promises of fines and forfeitures of particular persons before conviction are illegal and void.

13. And that for redress of all grievances, and for the amending, strengthening, and preserving of the laws, parliament ought to be held frequently.

And they do claim, demand, and insist upon all and singular the premises, as their undoubted rights and liberties. . . .

Having therefore an entire confidence that his said Highness the prince of Orange will perfect the deliverance so far advanced by him, and will still preserve them from the violation of their rights, which they have here asserted, and from all other attempt upon their religion, rights, and liberties:

The said lords spiritual and temporal, and commons, assembled at Westminster, do resolve that William and Mary, prince and princess of Orange, be, and be declared, king and queen of England, France, and Ireland. . . .

Upon which their said Majesties did accept the crown and royal dignity of the kingdoms of England, France, and Ireland, and the dominions thereunto belonging, according to the resolution and desire of the said lords and commons contained in the said declaration.

# III

# COMMERCE AND EMPIRE—THE WEST AND THE WORLD

*D*URING THE EIGHTEENTH *century a great expansion of European power in America and the Far East prepared the way for the eventual spread of Western ideas and institutions throughout the whole world. Among the old colonial powers Spain and Portugal continued to dominate South and Central America, and Spanish missionaries pushed northward into California. The Dutch retained their empire in the East Indies. England and France fought for power in North America and India, with England emerging as victor in both regions. A major development of the century was a vast increase in British wealth and power.*

*Different patterns of emigration, settlement, and relationships with indigenous peoples emerged in different parts of the world—often with decisive results for the future. Most of the settlers in North America were poor people seeking cheap or free land to farm. As they expanded westward they displaced or destroyed the native Indian populations. In India a small British aristocracy of merchants and bureaucrats came to dominate a vast native population. China retained a strong imperial government, quite capable of resisting foreign intrusions, but it seemed for a time that China might come under Western cultural influence through the influence of Jesuit missionaries. (The possibility ended when Pope Clement XI refused to accept any accommodation between Christianity and traditional Chinese culture.)*

*While the Western powers contended for overseas empires, a different kind of empire building was going on in Central and Eastern Europe. The old Holy Roman Empire exercised no effective government over all Germany, but the Hapsburg emperors retained a powerful state in Austria. Also, new powers were emerging in the region. Prussia, which would eventually provide a focus for German reunification, seized extensive territories from Austria. Russia expanded southward and eastward at the expense of the Turks. Finally Austria, Prussia, and Russia all added to their territorial empires by the dismemberment of Poland at the end of the century.*

# PATTERNS OF COMMERCE

## The Indies

*Simon de Pomponne, French ambassador to Holland, wrote an account of Dutch trade at the end of the seventeenth century.*

### From *Report of Simon de Pomponne*

Having struck down the Portuguese, the Dutch were for many years the sole masters of the Indies trade. The English had indeed established some trading posts after the Dutch example, but were content to confine their establishments to the lands of the princes with whom they traded, and their profits were moderate; hence the Dutch felt little rivalry with them. Since then the Royal [East India] Company which has been formed in London has grown larger; its ships now return in great numbers and with rich cargoes; and the trading establishments which it has already made in various places in the Indies, and to which it seeks to add, cause the Dutch much anxiety. This trade, to which both nations aspire equally, was the real cause of the war which broke out in 1653–1654 between Cromwell and the States General; it also caused the war between the Dutch and the king of England in 1665, which ended with the treaty of Breda; and in the future it will be a constant source of friction and disputes between them. . . .

Following their examples, the other nations of Europe have also wished to take their shares of the treasures and envisioned the profits to be made from sending their ships to such far-off places. The Danes made their efforts quite a while back and still maintain a fort and a colony on the Coromandel coast. The Swedes have also sent their ships to the Indies, but with repeated failure. Various French vessels have made the voyage at different times, but as these were only the endeavors of individuals or a small company too weak for great undertakings, even when they made a profit, it was not such as to arouse a desire in others to follow them upon such distant journeys. At the present time the East India Company [of France] which has been established under the authority of the King and enjoys his special protection, and in which His Majesty and individual persons have invested a considerable capital, gives hopes both great and legitimate, and perhaps not the least reason to anticipate its substantial success is that the Dutch have become concerned about its competition. . . .

The wares which they bring back are distributed upon their arrival among the cities of Holland, Zeeland and Friesland where the Company has its chambers. One part is sold publicly on days which are carefully publicized by notices distributed to the merchants of all Europe. The rest is kept in storehouses, and the Dutch shrewdly draw out only as much as other nations need, but not so much as would reduce prices.

The same cleverness which prompts this policy of restriction sometimes results in their selling wares in profusion. When another country, such as Spain or England, receives the same wares which they sell, the Dutch release their stores at a very low price, although they suffer considerable loss in doing so. They are satisfied if the loss is shared by those whose expansion in trade they fear, whom they compel to sell at the same price as themselves. They soon make good the loss which they suffer, and by discouraging competitors who do not have the same great wealth or the same head start as themselves, they remain the masters over a trade which others abandon to them.

This same desire to avoid a fall in the prices of their wares from the Indies as a result of oversupply has repeatedly caused them to throw overboard whole cargoes of pepper and to burn great piles of cinnamon, cloves and nutmeg which would have met the needs of all Europe for several years.

The profits from the sale of these goods provides the funds for refitting the ships which they send to the Indies. Apart from some cloth and brandy, they bring few wares from Europe. Trading there is conducted almost solely by means of gold, and as great quantities of gold are shipped there and little of it returns, we may say that with the passage of time the larger part of the gold which comes from America and Peru will pass on to the East Indies.

Once the Company has met its expenses, the remainder of its profits are distributed among those who share in its ownership. These dividends are greater or lesser depending on the value of the returning fleets and on whether or not wars, such as the last one with England [1665–1667], have prevented them from undertaking the voyage. During the time of my stay in Holland, I saw dividends issued amounting to 12 and 40 per cent upon the shares in the Company.

# The Atlantic

### From *The London Tradesman (1774)*

We export to *Jamaica*, and the rest of the Sugar Colonies, all manner of Materials for Wearing Appearel, Houshold Furniture of all Sorts, Cutlery and Haberdashery Wares, Watches, Jewels and Toys, *East-India* Goods of all sorts, some *French* Wines, *English* Malt Liquor, Linen Cloths of the Growth of *Scotland, Ireland*, and *Germany*, and our Ships generally touch in *Ireland* and take in Provisions, such as Beef, Pork, and Butter. The Returns from thence are Rums, Sugars, Cotton, Indigo, some fine Woods, such as Mahogany, Lignum Vitae, *&c*, and some Dying Woods, particularly Logwood.

We export to *New England, New York, Pensilvania*, and the rest of our Northern Colonies, the same Articles mentioned in the last Paragraph; in a word, every Article for the Use of Life, except Provisions: We have in return, Wood for Shipping, Corn and other Provisions for the Southern Colonies: Some Furs and Skins, Flax, Rice and Flax-Seed from the Provinces of *Georgia* and *Pensilvania*, and Fish from *New England*, for the *Levant* Market.

We export to *Virginia* and *Maryland* every Article mentioned before, and have in return Tobacco and Pig-Iron. From all the Colonies we have Ready Money, besides the Goods sent them, which they procure by the Illicite Trade carried on between our Island and the *Spanish Main*. . . .

To *Guinea* we send some Woollen and Linnen Goods, Cutlery Ware, Fire-Arms, Swords, Cutlasses, Toys of Glass and Metal, *&c.* and receive in return *Negroes* for the Use of our Plantations, Gold Dust, and Elephant's Teeth.

From R. Campbell, *The London Tradesman* (London, 1747), pp. 288–292.

*These instructions from a Rhode Island ship owner to a ship's captain describe a typical pattern of Atlantic trade.*

### Instructions to Captain Lindsay

Newport, June 10,1754

Captain David Lindsay:

Sir, You being master of our schooner *Sierra Leone*, and ready to sail, our orders are that you embrace the first opportunity of wind and weather and proceed for the coast of Africa, where, please God you arrive there, dispose of your cargo on the best terms you can for gold,

From George C. Mason, "The African Slave Trade in Colonial Times," *The American Historical Record*, Vol. 1 (1872), p. 340.

good slaves, etc. When you have finished your trade on the coast (which we desire may be with all convenient dispatch) proceed for the island of Barbados, where you will find letters lodged for you in the hands of Mr. Elias Merivielle, with whom consult in regard to the sale of your slaves, and if they will fetch 26 pounds sterling per head, round, you may dispose of them there, and invest the produce as per your orders you will find lodged there. But if you cannot sell at the above price, proceed without loss of time to St. Vincent, there dispose of your slaves if they will fetch nine hundred livres round in money, and in case you sell there, you may purchase as much cocoa as you can carry under your half deck and proceed to St. Eustatia, there load with molasses, and if an opportunity of freight, ship the remainder of the net proceeds in molasses to this port or to Boston. Should you find it will detain you long at St. Eustatia to accomplish this, send the schooner home as soon as possible after she is loaded and come passenger after you have finished your business. But if they will not fetch the above price, proceed directly for the island of Jamaica; there you will find orders lodged for you, and dispose of your slaves on the best terms you can and invest as much of the proceeds in good Muscovado sugar as will load you, in such casks as you can stow with most convenience, and proceed home with all possible dispatch. You are to have four out of 104 for your coast commission and five per cent for sale of your cargo in the West Indies and five per cent for the goods you purchase for return cargo. You are to have five slaves privilege, your chief mate two, if he can purchase them, and your second mate two.

We desire you will omit no opportunity of letting us hear from you. We wish you a good voyage and are your loving owners.

William Johnston & Co.

*This criticism of the slave trade is from an anonymous French author.*

## From *Diary of a Citizen*

As soon as the ships have lowered their anchors off the coast of Guinea, the price at which the captains have decided to buy the captives is announced to the Negroes who buy prisoners from various princes and sell them to the Europeans. Presents are sent to the sovereign who rules over that particular part of the coast, and permission to trade is given. Immediately the slaves are brought by inhuman brokers like so many victims dragged to a sacrifice. White men who covet

From Leon Apt and Robert E. Herzstein, *The Evolution of Western Society*, Vol. 2, Leon Apt, trans. (Hinsdale, Ill.: The Dryden Press, 1978), pp. 279–280. Copyright © 1978 by Leon Apt and Robert E. Herzstein. Reprinted by permission of Leon Apt.

that portion of the human race receive them in a little house they have erected on the shore, where they have entrenched themselves with two pieces of cannon and twenty guards. As soon as the bargain is concluded, the Negro is put in chains and led aboard the vessel, where he meets his fellow sufferers. Here sinister reflections come to his mind; everything shocks and frightens him and his uncertain destiny gives rise to the greatest anxiety. At first he is convinced that he is to serve as a repast to the white men, and the wine which the sailors drink confirms him in this cruel thought, for he imagines that this liquid is the blood of his fellows.

The vessel sets sail for the Antilles, and the Negroes are chained in a hold of the ship, a kind of lugubrious prison where the light of day does not penetrate, but into which air is introduced by means of a pump. Twice a day some disgusting food is distributed to them. Their consuming sorrow and the sad state to which they are reduced would make them commit suicide if they were not deprived of all the means for an attempt upon their lives. Without any kind of clothing it would be difficult to conceal from the watchful eyes of the sailors in charge any instrument apt to alleviate their despair. The fear of a revolt, such as sometimes happens on the voyage from Guinea, is the basis of a common concern and produces as many guards as there are men in the crew. The slightest noise or a secret conversation among two Negroes is punished with utmost severity. All in all, the voyage is made in a continuous state of alarm on the part of the white men, who fear a revolt, and in a cruel state of uncertainty on the part of the Negroes, who do not know the fate awaiting them.

When the vessel arrives at a port in the Antilles, they are taken to a warehouse where they are displayed, like any merchandise, to the eyes of buyers. The plantation owner pays according to the age, strength, and health of the Negro he is buying. He has him taken to his plantation, and there he is delivered to an overseer who then and there becomes his tormentor. In order to domesticate him, the Negro is granted a few days of rest in his new place, but soon he is given a hoe and a sickle and made to join a work gang. Then he ceases to wonder about his fate; he understands that only labor is demanded of him. But he does not know yet how excessive this labor will be. As a matter of fact, his work begins at dawn and does not end before nightfall; it is interrupted for only two hours at dinnertime. The food a full-grown Negro is given each week consists of two pounds of salt beef or cod and two pots of tapioca meal, amounting to about two pints of Paris. A Negro of twelve or thirteen years or under is given only one pot of meal and one pound of beef or cod. In place of food some planters give their Negroes the liberty of working for themselves every Saturday; others are even less generous and grant them this liberty only on Sundays and holidays.

*A Virginia settler defended slavery as a necessary economic fact of life.*

## From *Letter of Peter Fontaine (1757)*

As to your second query, if enslaving our fellow creatures be a practice agreeable to Christianity, it is answered in a great measure in many treatises at home, to which I refer you. I shall only mention something of our present state here.

Like Adam we are all apt to shift off the blame from ourselves and lay it upon others, how justly in our case you may judge. The Negroes are enslaved by the Negroes themselves before they are purchased by the masters of the ships who bring them here. It is to be sure at our choice whether we buy them or not, so this then is our crime, folly, or whatever you will please to call it. But, our Assembly, foreseeing the ill consequences of importing such numbers amongst us, hath often attempted to lay a duty upon them which would amount to a prohibition, such as ten or twenty pounds a head, but no governor dare pass such a law, having instructions to the contrary from the Board of Trade at home. By this means they are forced upon us, whether we will or will not. This plainly shows the African Company hath the advantage of the colonies, and may do as it pleases with the ministry. . . .

But to live in Virginia without slaves is morally impossible. Before our troubles, you could not hire a servant or slave for love or money, so that unless robust enough to cut wood, to go to mill, to work at the hoe, etc., you must starve, or board in some family where they both fleece and half starve you. There is no set price upon corn, wheat and provisions, so they take advantage of the necessities of strangers, who are thus obliged to purchase some slaves and land. . . . A common labourer, white or black, if you can be so much favoured as to hire one, is a shilling sterling or fifteen pence currency per day; a bungling carpenter two shillings or two shillings and sixpence per day; besides diet and lodging. That is, for a lazy fellow to get wood and water, £19. 16. 3, current per annum; add to this seven or eight pounds more and you have a slave for life.

From Ann Maury, ed., *Memoirs of a Huguenot Family* (New York: G. P. Putnam and Company, 1853), pp. 351–352.

# NORTH AMERICA—EXPLORATION AND IMMIGRATION

## Exploration

*Christian missionaries played a major role in exploring the North American continent. The French Jesuit Jacques Marquette and his party were the first Europeans to reach the Mississippi (1673).*

### From *Voyages of Marquette*

Here we are at Maskoutens. This Word may, in Algonquin, mean "the fire Nation,"—which, indeed, is the name given to this tribe. Here is the limit of the discoveries which the French have made, For they have not yet gone any farther. . . .

I took pleasure in observing the situation of this village. It is beautiful and very pleasing; For, from an Eminence upon which it is placed, one beholds on every side prairies, extending farther than the eye can see, interspersed with groves or with lofty trees. The soil is very fertile, and yields much indian corn. The savages gather quantities of plums and grapes, wherewith much wine could be made, if desired.

No sooner had we arrived than we, Monsieur Jollyet and I, assembled the elders together; and he told them that he was sent by Monsieur Our Governor to discover New countries, while I was sent by God to Illumine them with with the light of the holy Gospel. He told them that, moreover, The sovereign Master of our lives wished to be known by all the Nations; and that in obeying his will I feared not the death to which I exposed myself in voyages so perilous. He informed them that we needed two guides to show us the way; and We gave them a present, by it asking them to grant us the guides. To this they very Civilly consented; and they also spoke to us by means of a present, consisting of a Mat to serve us a bed during the whole of our voyage.

On the following day, the tenth of June, two Miamis who were given us as guides embarked with us, in the sight of a great crowd, who could not sufficiently express their astonishment at the sight of seven french-

From Reuben G. Thwaites, ed., *The Jesuit Relations and Allied Documents*, Vol. 59 (Cleveland, The Burrows Brothers Company, 1900), pp. 101–107.

men, alone and in two Canoes, daring to undertake so extraordinary and so hazardous an Expedition.

We knew that, at three leagues from Maskoutens, was a River which discharged into Missisipi. We knew also that the direction we were to follow in order to reach it was west-southwesterly. But the road is broken by so many swamps and small lakes that it is easy to lose one's way, especially as the River leading thither is so full of wild oats that it is difficult to find the Channel. For this reason we greatly needed our two guides, who safely Conducted us to a portage of 2,700 paces, and helped us to transport our Canoes to enter That river; after which they returned home, leaving us alone in this Unknown country, in the hands of providence.

Thus we left the Waters flowing to Quebeq, 4 or 500 Leagues from here, to float on Those that would thenceforward Take us through strange lands. Before embarking thereon, we Began all together a new devotion to the blessed Virgin Immaculate, which we practiced daily, addressing to her special prayers to place under her protection both our persons and the success of our voyage; and, after mutually encouraging one another, we entered our Canoes.

The River on which we embarked is called Meskousing [Wisconsin]. It is very wide; it has a sandy bottom, which forms various shoals that render its navigation very difficult. It is full of Islands Covered with Vines. On the banks one sees fertile land, diversified with woods, prairies, and Hills. There are oak, Walnut, and basswood trees; and another kind, whose branches are armed with long thorns. We saw there neither feathered game nor fish, but many deer, and a large number of cattle. Our Route lay to the southwest, and, after navigating about 30 leagues, we saw a spot presenting all the appearances of an iron mine; and, in fact, one of our party who had formerly seen such mines, assures us that The one which We found is very good and very rich. It is Covered with three feet of good soil, and is quite near a chain of rocks, the base of which is covered by very fine trees. After proceeding 40 leagues on This same route, we arrived at the mouth of our River; and, at 42 and a half degrees Of latitude, We safely entered Missisipi on The 17th of June, with a Joy that I cannot Express.

*Between March and July 1769, a Franciscan friar, Junipero Serra, journeyed from Loreto in Mexico to San Diego surveying sites for new missions.*

## From *Letters of Junipero Serra*

As to my own experiences, the whole trip was a very happy one without mishap or change in my health. As I crossed the frontier my leg and foot were in bad shape. But God was good to me. Every day I felt better, and kept up with the day's marches just as if nothing were wrong with me. At the present time the foot is as completely well as the other; but from the ankle half way up the leg, it is like the foot was before—one large wound, but without swelling or pain except a certain amount of itching. Anyway it is a matter of little moment.

I never went short of food or of anything; neither did the Indian neophytes with us; and so they all arrived in good health and in good condition. I kept a diary and I will send a copy of it to Your Reverence at the first opportunity. The missions, in the country we have seen, will be very good, as there is good land, good water supply, and neither here nor in much of the country behind us is it very rocky or choked with thorns. Mountains, yes, plenty of them—and big ones too—but of pure soil. The roads are both good and bad; the latter most of the time. But that's of no importance. Halfway on our journey or even before that, all the arroyos and valleys were dotted with groves of trees. Vines grow well and plentifully and in some places they are laden with grapes. In various arroyos along the way, and in the place where we are, besides the vines there are various kinds of Castilian roses. In short, it is a good country—distinctly better than Old California. . . .

[*Once arrived in San Diego, Serra planned a new chain of missions stretching north to San Francisco.*]

I can tell you that, over and above the ten new ones that are going to be founded—five between San Fernando de Velicatá and San Diego, and five, counting San Buenaventura, between San Diego and Monterey—and afterwards that of San Francisco, our Father, in his port, it is of vital interest that, as soon as possible, almost as many more should be founded, since from here to San Francisco at least two more are needed.

In the stretch between San Luis Obispo and San Buenaventura, three more are needed. They may be all on the Channel itself, to provide for that immense Indian population, living in so many large pueblos, and to prepare the way for the conversion of the islands facing them whose people maintain by means of their canoes a frequent intercourse with the inhabitants of the mainland, and vice versa; or at least two missions on the Channel and the third midway between the Channel and El Buchón, or San Luis. Furthermore, between San Buenaventura and San Gabriel, one, or better still, two. Another between San Gabriel and San Diego. The rest should be placed in the empty space between San Diego and Velicatá.

Such a plan would mean—over and above the great increase in Christianity, and an almost uninterrupted chain of missions covering an immense stretch of country, and that is our principal aim—that the religious who have to come would be saved the hardship of the ocean

From Antonine Tibesar, ed., *Writings of Junipero Serra*, Vol. 1 (Washington, D.C.: Academy of American Franciscan History, 1955). Reprinted by permission of Antonine Tibesar.

trip; the journey would be by land, and they would sleep at least every third day in a mission belonging to the College. This would make the whole trip easy, even if they had to go as far as San Francisco. There would only be the short sea crossing from San Blas to Loreto.

The gentleness and peaceful dispositions of the Indians are an incentive to travel by that route, and although in some parts they show signs of being troublesome, it is a matter of small importance; we all have to put up with some annoyance for God.

# Immigration

*In 1772 British customs officials interrogated Scottish emigrants about their motives for leaving home. The following responses are typical of many.*

## From *British Customs Report*

John Catanoch, aged fifty years, by trade a farmer, married, hath 4 children from 19 to 7 years old; resided last at Chabster in the parish of Rae in the county of Caithness, upon the estate of Mr. Alexander Nicolson, minister at Thurso, intends to go to Wilmington, North Carolina; left his own country because crops failed, bread became dear, the rents of his possession were raised from two to five pounds sterling; besides his pasture or common grounds were taken up by placing new tenants thereon, especially the grounds adjacent to his farm, which were the only grounds on which his cattle pastured. That this method of parking and placing tenants on the pasture grounds rendered his farm useless; his cattle died for want of grass, and his corn farm was unfit to support his family after paying the extravagant tack duty. That beside the rise of rents and scarcity of bread, the landlord exacted arbitrary and oppressive services, such as obliging the declarant to labor up his ground, cart, win, lead and stack his peats; mow, win and lead his hay, and cut his corn and lead it in the yard, which took up about 30 or 40 days of his servants and horses each year, without the least acknowledgment for it, and without victuals, save the men that mowed the hay who got their dinner only. That he was induced to emigrate by advices received from his friends in America; that provisions are extremely plenty and cheap, and the price of labour very high, so that people who are temperate and laborious have every chance of bettering their circumstances. Adds that the price of bread in the country he hath left is greatly enhanced by distilling, that being for so long a time so scarce and dear, and the price of cattle at the same time reduced full one half while the rents of lands have been

From *North Carolina Historical Review* 11 (1934), pp. 131–132. Reprinted by permission of the North Carolina Division of Archives and History.

raised nearly in the same proportion, all the smaller farms must inevitably be ruined.

Elizabeth McDonald, aged 29, unmarried, servant to James Duncan in Mointle in the parish of Farr in the county of Sutherland; intends to go to Wilmington in North Carolina, left her own country because several of her friends having gone to Carolina before her, had assured her that she would get much better service and greater encouragement in Carolina than in her own country.

John McBeath, aged 37, by trade a farmer and shoemaker, married; hath 5 children from 13 years to 9 months old. Resided last in Mault in the parish of Kildonnan in the county of Sutherland, upon the estate of Sutherland. Intends to go to Wilmington in North Carolina; left his own country because crops failed, he lost his cattle, the rent of his possession was raised, and bread had been long dear; he could get no employment at home whereby he could support himself and family, being unable to buy bread at the prices the factors on the estate of Sutherland and neighbouring estates exacted from him. That he was encouraged to emigrate by the accounts received from his own and his wife's friends already in America, assuring him that he would procure comfortable subsistence in that country for his wife and children, and that the price of labour was very high. He also assigns for the cause of bread being dear in his country that it is owing to the great quantities of corn consumed in brewing risquebah [whiskey].

*This account is by a Frenchman who lived for many years in America.*

# From J. Hector St. John de Crèvecoeur.
## What Is an American?

What attachment can a poor European emigrant have for a country where he had nothing? The knowledge of the language, the love of a few kindred as poor as himself, were the only cords that tied him: his country is now that which gives him land, bread, protection, and consequences: *Ubi panis ibi patria*, is the motto of all emigrants. What then is the American, this new man? He is either an European, or the descendant of an European, hence that strange mixture of blood, which you will find in no other country. I could point out to you a family whose grandfather was an Englishman, whose wife was Dutch, whose son married a French woman, and whose present four sons have now four wives of different nations. *He* is an American, who, leaving behind him all his ancient prejudices and manners, receives new ones from the new mode of life he has embraced, the new government he obeys, and the new rank he holds. He becomes an American

From M. G. J. de Crèvecouer, *Letters from an American Farmer* (Philadelphia: Matthew Carey, 1793), pp. 46–47.

by being received in the broad lap of our great *Alma Mater*. Here individuals of all nations are melted into a new race of men, whose labours and posterity will one day cause great changes in the world. Americans are the western pilgrims, who are carrying along with them that great mass of arts, sciences, vigour, and industry which began long since in the east; they will finish the great circle. The Americans were once scattered all over Europe; here they are incorporated into one of the finest systems of population which has ever appeared, and which will hereafter become distinct by the power of the different climates they inhabit. The American ought therefore to love this country much better than that wherein either he or his forefathers were born. Here the rewards of his industry follow with equal steps the progress of his labour; his labour is founded on the basis of nature, *self-interest*; can it want a stronger allurement? Wives and children, who before in vain demanded of him a morsel of bread, now, fat and frolicsome, gladly help their father to clear those fields whence exuberant crops are to arise to feed and to clothe them all; without any part being claimed, either by a despotic prince, a rich abbot, or a mighty lord. Here religion demands but little of him; a small voluntary salary to the minister and gratitude to God; can he refuse these? The American is a new man, who acts upon new principles; he must therefore entertain new ideas, and form new opinions. From involuntary idleness, servile dependence, penury, and useless labour, he has passed to toils of a very different nature, rewarded by ample subsistence.—This is an American. . . .

*The growth of settlements led to frequent clashes with native Indian population.*

## From *Remonstrance of the Pennsylvania Frontiersmen (1764)*

We, Matthew Smith and James Gibson, in behalf of ourselves and his Majesty's faithful and loyal subjects, the inhabitants of the frontier counties of Lancaster, York, Cumberland, Berks, and Northampton, humbly beg leave to remonstrate and lay before you the following grievances, which we submit to your wisdom for redress. . . .

During the late and present Indian War, the frontiers of this province had been repeatedly attacked and ravaged by skulking parties of the Indians, who have with the most savage cruelty murdered men, women, and children, without distinction, and have reduced near a thousand families to the most extreme distress. It grieves us to the very heart to see such of our frontier inhabitants as have escaped savage fury with the loss of their parents, their children, their wives or rela-

From *Minutes of the Provincial Council of Pennsylvania,* Vol. 9 (Philadelphia: J. Severns and Co., 1852), pp. 138–142.

tives, left destitute by the public, and exposed to the most cruel poverty and wretchedness, while upwards of an hundred and twenty of these savages, who are with great reason suspected of being guilty of these horrid barbarities, under the mask of friendship, have procured themselves to be taken under the protection of the government, with a view to elude the fury of the brave relatives of the murdered, and are now maintained at the public expense. Sone of these Indians now in the barracks of Philadelphia, are confessedly a part of the Wyalusing Indians, which tribe is now at war with us, and the others are the Moravian Indians, who, living with us under the cloak of friendship, carried on a correspondence with our known enemies on the Great Island. We cannot but observe, with sorrow and indignation, that some persons in this province are at pains to extenuate the barbarous cruelties practised by these savages on our murdered brethren and relatives, which are shocking to human nature, and must pierce every heart but that of the hardened perpetrators or their abettors; nor is it less distressing to hear others pleading that, although the Wyalusing Tribe is at war with us, yet that part of it which is under the protection of the government may be friendly to the English, and innocent. In what nation under the sun was it ever the custom that when a neighbouring nation took up arms, not an individual should be touched but only the persons that offered hostilities? Who ever proclaimed war with a part of a nation, and not with the whole? Had these Indians disapproved of the perfidy of their tribe, and been willing to cultivate and preserve friendship with us, why did they not give notice of the war before it happened, as it is known to be the result of long deliberations, and a preconcerted combination among them? Why did they not leave their tribe immediately and come among us before there was ground to suspect them, or war was actually waged with their tribe? No, they stayed amongst them, were privy to their murders and ravages, until we had destroyed their provisions, and when they could no longer subsist at home, they come, not as deserters, but as friends, to be maintained through the winter, that they may be able to scalp and butcher us in the spring. . . .

We humbly conceive that it is contrary to the maxims of good policy, and extremely dangerous to our frontiers, to suffer any Indians, of what tribe soever, to live within the inhabited parts of this province while we are engaged in an Indian war, as experience has taught us that they are all perfidious, and their claim to freedom and independency puts it in their power to act as spies, to entertain and give intelligence to our enemies, and to furnish them with provisions and warlike stores. To this fatal intercourse between our pretended friends and open enemies, we must ascribe the greatest of the ravages and murders that have been committed in the course of this and the last Indian war. We, therefore, pray that this grievance be taken under consideration and remedied. . . .

In the late Indian war this province, with others of his Majesty's colonies, gave rewards for Indian scalps, to encourage the seeking them in their own country as the most likely means of destroying or reducing them to reason, but no such encouragement has been given in this war, which has damped the spirits of many brave men who are willing to venture their lives in parties against the enemy. We, therefore, pray that public rewards may be proposed for Indian scalps, which may be adequate to the dangers attending enterprises of this nature. . . .

Signed on behalf of ourselves, and by appointment of a great number of the frontier inhabitants.

MATTHEW SMITH
JAMES GIBSON

# THE FAR EAST

## India—Wealth and Power

*After Robert Clive's victory over a Bengal army at the battle of Plassey (1757), the East India Company established its rule over large areas of India. Clive described some of the consequences in a speech to the House of Commons.*

### From Robert Clive. *Speech in Commons (1772)*

... Indostan was always an absolute despotic government. The inhabitants, especially of Bengal, in inferior stations, are servile, mean, submissive, and humble. In superior stations, they are luxurious, effeminate, tyrannical, treacherous, venal, cruel. The country of Bengal is called, by way of distinction, the paradise of the earth. It not only abounds with the necessaries of life to such a degree, as to furnish a great part of India with its superfluity, but it abounds in very curious and valuable manufactures, sufficient not only for its own use, but for the use of the whole globe. The silver of the west and the gold of the east have for many years been pouring into that country, and goods only have been sent out in return. This has added to the luxury and extravagance of Bengal.

From time immemorial it has been the custom of that country, for an inferior never to come into the presence of a superior without a present. It begins at the nabob, and ends at the lowest man that has an inferior. The nabob has told me, that the small presents he received amounted to 300,000l. a year; and I can believe him; because I know that I might have received as much during my last government. The Company's servants have ever been accustomed to receive presents. Even before we took part in the country troubles, when our possessions were very confined and limited, the governor and others used to receive presents; and I will take upon me to assert, that there has not been an officer commanding his Majesty's fleet; nor an officer commanding his Majesty's army; not a governor, not a member of council, not any other person, civil or military, in such a station as to have con-

From D. B. Horn and Mary Ransome, eds., *English Historical Documents, 1714–1783* (London: Eyre and Spottiswoode, 1957), pp. 809–811. Reprinted by permission of Methuen London.

*94*

nection with the country government, who has not received presents. With regard to Bengal, there they flow in abundance indeed. Let the House figure to itself a country consisting of 15 millions of inhabitants, a revenue of four millions sterling, and a trade in proportion. By progressive steps the Company have become sovereigns of that empire. Can it be supposed that their servants will refrain from advantages so obviously resulting from their situation? The Company's servants, however, have not been the authors of those acts of violence and oppression, of which it is the fashion to accuse them. Such crimes are committed by the natives of the country acting as their agents and for the most part without their knowledge. Those agents, and the banyans,[1] never desist, till, according to the ministerial phrase, they have dragged their masters into the kennel; and then the acts of violence begin. The passion for gain is as strong as the passion of love . . . Let us for a moment consider the nature of the education of a young man who goes to India. The advantages arising from the Company's service are now very generally known; and the great object of every man is to get his son appointed a writer to Bengal; which is usually at the age of 16. His parents and relations represent to him how certain he is of making a fortune; that my lord such a one, and my lord such a one, acquired so much money in such a time; and Mr. such a one, and Mr. such a one, so much in such a time. Thus are their principles corrupted at their very setting out, and as they generally go a good many together, they inflame one another's expectations to such a degree, in the course of the voyage, that they fix upon a period for their return before their arrival.

Let us now take a view of one of these writers arrived in Bengal, and not worth a groat. As soon as he lands, a banyan, worth perhaps 100,000l. desires he may have the honour of serving this young gentleman, at 4s. 6d. per month. The Company has provided chambers for him, but they are not good enough;—the banyan finds better. The young man takes a walk about the town, he observes that other writers, arrived only a year before him, live in splendid apartments or have houses of their own, ride upon fine prancing Arabian horses, and in palanqueens and chaises; that they keep seraglios, make entertainments, and treat with champaigne and claret. When he returns he tells the banyan what he has observed. The banyan assures him he may soon arrive at the same good fortune; he furnishes him with money; he is then at his mercy. The advantages of the banyan advance with the rank of his master, who in acquiring one fortune generally spends three. But this is not the worst of it: he is in a state of dependence under the banyan, who commits acts of violence and oppression, as his interest prompts him to, under the pretended sanction and authority of the Company's servant. Hence, Sir, arises the clamour against the

[1]Hindu traders or brokers.

English gentlemen in India. But look at them in a retired situation, when returned to England, when they are no longer nabobs and sovereigns of the east: see if there be any thing tyrannical in their disposition towards their inferiors: see if they are not good and humane masters: Are they not charitable? Are they not benevolent? Are they not generous? Are they not hospitable? If they are, thus far, not contemptible members of society, and if in all their dealings between man and man, their conduct is strictly honourable: if, in short, there has not yet been one character found amongst them sufficiently flagitious for Mr. Foote to exhibit on the theatre in the Haymarket, may we not conclude, that if they have erred, it has been because they were men, placed in situations subject to little or no controul?

*In 1773 the British government assumed a share of the responsibility for ruling British India. Lord North's "Regulating Act" set up a governor-general and council nominated partly by the East India Company and partly by the government.*

## From *Lord North's Regulating Act* (1773)

*An act for establishing certain regulations for the better management of the affairs of the* East India Company, *as well in* India *as in* Europe.

*Whereas the several powers and authorities granted by charters to the united company of merchants in* England *trading to the* East Indies *have been found, by experience, not to have sufficient force and efficacy to prevent various abuses which have prevailed in the government and administration of the affairs of the said united company, as well at home as in* India, *to the manifest injury of the publick credit, and of the commerical interests of the said company; and it is therefore become highly expedient that certain further regulations, better adapted to their present circumstances and condition, should be provided and established:* . . .

[The Act then lays down provisions governing the election of Directors.]

. . . *And, for the better management of the said united company's affairs in* India, be it further enacted by the authority aforesaid, That, for the government of the presidency of *Fort William* in *Bengal*, there shall be appointed a governor-general, and four counsellors; and that the whole civil and military government of the said presidency, and also the ordering, management and government of all the territorial acquisitions and revenues in the kingdoms of *Bengal, Bahar,* and *Orissa,* shall, during such time as the territorial acquisitions and revenues shall remain in the possession of the said united company, be, and are hereby vested in the said governor-general and council of the said

From D. B. Horn and Mary Ransome, eds., *English Historical Documents, 1714– 1783* (London: Eyre and Spottiswoode, 1957), pp. 811–812.

presidency of *Fort William* in *Bengal*, in like manner, to all intents and purposes whatsoever; as the same now are, or at any time heretofore might have been exercised by the president and council, or select committee, in the said kingdoms.

And be it enacted by the authority aforesaid, That in all cases whatsoever wherein any difference of opinion shall arise upon any question proposed in any consultation, the said governor-general and council shall be bound and concluded by the opinion and decision of the major part of those present: and if it shall happen that, by the death or removal, or by the absence, of any of the members of the said council, such governor-general and council shall happen to be equally divided; then, and in every such case, the said governor-general, or in his absence, the eldest counsellor present, shall have a casting voice, and his opinion shall be decisive and conclusive.

And be it further enacted by the authority aforesaid, That the said governor-general and council, or the major part of them, shall have, and they are hereby authorised to have, power of superintending and countrouling the government and management of the presidencies of *Madras, Bombay,* and *Bencoolen* respectively.

*Complaints of maladministration and corruption in India continued after North's Regulating Act.*

## From Edmund Burke. *Speech in Commons (1783)*

... Our conquest there, after twenty years, is as crude as it was the first day. The natives scarcely know what it is to see the grey head of an Englishman. Young men (boys almost) govern there, without society, and without sympathy with the natives. They have no more social habits with the people, than if they still resided in England; nor, indeed, any species of intercourse but that which is necessary to making a sudden fortune, with a view to a remote settlement. Animated with all the avarice of age, and all the impetuosity of youth, they roll in one after another; wave after wave; and there is nothing before the eyes of the natives but an endless, hopeless prospect of new flights of birds of prey and passage, with appetites continually renewing for a food that is continually wasting. Every rupee of profit made by an Englishman is lost for ever to India. With us are no retributory superstitions, by which a foundation of charity compensates, through ages, to the poor, for the rapine and injustice of a day. With us no pride erects stately monuments which repair the mischiefs which pride had produced, and

From D. B. Horn and Mary Ransome, eds., *English Historical Documents, 1714–1783* (London: Eyre and Spottiswoode, 1957), pp. 821–822 which adorn a country out of its own spoils. England has erected no churches, no hospitals, no palaces, no schools; England has built no bridges, made no high roads, cut no navigations, dug out no reservoirs. Every other conqueror of every other description has left some monument, either of state or beneficence, behind him. Were we to be driven out of India this day, nothing would remain, to tell that it had been possessed, during the inglorious period of our dominion, by any thing better than the ourang-outang or the tiger.

There is nothing in the boys we send to India worse, than in the boys whom we are whipping at school, or that we see trailing a pike, or bending over a desk at home. But as English youth in India drink the intoxicating draught of authority and dominion before their heads are able to bear it, and as they are full grown in fortune long before they are ripe in principle, neither nature nor reason have any opportunity to exert themselves for remedy of the excesses of their premature power. The consequences of their conduct, which in good minds, (and many of theirs are probably such,) might produce penitence or amendment, are unable to pursue the rapidity of their flight. Their prey is lodged in England; and the cries of India are given to seas and winds, to be blown about, in every breaking up of the monsoon, over a remote and unhearing ocean. In India all the vices operate by which sudden fortune is acquired; in England are often displayed by the same persons, the virtues which dispense hereditary wealth. Arrived in England, the destroyers of the nobility and gentry of a whole kingdom will find the best company in this nation, at a board of elegance and hospitality. Here the manufacturer and husbandman will bless the just and punctual hand that in India has torn the cloth from the loom, or wrested the scanty portion of rice and salt from the peasant of Bengal, or wrung from him the very opium in which he forgot his oppressions and his oppressor. They marry into your families; they enter into your senate; they ease your estates by loans; they raise their value by demand; they cherish and protect your relations which lie heavy on your patronage; and there is scarcely a house in the kingdom that does not feel some concern and interest, that makes all reform of our eastern government appear officious and disgusting; and, on the whole, a most discouraging attempt. In such an attempt you hurt those who are able to return kindness, or to resent injury. If you succeed, you save those who cannot so much as give you thanks. All these things show the difficulty of the work we have on hand; but they show its necessity too. Our Indian government is in its best state a grievance. It is necessary that the corrective should be uncommonly vigorous; and the work of men, sanguine, warm, and even impassioned in the cause. But it is an arduous thing to plead against abuses of a power which originates from your own country, and affects those whom we are used to consider as strangers. . . .

# China—Merchants and Missionaries

*A seventeenth-century Chinese official discussed the best ways of dealing with the Portuguese merchants at Macao.*

## From *Memorandum of Huo Ju-hsia*

There is a vast difference between peaceful trade and piratical raids. To be unable to pacify the barbarians who have come from afar to partake of our civilization is a reflection on our own goodness. To criticize them for their shortcomings while only too gladly collecting taxes from them is not what a righteous man should do. Without making any effort to observe their conduct or to differentiate the law-abiding from the evildoers, we indiscriminately call all of them bandits. Once we have branded them as bandits, we are obligated to exterminate them— only to see more of them come. Is this policy really wise?

What then should we do?

There are three measures we can take, each exclusive of the others. The best measure would be to govern them in the same manner as we govern our own people: to convert the territory they have occupied into a subprefecture and to place them under the jurisdictional control of duly appointed government officials. The next best measure would be to expel them and make sure that they never come back again. The worst measure would be to cut off their food supply, which would force them to revolt, and then use armed forces to exterminate them.

Ironical though it may seem, the best way to carry out the first measure is to threaten them with the adoption of the second. The government should issue an order addressed to them as follows: "It is reported by military authorities that you have gathered hooligans around yourselves and equipped yourselves with horses and cannons. We are afraid that some unprincipled, avaricious Chinese may incite you to illegal activities which will do harm to local communities. Therefore we have ordered the armed forces to demolish your dwellings and send you back to where you came from, to avoid trouble for all parties." While proclaiming this order, we should alert our troops for action. If the barbarians obey the order, they will leave China for other countries, where they are welcome to do whatever damage they choose. If on the other hand they beg us to let them stay and declare that they have no objection to being subject to Chinese administration, we should petition the imperial government to build cities for them and to govern them with Chinese officials. From then on they will be subject to Chinese law. This is the way barbarians have been transformed into Chinese; it is by far the best course to follow.

From *China in Transition, 1517–1911*, Dan J. Li, trans. (New York: Van Nostrand Reinhold Company, 1969), pp. 6–7. Reprinted by permission of Wadsworth Publishing Company.

Some people may say that once these barbarians are expelled from China, there will be no further disturbances on our frontier and our people will be much better off. How, they may ask, can expulsion be regarded as the second best course? I reply that to have confidence in the barbarians' natural goodness for our own defense is reflective of the greatness of the Son of Heaven, that to welcome all barbarians to partake of our civilization is indicative of the benign nature of the Celestial King, and that to provide food for our enemy so as to pacify the frontier betokens the farsightedness of a powerful nation. Besides, there are also practical considerations: (1) For the past hundred years the yearly revenue derived from overseas trade has been as large as the total revenue of a first-rate subprefecture, and this revenue has been used to support the armed forces in the Liangkwang region [Kwangtung and Kwangsi]. If this trade is cut off, where can we find funds to meet the military demand? (2) Macao has proved to be an effective buffer for Hsiangshan. Because it is there, pirates like Laowan, Tseng Yi-pen, and Ho Ya-pa have not dared to launch attacks, and the whole area has remained peaceful as a result. If the barbarians in Macao are expelled, Hsiangshan will have to defend itself. In short, to construct cities for them and to govern them with Chinese officials in accordance with the Chinese law will be the best policy to follow. It is best because it is a policy of kindness by which peace can be secured without great effort.

*The great emperor K'ang-hsi was at first friendly to the Jesuit missionaries working in China. By the end of the seventeenth century they had made many converts.*

## From *Decree of K'ang-hsi (1692)*

The Europeans are very quiet; they do not excite any disturbances in the provinces, they do no harm to anyone, they commit no crimes, and their doctrine has nothing in common with that of the false sects in the empire, nor has it any tendency to excite sedition . . . We decide therefore that all temples dedicated to the Lord of heaven, in whatever place they may be found, ought to be preserved, and that it may be permitted to all who wish to worship this God to enter these temples, offer him incense, and perform the ceremonies practised according to ancient custom by the Christians. Therefore let no one henceforth offer them any opposition.

*The Jesuits held that classical Chinese terms could be used to designate the Christian God. They also maintained that Confucian ceremonies were merely civil rites that Christians could attend and that Chinese ancestor worship was*

From S. Neill, *A History of Christian Missions* (Harmondsworth: Penguin Books, 1964), pp. 189–190.

*compatible with Christianity. Pope Clement XI condemned all these positions in 1715.*

## From *Decree of Pope Clement XI (1715)*

Pope Clement XI wishes to make the following facts permanently known to all the people in the world. . . .

I. The West calls *Deus* [God] the creator of Heaven, Earth, and everything in the universe. Since the word *Deus* does not sound right in the Chinese language, the Westerners in China and Chinese converts to Catholicism have used the term "Heavenly Lord" for many years. From now on such terms as "Heaven" and "Shang-ti" should not be used: *Deus* should be addressed as the Lord of Heaven, Earth, and everything in the universe. The tablet that bears the Chinese words "Reverence for Heaven" should not be allowed to hang inside a Catholic church and should be immediately taken down if already there.

II. The spring and autumn worship of Confucius, together with the worship of ancestors, is not allowed among Catholic converts. It is not allowed even though the converts appear in the ritual as bystanders, because to be a bystander in this ritual is as pagan as to participate in it actively.

III. Chinese officials and successful candidates in the metropolitan, provincial, or prefectural examinations, if they have been converted to Roman Catholicism, are not allowed to worship in Confucian temples on the first and fifteenth days of each month. The same prohibition is applicable to all the Chinese Catholics who, as officials, have recently arrived at their posts or who, as students, have recently passed the metropolitan, provincial, or prefectural examinations.

IV. No Chinese Catholics are allowed to worship ancestors in their familial temples.

V. Whether at home, in the cemetery, or during the time of a funeral, a Chinese Catholic is not allowed to perform the ritual of ancestor worship. He is not allowed to do so even if he is in company with non-Christians. Such a ritual is heathen in nature regardless of the circumstances.

Despite the above decisions, I have made it clear that other Chinese customs and traditions that can in no way be interpreted as heathen in nature should be allowed to continue among Chinese converts. The way the Chinese manage their households or govern their country should by no means be interfered with. As to exactly what customs should or should not be allowed to continue, the papal legate in China will make the necessary decisions. In the absence of the papal legate,

From *China in Transition, 1517–1911*, Dan. J. Li, trans. (New York: Van Nostrand Reinhold Company, 1969), pp. 22–24. Reprinted by permission of Wadsworth Publishing Company.

the responsibility of making such decisions should rest with the head of the China mission and the Bishop of China. In short, customs and traditions that are not contradictory to Roman Catholicism will be allowed, while those that are clearly contradictory to it will not be tolerated under any circumstances.

## From *Decree of K'ang-hsi (1721)*

Reading this proclamation, I have concluded that the Westerners are petty indeed. It is impossible to reason with them because they do not understand larger issues as we understand them in China. There is not a single Westerner versed in Chinese works, and their remarks are often incredible and ridiculous. To judge from this proclamation, their religion is no different from other small, bigoted sects of Buddhism or Taoism. I have never seen a document which contains so much nonsense. From now on, Westerners should not be allowed to preach in China, to avoid further trouble.

From *China in Transition, 1517–1911*, Dan J. Li, trans. (New York: Van Nostrand Reinhold Company, 1969), p. 22. Reprinted by permission of Wadsworth Publishing Company.

# THE OLD COLONIAL SYSTEM

## The System Defended

*During most of the eighteenth century it was taken for granted that the economic activities of colonies should be regulated in the interests of the mother country. Sir William Keith was governor of Pennsylvania from 1712 to 1726.*

### From Sir William Keith. *A Short Discourse*

When either by Conquest or Increase of People, foreign Provinces are possessed, and Colonies planted abroad, it is convenient, and often necessary, to substitute little dependant provincial Governments, whose People being infranchized, and made Partakers of the Liberties and Privileges belonging to the original Mother State, are justly bound by its Laws, and become subservient to its Interests, as the true End of their Incorporation.

Every Act of a dependant Provincial Government therefore ought to terminate in the Advantage of the Mother State, unto whom it owes its Being, and by whom it is protected in all its valuable Privileges: Hence it follows, that all advantageous Projects, or commercial Gains in any Colony, which are truly prejudicial to, and inconsistent with the Interest of the Mother State, must be understood to be illegal, and the Practice of them unwarrantable, because they contradict the End for which the Colony had a Being, and are incompatible with the Terms on which the People claim both Privilege and Protection....

It has ever been the Maxim of all polite Nations, to regulate their Government to the best Advantage of their trading Interest: wherefore it may be helpful to take a short View of the principal Benefits arising to *Great Britain* from the Trade of the Colonies.

1. The Colonies take off and consume above one sixth Part of the Woollen Manufactures exported from *Britain*, which is the chief Staple of *England*, and main support of the landed Interest.

2. They take off and consume more than double that Value in Linen and Callicoes, which is either the Product of *Britain* and *Ireland*,

From Sir William Keith, *A Collection of Papers and Other Tracts, Written Occasionally on Various Subjects* (London: J. Mechell, 1740), pp. 169–175.

or partly the profitable Returns made for that Product carried to foreign Countries.

3. The Luxury of the Colonies, which increases daily, consumes great Quantities of *English* manufactured Silk, Haberdashery, Houshold Furniture, and Trinkets of all Sorts; also a very considerable Value in *East-India* Goods.

4. A great Revenue is raised to the Crown of *Britain* by Returns made in the Produce of the Plantations, especially in Tobacco, which at the same time helps England to bring nearer to a Balance their unprofitable Trade with *France*.

5. Those Colonies promote the Interest and Trade of *Britain*, by a vast Increase of Shipping and Seamen, which enables them to carry great Quantities of Fish to *Spain, Portugal, Leghorn, &c.* Furs, Logwood, and Rice to *Holland*, whereby they help *Great Britain* considerably in the Ballance of Trade with those Countries.

6. If reasonably encouraged, the Colonies are now in a Condition to furnish *Britain* with as much of the following Commodities as it can demand, *viz.* Masting for the Navy, and all Sorts of Timber, Hemp, Flax, Pitch, Tar, Oil, Rosin, Copper Oar, with Pig and Bar Iron, by Means whereof the Ballance of Trade to *Russia* and the *Baltick* may be very much reduced in favour of *Great Britain*.

7. The Profits arising to all those Colonies by Trade is return'd in Bullion or other useful Effects to *Great Britain*, where the superflous Cash, and other Riches acquired in *America* must center, which is not one of the least Securities that *Britain* has to keep the Colonies always in due Subjection.

8. The Colonies upon the Main are the Granaries of *America*, and a necessary Support to the Sugar Plantations in the *West-Indies*, which could not subsist without them.

By this short View of Trade in general we may plainly understand, that those Colonies can be very beneficially employed both for *Great Britain* and themselves, without interfering with any of the staple Manufactures in *England*.

But in order to set this Point yet in a clearer Light, we will proceed to consider some of the obvious Regulations on the *American* Trade, for rendering the Colonies truly serviceable to *Great Britain*.

1. That all the Product of the Colonies, for which the Manufacture and Trade of *Britain* has a constant Demand, be enumerated among the Goods which by Law must be first transported to *Britain*, before they can be carried to any other Market.

2. That every valuable Merchandize to be found in the *English* Colonies, and but rarely any where else, and for which there is a constant Demand in *Europe*, shall also be enumerated, in order to assist *Great Britain* in the Ballance of Trade with other Countries.

3. That all Kinds of Woollen Manufactures for which the Colonies

have a Demand, shall continue to be brought from *Britain* only, and Linens from *Great Britain* and *Ireland*.

4. All other *European* Commodities to be carried to the Colonies, (Salt excepted) Entry thereof to be first made in *Britain*, before they can be transported to any of the *English* Colonies.

5. The Colonies to be absolutely restrained in their several Governments from laying any Manner of Duties on Shipping or Trade from *Europe*, or upon *European* Good transported from one Colony to another.

6. That the Acts of Parliament relating to the Trade and Government of the Colonies, be revised and collected into one distinct Body of Laws, for the Use of the Plantations, and such as Trade with them. . . .

Supposing these Things to be done, it will evidently follow, that the more extensive the Trade of the Colonies is, the greater will be the Advantages accruing to *Great Britain* therefrom; and consequently, that the Enlargement of the Colonies, and the Increase of their People, would still be an Addition to the national Strength. All smaller Improvements therefore pretended unto, and set up by lesser Societies for private Gain in *Great Britain*, or elsewhere, although they might have a just Pretence to bring some Sort of a publick Benefit along with them, yet if they shall appear to be more hurtful unto the much greater, and more national Concern of those useful trading Colonies, they ought in Justice to the Publick to be neglected in Favour of them; it being an unalterable Maxim, that a lesser publick Good must give place to a greater; and that it is of more Moment to maintain a greater, than a lesser Number of Subjects well employed to the Advantage of the State.

From what has been said of the Nature of Colonies, and the Restriction that ought to be laid on their Trade, it is plain that none of the *English* Plantations in *America* can with any Reason or good Sense pretend to claim an absolute legislative Power within themselves; so that let their several Constitutions be founded by antient Charters, Royal Patents, Customs by Prescription, or what other legal Authority you please; yet still they cannot be possessed of any rightful Capacity to contradict, or evade the true Intent and Force of any Act of Parliament, wherewith the Wisdom of *Great Britain* may think fit to affect them from Time to Time.

# The System Attacked

*During the year 1776 two different kinds of attack were launched against the "Old Colonial System." The grievances of the colonists finally led to the outbreak of the War of Independence in America. And in London Adam Smith published* The Wealth of Nations. *This work presented a powerful argument in favor of free enterprise and against all restrictions on trade.*

## From Adam Smith. *The Wealth of Nations*

. . . Every individual who employs his capital in the support of domestic industry, necessarily endeavours so to direct that industry, that its produce may be of the greatest possible value. . . .

But the annual revenue of every society is always precisely equal to the exchangeable value of the whole annual produce of its industry, or rather is precisely the same thing with that exchangeable value. As every individual, therefore, endeavors as much as he can both to employ his capital in the support of domestic industry, and so to direct that industry that its produce may be of the greatest value, every individual necessarily labours to render the annual revenue of the society as great as he can. He generally, indeed, neither intends to promote the public interest, nor knows how much he is promoting it. By preferring the support of domestic to that of foreign industry, he intends only his own security; and by directing that industry in such a manner as its produce may be of the greatest value, he intends only his own gain, and he is in this, as in many other cases, led by an invisible hand to promote an end which was no part of his intention. Nor is it always the worse for the society that it was no part of it. By pursuing his own interest he frequently promotes that of the society more effectually than when he really intends to promote it. I have never known much good done by those who affected to trade for the public good. It is an affectation, indeed, not very common among merchants, and very few words need be employed in dissuading them from it.

What is the species of domestic industry which his capital can employ, and of which the produce is likely to be of the greatest value, every individual, it is evident, can, in his local situation, judge much better than any statesman or lawgiver can do for him. The statesman, who should attempt to direct private people in what manner they ought to employ their capitals, would not only load himself with a most unnecessary attention, but assume an authority which could safely be trusted, not only to no single person, but to no council or senate whatever, and which would nowhere be so dangerous as in the hands of a man who had folly and presumption enough to fancy himself fit to exercise it.

The discovery of America, and that of a passage to the East Indies by the Cape of Good Hope, are the two greatest and most important events recorded in the history of mankind. Their consequences have

From Adam Smith, *An Enquiry into the Nature and Causes of the Wealth of Nations* (Oxford: Clarendon Press, 1880), Vol. 2, pp. 28–29, 208–213.

already been very great: but, in the short period of between two and three centuries which has elapsed since these discoveries were made, it is impossible that the whole extent of their consequences can have been seen. What benefits or what misfortunes to mankind may hereafter result from those great events, no human wisdom can foresee. By uniting, in some measure, the most distant parts of the world, by enabling them to relieve one another's wants, to increase one another's enjoyments, and to encourage one another's industry, their general tendency would seem to be beneficial. To the natives, however, both of the East and West Indies, all the commercial benefits which can have resulted from those events have been sunk and lost in the dreadful misfortunes which they have occasioned. These misfortunes, however, seem to have arisen rather from accident than from anything in the nature of those events themselves. At the particular time when these discoveries were made, the superiority of force happened to be so great on the side of the Europeans, that they were enabled to commit with impunity every sort of injustice in those remote countries. Hereafter, perhaps, the natives of those countries may grow stronger, or those of Europe may grow weaker, and the inhabitants of all the different quarters of the world may arrive at that equality of courage and force which, by inspiring mutual fear, can alone overawe the injustice of independent nations into some sort of respect for the rights of one another. But nothing seems more likely to establish this equality of force than that mutual communication of knowledge and of all sorts of improvements which an extensive commerce from all countries to all countries naturally, or rather necessarily, carries along with it.

In the meantime, one of the principal effects of those discoveries has been to raise the merchant system to a degree of splendour and glory which it could never otherwise have attained to. . . .

The countries which possess the colonies of America, and which trade directly to the East Indies, enjoy, indeed, the whole show and splendour of this great commerce. Other countries, however, not withstanding all the invidious restraints by which it is meant to exclude them, frequently enjoy a greater share of the real benefit of it. The colonies of Spain and Portugal, for example, give more real encouragement to the industry of other countries than to that of Spain and Portugal. In the single article of linen alone the consumption of those colonies amounts, it is said, but I do not pretend to warrant the quantity, to more than three millions sterling a year. But this great consumption is almost entirely supplied by France, Flanders, Holland, and Germany. Spain and Portugal furnish but a small part of it. The capital which supplies the colonies with this great quantity of linen is annually distributed among and furnishes a revenue to the inhabitants of those other countries. The profits of it only are spent in Spain and Portugal, where they help to support the sumptuous profusion of the merchants of Cadiz and Lisbon.

Even the regulations by which each nation endeavours to secure to itself the exclusive trade of its own colonies, are frequently more hurtful to the countries in favour of which they are established than to those against which they are established. The unjust oppression of the industry of other countries falls back, if I may say so, upon the heads of the oppressors, and crushes their industry more than it does that of those other countries. By those regulations, for example, the merchant of Hamburg must send the linen which he destines for the American market to London, and he must bring back from thence the tobacco which he destines for the German market; because he can neither send the one directly to America, nor bring back the other directly from thence. By this restraint he is probably obliged to sell the one somewhat cheaper, and to buy the other somewhat dearer than he otherwise might have done; and his profits are probably somewhat abridged by means of it. In this trade, however, between Hamburg and London, he certainly receives the returns of his capital much more quickly than he could possibly have done in the direct trade to America, even though we should suppose, what is by no means the case, that the payments of America were as punctual as those of London. In the trade, therefore, to which those regulations confine the merchant of Hamburg, his capital can keep in constant employment a much greater quantity of German industry than it possibly could have done in the trade from which he is excluded. Though the one employment, therefore, may to him perhaps be less profitable than the other, it cannot be less advantageous to his country. It is quite otherwise with the employment into which the monopoly naturally attracts, if I may say so, the capital of the London merchant. That employment may, perhaps, be more profitable to him than the greater part of other employments, but, on account of the slowness of the returns, it cannot be more advantageous to his country.

After all the unjust attempts, therefore, of every country in Europe to engross to itself the whole advantage of the trade of its own colonies, no country has yet been able to engross to itself anything but the expense of supporting in time of peace and of defending in time of war the oppressive authority which it assumes over them. The inconveniences resulting from the possession of its colonies, every country has engrossed to itself completely. The advantages resulting from their trade it has been obliged to share with many other countries.

At first sight, no doubt, the monopoly of the great commerce of America naturally seems to be an acquistion of the highest value. To the undiscerning eye of giddy ambition, it naturally presents itself amidst the confused scramble of politics and war as a very dazzling object to fight for. The dazzling splendour of the object, however, the immense greatness of the commerce, is the very quality which renders the monopoly of it hurtful. . . .

The private interests and passions of individuals naturally dispose them to turn their stock towards the employments which in ordinary cases are most advantageous to the society. . . . All the different regulations of the mercantile system necessarily derange more or less this natural and most advantageous distribution of stock. But those which concern the trade to America and the East Indies derange it, perhaps, more than any other; because the trade to those two great continents absorbs a greater quantity of stock than any two other branches of trade.

# EUROPEAN EMPIRES—GERMANY AND EASTERN EUROPE

## Germany

*At the end of the seventeenth century the political philosopher Samuel Pufendorf discussed the decentralization of power in the old Holy Roman Empire. (The dignity of Emperor was held by the Hapsburg rulers of Austria.)*

### From Samuel Pufendorf. *History of the Principal Kingdoms*

*Germany* has its particular Form of Government, the like is not to be met withal in any Kingdom of *Europe*, except that the ancient Form of Government in *France* came pretty near it. *Germany* acknowledges but one Supreme Head under the Title of the *Roman Emperor*; which Title did at first imply no more than the Sovereignty over the City of Rome, and the Protection of the Church of Rome and her Patrimony. This Dignity was first annexed to the *German* Empire by *Otto* I. but it is long ago since the Popes have robb'd the Kings of *Germany* of this Power, and only have left them the bare Name. But besides this, the Estates of *Germany* some of which have great and potent Countries in their possession, have a considerable share of the Sovereignty over their Subjects; and tho' they are Vassals of the Emperour and Empire, nevertheless they ought not to be consider'd as Subjects, or only as potent or rich Citizens in a Government; for they are actually possess'd of the supreme Jurisdiction in the Criminal Affairs; they have power to make Laws and to regulate Church Affairs, (which however is only to be understood of the Protestants) to dispose of the Revenues rising out of their Own Territories; to make Alliances, as well among themselves as with Foreign States, provided the same are not intended against the Emperour and Empire; they may build and maintain Fortresses and Armies of their own, Coin Money, and the like. This grandeur of the Estates, 'tis true, is a main obstacle that the Emperour cannot make himself absolute in the Empire, except it be in his Hereditary Countries.

Tho' it is certain that *Germany* within its self is so Potent, that it

From Samuel Pufendorf, *An Introduction to the History of the Principal Kingdoms and States of Europe* (London: Thomas Newborough and Martha Gilliflower, 1700), p. 303.

might be formidable to all its Neighbours, if its strength was well united and rightly employ'd; nevertheless this strong Body has also its infirmities, which weaken its strength, and slacken its vigour; its irregular Constitution of Government is one of the chief causes of its Distemper.

*Prussia's rise to power was made possible by the efficient army and bureaucracy built up under Frederick William I (1713–1740). (Count von Seckendorf was the Austrian ambassador in Berlin.)*

## From *Report of Count von Seckendorf*

It is certain that nowhere in the world one can see troops comparable with the Prussians for beauty, cleanliness, and order. Although in drill, training, and marching much is forced and affected, nearly everything is useful and efficient. Besides, it must be admitted that the army and the troops lack nothing that is needed. The soldiers number 70,000, and every regiment has at least a hundred more men than the normal figure. The Arsenal is superabundantly provided with field artillery and siege artillery, and only the teams are missing. Moreover, there is such an enormous store of powder, shot, and shells as if a great war was threatening. In Berlin and all about Brandenburg one sees as many troops moving as one saw in Vienna during the last war against the Turks. All this activity is directed by the King in person, and only by him. Besides, he looks after the whole public administration in all its branches with such care and thoroughness that not a thaler is spent unless he has given his signature. Those who do not see it cannot believe that there is any man in the world, however intelligent and able he may be, who can settle so many things personally in a single day as Frederick William the First, who works from 3 o'clock in the morning till 10, and spends the rest of the day in looking after and drilling his army. . . .

## From Isaac Isaacsohn. *History of the Prussian Civil Service*

The absolute subordination of the Civil Service from the highest to the lowest, their unquestioning obedience to the King, together with their absolute responsibility not only for their own actions, but also for those of their colleagues and their inferiors, created among them an extremely strong sense of professional honour, solidarity, and of professional pride. The influence of the nobility and of Society diminished unceasingly. The service of the King required undivided attention.

From *The Foundations of Germany*, J. Ellis Barker, trans. (New York: E. P. Dutton and Company, 1916), pp. 11, 15. Reprinted by permission of John Murray (Publishers) Ltd.

The King's uniform, which every Civil Servant had to wear when on duty, kept the feeling alive among them that they were the King's servants and had to represent the King's interests. The power of the officials and their independence, in case they were opposed by strong social influences, was increased by the fact that the officials were strangers in the districts in which they were employed, for Frederick William continued the policy of appointing only strangers to the district to official positions. . . .

*Frederick William's authoritarian temperament was in evidence in his relations with his son, the future Frederick II. This exchange of letters occurred when Frederick was sixteen.*

## From *Letters of Frederick II and Frederick William I*

Wusterhausen, September 11, 1728.

I have not ventured for a long time to present myself before my dear papa, partly because I was advised against it, but chiefly because I anticipated an even worse reception than usual and feared to vex my dear papa still further by the favor I have now to ask; so I have preferred to put it in writing.

I beg my dear papa that he will be kindly disposed toward me. I do assure him that after long examination of my conscience I do not find the slightest thing with which to reproach myself; but if, against my wish and will, I have vexed my dear papa, I hereby beg most humbly for forgiveness, and hope that my dear papa will give over the fearful hate which has appeared so plainly in his whole behavior and to which I cannot accustom myself. I have always thought hitherto that I had a kind father, but now I see the contrary. However, I will take courage and hope that my dear papa will think this all over and take me again into his favor. Meantime I assure him that I will never, my life long, willingly fail him, and in spite of his disfavor I am still, with most dutiful and childlike respect, my dear papa's

Most obedient and faithful servant and son,

FREDERICK

*Frederick William replied:*

A bad, obstinate boy, who does not love his father; for when one does one's best, and especially when one loves one's father, one does what he wishes not only when he is standing by but when he is not there to see. Moreover you know very well that I cannot stand an effeminate fellow who has no manly tastes, who cannot ride or shoot (to

From J. H. Robinson, *Readings in European History* (Boston: Ginn and Co., 1906), pp. 321–322.

his shame be it said!), is untidy about his person, and wears his hair curled like a fool instead of cutting it; and that I have condemned all these things a thousand times, and yet there is no sign of improvement. For the rest, haughty, offish as a country lout, conversing with none but a favored few instead of being affable and popular, grimacing like a fool, and never following my wishes out of love for me but only when forced into it, caring for nothing but to have his own way, and thinking nothing else is of any importance. This is my answer.

FREDERICK WILLIAM

*Frederick II (1740–1786) used the power accumulated by his father to increase the territory of Prussia. He began by attacking Silesia—in spite of a previous promise to respect Austrian territory.*

## From *Memoirs of Frederick II*

Posterity will perhaps see with surprise in these Memoirs accounts of treaties which have been concluded and broken. Although examples of broken treaties are common, the author of these Memoirs would require better reasons than precedent for explaining his conduct in breaking treaties. A sovereign must be guided by the interest of the State. In the following cases alliances may be broken:

(1) When one's ally does not fulfil his engagements;

(2) When one's ally wishes to deceive one, and when one cannot by any other means prevent him;

(3) When necessity (*force majeure*) compels one;

(4) When one lacks means to continue the war.

By the will of Fate wealth influences everything. Rulers are slaves of their means. To promote the interest of their State is a law to them, a law which is inviolable. If a ruler must be ready to sacrifice his life for the welfare of his subjects, he must be still more ready to sacrifice, for the benefit of his subjects, solemn engagements which he has undertaken if their observance would be harmful to his people. Cases of broken treaties may be encountered everywhere. It is not our intention to justify all breaches of treaty. Nevertheless, I venture to assert that there are cases when necessity or wisdom, prudence or consideration of the welfare of the people, oblige sovereigns to transgress because the violation of a treaty is often the only means whereby complete ruin can be avoided.

To me it seems clear and obvious that a private person must scrupulously observe the given word, even if he should have bound himself without sufficient thought. . . .

The word of a private person involves in misfortune only a single

From *The Foundations of Germany*, J. Ellis Barker, trans. (New York: E. P. Dutton, 1916), pp.35–36. Reprinted by permission of John Murray (Publishers) Ltd.

human being, while that of sovereigns can create calamities for entire nations. The question may therefore be summed up thus: Is it better that a nation should perish, or that a sovereign should break his treaty? Who can be stupid enough to hesitate in answering this question?

*Frederick took very seriously his duties as king.*

## From Frederick II. *Essay on the Forms of Government*

A sovereign must possess an exact and detailed knowledge of the strong and of the weak points of his country. He must be thoroughly acquainted with its resources, the character of the people, and the national commerce. . . .

Rulers should always remind themselves that they are men like the least of their subjects. The sovereign is the foremost judge, general, financier, and minister of his country, not merely for the sake of his prestige. Therefore, he should perform with care the duties connected with these offices. He is merely the principal servant of the State. Hence, he must act with honesty, wisdom, and complete disinterestedness in such a way that he can render an account of his stewardship to the citizens at any moment. Consequently, he is guilty if he wastes the money of the people, the taxes which they have paid, in luxury, pomp, and debauchery. He who should improve the morals of the people, be the guardian of the law, and improve their education should not pervert them by his bad example.

Princes, sovereigns, and king have not been given supreme authority in order to live in luxurious self-indulgence and debauchery. They have not been elevated by their fellow-men to enable them to strut about and to insult with their pride the simple-mannered, the poor, and the suffering. They have not been placed at the head of the State to keep around themselves a crowd of idle loafers whose uselessness drives them towards vice. The bad administration which may be found in monarchies springs from many different causes, but their principal cause lies in the character of the sovereign. A ruler addicted to women will become a tool of his mistresses and favourites, and these will abuse their power and commit wrongs of every kind, will protect vice, sell offices, and perpetrate every infamy. . . .

The sovereign is the representative of his State. He and his people form a single body. Ruler and ruled can be happy only if they are firmly united. The sovereign stands to his people in the same relation in which the head stands to the body. He must use his eyes and his brain for the whole community, and act on its behalf to the common advantage. If we wish to elevate monarchical above republican govern-

From *The Foundations of Germany*, J. Ellis Barker, trans. (New York: E. P. Dutton, 1916), pp. 22–23. Reprinted by permission of John Murray (Publishers) Ltd.

ment, the duty of sovereigns is clear. They must be active, hard-working, upright and honest, and concentrate all their strength upon filling their office worthily. That is my idea of the duties of sovereigns.

# Russia

*Catherine II (1762–1796), among her other achievements, added some 200,000 square miles to the territory of the Russian empire. The following letter was written by a perceptive French diplomat in Moscow.*

## From *Letter of Baron de Breteuil*

This princess seems to combine every kind of ambition in her person. Everything that may add luster to her reign will have some attraction for her. Science and the arts will be encouraged to flourish in the empire; projects useful for the domestic economy will be undertaken. She will endeavor to reform the administration of justice and to invigorate the laws; but her policies will be based on Machiavellianism; and I should not be suprised if in this field she rivals the king of Prussia. She will adopt the prejudices of her entourage regarding the superiority of her power and will endeavor to win respect not by the sincerity and probity of her actions but also by an ostentatious display of her strength. Haughty as she is, she will stubbornly pursue her undertakings and will rarely retrace a false step. Cunning and falsity appear to be vices in her character; woe to him who puts too much trust in her. Love affairs may become a stumbling block to her ambition and prove fatal for her peace of mind. This passionate princess, still held in check by the fear and consciousness of internal troubles, will know no restraint once she believes herself firmly established.

From *A Source Book for Russian History*, G. Vernadsky, trans. (New Haven: Yale University Press, 1972), Vol. 2. Reprinted by permission of Yale University Press.

*In 1767 Catherine summoned an assembly to draft a new code of laws for Russia and gave detailed instructions to the members about the principles they should apply. (The proposed code never went into effect.)*

## From Catherine II. *Proposals for a New Law Code*

6. Russia is an European State.

8. The Possessions of the Russian Empire extend upon the terrestrial Globe to 32 Degrees of Latitude, and to 165 of Longitude.

From *Documents of Catherine the Great*, W. F. Reddaway, trans. (Cambridge: Cambridge University Press, 1931), pp. 216, 219, 231, 241, 244, 258. Reprinted by permission of Cambridge University Press.

9. The Sovereign is absolute; for there is no other Authority but that which centers in his single Person, that can act with a Vigour proportionate to the Extent of such a vast Dominion.

10. The Extent of the Dominion requires an absolute Power to be vested in that Person who rules over it. It is expedient so to be, that the quick Dispatch of Affairs, sent from distant Parts, might make ample Amends for the Delay occasioned by the great Distance of the Places.

11. Every other Form of Government whatsoever would not only have been prejudicial to Russia, but would even have proved its entire Ruin.

12. Another Reason is; That it is better to be subject to the Laws under one Master, than to be subservient to many.

13. What is the true End of Monarchy? Not to deprive People of their natural Liberty; but to correct their Actions, in order to attain the *supreme Good*.

33. The Laws ought to be so framed, as to secure the Safety of every Citizen as much as possible.

34. The Equality of the Citizens consists in this; that they should all be subject to the same Laws.

38. A Man ought to form in his own Mind an exact and clear Idea of what Liberty is. *Liberty is the Right of doing whatsoever the Laws allow*: And if any one Citizen could do what the Laws forbid, there would be no more Liberty; because others would have an equal Power of doing the same.

39. The political Liberty of a Citizen is the Peace of Mind arising from the Consciousness, that every Individual enjoys his peculiar Safety; and in order that the People might attain this Liberty, the Laws ought to be so framed, that no one Citizen should stand in Fear of another; but that all of them should stand in Fear of the same Laws. . . .

123. The Usage of Torture is contrary to all the Dictates of Nature and Reason; even Mankind itself cries out against it, and demands loudly the total Abolition of it.

180. That Law, therefore, is highly beneficial to the Community where it is established, which ordains that every Man shall be judged by his Peers and Equals. For when the Fate of a Citizen is in Question, all Prejudices arising from the Difference of Rank or Fortune should be stifled; because they ought to have no Influence between the Judges and the Parties accused.

194. (1.) No Man ought to be looked upon as *guilty*, before he has received his judicial Sentence; nor can the Laws deprive him of *their* Protection, before it is proved that he has *forfeited all Right* to it. What Right therefore can Power give to any to inflict Punishment upon a Citizen at a Time, when it is yet dubious, whether he is *Innocent* or *guilty*?

269. It seems too, that the Method of exacting their Revenues, *newly*

invented by the Lords, diminishes both the *Inhabitants*, and the *Spirit of Agriculture* in Russia. Almost all the Villages are *heavily* taxed. The Lords, who seldom or never *reside* in their Villages, lay an Impost on every Head of one, two, and even five Rubles, without the least Regard to the *Means* by which their Peasants may be able to *raise* this Money.

270. It is highly necessary that the Law should prescribe a Rule to the Lords, for a more judicious Method of raising their Revenues; and oblige them to levy *such* a Tax, as *tends least* to separate the Peasant from his House and Family; this would be the Means by which Agriculture would become more extensive, and Population be more increased in the Empire.

*Although Catherine liked to use the liberal rhetoric of the Enlightenment, she actually ruled Russia with a heavy hand. Her government enacted this decree in the same year that the instructions about the proposed law code were issued.*

## From *Decree on Serfs (1767)*

The Governing Senate . . . has deemed it necessary to make known that the landlords' serfs and peasants . . . owe their landlords proper submission and absolute obedience in all matters, according to the laws that have been enacted from time immemorial by the autocratic forefathers of Her Imperial Majesty and which have not been repealed, and which provide that all persons who dare to incite serfs and peasants to disobey their landlords shall be arrested and taken to the nearest government office, there to be punished forthwith as disturbers of the public tranquility, according to the laws and without leniency. And should it so happen that even after the publication of the present decree of Her Imperial Majesty any serfs and peasants should cease to give the proper obedience to their landlords . . . and should make bold to submit unlawful petitions complaining of their landlords, and especially to petition Her Imperial Majesty personally, then both those who make the complaints and those who write up the petitions shall be punished by the knout and forthwith deported to Nerchinsk to penal servitude for life and shall be counted as part of the quota of recruits which their landlords must furnish to the army. And in order that people everywhere may know of the present decree, it shall be read in all the churches on Sundays and holy days for one month after it is received and therafter once every year during the great church festivals, lest anyone pretend ignorance.

From *A Source Book for Russian History*, G. Vernadsky, trans. (New Haven: Yale University Press, 1972), Vol. 2, pp. 453–454. Reprinted by permission of Yale University Press.

# Poland

*The territory of Poland was divided among its three great neighbors, Prussia, Austria, and Russia, in a series of partitions (1772, 1793, and 1795). The next readings illustrate the attitudes of the monarchs involved.*

## From *Memoirs of Frederick II*

The new claims [of Catherine II] aroused all Poland. The nobles of the kingdom appealed to the Turks for help. Soon a war broke out in which the Russians had only to show themselves to vanquish the Turks at every encounter. This war changed the whole political system of Europe. A new arena opened up and one would have had to be inept or stupidly dull not to have profited by such an advantageous chance. . . . I seized opportunity by the forelock and, by dint of negotiating and intriguing, I succeeded in indemnifying our monarchy for its past losses by incorporating Polish Prussia into my old provinces. This acquisition was one of the most important we could make because it joined Pomerania to East Prussia and, by making us masters of the Vistula, gained us the double advantage of being able to defend that kingdom [East Prussia] and of drawing considerable tolls from the Vistula, since all the trade of Poland goes by that river. This acquisition, which appears to me to mark an epoch in the annals of Prussia, seems remarkable enough for me to transmit the details of it to posterity, the more so as I was both witness and actor in the affair.

From *Oeuvres de Frédéric le Grand* (Berlin: Rodolphe Decker), Vol. 6, pp. 6–7.

## From *Letter of Maria Theresa*

. . . Firmian will receive a lengthy document with instructions in regard to our present situation, our engagements toward Russia, Prussia, and the Turks, but particularly in regard to this unfortunate partition of Poland, which is costing me ten years of my life. It will make plain the whole unhappy history of that affair. How many times have I refused to agree to it! But disaster after disaster heaped upon us by the Turks; misery, famine, and pestilence at home; no hope of assistance either from France or England, and the prospect of being left isolated and threatened with a war both with Russia and Prussia,—it was all these considerations that finally forced me to accede to that unhappy proposal, which will remain a blot on my whole reign. God grant that I be not held responsible for it in the other world! I confess that I cannot keep from talking about this affair. I have taken it so to heart that it poisons and imbitters all my days, which even without that are sad

From *Readings in European History*, J. H. Robinson, trans. (Boston: Ginn and Co., 1906), Vol. 2.

enough. I must stop writing about it at once, or I shall worry myself into the blackest melancholy. . . .

## From *Letter of Catherine II*

That dolt Hertzberg [a Prussian statesman] deserves a thorough thrashing all by himself; he has no more knowledge of history than my parrot. He has had the impudence to say that Russia, in taking possession of Polotsk, could produce no title to it; he should have said that Russia did not attach any importance to outdated titles. For Polotsk was given by Vladimir I to his eldest son Iziaslav. . . . The fifth son of Olgerd, Iagailo or Jacob, in 1386 became king of Poland and a convert to the Latin faith under the name of Wladyslaw, when he married Jadwiga, queen and heiress of Poland. Thus it was he who joined Lithuania to Poland, but the stupid, ignorant minister of state [Hertzberg] does not know this: arrogance makes him ignorant, stupid, and coarse like a Pomeranian ox. The underfed creature (the late king starved him, by his own admission) does not know that not only in Polotsk but in all of Lithuania up to the seventeenth century all governmental affairs were transacted in the Russian language; that all the Lithuanian archives are written in Russian; that all state documents were written with Russian characters in the Russian language; that all events since the creation of the world were dated according to the usage of our Greek church and that in this matter even the Greek ecclesiastical indictions were used as the authority—all this being proof that up to the seventeenth century the Greek religion was dominant not only in Polotsk but in all of Lithuania and had been the faith of the princes and grand dukes; that all the churches there, notably the cathedrals, have the altars placed eastward, according to the custom of the Eastern church. If you need still more evidence you have only to ask for it; it is not difficult to prove what is true. Moreover, Polotsk and Lithuania have been taken and retaken about twenty times, and no treaty was ever concluded without one side or the other claiming part or all of it, depending on circumstances. That fool of a minister of state deserves an even sounder thrashing for his ignorance regarding the peoples he lays claim to on behalf of his stupid master state [*Herresstaat*]. The silly ass!

From *A Source Book for Russian History*, G. Vernadsky, trans. (New Haven: Yale University Press, 1972), Vol. 2, pp. 409–410. Reprinted by permission of Yale University Press.

# IV

---

AGRICULTURE
**English and French Agriculture
Compared**
> From Arthur Young. *Travels
> During the Years 1787, 1788, and
> 1789 . . . in the Kingdom of
> France.*

**Feudal Practices in German
Agriculture**
> From William Jacob. *A View of the
> Agriculture . . . of Germany . . .*

**English Agriculture Transformed**
> 1743–1843 (A Poem)

**Agricultural Laborers**
> From David Davies. *The Case of
> Labourers in Husbandry . . .
> (1795)*

MANUFACTURE
**Spinning and Weaving**
> From William Radcliffe. *Origin of
> the . . . Power Loom (1828)*

**Families Disrupted**
> From *Observations . . . on the Loss
> of Woollen Spinning (c. 1794)*

**Machinery Attacked**
> *The Leeds Woollen Workers' Petition
> (1786)*

**Machinery Defended**
> *Letter from the Cloth Merchants of
> Leeds (1791)*

**The First Textile Factories**
> From Richard Guest. *Compendious
> History of the Cotton-Manufacture
> (1823)*

POPULATION
**Poverty and Population**
> From Thomas Malthus. *First Essay
> on Population (1798)*

# INDUSTRIAL REVOLUTION—AGRICULTURE, MANUFACTURE, POPULATION

*DURING THE EIGHTEENTH century major changes took place in agriculture and manufacturing. England was the home of both the agricultural and industrial revolutions, which introduced new technologies and altered traditional organizations of work. Farms were enclosed and expanded; crop rotations refertilized the soil and ended the uneconomical practice of leaving fields fallow; fertilizers were developed, which increased productivity even more. The new practices were accompanied by a dramatic social reorganization that pushed small farmers off their holdings and left them landless laborers, in the employ of large farmers, or in search of jobs in manufacturing. Indeed, agricultural changes in England helped provide the labor force for the new factories.*

*In manufacturing a parallel process occurred. New machinery and new ways of organizing industry produced goods more quickly and in greater quantity than ever before. At first, weavers brought the new looms into their cottages, but soon factories replaced households as the site of manufacturing activity. The new system not only displaced skilled workers, it disrupted family patterns of labor. Married women who had been able to combine work for wages with domestic chores found they had to choose between home and work. Skilled workers protested the impact of machinery on their livelihood, even destroying machines, but they were unable ultimately to prevail.*

*The increase in England's population of landless wage laborers, and in the poverty and size of the lower classes, turned attention to the causes and cures of poverty. Commentators debated the question of whether social reform was desirable or possible and whether the numbers of people looking for work in country and city should or could be controlled. Thomas Malthus enunciated his theory of population in the context of this debate.*

# AGRICULTURE

## English and French Agriculture Compared

*English publicists eager to applaud and promote agricultural innovation traveled to the Continent and sent home reports on the less productive arrangements they observed. Arthur Young (1741–1820) attributed the low return on French farming to two factors: the use of a system of field rotation that left one field fallow each year and the small size of farm holdings.*

### From Arthur Young. *Travels During the Years 1787, 1788, and 1789 . . . in the Kingdom of France*

If it be thought extraordinary, that land should sell for as high a price in France as in England, there are not wanted circumstances to explain the reason. In the first place, the net profit received from estates is greater. There are no poor rates in that kingdom; and tithes are much more moderately exacted. . . . Repairs, which form a considerable deduction with us, are a very trifling one with them. But what operates as much, or perhaps more than these circumstances, is the number of small properties. . . . All the savings which are made by the lower classes in France, are invested in land; but this practice is scarcely known in England, where such savings are usually lent on bond or mortgage, or invested in the public funds. This causes a competition for land in France, which, very fortunately for the prosperity of our agriculture, does not obtain here.

As to the next article, namely, the acreable produce of corn land, the difference will be found very great indeed; for in England, the average produce of wheat and rye . . . is twenty-four bushels, which form a vast superiority to eighteen, the produce of France; . . . But the superiority is greater than is apparent in the proportion of those two numbers; for the corn of England, as far as respects dressing, that is cleaning from dirt, chaff, seeds of weeds, &c. is as much better than that of France. . . . Another point, yet more important, is, that English wheat, in much the greater part of our kingdom, succeeds other preparatory crops; whereas the wheat of France follows almost universally a dead

From Arthur Young, *Travels During the Years 1787, 1788, and 1789 . . . in the Kingdom of France* (Dublin, 1793), Vol. 2, pp. 122–129, 381–384. (Spelling has been modernized by the editors.)

fallow, on which is spread all the dung of the farm. A circumstance, which ought to give a considerable superiority to the French crops, is that of climate, which in France is abundantly better for this production than in England; and, what is still of greater moment the spring corn of France, compared with that of England is absolutely contemptible, and indeed unworthy of any idea of comparison. While, therefore, in France, the wheat and rye are relied on for the almost total support of the farm and farmer, reason tells us, that the wheat ought to be much superior to the produce of a country, in which it does not bear an equally important part. Lastly, let me observe, that the soil of France is, for the most part, better than that of England. Under these various circumstances, for the average produce of the former, to be so much inferior, is truly remarkable. But eighteen bushels of wheat and rye, and miserable spring corn, afford as high a rent in France, as twenty-four in England, with the addition of our excellent spring corn; this forms a striking contrast, and leads to the explanation of the difference. It arises very much from the poverty of the French tenantry; for the political institutions and spirit of the government having, for a long series of ages, tended strongly to depress the lower classes, and favour the higher ones, the farmers in the greater part of France, are blended with the peasantry; and, in point of wealth, are hardly superior to the common labourers; these poor farmers are metayers, who find nothing towards stocking a farm but labour and implements; and being exceedingly miserable, there is rarely a sufficiency of the latter. The landlord is better able to provide live stock; but, engaged in a dissipated scene of life, probably at a distance from the farm, and being poor, like country gentlemen in many other parts of Europe, he stocks the farm not one penny beyond the most pressing necessity—from which system a wretched produce must unavoidably result. That the tenantry should generally be poor, will not be thought strange, when the taxes laid upon them are considered; their tallies and capitation are heavy in themselves; and the weight being increased by being laid arbitrarily, prosperity and good management are little more than signals for a higher assessment. Under such a system, a wealthy tenantry, on arable land, can hardly arise. With these farmers, and this management, it is not much to be wondered at that the land yields no more than eighteen bushels. Such a tenantry, contributing so little beyond the labour of their hands, are much more at the landlord's mercy than would be the case of wealthier farmers who, possessing a capital proper for their undertakings, are not content with a profit less than sufficient to return them a due interest for their money; and the consequence is, that the proprietor cannot have so high a rent as he had from metayers, who, possessing nothing are content merely to live. Thus, in the division of the gross produce, the landlord in France gets half, but in England, in the shape of rent only, from a fourth to a tenth; commonly from a fourth to a sixth. On some lands he gets a third, but that is uncommon. Nothing can be simpler than the principles upon which this is founded. The English tenant must not only be able to support himself and his family, but must be paid for his capital also,—upon which the future produce of the farm depends, as much as on the land itself.

The importance of a country producing twenty-five bushels per acre instead of eighteen, is prodigious; but it is an idle deception to speak of twenty-five, for the superiority of English spring corn (barley and oats) is doubly greater than that of wheat and rye, and would justify me in proportioning the corn products of England, in general, compared with those of France, as twenty-eight to eighteen; and I am well persuaded, that such a ratio would be no exaggeration. Ten millions of acres produce more corn than fifteen millions; consequently a territory of one hundred millions of acres more than equals another of one hundred and fifty millions. It is from such facts that we must seek for an explanation of the power of England, which has ventured to measure itself with that of a country so much more populous, extensive, and more favoured, by nature as France really is; and it is a lesson to all governments whatever, that if they would be powerful, they must encourage the only real and permanent basis of power, AGRICULTURE. By enlarging the quantity of the products of land in a nation, all those advantages flow which have been attributed to a great population; but which ought, with much more truth, to have been assigned to a great consumption; since it is not the mere number of people, but their ease and welfare, which constitute national prosperity. . . . In order the better to understand how the great difference of product between French and English crops may affect the agriculture of the two kingdoms it will be proper to observe, that the farmer in England will reap as much from his course of crops, in which wheat and rye occur but seldom, as the Frenchman can from his, in which they return often. . . .

The Englishman, in eleven years, gets three bushels more of wheat than the Frenchman. He gets three crops of barley, tares, or beans, which produce nearly twice as many bushels per acre, as what the three French crops of spring corn produce. And he farther gets, at the same time, three crops of turnips and two of clover, the turnips worth 40s. the acre, and the clover 60s. that is 121 for both. What an enormous superiority. More wheat; almost double of the spring corn; and above 20s. per acre per annum in turnips and clover. But farther; the Englishman's land, by means of the manure arising from the consumption of the turnips and clover is in a constant state of improvement, while the Frenchman's farm is stationary. . . .

Th[e] great populousness of France, I attribute very much to the division of the lands into small properties, which takes place in that country to a degree of which we have in England but little conception. Whatever promises the appearance even of subsistence, induces men to marry. The inheritance of ten or twelve acres to be divided among the children of the proprietor, will be looked to with the views of a permanent settlement, and either occasions a marriage, the infants of which die young for want of sufficient nourishment; or keeps children at home, distressing their relations, long after the time that they should have emigrated to towns. In districts that contain immense quantities of waste land of a certain degree of fertility, as in the roots of the Pyrenees, belonging to communities ready to sell them, economy and industry, animated with the views of settling and marrying, flourish greatly: in such neighbourhoods something like an American increase takes place; and, if the land be cheap, little distress is found. But as procreation goes on rapidly, under such circumstances, the least check to subsistence is attended with great misery; as wastes becoming dearer, or the best portions being sold; or difficulties arising in the acquisition; all which cases I met with in those mountains. The moment any impediment happens, the distress of such people will be proportioned to the activity and vigour which had animated population. It is obvious, that in the cases here referred to, no distress occurs, if the manufactures and commerce of the district are so flourishing as to demand all this superfluity of rural population as fast as it arises; for that is precisely the balance of employments which prevails in a well regulated society; the country breeding people to supply the demand and consumption of towns and manufactures. Population will, in every state, increase perhaps too fast for this demand. England is in this respect, from the unrivalled prosperity of her manufactures, in a better situation than any other country in Europe; but even in England population is sometimes too active, as we see clearly by the dangerous increase of poor's rates in country villages; and her manufactures being employed very much for supplying foreign consumption, they are often exposed to bad times; to a slack demand, which turns thousands out of employment, and sends them to their parishes for support. Since the conclusion of the American war, however, nothing of this kind has happened; and the seven years which have elapsed since that period, may be named as the most decisively prosperous which England ever knew. It has been said to me in France, "Would you leave uncultivated lands wastes, rather than let them be cultivated in small portions, through a fear of population?" I certainly would not: I would, on the contrary, encourage their culture; but I would prohibit the division of small farms, which is as mischievious to cultivation, as it is sure to be distressing to the people.... Go to districts where the properties are minutely divided, and you will find (at least I have done it universally), great distress, and even misery, and probably very bad agriculture. Go to others, where such sub-division has not taken place, and you will find a better cultivation, and infinitely less misery.... When you are engaged in this political tour, finish it by seeing England, and I will show you a set of peasants well cloathed, well nourished, tolerably drunken from superfluity, well-lodged, and at their ease; and yet amongst them, not one in a thousand has either land or cattle.

# Feudal Practices in German Agriculture

*William Jacob visited Germany, Holland, and France during 1819 and reported in great detail about agricultural practices in those countries. The contrast between feudal practices in the German states and the English system of land tenure and cultivation is an implicit one, although Jacob clearly favors changes in the German system that move it in the direction of the English.*

From William Jacob. *A view of the agriculture, manufactures, statistics and state of society, of Germany and parts of Holland and France . . .*

During my stay in Hanover, the early part of the mornings were spent in viewing some of the large farming establishments, within twelve or fourteen miles of it. I adopted the plan of riding, found the horses good, and was enabled to hire one for myself, and another for a groom, on very reasonable terms.

The immediate vicinity of the city is principally devoted to the production of culinary vegetables; and hence manure is so valuable, that the price of it, as I found by several inquiries, is considerably higher than in London.

On my way to Schulenburg, as soon as I was clear of the gardens and orchards, I observed the soil to be light, and apparently exhausted from over cropping; the villages were large, but looked poor, and the cattle very lean. As I was on horseback early, I saw some flocks of sheep before they had left the fold. I examined several, and talked with the shepherds; one of them under his care, a flock of three hundred and twenty, some ewes, and some taggs, all of the long-woolled kind; but in other respects, of a very mixed race. He complained bitterly of the dry summer, owing to which, though he had the range of the three thousand acres of land, the flock was in bad condition; and as they grow no turnips, and must be fed with straw or hay and a few potatoes, through the winter, there were no hopes of their improvement before next summer. Most of the other flocks were in a similar state. These sheep are not the property of the peasants who cultivate the soil, but of their feudal lords, to whom they are a kind of copyholders, and who retain the right, among many others, of turning their sheep over the corn land from harvest to the following spring

From William Jacob, *A View of the Agriculture, Manufactures, Statistics and State of Society, of Germany and Parts of Holland and France,* (London, 1820), pp. 118–121, 337–343.

seed-time. The whole of this first part that I passed over, is known in Germany by the term of *drei feld boden*, or three-course land; where a bastard fallow is succeeded by two corn crops. In approaching Schulenburg, the complexion of the land improved; it was of a less light texture, and with good culture was more adapted for wheat, than any land I had seen since entering Hanover. The common rotation is a fallow, with either pease, flax, or potatoes; then follow the two corn crops of rye and barley, or oats; between every other, or sometimes every third, rotation they make a clear fallow; thus in ten years they produce three green, and six corn, crops. It is manured once in three years, but the quality applied is very small. . . .

The amts, or manorial domains, that I visited, are the property of the king; but many similar ones belong to individual noblemen, whose chief tenant, like the king's, is dignified with the title of Amtman. They are a kind of farmers of the manorial rights, which, though frequently varying in extent and character, are of considerable latitude. Formerly they included the personal slavery of the bauers or peasants who held under the lord, according to the custom of the amt. Personal slavery is however, now universally abolished; but the rights to feed their cattle, to limited labour, and to many other privileges, which, in the grant of land to the tenants, the lords retained to themselves, still exist; and is the grant made to the Amtman, who usually occupies the large house and premises. The demesne land, sometimes a very extensive tract, is also in his hands, and, in some instances, furnish examples of superior husbandry, and new inventions or improvements, to the peasants under his influence. The influence of this officer is considerable, as he is usually the chief magistrate of an extensive district. The royal amts have by habit, rather than by any law, been considered as hereditary possessions; but of late, on the death of the Amtman, they have been granted, either to obtain increased rent, or for purposes of patronage and favouritism, to other persons. The peasants under this officer have usually only small portions of land, often at a distance from their houses, and generally scattered about in a common field. . . .

[*Jacob now travels to Weimar.*]

Agriculture is the principal pursuit of this duchy, the sovereign has an enthusiastic attachment to it, and takes such measures to promote it as he thinks best; whether they are, is more doubtful than the goodness of his intentions. The ancient laws and customs appear to me to be the principal impediments, and these he cannot alter; but others arise from being surrounded with great and powerful states, whose governments are jealous of each other. . . .

The Duke is generally beloved by his subjects, and the only complaints that are uttered against him originate in his attachments to the sports of the field, to which the comfort and the interests of all under him are too much sacrificed. His woods abound with both kinds of deer, and with wild swine, and are plentifully stocked with hares, pheasants, and partridges. The distinction betwixt different kinds of game is strictly marked, and deer, wild swine, and pheasants, under the name of the *hohe jagd*, must only be killed by those of noble blood. . . . In general these animals may be said to be exclusively preserved for the sport of the princes. The mode of hunting, (for so it is called, though the game is killed with guns), is by ordering the peasants of the villages in a certain district, to form an extensive circle and inclose the game; this circle is gradually contracted, till the whole enclosed within it, is driven towards the spot, where the party armed with guns, and accompanied by dogs, performs the operations of butchers, rather than of sportsmen. . . .

The liberties of England may be said in some measure to have originated from contests relating to the forest laws; and the tenacity of the King and the nobles respecting the chace, produced good effects, far beyond the ideas of those who were engaged in the struggle. In Germany, though I have heard much wild declamation about the rights of man, I have not heard those who assume the denomination of Liberals, turn their wrath against the game laws, or talk of them as some of their evils. They seem to me to be more ready to exclaim against evils that arise from the inevitable distinctions of society, and which must always exist, than against such as admit of a practical remedy.

A measure, adopted by the sovereigns of Prussia, Saxony, and some others, is beginning to produce a good effect, and may lead to important consequences at some future time,—I mean the permission to alienate estates, even those which could formerly be held by none but nobles. This enables the peasants or copy-holders to purchase those feudal rights of hunting, of personal service, and stipulated work for their cattle, which, though secured, and as sacred as any other property, are found more harassing to the peasantry than profitable to the lords. . . .

When the tenant or copyholder is bound to plough a certain quantity of land for his lord, or to execute any other work, it may be well imagined, that he will choose the most convenient time for himself, and perform it in the easiest, which is generally the worst, manner. If contentions arise, and it becomes the duty of the courts to decide, they usually do so in favour of the tenant. It may be easily supposed, that such a state of things very much favours the sale of those harassing claims to those tenants who are able to pay for them.

There can be no doubt but the converting these copyholders into freeholders would in time produce a considerable effect, if the progress of the operation were not checked by those ancient laws, which it is difficult in every country to alter. On the death of a peasant, his land must be disposed of, not according to his will, but among all his family; and thus, a number of small farms are created, often of ten or twelve acres, on which a family cannot subsist, except by living wholly on potatoes, and whose owner is superior in rank, but inferior in comforts, to a day-labourer. An alteration in this system seems to me indispensable, in order to give due effect to the permission to sell land and feudal rights to those who are not nobles.

## English Agriculture Transformed

*This poem describes the effect of the transformation of the organization and practice of agricultural cultivation in England over the course of a century.*

1743

Man, to the Plow
Wife, to the Cow
Girl, to the Yarn
Boy, to the Barn
And your Rent will be netted.

1843

Man, Tally-ho
Miss, Piano
Wife, Silk and Satin
Boy, Greek and Latin
And you'll all be Gazetted.

From Ivy Pinchbeck, *Women, Workers and the Industrial Revolution, 1750–1850* (Routledge, 1930; rpt. New York: Augustus Kelley, 1969), p. 37.

## Agricultural Laborers

*English observers sought explanations for the great increases in the population of the "dependent poor" during the late eighteenth and early nineteenth centuries. These were people who could not support themselves and their families without some form of charitable assistance. In this excerpt the author analyzes the situation of agricultural laborers.*

### From David Davies. *The Case of Labourers in Husbandry Stated and Considered (1795)*

III. *The practice of enlarging and engrossing of farms, and especially that of depriving the peasantry of all landed property, have contributed greatly to increase the number of dependent poor.*

The *Land-owner*, to render his income adequate to the increased expence of living, unites several small farms into one, raises the rent to

From David Davies, *The Case of Labourers in Husbandry Stated and Considered* (London, 1795), pp. 55–56.

the utmost, and avoids the expence of repairs. The rich farmer also engrosses as many farms as he is able to stock; lives in more credit and comfort than he could otherwise do; and out of the profits of *several farms*, makes an ample provision for *one family*. Thus thousands of families, which formerly gained an independent livelihood on those separate farms, have been gradually reduced to the class of day-labourers. But day-labourers are sometimes in want of work, and are sometimes unable to work; and in either case their sole resource is the parish. It is a fact, that thousands of parishes have not now half the number of farmers which they had formerly. And in proportion as the number of farming families has decreased, the number of poor families has increased.

The depriving the peasantry of all landed property has beggared multitudes. It is plainly agreeable to sound policy, that as many individuals as possible in a state should possess an interest in the soil; because this attaches them strongly to the country and its constitution, and makes them zealous and resolute in defending them. But the gentry of this kingdom seem to have lost sight of this wise and salutary policy. Instead of giving to labouring people a valuable stake in the soil, the opposite measure has so long prevailed, that but few cottages, comparatively, have now *any* land about them. Formerly many of the lower sort of people occupied tenements of their own, with parcels of land about them, or they rented such of others. On these they raised for themselves a considerable part of their subsistence, without being obliged, as now, to buy all they want at shops. And this kept numbers from coming to the parish. But since those small parcels of ground have been swallowed up in the contiguous farms and inclosures, and the cottages themselves have been pulled down; the families which used to occupy them are crouded together in decayed farm-houses, with hardly ground enough about them for a cabbage garden: and being thus reduced to be *mere* hirelings, they are of course very liable to come to want. And not only the *men* occupying those tenements, but *their wives and children* too, could formerly, when they wanted work abroad, employ themselves profitably at home; whereas now, few of *these* are constantly employed, except in harvest; so that almost the whole burden of providing for their families rests upon the *men*. Add to this, that the former occupiers of small farms and tenements, though poor themselves, gave away something in alms to their poorer neighbours; a resource which is now much diminished.

Thus an amazing number of people have been reduced from a comfortable state of partial independence to the precarious condition of hirelings, who, when out of work, must immediately come to their parish. And the great plenty of working hands always to be had when wanted, having kept down the price of labour below its proper level, the consequence is universally felt in the increased number of dependent poor.

# MANUFACTURE

## Spinning and Weaving

*The use of new machinery for cotton spinning stimulated the expansion of handloom weaving during the last decades of the eighteenth century in England. The period of expansion ended with the introduction of power looms in the early 1800s.*

### From William Radcliffe. *Origin of the New System of Manufacture, Commonly Called Power Loom Weaving (1828)*

. . . The principal estates being gone from the family, my father resorted to the common but never-failing resource for subsistence at that period, viz.—the loom for men, and the cards and hand-wheel for women and boys. He married a spinster, (in my etymology of the word) and my mother taught me (while too young to weave) to earn my bread by carding and spinning cotton, winding linen or cotton weft for my father and elder brothers at the loom, until I became of sufficient age and strength for my father to put me into a loom. After the practical experience of a few years, any young man who was industrious and careful, might then from his earnings as a weaver, lay by sufficient to set him up as a manufacturer, and though but few of the great body of weavers had the courage to embark in the attempt, I was one of those few. Availing myself of the improvements that came out while I was in my teens, by the time I was married, (at the age of 24, in 1785,) with my little savings, and a practical knowledge of every process from the cotton-bag to the piece of cloth, such as carding by hand or by the engine, spinning by the hand-wheel or jenny, winding, warping, sizing, looming the web, and weaving either by hand or fly-shuttle, I was ready to commence business for myself; and by the year 1789, I was well established, and employed many hands both in spinning and weaving, as a master manufacturer.

From 1789 to 1794, my chief business was the sale of muslin warps, sized and ready for the loom, (being the first who sold cotton twist in

From William Radcliffe, *Origin of the New System of Manufacture, Commonly Called Power Loom Weaving* (London, 1828), pp. 9–10, 59–67; reprinted in J. F. C. Harrison, *Society and Politics in England, 1780–1960* (New York: Harper & Row, 1965), pp. 58–61.

that state, chiefly to Mr Oldknow, the father of the muslin trade in our country.) Some warps I sent to Glasgow and Paisley. I also manufactured a few muslins myself, and had a warehouse in Manchester for my general business. . . .

In the year 1770, the land in our township was occupied by between fifty to sixty farmers; rents, to the best of my recollection, did not exceed 10s. per statute acre, and out of these fifty or sixty farmers, there were only six or seven who raised their rents directly from the produce of their farms; all the rest got their rent partly in some branch of trade, such as spinning and weaving woollen, linen, or cotton. The cottagers were employed entirely in this manner, except for a few weeks in the harvest. Being one of those cottagers, and intimately acquainted with all the rest, as well as every farmer, I am the better able to relate particularly how the change from the old system of hand-labour to the new one of machinery operated in raising the price of land in the subdivision I am speaking of. Cottage rents at that time, with convenient loom-shop and a small garden attached, were from one and a-half to two guineas per annum. The father of a family would earn from eight shillings to half a guinea at his loom, and his sons, if he had one, two, or three along side of him, six or eight shillings each per week; but the great sheet anchor of all cottages and small farms, was the labour attached to the hand-wheel, and when it is considered that it required six to eight hands to prepare and spin yarn, of any of the three materials I have mentioned, sufficient for the consumption of one weaver,—this shews clearly the inexhaustible source there was for labour for every person from the age of seven to eighty years (who retained their sight and could move their hands) to earn their bread, say one to three shillings per week without going to the parish. The better class of cottagers and even small farmers also helped to earn what might aid in making up their rents, and supporting their families respectably. . . .

From the year 1770 to 1788 a complete change had gradually been effected in the spinning of yarns,—that of wool had disappeared altogether, and that of linen was also nearly gone,—cotton, cotton, cotton, was become the almost universal material for employment, the hand-wheels, with the exception of one establishment were all thrown into lumber-rooms, the yarn was all spun on common jennies, the carding for all numbers, up to 40 hanks in the pound, was done on carding engines; but the finer numbers of 60 to 80 were still carded by hand, it being a general opinion at that time that machine-carding would never answer for fine numbers. In weaving no great alteration had taken place during these 18 years, save the introduction of the fly-shuttle, a change in the woollen looms to fustians and calico, and the linen nearly gone, except the few fabrics in which there was a mixture of cotton. To the best of my recollection there was no increase of looms during this period,—but rather a decrease. Although our family and some others in the neighbourhood during the latter half of the time, earned from three to four fold-wages to what the same families had heretofore done, yet, upon the whole, the district was not much benefited by the change; for what was gained by some families who had the advantage of machinery, might, in a great measure, be said to be lost to the others, who had been compelled to throw their old cards and hand-wheels aside as lumber.

One of the formidable consequences of this change now began to make its appearance, the poor's rate, which previous to this change had only been known in a comparatively nominal way by an annual meeting at Easter to appoint a new overseer, and the old one to make up his accounts which nobody thought it worth while to look into, as they only contained the expenses of his journey to a petty sessions at a distance, and a few cases of very old persons, 70 to 90 years of age, (whose eyes or hands failed them) having had a weekly allowance. Relief to persons who could not get employment, or bastardy, were alike unknown on their books,—this I state partly traditionally, and partly from many years under my own observance. There was no material advance in the rent of land or cottages during this period, but in the articles of butcher's meat, butter, cheese, and sundry necessaries of life, there had been some increase of price.

The next fifteen years, viz. from 1788 to 1803, which fifteen years I will call the golden age of this great trade, which has been ever since in a gradual decline. . . .

. . . I shall confine myself to the families in my own neighbourhood. These families, up to the time I have been speaking of, whether as cottagers or small farmers, had supported themselves by the different occupations I have mentioned in spinning and manufacturing, as their progenitors from the earliest institutions of society had done before them. But the mule-twist now coming into vogue, for the warp, as well as weft, added to the water-twist and common jenny yarns, with an increasing demand for every fabric the loom could produce, put all hands in request of every age and description. The fabrics made from wool or linen vanished, while the old loom-shops being insufficient, every lumber-room, even old barns, cart-houses, and outbuildings of any description were repaired, windows broke through the old blank walls, and all fitted up for loom-shops. This source of making room being at length exhausted, new weavers' cottages with loom-shops rose up in every direction; all immediately filled, and when in full work the weekly circulation of money as the price of labour only rose to five times the amount ever before experienced in this sub-division, every family bringing home weekly 40, 60, 80, 100, or even 120 shillings per week!!! . . .

. . . the operative weavers on *machine yarns*, both as cottagers and small farmers, even with three times their former rents, they might be truly said to be placed in a higher state of "wealth, peace, and godliness," by the great demand for, and high price of, their labour, than they had ever before experienced. Their dwellings and small gardens clean and neat,—all the family well clad,—the men with each a watch in his pocket, and the women dressed to their own fancy,—*the church crowded to excess every Sunday,*—every house well furnished with a clock in elegant mahogany or fancy case,—handsome tea services in Staffordshire ware, with silver or plated sugar-tongs and spoons,—Birmingham, Potteries, and Sheffield wares for necessary use and ornament, wherever a corner cupboard or shelf could be placed to *shew them off,*—many cottage families had their cow, paying so much for the summer's grass, and about a statute acre of land laid out for them in some croft or corner, which they dressed up as a meadow for hay in the winter.

# Families Disrupted

*This account reports on the impact of mechanization on the family economy of those engaged in cottage manufacture.*

## From *Observations . . . on the Loss of Woollen Spinning* (c.1794)

The Combers being men and boys may possibly turn to some other work, but it is not so with the wife and daughters of the day-labourers, whose occupation in a country parish where no particular manufactory is carried on, must be within their own dwelling; who deprived of Woollen Spinning have no other employment, (except when they can go into the fields) to bring in any money towards the support of the Family. To tell a poor woman with three, four or five children, all under the age at which farmers will employ them to set her children to work, where no Wool is to be had is a mockery of misery, and if it is in a neighborhood distant from Machines, where some hand-work is still put out, the low price that is paid for her unwearied labour, of running with her children all day at the Wheel, disheartens her. The scanty fare it enables them to eat when the day's work is done, with want of firing makes her at length prefer breaking a hedge for her own fuel, and often for sale to the Village Tradesman, and bringing up her children to the same idle habits.

Many things combine to make the Hand Spinning of Wool, the most desirable work for the cottager's wife and children.—A Wooden Wheel costing 2s. for each person, with one Reel costing 3s. set up the family. The Wool-man either supplies them with Wool by the pound or more at a time, as he can depend on their care, or they take it on his account from the chandler's shop, where they buy their food and raiment. No stock is required, and when they carry back their pound of Wool spun, they have no further concern in it. Children from five years old can run at the Wheel, it is a very wholesome employment for them, keeps them in constant exercise, and upright: persons can work at it till a very advanced age.

But from the establishment of the Spinning Machines in many Counties where I was last Summer, no Hand Work could be had, the consequence of which is the whole maintenance of the family devolves on the father, and instead of six or seven shillings a week, which a wife and four children could add by their wheels, *his* weekly pay is *all* they have to depend upon. . . .

. . . another advantage of this work was, that until these Machines were introduced, it was equally to be obtained in every County, unlike every manufactory, a child with a Wheel was never thrown absolutely out of bread, by change of place when grown up.—But all this is altered. . . .

I then walked to the Machines, and with some difficulty gained ad mittance: there I saw both the Combing Machine and Spinning Jenny. The Combing Machine was put in motion by a Wheel turned by four men, but which I am sure could be turned either by water or steam. The frames were supplied by a child with Wool, and as the wheel turned, flakes of ready combed Wool dropped off a cylinder into a trough, these were taken up by a girl of about fourteen years old, who placed them on the Spinning Jenny, which has a number of horizontal beams of wood, on each of which may be fifty bobbins. One such girl sets these bobbins all in motion by turning a wheel at the end of the beam, a wire then catches up a flake of Wool, spins it, and gathers it upon each bobbin. The girl again turns the wheel, and another fifty flakes are taken up and Spun. This is done every minute without in- termission, so that probably one girl turning that wheel, may do the work of One Hundred Hand Wheels at the least. About twenty of these sets of bobbins, were I judge at work in one room. Most of these Manufactories are many stories high, and the rooms much larger than this I was in. Struck with the impropriety of even so many as the twenty girls I saw, without any woman presiding over them, I enquired of the Master if he was married, why his Wife was not present? He said he was not a married man, and that many parents *did* object to send their girls, but that the poverty of others, and not having any work to set them to, left him not at any loss for hands. I must do all the parties the justice to say, that these girls appeared neat and orderly: yet at best, I cannot but fear the taking such young persons from the eyes of their parents, and thus herding them together with only men and boys, must bring up a dissolute race of poor.

These Machines then once set up, and the expence of them does not appear very great, 20 Girls do the work of 2,000 Women and Children, and when these Girls are of age to go into a Farmer's Service, how can they endure the fatigue and exposure to weather, necessary to their situation. Numbers confined together in one room cannot make them so hardy and strong, as running at the wheel in a cold cottage, and frequently at the outside of their door in the open air.—If they marry, they can neither teach their children to work, or spin, or bring in any earnings to maintain them. Who then shall patch the cloaths, mend the shoes, and economize their little store?

Shut up from morning till night, except when they are sent home for their meals, these girls are ignorant of, and unhandy at every domestic employment, whereas if at her wheel in her mother's cottage, the girl assists in every occupation of the family. She lights the faggot, nurses the young children, gleans in the harvest, takes charge of the house in her mother's necessary absence to the shop, or when she can get work at neighbouring houses, becoming an assistant to her parents in sickness and old age, and in *her* turn a good wife to a day labourer, a fit mother for his family she lives with those to whom she ought to be attached, and therefore will feel an affection towards them: but a girl taken from six years old to sixteen, and employed at the machines, can know none of these habits. . . .

If these are the miseries that result from the Machines to the day-labourer's *wife and children* during his life, what must be their lot when deprived by his death of all support, but the pittance their own industry affords them. A widow could assist to maintain herself and her children by her spinning when she was paid 1d. for every skain; but now, she must become a parish pauper, a wretched inhabitant of a Workhouse. . . .

The manufacturing of Cotton and Wool by Machines bear no resemblance as to the detriment to the poor. Wool being in its raw state the produce of every parish, Wool-staplers were consequently to be found in every Market Town; Combers were set to work by them, to prepare it for every Cottager, who was glad at the expence of 2s. to find a wholesome employment within her own house for herself, and all those children who were able to stand to the wheel, and whom she could not place out. Thus from time immemorial the Hand or Jazey Wheel, has been the pride of the English Housewife. In bad and good weather it equally was a resource, and a better fated neighbour, would lend her a trifle on a sick or lying-in bed, she mortgaging the next hand-work her children should carry to the shop. But now the Wheel must be laid aside as a useless thing!—No Yarn is spun out of the ends to mend or knit a stocking, or darn a woollen garment, all is bought ready made at the shop, worn while it will hang together, and a lifeless slatternly race of young people will swarm in every village. . . .

The assistance women and girls may be of in husbandry is sometimes proposed as a remedy for the loss of spinning: but for the mothers of families, common humanity will point without need of much argument, how frequently they must be unfit for working in the fields either when big with child, or with an infant at the breast. If from dire necessity they are thus obliged to expose themselves and infants in all the seasons of our varying year, what must be the consequence to their domestic happiness?

# Machinery Attacked

*In this petition Yorkshire wool workers demand that machines not be used to prepare wool for spinning. It was printed in local newspapers in 1786.*

### The Leeds Woollen Workers' Petition (1786)

To the Merchants, Clothiers and all such as wish well to the Staple Manufactory of this Nation.

The Humble ADDRESS and PETITION of Thousands, who labour in the Cloth Manufactory.

SHEWETH, That the Scribbling-Machines have thrown thousands of your petitioners out of employ, whereby they are brought into great distress, and are not able to procure a maintenance for their families, and deprived them of the opportunity of bringing up their children to labour: We have therefore to request, that prejudice and self-interest may be laid aside, and that you may pay that attention to the following facts, which the nature of the case requires.

The number of Scribbling-Machines extending about seventeen miles south-west of LEEDS, exeed all belief, being no less than *one hundred and seventy*! and as each machine will do as much work in twelve hours, as ten men can in that time do by hand, (speaking within bounds) and they working night-and day, one machine will do as much work in one day as would otherwise employ twenty men.

As we do not mean to assert any thing but what we can prove to be true, we allow four men to be employed at each machine twelve hours, working night and day, will take eight men in twenty-four hours; so that, upon a moderate computation twelve men are thrown out of employ for every single machine used in scribbling; and as it may be supposed the number of machines in all the other quarters together, nearly equal those in the South-West, full four thousand men are left to shift for a living how they can, and must of course fall to the Parish, if not timely relieved. Allowing one boy to be bound apprentice from each family out of work, eight thousand hands are deprived of the opportunity of getting a livelihood.

We therefore hope, that the feelings of humanity will lead those who have it in their power to prevent the use of those machines, to give

From J. F. C. Harrison, *Society and Politics in England, 1780–1960* (New York: Harper & Row, 1965), pp. 70–72.

every discouragement they can to what has a tendency so prejudicial to their fellow-creatures.

This is not all; the injury to the Cloth is great, in so much that in Frizing, instead of leaving a nap upon the cloth, the wool is drawn out, and the Cloth is left thread-bare.

Many more evils we could enumerate, but we would hope, that the sensible part of mankind, who are not biassed by interest, must see the dreadful tendancy of their continuance; a depopulation must be the consequence; trade being then lost, the landed interest will have no other satisfaction but that of being *last devoured*.

We wish to propose a few queries to those who would plead for the further continuance of these machines:

Men of common sense must know, that so many machines in use, take the work from the hands employed in Scribbling,—and who did that business before machines were invented.

How are those men, thus thrown out of employ to provide for their families;—and what are they to put their children apprentice to, that the rising generation may have something to keep them at work, in order that they may not be like vagabonds strolling about in idleness? Some say, Begin and learn some other business.—Suppose we do; who will maintain our families, whilst we undertake the arduous task; and when we have learned it, how do we know we shall be any better for all our pains; for by the time we have served our second apprenticeship, another machine may arise, which may take away that business also; so that our families, being half pined whilst we are learning how to provide them with bread, will be wholly so during the period of our third apprenticeship.

But what are our children to do; are they to be brought up in idleness? Indeed as things are, it is no wonder to hear of so many executions; for our parts, though we may be thought illiterate men, our conceptions are, that bringing children up to industry, and keeping them employed, is the way to keep them from falling into those crimes, which an idle habit naturally leads to.

These things impartially considered will we hope, be strong advocates in our favour; and we conceive that men of sense, religion and humanity, will be satisfied of the reasonableness, as well as necessity of this address, and that their own feelings will urge them to espouse the cause of us and our families—

Signed, in behalf of THOUSANDS, by

Joseph Hepworth    Thomas Lobley
Robert Wood         Thos. Blackburn


# Machinery Defended

*In this statement, Leeds woollen merchants defended their use of machinery.*

## Letter from the Cloth Merchants of Leeds (1791)

At a time when the People, engaged in every other Manufacture in the Kingdom, are exerting themselves to bring their Work to Market at reduced Prices, which can alone be effected by the Aid of Machinery, it certainly is not necessary that the Cloth Merchants of Leeds, who depend chiefly on a Foreign Demand, where they have for Competitors the Manufacturers of other Nations, whose Taxes are few, and whose manual Labour is only Half the Price it bears here, should have Occasion to defend a Conduct, which has for its Aim the Advantage of the Kingdom in general, and of the Cloth Trade in particular; yet anxious to prevent Misrepresentations, which have usually attended the Introduction of the most useful Machines, they wish to remind the Inhabitants of this Town, of the Advantages derived to every flourishing Manufacture from the Application of Machinery; they instance that of Cotton in particular, which in its internal and foreign Demand is nearly alike to our own, and has in a few Years by the Means of Machinery advanced to its present Importance, and is still increasing.

If then by the Use of Machines, the Manufacture of Cotton, an Article which we import, and are supplied with from other Countries, and which can every where be procured on equal Terms, has met with such amazing Success, may not greater Advantages be reasonably expected from cultivating to the utmost the Manufacture of Wool, the Produce of our own Island, an Article in Demand in all Countries, almost the universal Cloathing of Mankind?

In the Manufacture of Woollens, the Scribbling Mill, the Spinning Frame, and the Fly Shuttle, have reduced manual Labour nearly One-third, and each of them at its first Introduction carried an Alarm to the Work People, yet each has contributed to advance the Wages and to increase the Trade, so that if an Attempt was now made to deprive us of the Use of them, there is no Doubt, but every Person engaged in the Business, would exert himself to defend them.

From these Premises, we the undersigned Merchants, think it a Duty we owe to ourselves, to the Town of Leeds, and to the Nation at large, to declare that we will protect and support the free Use of the proposed Improvements in Cloth-Dressing, by every legal Means in our Power; and if after all, contrary to our Expectations, the Introduction of Machinery should for a Time occasion a Scarcity of Work in the Cloth Dressing Trade, we have unanimously agreed to give a Preference to such Workmen as are now settled Inhabitants of this Parish, and who give no Opposition to the present Scheme.

Appleby & Sawyer
Bernard Bischoff & Sons
[and 59 other names]

From J. F. C. Harrison, *Society and Politics in England, 1780–1960* (New York: Harper & Row, 1965), pp. 72–74.

# The First Textile Factories

*The use of power machinery led manufacturers to centralize textile production in factories. The machinery also reduced the skill requirements for spinners and weavers, leading to the substitution of children and women for skilled adults. Output increased dramatically at the same time that labor costs were lowered. Employers found the new system profitable and satisfactory. Skilled workers who found themselves without work as a result of the new system demanded that the machines be banished and their jobs restored.*

## From Richard Guest. *Compendious History of the Cotton-Manufacture (1823)*

### The Steam Loom

The same powerful agent which so materially forwarded and advanced the progress of the Cotton Manufacture in the concluding part of the last century, has lately been further used as a substitute for manual labour, and the Steam Engine is now applied to the working of the loom as well as to the preparatory processes. . . .

In 1785, the Rev. E. Cartwright invented a Loom to be worked by water or steam. The following account of this invention is taken from the Supplement to the Encyclopædia Britannica:—"Happening to be at Matlock, in the summer of 1784, I fell in company with some gentlemen of Manchester, when the conversation turned on Arkwright's spinning machinery. One of the company observed, that as soon as Arkwright's patent expired, so many mills would be erected, and so much cotton spun, that hands never could be found to weave it. To this observation I replied that Arkwright must then set his wits to work to invent a weaving mill. This brought on a conversation on the subject, in which the Manchester gentlemen unanimously agreed that the thing was impracticable; and in defence of their opinion, they adduced arguments which I certainly was incompetent to answer or even to comprehend, being totally ignorant of the subject, having never at that time seen a person weave. I controverted, however, the impracticability of the thing, by remarking that there had lately been exhibited in London, an automaton figure, which played at chess. Now you will not assert, gentlemen, said I, that it is more difficult to construct a machine that shall weave, than one which shall make all the variety of moves which are required in that complicated game.

"Some little time afterwards, a particular circumstance recalling this conversation to my mind, it struck me, that, as in plain weaving, ac-

From Richard Guest, *Compendious History of the Cotton Manufacture* (Manchester, 1823), pp. 44–48.

cording to the conception I then had of the business, there could only be three movements, which were to follow each other in succession, there would be little difficulty in producing and repeating them. Full of these ideas, I immediately employed a carpenter and smith to carry them into effect. As soon as the machine was finished, I got a weaver to put in the warp, which was of such materials as sail cloth is usually made of. To my great delight, a piece of cloth, such as it was, was the produce.

"As I had never before turned my thoughts to any thing mechanical, either in theory or practice, nor had ever seen a loom at work, or knew any thing of its construction, you will readily suppose that my first Loom must have been a most rude piece of machinery.

"The warp was placed perpendicularly, the reed fell with a force of at least half an hundred weight, and the springs which threw the shuttle were strong enough to have thrown a Congreve rocket. In short, it required the strength of two powerful men to work the machine at a slow rate, and only for a short time. Conceiving in my great simplicity, that I had accomplished all that was required, I then secured what I thought a most valuable property, by a patent, 4th April, 1785. This being done, I then condescended to see how other people wove; and you will guess my astonishment, when I compared their easy modes of operation with mine. Availing myself, however, of what I then saw, I made a Loom in its general principles, nearly as they are now made. But it was not till the the year 1787, that I completed my invention, when I took out my last weaving patent, August 1st, of that year."

Mr. Cartwright erected a weaving mill at Doncaster, which he filled with Looms. This concern was unsuccessful, and at last was abandoned, and some years afterwards, upon an application from a number of manufacturers at Manchester, Parliament granted Mr. Cartwright a sum of money as a remuneration for his ingenuity and trouble.

About 1790, Mr. Grimshaw, of Manchester, under a licence from Mr. Cartwright, erected a weaving factory turned by a Steam Engine. The great loss of time experienced in dressing the warp, which was done in small portions as it unrolled from the beam, and other difficulties arising from the quality of the yarn then spun, were in this instance formidable obstacles to success; the factory, however, was burnt down before it could be fully ascertained whether the experiment would succeed or not, and for many years no further attempts were made in Lancashire to weave by steam.

Mr. Austin, of Glasgow, invented a similar Loom, in 1789, which he still further improved in 1798, and a building to contain two hundred of these Looms was erected by Mr. Monteith, of Pollockshaws, in 1800.

In the year 1803, Mr. Thomas Johnson, of Bradbury, in Cheshire, invented the Dressing Frame. Before this invention the warp was dressed in the Loom in small portions as it unrolled from the beam, the Loom ceasing to work during the operation. Mr. Johnson's machine dresses the whole warp at once; when dressed the warp is placed in the Loom which now works without intermission. A factory for Steam Looms was built in Manchester, in 1806. Soon afterwards two others were erected at Stockport, and about 1809, a fourth was completed in Westhoughton. In these renewed attempts to weave by steam, considerable improvements were made in the structure of the Looms, in the mode of warping, and in preparing the weft for the shuttle. With these improvements, aided by others in the art of spinning, which enabled the spinners to make yarn much superior to that made in 1790, and assisted by Johnson's machine, which is peculiarly adapted for the dressing of warps for Steam Looms, the experiment succeeded. Before the invention of the Dressing Frame, one Weaver was required to each Steam Loom, at present a boy or girl, fourteen or fifteen years of age, can manage two Steam Looms, and with their help can weave three and a half times as much cloth as the best hand Weaver. The best hand Weavers seldom produce a piece of uniform evenness; indeed, it is next to impossible for them to do so, because a weaker or stronger blow with the lathe immediately alters the thickness of the cloth, and after an interruption of some hours, the most experienced weaver finds it difficult to recommence with a blow of precisely the same force as the one with which he left off. In Steam Looms, the lathe gives a steady, certain blow, and when once regulated by the engineer, moves with the greatest precision from the beginning to the end of the piece. Cloth made by these Looms, when seen by those manufacturers who employ hand Weavers, at once excites admiration and a consciousness that their own workmen cannot equal it. The increasing number of Steam Looms is a certain proof of their superiority over the Hand Looms. In 1818, there were in Manchester, Stockport, Middleton, Hyde, Stayley Bridge, and their vicinities, fourteen factories, containing about two thousand Looms. In 1821, there were in the same neighbourhoods thirty-two factories, containing five thousand seven hundred and thirty-two Looms. Since 1821, their number has still farther increased, and there are at present not less than ten thousand Steam Looms at work in Great Britain.

It is a curious circumstance, that, when the Cotton Manufacture was in its infancy, all the operations, from the dressing of the raw material to its being finally turned out in the state of cloth, were completed under the roof of the weaver's cottage. The course of improved manufacture which followed, was to spin the yarn in factories and to weave it in cottages. At the present time, when the manufacture has attained a mature growth, all the operations, with vastly increased means and more complex contrivances, are again performed in a single building. The Weaver's cottage with its rude apparatus of peg warping, hand cards, hand wheels, and imperfect looms, was the Steam Loom factory in miniature. Those vast brick edifices in the vicinity of all the great manufacturing towns in the south of Lancashire, towering to the height of seventy or eighty feet, which strike the attention and excite the curiosity of the traveller, now perform labours which formerly employed whole villages. In the Steam Loom factories, the cotton is carded, roved, spun, and woven into cloth, and the same quantum of labour is now performed in one of these structures which formerly occupied the industry of an entire district.

A very good Hand Weaver, a man twenty-five or thirty years of age, will weave two pieces of nine-eighths shirting per week, each twenty-four yards long, and containing one hundred and five shoots of weft in an inch, the reed of the cloth being a forty-four, Bolton count, and the warp and weft forty hanks to the pound. A Steam Loom Weaver, fifteen years of age, will in the same time weave seven similar pieces. A Steam Loom factory containing two hundred Looms, with the assistance of one hundred persons under twenty years of age, and of twenty-five men, will weave seven hundred pieces per week, of the length and quality before described. To manufacture one hundred similar pieces per week by the hand, it would be necessary to employ at least one hundred and twenty-five Looms, because many of the Weavers are females, and have cooking, washing, cleaning and various other duties to perform; others of them are children and, consequently, unable to weave as much as the men. It requires a man of mature age and a very good Weaver to weave two of the pieces in a week, and there is also an allowance to be made for sickness and other incidents. Thus, eight hundred and seventy-five hand Looms would be required to produce the seven hundred pieces per week; and reckoning the weavers, with their children, and the aged and infirm belonging to them at two and a half to each loom, it may very safely be said, that the work done in a Steam Factory containing two hundred Looms, would, if done by hand Weavers, find employment and support for a population of more than two thousand persons.

The Steam Looms are chiefly employed in Weaving printing cloth and shirtings; but they also weave thicksetts, fancy cords, dimities, cambrics and quiltings, together with silks, worsteds, and fine woollen or broad cloth. Invention is progressive, every improvement that is made is the foundation of another, and as the attention of hundreds of skilful mechanics and manufacturers is now turned to the improvement of the Steam Loom, it is probable that its application will become as general, and its efficiency as great, in Weaving, as the Jenny, Water Frame and Mule, are in Spinning, and that it will, in this country at least, entirely supersede the hand Loom.

# POPULATION

## Poverty and Population

*The Rev. Thomas R. Malthus (1766–1834) offered his analysis of the "laws" of population in 1798. His interpretation was meant to counter the arguments of reformers of the day, represented by William Godwin (1756–1836). Godwin's* Enquiry Concerning Political Justice *suggested that a more egalitarian social and economic organization could end the poverty that seemed to have deepened and increased during the eighteenth century.*

### From Thomas Malthus. *First Essay on Population (1798)*

The following Essay owes its origin to a conversation with a friend, on the subject of Mr. Godwin's Essay, on avarice and profusion, in his Enquirer. The discussion, started the general question of the future improvement of society; and the Author at first sat down with an intention of merely stating his thoughts to his friend, upon paper, in a clearer manner than he thought he could do, in conversation. But as the subject opened upon him, some ideas occurred, which he did not recollect to have met with before; and as he conceived, that every, the least light, on a topic so generally interesting, might be received with candour, he determined to put his thoughts in a form for publication. . . .

I think I may fairly make two postulata.

First, That food is necessary to the existence of man.

Secondly, That the passion between the sexes is necessary, and will remain nearly in its present state.

These two laws ever since we have had any knowledge of mankind, appear to have been fixed laws of our nature; and, as we have not hitherto seen any alteration in them, we have no right to conclude that they will ever cease to be what they now are, without an immediate act of power in that Being who first arranged the system of the universe; and for the advantage of his creatures, still executes, according to fixed laws, all its various operations.

I do not know that any writer has supposed that on this earth man will ultimately be able to live without food. But Mr. Godwin has con-

From Thomas R. Malthus, *First Essay on Population* (London: Macmillan and Co., 1926), pp. i, 11–17, 26–31, 37–38.

jectured that the passion between the sexes may in time be extinguished. As, however, he calls this part of his work, a deviation into the land of conjecture, I will not dwell longer upon it at present, than to say, that the best arguments for the perfectibility of man, are drawn from a contemplation of the great progress that he has already made from the savage state, and the difficulty of saying where he is to stop. But towards the extinction of the passion between the sexes, no progress whatever has hitherto been made. It appears to exist in as much force at present as it did two thousand, or four thousand years ago. There are individual exceptions now as there always have been. But, as these exceptions do not appear to increase in number, it would surely be a very unphilosophical mode of arguing, to infer merely from the existence of an exception, that the exception would, in time, become the rule, and the rule the exception.

Assuming then, my postulata as granted, I say, that the power of population is indefinitely greater than the power in the earth to produce subsistence for man.

Population, when unchecked, increases in a geometrical ratio. Subsistence increases only in an arithmetical ratio. A slight acquaintance with numbers will shew the immensity of the first power in comparison of the second.

By that law of our nature which makes food necessary to the life of man, the effects of these too unequal powers must be kept equal.

This implies a strong and constantly operating check on population from the difficulty of subsistence. This difficulty must fall some where; and must necssarily be severely felt by a large portion of mankind.

Through the animal and vegetable kingdoms, nature has scattered the seeds of life abroad with the most profuse and liberal hand. She has been comparatively sparing in the room, and the nourishment necessary to rear them. The germs of existence contained in this spot of earth, with ample food, and ample room to expand in, would fill millions of worlds in the course of a few thousand years. Necessity, that imperious all pervading law of nature, restrains them within the prescribed bounds. The race of plants, and the race of animals shrink under this great restrictive law. And the race of man cannot, by any efforts of reason, escape from it. Among plants and animals its effects are waste of seed, sickness, and premature death. Among mankind, misery and vice. The former, misery, is an absolutely necessary consequence of it. Vice is a highly probable consequence, and we therefore see it abundantly prevail; but it ought not, perhaps, to be called an absolutely necessary consequence. The ordeal of virtue is to resist all temptation to evil.

This natural inequality of the two powers of population, and of production in the earth, and that great law of our nature which must constantly keep their effects equal, form the great difficulty that to me appears insurmountable in the way to the perfectibility of society. All other arguments are of slight and subordinate consideration in comparison of this. I see no way by which man can escape from the weight of this law which pervades all animated nature. No fancied equality, no agrarian regulations in their utmost extent, could remove the pressure of it even for a single century. And it appears, therefore, to be decisive against the possible existence of a society, all the members of which, should live in ease, happiness, and comparative leisure; and feel no anxiety about providing the means of subsistence for themselves and families.

Consequently, if the premises are just, the argument is conclusive against the perfectibility of the mass of mankind.

I have thus sketched the general outline of the argument; but I will examine it more particularly; and I think it will be found that experience, the true source and foundation of all knowledge, invariably confirms its truth. . . .

No limits whatever are placed to the productions of the earth; they may increase for ever and be greater than any assignable quantity; yet still the power of population being a power of a superior order, the increase of the human species can only be kept commensurate to the increase of the means of subsistence, by the constant operation of the strong law of necessity acting as a check upon the greater power.

The effects of this check remain now to be considered.

Among plants and animals the view of the subject is simple. They are all impelled by a powerful instinct to the increase of their species; and this instinct is interrupted by no reasoning, or doubts about providing for their offspring. Wherever therefore there is liberty, the power of increase is exerted; and the superabundant effects are repressed afterwards by want of room and nourishment, which is common to animals and plants; and among animals, by becoming the prey of others.

The effects of this check on man are more complicated.

Impelled to the increase of his species by an equally powerful instinct, reason interrupts his career, and asks him whether he may not bring beings into the world, for whom he cannot provide the means of subsistence. In a state of equality, this would be the simple question. In the present state of society, other considerations occur. Will he not lower his rank in life? Will he not subject himself to greater difficulties than he at present feels? Will he not be obliged to labour harder? and if he has a large family, will his utmost exertions enable him to support them? May he not see his offspring in rags and misery, and clamouring for bread that he cannot give them? And may he not be reduced to the grating necessity of forfeiting his independence, and of being obliged to the sparing hand of charity for support?

These considerations are calculated to prevent, and certainly do prevent, a very great number in all civilized nations from pursuing the dictate of nature in an early attachment to one woman. And this restraint almost necessarily, though not absolutely so, produces vice. Yet in all societies, even those that are most vicious, the tendency to a virtuous attachment is so strong, that there is a constant effort towards an increase of population. This constant effort as constantly tends to subject the lower classes of the society to distress, and to prevent any great permanent amelioration of their condition.

The way in which these effects are produced seems to be this.

We will suppose the means of subsistence in any country just equal to the easy support of its inhabitants. The constant effort towards population, which is found to act even in the most vicious societies, increases the number of people before the means of subsistence are increased. The food therefore which before supported seven millions, must now be divided among seven millions and a half or eight millions. The poor consequently must live much worse, and many of them be reduced to severe distress. The number of labourers also being above the proportion of the work in the market, the price of labour must tend toward a decrease; while the price of provisions would at the same time tend to rise. The labourer therefore must work harder to earn the same as he did before. During this season of distress, the discouragements to marriage, and the difficulty of rearing a family are so great, that population is at a stand. In the mean time the cheapness of labour, the plenty of labourers, and the necessity of an increased industry amongst them, encourage cultivators to employ more labour upon their land; to turn up fresh soil, and to manure and improve more completely what is already in tillage; till ultimately the means of subsistence become in the same proportion to the population as at the period from which we set out. The situation of the labourer being then again tolerably comfortable, the restraints to population are in some degree loosened; and the same retrograde and progressive movements with respect to happiness are repeated. . . .

The theory, on which the truth of this position depends, appears to me so extremely clear; that I feel at a loss to conjecture what part of it can be denied.

That population cannot increase without the means of subsistence, is a proposition so evident, that it needs no illustration.

That population does invariably increase, where there are the means of subsistence, the history of every people that have ever existed will abundantly prove.

And, that the superior power of population cannot be checked, without producing misery or vice, the ample portion of these too bitter ingredients in the cup of human life, and the continuance of the physical causes that seem to have produced them bear too convincing a testimony.

# V

# THE ENLIGHTENMENT—NATURE, REASON, AND PROGRESS

*THE PHILOSOPHERS OF the eighteenth-century Enlightenment were very confident about the intellectual achievement of their age. They believed that Newtonian physics had carried human understanding of the universe beyond anything achieved in the ancient world, and they expected the progress of scientific thought to continue indefinitely on into the future. But, at the same time, the Enlightenment thinkers were sharply conscious of the anomalies and cruelties that persisted in their society. (In eighteenth-century France, and in other countries, men and women were still subjected to brutal punishment for trifling crimes, or for none at all except offending someone in power.) Voltaire's slogan,* Ecrasez l'infâme, *could have stood as a motto for the whole Enlightenment. The "infamy" that Voltaire wanted to "crush" was the intolerance and superstition and cruelty associated with the existing institutions of church and state.*

*In seeking remedies for the evils of the times Enlightenment thinkers appealed above all to Reason and to Nature. Reason could sweep away outworn superstitions. Nature could provide universal principles of morality to correct the artificialities and abuses of society. Within this widely accepted framework of thought were many currents and countercurrents of argument. Most of the Enlightenment philosophers were deists, but a few professed atheism. Most believed that reason could establish universal principles of morality, but one leading thinker, David Hume, denied this. Some writers admired English constitutionalism; others favored enlightened absolutism. Virtually all Enlightenment thinkers supported in different ways the causes of rationalism and reform.*

*We cannot understand the Enlightenment fully without knowing something of the social life of the* philosophes. *They did not live in individual ivory towers but met frequently at the salons of prominent women. These salons served as centers of culture, where philosophers debated their ideas, politicians planned strategies, and poets read from their work. They were also social centers where relationships of friendship and love were established.*

# NATURE AND MAN

## Natural Right

*John Locke (1632–1704) turned away from seventeenth-century doctrines of patriarchal authority to build a political theory based on natural rights and free consent.*

### From John Locke. *Second Treatise of Civil Government (1690)*

I think it may not be amiss to set down what I take to be political power; that the power of a magistrate over a subject may be distinguished from that of a father over his children, a master over his servants, a husband over his wife, and a lord over his slave. All which distinct powers happening sometimes together in the same man, if he be considered under these different relations, it may help us to distinguish these powers one from another, and show the difference betwixt a ruler of a commonwealth, a father of a family, and a captain of a galley.

Political power, then, I take to be a right of making laws with penalties of death and, consequently, all less penalties for the regulating and preserving of property, and of employing the force of the community in the execution of such laws, and in the defence of the commonwealth from foreign injury, and all this only for the public good.

### Of the State of Nature

To understand political power right, and derive it from its original, we must consider what state all men are naturally in, and that is a state of perfect freedom to order their actions and dispose of their possessions and persons as they think fit, within the bounds of the law of nature, without asking leave or depending upon the will of any other man.

A state also of equality, wherein all the power and jurisdiction is reciprocal, no one having more than another; there being nothing more evident than that creatures of the same species and rank, promiscuously born to all the same advantages of nature and the use of the

From John Locke, *Of Civil Government and Toleration*, J. Morley, ed. (New York: Cassell and Co., 1905), pp. 9–12, 22–26, 60, 64–65, 71, 75–76, 127–128.

same faculties, should also be equal one amongst another without subordination or subjection. . . .

But though this be a state of liberty, yet it is not a state of licence. . . . The state of nature has a law of nature to govern it which obliges every one; and reason, which is that law, teaches all mankind who will but consult it that, being all equal and independent, no one ought to harm another in his life, health, liberty, or possessions; for men being all the workmanship of one omnipotent and infinitely wise Maker—all the servants of one sovereign master, sent into the world by his order, and about his business—they are his property whose workmanship they are, made to last during his, not one another's, pleasure; and being furnished with like faculties, sharing all in one community of nature, there cannot be supposed any such subordination among us that may authorize us to destroy another, as if we were made for one another's uses as the inferior ranks of creatures are for ours. . . .

And that all men may be restrained from invading others' rights and from doing hurt to one another, and the law of nature be observed which willeth the peace and preservation of all mankind, the execution of the law of nature is, in that state, put into every man's hands, whereby everyone has a right to punish the transgressors of that law to such a degree as may hinder its violation; for the law of nature would, as all other laws that concern men in this world, be in vain, if there were nobody that in the state of nature had a power to execute that law and thereby preserve the innocent and restrain offenders. And if any one in the state of nature may punish another for any evil he has done, every one may do so; for in that state of perfect equality where naturally there is no superiority or jurisdiction of one over another, what any may do in prosecution of that law, every one must needs have a right to do.

## Of Property

Whether we consider natural reason, which tells us that men, being once born, have a right to their preservation, and consequently to meat and drink and such other things as nature affords for their subsistence; or revelation, which gives us an account of those grants God made of the world to Adam, and to Noah and his sons; it is very clear that God, as King David says (Psal. cxv. 16), "has given the earth to the children of men," given it to mankind in common. . . . But this being supposed, it seems to some a very great difficulty how any one should ever come to have a property in anything. . . .

Though the earth and all inferior creatures be common to all men, yet every man has a property in his own person; this nobody has any right to but himself. The labour of his body and the work of his hands, we may say, are properly his. Whatsoever then he removes out of the state that nature hath provided and left it in, he hath mixed his labour with, and joined to it something that is his own, and thereby makes it his property. . . . Thus this law of reason makes the deer that Indian's who hath killed it; it is allowed to be his goods who hath bestowed his labour upon it, though before it was the common right of every one. . . . As much land as a man tills, plants, improves, cultivates, and can use the product of, so much is his property. . . . God gave the world to men in common; but since he gave it them for their benefit and the greatest conveniences of life they were capable to draw from it, it cannot be supposed he meant it should always remain common and uncultivated. He gave it to the use of the industrious and rational—and labour was to be his title to it—not to the fancy or covetousness of the quarrelsome and contentious.

## Of the Beginning of Political Societies

Men being, as has been said, by nature all free, equal, and independent, no one can be put out of this estate and subjected to the political power of another without his own consent. The only way whereby any one divests himself of his natural liberty, and puts on the bonds of civil society, is by agreeing with other men to join and unite into a community for their comfortable, safe, and peaceable living one amongst another, in a secure enjoyment of their properties and a greater security against any that are not of it. This any number of men may do, because it injures not the freedom of the rest; they are left as they were in the liberty of the state of nature. When any number of men have so consented to make one community or government, they are thereby presently incorporated and make one body politic wherein the majority have a right to act and conclude the rest. . . .

I will not deny that, if we look back as far as history will direct us towards the original of commonwealths, we shall generally find them under the government and administration of one man. And I am also apt to believe that where a family was numerous enough to subsist by itself, and continued entire together without mixing with others, as it often happens where there is much land and few people, the government commonly began in the father. . . . yet it destroys not that which I affirm—viz., that the beginning of politic society depends upon the consent of the individuals to join into and make one society . . . though perhaps the father's pre-eminence might in the first institution of some commonwealth give rise to, and place in the beginning the power in one hand; yet it is plain that the reason that continued the form of government in a single person was not any regard or respect to paternal authority, since all petty monarchies, that is, almost all monarchies, near their original, have been commonly, at least upon occasion, elective. . . . It was not the natural right of the father descending to his heirs that made governments in the beginning, since it was impossible, upon that ground, there should have been so many little kingdoms; all must have been but only one universal monarchy if men had not been at liberty to separate themselves from their families and the government, be it what it will; that was set up in it, and go and make distinct commonwealths and other governments as they thought fit.

## Of the Ends of Political Society and Government

If man in the state of nature be so free, as has been said, if he be absolute lord of his own person and possessions, equal to the greatest, and subject to nobody, why will he part with his freedom, why will he give up his empire and subject himself to the dominion and control of any other power? To which it is obvious to answer that though in the state of nature he hath such a right, yet the enjoyment of it is very uncertain and constantly exposed to the invasion of others; for all being kings as much as he, every man his equal, and the greater part no strict observers of equity and justice, the enjoyment of the property he has in this state is very unsafe, very unsecure. This makes him willing to quit a condition which, however free, is full of fears and continual dangers; and it is not without reason that he seeks out and is willing to join in society with others who are already united, or have a mind to unite, for the mutual preservation of their lives, liberties, and estates, which I call by the general name "property."

The great and chief end, therefore, of men's uniting into commonwealths and putting themselves under government is the preservation of their property.

## Of the Dissolution of Government

The reason why men enter into society is the preservation of their property; and the end why they choose and authorize a legislative is that there may be laws made and rules set as guards and fences to the properties of all the members of the society, to limit the power and moderate the dominion of every part and member of the society; for since it can never be supposed to be the will of the society that the legislative should have a power to destroy that which every one designs to secure by entering into society, and for which the people submitted themselves to legislators of their own making, whenever the legislators endeavour to take away and destroy the property of the people, or to reduce them to slavery under arbitrary power, they put themselves into a state of war with the people who are thereupon absolved from any further obedience, and are left to the common refuge which God hath provided for all men against force and violence. Whensoever, therefore, the legislative shall trangress this fundamental rule of society, and either by ambition, fear, folly, or corruption, endeavour to grasp themselves, or put into the hands of any other, an absolute power over the lives, liberties, and estates of the people, by this breach of trust they forfeit the power the people had put into their hands for quite contrary ends, and it devolves to the people who have a right to resume their original liberty, and by the establishment of a new legislative, such as they shall think fit, provide for their own safety and security, which is the end for which they are in society.

## Human Nature

*Locke's theory of cognition could have radical implications. If everyone's mind to begin with was a "white sheet of paper," then perhaps there was no essential difference between an aristocrat and a peasant.*

### From John Locke. *An Essay Concerning Human Understanding (1690)*

It is an established opinion amongst some men, that there are in the understanding certain *innate principles*; some primary notions, characters, as it were stamped upon the mind of man; which the soul receives in its very first being, and brings into the world with it. It would be sufficient to convince unprejudiced readers of the falseness of this supposition, if I should only show (as I hope I shall in the following parts of this Discourse) how men, barely by the use of their natural faculties, may attain to all the knowledge they have, without the help of any innate impressions; and may arrive at certainty, without any such original notions or principles. . . .

Let us then suppose the mind to be, as we say, white paper, void of all characters, without any ideas:—How comes it to be furnished? Whence comes it by that vast store which the busy and boundless fancy of man has painted on it with an almost endless variety? Whence has it all the *materials* of reason and knowledge? To this I answer, in one word, from EXPERIENCE. In that all our knowledge is founded; and from that it ultimately derives itself. Our observation employed either, about external sensible objects, or about the internal operations of our minds perceived and reflected on by ourselves, is that which supplies our understandings with all the *materials* of thinking. These two are the fountains of knowledge, from whence all the ideas we have, or can naturally have, do spring.

First, our Senses, conversant about particular sensible objects, do convey into the mind several distinct perceptions of things, according to those various ways wherein those objects do affect them. And thus we come by those *ideas* we have of *yellow, white, heat, cold, soft, hard, bit-*

From John Locke, *An Essay Concerning Human Understanding*, A. C. Fraser, ed. (Oxford: Clarendon Press, 1894), Vol. 1, pp. 37–38, 121–124.

*ter, sweet,* and all those which we call sensible qualities; which when I say the senses convey into the mind, I mean, they from external objects convey into the mind what produces there those perceptions. This great source of most of the ideas we have, depending wholly upon our senses, and derived by them to the understanding, I call SENSATION.

Secondly, the other fountain from which experience furnisheth the understanding with ideas is,—the perception of the operations of our own mind within us, as it is employed about the ideas it has got;—which operations, when the soul comes to reflect on and consider, do furnish the understanding with another set of ideas, which could not be had from things without. And such are *perception, thinking, doubting, believing, reasoning, knowing, willing,* and all the different actings of our own minds;—which we being conscious of, and observing in ourselves, do from these receive into our understandings as distinct ideas as we do from bodies affecting our senses. This source of ideas every man has wholly in himself; and though it be not sense, as having nothing to do with external objects, yet it is very like it, and might properly enough be called *internal sense.* But as I call the other Sensation, so I call this REFLECTION, the ideas it affords being such only as the mind gets by reflecting on its own operations within itself. . . .

The understanding seems to me not to have the least glimmering of any ideas which it doth not receive from one of these two. *External objects* furnish the mind with the ideas of sensible qualities, which are all those different perceptions they produce in us; and *the mind* furnishes the understanding with ideas of its own operations.

# GOD AND NATURE

## Theism

### From Voltaire. *Elements of the Philosophy of Newton*

The whole of the philosophy of Newton leads necessarily to the knowledge of a supreme Being, who has created all things, and disposed of them with perfect liberty. For if the universe be finite, or if there be a vacuum, matter exists not by necessity; it has therefore received existence from a freely acting cause. If matter gravitates, as is demonstrable, it does not appear to gravitate of its own nature, in like manner as it is extended of its own nature; it has, therefore, received the power or quality of gravitation from God. If the planets revolve in one direction rather than another, in a non-resisting space, the hand of their Creator must have directed their motions in that direction with an absolute liberty. . . .

Many will perhaps be surprised that, of all the proofs of the existence of a God, that which is deduced from final causes should appear the strongest in the eyes of Newton. The design, or rather the designs varied to infinity, which shine forth in the most vast as well as in the most minute parts of the universe, form a demonstration, which, because dependent on sense, is almost despised by some philosophers; but in short, Newton concluded that the infinity of arguments, of which he saw more than any other man, were the work of an infinitely skilful artist. . . .

In a word, I do not know if there be a proof in metaphysics, more striking to the mind of man, than that admirable order that reigns throughout the world, or if there be a more convincing argument than this verse, *the heavens declare the glory of God*. And thus you see that Newton uses no other at the end of his Optics and his Principia. He found no reasoning more convincing and admirable in favour of the Divinity than that of Plato, who makes one of the persons in his dialogues say, You conclude that I have an intelligent soul, because you perceive order in my speech, and actions; believe then from the order you see in the world, that there is a sovereign and intelligent mind.

From Voltaire, *Elements of the Philosophy of Newton,* trans. D. Williams et al. (London: Fielding and Walker, 1780), Vol. 63, pp. 2–4.

## From Alexander Pope. *An Essay on Man*

All are but parts of one stupendous whole,
Whose body Nature is, and God the soul;
That, chang'd thro' all, and yet in all the same;
Great in the earth, as in th' ethereal frame;
Warms in the sun, refreshes in the breeze,
Glows in the stars, and blossoms in the trees,
Lives thro' all life, extends thro' all extent,
Spreads undivided, operates unspent;
Breathes in our soul, informs our mortal part,
As full, as perfect, in a hair as heart:
As full, as perfect, in vile Man that mourns,
As the rapt Seraph that adores and burns:
To him no high, no low, no great, no small;
He fills, he bounds, connects, and equals all.

Cease then, nor Order Imperfection name:
Our proper bliss depends on what we blame.
Know thy own point: This kind, this due degree
Of blindness, weakness, Heav'n bestows on thee;
Submit.—In this, or any other sphere,
Secure to be as blest as thou canst bear:
Safe in the hand of one disposing Pow'r,
Or in the natal, or the mortal hour.
All Nature is but Art, unknown to thee;
All Chance, Direction, which thou canst not see;
All Discord, Harmony not understood;
All partial Evil, universal Good:
And, spite of Pride, in erring Reason's spite,
One truth is clear, WHATEVER IS, IS RIGHT.

From A. W. Ward, ed., *The Poetical Works of Alexander Pope* (London: Macmillan and Co., 1879), pp. 199–200.

# Atheism

## From Baron d'Holbach. *Common Sense*

To annihilate religious prejudices it would be sufficient to show that what is inconceivable to man can not be of any use to him. Does it need, then, anything but simple common sense to perceive that a being

From Baron d'Holbach, *Common Sense*, Anna Knoop, trans. (New York: Miss A. Knoop, 1884), pp. 42–43, 55–56, 63–65, 69–70.

most clearly irreconcilable with the notions of mankind, that a cause continually opposed to the effects attributed to him; that a being of whom not a word can be said without falling into contradictions; that a being who, far from explaining the mysteries of the universe, only renders them more inexplicable; that a being to whom for so many centuries men addressed themselves so vainly to obtain their happiness and deliverance from their sufferings; does it need, I say, more than simple common sense to understand that the idea of such a being is an idea without model, and that he is himself evidently not a reasonable being? Does it require more than common sense to feel that there is at least delirium and frenzy in hating and tormenting each other for unintelligible opinions of a being of this kind? Finally, does it not all prove that morality and virtue are totally incompatible with the idea of a God, whose ministers and interpreters have painted him in all countries as the most fantastic, the most unjust, and the most cruel of tyrants, whose pretended wishes are to serve as rules and laws for the inhabitants of the earth? To discover the true principles of morality, men have no need of theology, of revelation, or of Gods; they need but common sense; they have only to look within themselves, to reflect upon their own nature, to consult their obvious interests, to consider the object of society and of each of the members who compose it, and they will easily understand that virtue is an advantage, and that vice is an injury to beings of their species.

By metaphysics, God is made a pure spirit, but has modern theology advanced one step further than the theology of the barbarians? They recognized a grand spirit as master of the world. The barbarians, like all ignorant men, attribute to spirits all the effects of which their inexperience prevents them from discovering the true causes. Ask a barbarian what causes your watch to move, he will answer, "a spirit!" Ask our philosophers what moves the universe, they will tell you "it is a spirit."

Is it not more natural and more intelligible to deduce all which exists, from the bosom of matter, whose existence is demonstrated by all our senses, whose effects we feel at every moment, which we see act, move, communicate, motion, and constantly bring living beings into existence, than to attribute the formation of things to an unknown force, to a spiritual being, who can not draw from his ground that which he has not himself, and who, by the spiritual essence claimed for him, is incapable of making anything, and of putting anything in motion?

We are assured that the wonders of nature are sufficient to a belief in the existence of a God, and to convince us fully of this important truth. . . . The unprejudiced philospher sees nothing in the wonders of nature but permanent and invariable law; nothing but the necessary effects of different combinations of diversified substance.

Whence comes man? What is his origin? Is he the result of the fortuitous meeting of atoms? Was the first man formed of the dust of the earth? I do not know! Man appears to me to be a production of nature like all others she embraces. I should be just as much embarrassed to tell you whence came the first stones, the first trees, the first elephants, the first ants, the first acorns, as to explain the origin of the human species. Recognize, we are told, the hand of God, of an infinitely intelligent and powerful workman, in a work so wonderful as the human machine. I would admit without question that the human machine appears to me surprising; but since man exists in nature, I do not believe it right to say that his formation is beyond the forces of nature. . . . I see that this admirable machine is subject to derangement; that at that time this wonderful intelligence is disordered, and sometimes totally disappears; from this I conclude that human intelligence depends upon a certain disposition of the material organs of the body, and that, because man is an intelligent being, it is not well to conclude that God must be an intelligent being, any more than because man is material, we are compelled to conclude that God is material. The intelligence of man no more proves the intelligence of God than the malice of men proves the malice of this God, of whom they pretend that man is the work. In whatever way theology is taken, God will always be a cause contradicted by its effects, or of whom it is impossible to judge by His works. We shall always see evil, imperfections, and follies resulting from a cause claimed to be full of goodness, of perfections, and of wisdom.

# PROGRESS AND REFORM

## The Idea of Progress

*Edward Gibbon's contemplation of the "decline and fall" of ancient Rome did not make him pessimistic about the prospects of European society in his own age.*

### From Edward Gibbon. *The Decline and Fall of the Roman Empire*

It is the duty of a patriot to prefer and promote the exclusive interest and glory of his native country; but a philosopher may be permitted to enlarge his views, and to consider Europe as one great republic, whose various inhabitants have attained almost the same level of politeness and cultivation. The balance of power will continue to fluctuate, and the prosperity of our own, or the neighbouring kingdoms, may be alternately exalted or depressed; but these partial events cannot essentially injure our general state of happiness, the system of arts, and laws, and manners, which so advantageously distinguish, above the rest of mankind, the Europeans and their colonies. The savage nations of the globe are the common enemies of civilised society; and we may inquire, with anxious curiosity, whether Europe is still threatened with a repetition of those calamities, which formerly oppressed the arms and institutions of Rome. Perhaps the same reflections will illustrate the fall of that mighty empire, and explain the probable causes of our actual security. . . .

The military art has been changed by the invention of gunpowder; which enables man to command the two most powerful agents of nature, air and fire. Mathematics, chemistry, mechanics, architecture, have been applied to the service of war; and the adverse parties oppose to each other the most elaborate modes of attack and of defence. Historians may indignantly observe, that the preparation of a siege would found and maintain a flourishing colony; yet we cannot be displeased, that the subversion of a city should be a work of cost and difficulty: or that an industrious people should be protected by those arts, which

From Edward Gibbon, *The History of the Decline and Fall of the Roman Empire,* J. B. Bury, ed. (London: Methuen and Co., 1901), Vol. 4, pp. 163–169.

survive and supply the decay of military virtue. Cannon and fortifications now form an impregnable barrier against the Tartar horse; and Europe is secure from any future irruption of Barbarians; since, before they can conquer, they must cease to be barbarous. Their gradual advances in the science of war would always be accompanied, as we may learn from the example of Russia, with a proportionable improvement in the arts of peace and civil policy; and they themselves must deserve a place among the polished nations whom they subdue.

Should these speculations be found doubtful or fallacious, there still remains a more humble source of comfort and hope. The discoveries of ancient and modern navigators, and the domestic history, or tradition, of the most enlightened nations, represent the *human savage*, naked both in mind and body, and destitute of laws, of arts, of ideas, and almost of language. From this abject condition, perhaps the primitive and universal state of man, he has gradually arisen to command the animals, to fertilise the earth, to traverse the ocean, and to measure the heavens. His progress in the improvement and exercise of his mental and corporeal faculties had been irregular and various; infinitely slow in the beginning, and increasing by degrees with redoubled velocity: ages of laborious ascent have been followed by a moment of rapid downfall; and the several climates of the globe have felt the vicissitudes of light and darkness. Yet the experience of four thousand years should enlarge our hopes, and diminish our apprehensions: we cannot determine to what height the human species may aspire in their advances towards perfection; but it may safely be presumed, that no people, unless the face of nature is changed, will relapse into their original barbarism. . . . Fortunately for mankind, the more useful, or, at least, more necessary arts, can be performed without superior talents, or national subordination; without the powers of *one*, or the union of *many*. Each village, each family, each individual, must always possess both ability and inclination, to perpetuate the use of fire and of metals; the propagation and service of domestic animals; the methods of hunting and fishing; the rudiments of navigation; the imperfect cultivation of corn, or other nutritive grain; and the simple practice of the mechanic trades. Private genius and public industry may be extirpated; but these hardy plants survive the tempest, and strike an everlasting root into the most unfavourable soil. The splendid days of Augustus and Trajan were eclipsed by a cloud of ignorance: and the Barbarians subverted the laws and palaces of Rome. But the scythe, the invention or emblem of Saturn, still continued annually to mow the harvests of Italy; and the human feasts of the Laestrigons have never been renewed on the coast of Campania.

Since the first discovery of the arts, war, commerce, and religious zeal have diffused, among the savages of the Old and New World, these inestimable gifts: they have been successively propagated: they can never be lost. We may therefore acquiesce in the pleasing conclusion, that every age of the world has increased, and still increases, the real wealth, the happiness, the knowledge, and perhaps the virtue, of the human race.

*Condorcet, a distinguished mathematician and philosopher, is remembered especially for his vision of human progress.*

# From Marquis de Condorcet. *Progress of the Human Mind*

All the causes which contribute to the improvement of the human species, all the means we have enumerated that insure its progress, must, from their very nature, exercise an influence always active, and acquire an extent forever increasing. The proofs of this have been exhibited, and from their development in the work itself they will derive additional force: accordingly we may already conclude, that the perfectibility of man is indefinite. Meanwhile we have hitherto considered him as possessing only the same natural faculties, as endowed with the same organization. How much greater would be the certainty, how much wider the compass of our hopes, could we prove that these natural faculties themselves, that this very organization, are also susceptible of melioration? And this is the last question we shall examine.

The organic perfectibility or deterioration of the classes of the vegetable, or species of the animal kingdom, may be regarded as one of the general laws of nature.

This law extends itself to the human race; and it cannot be doubted that the progress of the sanative art, that the use of more wholesome food and more comfortable habitations, that a mode of life which shall develop the physical powers by exercise, without at the same time impairing them by excess; in fine that the destruction of the two most active causes of deterioration, penury and wretchedness on the one hand, and enormous wealth on the other, must necessarily tend to prolong the common duration of man's existence, and secure him a more constant health and a more robust constitution. It is manifest that the improvement of the practice of medicine, become more efficacious in consequence of the progress of reason and the social order, must in the end put a period to transmissible or contagious disorders, as well to those general maladies resulting from climate, aliments, and the nature of certain occupations. Nor would it be difficult to prove that this hope might be extended to almost every other malady, of which it is probable we shall hereafter discover the most remote causes. Would it even be absurd to suppose this quality of melioration in the human

From Marquis de Condorcet, *Outlines of a Historical View of the Progress of the Human Mind* (Philadelphia: M. Carey et al., 1796), pp. 289–293.

species as susceptible of an indefinite advancement; to suppose that a period must one day arrive when death will be nothing more than the effect either of extraordinary accidents, or of the flow and gradual decay of the vital powers; and that the duration of the middle space, of the interval between the birth of man and this decay, will itself have no assignable limit? Certainly man will not become immortal; but may not the distance between the moment in which he draws his first breath and the common term when, in the course of nature, without malady, without accident, he finds it impossible any longer to exist, be necessarily protracted? . . .

May not our physical faculties, the force, the sagacity, the acuteness of the senses, be numbered among the qualities, the individual improvement of which it will be practicable to transmit? An attention to the different breeds of domestic animals must lead us to adopt the affirmative of this question, and a direct observation of the human species itself will be found to strengthen the opinion.

Lastly, may we not include in the same circle the intellectual and moral faculties? May not our parents, who transmit to us the advantages or defects of their conformation, and from whom we receive our features and shape, as well as our propensities to certain physical affections, transmit to us also that part of organization upon which intellect, strength of understanding, energy of soul or moral sensibility depend? Is it not probable that education by improving these qualities will at the same time have an influence upon, will modify and improve this organization itself? Analogy, an investigation of the human faculties, and even some facts, appear to authorize these conjectures, and thereby to enlarge the boundary of our hopes.

Such are the questions with which we shall terminate the last division of our work. And how admirably calculated is this view of the human race, emancipated from its chains, released alike from the dominion of chance, as well as from that of the enemies of its progress, and advancing with a firm and ineviate step in the paths of truth, to console the philosopher lamenting the errors, the flagrant acts of injustice, the crimes with which the earth is still polluted? It is the contemplation of this prospect that rewards him for all his efforts to assist the progress of reason and the establishment of liberty.

# Legal Reform

*Progress required reform, and the philosophers of the Enlightenment were especially concerned with the reform of archaic legal systems. Cesare Beccaria was the outstanding thinker in this area.*

## From Cesare Beccaria. *Essay on Crimes and Punishments*

If we look into history we shall find that laws, which are, or ought to be, conventions between men in a state of freedom, have been, for the most part the work of the passions of a few, or the consequences of a fortuitous or temporary necessity; not dictated by a cool examiner of human nature, who knew how to collect in one point the actions of a multitude, and had this only end in view, *the greatest happiness of the greatest number.*

Observe that by *justice* I understand nothing more than that bond which is necessary to keep the interest of individuals united, without which men would return to their original state of barbarity. All punishments which exceed the necessity of preserving this bond are in their nature unjust.

The end of punishment, therefore, is no other than to prevent the criminal from doing further injury to society, and to prevent others from committing the like offence. Such punishments, therefore, and such a mode of inflicting them, ought to be chosen, as will make the strongest and most lasting impressions on the minds of others, with the least torment to the body of the criminal.

The torture of a criminal during the course of his trial is a cruelty consecrated by custom in most nations. It is used with an intent either to make him confess his crime, or to explain some contradiction into which he had been led during his examination, or discover his accomplices, or for some kind of metaphysical and incomprehensible purgation of infamy, or, finally, in order to discover other crimes of which he is not accused, but of which he may be guilty.

No man can be judged a criminal until he be found guilty; nor can society take from him the public protection until it have been proved that he has violated the conditions on which it was granted. What right, then, but that of power, can authorise the punishment of a citizen so long as there remains any doubt of his guilt? This dilemma is frequent. Either he is guilty, or not guilty. If guilty, he should only suffer the punishment ordained by the laws, and torture becomes useless, as his confession is unnecessary. If he be not guilty, you torture the innocent; for, in the eye of the law, every man is innocent whose crime has not been proved.

Crimes are more effectually prevented by the *certainty* than the *severity* of punishment.

In proportion as punishments become more cruel, the minds of men, as a fluid rises to the same height with that which surrounds it,

From Cesare Beccaria, *An Essay on Crimes and Punishments*, E. D. Ingraham, trans. (Philadelphia: H. Nicklin, 1819), pp. xii, 18–19, 47, 59–60, 93–94, 104–105, 148–149.

grow hardened and insensible; and the force of the passions still continuing, in the space of an hundred years the *wheel* terrifies no more than formerly the *prison*. That a punishment may produce the effect required, it is sufficient that the evil it occasions should exceed the *good* expected from the crime, including in the calculation the certainty of the punishment, and the privation of the expected advantage. All severity beyond this is superfluous, and therefore tyrannical.

The punishment of death is pernicious to society, from the example of barbarity it affords. If the passions, or the necessity of war, have taught men to shed the blood of their fellow creatures, the laws, which are intended to moderate the ferocity of mankind, should not increase it by examples of barbarity, the more horrible as this punishment is usually attended with formal pageantry. Is it not absurd, that the laws, which detest and punish homicide, should, in order to prevent murder, publicly commit murder themselves?

It is better to prevent crimes than to punish them. This is the fundamental principle of good legislation, which is the art of conducting men to the *maximum* of happiness, and to the *minimum* of misery, if we may apply this mathematical expression to the good and evil of life. . . .

Would you prevent crimes? Let the laws be clear and simple, let the entire force of the nation be united in their defence, let them be intended rather to favour every individual than any particular classes of men; let the laws be feared, and the laws only. The fear of the laws is salutary, but the fear of men is a fruitful and fatal source of crimes.

# SKEPTICISM AND SATIRE

## Skepticism—Miracles and Morality

*David Hume (1711–1776) used his powerful critical intelligence not only to question conventional religious beliefs but also to attack a favorite doctrine of other enlightenment thinkers—that principles of morality could be discerned by pure reason.*

### From David Hume. *An Enquiry Concerning Human Understanding*

A miracle is a violation of the laws of nature; and as a firm and unalterable experience has established these laws, the proof against a miracle, from the very nature of the fact, is as entire as any argument from experience can possibly be imagined. Why is it more than probable, that all men must die; that lead cannot, of itself, remain suspended in the air; that fire consumes wood, and is extinguished by water; unless it be, that these events are found agreeable to the laws of nature, and there is required a violation of these laws, or in other words, a miracle to prevent them? Nothing is esteemed a miracle, if it ever happen in the common course of nature. It is no miracle that a man, seemingly in good health, should die on a sudden: because such a kind of death, though more unusual than any other, has yet been frequently observed to happen. But it is a miracle, that a dead man should come to life; because that has never been observed in any age or country. There must, therefore, be a uniform experience against every miraculous event, otherwise the event would not merit that appellation. . . .

The plain consequence is (and it is a general maxim worthy of our attention), 'That no testimony is sufficient to establish a miracle, unless the testimony be of such a kind, that its falsehood would be more miraculous, than the fact, which it endeavours to establish. . . .' When anyone tells me, that he saw a dead man restored to life, I immediately consider with myself, whether it be more probable, that this person should either deceive or be deceived, or that the fact, which he relates,

From David Hume, *An Enquiry Concerning Human Understanding*, L. A. Selby-Bigge, ed. (Oxford: Clarendon Press, 1902), pp. 114–116.

should really have happened. I weigh the one miracle against the other; and according to the superiority, which I discover, I pronounce my decision, and always reject the greater miracle. If the falsehood of his testimony would be more miraculous, than the event which he relates; then, and not till then, can he pretend to command my belief or opinion.

In the foregoing reasoning we have supposed, that the testimony, upon which a miracle is founded, may possibly amount to an entire proof, and that the falsehood of that testimony would be a real prodigy: But it is easy to shew, that we have been a great deal too liberal in our concession, and that there never was a miraculous event established on so full an evidence.

## From David Hume. *A Treatise of Human Nature*

Those who affirm that virtue is nothing but a conformity to reason; that there are eternal fitnesses and unfitnesses of things, which are the same to every rational being that considers them; that the immutable measures of right and wrong impose an obligation, not only on human creatures, but also on the Deity himself: All these systems concur in the opinion, that morality, like truth, is discern'd merely by ideas, and by their juxta-position and comparison. In order, therefore, to judge of these systems, we need only consider, whether it be possible, from reason alone, to distinguish betwixt moral good and evil, or whether there must concur some other principles to enable us to make that distinction. . . .

Reason is the discovery of truth or falshood. Truth or falshood consists in an agreement or disagreement either to the *real* relations of ideas, or to *real* existence and matter of fact. Whatever, therefore, is not susceptible of this agreement or disagreement, is incapable of being true or false, and can never be an object of our reason. . . .

But to make these general reflections more clear and convincing, we may illustrate them by some particular instances, wherein this character of moral good or evil is the most universally acknowledged. . . . I would fain ask any one, why incest in the human species is criminal, and why the very same action, and the same relations in animals have not the smallest moral turpitude and deformity? If it be answer'd that this action is innocent in animals, because they have not reason sufficient to discover its turpitude; but that man, being endow'd with that faculty, which *ought* to restrain him to his duty, the same action instantly becomes criminal to him; should this be said, I would reply, that this is evidently arguing in a circle. For before reason can perceive this turpitude, the turpitude must exist; and consequently is independent

From David Hume, *A Treatise of Human Nature*, L. A. Selby-Bigge, ed. (Oxford: Clarendon Press, 1888), pp. 466–470.

of the decisions of our reason, and is their object more properly than their effect. . . . The duties and obligations of morality must antecedently exist, in order to their being perceiv'd. Reason must find them, and can never produce them. This argument deserves to be weigh'd, as being, in my opinion, entirely decisive.

Nor does this reasoning only prove, that morality consists not in any relations, that are the objects of science; but if examin'd, will prove with equal certainty, that it consists not in any *matter of fact*, which can be discover'd by the understanding. This is the *second* part of our argument; and if it can be made evident, we may conclude, that morality is not an object of reason. But can there be any difficulty in proving, that vice and virtue are not matters of fact, whose existence we can infer by reason? Take any action allow'd to be vicious: Wilful murder, for instance. Examine it in all lights, and see if you can find that matter of fact, or real existence, which you call *vice*. In which-ever way you take it, you find only certain passions, motives, volitions and thoughts. There is no other matter of fact in the case. The vice entirely escapes you, as long as you consider the object. You never can find it, till you turn your reflection into your own breast, and find a sentiment of disapprobation, which arises in you, towards this action. Here is a matter of fact; but 'tis the object of feeling, not of reason. It lies in yourself, not in the object. So that when you pronounce any action or character to be vicious, you mean nothing, but that from the constitution of your nature you have a feeling or sentiment of blame from the contemplation of it. Vice and virtue, therefore, may be compar'd to sounds, colours, heat and cold, which, according to modern philosophy, are not qualities in objects, but perceptions in the mind: And this discovery in morals, like that other in physics, is to be regarded as a considerable advancement of the speculative sciences; tho', like that too, it has little or no influence on practice. Nothing can be more real, or concern us more, than our own sentiments of pleasure and uneasiness; and if these be favourable to virtue, and unfavourable to vice, no more can be requisite to the regulation of our conduct and behaviour.

I cannot forbear adding to these reasonings an observation, which may, perhaps, be found of some importance. In every system of morality, which I have hitherto met with, I have always remark'd, that the author proceeds for some time in the ordinary way of reasoning, and establishes the being of a God, or makes observations concerning human affairs; when of a sudden I am surpriz'd to find, that instead of the usual copulations of propositions, *is*, and *is not*, I meet with no proposition that is not connected with an *ought*, or an *ought not*. This change is imperceptible; but is, however, of the last consequence. For as this *ought*, or *ought not*, expresses some new relation or affirmation, 'tis necessary that it shou'd be observ'd and explain'd; and at the same time that a reason should be given, for what seems altogether inconceivable, how this new relation can be a deduction from others, which are entirely different from it. But as authors do not commonly use this precaution, I shall presume to recommend it to the readers; and am persuaded, that this small attention wou'd subvert all the vulgar systems of morality, and let us see, that the distinction of vice and virtue is not founded merely on the relations of objects, nor is perceiv'd by reason.

## Satire—Candide and Figaro

*Voltaire did not share the facile optimism of some of his contemporaries. He made this abundantly clear in the story of Candide.*

### From Voltaire. *Candide, or the Optimist*

How Candide was Brought Up in a Magnificent Castle and How He was Driven Thence.

In the country of Westphalia, in the castle of the most noble baron of Thunder-ten-tronckh, lived a youth whom nature had endowed with a most sweet disposition. His face was the true index of his mind. He had a solid judgment joined to the most unaffected simplicity; and hence, I presume, he had his name of Candide. . . .

The baron was one of the most powerful lords in Westphalia; for his castle had not only a gate, but even windows; and his great hall was hung with tapestry. . . . My lady baroness weighed three hundred and fifty pounds, consequently was a person of no small consideration; and then she did the honors of the house with a dignity that commanded universal respect. Her daughter was about seventeen years of age, fresh colored, comely, plump, and desirable. The baron's son seemed to be a youth in every respect worthy of the father he sprung from. Pangloss, the preceptor, was the oracle of the family, and little Candide listened to his instructions with all the simplicity natural to his age and disposition.

Master Pangloss taught the metaphysico-theologo-cosmolo-nigology. He could prove to admiration that there is no effect without a cause; and, that in this best of all possible worlds, the baron's castle was the most magnificent of all castles, and my lady the best of all possible baronesses.

It is demonstrable, said he, that things cannot be otherwise than as they are; for as all things have been created for some end, they must necessarily be created for the best end. Observe, for instance, the nose

From Voltaire, *Candide; or, The Optimist* in *Works*, W. F. Fleming, trans. (New York: E. R. Dumont, 1901), Vol. 1, pp. 61–63, 69–82 (revised).

is formed for spectacles, therefore we wear spectacles. The legs are visibly designed for stockings, accordingly we wear stockings. Stones were made to be hewn, and to construct castles, therefore My Lord has a magnificent castle; for the greatest baron in the province ought to be the best lodged. Swine were intended to be eaten, therefore we eat pork all the year round: and they, who assert that everything is *right*, do not express themselves correctly; they should say that everything is *best.*

Candide listened attentively, and believed implicitly; for he thought Miss Cunegund excessively handsome, though he never had the courage to tell her so. He concluded that next to the happiness of being baron of Thunder-ten-tronckh, the next was that of being Miss Cunegund, the next that of seeing her every day, and the last that of hearing the doctrine of Master Pangloss, the greatest philosopher of the whole province and consequently of the whole world.

[*Candide is expelled from the castle for kissing Cunegund. After various misadventures he arrives in Holland.*]

When he arrived in Holland his provision failed him; but having heard that the inhabitants of that country were all rich and Christians, he made himself sure of being treated by them in the same manner as at the baron's castle, before he had been driven thence through the power of Miss Cunegund's bright eyes.

He asked charity of several grave-looking people, who one and all answered him, that if he continued to follow this trade they would have him sent to the house of correction, where he should be taught to get his bread.

He next addressed himself to a person who had just come from haranguing a numerous assembly for a whole hour on the subject of charity. The orator, squinting at him under his broad-brimmed hat, asked him sternly, what brought him thither and whether he was for the good old cause? "Sir," said Candide, in a submissive manner, "I conceive there can be no effect without a cause; everything is necessarily concatenated and arranged for the best. It was necessary that I should be banished from the presence of Miss Cunegund; that I should afterwards run the gauntlet; and it is necessary I should beg my bread, till I am able to get it: all this could not have been otherwise." "Hark ye, friend," said the orator, "do you hold the pope to be Antichrist?" "Truly, I never heard anything about it," said Candide, "but whether he is or not, I am in want of something to eat." "Thou deservest not to eat or to drink," replied the orator, "wretch, monster, that thou art! hence! avoid my sight, nor ever come near me again while thou livest." The orator's wife happened to put her head out of the window at that instant, when, seeing a man who doubted whether the pope was Antichrist, she discharged upon his head a utensil full of. . . . Good heavens, to what excess does religious zeal transport womankind!

A man who had never been christened, an honest anabaptist named James, was witness to the cruel and ignominious treatment showed to one of his brethren, to a rational, two-footed, unfledged being. Moved with pity he carried him to his own house, caused him to be cleaned, gave him meat and drink, and made him a present of two florins, at the same time proposing to instruct him in his own trade of weaving Persian silks, which are fabricated in Holland. Candide, penetrated with so much goodness, threw himself at his feet, crying, "Now I am convinced that my Master Pangloss told me truth when he said that everything was for the best in this world; for I am infinitely more affected with your extraordinary generosity than with the inhumanity of that gentleman in the black cloak, and his wife." The next day, as Candide was walking out, he met a beggar all covered with scabs, his eyes sunk in his head, the end of his nose eaten off, his mouth drawn on one side, his teeth as black as a cloak, snuffling and coughing most violently, and every time he attempted to spit out dropped a tooth.

### How Candide Found His Old Master Pangloss Again and What Happened to Him.

Candide, divided between compassion and horror, but giving way to the former, bestowed on this shocking figure the two florins which the honest anabaptist, James, had just before given to him. The spectre looked at him very earnestly, shed tears and threw his arms about his neck. Candide started back aghast. "Alas!" said the one wretch to the other, "don't you know your dear Pangloss?" "What do I hear? Is it you, my dear master! you I behold in this piteous plight? What dreadful misfortune has befallen you? What has made you leave the most magnificent and delightful of all castles? What has become of Miss Cunegund, the mirror of young ladies, and nature's masterpiece?" "Oh Lord!" cried Pangloss, "I am so weak I cannot stand," upon which Candide instantly led him to the anabaptist's stable, and procured him something to eat. As soon as Pangloss had a little refreshed himself, Candide began to repeat his inquiries concerning Miss Cunegund. "She is dead," replied the other. "Dead!" cried Candide, and immediately fainted away; his friend restored him by the help of a little bad vinegar, which he found by chance in the stable. Candide opened his eyes, and again repeated: "Dead! is Miss Cunegund dead? Ah, where is the best of worlds now? But of what illness did she die? Was it of grief on seeing her father kick me out of his magnificent castle?" "No," replied Pangloss, "her belly was ripped open by the Bulgarian soldiers, after they had raped her as much as a damsel could survive; they knocked the baron, her father, on the head for attempting to defend her; my lady, her mother, was cut in pieces; my poor pupil was served just in the same manner as his sister, and as for the castle, they have not left one stone upon another; they have destroyed all the ducks, and the sheep, the barns, and the trees; but we have had our revenge, for the Abares have done the very same thing in a neighboring barony, which belonged to a Bulgarian lord."

At hearing this, Candide fainted away a second time, but, having come to himself again, he said all that it became him to say; he inquired into the cause and effect, as well as into the sufficing reason that had reduced Pangloss to so miserable a condition. "Alas," replied the preceptor, "it was love; love, the comfort of the human species; love, the preserver of the universe; the soul of all sensible beings; love! tender love!" "Alas," cried Candide, "I have had some knowledge of love myself, this sovereign of hearts, this soul of souls; yet it never cost me more than a kiss and twenty kicks on the backside. But how could this beautiful cause produce in you so hideous an effect?"

Pangloss made answer in these terms: "O my dear Candide, you must remember Pacquette, that pretty wench, who waited on our noble baroness; in her arms I tasted the pleasures of paradise, which produced these hell-torments with which you see me devoured. She was infected with an ailment, and perhaps has since died of it; she received this present of a learned cordelier, who derived it from the fountain head; he was indebted for it to an old countess, who had it of a captain of horse, who had it of a marchioness, who had it of a page, the page had it of a Jesuit, who, during his novitiate, had it in a direct line from one of the fellow-adventurers of Christopher Columbus; for my part I shall give it to nobody, I am a dying man."

"O sage Pangloss," cried Candide, "what a strange genealogy is this! Is not the devil the root of it?" "Not at all," replied the great man, "it was a thing unavoidable, a necessary ingredient in the best of worlds; for if Columbus had not caught in an island in America this disease, which contaminates the source of generation, and frequently impedes propagation itself, and is evidently opposed to the great end of nature, we should have had neither chocolate nor cochineal. . . ."

[*Later, Candide and Pangloss arrive in Lisbon just in time for the great earthquake of 1756.*]

### A Tempest, a Shipwreck, An Earthquake; and What Else Befell

. . . The next day, in searching among the ruins, they found some eatables with which they repaired their exhausted strength. After this they assisted the inhabitants in relieving the distressed and wounded . . . Pangloss endeavored to comfort them under this affliction by affirming that things could not be otherwise than they were: "For," said he, "all this is for the very best end, for if there is a volcano at Lisbon it could be in no other spot; and it is impossible but things should be as they are, for everything is for the best."

By the side of the preceptor sat a little man dressed in black, who was one of the *familiars* of the Inquisition. This person, taking him up with great complaisance, said, "Possibly, my good sir, you do not believe in original sin; for, if everything is best, there could have been no such thing as the fall or punishment of man."

"I humbly ask your excellency's pardon," answered Pangloss, still more politely; "for the fall of man and the curse consequent thereupon necessarily entered into the system of the best of worlds." "That is as much as to say, sir," rejoined the *familiar*, "you do not believe in free will." "Your excellency will be so good as to excuse me," said Pangloss, "free will is consistent with absolute necessity; for it was necessary we should be free, for in that the will—"

Pangloss was in the midst of his proposition, when the inquisitor beckoned to this attendant to help him to a glass of port wine.

## How the Portuguese Made a Superb Auto-Da-Fé to Prevent Any Future Earthquakes, and How Candide Underwent Public Flagellation.

After the earthquake, which had destroyed three-fourths of the city of Lisbon, the sages of that country could think of no means more effectual to preserve the kingdom from utter ruin than to entertain the people with an *auto-da-fé*, it having been decided by the University of Coimbra, that the burning of a few people alive by a slow fire, and with great ceremony, is an infallible preventive of earthquakes.

In consequence thereof they had seized on a Biscayan for marrying his godmother, and on two Portuguese for taking out the bacon of a larded pullet they were eating; after dinner they came and secured Doctor Pangloss, and his pupil Candide, the one for speaking his mind, and the other for seeming to approve what he had said. They were conducted to separate apartments, extremely cool, where they were never incommoded with the sun. Eight days afterwards they were each dressed in a *sanbenito*, and their heads were adorned with paper mitres. The mitre and *sanbenito* worn by Candide were painted with flames reversed and with devils that had neither tails nor claws; but Doctor Pangloss's devils had both tails and claws, and his flames were upright. In these habits they marched in procession, and heard a very pathetic sermon, which was followed by an anthem in a droning plainsong. Candide was flogged in time to the music, while the anthem was being sung; the Biscayan and the two men who would not eat bacon were burned, and Pangloss was hanged, which is not a common custom at these solemnities. The same day there was another earthquake, which made most dreadful havoc. . . . Candide, amazed, terrified, confounded, astonished, all bloody, and trembling from head to foot, said to himself, "If this is the best of all possible worlds, what are the others like?"

*Although Beaumarchais' The Marriage of Figaro was a farcical comedy, the Paris censors found it so subversive that they banned it from the stage for six years. In this scene Figaro suspects that his master, the Count of Almaviva, has seduced his young bride, Susanna.*

## From Beaumarchais. *The Marriage of Figaro*

*Manent* Figaro *and* Doctor.

Figaro.   Oh Woman, Woman, Woman! Inconstant, weak, deceitful Woman!—But each Animal is obliged to follow the instinct of its Nature; and it is thine to betray!—What, after swearing this very Morning to remain for ever Faithful; and on the identical Day! The bridal Day!—

*Doctor.*   Patience.

*Figaro.*   I even saw her laugh with Delight, while he read her Billet!—They think themselves secure, but perhaps they yet may be deceived.—No, my very worthy Lord and Master, you have not got her yet.—What! Because you are a great Man, you fancy yourself a great Genius.—Which way?—How came you to be the rich and mighty Count Almaviva? Why truly, you gave yourself the Trouble to be born! While the obscurity in which I have been cast demanded more Abilities to gain a mere Subsistence than are requisite to govern Empires. And what, most noble Count, are your Claims to Distinction, to pompous Titles, and immense Wealth, of which you are so proud, and which, by Accident, you possess? For which of your virtues? Your wisdom? Your Generosity? Your Justice?—The Wisdom you have acquired consists in vile Arts, to gratify vile Passions; your Generosity is lavished on your hireling Instruments, but whose Necessities make them far less Contemptible than yourself; and your Justice is the inveterate Persecution of those who have the Will and the Wit to resist your Depredations. But this has ever been the Practice of the *little* Great; those they cannot degrade, they endeavour to crush.

*Doctor.*   Be advised, Figaro—be calm—there has ever been a Respect paid— . . . *(Exit).*

*Figaro.*   Oh, how easy it is for the prayer mumbling Priest to bid the Wretch on the Rack suffer patiently. *(Figaro listens.)* I hear nothing—all is silent—and dark as their designs. Why, what a

From Pierre de Beaumarchais, *The Marriage of Figaro*, T. Holcroft, trans. (London: G. G. J. and J. Robinson, 1785), pp. 91–94.

Destiny is mine—Am I for ever doom'd to be the foot-ball of Fortune?—Son of I knew not who, stol'n I knew not how, and brought up to I knew not what, lying and thieving excepted, I had the sense, tho' young, to despise a life so base, and fled such infernal Tutors. My Genius, tho' cramp'd, could not be totally subdued, and I spent what little time and money I could spare in Books and Study. Alas! it was but time and money thrown away. Desolate in the world, unfriended, unprotected, my poor stock of knowledge not being whip'd into me by the masculine hic haec hoc hand of a School-master, I could not get Bread, much less Preferment.—Disheartened by the failure of all my projects, I yet had the audacity to attempt a Comedy, but as I had the still greater audacity to attack the favorite Vice of the favorite Mistress, of the favorite Footman of the Favorite minister, I could not get it licensed.—It happened about that time, that the fashionable Question of the day was an enquiry into the real and imaginary Wealth of Nations; and, as it is not necessary to possess the thing you write about, I, with lank Cheeks, pennyless Purse, and all the simplicity of a Boy, or a Philosopher, freely described the true causes of national Poverty: when suddenly I was awaken'd in my bed at Mid-night, and entrusted to the tender care of his Catholic Majesty's Mirmidons, whose Magic-power caused the heavy gates of an old Castle to fly open at my approach, where I was graciously received, lodged, and ornamented, according to the fashion of the place, and provided with Straw, and Bread, and Water gratis. My ardor for Liberty sufficiently cool'd. I was once more turned adrift in the wide World, with leave to provide Straw and Bread and Water for myself.—On this my second birth, I found all Madrid in Raptures, concerning a most generous Royal Edict, lately published, in favor of the Liberty of the press: and I soon learnt, that, provided I neither spoke of the Wealth of Nations in my writings, nor of the Government, nor of Religion, nor of any Corporate-Companies, nor offended the favorite Mistress of the Minister's Favorite Footman, nor said any one thing which could be twisted into a reference, or hint, derogatory to any one Individual, who had more powerful friends than I had, I was at liberty to write, freely, all, and whatever I pleased, under the inspection of some two or three Censors!

# POLITICAL IDEAS

## The English Model

*Some eighteenth-century thinkers admired English constitutional government. Others thought that only an enlightened despot could carry through the reforms they favored.*

### From Voltaire. *Philosophical Dictionary*

. . . The English constitution has, in fact, arrived at that point of excellence, in consequence of which all men are restored to those natural rights, which, in nearly all monarchies, they are deprived of. These rights are, entire liberty of person and property; freedom of the press; the right of being tried in all criminal cases by a jury of independent men—the right of being tried only according to the strict letter of the law; and the right of every man to profess, unmolested, what religion he chooses, while he renounces offices, which the members of the Anglican or established church alone can hold. These are denominated privileges. And, in truth, invaluable privileges they are in comparison with the usages of most other nations of the world! To be secure on lying down that you shall rise in possession of the same property with which you retired to rest; that you shall not be torn from the arms of your wife, and from your children, in the dead of night, to be thrown into a dungeon, or buried in exile in a desert; that, when rising from the bed of sleep, you will have the power of publishing all your thoughts; and that, if you are accused of having either acted, spoken, or written wrongly, you can be tried only according to law. These privileges attach to every one who sets his foot on English ground. A foreigner enjoys perfect liberty to dispose of his property and person; and, if accused of any offence, he can demand that half the jury shall be composed of foreigners.

I will venture to assert, that, were the human race solemnly assembled for the purpose of making laws, such are the laws they would make for their security.

From Voltaire, *Philosophical Dictionary*, in *Works*, W. F. Fleming, trans. (New York: E. R. Dumont, 1901), Vol. 5, pp. 293–294.

## From Montesquieu. *Spirit of the Laws*

### Of Political Liberty

Democratic and aristocratic states are not in their own nature free. Political liberty is to be found only in moderate governments; and even in these it is not always found. It is there only when there is no abuse of power: but constant experience shews us that every man invested with power is apt to abuse it, and to carry his authority as far as it will go. Is it not strange, though true, to say, that virtue itself has need of limits?

To prevent this abuse, it is necessary, from the very nature of things, power should be a check to power. A government may be so constituted as no man shall be compelled to do things to which the law does not oblige him, nor forced to abstain from things which the law permits. . . .

### The Constitution of England

The political liberty of the subject is a tranquility of mind arising from the opinion each person has of his safety. In order to have this liberty, it is requisite the government be so constituted as one man need not be afraid of another.

When the legislative and executive powers are united in the same person, or in the same body of magistrates, there can be no liberty; because apprehensions may arise, lest the same monarch or senate should enact tyrannical laws, to execute them in a tyrannical manner.

Again, there is no liberty if the judiciary power be not separated from the legislative and executive. Were it joined with the legislative, the life and liberty of the subject would be exposed to arbitrary control; for the judge would be then the legislator. Were it joined to the executive power, the judge might behave with violence and oppression.

There would be an end of everything, were the same man, or the same body, whether of the nobles or of the people, to exercise those three powers, that of enacting laws, that of executing the public resolutions, and of trying the causes of individuals.

# Enlightened Absolutism

*Mercier de la Rivière distinguished between a bad form of absolutism, which he called "arbitrary," and a good form, which he called "legal."*

From *The Complete Works of M. de Montesquieu* (London: T. Evans, 1777), Vol. 1, pp. 197–198.

## From Mercier de la Rivière. *The Natural Order*

Under *legal* despotism, the majesty of the Sovereign and his despotic authority are constantly represented everywhere in his kingdom, no matter how far the king himself may be, by immutable laws which are manifestly just and necessary. As the sovereign's will is only the expression of the public order, to be obeyed it needs only to be known; and the sovereign governs his state by means of laws whose wisdom is manifest, in the same way that God, whose image he is, governs the universe, in which, as we see, all secondary causes are subject *without variation* to laws from which they cannot depart. Hence such a Monarch devotes his attention solely to the good works which cannot be performed except by him and through him. The peace which reigns constantly within his person bestows its priceless benefits upon the world without; and the more these benefits multiply for others, the more they multiply for him.

What an enormous difference there is between the situation of a Sovereign whom every one regards as a good which he fears to lose, and that of an arbitrary despot whom every one looks upon as an evil to be suffered only as long as it cannot be thrown off. The authority of an *arbitrary* despot cannot help but be precarious and unstable, because it is impossible to hold in steady balance the diverse opinions, interests and claims upon which it rests; that of the *legal* despot is unshakeable, because its principle, which is manifest justice and necessity, is invariable and always produces the same effects. . . .

Euclid is a true despot, and the geometric laws which he has handed down to us are truly despotic laws: their legal despotism and the personal despotism of this Lawmaker are one and the same thing, the irresistible force of manifest truth. This is the means by which Euclid the despot has ruled for centuries without contradiction over all enlightened peoples; and he will not cease to exercise the same despotism over them so long as there is no contradiction to meet from the side of ignorance.

If the kings are truly great, truly kings, it is only through a government of this kind—all authority belongs to them and to no others: and because all their purposes are dictated by manifest justice and necessity, it can be said, in a way, that they are associated with *supreme reason* in the government of the earth; that in this quality his divine wisdom, which is communicated to them in the quality of manifest justice and necessity, and which always dwells within them, compels them to do good and makes them unable to do evil; so that, by their mediation, heaven and earth touch and the justice and goodness of God does not

From Mercier de la Rivière, *L'ordre naturel et essentiel des sociétés politiques,* Herbert H. Rowen, trans., in *From Absolutism to Revolution, 1648–1848,* 2nd ed. (New York: Macmillan Co., 1963), pp. 159–161. Copyright © 1963, 1968 by Macmillan Publishing Co., Inc. Reprinted by permission of the publisher.

cease to be made manifest to men, being present to them in the Agents of his authority. . . .

How happy are the nations which enjoy the despotism of manifest justice and necessity: peace, justice, abundance, the purest felicity dwell endlessly among them; happier still are the Sovereigns to whom one can say without offending them: "Powerful masters of the earth, *your power* comes from God; it is from him that you hold your absolute authority because it is the authority of the manifest justice and necessity which God has instituted. Take care not to exchange this sacred authority for a power which can be arbitrary in you only insofar as it is so in its origins: your power, which is natural, absolute, independent, would be no more than an artificial, uncertain authority, dependent upon the very people whom it is supposed to govern. You are kings, but you are men—as men, you can make laws *arbitrarily;* as kings, you can only proclaim laws already established by the deity whose agents you are. . . . Like him you are despots; like him, you will always be despots, because it is not in the nature of manifest justice and necessity that you should cease to be so; and your despotism will lavish glory and prosperity of every kind upon you; but it does not lie within order, in which you are instructed by manifest justice and necessity, that the best possible condition of the peoples should not be the best possible condition of Sovereigns."

# Totalitarian Democracy

*Jean Jacques Rousseau developed a theory of politics that has been called "totalitarian democracy."*

## From Jean Jacques Rousseau. *The Social Contract*

### Subject of the First Book

Man is born free; and everywhere he is in chains. One thinks himself the master of others, and still remains a greater slave than they. How did this change come about? I do not know. What can make it legitimate? That question I think I can answer.

If I took into account only force, and the effects derived from it, I should say: 'As long as a people is compelled to obey, and obeys, it does well; as soon as it can shake off the yoke, and shakes it off, it does still better; for, regaining its liberty by the same right as took it away,

From Jean Jacques Rousseau, *The Social Contract and Discourses* (New York: E. P. Dutton and Co., Inc., 1913), pp. 3–4, 10–13, 14–15, 16. Reprinted by permission of J. M. Dent and Sons Ltd.

either it is justified in resuming it, or there was no justification for those who took it away.' But the social order is a sacred right which is the basis of all other rights. Nevertheless, this right does not come from nature, and must therefore be founded on conventions. Before coming to that, I have to prove what I have just asserted.

## The Social Compact

I suppose men to have reached the point at which the obstacles in the way of their preservation in the state of nature show their power of resistance to be greater than the resources at the disposal of each individual for his maintenance in that state. That primitive condition can then subsist no longer; and the human race would perish unless it changed its manner of existence.

But, as men cannot engender new forces, but only unite and direct existing ones, they have no other means of preserving themselves than the formation, by aggregation, of a sum of forces great enough to overcome the resistance. These they have to bring into play by means of a single motive power, and cause to act in concert.

This sum of forces can arise only where several persons come together: but, as the force and liberty of each man are the chief instruments of his self-preservation, how can he pledge them without harming his own interests, and neglecting the care he owes to himself? This difficulty, in its bearing on my present subject, may be stated in the following terms:

'The problem is to find a form of association which will defend and protect with the whole common force the person and goods of each associate, and in which each, while uniting himself with all, may still obey himself alone, and remain as free as before.' This is the fundamental problem of which the *Social Contract* provides the solution.

The clauses of this contract are so determined by the nature of the act that the slightest modification would make them vain and ineffective; so that, although they have perhaps never been formally set forth, they are everywhere the same and everywhere tacitly admitted and recognized, until, on the violation of the social compact, each regains his original rights and resumes his natural liberty, while losing the conventional liberty in favour of which he renounced it.

These clauses, properly understood, may be reduced to one—the total alienation of each associate, together with all his rights, to the whole community; for, in the first place, as each gives himself absolutely, the conditions are the same for all; and, this being so, no one has any interest in making them burdensome to others.

Moreover, the alienation being without reserve, the union is as perfect as it can be, and no associate has anything more to demand: for, if the individuals retained certain rights, as there would be no common superior to decide between them and the public, each, being on one point his own judge, would ask to be so on all; the state of nature would thus continue, and the association would necessarily become inoperative or tyrannical.

Finally, each man, in giving himself to all, gives himself to nobody; and as there is no associate over which he does not acquire the same right as he yields others over himself, he gains an equivalent for everything he loses, and an increase of force for the preservation of what he has.

If then we discard from the social compact what is not of its essence, we shall find that it reduces itself to the following terms:

*'Each of us puts his person and all his power in common under the supreme direction of the general will, and, in our corporate capacity, we receive each member as an indivisible part of the whole.'*

At once, in place of the individual personality of each contracting party, this act of association creates a moral and collective body, composed of as many members as the assembly contains voters, and receiving from this act its unity, its common identity, its life, and its will. This public person, so formed by the union of all other persons, formerly took the name of *city*, and now takes that of *Republic* or *body politic*; it is called by its members *State* when passive, *Sovereign* when active, and *Power* when compared with others like itself. Those who are associated in it take collectively the name of *people*, and severally are called *citizens*, as sharing in the sovereign power, and *subjects*, as being under the laws of the State. But these terms are often confused and taken one for another: it is enough to know how to distinguish them when they are being used with precision.

## The Sovereign

If the State is a moral person whose life is in the union of its members, and if the most important of its cares is the care for its own preservation, it must have a universal and compelling force, in order to move and dispose each part as may be most advantageous to the whole. As nature gives each man absolute power over all his members, the social compact gives the body politic absolute power over all its members also; and it is this power which, under the direction of the general will, bears, as I have said, the name of Sovereignty.

Again, the Sovereign, being formed wholly of the individuals who compose it, neither has nor can have any interest contrary to theirs; and consequently the sovereign power need give no guarantee to its subjects, because it is impossible for the body to wish to hurt all its members. We shall also see later on that it cannot hurt any in particular. The Sovereign, merely by virtue of what it is, is always what it should be.

This, however, is not the case with the relation of the subjects to the

Sovereign, which, despite the common interest, would have no security that they would fulfil their undertakings, unless it found means to assure itself of their fidelity.

In fact, each individual, as a man, may have a particular will contrary or dissimilar to the general will which he has as a citizen. His particular interest may speak to him quite differently from the common interest: his absolute and naturally independent existence may make him look upon what he owes to the common cause as a gratuitous contribution, the loss of which will do less harm to others than the payment of it is burdensome to himself; and, regarding the moral person which constitutes the State as a *persona ficta*, because not a man, he may wish to enjoy the rights of citizenship without being ready to fulfil the duties of a subject. The continuance of such an injustice could not but prove the undoing of the body politic.

In order then that the social compact may not be an empty formula, it tacitly includes the undertaking, which alone can give force to the rest, that whoever refuses to obey the general will shall be compelled to do so by. the whole body. This means nothing less than that he will be forced to be free; for this is the condition which, by giving each citizen to his country, secures him against all personal dependence. In this lies the key to the working of the political machine; this alone legitimizes civil undertakings, which, without it, would be absurd, tyrannical, and liable to the most frightful abuses.

## The Civil State

. . . Let us draw up the whole account in terms easily commensurable. What man loses by the social contract is his natural liberty and an unlimited right to everything he tries to get and succeeds in getting; what he gains is civil liberty and the proprietorship of all he possesses. If we are to avoid mistake in weighing one against the other, we must clearly distinguish natural liberty, which is bounded only by the strength of the individual, from civil liberty, which is limited by the general will; and possession, which is merely the effect of force or the right of the first occupier, from property, which can be founded only on a positive title.

We might, over and above all this, add, to what man acquires in the civil state, moral liberty, which alone makes him truly master of himself; for the mere impulse of appetite is slavery, while obedience to a law which we prescribe to ourselves is liberty. But I have already said too much on this head, and the philosophical meaning of the word liberty does not now concern us.

# LOVE AND FRIENDSHIP

## The Salons

*This reading presents a modern account of salon society.*

### From *Not in God's Image*

One of the few scenes—apart from their kitchens—where women were consistently in control was the French drawing room of the seventeenth and eighteenth centuries. Salon society was one of the acknowledged triumphs of the *ancien régime*; elitist and necessarily transient, its prime product was the 'art of conversation' and, more vaguely, that sweetness of life which, Talleyrand assured, no one who had not lived before the Revolution could ever know. For the historian of women, it provides an instance when a few women of birth plucked the prize which the world of social hierarchies and double standards constantly dangled and rarely delivered. 'Stay at home,' the manuals of that society had been advising for centuries. 'Be feminine. Use your charm, and men will bring you the best of themselves and leave the rest in the crude world outside your doors.' For this promise to be kept, conditions had to be right, and in Paris, for the rich and clever, for a century and a half, they were. Education for women was new enough to excite them still and general enough in the upper classes to make for discussions on a wide variety of topics. Money, leisure, and the ingenuity of satellite men of letters went into the preparation of elaborate games and *tableaux vivants*. Houses were remodeled and alcoves created which favored casual and intimate talk. This talk throbbed with sex ('Platonic love'); husbands were notably absent; the notion—first formulated by Castiglione—was thrillingly debated that perhaps a woman might, with propriety, enjoy an intellectual relationship with an admirer while keeping her body for her husband. Could she give her hand to one man, her heart to another? The question had more resonance than may appear. In asking it, young women, who had been disposed of as

From Julia O'Faolain and Lauro Martines, *Not in God's Image* (New York: Harper & Row, 1973), pp. 276–277, 280–281. Reprinted by permission of Harper & Row, Publishers, Inc.

brood mares are brought to stud, were groping for a way of affirming their identity. . . .

Platonic love went out of fashion, but salons survived. There were political salons, learned salons, literary, atheistic, and epicurean salons. Women nearly always presided. Prudery abated. Ninon de Lenclos, although her lovers were countless and some paid her rent, was visited by the most brilliant and fashionable people in France. Mademoiselle de Lespinasse lived more or less openly with d'Alembert, and articles for the great encyclopedia were prepared and discussed in her salon. Madame Geoffrin, a middle-class woman, received visits from King Gustave of Sweden and the Emperor Joseph II. She went to Poland to visit King Stanislas Augustus and to Vienna to see Maria Theresa. Hume, Walpole, Benjamin Franklin visited. The list is endless.

# Julie de Lespinasse

*Each of the leading hostesses had her own special qualities. One, for instance, was noted for her conversation and her love affairs, another for her kindness and generosity.*

## From *Memoir of Baron de Grimm*

Her circle met daily from five o'clock until nine in the evening. There we were sure to find choice men of all orders in the State, the Church, the Court,—military men, foreigners, and the most distinguished men of letters. Every one agrees that though the name of M. d'Alembert may have drawn them thither, it was she alone who kept them there. Devoted wholly to the care of preserving that society, of which she was the soul and the charm, she subordinated to this purpose all her tastes and all her personal intimacies. She seldom went to the theatre or into the country, and when she did make an exception to this rule it was an event of which all Paris was notified in advance. . . . Politics, religion, philosophy, anecdotes, news, nothing was excluded from the conversation, and, thanks to her care, the most trivial little narrative gained, as naturally as possible, the place and notice it deserved. News of all kinds was gathered there in its first freshness.

## From *Memoir of Marmontel*

The circle was formed of persons who were not bound together. She had taken them here and there in society, but so well assorted were

From *Letters of Julie de Lespinasse*, Katherine P. Wormley, trans. (Boston: Hardy, Pratt and Co., 1903), pp. 34–35.

they that once there they fell into harmony like the strings of an instrument touched by an able hand. Following out that comparison, I may say that she played the instrument with an art that came of genius; she seemed to know what tone each string would yield before she touched it; I mean to say that our minds and our natures were so well known to her that in order to bring them into play she had but to say a word. Nowhere was conversation more lively, more brilliant, or better regulated than at her house. It was a rare phenomenon indeed, the degree of tempered, equable heat which she knew so well how to maintain, sometimes by moderating it, sometimes by quickening it. The continual activity of her soul was communicated to our souls, but measurably; her imagination was the mainspring, her reason the regulator. Remark that the brains she stirred at will were neither feeble nor frivolous: the Coudillacs and Turgots were among them; d'Alembert was like a simple, docile child beside her. Her talent for casting out a thought and giving it for discussion to men of that class, her own talent in discussing it with precision, sometimes with eloquence, her talent for bringing forward new ideas and varying the topic—always with the facility and ease of a fairy, who, with one touch of her wand, can change the scene of her enchantment—these talents, I say, were not those of an ordinary woman. It was not with the follies of fashion and vanity that daily, during four hours of conversation, without languor and without vacuum, she knew how to make herself interesting to a wide circle of strong minds.

*The letters of Julie de Lespinasse to her lovers are full of passion as well as intelligence. (A contemporary, referring to Rousseau's popular love story, called her "La Nouvelle Heloise in action.") This excerpt is from a letter written to the Comte de Guibert.*

## From *Letter of Julie de Lespinasse*

I love you too well to impose the least restraint upon myself; I prefer to have to ask your pardon rather than commit no faults. I have no self-love with you; I do not comprehend those rules of conduct that make us so content with self and so cold to those we love. I detest prudence, I even hate (suffer me to say so) those "duties of friendship" which substitute propriety for interest, and circumspection for feeling. How shall I say it? I love the abandonment to impulse, I act from impulse only, and I love to madness that others do the same by me.

Ah! *mon Dieu!* how far I am from being equal to you! I have not your virtues, I know no duties with my friend; I am closer to the state of nature; savages do not love with more simplicity and good faith.

From *Letters of Julie de Lespinasse*, Katherine P. Wormley, trans. (Boston: Hardy, Pratt and Co., 1903), p. 75.

The world, misfortunes, evils, nothing has corrupted my heart. I shall never be on my guard against you; I shall never suspect you. You say that you have friendship for me; you are virtuous; what can I fear? I will let you see the trouble, the agitation of my soul, and I shall not blush to seem to you weak and inconsistent. I have already told you that I do not seek to please you; I do not wish to usurp your esteem. I prefer to deserve your indulgence—in short, I want to love you with all my heart and to place in you a confidence without reserve. . . .

# Madame Geoffrin

*Madame Geoffrin had the good fortune to marry a rich husband; she used her wealth generously to help her friends among the* philosophes.

## From *Memoir of d'Alembert*

Much has been said respecting Madame Geoffrin's goodness, to what a point it was active, restless, obstinate. But it has not been added, and which reflects the greatest honour upon her, that, as she advanced in years, this habit constantly increased. For the misfortune of society, it too often happens that age and experience produce a directly contrary effect, even in very virtuous characters, if virtue be not in them a powerful sentiment indeed, and of no common stamp. The more disposed they have been at first to feel kindness towards their fellow creatures, the more, finding daily their ingratitude, do they repent of having served them, and even consider it almost as a reproach to themselves to have loved them. Madame Geoffrin had learnt, from a more reflected study of mankind, from taking a view of them more enlightened by reason and justice, that they are more weak and vain than wicked; that we ought to compassionate their weakness, and bear with their vanity, that they may bear with ours. . . .

The passion of *giving*, which was an absolute necessity to her, seemed born with her, and tormented her, if I may say so, even from her earliest years. While yet a child, if she saw from the window any poor creature asking alms, she would throw whatever she could lay her hands upon to them; her bread, her linen, and even her clothes. She was often scolded for this *intemperance* of charity, sometimes even punished, but nothing could alter the disposition, she would do the same the very next day. . . .

Always occupied with those whom she loved, always anxious about them, she even anticipated every thing which might interrupt their happiness. A young man,[1] for whom she interested herself very much,

[1]This young man was M. d'Alembert himself.

From Baron de Grimm, *Historical and Literary Memoirs and Anecdotes* (London: Henry Colburn, 1815), Vol. 3, pp. 400–405, 52–53.

who had till that moment been wholly absorbed in his studies, was suddenly seized with an unfortunate passion, which rendered study, and even life itself insupportable to him. She succeeded in curing him. Some time after she observed that the same young man, mentioned to her, with great interest, an amiable woman with whom he had recently become acquainted. Madame Geoffrin, who knew the lady, went to her. "I am come," she said, "to intreat a favour of you. Do not evince too much friendship for * * * * or too much desire to see him, he will be soon in love with you, he will be unhappy, and I shall be no less so to see him suffer; nay, you yourself will be a sufferer, from consciousness, of the sufferings you occasion him." This woman, who was truly amiable, promised what Madame Geoffrin desired, and kept her word.

As she had always among the circle of her society persons of the highest rank and birth, as she appeared even to seek an acquaintance with them, it was supposed that this flattered her vanity. But here a very erroneous opinion was formed of her; she was in no respect the dupe of such prejudices, but she thought that by managing the humours of these people, she could render them useful to her friends. "You think," said she, to one of the latter, for whom she had a particular regard, "that it is for my own sake I frequent ministers and great people. Undeceive yourself,—it is for the sake of you, and those like you who may have occasion for them. . . ."

*Husbands were usually not much in evidence at their wives' salons.*


## From *Memoir of Baron de Grimm*

Whether from malice or inattention, one who was in the habit of lending books to the husband of Madame Geoffrin, sent him several times in succession the first volume of the *Travels of Father Labbat.* M. Geoffrin with all the composure possible, always read the book over again without perceiving the mistake. *"How do you like these Travels, Sir?"*— *"They are very interesting, but the author seems to me somewhat given to repetition."*—He read Bayle's Dictionary with great attention, following the line with his finger along the two columns. *"What an excellent work,* he said, *if it were only a little less abstruse."*—*"You were at the play this evening, M. Geoffrin,* said one, *pray what was the performance?"*—*"I really cannot say, I was in a great hurry to get in and had no time to look at the bill."*— However deficient the poor man was, he was permitted to sit down to dinner, at the end of the table, upon condition that he never attempted to join in conversation. A foreigner who was very assiduous in his visits to Madame Geoffrin, one day, not seeing him as usual at table, enquired after him: *"What have you done, Madam, with the poor man whom I always used to see here, and who never spoke a word?"*—*"Oh, that was my husband!—he is dead."*

# VI

# THE FRENCH REVOLUTION

*THE FRENCH REVOLUTION began as a dispute between the king and the nobility over the question of the nobles' privileged exemption from taxes. It quickly escalated into a major political and social upheaval that rocked the foundations of European society. The revolutionaries first substituted a constitutional monarchy for the absolutism of the Bourbon kings. They abolished feudalism and proclaimed the rights to life, liberty, and property, enshrining Enlightenment ideas in the new political order. When the monarchs of Europe threatened the new government, France declared war on them and promised to bring revolutionary liberties to all corners of the continent. When Louis XVI sought to undermine the new representative assembly and collaborate with France's enemies, he was tried and executed and a republican form of government replaced rule by a king.*

*The fact of major change in political and social organization led many different groups in French society to demand recognition of their needs and rights. French women argued unsuccessfully that, as individuals, they ought to be allowed to choose their representatives and participate in politics. Workers, shopkeepers, and craftsmen in Paris insisted that direct democracy was the only way to run a republic. When government officials were slow to heed their message, these sans-culottes took to the streets to insist on the validity of their point of view. From the fall of the Bastille to the fall of Robespierre and the Jacobins (1789–1794), crowds of sans-culottes pushed the revolution to the left. Among radical groups were those who, with Robespierre, justified severe represssion of "enemies" of the revolution, judged so by their lack of "virtue." Others, among them Babeuf, demanded not only political, but economic equality—an end to all distinctions between rich and poor.*

*The disorder and political uncertainty spawned by revolutionary conflict was ended when Napoleon Bonaparte took over in a coup d'etat in 1799. The general imposed order and issued a new constitution, which he overturned in 1800 and again in 1804, when he was crowned emperor in the Cathedral of Notre Dame. Despite the ending of republican institutions, French society under Napoleon and, indeed, under the Restoration (1814–1830), retained its belief in many of the principles and the practices that the revolution introduced.*

# THE DEBATE OVER NOBLE PRIVILEGE

## Royal Power Asserted

*In response to claims by the royal courts (the parlements) that they had a right to review and even refuse royal legislation, King Louis XV called the members of the courts before him to remind them of his absolute sovereign power.*

### From *The Official Transcript of the Session of the Scourging (March 3, 1766)*

This day, after the report on several cases, the king's guards having seized control of the doors, the court, informed that the king was coming to parlement, deputized messieurs . . . to go and receive him, who . . . met the said lord king at the foot of the steps, opposite the Sainte-Chapelle, and accompanied him. . . .

When the king had been elevated to his high place, had seated himself and put on his hat, he said "I wish the present session to be an exceptional one. Monsieur the President, have the chambers assemble." The President, having put on his hat, said, "Go to the Tournelle, to the Chambers, and send for the Courts of Requests of the Palace." When all these gentlemen had entered, taken their ordained places, and sat down, the king removed his hat, and, having put it on again, said:

"Gentlemen, I have come in person to reply to your remonstrances. Monsieur de Saint-Florentin, have this answer read by one of you."

Whereupon the Count de Saint-Florentin, having approached the king and knelt, took from the hands of H.M. the reply, and, having resumed his place, had it handed to Joly de Fleury, named above, who read it as follows:

"What has happened in my parlements of Pau and Rennes is no concern of my other parlements; I have acted with regard to these two courts as my authority required, and I owe an explanation to nobody.

From *The Brittany Affair and the Crisis of the Ancien Regime*, John Rothney, ed. (New York: Oxford University Press, 1969). Copyright © 1969 by Oxford University Press, Inc. Reprinted by permission of the publisher.

"I would have no other answer to give to the numerous remonstrances made to me on this subject, if their combination, the impropriety of their style, the rashness of the most erroneous principles, and the pretension of the new expressions which characterize them had not revealed the pernicious consequences of that idea of unity which I have already prohibited, and which people wish to establish as a principle at the same moment in which they dare to put it into practice.

"I shall not tolerate in my kingdom the formation of an association which would cause the natural bond of similar duties and common responsibilities to degenerate into a confederation for resistance, nor the introduction into the monarchy of an imaginary body which could only upset its harmony; the magistracy does not form a body, nor a separate order in the three orders of the kingdom; the magistrates are my officers, responsible for carrying out my truly royal duty of rendering justice to my subjects, a function which attaches them to my person and which will always render them praiseworthy in my eyes. I recognize the importance of their services; it is an illusion, which can only tend to shake confidence by a series of false alarms, to imagine that a plan has been drawn up to annihilate the magistracy, or to claim that it has enemies close to the throne; its real, its only enemies are those within it who persuade it to speak a language opposed to its principles; who lead it to claim that all the parlements together are but one and the same body, distributed in several classes; that this body, necessarily indivisible, is the essence and basis of the monarchy; that it is the seat, the tribunal, the spokesman of the nation; that it is the protector and the essential depository of the nation's liberties, interests, and rights; that it is responsible to the nation for this trust and that it would be criminal to abandon it; that it is responsible, in all concerns of the public welfare, not only to the king, but also to the nation; that it is a judge between the king and his people; that as a reciprocal guardian, it maintains the balance of government, repressing equally the excesses of liberty and the abuses of authority; that the parlements co-operate with the sovereign power in the establishment of laws; that they can sometimes on their own authority free themselves from a registered law and legally regard it as nonexistent; that they must oppose an insurmountable barrier to decisions which they attribute to arbitrary authority, and which they call illegal acts, as well as to orders which they claim to be surprises, and that, if a conflict of authority arises, it is their duty to abandon their functions and to resign from their offices, even if their resignations are not accepted. To try to make principles of such pernicious novelties is to injure the magistracy, to deny its institutional position, to betray its interests and to disregard the fundamental laws of the state; as if anyone could forget that the sovereign power resides in my person only, that sovereign power of which the natural characteristics are the spirit of consultation, justice, and reason; that my courts derive their existence and their authority from me alone; that the plenitude of that authority, which they only exercise in my name, always remains with me, and that it can never be employed against me; that to me alone belongs legislative power without subordination and undivided; that it is by my authority alone that the officers of my courts proceed, not to the formation, but to the registration, the publication, the execution of the law, and that it is permitted for them to remonstrate only within the limits of the duty of good and useful councilors; that public order in its entirety emanates from me, and that the rights and interests of the nation, which some dare to regard as a separate body from the monarch, are necessarily united with my rights and interests, and repose only in my hands.

"I am convinced that the officers of my courts will never lose sight of these sacred and immutable maxims, which are engraved on the hearts of all faithful subjects, and that they will disavow these extraneous ideas, that spirit of independence and these errors, the consequences of which they could not envisage without terror.

"Remonstrances will always be received favorably when they reflect only the moderation proper to the magistrate and to truth, when their secrecy keeps them decent and useful, and when this method [of remonstrance] so wisely established is not made a travesty of libelous utterances, in which submission to my will is presented as a crime and the accomplishment of the duties I have ordered as a subject for condemnation; in which it is supposed that the whole nation is groaning at seeing its rights, its liberty, its security on the point of perishing under a terrible power, and in which it is announced that the bonds of obedience may soon be broken; but if, after I have examined these remonstrances, and, knowing the case, I have maintained my will, my courts should persevere in their refusal to submit, and, instead of registering at the very express command of the king (an expression chosen to reflect the duty of obedience) if they undertook to annul on their own authority laws solemnly registered, and if, finally, when my authority has been compelled to be employed to its full extent, they dared still in some fashion to battle against it, by decrees of prohibition, by suspensive opposition or by irregular methods such as ceasing their service or resigning, then confusion and anarchy would take the place of legitimate order, and the scandalous spectacle of an open contradiction to my sovereign power would reduce me to the unhappy necessity of using all the power which I have received from God in order to preserve my peoples from the terrible consequences of such enterprises.

"Let the officers of my courts, then, weigh carefully what my good will deigns once again to recall to their attention; let them, in obedience only to their own sentiments, dismiss all prospects of association, all new ideas and all these expressions invented to give credit to the most false and dangerous conceptions; let them, in their decrees and remonstrances, keep within the limits of reason and of the respect which is due me; let them keep their deliberations secret and let them consider how indecent it is and how unworthy of their character to broadcast invective against the members of my council to whom I have given my orders and who have shown themselves so worthy of my confidence; I shall not permit the slightest infraction of the principles set forth in this response. I would expect to find these principles obeyed in my Parlement of Paris, even if they should be disregarded in the others; let it never forget what it has so often done to maintain these principles in all their purity, and that the court of Paris should be an example to the other courts of the kingdom. . . ."

# Noble Privilege Defended

*In response to Louis XV's insistence on royal power, the noble courts, the* parlements, *insisted on their historic right to review legislation. The constitutional dispute reached a crisis in 1771, when Chancellor Maupeou dissolved the parlements. In this document, the Parlement of Bordeaux protests against his action.*

## From *Remonstrance of the Parlement of Bordeaux (1771)*

Our system, Sire, (your Courts of Parliament have never known any other) was and always will be to cause justice to reign, to see to the happiness of the population, to the observation of the laws and to keep intact the sacred depository confided to us and to punish anyone who dares to violate it.

Our principles exist with the monarchy, monarchy cannot exist without them.

Before subjugating the Gauls, the Franks had laws or rather tacit agreements under which they had formed an association, and which usage had consecrated. We find these laws and customs [still in use] after the conquest of the Gauls; they form the constitution of the French monarchy. They assure the nation the rights to assist in the formation of new laws.

We find, under the first race of our kings, several references to the Assemblies of the Champ de Mars, which prove the assistance [given] by the nation.

The kings of the second race maintained the right of the nation to assist in the exercise of legislative power. . . .

[Charles the Bald] recognized that the orders of kings could only be considered to be laws in so far as the French had accepted them and ordered that they be observed. . . .

The terrible mixture of anarchy and tyranny created by feudal government and the strange ignorance into which all the orders of the state fell for several centuries caused all the laws to go unobserved. For a long time, no public power was known in the realm; the rights of the prince and of the nation were indeterminate. Nevertheless, one sees the parliament assembled several times in this era of disorder and confusion; and its right to assist in framing legislation is almost the only one of the fundamental laws to survive this chaos.

Thus, from the foundation of the monarchy to the reign of Philip the Fair, the nation was maintained in its right to assist in passing legislation: there is no law without its consent. . . . Even if your Courts of parliament, Sire, hadn't the right to examine and verify such new laws as it may please your majesty to propose, this right could not be lost to the nation. It is imprescriptible and inalienable. To attack this principle is to betray not only the nation but kings themselves; it is to overthrow the constitution of the kingdom, to destroy the foundation of the monarch's authority. Can it be believed that verification of new laws in the Courts of parliament does not fulfil this original right of the nation? Could public order profit from its being exercised once again by the nation? As soon as your Majesty deigns to reestablish the nation in the enjoyment of its rights, we shall no longer demand the sort of authority which your royal predecessors have granted us.

But until then, Sire, be so kind as to consider that the verification of new laws is a duty inseparable from our functions: there is no law without verification, as there could be none without the consent of the nation assembled.

Is this rule of state merely an empty formula? Has the population been told of an examination, a verification of the laws to which they are to be subject only as a means of fooling them more surely, by forcing your Courts of Parliament to register them without examination or against their conscience? Do entries of laws on the court registers carried out by order of the king suffice to give the king's will the sanction and character of law? Would it then be possible to order the magistrates to approve, by their silence or their presence, the infringement of fundamental laws? Could they fail to speak the truth without betraying the state and the sovereign? Could they be forced to fool the population themselves, by allowing it to believe that they have verified and registered [an edict] when there has been neither examination nor deliberation?

A long time ago it was said in your name and presence "that the Courts of parliament were the depositories of the sacred rights of the crown and of the liberties of the realm; that the king had confided this portion of his authority to them". They were ordered to use it with the steadfastness that their consciences demanded.

In the very first moments of your reign you recognized, Sire, that you could do nothing more advantageous for your service than to re-establish the ancient freedom of verification of parliament. Oh! how could the laws be verified without this freedom? Verification necessarily supposes examination and deliberation, and there can be no deliberation without freedom of choice.

We will not hide from you the fact, Sire, that this freedom has been infringed more than once; but the protests of your Courts of Parliament have always maintained the fundamental law of free verification. The numerous efforts of arbitrary power have always failed or, at least, its temporary successes have served only to prove the wisdom and utility of the established way of doing things; these very successes have strengthened the dominion of the fundamental law.

Such is the dominion of the fundamental law in your realm, Sire, that it sustains and perpetuates itself by its own strength. The greatest, wisest and best kings, the very ones who were most jealous of their authority, have not hesitated to recognize this fact. The more attacks have been made against the fundamental law, the more it has been proven that it is bound to the monarchy and can perish only with the monarchy.

Your Courts of parliament, Sire, have always used the freedom the fundamental law gives them for the welfare of the state and the glory of the king. If they have resisted [your orders] it was to defend your rights or those of your predecessors; and never have they shown more zeal and fidelity than when they seemed to oppose the will of those who held the reins of state.

[The king's evil advisors] do not wish to recognize any of the fundamental principles of the monarchy. The new law presented on your behalf [to destroy the authority of parliament] excludes them all. It establishes a law that destroys all laws. It is desired that your Parliament sitting in Paris should receive and have executed, as laws, all the wishes that will seem to emanate from Your Majesty, even when just motives keep them from proceeding freely to their registration. Remonstrances are permitted, and they may be reiterated. But to order at the same time that, in case of a persevering royal will, the transcription of the edicts on the registers of your courts, done in your presence or by bearers of your orders, replace and have the same effect as a free and thoughtful verification—is this not to destroy the apparent freedom we have to speak to you of the needs of your people? Is this not to render vain and fruitless our right to make you hear their groaning? And, finally, it is not, under the guise of the specious mildness of monarchical government, really to exercise the rigors of despotism?

# Noble Privilege Challenged

*Emmanuel Joseph Sieyès (1748–1836), an abbé, became famous with the publication in 1789 of his pamphlet,* What Is the Third Estate? *Sieyès justified the attack on noble privilege and offered a plan for the creation of a National Assembly.*

## From Abbé Sieyès. *What Is the Third Estate?*

What is necessary that a nation should subsist and prosper? Individual effort and public functions.

All individual efforts may be included in four classes: 1. Since the earth and the waters furnish crude products for the needs of man, the first class, in logical sequence, will be that of all families which devote themselves to agricultural labor. 2. Between the first sale of products and their consumption or use, a new manipulation, more or less repeated, adds to these products a second value more or less composite. In this manner human industry succeeds in perfecting the gifts of nature, and the crude product increases two-fold, ten-fold, one hundred-fold in value. Such are the efforts of the second class. 3. Between production and consumption, as well as between the various stages of production, a group of intermediary agents establish themselves, useful both to producers and consumers; these are the merchants and brokers: the brokers who, comparing incessantly the demands of time and place, speculate upon the profit of retention and transportation; merchants who are charged with distribution, in the last analysis, either at wholesale or at retail. This species of utility characterizes the third class. 4. Outside of these three classes of productive and useful citizens, who are occupied with real objects of consumption and use, there is also need in a society of a series of efforts and pains, whose objects are directly useful or agreeable to the individual. This fourth class embraces all those who stand between the most distinguished and liberal professions and the less esteemed services of domestics.

From *Translations and Reprints from the Original Sources of European History* (Philadelphia: Department of History, University of Pennsylvania, 1900), Vol. 6, No. 1, pp. 32–35.

Such are the efforts which sustain society. Who puts them forth? The Third Estate.

Public functions may be classified equally well, in the present state of affairs, under four recognized heads; the sword, the robe, the church and the administration. It would be superfluous to take them up one by one, for the purpose of showing that everywhere the Third Estate attends to nineteen-twentieths of them, with this distinction; that it is laden with all that which is really painful, with all the burdens which the privileged classes refuse to carry. Do we give the Third Estate credit for this? That this might come about, it would be necessary that the Third Estate should refuse to fill these places, or that is should be less ready to exercise their functions. The facts are well known. Meanwhile they have dared to impose a prohibition upon the order of the Third Estate. They have said to it: "Whatever may be your services, whatever may be your abilities, you shall go thus far; you may not pass beyond!" Certain rare exceptions, properly regarded, are but a mockery, and the terms which are indulged in on such occasions, one insult the more.

If this exclusion is a social crime against the Third Estate; if it is a veritable act of hostility, could it perhaps be said that it is useful to the public weal? Alas! who is ignorant of the effects of monopoly? If it discourages those whom it rejects, is it not well known that it tends to render less able those whom it favors? Is it not understood that every employment from which free competition is removed, becomes dearer and less effective?

In setting aside any function whatsoever to serve as an appanage for a distinct class among citizens, is it not to be observed that it is no longer the man alone who does the work that it is necessary to reward, but all the unemployed members of that same caste, and also the entire families of those who are employed as well as those who are not? Is it not to be remarked that since the government has become the patrimony of a particular class, it has been distended beyond all measure; places have been created, not on account of the necessities of the governed, but in the interests of the governing, etc., etc.? Has not attention been called to the fact that this order of things, which is basely and—I even presume to say—beastly respectable with us, when we find it in reading the History of Ancient Egypt or the accounts of Voyages to the Indies, is despicable, monstrous, destructive of all industry, the enemy of social progress; above all degrading to the human race in general, and particularly intolerable to Europeans, etc., etc.? But I must leave these considerations, which, if they increase the importance of the subject and throw light upon it, perhaps, along with the new light, slacken our progress.

It suffices here to have made it clear that the pretended utility of a privileged order for the public service is nothing more than a chimera;

that with it all that which is burdensome in this service is performed by the Third Estate; that without it the superior places would be infinitely better filled; that they naturally ought to be the lot and the recompense of ability and recognized services, and that if privileged persons have come to usurp all the lucrative and honorable posts, it is a hateful injustice to the rank and file of citizens and at the same time a treason to the public weal.

Who then shall dare to say that the Third Estate has not within itself all that is necessary for the formation of a complete nation? It is the strong and robust man who has one arm still shackled. If the privileged order should be abolished, the nation would be nothing less, but something more. Therefore, what is the Third Estate? Everything, but an everything shackled and oppressed. What would it be without the privileged order? Everything, but an everything free and flourishing. Nothing can succeed without it, everything would be infinitely better without the others.

It is not sufficient to show that privileged persons, far from being useful to the nation, cannot but enfeeble and injure it; it is necessary to prove further that the noble order does not enter at all into the social organization; that it may indeed be a burden upon the nation, but that it cannot of itself constitute a nation.

In the first place, it is not possible in the number of all the elementary parts of a nation to find a place for the *caste* of nobles. I know that there are individuals in great number whom infirmities, incapacity, incurable laziness, or the weight of bad habits render strangers to the labors of society. The exception and the abuse are everywhere found beside the rule. But it will be admitted that the less there are of these abuses, the better it will be for the State. The worst possible arrangement of all would be where not alone isolated individuals, but a whole class of citizens should take pride in remaining motionless in the midst of the general movement, and should consume the best part of the product without bearing any part in its production. Such a class is surely estranged to the nation by its indolence.

The noble order is not less estranged from the generality of us by its civil and political prerogatives.

What is a nation? A body of associates, living under a common law, and represented by the same legislature, etc.

Is it not evident that the noble order has privileges and expenditures which it dares to call its rights, but which are apart from the rights of the great body of citizens? It departs there from the common order, from the common law. So its civil rights make of it an isolated people in the midst of the great nation. This is truly *imperium in imperio*.

In regard to its political rights, these also it exercises apart. It has its special representatives, which are not charged with securing the interests of the people. The body of its deputies sit apart; and when it is assembled in the same hall with the deputies of simple citizens, it is none the less true that its representation is essentially distinct and separate: it is a stranger to the nation, in the first place, by its origin, since its commission is not derived from the people; then by its object, which consists of defending not the general, but the particular interest.

The Third Estate embraces then all that which belongs to the nation; and all that which is not the Third Estate, cannot be regarded as being of the nation. What is the Third Estate? It is the whole.

# THE THIRD ESTATE TRIUMPHANT

## The Fall of the Bastille

*On July 14, 1789, crowds of Parisians, in search of arms to protect their revolution, captured the old prison, the Bastille. Though it contained few prisoners, the building symbolized the despotism of the old regime. Its fall marked the triumph of "liberty" and the intervention of the Parisian populace into the turbulent events of the revolution.*

### From *A Parisian Newspaper Account, July 14, 1789*

Tuesday 14 July

The night of Monday to Tuesday was extremely quiet, apart from the arrest by the citizen militia of some thirty-four unauthorised persons, who had plundered and caused a great deal of damage at St.-Lazare; they have been taken into custody. . . .

But a victory of outstanding significance, and one which will perhaps astonish our descendants, was the taking of the Bastille, in four hours or so.

First, the people tried to enter this fortress by the Rue St.-Antoine, this fortress, which no one has ever penetrated against the wishes of this frightful despotism and where the monster still resided. The treacherous governor had put out a flag of peace. So a confident advance was made; a detachment of French Guards, with perhaps five to six thousand armed bourgeois, penetrated the Bastille's outer courtyards, but as soon as some six hundred persons had passed over the first drawbridge, the bridge was raised and artillery fire mowed down several French Guards and some soldiers; the cannon fired on the town, and the people took fright; a large number of individuals were killed or wounded; but then they rallied and took shelter from the fire; a row of bayonets, fixed in the wall, enabled some brave individual to cut through a post that locked the drawbridge; immediately it fell and they came to the second ditch, near which lay the first victims; mean-

From J. Gilchrist and W. Murray, *The Press in the French Revolution: A Selection of Documents Taken from the Press of the Revolution for the Years 1789–1794* (London: St. Martin's, 1971), pp. 53–55. Reprinted by permission of Ginn and Company Ltd.

while, they tried to locate some cannon; they attacked from the water's edge through the gardens of the arsenal, and from there made an orderly siege; they advanced from various directions, beneath a ceaseless round of fire. It was a terrible scene. The brave French Guard did wonders. About three o'clock they captured the overseer of the gunpowder store, whose uniform made them mistake him for the Governor of the Bastille; he was manhandled and taken to the town, where he was recognised and set free. The fighting grew steadily more intense; the citizens had become hardened to the fire; from all directions they clambered onto the roofs or broke into the rooms; as soon as an enemy appeared among the turrets on the tower, he was fixed in the sights of a hundred guns and mown down in an instant; meanwhile cannon fire was hurriedly directed against the second drawbridge, which it pierced, breaking the chains; in vain did the cannon on the tower reply, for most people were sheltered from it; the fury was at its height; people bravely faced death and every danger; women, in their eagerness, helped us to the utmost; even the children, after the discharge of fire from the fortress, ran here and there picking up the bullets and shot; [and so the Bastille fell and the governor, De Launay, was captured] . . . they strip him of his badges of rank; they treat him shamelessly; he is dragged through the crowd . . . Serene and blessed liberty, for the first time, has at last been introduced into this abode of horrors, this frightful refuge of monstrous despotism and its crimes.

Meanwhile, they get ready to march; they leave amidst an enormous crowd; the applause, the outbursts of joy, the insults, the oaths hurled at the treacherous prisoners of war; everything is confused; cries of vengeance and of pleasure issue from every heart; the conquerors, glorious and covered in honour, carry their arms and the spoils of the conquered, the flags of victory, the militia mingling with the soldiers of the fatherland, the victory laurels offered them from every side,—all this created a frightening and splendid spectacle. On arriving at the square, the people, anxious to avenge themselves, allowed neither De Launay nor the other officers to reach the place of trial; they seized them from the hands of their conquerors, and trampled them underfoot one after the other. De Launay was struck by a thousand blows, his head was cut off and hoisted on the end of a pike with blood streaming down all sides. . . . This glorious day must amaze our enemies, and finally usher in for us the triumph of justice and liberty. In the evening, there were celebrations.

## Feudal Rights Abolished

*On the night of August 4, 1789, after hearing reports of peasant uprisings in the countryside, the delegates to the National Assembly voted to destroy noble rights and privileges that still existed. The declarations of that long and dramatic session were set forth more soberly in the decree of August 11. On*

*August 26, the Assembly voted for the Declaration of the Rights of Man and Citizen, which was to serve as a preamble to the new constitution. A year later, the Assembly turned its attention to the Catholic church and, in its most controversial early legislation, it confiscated church lands, stripped church officials of special privileges, and established the clergy as paid servants of the French state.*

## The August 4th Decrees (4–11 August, 1789)

1. The National Assembly abolishes the feudal regime entirely, and decreees that both feudal and *censuel* rights and dues deriving from real or personal *mainmorte* and personal servitude, and those representative thereof, are abolished without indemnity, and all others declared redeemable; and that the price and manner of redemption shall be established by the National Assembly. Those of the said dues which are not suppressed by the present decree, however, shall continue to be collected until reimbursement has been made.

2. The exclusive right to *fuies* and *colombiers* is abolished; pigeons shall be confined at times determined by the communities; and during such periods they shall be regarded as game, and everyone shall have the right to kill them on his own land.

3. The exclusive right of hunting and open warrens is likewise abolished; and every proprietor has the right to destroy and to have destroyed, on his own property only, every kind of game, conditional upon conformity with police regulations relative to public security.

All *capitaineries*, even royal ones, and all hunting preserves, under whatever denomination, are likewise abolished; and provision shall be made, by means compatible with the respect due property and liberty, for the preservation of the personal diversions of the King.

The President shall be charged with requesting the King for the recall of persons exiled and consigned to the galleys simply for hunting, the release of prisoners now detained, and the cancellation of existing proceedings in that connection.

4. All seigneurial courts of justice are suppressed without any indemnity; nevertheless, the officials of such courts shall continue in office until the National Assembly has provided for the establishment of a new judicial organization.

5. Tithes of every kind and dues which take the place thereof, under whatever denomination they are known and collected, even by subscription, *possessed by secular and regular bodies*, by beneficed clergymen, *fabriques* and all persons in *mainmorte*, even by the Order of Malta and

other religious and military orders, even those abandoned to laity in substitution for and option of *portion congruë*, are abolished, subject to the devising of means for providing in some other manner for the expenses of divine worship, the maintenance of ministers of religion, relief of the poor, repairs and rebuilding of churches and parsonages, and for all establishments, seminaries, schools, colleges, hospitals, communities and others, to the maintenance of which they are now assigned. Meanwhile, until such provision is made and the former possessors are furnished with their equivalent, the National Assembly orders that collection of the said tithes shall continue according to law and in the usual manner. Other tithes, of whatever nature, shall be redeemable according to the regulations of the Assembly; and until such regulations are made, the National Assembly orders that the collection thereof also be continued.

6. All perpetual ground rents, either in kind or in money, of whatever species, whatever their origin, to whatever persons they are due . . . shall be redeemable; *champarts* of every kind and denomination likewise shall be redeemable at a rate established by the Assembly. No nonredeemable due may be created henceforth.

7. Venality of judicial and municipal offices is suppressed henceforth. Justice shall be rendered gratuitously; nevertheless, the incumbents of said offices shall continue to perform their duties and to collect the emoluments thereof until the Assembly has provided means of procuring their reimbursement.

8. The contingent fees of country *curés* are suppressed, and shall cease to be paid as soon as provision has been made for the increase of the *portions congruës* and for the payment of vicars; and a regulation determining the lot of the town *curés* shall be made.

9. Pecuniary privileges, personal or real, in matters of taxation are abolished forever. Collection shall be made from all citizens and on all property, in the same manner and in the same form; and means of effecting proportional payment of all taxes, even for the last six months of the current year, shall be considered.

10. Since a national constitution and public liberty are more advantageous to the provinces than the privileges which some of them enjoy, and the sacrifice of which is necessary for the close union of all parts of the realm, all special privileges of provinces, principalities, *pays*, cantons, cities, and communities of inhabitants, whether pecuniary or of any other kind, are declared abolished forever, and shall be absorbed into the law common to all Frenchmen.

11. All citizens may be admitted, without distinction of birth, to all ecclesiastical, civil, and military employments and offices, and no useful profession shall entail forfeiture.

12. In future no *deniers* for annates or for any other cause whatsoever shall be dispatched to the court of Rome, the vice-legation at Avignon, or the nunciature at Lucerne; diocesans shall address them-

selves to their bishops for all provisions of benefices and dispensations, which shall be granted gratuitously . . .

13. The *déports,* rights of *côte-morte, dépouilles, vacat, censuel* dues, Peter's pence, and others of the same kind established in favor of bishops, archdeacons, archpriests, chapters, *curés primitifs,* and all others, under any name whatsoever, are abolished, subject to suitable provision for the endowment of insufficiently endowed archdeacons and archpriests.

14. Plurality of benefices shall no longer exist when the revenues of the benefice or benefices of an incumbent exceed the sum of 3,000 *livres.* Possession of several pensions on a benefice, or a pension and a benefice, shall no longer be permitted if the revenue from those already held exceeds the said sum of 3,000 *livres.*

15. On the basis of the account to be rendered concerning the state of pensions, favors, and stipends, the National Assembly, in concert with the King, shall undertake the suppression of those which are not merited, and the reduction of those which are excessive, subject to determining for the future a sum which the King may use for such purpose.

16. The National Assembly decrees that, in memory of the impressive and momentous deliberations just held for the welfare of France, a medal shall be struck, and that, as an expression of gratitude, a *Te Deum* shall be sung in all parishes and churches of the kingdom.

17. The National Assembly solemnly proclaims King Louis XVI *Restorer of French Liberty.*

18. The National Assembly shall repair *en masse* to the King to present to His Majesty the decree just pronounced, to bear him the homage of its most respectful gratitude, and to supplicate him to permit the *Te Deum* to be sung in his chapel, and to be present there himself.

19. Immediately after the Constitution, the National Assembly shall undertake the drafting of laws necessary for the development of the principles established by the present decree, which, with the decree of the tenth of this month, shall be dispatched immediately by the deputies into all the provinces, there to be printed, proclaimed also at the parish sermons, and posted wherever necessary.

## Declaration of the Rights of Man and Citizen
### (27 August, 1789)

The representatives of the French people, organized in National Assembly, considering that ignorance, forgetfulness, or contempt of the rights of man are the sole causes of public misfortunes and of the corruption of governments, have resolved to set forth in a solemn declaration the natural, inalienable, and sacred rights of man, in order that such declaration, continually before all members of the social body, may be a perpetual reminder of their rights and duties; in order that the acts of the legislative power and those of the executive power may constantly be compared with the aim of every political institution and may accordingly be more respected; in order that the demands of the citizens, founded henceforth upon simple and incontestable principles, may always be directed towards the maintenance of the Constitution and the welfare of all.

Accordingly, the National Assembly recognizes and proclaims, in the presence and under the auspices of the Supreme Being, the following rights of man and citizen.

1. Men are born and remain free and equal in rights; social distinctions may be based only upon general usefulness.

2. The aim of every political association is the preservation of the natural and inalienable rights of man; these rights are liberty, property, security, and resistance to oppression.

3. The source of all sovereignty resides essentially in the nation; no group, no individual may exercise authority not emanating expressly therefrom.

4. Liberty consists of the power to do whatever is not injurious to others; thus the enjoyment of the natural rights of every man has for its limits only those that assure other members of society the enjoyment of those same rights; such limits may be determined only by law.

5. The law has the right to forbid only actions which are injurious to society. Whatever is not forbidden by law may not be prevented, and no one may be constrained to do what it does not prescribe.

6. Law is the expression of the general will; all citizens have the right to concur personally, or through their representatives, in its formation; it must be the same for all, whether it protects or punishes. All citizens, being equal before it, are equally admissible to all public offices, positions, and employments, according to their capacity, and without other distinction than that of virtues and talents.

7. No man may be accused, arrested, or detained except in the cases determined by law, and according to the forms prescribed thereby. Whoever solicit, expedite, or execute arbitrary orders, or have them executed, must be punished; but every citizen summoned or apprehended in pursuance of the law must obey immediately; he renders himself culpable by resistance.

8. The law is to establish only penalties that are absolutely and obviously necessary; and no one may be punished except by virtue of a law established and promulgated prior to the offence and legally applied.

9. Since every man is presumed innocent until declared guilty, if arrest be deemed indispensable, all unnecessary severity for securing the person of the accused must be severely repressed by law.

10. No one is to be disquieted because of his opinions, even religious, provided their manifestation does not disturb the public order established by law.

11. Free communication of ideas and opinions is one of the most precious of the rights of man. Consequently, every citizen may speak, write, and print freely, subject to responsibility for the abuse of such liberty in the cases determined by law.

12. The guarantee of the rights of man and citizen necessitates a public force; such a force, therefore, is instituted for the advantage of all and not for the particular benefit of those to whom it is entrusted.

13. For the maintenance of the public force and for the expenses of administration a common tax is indispensable; it must be assessed equally on all citizens in proportion to their means.

14. Citizens have the right to ascertain, by themselves or through their representatives, the necessity of the public tax, to consent to it freely, to supervise its use, and to determine its quota, assessment, payment, and duration.

15. Society has the right to require of every public agent an accounting of his administration.

16. Every society in which the guarantee of rights is not assured or the separation of powers not determined has no constitution at all.

17. Since property is a sacred and inviolable right, no one may be deprived thereof unless a legally established public necessity obviously requires it, and upon condition of a just and previous indemnity.

## From *The Civil Constitution of the Clergy (July 12, 1790)*

### Title I. Of Ecclesiastical Offices

1. Each and every department shall constitute a single diocese . . . and every diocese shall have the same extent and limits as the department. . . .

4. No church or parish of France, and no French citizen, may, under any circumstances or on any pretext whatsoever, acknowledge the authority of an ordinary bishop or archbishop whose see is established under the name of a foreign power, or that of its delegates residing in France or elsewhere; without prejudice, however, to the unity of faith and communion, which shall be maintained with the Visible Head of the Universal Church as hereinafter provided. . .

6. A new organization and division of all parishes of the kingdom shall be undertaken immediately, upon the advice of the diocesan bishop and the district administrations; the number and extent thereof shall be determined according to rules to be established. . .

From John Hall Stewart, ed., *A Documentary Survey of the French Revolution* (New York: Macmillan, 1951), pp. 169–181. Copyright 1951 by Macmillan Publishing Co., Inc., renewed 1979 by John Hall Stewart. Reprinted by permission of the publishers.

9. There shall be sixteen vicars of the cathedral church in cities of more than 10,000 inhabitants, but only twelve where the population is fewer than 10,000 inhabitants.

10. In each and every diocese one seminary only shall be preserved or established for preparation for orders, without intending any prejudice for the present with regard to other houses of instruction and education. . . .

15. In all cities and towns of not more than 6,000 inhabitants there shall be only one parish; other parishes shall be suppressed and united with the principal church.

16. In cities of more than 6,000 inhabitants every parish may include a greater number of parishioners, and as many parishes shall be preserved or established as the needs of the people and the localities require.

17. The administrative assemblies, in concert with the diocesan bishop, shall indicate to the next legislature the parishes and annexes or chapels of ease in town and country which it is fitting to preserve, extend, establish, or suppress; and they shall indicate the limits thereof according to the needs of the people and the different localities, and as befits the dignity of religion. . . .

20. All titles and offices, other than those mentioned in the present constitution, dignities, canonries, prebends, half prebends, chapels, chaplaincies, in both cathedral and collegiate churches, and all regular and secular chapters of either sex, abbeys and priories, regular or *in commendam,* of either sex, and all other benefices and *prestimonies* in general of whatever kind and under whatever denomination, are abolished and suppressed dating from the day of publication of the present decree, and similar ones may never be established. . . .

## Title II. Of Appointment to Benefices

1. Dating from the day of publication of the present decree, appointments to bishoprics and cures are to be made by election only.

2. All elections shall be by ballot and absolute majority of votes.

3. The election of bishops shall take place according to the form prescribed by, and by the electoral body designated in, the decree of 22 December, 1789, for the appointment of members of the departmental assembly. . . .

6. The election of the bishop may take place or be initiated only on a Sunday, in the principal church of the chief town of the department, following the parochial mass, at which all electors are required to be present. . . .

19. The new bishop may not apply to the Pope for confirmation, but shall write to him as the Visible Head of the Universal Church, in testimony of the unity of faith and communion which he is to maintain therewith.

20. The consecration of a bishop may be performed only in his ca-

thedral church by his metropolitan or, failing him, by the oldest bishop in the *arrondissement* of the metropolitan see, assisted by the bishops of the two nearest dioceses, on a Sunday, during the parochial mass, in the presence of the people and the clergy.

21. Before the ceremony of consecration begins, the bishop-elect shall take a solemn oath, in the presence of the municipal officials, the people, and the clergy, to watch with care over the faithful of the diocese entrusted to him, to be faithful to the nation, to the law, and to the King, and to maintain with all his power the Constitution decreed by the National Assembly and accepted by the King.

22. The bishop shall have the liberty of choosing the vicars of his cathedral church from among all the clergy of his diocese, provided that he names only priests who have performed ecclesiastical duties for at least ten years. He may remove them only upon the advice of his council, and by a resolution decided by majority vote and with full knowledge of the circumstances. . . .

25. The election of *curés* shall be conducted according to the forms prescribed by, and by the electors designated in, the decree of 22 December, 1789, for the election of members of the district administrative assembly. . . .

30. The election of *curés* may be held or initiated only on a Sunday, in the principal church of the chief town of the district, at the close of the parish mass, at which all electors are required to be present.

31. The announcement of those elected shall be made by the president of the electoral body, in the principal church, before the solemn mass which is to be celebrated for such purpose, and in the presence of the people and the clergy.

# Exporting the Revolution

*As France entered wars with the European monarchies, it defined its fight as a crusade of liberty against the tyranny of despots and it appealed to people in those countries where French armies fought to rise up and create a revolution of their own. The Propagandist Decrees, drawn up in November and December of 1792, stated the position of the National Convention.*

## The Propagandist Decrees (1792)

### The First Propagandist Decree
### November 19, 1792

The National Convention declares, in the name of the French nation, that it will grant fraternity and aid to all peoples who wish to recover their liberty; and it charges the executive power with giving the generals the orders necessary for bringing aid to such peoples and for defending citizens who have been, or who might be, harassed for the cause of liberty.

## The Second Propagandist Decree
## December 15, 1792

The National Convention, having heard the report of its combined Committees of Finance, War, and Diplomacy; faithful to the principles of the sovereignty of the people, which do not permit it to recognize any institutions detrimental thereto, and wishing to establish the rules to be followed by the generals of the armies of the Republic in territories where they bear arms, decrees:

1. In territories which are or may be occupied by the armies of the Republic, the generals shall proclaim immediately, in the name of the French nation, the sovereignty of the people, the suppression of all established authorities and of existing imposts or taxes, the abolition of the tithe, of feudalism, of seigneurial rights, both feudal and *censuel,* fixed or contingent, of *banalités,* of real and personal servitude, of hunting and fishing privileges, of *corvées,* of nobility, and generally of all privileges.

2. They shall announce to the people that they bring it peace, aid, fraternity, liberty, and equality, and they shall convoke it thereafter in primary or communal assemblies, in order to create and organize a provisional administration and justice; they shall supervise the security of persons, and property; they shall have the present decree and the proclamation annexed thereto printed in the language or idiom of the territory and posted and executed without delay in every commune.

3. All agents and civil or military officials of the former government, as well as individuals heretofore considered noble, or members of any corporation heretofore privileged, shall be, for this time only, inadmissible to vote in the primary or communal assemblies, and they may not be elected to positions in the provisional administration or judiciary.

4. The generals shall place, consecutively, under the safeguard and protection of the French Republic all real and personal property belonging to the public treasury, to the prince, his abettors, adherents, and voluntary satellites, to public establishments, and to lay and ecclesiastical bodies and communities; they shall have a detailed statement thereof drafted promptly and dispatched to the Executive Council, and they shall take all measures within their power in order that such properties be respected.

From John Hall Stewart, ed., *A Documentary Survey of the French Revolution* (New York: Macmillan, 1951), pp. 381–384. Copyright 1951 by Macmillan Publishing Company, renewed 1979 by John Hall Stewart. Reprinted by permission of the publishers.

5. The provisional administration, elected by the people, shall be responsible for the surveillance and administration of matters placed under the safeguard and protection of the French Republic; it shall supervise the security of persons and property; it shall have the laws now in force relative to the trial of civil and criminal suits, to the police, and to public security put into effect; it shall be in charge of regulating and paying local expenses and those necessary for the common defence; it may institute taxes, provided, however, that they are not borne by the indigent and hard-working portion of the population.

6. As soon as the provisional administration has been organized, the National Convention shall appoint commissioners from within its own body to go to fraternize with it.

7. The Executive Council also shall appoint national commissioners who shall go, consecutively, to the places, to consult the generals and the provisional administration elected by the people concerning measures to be taken for the common defence and concerning the means to be employed to procure the clothing and provisions necessary for the armies, and to pay their [i.e., the armies] expenses during their sojourn on its territory.

8. The national commissioners appointed by the Executive Council shall render it a fortnightly account of their activities. The Executive Council shall approve, modify, or reject same, and, in turn, shall render account thereof to the Convention.

9. The provisional administration elected by the people, and the functions of the national commissioners shall terminate as soon as the inhabitants, after having declared the sovereignty and independence of the people, liberty, and equality, have organized a form of free and popular government.

10. A statement shall be made of the expenses which the French Republic has incurred for the common defence, and of the sums which it may have received, and the French nation shall make arrangements with the established government for whatever is due; and, in case the common interest requires the troops of the Republic to remain upon foreign territory beyond that time, it shall take suitable measures to provide for their maintenance.

11. The French nation declares that it will treat as an enemy of the people anyone who, refusing liberty and equality, or renouncing them, might wish to preserve, recall, or treat with the prince and the privileged castes; it promises and engages itself not to subscribe to any treaty, and not to lay down its arms until after the establishment of the sovereignty and independence of the people upon whose territory the troops of the Republic have entered, who shall have adopted the principles of equality and established a free and popular government.

12. The Executive Council shall dispatch the present decree by special messengers to all generals, and shall take the necessary measures for assuring its execution.

Brothers and friends, we have gained liberty and we shall maintain it. We offer to help you enjoy this inestimable good which has always belonged to us, and of which our oppressors have not been able to deprive us without crime.

We have expelled your tyrants; show yourselves free men, and we will guarantee you from their vengeance, their designs, and their return.

Henceforth the French nation proclaims the sovereignty of the people, the suppression of all civil and military authorities which have governed you up to the present, and of all taxes which you sustain, in whatever form they exist; the abolition of the tithe, of feudalism, of seigneurial rights, both feudal and *censuel,* fixed or contingent, of *banalités,* of real and personal servitude, of hunting and fishing privileges, of *corvées,* of the *gabelle,* of tolls, of *octrois,* and generally of every species of contributions with which you have been burdened by your usurpers; it proclaims also the abolition among you of every corporation, noble, sacerdotal, and others, of all prerogatives and privileges that are contrary to equality. You are henceforth, brothers and friends, all citizens, all equal in rights, and all equally summoned to govern, to serve, and to defend your *Patrie.*

Assemble immediately in primary or communal assemblies, hasten to establish your provisional administrations and courts, conforming therein to the provisions of article 3 of the above decree. The agents of the French Republic will consult you in order to assure your welfare and the fraternity which is to exist henceforth between us.

# CHALLENGES TO LIBERAL
# REVOLUTIONARIES

## Are Women Citizens?

*During the Revolution some women formed clubs and republican societies; others supported the claims of the third estate and sans-culottes by engaging in street demonstrations and attending political meetings. A small group of women demanded the right to vote and enjoy the liberties of citizens. Olympe de Gouges wrote a declaration of women's rights to parallel the Declaration of the Rights of Man and Citizen. In 1793, the National Convention denied the women's appeal and, indeed, ruled that women had no political role in the new society the revolution was creating.*

### From Olympe de Gouges. *Declaration of the Rights of Woman and the Female Citizen (1791)*

Man, are you capable of being just? It is a woman who poses the question; you will not deprive her of that right at least. Tell me, what gives you sovereign empire to oppress my sex? Your strength? Your talents? Observe the Creator in his wisdom; survey in all her grandeur that nature with whom you seem to want to be in harmony, and give me, if you dare, an example of this tyrannical empire. Go back to animals, consult the elements, study plants, finally glance at all the modifications of organic matter, and surrender to the evidence when I offer you the means; search, probe, and distinguish, if you can, the sexes in the administration of nature. Everywhere you will find them mingled; everywhere they cooperate in harmonious togetherness in this immortal masterpiece.

Man alone has raised his exceptional circumstances to a principle. Bizarre, blind, bloated with science and degenerated—in a century of enlightenment and wisdom—into the crassest ignorance, he wants to command as a despot a sex which is in full possession of its intellectual faculties; he pretends to enjoy the Revolution and to claim his rights to equality in order to say nothing more about it.

From Darlene Levy, H. Applewhite, and M. Johnson, eds., *Women in Revolutionary Paris, 1785–1795* (Champaign, Ill.: University of Illinois Press, 1979), pp. 89–93. Reprinted by permission of the publisher.

## Declaration of the Rights of Woman and the Female Citizen

For the National Assembly to decree in its last sessions, or in those of the next legislature:

### Preamble

Mothers, daughters, sisters [and] representatives of the nation demand to be constituted into a national assembly. Believing that ignorance, omission, or scorn for the rights of woman are the only causes of public misfortunes and of the corruption of governments, [the women] have resolved to set forth in a solemn declaration the natural, inalienable, and sacred rights of woman in order that this declaration, constantly exposed before all the members of the society, will ceaselessly remind them of their rights and duties; in order that the authoritative acts of women and the authoritative acts of men may be at any moment compared with and respectful of the purpose of all political institutions; and in order that citizens' demands, henceforth based on simple and incontestable principles, will always support the constitution, good morals, and the happiness of all.

Consequently, the sex that is as superior in beauty as it is in courage during the sufferings of maternity recognizes and declares in the presence and under the auspices of the Supreme Being, the following Rights of Woman and of Female Citizens.

### Article I

Woman is born free and lives equal to man in her rights. Social distinctions can be based only on the common utility.

### Article II

The purpose of any political association is the conservation of the natural and imprescriptible rights of woman and man; these rights are liberty, property, security, and especially resistance to oppression.

### Article III

The principle of all sovereignty rests essentially with the nation, which is nothing but the union of woman and man; no body and no individual can exercise any authority which does not come expressly from it [the nation].

### Article IV

Liberty and justice consist of restoring all that belongs to others; thus, the only limits on the exercise of the natural rights of woman are perpetual male tyranny; these limits are to be reformed by the laws of nature and reason.

## Article V

Laws of nature and reason proscribe all acts harmful to society; everything which is not prohibited by these wise and divine laws cannot be prevented, and no one can be constrained to do what they do not command.

## Article VI

The law must be the expression of the general will; all female and male citizens must contribute either personally or through their representatives to its formation; it must be the same for all: male and female citizens, being equal in the eyes of the law, must be equally admitted to all honors, positions, and public employment according to their capacity and without other distinctions besides those of their virtues and talents.

## Article VII

No woman is an exception; she is accused, arrested, and detained in cases determined by law. Women, like men, obey this rigorous law.

## Article VIII

The law must establish only those penalties that are strictly and obviously necessary, and no one can be punished except by virtue of a law established and promulgated prior to the crime and legally applicable to women.

## Article IX

Once any woman is declared guilty, complete rigor is [to be] exercised by the law.

## Article X

No one is to be disquieted for his very basic opinions; woman has the right to mount the scaffold; she must equally have the right to mount the rostrum, provided that her demonstrations do not disturb the legally established public order.

## Article XI

The free communication of thoughts and opinions is one of the most precious rights of woman, since that liberty assures the recognition of children by their fathers. Any female citizen thus may say freely, I am the mother of a child which belongs to you, without being forced by a barbarous prejudice to hide the truth; [an exception may be made] to respond to the abuse of this liberty in cases determined by the law.

## Article XII

The guarantee of the rights of woman and the female citizen implies a major benefit; this guarantee must be instituted for the advantage of all, and not for the particular benefit of those to whom it is entrusted.

## Article XIII

For the support of the public force and the expenses of administration, the contributions of woman and man are equal; she shares all the duties [*corvées*] and all the painful tasks; therefore, she must have the same share in the distribution of positions, employment, offices, honors, and jobs [*industrie*].

## Article XIV

Female and male citizens have the right to verify, either by themselves or through their representatives, the necessity of the public contribution. This can only apply to women if they are granted an equal share, not only of wealth, but also of public administration, and in the determination of the proportion, the base, the collection, and the duration of the tax.

## Article XV

The collectivity of women, joined for tax purposes to the aggregate of men, has the right to demand an accounting of his administration from any public agent.

## Article XVI

No society has a constitution without the guarantee of rights and the separation of powers; the constitution is null if the majority of individuals comprising the nation have not cooperated in drafting it.

### Article XVII

Property belongs to both sexes whether united or separate; for each it is an inviolable and sacred right; no one can be deprived of it, since it is the true patrimony of nature, unless the legally determined public need obviously dictates it, and then only with a just and prior indemnity.

### Postscript

Woman, wake up; the tocsin of reason is being heard throughout the whole universe; discover your rights. The powerful empire of nature is no longer surrounded by prejudice, fanaticism, superstition, and lies. The flame of truth has dispersed all the clouds of folly and usurpation. Enslaved man has multiplied his strength and needs recourse to yours to break his chains. Having become free, he has become unjust to his companion. Oh, women, women! When will you cease to be blind? What advantages have you received from the Revolution? A more pronounced scorn, a more marked disdain. In the centuries of corruption you ruled only over the weakness of men. The reclamation of your patrimony, based on the wise decrees of nature—what have you to dread from such a fine undertaking? . . . Do you fear that our French legislators, correctors of that morality, long ensnared by political practices now out of date, will only say again to you: women, what is there in common between you and us? Everything, you will have to answer. If they persist in their weakness in putting this non sequitur in contradiction to their principles, courageously oppose the force of reason to the empty pretentions of superiority; unite yourselves beneath the standards of philosophy; deploy all the energy of your character, and you will soon see these haughty men, not groveling at your feet as servile adorers, but proud to share with you the treasures of the Supreme Being. Regardless of what barriers confront you, it is in your power to free yourselves; you have only to want to. . . .

## From *Debates in the National Convention of Clubs and Popular Societies for Women (1793)*

**National Convention**
**Moise Bayle, Presiding**
**Session of 9 Brumaire**

. . . *Amar, for the Committee of General Security:* Citizens, your Committee has been working without respite on means of warding off the con-

From Darlene Levy, H. Applewhite, and M. Johnson, eds., *Women in Revolutionary Paris, 1789–1795* (Champaign, Ill.: University of Illinois Press, 1979), pp. 214–217. Reprinted by permission of the publisher.

sequences of disorders which broke out the day before yesterday in Paris at the Marché des Innocents, near Saint-Eustache. It [the Committee] spent the night receiving deputations, listening to various reports which were made to it, and taking measures to maintain public order. Several women, calling themselves Jacobines, from an alledgedly revolutionary society, were going about in the morning, in the market and under the ossuaries of les Innocents, in pantaloons and red bonnets. They intended to force other *citoyennes* to wear the same costume; several [of the latter] testified that they had been insulted by them. A mob of nearly six thousand women gathered. All the women were in agreement that violence and threats would not make them dress in a costume [which] they respected but which they believed was intended for men; they would obey laws passed by the legislators and acts of the people's magistrates, but they would not give in to the wishes and caprices of a hundred lazy and suspect women. They all cried out, *"Vive la République, une et indivisible!"*

Municipal officers and members of the Revolutionary Committee of the Section du Contrat Social quieted people down and dispersed the mobs. In the evening the same disturbance broke out with greater violence. A brawl started. Several self-proclaimed Revolutionary Women were roughed up. Some members of the crowd indulged themselves in acts of violence towards them which decency ought to have proscribed. Several remarks reported to your Committee show that this disturbance can be attributed only to a plot by enemies of the state. Several of these self-proclaimed Revolutionary Women may have been led astray by an excess of patriotism, but others, doubtless, were motivated only by malevolence.

Right now, when Brissot and his accomplices are being judged, they want to work up some disorders in Paris, as was the case whenever you [the Convention] were about to consider some important matter and when it was a question of making measures useful for the Fatherland.

The Section des Marchés, informed of these events, drew up a resolution in which it informs your Committee that it believes several malevolent persons have put on the mask of an exaggerated patriotism to foment disturbances in the Section and a kind of counterrevolution in Paris. This Section requests that it be illegal to hinder anyone's freedom of dress and that popular societies of women be strictly prohibited, at least during the revolution.

The committee thought it should carry its investigation further. It raised the following questions: (1) Is it permissible for citizens or for an individual society to force other citizens to do what the law does not prescribe? (2) Should meetings of women gathered together in popular societies in Paris be allowed? Don't the disorders already occasioned by these societies argue against tolerating their existence any longer?

Naturally, these questions are complicated, and their resolution must be preceded by two more general questions, which are: (1) Can women exercise political rights and take an active part in affairs of government? (2) Can they deliberate together in political associations or popular societies?

With respect to these two questions, the Committee decided in the negative. Time does not allow for the full development to which these major questions—and the first, above all—lend themselves. We are going to put forward a few ideas which may shed light on them [these questions]. In your wisdom you will know how to submit them to thorough examination.

1. Should women exercise political rights and meddle in affairs of government? To govern is to rule the commonwealth by laws, the preparation of which demands extensive knowledge, unlimited attention and devotion, a strict immovability, and self-abnegation; again, to govern is to direct and ceaselessly to correct the action of constituted authorities. Are women capable of these cares and of the qualities they call for? In general, we can answer, no. Very few examples would contradict this evaluation.

The citizen's political rights are to debate and to have resolutions drawn up, by means of comparative deliberations, that relate to the interest of the state, and to resist oppression. Do women have the moral and physical strength which the exercise of one and the other of these rights calls for? Universal opinion rejects this idea.

2. Should women meet in political associations? The goal of popular associations is this: to unveil the maneuvers of the enemies of the commonwealth; to exercise surveillance both over citizens as individuals and over public functionaries—even over the legislative body; to excite the zeal of one and the other by the example of republican virtues; to shed light by public and in-depth discussion concerning the lack or reform of political laws. Can women devote themselves to these useful and difficult functions? No, because they would be obliged to sacrifice the more important cares to which nature calls them. The private functions for which women are destined by their very nature are related to the general order of society; this social order results from the differences between man and woman. Each sex is called to the kind of occupation which is fitting for it; its action is circumscribed within this circle which it cannot break through, because nature, which has imposed these limits on man, commands imperiously and receives no law.

Man is strong, robust, born with great energy, audacity, and courage; he braves perils [and] the intemperance of seasons because of his constitution; he resists all the elements; he is fit for the arts, difficult labors; and as he is almost exclusively destined for agriculture, commerce, navigation, voyages, war—everything that calls for force, intelligence, capability, so in the same way, he alone seems to be equipped for profound and serious thinking which calls for great intellectual effort and long studies which it is not granted to women to pursue.

What character is suitable for woman? Morals and even nature have assigned her functions to her. To begin educating men, to prepare children's mind and hearts for public virtues, to direct them early in life towards the good, to elevate their souls, to educate them in the political cult of liberty: such are their functions, after household cares. Woman is naturally destined to make virtue loved. When they have fulfilled all these obligations, they will have deserved well of the Fatherland. Doubtless they must educate themselves in the principles of liberty in order to make their children cherish it; they can attend the deliberations of the Sections [and] discussions of the popular societies, but as they are made for softening the morals of man, should they take an active part in discussions the passion of which is incompatible with the softness and moderation which are the charm of their sex?

We must say that this question is related essentially to morals, and without morals, no republic. Does the honesty of woman allow her to display herself in public and to struggle against men? to argue in full view of a public about questions on which the salvation of the republic depends? In general, women are ill suited for elevated thoughts and serious meditations, and if, among ancient peoples, their natural timidity and modesty did not allow them to appear outside their families, then in the French Republic do you want them to be seen coming into the gallery to political assemblies as men do? abandoning both reserve—source of all the virtues of their sex—and the care of their family?

They have more than one alternative way of rendering service to the Fatherland; they can enlighten their husbands, communicating precious reflections, the fruit of the quiet of a sedentary life, [and] work to fortify their love of country by means of everything which intimate love gives them in the way of empire. And the man, enlightened by peaceful family discussions in the midst of his household, will bring back into society the useful ideas imparted to him by an honest woman.

We believe, therefore, that a woman should not leave her family to meddle in affairs of government.

There is another sense in which women's associations seem dangerous. If we consider that the political education of men is at its beginning, that all its principles are not developed, and that we are still stammering the word liberty, then how much more reasonable is it for women, whose moral education is almost nil, to be less enlightened concerning principles? Their presence in popular societies, therefore, would give an active role in government to people more exposed to error and seduction. Let us add that women are disposed by their organization to an over-excitation which would be deadly in public affairs and that interests of state would soon be sacrificed to everything which ardor in passions can generate in the way of error and disorder. Delivered over to the heat of public debate, they would teach their children not love of country but hatreds and suspicions.

We believe, therefore, and without any doubt you will think as we do, that it is not possible for women to exercise political rights. You will destroy these alleged popular societies of women which the aristocracy would want to set up to put them [women] at odds with men, to divide the latter by forcing them to take sides in these quarrels, and to stir up disorder. . . .

The National Convention, after having heard the report of its Committee of General Security, decrees:

Article I: Clubs and popular societies of women, whatever name they are known under, are prohibited. . . .

# Revolutionary Morality

*As the revolution moved to the left, its supporters attempted to articulate standards of conduct that exemplified republican dedication. The next three documents illustrate the connections made between personal conduct, economic values, and political "morality." In the first document the* sans-culottes *of Paris define themselves. The term* sans-culottes *referred to the trousers worn by ordinary workers and shopkeepers, in contrast to the knee breeches favored by aristocrats. As the document indicates, the Parisians who considered themselves* sans-culottes *believed in democracy, in virtuous conduct, and in direct action to support a revolution that took power from the rich and privileged. In the second document, Maximilien Robespierre (1758–1794) urges the Convention to remove any opponents of the revolution from its midst. He delivered this speech as a representative of the Committee of Public Safety, the executive body of twelve men that effectively ruled France in this period. The speech offers justification for what became known as the "reign of terror" during 1793–1794. In the third document, "Gracchus" Babeuf (1760–1797) insists that the revolution ought to end economic as well as political inequality. The editor of the newspaper* The Tribune of the People, *Babeuf represents a socialist strand in the French Revolution. In 1796 he led a group determined to overthrow the Directory and replace it with leaders committed to economic reform. He was arrested and executed in 1797.*

## What Is a Sans-Culotte?

The sans-culotte '. . .is someone who goes everywhere on foot . . . and who lives quite simply with his wife and children, if he has any, on the fourth or fifth floor.' . . . 'If you wish to meet the cream of the sans-culotterie, then visit the garrets of the workers (ouvriers).' The sans-culotte is useful 'because he knows how to plough a field, how to forge,

From Albert Soboul, *The Parisian Sans-Culottes and the French Revolution, 1793–1794,* Gwynne Lewis, trans. (London: Oxford University Press, 1964), pp. 37–38. This is a composite Soboul drew from newspapers and archives.

to saw, to file, to cover a roof and how to make shoes. . . . And since he works, it is certain that you will not find him at the café de Chartres, nor in the dens where people gamble and plot, nor at the théatre de la Nation where they are performing *l'Ami des lois.* . . . In the evening, he goes to his Section, not powdered and perfumed not elegantly dressed in the hope of catching the eye of the citizens in the galleries, but to give his unreserved support to sound resolutions. . . . Besides this, the sans-culotte always has his sword with the edge sharpened to give a salutary lesson to all trouble-makers. Sometimes he carries his pike with him, and at the first beat of the drum, he will be seen leaving for the Vendée, for the *armée des Alpes* or the *armée du Nord.*'

## From Maximilien Robespierre. *On the Principles of Political Morality (February 1794)*

Citizens, Representatives of the People:

Some time since we laid before you the principles of our exterior political system, we now come to develop the principles of political morality which are to govern the interior. After having long pursued the path which chance pointed out, carried away in a manner by the efforts of contending factions, the Representatives of the People at length acquired a character and produced a form of government. A sudden change in the success of the nation announced to Europe the regeneration which was operated in the national representation. But to this point of time, even now that I address you, it must be allowed that we have been impelled thro' the tempest of a revolution, rather by a love of right and a feeling of the wants of our country, than by an exact theory, and precise rules of conduct, which we had not even leisure to sketch.

It is time to designate clearly the purposes of the revolution and the point which we wish to attain: It is time we should examine ourselves the obstacles which yet are between us and our wishes, and the means most proper to realize them: A consideration simple and important which appears not yet to have been contemplated. Indeed, how could a base and corrupt government have dared to view themselves in the mirror of political rectitude? A king, a proud senate, a Caesar, a Cromwell; of these the first care was to cover their dark designs under the cloak of religion, to covenant with every vice, caress every party, destroy men of probity, oppress and deceive the people in order to attain the end of their perfidious ambition. If we had not had a task of the first magnitude to accomplish; if all our concern had been to raise a party or create a new aristocracy, we might have believed, as certain

From M. Robespierre, *Report upon the Principles of Political Morality Which Are to Form the Basis of the Administration of the Interior Concerns of the Republic* (Philadelphia, 1794).

writers more ignorant than wicked asserted, that the plan of the French revolution was to be found written in the works of Tacitus and of Machiavel; we might have sought the duties of the representatives of the people in the history of Augustus, of Tiberius, or of Vespasian, or even in that of certain French legislators; for tyrants are substantially alike and only differ by trifling shades of perfidy and cruelty.

For our part we now come to make the whole world partake in your political secrets, in order that all friends of their country may rally at the voice of reason and public interest, and that the French nation and her representatives be respected in all countries which may attain a knowledge of their true principles; and that intriguers who always seek to supplant other intriguers may be judged by public opinion upon settled and plain principles.

Every precaution must early be used to place the interests of freedom in the hands of truth, which is eternal, rather than in those of men who change; so that if the government forgets the interests of the people or falls into the hands of men corrupted, according to the natural course of things, the light of acknowledged principles should unmask their treasons, and that every new faction may read its death in the very thought of a crime.

Happy the people that attains this end; for, whatever new machinations are plotted against their liberty, what resources does not public reason present when guaranteeing freedom!

What is the end of our revolution? The tranquil enjoyment of liberty and equality; the reign of that eternal justice, the laws of which are graven, not on marble or stone, but in the hearts of men, even in the heart of the slave who has forgotten them, and in that of the tyrant who disowns them.

We wish that order of things where all the low and cruel passions are enchained, all the beneficent and generous passions awakened by the laws; where ambition subsists in a desire to deserve glory and serve the country: where distinctions grow out of the system of equality, where the citizen submits to the authority of the magistrate, the magistrate obeys that of the people, and the people are governed by a love of justice; where the country secures the comfort of each individual, and where each individual prides himself on the prosperity and glory of his country; where every soul expands by a free communication of republican sentiments, and by the necessity of deserving the esteem of a great people: where the arts serve to embellish that liberty which gives them value and support, and commerce is a source of public wealth and not merely of immense riches to a few individuals.

We wish in our country that morality may be substituted for egotism, probity for false honour, principles for usages, duties for good manners, the empire of reason for the tyranny of fashion, a contempt of vice for a contempt of misfortune, pride for insolence, magnanimity for vanity, the love of glory for the love of money, good people for good company, merit for intrigue, genius for wit, truth for tinsel show, the attractions of happiness for the ennui of sensuality, the grandeur of man for the littleness of the great, a people magnanimous, powerful, happy, for a people amiable, frivolous and miserable; in a word, all the virtues and miracles of a Republic instead of all the vices and absurdities of a Monarchy.

We wish, in a word, to fulfill the intentions of nature and the destiny of man, realize the promises of philosophy, and acquit providence of a long reign of crime and tyranny. That France, once illustrious among enslaved nations, may, by eclipsing the glory of all free countries that ever existed, become a model to nations, a terror to oppressors, a consolation to the oppressed, an ornament of the universe and that, by sealing the work with our blood, we may at least witness the dawn of the bright day of universal happiness. This is our ambition,—this is the end of our efforts. . . .

Since virtue and equality are the soul of the republic, and that your aim is to found, to consolidate the republic, it follows, that the first rule of your political conduct should be, to let all your measures tend to maintain equality and encourage virtue, for the first care of the legislator should be to strengthen the principles on which the government rests. Hence all that tends to excite a love of country, to purify manners, to exalt the mind, to direct the passions of the human heart towards the public good, you should adopt and establish. All that tends to concenter and debase them into selfish egotism, to awaken an infatuation for littlenesses, and a disregard for greatness, you should reject or repress. In the system of the French revolution that which is immoral is impolitic, and what tends to corrupt is counter-revolutionary. Weaknesses, vices, prejudices are the road to monarchy. Carried away, too often perhaps, by the force of ancient habits, as well as by the innate imperfection of human nature, to false ideas and pusillanimous sentiments, we have more to fear from the excesses of weakness, than from excesses of energy. The warmth of zeal is not perhaps the most dangerous rock that we have to avoid; but rather that languour which ease produces and a distrust of our own courage. Therefore continually wind up the sacred spring of republican government, instead of letting it run down. I need not say that I am not here justifying any excess. Principles the most sacred may be abused: the wisdom of government should guide its operations according to circumstances, it should time its measures, choose its means; for the manner of bringing about great things is an essential part of the talent of producing them, just as wisdom is an essential attribute of virtue. . . .

It is not necessary to detail the natural consequences of the principle of democracy, it is the principle itself, simple yet copious, which deserves to be developed.

Republican virtue may be considered as it respects the people and as it respects the government. It is necessary in both. When however, the government alone want it, there exists a resource in that of the people; but when the people themselves are corrupted liberty is already lost.

Happily virtue is natural in the people, [despite] aristocratical prejudices. A nation is truly corrupt, when, after having, by degrees lost its character and liberty, it slides from democracy into aristocracy or monarchy; this is the death of the political body by decrepitude. . . .

But, when, by prodigious effects of courage and of reason, a whole people break asunder the fetters of despotism to make of the fragments trophies to liberty; when, by their innate vigor, they rise in a manner from the arms of death, to resume all the strength of youth when, in turns forgiving and inexorable, intrepid and docile, they can neither be checked by impregnable ramparts, nor by innumerable armies of tyrants leagued against them, and yet of themselves stop at the voice of the law; if then they do not reach the heights of their destiny it can only be the fault of those who govern.

Again, it may be said, that to love justice and equality the people need no great effort of virtue; it is sufficient that they love themselves. . . .

If virtue be the spring of a popular government in times of peace, the spring of that government during a revolution is virtue combined with terror: virtue, without which terror is destructive; terror, without which virtue is impotent. Terror is only justice prompt, severe and inflexible; it is then an emanation of virtue; it is less a distinct principle than a natural consequence of the general principle of democracy, applied to the most pressing wants of the country.

It has been said that terror is the spring of despotic government. Does yours then resemble despotism? Yes, as the steel that glistens in the hands of the heroes of liberty resembles the sword with which the satellites of tyranny are armed. Let the despot govern by terror his debased subjects; he is right as a despot: conquer by terror the enemies of liberty and you will be right as founders of the republic. The government in a revolution is the despotism of liberty against tyranny. Is force only intended to protect crime? Is not the lightning of heaven made to blast vice exalted?

The law of self-preservation, with every being whether physical or moral, is the first law of nature. Crime butchers innocence to secure a throne, and innocence struggles with all its might against the attempts of crime. If tyranny reigned one single day not a patriot would survive it. How long yet will the madness of despots be called justice, and the justice of the people barbarity or rebellion?—How tenderly oppressors and how severely the oppressed are treated! Nothing more natural: whoever does not abhor crime cannot love virtue. Yet one or the other must be crushed. Let mercy be shown the royalists exclaim some men. Pardon the villains! No: be merciful to innocence, pardon the unfortunate, show compassion for human weakness.

The protection of government is only due to peaceable citizens; and all citizens in the republic are republicans. The royalists, the conspirators, are strangers, or rather enemies. Is not this dreadful contest, which liberty maintains against tyranny, indivisible? Are not the internal enemies the allies of those in the exterior? The assassins who lay waste the interior; the intriguers who purchase the consciences of the delegates of the people: the traitors who sell them; the mercenary libellists paid to dishonor the cause of the people, to smother public virtue, to fan the flame of civil discord, and bring about a political counter revolution by means of a moral one; all these men, are they less culpable or less dangerous than the tyrants whom they serve? . . .

To punish the oppressors of humanity is clemency; to forgive them is cruelty. The severity of tyrants has barbarity for its principle; that of a republican government is founded on beneficence. Therefore let him beware who should dare to influence the people by that terror which is made only for their enemies! Let him beware, who, regarding the inevitable errors of civism in the same light, with the premeditated crimes of perfidiousness, or the attempts of conspirators, suffers the dangerous intriguer to escape and pursues the peaceable citizen! Death to the villain who dares abuse the sacred name of liberty or the powerful arms intended for her defence, to carry mourning or death to the patriotic heart. . . .

## From "Gracchus" Babeuf. *Manifesto of the Equals*

People of France!

For fifteen centuries you have lived slaves, and therefore unhappy. It is now scarcely six years since you have begun to revive in the hope of independence, happiness and equality. . . .

Equality! First need of nature, first demand of man, and chief bond of all legitimate society! French people! you have not been more favoured than the other nations that vegetate on this wretched globe! Always and everywhere poor humanity, in the hands of more or less adroit cannibals is the tool of every ambition, the pasture of every tyranny. Always and everywhere men were lulled by fine phrases; never and nowhere did they receive the fulfilment with the promise. From time immemorial we have been hypocritically told: *Men are equal:* and from time immemorial the insolent weight of the most degrading and most monstrous inequality has weighed down the human race. Since civilised society began, this finest possesion of humanity has been unanimously recognised, yet not once realised; equality was only a fair and sterile fiction of the law. To-day when it is more loudly claimed,

From Raymond Postgate, *Revolution from 1789–1906* (New York: Harper & Row, 1962), pp 54–56.

we are answered: Silence, wretches! real equality is but a chimera: be content with constitutional equality: you are all equal before the law. *Canaille*, what more do you want?—What more do we want? Legislators, governors, rich proprietors, listen in your turn.

We are all equal, are we not? This principle is uncontested: for without being mad one cannot say it is night when it is day.

Well, henceforward we are going to live and die equal as we were born; we desire real equality or death: that is what we want.

And we shall have this real equality at all costs. Woe to those who stand between it and us! Woe to those who resist so strong a desire!

The French Revolution is but the precursor of another revolution, far greater, far more solemn, which will be the last. . . .

What do we want more than equality in law?

We want this equality not merely written down in the Declaration of the Rights of Man and the Citizen: we want it in our midst, beneath the roofs of our houses. We will consent to everything for it; we will make a clean sweep to hold to it alone. Perish, if need be, all the arts as long as we have real equality! . . .

We aim at . . . the COMMON good or the COMMUNITY OF GOODS! No more private property in land: *The earth is nobody's.* We claim, we will the common use of the fruits of the earth: *its fruits are everybody's.* . . .

Ancient habits, archaic prejudices again try to prevent the establishment of the *Republic of Equals.* The organizing of real equality, the only state which answers all requirements without making victims or costing sacrifices, perhaps will not at first please everyone. The egoist and ambitious man will scream with rage. Those who possess unjustly will cry out, injustice! Their exclusive delights, their solitary pleasures, their personal ease will leave bitter longings in the hearts of some individuals who have grown effete by their neighbour's toil. Lovers of absolute power, and worthless tools of arbitrary authority, will find it hard to bring their proud chiefs to the level of equality. Their short-sight cannot penetrate into the near future of the common good; but what is the power of a few thousand malcontents against the mass of men, entirely happy and wondering that they sought so long for what was beneath their hand.

On the morrow of this true revolution they will say: What, was the common good so easy? We had but to will it. Ah, why did we not will it sooner? Was it necessary to repeat it to us so often? Yes, without doubt, but one man on earth more rich and powerful than his fellows, his equals, shatters the equilibrium; and crime and unhappiness arise on earth. . . .

People of France,
Open your eyes and hearts to the fulness of joy. Recognize and proclaim with us THE REPUBLIC OF EQUALS.

# NAPOLEONIC CONSOLIDATION

## The End of the Revolution

*Having established his reputation as a general with the revolutionary armies, Napoleon Bonaparte returned to France and, in 1799, took over the government. With the help of Sieyès and others, he replaced the Directory with a Consulate and proclaimed a constitution designed to restore order and end the revolution.*

### Proclamation to the French Nation (November 10, 1799)

Paris, 19 Brumaire, Year VIII, 11 P.M.

On my return to Paris I found all authority in chaos and agreement only on the one truth that the Constitution was half destroyed and incapable of preserving liberty.

Men of every party came to me, confided their plans, disclosed their secrets and asked for my support: I refused to be a man of party.

The Council of the Ancients called upon me and I responded to its appeal. A plan for general reform has been drawn up by men upon whom the nation is accustomed to look as the defenders of liberty, equality and property. That plan needed calm examination, free from all fear and partisan influence. Therefore, the Council of the Ancients resolved to transfer the legislative body to Saint-Cloud and charged me to deploy the force necessary to ensure its independence. I believed it my duty to my fellow-citizens, to the soldiers laying down their lives in our armies, to the national glory gained at the price of their blood to accept this command.

The Councils reassembled at Saint-Cloud. The troops of the Republic guaranteed their security from without. But assassins created terror within. Several Deputies of the Council of Five Hundred, bearing daggers and fire-arms, uttered threats of death all around them. Discussion of the plans was halted, the majority became disorganized, the most intrepid orators hesitated and the hopelessness of any wise proposal was evident.

From John E. Howard, *Letters and Documents of Napoleon* (London: Cresset Press, 1961), Vol. 1, pp. 313–314, 314–315, 323. Reprinted by permission of Hutchinson Publishers.

I carried my indignation and sorrow to the Council of the Ancients. I urged it to ensure the execution of its liberal designs. I recalled to it the ills of the nation which had led it to conceive them. The Council joined with me in renewed assurance of its steadfast resolve.

I then appeared before the Council of Five Hundred, alone, unarmed, bareheaded, just as the Ancients had received and applauded me. I came to recall the majority to its purpose and assure it of its power.

The daggers which threatened the deputies were immediately raised against their liberator: a score of assassins threw themselves upon me, seeking my breast. The grenadiers of the legislative guard, whom I had left at the door of the chamber, ran up, came between us and bore me out. One of the grenadiers had his coat pierced by a dagger.

At that moment cries of "outlaw" were heard against the defender of the law, the savage cry of the assassins against the force destined to crush them. They pressed round the president, threatening, arms in their hands, ordering him to declare my outlawry. Told of this, I ordered him to be saved from their fury and six grenadiers rescued him. Immediately afterwards the legislative guard entered at the charge and cleared the chamber.

Intimidated, the seditious dispersed and disappeared. The majority, safe from their threats, returned freely and peacefully to the chamber, heard the proposals made to them for the public good, debated and prepared the salutary resolution which must become the new, provisional law of the Republic.

Frenchmen, you will no doubt recognize in my conduct the zeal of a soldier of liberty and of a devoted citizen of the Republic. Liberal, beneficent and traditional ideas have returned to their rightful place through the dispersal of the odious and despicable factions which sought to overawe the Councils.

BONAPARTE

## Proclamation to the French Nation (November 12, 1799)

Paris, 21 Brumaire, Year VIII

The Constitution of the Year III was dying. It was incapable of protecting your rights, even of protecting itself. Through repeated assaults it was losing beyond recall the respect of nations. Malignant and selfish factions were despoiling the Republic. France, indeed, was entering the last stage of general disorganization.

But patriots have made themselves heard. All who could harm you have been cast aside. All who can serve you, all those representatives who have remained pure have come together under the banner of liberty.

Frenchmen, the Republic, strengthened and restored to that rank in Europe which should never have been lost, will realize all the hopes of her citizens and will accomplish her glorious destiny.

Swear with us the oath we have taken to be faithful to the Republic, one and indivisible, founded on equality, liberty and the representative system.

The Consuls of the Republic
BONAPARTE. ROGER DUCOS. SIEYÈS

## Proclamation to the French Nation (December 15, 1799)

Paris, 24 Frimaire, Year VIII

A Constitution is laid before you.

It ends the uncertainty which the provisional nature of the government was bringing to foreign affairs and to the internal and military situation of the Republic. It appoints to the offices it establishes chief magistrates whose devotion will make it effective.

The Constitution is based on the true principles of representative government and on the sacred rights of property, equality and liberty. The powers which it sets up will be strong and stable, as they must be in order to guarantee the rights of the citizens and the interests of the State.

Citizens, the revolution is established on the principles with which it began. It is complete.

The Consuls of the Republic
BONAPARTE. ROGER DUCOS. SIEYÈS

# VII

*230*

# RESPONSES TO REVOLUTION— THEORY AND POLITICS (1790–1832)

*THE FRENCH REVOLUTION affected the thinking of Europeans long after the defeat of Napoleon. Whether they condemned its excesses or praised its accomplishments, politicians and poets took inspiration from France's recent history. Leaders of the European states who assembled at the Congress of Vienna endorsed generally conservative principles. They vowed to restore order, protect monarchy, and prevent the outbreak of new revolutions. Some argued that the organization of society was not merely natural, but divinely ordained.*

*In literature, philosophy, and the arts, the rationalism of the Enlightenment was rejected for a more emotional, spiritual vision of human existence. Whether conservative or radical in politics, the Romantics stressed human subjectivity and the ultimate inability of men and women to conquer the great forces of nature, God, or history.*

*The Romantic view informed early nationalist movements, which had also been ignited by the armies of the French Revolution. Poles and Italians dreamed of fulfilling their national and religious destinies by restoring a Polish kingdom or creating an Italian republic. The French abolition of feudalism and the creation of a more democratic state inspired movements of reform in other countries. These movements met with varying success during the 1820s and 1830s. In England, a movement for universal manhood suffrage was defeated, but a measure of electoral reform was granted in 1832. Middle-class men were enfranchised at least in part because the government sought to quash the more radical demands for popular democracy.*

# CONSERVATISM

## A Reaffirmation of Aristocracy

*Even before the French Revolution entered its most radical phase, Edmund Burke (1729–1797) condemned it. A member of parliament from Ireland, Burke offered his* Reflections *in 1790 as "A Letter Intended to Have Been Sent to a Gentleman in Paris." His statement represents the philosophy of political conservatism: an attack on liberal reforms based on abstract ideas and a defense of traditional historical evolution and the rule of the natural (aristocratic) elite.*

### From Edmund Burke. *Reflections on the Revolution in France* (1790)

France, by the perfidy of her leaders, has utterly disgraced the tone of lenient council in the cabinets of princes, and disarmed it of its most potent topics. She has sanctified the dark suspicious maxims of tyrannous distrust; and taught kings to tremble at (what will hereafter be called) the delusive plausibilities, of moral politicians. Sovereigns will consider those who advise them to place an unlimited confidence in their people, as subverters of their thrones; as traitors who aim at their destruction, by leading their easy good nature, under specious pretences, to admit combinations of bold and faithless men into a participation of their power. This alone (if there were nothing else) is an irreparable calamity to you and to mankind. . . .

. . . Laws overturned; tribunals subverted; industry without vigor; commerce expiring; the revenue unpaid, yet the people impoverished; a church pillaged, and a state not relieved; civil and military anarchy made the constitution of the kingdom; every thing human and divine sacrificed to the idol of public credit, and national bankruptcy the consequence; and to crown all, the paper securities of new, precarious, tottering power, the discredited paper securities of impoverished fraud, and beggared rapine, held out as a currency for the support of an empire, in lieu of the two great recognised species that represent the lasting conventional credit of mankind, which disappeared and hid them-

From Edmund Burke, *The Works of Edmund Burke* (Boston: Chas. C. Little and James Brown, 1839), Vol. 3, pp. 57–62, 71–73, 81–83, 97–101.

selves in the earth from whence they came, when the principle of property, whose creatures and representatives they are, was systematically subverted.

Were all these dreadful things necessary? Were they the inevitable results of the desperate struggle of determined patriots, compelled to wade through blood and tumult, to the quiet shore of a tranquil and prosperous liberty? No! nothing like it. The fresh ruins of France, which shock our feelings wherever we can turn our eyes, are not the devastation of civil war; they are the sad but instructive monuments of rash and ignorant counsel in time of profound peace. They are the display of inconsiderate and presumptuous, because unresisted and irresistible authority.

This unforced choice, this fond election of evil, would appear perfectly unaccountable, if we did not consider the composition of the national assembly; I do not mean its formal constitution, which, as it now stands, is exceptionable enough, but the materials of which, in a great measure, it is composed, which is of ten thousand times greater consequence than all the formalities in the world. If we were to know nothing of this assembly but by its title and function, no colors could paint to the imagination any thing more venerable. . . .

After I had read over the list of the persons and descriptions elected into the *Tiers Etat,* nothing which they afterwards did could appear astonishing. Among them, indeed, I saw some of known rank; some of shining talents; but of any practical experience in the state, not one man was to be found. The best were only men of theory. But whatever the distinguished few may have been, it is the substance and mass of the body which constitutes its character, and must finally determine its direction. . . .

Judge, sir, of my surprise, when I found that a very great proportion of the assembly (a majority, I believe, of the members who attended,) was composed of practitioners in the law. It was composed, not of distinguished magistrates, who had given pledges to their country of their science, prudence, and integrity; not of leading advocates, the glory of the bar; not of renowned professors in universities; but for the far greater part, as it must in such a number, of the inferior, unlearned, mechanical, merely instrumental members of the profession. There were distinguished exceptions; but the general composition was of obscure provincial advocates, of stewards of petty local jurisdictions, country attorneys, notaries, and the whole train of the ministers of municipal litigation, the fomenters and conductors of the petty war of village vexation. From the moment I read the list, I saw distinctly, and very nearly as it has happened, all that was to follow. . . .

Whenever the supreme authority is vested in a body so composed, it must evidently produce the consequences of supreme authority placed in the hands of men not taught habitually to respect themselves; who had no previous fortune in character at stake; who could not be expected to bear with moderation, or to conduct with discretion, a power, which they themselves, more than any others, must be surprised to find in their hands. . . .

Nothing is a due and adequate representation of a state, that does not represent its ability, as well as its property. But as ability is a vigorous and active principle, and as property is sluggish, inert and timid, it never can be safe from the invasions of ability, unless it be, out of all proportion, predominant in the representation. It must be represented too in great masses of accumulation, or it is not rightly protected. The characteristic essence of property, formed out of the combined principles of its acquisition and conservation, is to be *unequal*. . . .

The power of perpetuating our property in our families is one of the most valuable and interesting circumstances belonging to it, and that which tends the most to the perpetuation of society itself. It makes our weakness subservient to our virtue; it grafts benevolence even upon avarice. The possessors of family wealth, and of the distinction which attends hereditary possession (as most concerned in it) are the natural securities for this transmission. With us, the house of peers is formed upon this principle. It is wholly composed of hereditary property and hereditary distinction; and made therefore the third of the legislature; and in the last event, the sole judge of all property in all its subdivisions. The house of commons too, though not necessarily, yet in fact, is always so composed in the far greater part. Let those large proprietors be what they will, and they have their chance of being among the best, they are at the very worst, the ballast in the vessel of the commonwealth. For though hereditary wealth, and the rank which goes with it, are too much idolized by creeping sycophants, and the blind abject admirers of power, they are too rashly slighted in shallow speculations of the petulant, assuming, short-sighted coxcombs of philosophy. Some decent regulated preëminence, some preference (not exclusive appropriation) given to birth, is neither unnatural, nor unjust, nor impolitic.

It is said, that twenty-four millions ought to prevail over two hundred thousand. True; if the constitution of a kingdom be a problem of arithmetic. This sort of discourse does well enough with the lamp-post for its second: to men who *may* reason calmly, it is ridiculous. The will of the many, and their interest, must very often differ; and great will be the difference when they make an evil choice. A government of five hundred country attorneys and obscure curates is not good for twenty-four millions of men, though it were chosen by eight and forty millions; nor is it the better for being guided by a dozen of persons of quality, who have betrayed their trust in order to obtain that power. At present, you seem in every thing to have strayed out of the high-road of nature. The property of France does not govern it. Of course property is destroyed, and rational liberty has no existence. All you have got for the present is a paper circulation, and a stock-jobbing constitution: and as to the future, do you seriously think that the territory of France, upon the republican system of eighty-three independent municipalities (to say nothing of the parts that compose them) can ever be governed as one body, or can ever be set in motion by the impulse of one mind? When the national assembly has completed its work, it will have accomplished its ruin. . . .

Government is not made in virtue of natural rights, which may and do exist in total independence of it; and exist in much greater clearness, and in a much greater degree of abstract perfection: but their abstract perfection is their practical defeat. By having a right to every thing, they want every thing. Government is a contrivance of human wisdom to provide for human *wants*. Men have a right that these wants should be provided for by this wisdom. Among these wants is to be reckoned the want, out of civil society, of a sufficient restraint upon their passions. Society requires not only that the passions of individuals should be subjected, but that even in the mass and body as well as in the individuals, the inclinations of men should frequently be thwarted, their will controlled, and their passions brought into subjection. This can only be done *by a power out of themselves*; and not, in the exercise of its function, subject to that will and to those passions which it is its office to bridle and subdue. In this sense the restraints on men, as well as their liberties, are to be reckoned among their rights. But as the liberties and the restrictions vary with times and circumstances, and admit of infinite modifications, they cannot be settled upon any abstract rule; and nothing is so foolish as to discuss them upon that principle.

The moment you abate any thing from the full rights of men, each to govern himself, and suffer any artificial positive limitation upon those rights, from that moment the whole organization of government becomes a consideration of convenience. This it is which makes the constitution of a state, and the due distribution of its powers, a matter of the most delicate and complicated skill. It requires a deep knowledge of human nature and human necessities, and of the things which facilitate or obstruct the various ends which are to be pursued by the mechanism of civil institutions. The state is to have recruits to its strength, and remedies to its distempers. What is the use of discussing a man's abstract right to food or medicine? The question is upon the method of procuring and administering them. In that deliberation I shall always advise to call in the aid of the farmer and the physician, rather than the professor of metaphysics.

The science of constructing a commonwealth, or renovating it, or reforming it, is, like every other experimental science, not to be taught *a priori*. Nor is it a short experience that can instruct us in that practical science; because the real effects of moral causes are not always immediate; but that which in the first instance is prejudicial may be excellent in its remoter operation; and its excellence may arise even from the ill effects it produces in the beginning. . . .

The nature of man is intricate; the objects of society are of the greatest possible complexity: and therefore no simple disposition or direction of power can be suitable either to man's nature, or to the quality of his affairs. When I hear the simplicity of contrivance aimed at and boasted of in any new political constitutions, I am at no loss to decide that the artificers are grossly ignorant of their trade, or totally negligent of their duty. The simple governments are fundamentally defective, to say no worse of them. If you were to contemplate society in but one point of view, all these simple modes of polity are infinitely captivating. In effect each would answer its single end much more perfectly than the more complex is able to attain all its complex purposes. But it is better that the whole should be imperfectly and anomalously answered, than that, while some parts are provided for with great exactness, others might be totally neglected, or perhaps materially injured, by the over-care of a favorite member. . . .

[*Burke then turns to the events of the French Revolution and their impact on the royal family*]

It is now sixteen or seventeen years since I saw the queen of France, then the dauphiness, at Versailles; and surely never lighted on this orb, which she hardly seemed to touch, a more delightful vision. I saw her just above the horizon, decorating and cheering the elevated sphere she just began to move in,—glittering like the morning-star; full of life, and splendor, and joy. Oh! what a revolution! and what an heart must I have, to contemplate without emotion that elevation and that fall! Little did I dream when she added titles of veneration to those of enthusiastic, distant, respectful love, that she should ever be obliged to carry the sharp antidote against disgrace concealed in that bosom; little did I dream, that I should have lived to see such disasters fallen upon her in a nation of gallant men, in a nation of men of honor and of cavaliers. I thought ten thousand swords must have leaped from their scabbards to avenge even a look that threatened her with insult. But the age of chivalry is gone: that of sophisters, economists, and calculators has succeeded; and the glory of Europe is extinguished for ever. Never, never more, shall we behold that generous loyalty to rank and sex, that proud submission, that dignified obedience, that subordination of the heart, which kept alive, even in servitude itself, the spirit of an exalted freedom. The unbought grace of life, the cheap defence of nations, the nurse of manly sentiment and heroic enterprise is gone! It is gone, that sensibility of principle, that chastity of honor, which felt a stain like a wound, which inspired courage whilst it mitigated ferocity, which ennobled whatever it touched, and under which vice itself lost half its evil, by losing all its grossness.

This mixed system of opinion and sentiment had its origin in the ancient chivalry; and the principle, though varied in its appearance by the varying state of human affairs, subsisted and influenced through a long succession of generations, even to the time we live in. If it should ever be totally extinguished, the loss I fear will be great. It is this which has given its character to modern Europe. It is this which has distinguished it under all its forms of government, and distinguished it to its advantage, from the states of Asia, and possibly from those states which flourished in the most brilliant periods of the antique world. It was this, which, without confounding ranks, had produced a noble equality, and handed it down through all the gradations of social life. It was this opinion which mitigated kings into companions, and raised private men to be fellows with kings. Without force, or opposition, it subdued the fierceness of pride and power; it obliged sovereigns to submit to the soft collar of social esteem, compelled stern authority to submit to elegance, and gave a domination vanquisher of laws, to be subdued by manners.

But now all is to be changed. All the pleasing illusions, which made power gentle, and obedience liberal, which harmonized the different shades of life, and which, by a bland assimilation, incorporated into politics the sentiments which beautify and soften private society, are to be dissolved by this new conquering empire of light and reason. All the decent drapery of life is to be rudely torn off. All the superadded ideas, furnished from the wardrobe of a moral imagination, which the heart owns, and the understanding ratifies, as necessary to cover the defects of our naked shivering nature, and to raise it to dignity in our own estimation, are to be exploded as a ridiculous, absurd, and antiquated fashion.

On this scheme of things, a king is but a man, a queen is but a woman; a woman is but an animal; and an animal not of the highest order. All homage paid to the sex in general as such, and without distinct views, is to be regarded as romance and folly. Regicide, and parricide, and sacrilege, are but fictions of superstition, corrupting jurisprudence by destroying its simplicity. The murder of a king, or a queen, or a bishop, or a father, are only common homicide; and if the people are by any chance, or in any way gainers by it, a sort of homicide much the most pardonable, and into which we ought not to make too severe a scrutiny.

On the scheme of this barbarous philosophy, which is the offspring of cold hearts and muddy understandings, and which is as void of solemn wisdom, as it is destitute of all taste and elegance, laws are to be supported only by their own terrors, and by the concern, which each individual may find in them, from his own private speculations, or can spare to them from his own private interests. In the groves of *their* academy, at the end of every vista, you see nothing but the gallows. Nothing is left which engages the affections on the part of the commonwealth. On the principles of this mechanic philosophy, our institutions can never be embodied, if I may use the expression, in persons; so as to create in us love, veneration, admiration, or attachment. But that sort of reason which banishes the affections is incapable of filling their place. These public affections, combined with manners, are required sometimes as supplements, sometimes as correctives, always as aids to law. . . .

There ought to be a system of manners in every nation which a well-formed mind would be disposed to relish. To make us love our country, our country ought to be lovely

# The Divine Origin of Constitutions

*The French count Joseph de Maistre (1754–1821) emphasized the importance of religion for the philosophy and politics of conservatism. In this essay, de Maistre addresses the question of constitutions; in 1819, in another essay, he insists on the role of the pope in preserving international stability.*

## From Joseph de Maistre. *Essay on the Generative Principle of Political Constitutions (1810)*

The more we examine the influence of human agency in the formation of political constitutions, the greater will be our conviction that it enters there only in a manner infinitely subordinate, or as a simple instrument; and I do not believe there remains the least doubt of the incontestable truth of the following propositions:—

1. That the fundamental principles of political constitutions exist before all written law.

2. That a constitutional law is, and can only be, the development or sanction of an unwritten pre-existing right.

3. That which is most essential, most intrinsically constitutional, and truly fundamental, is never written, and could not be, without endangering the state.

4. That the weakness and fragility of a constitution are actually in direct proportion to the multiplicity of written constitutional articles.
. . .

To this general rule, *that no constitution can be made or written, à priori,* we know of but one single exception; that is, the legislation of Moses. This alone was *cast,* so to speak, like a statue, and written out, even to its minutest details, by a wonderful man, who said, Fiat! without his work ever having need of being corrected, improved, or in any way modified, by himself or others. This, alone, has set time at defiance, because it owed nothing to time, and expected nothing from it; this alone has lived fifteen hundred years; and even after eighteen new centuries have passed over it, since the great anathema which smote it on the fated day, we see it, enjoying, if I may say so, a second life,

From M. Le Comte Joseph de Maistre, *Essay on the Generative Principle of Political Constitutions* (Boston: Little, Brown, 1847), pp. 41–42, 93–95, 129–130, 171–173.

binding still, by I know not what mysterious bond, which has no human name, the different families of a people, which remain dispersed without being disunited. So that, like attraction, and by the same power, it acts at a distance, and makes one whole, of many parts widely separated from each other. Thus, this legislation lies evidently, for every intelligent conscience, beyond the circle traced around human power; and this magnificent exception to a general law, which has only yielded once, and yielded only to its Author, alone demonstrates the Divine mission of the great Hebrew Lawgiver. . . .

But, since every constitution is divine in its principle, it follows, that man can do nothing in this way, unless he reposes himself upon God, whose instrument he then becomes. Now, this is a truth, to which the whole human race in a body have ever rendered the most signal testimony. Examine history, which is experimental politics, and we shall there invariably find the cradle of nations surrounded by priests, and the Divinity constantly invoked to the aid of human weakness. . . .

Man in relation with his Creator is sublime, and his action is creative: on the contrary, so soon as he separates himself from God, and acts alone, he does not cease to be powerful, for this is a privilege of his nature; but his action is negative, and tends only to destroy. . . .

There is not in the history of all ages a single fact which contradicts these maxims. No human institution can endure unless supported by the Hand which supports all; that is to say, if it is not especially consecrated to Him at its origin. The more it is penetrated with the Divine principle, the more durable it will be.

# A Call for Monarchical Solidarity

*Prince Klemens von Metternich (1773–1859), an Austrian diplomat, was the architect of an alliance system among the European powers after Napoleon's defeat. In 1820, using arguments contained in this document, he convinced the Russian Tsar, Alexander I, to endorse a protocol uniting the Great Powers against reform and disorder. Issued at the Congress of Troppau, the protocol was also signed by Prussia; Great Britain and France refused to endorse it.*

## From Prince Klemens von Metternich. *Political Confession of Faith (1820)*

### The Source of the Evil

Man's nature is immutable. The first needs of society are and remain

From Prince Klemens von Metternich, *Memoirs of Prince Metternich, 1815–1829*, ed. Prince Richard Metternich (New York: Howard Fertig, 1970; photoreprint of a Scribner and Sons 1881 edition), Vol. 3, pp. 456–463, 469–471, 473–476.

the same, and the differences which they seem to offer find their explanation in the diversity of influences, acting on the different races by natural causes, such as the diversity of climate, barrenness or richness of soil, insular or continental position, &c. &c. These local differences no doubt produce effects which extend far beyond purely physical necessities; they create and determine particular needs in a more elevated sphere; finally, they determine the laws, and exercise an influence even on religions.

It is, on the other hand, with institutions as with everything else. Vague in their origin, they pass through periods of development and perfection, to arrive in time at their decadence; and, conforming to the laws of man's nature, they have, like him, their infancy, their youth, their age of strength and reason, and their age of decay.

Two elements alone remain in all their strength, and never cease to exercise their indestructible influence with equal power. These are the precepts of morality, religious as well as social, and the necessities created by locality. From the time that men attempt to swerve from these bases, to become rebels against these sovereign arbiters of their destinies, society suffers from a malaise which sooner or later will lead to a state of convulsion. The history of every country, in relating the consequences of such errors, contains many pages stained with blood; but we dare to say, without fear of contradiction, one seeks in vain for an epoch when an evil of this nature has extended its ravages over such a vast area as it has done at the present time.

The progress of the human mind has been extremely rapid in the course of the last three centuries. This progress having been accelerated more rapidly than the growth of wisdom (the only counterpoise to passions and to error); a revolution prepared by the false systems, the fatal errors into which many of the most illustrious sovereigns of the last half of the eighteenth century fell, has at last broken out in a country advanced in knowledge, and enervated by pleasure, in a country inhabited by a people whom one can only regard as frivolous, from the facility with which they comprehend and the difficulty they experience in judging calmly.

Having now thrown a rapid glance over the first causes of the present state of society, it is necessary to point out in a more particular manner the evil which threatens to deprive it, at one blow, of the real blessings, the fruits of genuine civilisation, and to disturb it in the midst of its enjoyments. This evil may be described in one word—presumption; the natural effect of the rapid progression of the human mind towards the perfecting of so many things. This it is which at the present day leads so many individuals astray, for it has become an almost universal sentiment. . . .

The causes of the deplorable intensity with which this evil weighs on society appear to us to be of two kinds. . . .

... We will place among the first the feebleness and the inertia of Governments.

It is sufficient to cast a glance on the course which the Governments followed during the eighteenth century, to be convinced that not one among them was ignorant of the evil or of the crisis towards which the social body was tending. ...

France had the misfortune to produce the greatest number of these men. It is in her midst that religion and all that she holds sacred, that morality and authority, and all connected with them, have been attacked with a steady and systematic animosity, and it is there that the weapon of ridicule has been used with the most ease and success.

Drag through the mud the name of God and the powers instituted by His divine decrees, and the revolution will be prepared! Speak of a social contract, and the revolution is accomplished! The revolution was already completed in the palaces of Kings, in the drawing-rooms and boudoirs of certain cities, while among the great mass of the people it was still only in a state of preparation. ...

The scenes of horror which accompanied the first phases of the French Revolution prevented the rapid propagation of its subversive principles beyond the frontiers of France, and the wars of conquest which succeeded them gave to the public mind a direction little favourable to revolutionary principles. Thus the Jacobin propaganda failed entirely to realise criminal hopes.

Nevertheless the revolutionary seed had penetrated into every country and spread more or less. It was greatly developed under the *régime* of the military despotism of Bonaparte. His conquests displaced a number of laws, institutions, and customs; broke through bonds sacred among all nations, strong enough to resist time itself; which is more than can be said of certain benefits conferred by these innovators. From these perturbations it followed that the revolutionary spirit could in Germany, Italy, and later on in Spain, easily hide itself under the veil of patriotism. ...

We are convinced that society can no longer be saved without strong and vigorous resolutions on the part of the Governments still free in their opinions and actions.

We are also convinced that this may yet be, if the Governments face the truth, if they free themselves from all illusion, if they join their ranks and take their stand on a line of correct, unambiguous, and frankly announced principles.

By this course the monarchs will fulfil the duties imposed upon them by Him who, by entrusting them with power, has charged them to watch over the maintenance of justice, and the rights of all, to avoid the paths of error, and tread firmly in the way of truth. Placed beyond the passions which agitate society, it is in days of trial chiefly that they are called upon to despoil realities of their false appearances, and to show themselves as they are, fathers invested with the authority belonging by right to the heads of families, to prove that, in days of mourning, they know how to be just, wise, and therefore strong, and that they will not abandon the people whom they ought to govern to be the sport of factions, to error and its consequences, which must involve the loss of society. The moment in which we are putting our thoughts on paper is one of these critical moments. The crisis is great; it will be decisive according to the part we take or do not take. . . .

Union between the monarchs is the basis of the policy which must now be followed to save society from total ruin. . . .

The first principle to be followed by the monarchs, united as they are by the coincidence of their desires and opinions, should be that of maintaining the stability of political institutions against the disorganised excitement which has taken possession of men's minds; the immutability of principles against the madness of their interpretation; and respect for laws actually in force against a desire for their destruction. . . .

Let [the Governments] in these troublous times be more than usually cautious in attempting real ameliorations, not imperatively claimed by the needs of the moment, to the end that good itself may not turn against them—which is the case whenever a Government measure seems to be inspired by fear.

Let them not confound concessions made to parties with the good they ought to do for their people, in modifying, according to their recognised needs, such branches of the administration as require it.

Let them give minute attention to the financial state of their kingdoms, so that their people may enjoy, by the reduction of public burdens, the real, not imaginary, benefits of a state of peace.

Let them be just, but strong; beneficent, but strict.

Let them maintain religious principles in all their purity, and not allow the faith to be attacked and morality interpreted according to the *social contract* or the visions of foolish sectarians.

Let them suppress Secret Societies, that gangrene of society.

In short, let the great monarchs strengthen their union, and prove to the world that if it exists, it is beneficent, and ensures the political peace of Europe: that it is powerful only for the maintenance of tranquillity at a time when so many attacks are directed against it; that the principles which they profess are paternal and protective, menacing only the disturbers of public tranquillity. . . .

To every great State determined to survive the storm there still remain many chances of salvation, and a strong union between the States on the principles we have announced will overcome the storm itself.

# ROMANTICISM

## "Nature . . . the Guardian of My Heart"

*The English poet William Wordsworth (1770–1850) represents one of the great voices of the Romantic Movement in his emphasis on the senses and on nature.*

### From William Wordsworth. *Lines Composed a Few Miles Above Tintern Abbey*

> . . . I have learned
> To look on nature, not as in the hour
> Of thoughtless youth; but hearing oftentimes
> The still, sad music of humanity,
> Nor harsh nor grating, though of ample power
> To chasten and subdue. And I have felt
> A presence that disturbs me with the joy
> Of elevated thoughts; a sense sublime
> Of something far more deeply interfused,
> Whose dwelling is the light of setting suns,
> And the round ocean and the living air,
> And the blue sky, and in the mind of man:
> A motion and a spirit, that impels
> All thinking things, all objects of all thought,
> And rolls through all things. Therefore am I still
> A lover of the meadows and the woods,
> And mountains; and of all that we behold
> From this green earth; of all the mighty world
> Of eye, and ear,—both what they half create,
> And what perceive; well pleased to recognise
> In nature and the language of the sense
> The anchor of my purest thoughts, the nurse,
> The guide, the guardian of my heart, and soul
> Of all my moral being.

# The Inner Spiritual Life

*Friedrich von Schlegel (1772–1829) in this document elaborates some of the tenets of German romanticism.*

## From Friedrich von Schlegel. *The Philosophy of Life and Philosophy of Language*

The object therefore of philosophy is the inner mental life *(geistige Leben)*, not merely this or that individual faculty in any partial direction, but man's spiritual life with all its rich and manifold energies. With respect to form and method: the philosophy of life sets out from a single assumption—that of life, or in other words, of a consciousness to a certain degree awakened and manifoldly developed by experience— since it has for its object, and purposes to make known the entire consciousness and not merely a single phase of it. Now, such an end would be hindered rather than promoted by a highly elaborate or minutely exhaustive form and a painfully artificial method; and it is herein that the difference lies between a philosophy of life and the philosophy of the school. . . .

Now, the distinction between the philosophy of life and the philosophy of the school will appear in very different lights according to the peculiarity of view which predominates in the several philosophical systems. That species of philosophy which revolves in the dialectical orbit of abstract ideas, according to its peculiar character presupposes and requires a well-practised talent of abstraction, perpetually ascending through higher grades to the very highest, and even then boldly venturing a step beyond. In short, as may be easily shown in the instance of modern German science, the being unintelligible is set up as a kind of essential characteristic of a true and truly scientific philosophy. I, for my part, must confess, that I feel a great distrust of that philosophy which dwells in inaccessible light, where the inventor indeed asserts of himself, that he finds himself in an unattainable certainty and clearness of insight, giving us all the while to understand thereby, that he does see well enough how of all other mortals scarcely any, or perhaps, strictly speaking, no one, understands or is capable of understanding him. In all such cases it is only the false light of some internal *ignis fatuus* that produces this illusion of the unintelligible, or rather of nonsense. In this pursuit of wholly abstract and unintelligible thought, the philosophy of the school is naturally enough esteemed above every other, and regarded as pre-eminently the true science—*i.e.,* the unintelligible. . . .

From F. Von Schlegel, *The Philosophy of Life and Philosophy of Language in a Course of Lectures,* trans. A. J. W. Morrison (London: Henry G. Bohn, 1847), pp. 4–6, 8–12, 16–17, 21–22.

But the true living philosophy has no relation or sympathy with this continuous advance up to the unintelligible heights of empty abstraction. Since the objects it treats of are none other than those which every man of a cultivated mind and in any degree accustomed to observe his own consciousness, both has and recognizes within himself, there is nothing to prevent its exposition being throughout clear, easy, and forcible. Here the relation is reversed. In such a system the philosophy of life is the chief and paramount object of interest; while the philosophy of the school, or the scientific teaching of it in the schools, however necessary and valuable in its place, is still, as compared with the whole thing itself, only secondary and subordinate. In the philosophy of life, moreover, the method adopted must also be a living one. Consequently it is not, by any means, a thing to be neglected. But still it need not to be applied with equal rigour throughout, or to appear prominently in every part, but on all occasions must be governed in these respects by what the particular end in view may demand. . . .

. . . But in order to illustrate this simple method of studying life from its true central point, which is intermediate between the two wrong courses already indicated, and in order to make by contrast my meaning the plainer, I would here in a few words, characterize the false starting-point from which the prevailing philosophy of a day—whether that of France in the eighteenth century or the more recent systems of Germany—has hitherto for the most part proceeded. False do I call it, both on account of the results to which it has led, and also of its own intrinsic nature. In one case as well as in the other, the starting-point was invariably some controverted point of the reason— some opposition or other to the legitimacy of the reason; under which term, however, little else generally was understood, than an opposition of the reason itself to some other principle equally valid and extensive. The principal, or rather only way which foreign philosophy took in this pursuit, was to reduce every thing to sensation as opposed to reason, and to derive every thing from it alone, so as to make the reason itself merely a secondary faculty, no original and independent power, and ultimately nothing else than a sort of chemical precipitate and residuum from the material impressions. . . .

Briefly to recapitulate what has been said: The existence of the brutes is simple, because in them the soul is completely mixed up and merged in the organic body, and is one with it; on the destruction of the latter it reverts to the elements, or is absorbed in the general soul of nature. Twofold, however, is the nature of created spirits, who besides this ethereal body of light are nothing but mind or spirit; but threefold is the nature of man, as consisting of spirit, soul, and body. And this triple constitution and property, this threefold life of man, is, indeed, not in itself that pre-eminence, although it is closely connected with that superior excellence which ennobles and distinguishes man from all other created beings. I allude to that prerogative by which he alone of all created beings is invested with the Divine image and likeness. This threefold principle is the simple basis of all philosophy; and the philosophical system which is constructed on such a foundation is the philosophy of life, which therefore has even "words of life." It is no idle speculation, and no unintelligible hypothesis. It is not more difficult, and needs not to be more obscure, than any other discourse on spiritual subjects; but it can and may be as easy and as clear as the reading of a writing, the observation of nature, and the study of history. For it is in truth nothing else than a simple theory of spiritual life, drawn from life itself, and the simple understanding thereof. If, however, it becomes abstract and unintelligible, this is invariably a consequence, and for the most part an infallible proof of its having fallen into error. When in thought we place before us the whole composite human individual, then, after spirit and soul, the organic body is the third constituent, or the third element out of which, in combination with the other two, the whole man consists and is compounded. But the structure of the organic body, its powers and laws, must be left to physical science to investigate. Philosophy is the science of consciousness alone; it has, therefore, primarily to occupy itself with soul and spirit or mind, and must carefully guard against transgressing its limits in any respect. But the third constituent beside mind and soul, in which these two jointly carry on their operations, needs not always, as indeed the above instance proves, to be an organic body. In other relations of life, this third, in which both are united, or which they in unison produce, may be the word, the deed, life itself, or the divine order on which both are dependent. These, then, are the subjects which I have proposed for consideration. But in order to complete this scale of life, I will further observe: triple is the nature of man, but four-fold is the human consciousness. For the spirit or mind, like the soul, divides and falls asunder, or rather is split and divided into two powers or halves—the mind, namely, into understanding and will, the soul into reason and fancy. These are the four extreme points, or, if the expression be preferred, the four quarters of the inner world of consciousness. All other faculties of the soul, or powers of mind, are merely subordinate ramifications of the four principal branches; but the living centre of the whole is the thinking soul.

# The Romantic Sensibility

*Mary Shelley (1797–1851) was the daughter of Mary Wollstonecraft and William Godwin. She was the wife of the poet Percy Bysshe Shelley and a member of the circle of young English Romantic writers. Mary Shelley was the author of* Frankenstein *as well as* The Last Man, *written as an expression of her grief after Shelley's death in 1822.*

## From Mary Shelley. *The Last Man*

I AWOKE in the morning, just as the higher windows of the lofty houses received the first beams of the rising sun. The birds were chirping, perched on the window sills and deserted thresholds of the doors. I awoke, and my first thought was, Adrian and Clara are dead. I no longer shall be hailed by their good-morrow—or pass the long day in their society. I shall never see them more. The ocean has robbed me of them—stolen their hearts of love from their breasts, and given over to corruption what was dearer to me than light, or life, or hope.

I was an untaught shepherd-boy, when Adrian deigned to confer on me his friendship. The best years of my life had been passed with him. All I had possessed of this world's goods, of happiness, knowledge, or virtue—I owed to him. He had, in his person, his intellect, and rare qualities, given a glory to my life, which without him it had never known. Beyond all other beings he had taught me, that goodness, pure and single, can be an attribute of man. It was a sight for angels to congregate to behold, to view him lead, govern, and solace, the last days of the human race.

My lovely Clara also was lost to me—she who last of the daughters of man, exhibited all those feminine and maiden virtues, which poets, painters, and sculptors, have in their various languages strove to express. Yet, as far as she was concerned, could I lament that she was removed in early youth from the certain advent of misery? Pure she was of soul, and all her intents were holy. But her heart was the throne of love, and the sensibility her lovely countenance expressed, was the prophet of many woes, not the less deep and drear, because she would have for ever concealed them.

These two wondrously endowed beings had been spared from the universal wreck, to be my companions during the last year of solitude. I had felt, while they were with me, all their worth. I was conscious that every other sentiment, regret, or passion had by degrees merged into a yearning, clinging affection for them. I had not forgotten the sweet partner of my youth, mother of my children, my adored Idris; but I saw at least a part of her spirit alive again in her brother; and after, that by Evelyn's death I had lost what most dearly recalled her to me; I enshrined her memory in Adrian's form, and endeavoured to confound the two dear ideas. I sound the depths of my heart, and try in vain to draw thence the expressions that can typify my love for these remnants of my race. If regret and sorrow came athwart me, as well it might in our solitary and uncertain state, the clear tones of Adrian's voice, and his fervent look, dissipated the gloom; or I was cheered unaware by the mild content and sweet resignation Clara's cloudless brow and deep blue eyes expressed. They were all to me—the suns of my

From Mary Shelley, *The Last Man*, ed. Hugh J. Lake, Jr. (Lincoln, Neb.: University of Nebraska Press, 1965), pp. 328–330.

benighted soul—repose in my weariness—slumber in my sleepless woe. Ill, most ill, with disjointed words, bare and weak, have I expressed the feeling with which I clung to them. I would have wound myself like ivy inextricably round them, so that the same blow might destroy us. I would have entered and been a part of them—so that

> If the dull substance of my flesh were thought,

even now I had accompanied them to their new and incommunicable abode.

Never shall I see them more. I am bereft of their dear converse—bereft of sight of them. I am a tree rent by lightning; never will the bark close over the bared fibres—never will their quivering life, torn by the winds, receive the opiate of a moment's balm. I am alone in the world—but that expression as yet was less pregnant with misery, than that Adrian and Clara are dead.

The tide of thought and feeling rolls on for ever the same, though the banks and shapes around, which govern its course, and the reflection in the wave, vary. Thus the sentiment of immediate loss in some sort decayed, while that of utter, irremediable loneliness grew on me with time. Three days I wandered through Ravenna—now thinking only of the beloved beings who slept in the oozy caves of ocean—now looking forward on the dread blank before me; shuddering to make an onward step—writhing at each change that marked the progress of the hours.

For three days I wandered to and fro in this melancholy town. I passed whole hours in going from house to house, listening whether I could detect some lurking sign of human existence. Sometimes I rang at a bell; it tinkled through the vaulted rooms, and silence succeeded to the sound. I called myself hopeless, yet still I hoped; and still disappointment ushered in the hours, intruding the cold, sharp steel which first pierced me, into the aching festering wound. I fed like a wild beast, which seizes its food only when stung by intolerable hunger. I did not change my garb, or seek the shelter of a roof, during all those days. Burning heats, nervous irritation, a ceaseless, but confused flow of thought, sleepless nights, and days instinct with a frenzy of agitation, possessed me during that time.

As the fever of my blood increased, a desire of wandering came upon me. I remember, that the sun had set on the fifth day after my wreck, when, without purpose or aim, I quitted the town of Ravenna. I must have been very ill. Had I been possessed by more or less of delirium, that night had surely been my last; for, as I continued to walk on the banks of the Mantone, whose upward course I followed, I looked wistfully on the stream, acknowledging to myself that its pellucid waves could medicine my woes for ever, and was unable to account to myself for my tardiness in seeking their shelter from the poisoned arrows of thought, that were piercing me through and through. I walked a considerable part of the night, and excessive weariness at length conquered my repugnance to the availing myself of the deserted habitations of my species. The waning moon, which had just risen, shewed me a cottage, whose neat entrance and trim garden reminded me of my own England. I lifted up the latch of the door and entered. A kitchen first presented itself, where, guided by the moon beams, I found materials for striking a light. Within this was bed room; the couch was furnished with sheets of snowy whiteness; the wood piled on the hearth, and an array as for a meal, might almost have deceived me into the dear belief that I had here found what I had so long sought—one survivor, a companion for my loneliness, a solace to my despair. I steeled myself against the delusion; the room itself was vacant: it was only prudent, I repeated to myself, to examine the rest of the house. I fancied that I was proof against the expectation; yet my heart beat audibly, as I laid my hand on the lock of each door, and it sunk again, when I perceived in each the same vacancy. Dark and silent they were as vaults; so I returned to the first chamber, wondering what sightless host had spread the materials for my repast, and my repose. I drew a chair to the table, and examined what the viands were of which I was to partake. In truth it was a death feast! The bread was blue and mouldy; the cheese lay a heap of dust. I did not dare examine the other dishes; a troop of ants passed in a double line across the table cloth; every utensil was covered with dust, with cobwebs, and myriads of dead flies: these were objects each and all betokening the fallaciousness of my expectations. Tears rushed into my eyes; surely this was a wanton display of the power of the destroyer. What had I done, that each sensitive nerve was thus to be anatomized? Yet why complain more now than ever? This vacant cottage revealed no new sorrow—the world was empty; mankind was dead—I knew it well—why quarrel therefore with an acknowledged and stale truth? Yet, as I said, I had hoped in the very heart of despair, so that every new impression of the hard-cut reality on my soul brought with it a fresh pang, telling me the yet unstudied lesson, that neither change of place nor time could bring alleviation to my misery, but that, as I now was, I must continue, day after day, month after month, year after year, while I lived. I hardly dared conjecture what space of time that expression implied. It is true, I was no longer in the first blush of manhood; neither had I declined far in the vale of years—men have accounted mine the prime of life: I had just entered my thirty-seventh year; every limb was as well knit, every articulation as true, as when I had acted the shepherd on the hills of Cumberland; and with these advantages I was to commence the train of solitary life. Such were the reflections that ushered in my slumber on that night.

# NATIONALISM

*The desire for nationhood was expressed in many forms. Adam Mickiewicz (1798–1855), the Polish Romantic poet, saw a parallel between the sufferings of Christ and of Poland, repeatedly divided among warring powers. In Russia, the death of Alexander I was the occasion for the Decembrist uprising by groups seeking to establish a constitutional monarchy and bring an end to feudalism. Giuseppe Mazzini (1805–1872) organized Young Italy, a revolutionary society that sought a unified, republican Italy as a prelude to a Christian brotherhood of European nations.*

## Poland

### From Adam Mickiewicz. *The Books of the Polish Nation from the Beginning of the World to the Martydom of the Polish Nation*

In the beginning there was belief in one God, and there was freedom in the world. And there were no laws, only the will of God, and there were no lords and slaves, only patriarchs and their children.

But later the people denied the one God, and made for themselves idols, and bowed themselves down to them, and slew in their honor bloody offerings, and waged war for the honor of their idols.

Therefore God sent upon the idolaters the greatest punishment, which is slavery.

And it came to pass that when slavery had grown strong in the world, there came on a turning point for it; even as the solstice, the turning point of night, in the longest and darkest night, such was the turning point of slavery in the time of the Roman bondage.

At that time there came to earth Jesus Christ, the Son of God, teaching men that all are born brothers, children of one God.

And that he is the greatest among men, who serveth them and who sacrificeth himself for their good. And whosoever is better in any way, so much the more ought he to sacrifice. But Christ, being best of all, was to sacrifice his blood for them through the bitterest suffering.

So Christ taught that naught is to be held in respect on earth, nei-

From Adam Mickiewicz, *Konrad Wallenrod and Other Writings of Adam Mickiewicz*, trans. Jewell Parish *et al.* (Berkeley: University of California Press, 1925), pp. 133–136, 138, 140–143.

ther human wisdom, nor office, nor riches, nor a crown; but that sacrificing oneself for the good of men is alone to be held in respect.

And whosoever sacrificeth himself for others shall find wisdom and riches and a crown on earth, in heaven, and everywhere.

But whosoever sacrificeth others for himself, that he may have wisdom, and office, and riches, shall find folly and wretchedness and damnation on earth, in hell, and everywhere.

And finally Christ said: "Whosoever will follow after me shall be saved, for I AM TRUTH AND JUSTICE." And when Christ taught in this manner, the judges, who judged in the name of the Roman Emperor, were terrified; and they said: "We drove out justice from the earth, and behold it returneth: let us slay it and bury it in the earth."

Then they martyred the holiest and most innocent of men, and laid him in the tomb, and they cried out: "Justice and truth are in the world no longer; who now will rise against the Roman Emperor?"

But they cried out foolishly, for they knew not that having committed the greatest sin, they had already filled up the measure of their iniquities; and their power came to an end in the time when they exulted most.

For Christ arose from the dead, and, having driven out the Emperors, set up his cross in their capital city; and at that time the lords freed their slaves and acknowledged them as brothers, and the kings, anointed in the name of God, acknowledged that the law of God was over them, and justice returned to the earth.

And all the nations that believed, whether they were Germans, or Italians, or French, or Poles, looked upon themselves as one nation, and this nation was called Christendom.

And the kings of the different nations looked upon themselves as brothers, and marched under the one sign of the cross.

And he who was a man of knightly rank rode out to war against the heathen in Asia, that he might protect the Christians in Asia and win back the sepulcher of the Savior.

And they called this war in Asia the war of the cross.

And although the Christians did not make war either for glory or for the conquest of lands or for riches, but for the deliverance of the Holy Land, yet God rewarded them for this war with glory and lands and riches and wisdom. And Europe became enlightened and set in order and enriched. And God rewarded her for that she had made a sacrifice of herself for the good of others.

And freedom spread abroad in Europe slowly but steadily and in order; from the kings freedom passed to the great lords, and, these being free, they bestowed freedom upon the nobility, and from the nobility freedom passed to the cities, and soon it would have come down to the people, and all Christendom would have been free, and all Christians, like brothers, equal with one another.

But the kings corrupted all.

For the kings became evil and Satan entered into them and they said in their hearts: "Let us take heed: lo, the people are attaining understanding and plenty, and they live uprightly, so that we cannot punish them, and the sword rusteth in our hands; but the people are attaining freedom and our power weakeneth, and as soon as they mature and become wholly free, our power will be at an end."

But the kings in so thinking thought foolishly, for if kings are the fathers of the nations, then the nations, like children, on coming of age go out from under the rod and guardianship. . . .

Then the kings, renouncing Christ, made ready new gods that were idols, and set them up in the sight of the people, and bade them bow down to them and fight for them.

And so the kings made an idol for the French and called it *honor;* and this was the same idol that in pagan times was called the golden calf.

Then their king made an idol for the Spaniards, which he called *political preponderance,* or *political influence,* or power and authority, and this was the same idol that the Assyrians had worshiped under the name of Baal, and the Philistines under the name of Dagon, and the Romans under the name of Jupiter.

And then their king made an idol for the English that he called *sea power and commerce,* and this was the same idol that of old was called Mammon.

And then an idol was made for the Germans that was called *Brotsinn* or *welfare,* and this was the same idol that of old had been called Moloch and Comus. . . .

. . . The Italians devised for themselves an idol goddess, whom they called *Political Balance of Power.* And this idol the pagans of old had not known, but the Italians were the first to establish its worship among themselves, and fighting over it they became weak and foolish and fell into the hands of tyrants.

Then the kings of Europe, seeing that the worship of this goddess *Balance of Power* had exhausted the Italian nation, introduced her quickly into their kingdoms, and spread abroad her worship and bade men fight for her.

And the Prussian king drew a *circle* and said: "Lo, here is a new God." And they bowed down to this *circle* and called this worship *political rounding.* . . .

Finally in idolatrous Europe there rose three rulers; the name of the first was *Frederick the Second* of Prussia, the name of the second was *Catherine the Second* of Russia, the name of the third was *Maria Theresa* of Austria.

And this was a Satanic trinity, contrary to the Divine Trinity, and was in the manner of a mock and a derision of all that is holy. . . .

Meanwhile all nations were bowing down to *Interest.* And the kings said: "If we spread abroad the worship of this idol, then as nation fighteth with nation, so afterwards city will fight with city, and then man with man.

"And people will again become savage, and we shall again have such power as the savage kings had of old, idolaters, and such as the Moorish kings and the cannibal kings now have, that they may eat their subjects."

But the Polish nation alone did not bow down to the new idol, and did not have in its language the expression for christening it in Polish, neither for christening its worshipers, whom it calls by the French word *egoists*.

The Polish nation worshiped God, knowing that he who honoreth God giveth honor to everything that is good.

The Polish nation then from the beginning to the end was true to the God of its ancestors.

Its kings and men of knightly rank never assaulted any believing nation, but defended Christendom from the pagans and barbarians who brought slavery.

And the Polish kings went to the defense of Christians in distant lands, King Wladislaw to Varna, and King Jan to Vienna, to the defense of the east and the west.

And never did their kings and men of knightly rank seize neighboring lands by force, but they received the nations into brotherhood, uniting them with themselves by the gracious gift of faith and freedom.

And God rewarded them, for a great nation, Lithuania, united itself with Poland, as husband with wife, two souls in one body. And there was never before this such a union of nations. But hereafter there shall be.

For that union and marriage of Lithuania and Poland is the symbol of the future union of all Christian peoples in the name of faith and freedom.

And God gave unto the Polish kings and knights freedom, that all might be called brothers, both the richest and the poorest. And such freedom never was before. But hereafter there shall be.

The king and the men of knightly rank received into their brotherhood still more people; they received whole armies and whole tribes. And the number of brothers became as great as a nation, and in no nation were there so many people free and calling each other brothers as in Poland.

And finally, on the Third of May, the king and the knightly body determined to make all Poles brothers, at first the burghers and later the peasants.

And they called the brothers the nobility, because they had become noble, that is had become brothers with the Lachs, who were men free and equal.

And they wished to bring it about that every Christian in Poland should be ennobled and called a Nobleman, for a token that he should have a noble soul and always be ready to die for freedom. . . .

Nobility then was to be the baptism of freedom, and every one who was ready to die for freedom was to be baptized of the law and of the sword.

And finally Poland said: "Whosoever will come to me shall be free and equal, for *I am Freedom.*"

But the kings when they heard of this were terrified in their hearts and said: "We banished freedom from the earth; but lo, it returneth in the person of a just nation, that doth not bow down to our idols! Come, let us slay this nation." And they plotted treachery among themselves. . . .

And they martyred the Polish Nation and laid it in the grave, and the kings cried out: "We have slain and we have buried Freedom."

But they cried out foolishly, for in committing the last sin they filled up the measure of their iniquities, and their power was coming to an end at the time when they exulted most.

For the Polish Nation did not die: its body lieth in the grave, but its spirit hath descended from the earth, that is from public life, to the abyss, that is to the private life of people who suffer slavery in their country and outside of their country, that it may see their sufferings.

But on the third day the soul shall return to the body, and the Nation shall arise and free all the peoples of Europe from slavery.

And already two days have gone by. One day passed with the first capture of Warsaw, and the second day passed with the second capture of Warsaw, and the third day shall begin, but shall not pass.

And as after the resurrection of Christ bloody offerings ceased in all the world, so after the resurrection of the Polish Nation wars shall cease in all Christendom.

# Russia

## From Peter Kakhovsky. *Letter To General Levashev (February 1826)*

Your Excellency,
Dear Sir!

The uprising of December 14 is a result of causes related above. I see, Your Excellency, that the Committee established by His Majesty is making a great effort to discover all the members of the secret Society.

From Anatole G. Mazour, *The First Russian Revolution 1825: The Decembrist Movement* (Palo Alto, Calif.: Stanford University Press, 1963), pp. 274–277.

But the government will not derive any notable benefit from that. We were not trained within the Society but were already ready to work when we joined it. The origin and the root of the Society one must seek in the spirit of the time and in our state of mind. I know a few belonging to the secret Society but am inclined to think the membership is not very large. Among my many acquaintances who do not adhere to secret societies very few are opposed to my opinions. Frankly I state that among thousands of young men there are hardly a hundred who do not passionately long for freedom. These youths, striving with pure and strong love for the welfare of their Fatherland, toward true enlightenment, are growing mature.

The people have conceived a sacred truth—that they do not exist for governments, but that governments must be organized for them. This is the cause of struggle in all countries; peoples, after tasting the sweetness of enlightenment and freedom, strive toward them; and governments, surrounded by millions of bayonets, make efforts to repel these peoples back into the darkness of ignorance. But all these efforts will prove in vain; impressions once received can never be erased. Liberty, that torch of intellect and warmth of life, was always and everywhere the attribute of peoples emerged from primitive ignorance. We are unable to live like our ancestors, like barbarians or slaves. . . .

Emperor Alexander promised us much; he, it could be said, enormously stirred the minds of the people toward the sacred rights of humanity. Later he changed his principles and intentions. The people became frightened, but the seed had sprouted and the roots grew deep. So rich with various revolutions are the latter half of the past century and the events of our own time that we have no need to refer to distant ones. We are witnesses of great events. The discovery of the New World and the United States, by virtue of its form of government, have forced Europe into rivalry with her. The United States will shine as an example even to distant generations. The name of Washington, the friend and benefactor of the people, will pass from generation to generation; the memory of his devotion to the welfare of the Fatherland will stir the hearts of citizens. In France the revolution which began so auspiciously turned, alas, at the end from a lawful into a criminal one. However, not the people but court intrigues and politics were responsible for that. The revolution in France shook all the thrones of Europe and had a greater influence upon the governments and peoples than the establishment of the United States.

The dominance of Napoleon and the war of 1813 and 1814 united all the European nations, summoned by their monarchs and fired by the call to freedom and citizenship. By what means were countless sums collected among citizens? What guided the armies? They preached freedom to us in Manifestoes, Appeals, and in Orders! We were lured and, kindly by nature, we believed, sparing neither blood nor property. Napoleon was overthrown! The Bourbons were called back to the throne of France and, submitting to circumstances, gave that brave, magnanimous nation a constitution, pledging themselves to forget the past. The Monarchs united into a Holy Alliance; congresses sprang into existence, informing the nations that they were assembled to reconcile all classes and introduce political freedom. But the aim of these congresses was soon revealed; the nations learned how greatly they had been deceived. The Monarchs thought only of how to retain their unlimited power, to support their shattered thrones, and to extinguish the last spark of freedom and enlightenment.

Offended nations began to demand what belonged to them and had been promised to them—chains and prisons became their lot! Crowns transgressed their pledges, the constitution of France was violated at its very base. Manuel, the representative of the people, was dragged from the Chamber of Deputies by gendarmes! Freedom of the press was restricted, the army of France, against its own will, was sent to destroy the lawful liberty of Spain. Forgetting the oath given by Louis XVIII, Charles X compensates *émigrés* and for that purpose burdens the people with new taxes. The government interferes with the election of deputies, and in the last elections, among the deputies only thirty-three persons were not in the service and payment of the King, the rest being sold to the Ministers. The firm, courageous Spanish people at the cost of blood rose for the liberty of their country, saved the King, the Monarchy, and the honor of the Fatherland; of their own volition the people themselves received Ferdinand as King. The King took the oath to safeguard the rights of the people. As early as the year 1812, Alexander I recognized the constitution of Spain.

Then the Alliance itself assisted France by sending her troops, and thus aided in dishonoring her army in the invasion of Spain. Ferdinand, arrested in Cadiz, was sentenced to death. He summoned Riego, swore to be once more loyal to the constitution and to expel the French troops from his territory, and begged Riego to spare his life. Honest men are apt to be trustful. Riego gave guaranty to the Cortes for the King, and he was freed. And what was the first step of Ferdinand? By his order Riego was seized, arrested, poisoned and, half-alive, that saint-martyr hero who renounced the throne offered to him, friend of the people, savior of the King's life, by the King's order is now taken through the streets of Madrid in the shameful wagon pulled by a donkey, and is hanged like a criminal. What an act! Whose heart would not shudder at it? Instead of the promised liberty the nations of Europe found themselves oppressed and their educational facilities curtailed. The prisons of Piedmont, Sardinia, Naples, and, in general, of the whole of Italy and Germany were filled with chained citizens. The lot of the people became so oppressive that they began to regret the past and to bless the memory of Napoleon the conqueror! These are the incidents which enlightened their minds and made them realize that it was impossible to make agreements with Sovereigns. . . .

The events of December are calamitous for us and, of course, must be distressing to the Emperor. Yet the events of this date should be fortunate for His Imperial Highness. After all, it was necessary sometime for the Society to begin its activities, but hardly could it have been so precipitate as in this instance. I swear to God, I wish the kind Sovereign prosperity! May God aid him in healing the wounds of our Fatherland and to become a friend and benefactor of the people. . . .

Most obedient and devoted servant of Your Excellency,

1826                                 PETER KAKHOVSKY

February, 24th day

# Italy

## From Giuseppe Mazzini. *Young Italy (1832)*

We have beheld Italy—Italy, the purpose, the soul, the consolation of our thoughts, the country chosen of God and oppressed by men, twice queen of the world and twice fallen through the infamy of foreigners and the guilt of her citizens, yet lovely still though she be dust, unmatched by any other nation whatever fortune has decreed; and Genius returns to seek in this dust the word of eternal life, and the spark that creates the future. We have tried to see her with an objectivity as cool as intense longing and the need to grasp her internal nature will allow—and our hearts beat strong within our breasts, for we have young passions, and pride in the name Italian lifts our souls within—but we enjoined our hearts to silence, and saw her as she was—vast, strong, intelligent, fertile with the elements of rebirth, beautiful in memories such as could create a second universe, peopled with spirits great in sacrifice, and great in victory—but laid to waste, divided, mistrustful, ignorant, wavering irresolute between the threats of tyranny and the treacherous flattery of the many who with their adulation of her antique grandeur put her to sleep lest she seek new grandeur—and all the forces of her several parts counterbalanced against one another, neutralized by lack of unity and lack of faith—qualities which neither the ten centuries of wretchedness that resulted from provincial jealousies, nor the power of intellect, nor the fervor of imagination, have so far made to prevail among us—and to create them, what is wanted more than anything else is the authority of a principle

From Mack Walker, ed. and trans., *Metternich's Europe* (New York: Harper & Row, 1968), pp. 160–165, 167–169. Reprinted by permission of Mack Walker.

that is lofty, regenerative, universal, applicable to all the parts of Italian civilization, and that reforms and purifies them all into one design—of a single and potent principle in which are focused all the rays, all the elements of life, a faith in which souls may be made virginal again, and conscience may whisper destiny to the masses—because what we lack today is not the means for action, but accord and ties among the means: not substance, but motion to impel it, not power, but the conviction that we are powerful. . . .

And we looked at the past, to see whether we could find the remedy there. Now the past has taught us not to despair, the past has taught us how many things and which things are only artifices of tyranny and relics of servitude of the spirit—no more than that. The learning of our forefathers was exercised more in the realm of principles than of application. Perhaps the flame of fatherland and liberty with which they burned showed them how vast the arena was. But circumstances stifled the conception, and their efforts took on neither the energy, nor the magnitude, nor the harmony that such work requires. . . .

. . . All the tendencies that seem visible in the age, . . . we shall develop in our journals with all the ardor of people who expect nothing and fear nothing from political parties, and who seek nothing on earth but a goal and a way to attain it. And from these tendencies which now exist in embryo, from all the inevitability clearly apparent in past events, and from all the inspirations of the age will come, let us hope, a system that will gather within itself the coming generation. It is simply a system, let us say it again, that we have tried to identify with the name *Young Italy;* but we chose this term because the one term seems to marshal before the youth of Italy the magnitude of its duties and the solemnity of the mission that circumstances have entrusted to it, so that it will be ready when the hour has struck to arise from its slumber to a new life of action and regeneration. And we chose it because we wanted to show ourselves, writing it, as what we are, to do battle with raised visors, to bear our faith before us, as the knights of medieval times bore their faith on their shields. For while we pity men who do not know the truth, we despise men who, though they know the truth, do not dare to speak it.

Undefiled by connections or by private grudges, hearts burning with generous wrath but open to love, with no other desire than to die for the progress of humanity and for the liberty of the fatherland, we need not be suspected of personal ambition or of envy.

. . . We raise our banner between the old world and the new. Let him who will, rally to this banner; let him who will not, live on memories. . . .

Peace then! To peace our souls are devoted. In the name of the fatherland—in the name of all that is most sacred—we cry peace! Let the charge of sowing discord fall upon the heads of those men who proclaim themselves free, but allow no progress in human affairs, who talk

of concord and then smother ideas frankly offered under malign interpretations and suspicions, who preach unity and spatter venom on efforts to achieve it. With these, there can be no accord.

Youth, my brothers—take comfort and be great! Faith in God, in the
right, and in ourselves!—that was the cry of Luther, and it moved half
Europe. Raise this cry—and forward! Events will show whether we are
mistaken when we say the future is ours.

# REFORM

## England

*In England the movement for parliamentary reform emerged after 1815. Its members, organized in societies all over the country, called for annual parliaments, repeal of the corn laws, and universal manhood suffrage. Samuel Bamford (1788–1872), a silk weaver and radical, took part in the demonstration at St. Peter's Fields, Manchester, in August 1819, and detailed what happened when troops dispersed the unarmed crowd. The "Peterloo Massacre" was followed by government restriction of the radical press and other repressive legislation. In the late 1820s, the movement for reform found advocates within parliament, especially among Whigs who sought to break the power of their Tory opponents. When a Reform Bill was passed in 1832, it enfranchised the middle classes only, for reasons set forth in the speech by the historian and Whig member of parliament, Thomas Babington Macaulay (1800–1859).*

### From Samuel Bamford. *Passages in the Life of a Radical—on the Peterloo Massacre*

WITH the restoration of the Habeas Corpus Act, the agitation for reform was renewed. A public meeting on the subject was held at Westminster, on the 28th of March and in June [1819] Sir Francis Burdett's motion for reform was negatived in the House of Commons.

Numerous meetings followed in various parts of the country; and Lancashire, and the Stockport borders of Cheshire, were not the last to be concerned in public demonstrations for reform. At one of these meetings, which took place at Lydgate, in Saddleworth, and at which Bagguley, Drummond, Fitton, Haigh, and others were the principal speakers, I, in the course of an address, insisted on the right, and the propriety also, of females who were present at such assemblages voting by a show of hand for or against the resolutions. This was a new idea; and the women, who attended numerously on that bleak ridge, were mightily pleased with it. The men being nothing dissentient, when the resolution was put the women held up their hands amid much laugh-

From Henry Dunckley, *Bamford's Passages in the Life of a Radical and Early Days* (London: Unwin, 1893), Vol. 2, pp. 141–142, 149–153, 155–156.

ter; and ever from that time females voted with the men at the Radical meetings. I was not then aware that the new impulse thus given to political movement would in a short time be applied to charitable and religious purposes. But it was so; our females voted at every subsequent meeting; it became the practice, female political unions were formed, with their chairwoman, committees, and other officials; and from us the practice was soon borrowed, very judiciously no doubt, and applied in a greater or less degree to the promotion of religious and charitable institutions.

Amongst the meetings for reform held in the early part of the summer of 1819 were the one which took place on Spa Fields, London, at which Mr. Hunt was chairman, and another held at Birmingham, at which Major Cartwright and Sir Charles Wolseley were elected to act as legislatorial attornies for that town in Parliament.

It would seem that these movements in the country induced our friends at Manchester to adopt a course similar to that at Birmingham, and it was accordingly arranged that a meeting for that purpose should be held on St. Peter's Field on the 9th of August. But the object of that meeting having been declared illegal by the authorities, it was countermanded, and another was appointed to be held on the 16th of the same month. . . .

By eight o'clock on the morning of Monday, the 16th of August, 1819, the whole town of Middleton might be said to be on the alert: some to go to the meeting, and others to see the procession, the like of which, for such a purpose, had never before taken place in that neighbourhood.

First were selected twelve of the most comely and decent-looking youths, who were placed in two rows of six each, with each a branch of laurel held presented in his hand, as a token of amity and peace; then followed the men of several districts in fives; then the band of music, an excellent one; then the colours: a blue one of silk, with inscriptions in golden letters, "Unity and Strength," "Liberty and Fraternity"; a green one of silk, with golden letters, "Parliaments Annual," "Suffrage Universal"; and betwixt them, on a staff, a handsome cap of crimson velvet with a tuft of laurel, and the cap tastefully braided, with the word *"Libertas"* in front. Next were placed the remainder of the men of the districts in fives.

Every hundred men had a leader, who was distinguished by a sprig of laurel in his hat; others similarly distinguished were appointed over these, and the whole were to obey the directions of a principal conductor, who took his place at the head of the column, with a bugleman to sound his orders. Such were our dispositions on the ground at Barrowfields. At the sound of the bugle not less than three thousand men formed a hollow square, with probably as many people around them, and, an impressive silence having been obtained, I reminded them that they were going to attend the most important meeting that had ever been held for Parliamentary Reform, and I hoped their conduct would be marked by a steadiness and seriousness befitting the occasion, and such as would cast shame upon their enemies, who had always represented the reformers as a mob-like rabble; ... I requested they would not leave their ranks, nor show carelessness, nor inattention to the order of their leaders; but that they would walk comfortably and agreeably together. Not to offer any insult or provocation by word or deed; nor to notice any persons who might do the same by them, but to keep such persons as quiet as possible; for if they began to retaliate, the least disturbance might serve as a pretext for dispersing the meeting. If the peace officers should come to arrest myself or any other person, they were not to offer any resistance, but suffer them to execute their office peaceably. . . .

... I also said that, in conformity with a rule of the committee, no sticks, nor weapons of any description, would be allowed to be carried in the ranks; and those who had such were requested to put them aside, or leave them with some friend until their return. In consequence of this order many sticks were left behind; and a few only of the oldest and most infirm amongst us were allowed to carry their walking staves. I may say with truth that we presented a most respectable assemblage of labouring men; all were decently, though humbly attired; and I noticed not even one who did not exhibit a white Sunday's shirt, a neck-cloth, and other apparel in the same clean, though homely condition. . . .

From all that I had heard of the disposition of the authorities, I had scarcely expected that we should be allowed to enter Manchester in a body. I had thought it not improbable that they, or some of them, would meet us with a civil and military escort; would read the Riot Act, if they thought proper, and warn us from proceeding, and that we should then have nothing to do but turn back and hold a meeting in our town. I had even fancied that they would most likely stop us at the then toll-gate, where the roads forked towards Collyhurst and Newtown; but when I saw both those roads open, with only a horseman or two prancing before us, I began to think that I had over-estimated the forethought of the authorities, and I felt somewhat assured that we should be allowed to enter the town quietly, when, of course, all probability of interruption would be at an end. . .

Having squeezed ourselves through the gully of a road below St. Michael's Church, we traversed Blackley Street and Miller's Lane, and went along Swan Street and Oldham Street, frequently hailed in our progress by the cheers of the townspeople. We learned that other parties were on the field before us, and that the Lees and Saddleworth Union had been led by Doctor Healey, walking before a pitch-black flag, with staring white letters, forming the words, "Equal Representation or Death," "Love"—two hands joined and a heart; . . .

... The meeting was indeed a tremendous one.... Mr. Hunt, stepping towards the front of the stage, took off his white hat, and addressed the people.

Whilst he was doing so, I proposed to an acquaintance that, as the speeches and resolutions were not likely to contain anything new to us, and as we could see them in the papers, we should retire awhile and get some refreshment, of which I stood much in need, being not in very robust health. He assented, and we had got to nearly the outside of the crowd, when a noise and strange murmur arose towards the church. Some persons said it was the Blackburn people coming, and I stood on tip-toe and looked in the direction whence the noise proceeded, and saw a party of cavalry in blue and white uniform come trotting, sword in hand, round the corner of a garden-wall, and to the front of a row of new houses, where they reined up in a line.

"The soldiers are here," I said; "we must go back and see what this means." "Oh," some one made reply, "they are only come to be ready if there should be any disturbance in the meeting." "Well, let us go back," I said, and we forced our way towards the colours.

On the cavalry drawing up they were received with a shout of good-will, as I understood it. They shouted again, waving their sabres over their heads; and then, slackening rein, and striking spur into their steeds, they dashed forward and began cutting the people....

On the breaking of the crowd the yeomanry wheeled, and, dashing whenever there was an opening, they followed, pressing and wounding. Many females appeared as the crowd opened; and striplings or mere youths also were found. Their cries were piteous and heart-rending, and would, one might have supposed, have disarmed any human resentment: but here their appeals were in vain. Women, white-vested maids, and tender youths, were indiscriminately sabred or trampled; and we have reason for believing that few were the instances in which that forbearance was vouchsafed which they so earnestly implored.

In ten minutes from the commencement of the havoc the field was an open and almost deserted space.

# From Thomas Babington Macaulay. *Speeches (March 2, 1831)—On The Reform Bill of 1832*

*On Lord John Russell's motion for leave to bring in a Bill to amend the Representation of the People of England and Wales.*

IT is a circumstance, sir, of happy augury for the measure before the House, that almost all those who have opposed it have declared them-

From Thomas Babington Macaulay, *Speeches, Parliamentary and Miscellaneous* (London: H. Vizetelly, 1853), Vol. 1, pp. 11–14, 20–21, 25–26.

selves altogether hostile to the principle of Reform. Two members, I think, have professed, that though they disapprove of the plan now submitted to us, they yet conceive some alteration of the representative system to be advisable. Yet even those gentlemen have used, so far as I have observed, no arguments which would not apply as strongly to the most moderate change as to that which has been proposed by his Majesty's Government. I say, sir, that I consider this as a circumstance of happy augury. For what I feared was, not the opposition of those who shrink from all reform, but the disunion of reformers. I knew that during three months every reformer had been employed in conjecturing what the plan of the Government would be. I knew that every reformer had imagined in his own mind a scheme differing, doubtless, in some points from that which my noble friend the Paymaster of the Forces (Lord John Russell) has developed. I felt, therefore, great apprehension that one person would be dissatisfied with one part of the Bill, that another person would be dissatisfied with another part, and that thus our whole strength would be wasted in internal dissensions. That apprehension is now at an end. I have seen with delight the perfect concord which prevails among all who deserve the name of reformers in this House, and I trust that I may consider it as an omen of the concord which will prevail among reformers throughout the country.

I will not, sir, at present express any opinion as to the details of the Bill; but having during the last twenty-four hours given the most diligent consideration to its general principles, I have no hesitation in pronouncing it a wise, noble, and comprehensive measure, skilfully framed for the healing of great distempers, for the securing at once of the public liberties and of the public repose, and for the reconciling and knitting together of all the orders of the State. The hon. baronet (Sir John Walsh) who has just sat down has told us that the Ministers have attempted to unite two inconsistent principles in one abortive measure. He thinks, if I understand him rightly, that they ought either to leave the representative system such as it is, or to make it symmetrical. I think, sir, that they would have acted unwisely if they had taken either of these courses. Their principle is plain, rational, and consistent. It is this—to admit the middle class to a large and direct share in the representation, without any violent shock to the institutions of our country. . . .

. . . I praise the Ministers for not attempting, under existing circumstances, to make the representation uniform—I praise them for not effacing the old distinction between the towns and the counties—for not assigning members to districts, according to the American practice, by the rule of three. They have done all that was necessary for the removing of a great practical evil, and no more than was necessary. . . .

. . . I believe that there are societies in which every man may safely be admitted to vote. . . . I say, sir, that there are countries in which the condition of the labouring-classes is such that they may safely be intrusted with the right of electing members of the Legislature. If the labourers of England were in that state in which I, from my soul, wish to see them—if employment were always plentiful, wages always high, food always cheap—if a large family were considered not as an incumbrance but as a blessing—the principal objections to universal suffrage would, I think, be removed. Universal suffrage exists in the United States without producing any very frightful consequences; and I do not believe that the people of those States, or of any part of the world, are in any good quality naturally superior to our own countrymen. But, unhappily, the lower orders in England, and in all old countries, are occasionally in a state of great distress. . . .

For the sake, therefore, of the whole society, for the sake of the labouring-classes themselves, I hold it to be clearly expedient that, in a country like this, the right of suffrage should depend on a pecuniary qualification. Every argument, sir, which would induce me to oppose universal suffrage, induces me to support the measure which is now before us. I oppose universal suffrage, because I think that it would produce a destructive revolution. I support this measure, because I am sure that it is our best security against a revolution. . . .

. . . I support this measure as a measure of reform; but I support it still more as a measure of conservation. That we may exclude those whom it is necessary to exclude, we must admit those whom it may be safe to admit. . . .

My hon. friend the member of the University of Oxford tells us that, if we pass this law, England will soon be a Republic. The reformed House of Commons will, according to him, before it has sat ten years, depose the King, and expel the Lords from their House. Sir, if my hon. friend could prove this, he would have succeeded in bringing an argument for democracy infinitely stronger than any that is to be found in the works of Paine. His proposition is, in fact, this—that our monarchical and aristocratical institutions have no hold on the public mind of England; that these institutions are regarded with aversion by a decided majority of the middle class. . . . Now, sir, if I were convinced that the great body of the middle class in England look with aversion on monarchy and aristocracy, I should be forced, much against my will, to come to this conclusion, that monarchical and aristocratical institutions are unsuited to this country. Monarchy and aristocracy, valuable and useful as I think them, are still valuable and useful as means, and not as ends. The end of government is the happiness of the people; and I do not conceive that, in a country like this, the happiness of the people can be promoted by a form of government in which the middle classes place no confidence, and which exists only because the middle classes have no organ by which to make their sentiments known. But, sir, I am fully convinced that the middle classes sincerely wish to uphold the royal prerogatives, and the constitutional rights of the Peers. . . .

. . . Is it possible that gentlemen long versed in high political affairs cannot read these signs? Is it possible that they can really believe that the representative system of England, such as it now is, will last till the year 1860? If not, for what would they have us wait? Would they have us wait merely that we may show to all the world how little we have profited by our own recent experience? Would they have us wait that we may once again hit the exact point where we can neither refuse with authority nor concede with grace? Would they have us wait that the numbers of the discontented party may become larger, its demands higher, its feelings more acrimonious, its organisation more complete? Would they have us wait till the whole tragi-comedy of 1827 has been acted over again—till they have been brought into office by a cry of "No Reform!" to be reformers, as they were once before brought into office by a cry of "No Popery!" to be emancipators? Have they obliterated from their minds—gladly, perhaps, would some among them obliterate from their minds—the transactions of that year? And have they forgotten all the transactions of the succeeding year? Have they forgotten how the spirit of liberty in Ireland, debarred from its natural outlet, found a vent by forbidden passages? Have they forgotten how we were forced to indulge the Catholics in all the license of rebels, merely because we chose to withhold from them the liberties of subjects? Do they wait for associations more formidable than that of the Corn Exchange, for contributions larger than the rent—for agitators more violent than those who, three years ago, divided, with the King and the Parliament, the sovereignty of Ireland? Do they wait for that last and most dreadful paroxysm of popular rage—for that last and most cruel test of military fidelity? Let them wait, if their past experience shall induce them to think that any high honour or any exquisite pleasure is to be obtained by a policy like this. Let them wait, if this strange and fearful infatuation be indeed upon them, that they should not see with their eyes, or hear with their ears, or understand with their heart.

But let us know our interest and our duty better. Turn where we may—within, around—the voice of great events is proclaiming to us, "Reform, that you may preserve." Now, therefore, while everything at home and abroad forebodes ruin to those who persist in a hopeless struggle against the spirit of the age; now, while the crash of the proudest throne of the Continent is still resounding in our ears; . . . now, while the heart of England is still sound; now, while the old feelings and the old associations retain a power and a charm which may too soon pass away; now, in this your accepted time; now, in this your day of salvation, take counsel, not of prejudice, not of party spirit, not of the ignominious pride of a fatal consistency, but of history, of reason, of the ages which are past, of the signs of this most portentous time. Pronounce in a manner worthy of the expectation with which this great debate has been anticipated, and of the long remembrance which it will leave behind. Renew the youth of the State. Save property divided against itself. Save the multitude, endangered by their own ungovernable passions. Save the aristocracy, endangered by its own unpopular power. Save the greatest, and fairest, and most highly civilised community that ever existed, from calamities which may in a few days sweep away all the rich heritage of so many ages of wisdom and glory. The danger is terrible. The time is short. If this Bill should be rejected, I pray to God that none of those who concur in rejecting it may ever remember their votes with unavailing regret, amidst the wreck of laws, the confusion of ranks, the spoliation of property, and the dissolution of social order.

# VIII

# INDUSTRIALIZATION AND SOCIAL UPHEAVAL

*A*S THE FACTORY *system spread, with its new technology and organization of production, it brought dramatic changes in its wake. Capitalist manufacturers, seeking to cut labor costs, hired women and children to run the new machines. Employers sought to standardize not only the products manufactured, but also the efforts put into production. They imposed strict rules on their factory workers (male and female), which regulated the work day and the way time at work was spent.*

*In many areas, employers constructed housing for their workers close to factories. Workers migrated to these new industrial centers, moved into crowded tenements, and adapted their life-styles to urban conditions. In order to make ends meet and to pay for food, clothing, fuel, and rent, families sent all able-bodied members into the workforce. In sharp contrast to middle-class families, where women stayed at home and children were sent to school, working-class families expected wives and children to earn wages when the household needed money.*

*Factory owners, middle-class professionals, and politicians praised the industrial system and argued that success and wealth were attainable by individual self-help. In response, representatives of the working classes argued that major political and economic reforms were necessary if workers were to enjoy the fruits of industrial growth. Movements for reform grew during the 1840s, a period of economic depression, and culminated in the revolutions that swept European capitals in the spring of 1848. No revolution occurred in England in 1848, however. The Reform Bill of 1832 had effectively broken the coalition between workers and the middle classes and insured political representation for middle-class interests.*

# THE FACTORY SYSTEM

## Principles

*Andrew Ure (1778–1857) was a professor of applied science in Glasgow. He was among the most enthusiastic exponents of the new factory system.*

### From Andrew Ure. *The Philosophy of Manufactures*

This island is pre-eminent among civilized nations for the prodigious development of its factory wealth, and has been therefore long viewed with a jealous admiration by foreign powers. This very pre-eminence, however, has been contemplated in a very different light by many influential members of our own community, and has been even denounced by them as the certain origin of innumerable evils to the people, and of revolutionary convulsions to the state. If the affairs of the kingdom be wisely administered, I believe such allegations and fears will prove to be groundless, and to proceed more from the envy of one ancient and powerful order of the commonwealth, towards another suddenly grown into political importance, than from the nature of things. . . .

The blessings which physio-mechanical science has bestowed on society, and the means it has still in store for ameliorating the lot of mankind, have been too little dwelt upon; while, on the other hand, it has been accused of lending itself to the rich capitalists as an instrument for harassing the poor, and of exacting from the operative an accelerated rate of work. It has been said, for example, that the steam-engine now drives the power-looms with such velocity as to urge on their attendant weavers at the same rapid pace; but that the hand-weaver, not being subjected to this restless agent, can throw his shuttle and move his treddles at his convenience. There is, however, this difference in the two cases, that in the factory, every member of the loom is so adjusted, that the driving force leaves the attendant nearly nothing at all to do, certainly no muscular fatigue to sustain, while it procures for him good, unfailing wages, besides a healthy workshop *gratis:* whereas the non-factory weaver, having everything to execute by muscular ex-

From Andrew Ure, *The Philosophy of Manufactures* (London: Chas. Knight, 1835), pp. 5–8, 14–15, 20–21, 23, 29–31.

ertion, finds the labour irksome, makes in consequence innumerable short pauses, separately of little account, but great when added together; earns therefore proportionally low wages, while he loses his health by poor diet and the dampness of his hovel. . . .

The constant aim and effect of scientific improvement in manufactures are philanthropic, as they tend to relieve the workmen either from niceties of adjustment which exhaust his mind and fatigue his eyes, or from painful repetition of efforts which distort or wear out his frame. At every step of each manufacturing process described in this volume the humanity of science will be manifest. . . .

In its precise acceptation, the Factory system is of recent origin, and may claim England for its birthplace. The mills for throwing silk, or making organzine, which were mounted centuries ago in several of the Italian states, and furtively transferred to this country by Sir Thomas Lombe in 1718, contained indeed certain elements of a factory, and probably suggested some hints of those grander and more complex combinations of self-acting machines, which were first embodied half a century later in our cotton manufacture by Richard Arkwright, assisted by gentlemen of Derby, well acquainted with its celebrated silk establishment. But the spinning of an entangled flock of fibres into a smooth thread, which constitutes the main operation with cotton, is in silk superfluous; being already performed by the unerring instinct of a worm, which leaves to human art the simple task of doubling and twisting its regular filaments. The apparatus requisite for this purpose is more elementary, and calls for few of those gradations of machinery which are needed in the carding, drawing, roving, and spinning processes of a cotton-mill.

When the first water-frames for spinning cotton were erected at Cromford, in the romantic valley of the Derwent, about sixty years ago, mankind were little aware of the mighty revolution which the new system of labour was destined by Providence to achieve, not only in the structure of British society, but in the fortunes of the world at large. Arkwright alone had the sagacity to discern, and the boldness to predict in glowing language, how vastly productive human industry would become, when no longer proportioned in its results to muscular effort, which is by its nature fitful and capricious, but when made to consist in the task of guiding the work of mechanical fingers and arms, regularly impelled with great velocity by some indefatigable physical power. What his judgment so clearly led him to perceive, his energy of will enabled him to realize with such rapidity and success, as would have done honour to the most influential individuals, but were truly wonderful in that obscure and indigent artisan. . . .

The principle of the factory system then is, to substitute mechanical science for hand skill, and the partition of a process into its essential constituents, for the division or graduation of labour among artisans. On the handicraft plan, labour more or less skilled was usually the most expensive element of production. . . . but on the automatic plan, skilled labour gets progressively superseded, and will, eventually, be replaced by mere overlookers of machines.

By the infirmity of human nature it happens, that the more skilful the workman, the more self-willed and intractable he is apt to become, and, of course, the less fit a component of a mechanical system, in which, by occasional irregularities, he may do great damage to the whole. The grand object therefore of the modern manufacturer is, through the union of capital and science, to reduce the task of his work-people to the exercise of vigilance and dexterity,—faculties, when concentred to one process, speedily brought to perfection in the young. In the infancy of mechanical engineering, a machine-factory displayed the division of labour in manifold gradations—the file, the drill, the lathe, having each its different workmen in the order of skill: but the dextrous hands of the filer and driller are now superseded by the planing, the keygroove cutting, and the drilling-machines; and those of the iron and brass turners, by the self-acting slide-lathe. . . .

It is, in fact, the constant aim and tendency of every improvement in machinery to supersede human labour altogether, or to diminish its cost, by substituting the industry of women and children for that of men; or that of ordinary labourers for trained artisans. In most of the water-twist, or throstle cotton-mills, the spinning is entirely managed by females of sixteen years and upwards. The effect of substituting the self-acting mule for the common mule, is to discharge the greater part of the men spinners, and to retain adolescents and children. The proprietor of a factory near Stockport states, in evidence to the commissioners, that, by such substitution, he would save 50*l.* a week in wages, in consequence of dispensing with nearly forty male spinners, at about 25*s.* of wages each. . . .

Steam-engines furnish the means not only of their support but of their multiplication. They create a vast demand for fuel; and, while they lend their powerful arms to drain the pits and to raise the coals, they call into employment multitudes of miners, engineers, shipbuilders, and sailors, and cause the construction of canals and railways. Thus therefore, in enabling these rich fields of industry to be cultivated to the utmost, they leave thousands of fine arable fields free for the production of food to man, which must have been otherwise allotted to the food of horses. Steam-engines moreover, by the cheapness and steadiness of their action, fabricate cheap goods, and procure in their exchange a liberal supply of the necessaries and comforts of life produced in foreign lands.

Improvements in the machinery have a three-fold bearing:—

1st. They make it possible to fabricate some articles which, but for them, could not be fabricated at all.

2nd. They enable an operative to turn out a greater quantity of work than he could before,—time, labour, and quality of work remaining constant.

3rd. They effect a substitution of labour comparatively unskilled, for that which is more skilled.

# Discipline

*As factory owners centralized production and sought to make it more efficient, they found they had to teach their employees to accommodate the new system. The former peasants or skilled workers were used to regulating their own time, pacing a production schedule over a week or two. In the new factories employers expected uniform input each day.*

## Factory Rules in Berlin (1844)

In every large works, and in the co-ordination of any large number of workmen, good order and harmony must be looked upon as the fundamentals of success, and therefore the following rules shall be strictly observed.

Every man employed in the concern named below shall receive a copy of these rules, so that no one can plead ignorance. Its acceptance shall be deemed to mean consent to submit to its regulations.

(1) The normal working day begins at all seasons at 6 a.m. precisely and ends, after the usual break of half an hour for breakfast, an hour for dinner and half an hour for tea, at 7 p.m., and it shall be strictly observed.

Five minutes before the beginning of the stated hours of work until their actual commencement, a bell shall ring and indicate that every worker employed in the concern has to proceed to his place of work, in order to start as soon as the bell stops.

The doorkeeper shall lock the door punctually at 6 a.m., 8.30 a.m., 1 p.m. and 4.30 p.m.

Workers arriving 2 minutes late shall lose half an hour's wages; whoever is more than 2 minutes late may not start work until after the next break, or at least shall lose his wages until then. Any disputes about the correct time shall be settled by the clock mounted above the gatekeeper's lodge.

These rules are valid both for time- and for piece-workers, and in cases of breaches of these rules, workmen shall be fined in proportion

From Sidney Pollard and Colin Holmes, *Documents of European Economic History*, (New York: St. Martin's Press, 1968), Vol. 1, pp. 534–536. Reprinted courtesy of the authors.

to their earnings. The deductions from the wage shall be entered in the wage-book of the gatekeeper whose duty they are; they shall be unconditionally accepted as it will not be possible to enter into any discussions about them.

(2) When the bell is rung to denote the end of the working day, every workman, both on piece- and on day-wage, shall leave his workshop and the yard, but is not allowed to make preparations for his departure before the bell rings. Every breach of this rule shall lead to a fine of five silver groschen to the sick fund. Only those who have obtained special permission by the overseer may stay on the workshop in order to work.—If a workman has worked beyond the closing bell, he must give his name to the gatekeep on leaving, on pain of losing his payment for the overtime.

(3) No workman, whether employed by time or piece, may leave before the end of the working day, without having first received permission from the overseer and having given his name to the gatekeeper. Omission of these two actions shall lead to a fine of ten silver groschen payable to the sick fund.

(4) Repeated irregular arrival at work shall lead to dismissal. This shall also apply to those who are found idling by an official or overseer, and refuse to obey their order to resume work.

(5) Entry to the firm's property by any but the designated gateway, and exit by any prohibited route, e.g. by climbing fences or walls, or by crossing the Spree, shall be punished by a fine of fifteen silver groschen to the sick fund for the first offences, and dismissal for the second.

(6) No worker may leave his place of work otherwise than for reasons connected with his work.

(7) All conversation with fellow-workers is prohibited; if any worker requires information about his work, he must turn to the overseer, or to the particular fellow-worker designated for the purpose.

(8) Smoking in the workshops or in the yard is prohibited during working hours; anyone caught smoking shall be fined five silver groschen for the sick fund for every such offence.

(9) Every worker is responsible for cleaning up his space in the workshop, and if in doubt, he is to turn to his overseer.—All tools must always be kept in good condition, and must be cleaned after use. This applies particularly to the turner, regarding his lathe.

(10) Natural functions must be performed at the appropriate places, and whoever is found soiling walls, fences, squares, etc., and similarly, whoever is found washing his face and hands in the workshop and not in the places assigned for the purpose, shall be fined five silver groschen for the sick fund.

(11) On completion of his piece of work, every workman must hand it over at once to his foreman or superior, in order to receive a fresh piece of work. Pattern makers must on no account hand over their pat-

terns to the foundry without express order of their supervisors. No workman may take over work from his fellow-workman without instruction to that effect by the foreman.

(12) It goes without saying that all overseers and officials of the firm shall be obeyed without question, and shall be treated with due deference. Disobedience will be punished by dismissal.

(13) Immediate dismissal shall also be the fate of anyone found drunk in any of the workshops.

(14) Untrue allegations against superiors or officials of the concern shall lead to stern reprimand, and may lead to dismissal. The same punishment shall be meted out to those who knowingly allow errors to slip through when supervising or stocktaking.

(15) Every workman is obliged to report to his superiors any acts of dishonesty or embezzlement on the part of his fellow workmen. If he omits to do so, and it is shown after subsequent discovery of a misdemeanour that he knew about it at the time, he shall be liable to be taken to court as an accessory after the fact and the wage due to him shall be retained as punishment. Conversely, anyone denouncing a theft in such a way as to allow conviction of the thief shall receive a reward of two Thaler, and, if necessary, his name shall be kept confidential.—Further, the gatekeeper and the watchman, as well as every official, are entitled to search the baskets, parcels, aprons etc. of the women and children who are taking the dinners into the works, on their departure, as well as search any worker suspected of stealing any article whatever. . . .

(18) Advances shall be granted only to the older workers, and even to them only in exceptional circumstances. As long as he is working by the piece, the workman is entitled merely to his fixed weekly wage as subsistence pay; the extra earnings shall be paid out only on completion of the whole piece contract. If a workman leaves before his piece contract is completed, either of his own free will, or on being dismissed as punishment, or because of illness, the partly completed work shall be valued by the general manager with the help of two overseers, and he will be paid accordingly. There is no appeal against the decision of these experts.

(19) A free copy of these rules is handed to every workman, but whoever loses it and requires a new one, or cannot produce it on leaving, shall be fined 2½ silver groschen, payable to the sick fund.

Moabit, August, 1844.

# THE INDUSTRIAL CITY

## "Outrage Done to Nature"

*William Wordsworth's (1770–1850) depiction of the new industrial cities was echoed by social critics such as Friedrich Engels (1820–1895). Engels' description of the city of Manchester, one of the creations of the industrial age, is a classic commentary on the physical and social effects of the industrial revolution.*

### From William Wordsworth. *The Excursion (1814)*

Meanwhile, at social Industry's command,
How quick, how vast an increase. From the germ
Of some poor hamlet, rapidly produced
Here a huge town, continuous and compact,
Hiding the face of earth for leagues—and there,
Where not a habitation stood before,
Abodes of men irregularly massed
Like trees in forests,—spread through spacious tracts,
O'er which the smoke of unremitting fires
Hangs permanent, and plentiful as wreaths
Of vapour glittering in the morning sun.
And, wheresoe'er the traveller turns his steps,
He sees the barren wilderness erased,
Or disappearing; triumph that proclaims
How much the mild Directress of the plough
Owes to alliance with these new-born arts!
—Hence is the wide sea peopled,—hence the shores
Of Britain are resorted to by ships
Freighted from every climate of the world
With the world's choicest produce. Hence that sum
Of keels that rest within her crowded ports,
Or ride at anchor in her sounds and bays;
That animating spectacle of sails
That, through her inland regions, to and fro
Pass with the respirations of the tide,
Perpetual, multitudinous! . . .

... I grieve, when on the darker side
Of this great change I look; and there behold
Such outrage done to nature as compels
The indignant power to justify herself;
Yea, to avenge her violated rights.
For England's bane.

## From Friedrich Engels. *The Condition of the Working-Class in England in 1844*

Manchester lies at the foot of the southern slope of a range of hills, which stretch hither from Oldham, their last peak, Kersallmoor, being at once the racecourse and the Mons Sacer of Manchester. Manchester proper lies on the left bank of the Irwell, between that stream and the two smaller ones, the Irk and the Medlock, which here empty into the Irwell. On the left bank of the Irwell, bounded by a sharp curve of the river, lies Salford, and farther westward Pendleton; northward from the Irwell lie Upper and Lower Broughton; northward of the Irk, Cheetham Hill; south of the Medlock lies Hulme; farther east Chorlton on Medlock; still farther, pretty well to the east of Manchester, Ardwick. The whole assemblage of buildings is commonly called Manchester, and contains about four hundred thousand inhabitants, rather more than less. The town itself is peculiarly built, so that a person may live in it for years, and go in and out daily without coming into contact with a working-people's quarter or even with workers, that is, so long as he confines himself to his business or to pleasure walks. This arises chiefly from the fact, that by unconscious tacit agreement, as well as with outspoken conscious determination, the working-people's quarters are sharply separated from the sections of the city reserved for the middle-class; ...

I may mention just here that the mills almost all adjoin the rivers or the different canals that ramify throughout the city, before I proceed at once to describe the labouring quarters. First of all, there is the old town of Manchester, which lies between the northern boundary of the commercial district and the Irk. Here the streets, even the better ones, are narrow and winding, as Todd Street, Long Millgate, Withy Grove, and Shude Hill, the houses dirty, old, and tumble-down, and the construction of the side streets utterly horrible. Going from the Old Church to Long Millgate, the stroller has at once a row of old-fashioned houses at the right, of which not one has kept its original level; these are remnants of the old pre-manufacturing Manchester, whose

From Friedrich Engels, *The Condition of the Working-Class in England in 1844* (London: Swan Sonnenschein & Co., 1892), pp. 45, 48–53.

former inhabitants have removed with their descendants into better-built districts, and have left the houses, which were not good enough for them, to a population strongly mixed with Irish blood. Here one is in an almost undisguised working-men's quarter, for even the shops and beerhouses hardly take the trouble to exhibit a trifling degree of cleanliness. But all this is nothing in comparison with the courts and lanes which lie behind, to which access can be gained only through covered passages, in which no two human beings can pass at the same time. Of the irregular cramming together of dwellings in ways which defy all rational plan, of the tangle in which they are crowded literally one upon the other, it is impossible to convey an idea. And it is not the buildings surviving from the old times of Manchester which are to blame for this; the confusion has only recently reached its height when every scrap of space left by the old way of building has been filled up and patched over until not a foot of land is left to be further occupied.

The south bank of the Irk is here very steep and between fifteen and thirty feet high. On this declivitous hillside there are planted three rows of houses, of which the lowest rise directly out of the river, while the front walls of the highest stand on the crest of the hill in Long Millgate. Among them are mills on the river, in short, the method of construction is as crowded and disorderly here as in the lower part of Long Millgate. Right and left a multitude of covered passages lead from the main street into numerous courts, and he who turns in thither gets into a filth and disgusting grime, the equal of which is not to be found—especially in the courts which lead down to the Irk, and which contain unqualifiedly the most horrible dwellings which I have yet beheld. In one of these courts there stands directly at the entrance, at the end of the covered passage, a privy without a door, so dirty that the inhabitants can pass into and out of the court only by passing through foul pools of stagnant urine and excrement. This is the first court on the Irk above Ducie Bridge—in case any one should care to look into it. Below it on the river there are several tanneries which fill the whole neighbourhood with the stench of animal putrefaction. Below Ducie Bridge the only entrance to most of the houses is by means of narrow, dirty stairs and over heaps of refuse and filth. The first court below Ducie Bridge, known as Allen's Court, was in such a state at the time of the cholera that the sanitary police ordered it evacuated, swept, and disinfected with chloride of lime. Dr. Kay gives a terrible description of the state of this court at that time. Since then, it seems to have been partially torn away and rebuilt; at least looking down from Ducie Bridge, the passer-by sees several ruined walls and heaps of débris with some newer houses. The view from this bridge, mercifully concealed from mortals of small stature by a parapet as high as a man, is characteristic for the whole district. At the bottom flows, or rather stagnates, the Irk, a narrow, coal-black, foul-smelling stream, full of débris and refuse, which it deposits on the shallower right bank.

In dry weather, a long string of the most disgusting, blackish-green, slime pools are left standing on this bank, from the depths of which bubbles of miasmatic gas constantly arise and give forth a stench unendurable even on the bridge forty or fifty feet above the surface of the stream. But besides this, the stream itself is checked every few paces by high weirs, behind which slime and refuse accumulate and rot in thick masses. Above the bridge are tanneries, bonemills, and gasworks, from which all drains and refuse find their way into the Irk, which receives further the contents of all the neighbouring sewers and privies. It may be easily imagined, therefore, what sort of residue the stream deposits. Below the bridge you look upon the piles of débris, the refuse, filth, and offal from the courts on the steep left bank; here each house is packed close behind its neighbour and a piece of each is visible, all black, smoky, crumbling, ancient, with broken panes and window frames. The background is furnished by old barrack-like factory buildings. On the lower right bank stands a long row of houses and mills; the second house being a ruin without a roof, piled with débris; the third stands so low that the lowest floor is uninhabitable, and therefore without windows or doors. Here the background embraces the pauper burial-ground, the station of the Liverpool and Leeds railway, and, in the rear of this, the Workhouse, the "Poor-Law Bastille" of Manchester, which, like a citadel, looks threateningly down from behind its high walls and parapets on the hilltop, upon the working-people's quarter below.

Above Ducie Bridge, the left bank grows more flat and the right bank steeper, but the condition of the dwellings on both banks grows worse rather than better. He who turns to the left here from the main street, Long Millgate, is lost; he wanders from one court to another, turns countless corners, passes nothing but narrow, filthy nooks and alleys, until after a few minutes he has lost all clue, and knows not whither to turn. Everywhere half or wholly ruined buildings, some of them actually uninhabited, which means a great deal here; rarely a wooden or stone floor to be seen in the houses, almost uniformly broken, ill-fitting windows and doors, and a state of filth! Everywhere heaps of débris, refuse, and offal; standing pools for gutters, and a stench which alone would make it impossible for a human being in any degree civilised to live in such a district. The newly-built extension of the Leeds railway, which crosses the Irk here, has swept away some of these courts and lanes, laying others completely open to view. Immediately under the railway bridge there stands a court, the filth and horrors of which surpass all the others by far, just because it was hitherto so shut off, so secluded that the way to it could not be found without a good deal of trouble. I should never have discovered it myself, without the breaks made by the railway, though I thought I knew this whole region thoroughly. Passing along a rough bank, among stakes and washing-lines, one penetrates into this chaos of small one-storied, one-roomed huts, in most of which there is no artificial floor; kitchen, living and sleeping-room all in one. In such a hole, scarcely five feet long by six broad, I found two beds—and such bedsteads and beds!— which, with a staircase and chimney-place, exactly filled the room. In several others I found absolutely nothing, while the door stood open, and the inhabitants leaned against it. Everywhere before the doors refuse and offal; that any sort of pavement lay underneath could not be seen but only felt, here and there, with the feet. This whole collection of cattle-sheds for human beings was surrounded on two sides by houses and a factory, and on the third by the river, and besides the narrow stair up the bank, a narrow doorway alone led out into another almost equally ill-built, ill-kept labyrinth of dwellings. . . .

If we leave the Irk and penetrate once more on the opposite side from Long Millgate into the midst of the working-men's dwellings, we shall come into a somewhat newer quarter, which stretches from St. Michael's Church to Withy Grove and Shude Hill. Here there is somewhat better order. In place of the chaos of buildings, we find at least long straight lanes and alleys or courts, built according to a plan and usually square. But if, in the former case, every house was built according to caprice, here each lane and court is so built, without reference to the situation of the adjoining ones. . . .

. . . Here, as in most of the working-men's quarters of Manchester, the pork-raisers rent the courts and build pig-pens in them. In almost every court one or even several such pens may be found, into which the inhabitants of the court throw all refuse and offal, whence the swine grow fat; and the atmosphere, confined on all four sides, is utterly corrupted by putrefying animal and vegetable substances. . . .

Such is the Old Town of Manchester, and on re-reading my description, I am forced to admit that instead of being exaggerated, it is far from black enough to convey a true impression of the filth, ruin, and uninhabitableness, the defiance of all considerations of cleanliness, ventilation, and health which characterise the construction of this single district, containing at least twenty to thirty thousand inhabitants. And such a district exists in the heart of the second city of England, the first manufacturing city of the world. If any one wishes to see in how little space a human being can move, how little air—and *such* air!—he can breathe, how little of civilisation he may share and yet live, it is only necessary to travel hither. True, this is the *Old* Town, and the people of Manchester emphasise the fact whenever any one mentions to them the frightful condition of this Hell upon Earth; but what does that prove? Everything which here arouses horror and indignation is of recent origin, belongs to the *industrial epoch*.

# FAMILY ORGANIZATION

## The Working-Class Family Economy

*The industrial revolution intensified economic pressures on working-class families. To make ends meet, all members of the family went to work to earn a wage. Young children were expected to help out as soon as they could find work; and women as well as men contributed to the household purse. In textile towns women and girls found jobs in factories; in cities they more often took up typically female occupations such as domestic service or garment sewing. Mrs. Layton's autobiography offers detailed insight into urban working-class family life in the second half of the nineteenth century.*

### From Mrs. Layton. *Memories of Seventy Years*

I was born in Bethnal Green, April 9th, 1855, a tiny scrap of humanity. I was my mother's seventh child, and seven more were born after me—fourteen in all—which made my mother a perfect slave. Generally speaking, she was either expecting a baby to be born or had one at the breast. At the time there were eight of us the oldest was not big enough to get ready to go to school without help. . . .

My eldest sister, who has been all through my life one of my best friends, went into service at the age of twelve years old and always did well. When I was eight years old she was nurse to twin boys, whose smart clothes and fine perambulator set me longing to be a children's nurse when I grew up, and it was the delight of my life when one day some of the fine clothes cast off by the twins descended to my little brother. I shall never forget how well he looked in a pretty blue pelisse and cape, and I thought he was ever so much nicer looking than the previous wearer. I *was* proud of my little brother and I *did* wish he could always have nice clothes.

My fourth sister and I always stayed away from school on washing day to mind the babies. In the summer it was real sport, because so many people did their washing on the same day, and everybody had

From Co-Operative Working Women, Margaret Llewelyn Davies, ed., *Life As We Have Known It* (New York: W. W. Norton, 1975), pp. 1, 3–4, 6–8, 20, 22, 34–37. Copyright 1931 by The Hogarth Press Ltd.; Norton Library Edition published 1975. Reprinted by permission of W. W. Norton and Company, Inc., the author's Literary Estate, and The Hogarth Press.

large families and generally kept the elder girls, and sometimes boys, at home to mind the little ones. . . .

My father, a well-educated man, was employed in a government situation, working from 10 a.m. to 4 p.m. He was always steady and industrious, was a fine singer and very musical. . . . In his spare time he learnt the trade of a tailor and was able to augment his small salary by doing work for people who knew him and by growing nearly all the vegetables the family consumed. . . . A good father and husband up to a point, he left the responsibility of the whole family to my mother. She it was who had to start us all out in life.

As our family increased and my father's wages remained stationary, it was necessary for my mother to earn money to help to keep us in food and clothing. The clergyman's wife was very fond of her, and always had her to nurse her whenever there was a baby born or illness of any kind. My eldest sister had to stay at home whenever there was a new baby at the parsonage, and we took it in turns to take my mother's baby there for her to feed at the breast three or four times a day, for it generally happened that my mother had a baby dependent on her for the breast when our clergyman's wife had her babies. When my mother was away, my father gave out each morning before he went to his work the portion of food for each one of us for the day. We were all allowed a teaspoonful of sugar except "baby Lizzie"—myself—who had a teaspoonful and a half, much to my brother's disgust.

When I think of my poor overworked, tired mother I wonder that she lived as long as she did. She was kindness itself, the friend of everybody, and her own enemy, for her good nature was her downfall. She would get into debt to get nourishment for a sick neighbour or food for a family in distress. . . .

When I was ten years old I began to earn my own living. I went to mind the baby of a person who kept a small general shop. My wages were 1/6 a week and my tea, and 2d. a week for myself. I got to work at eight in the morning and left at eight at night, with the exception of two nights a week when I left at seven o'clock to attend a night school, one of a number started by Lord Shaftesbury, called Ragged Schools. I was very happy in my place and was very fond of the baby. . . .

When I was thirteen years old I went into service at Hampstead where I stayed twelve months. I had a very kind mistress and plenty of good food. I was fairly happy, but had to sleep in the basement kitchen which swarmed with black-beetles, and this made me very wretched at nights. I was only allowed out on Sundays to go to church. Sometimes I got a change by going on to the heath with the three children. The tie was almost too much for me at times, and on more than one occasion on a fine Sunday, instead of going to church, I went to see my married sister who lived about a mile away.

. . . [I was] married on December 2nd, 1882, he being twenty-seven and I twenty-six years of age.

For eight months my husband tramped from early morn till late at night looking for work, and during all that time he did small jobs which brought in £3 in all. The little money I had saved had dwindled down to a few pounds. I had tried to help the situation by first going out to work and then by doing washing at home. I turned my hand to anything that would honestly bring in money. My health was becoming impaired with work and worry and I was expecting a baby which made it very hard for me. But I made the best of what every one of my friends called a bad job, and like Mr. Micawber was always hoping for something to turn up. It did at last, just a month before my baby was born. My husband got a job on the Midland Railway as carriage cleaner at St. Pancras. He worked on nights, twelve hours a night, six nights a week, at the large wage of 19/- a week. It was very dirty work, but we were thankful for that amount of money, for I was beginning to wonder how my confinement was to be paid for when I had to give up work. . . .

When my baby was three months old my husband lost his job, and was out of work again. When he came home and told me I did not know what to do. I was weak and my baby was cross and poorly. I had never given in with all the previous troubles but now I could not help giving way. I had never parted with any of my clothes or furniture by pawning, as I had been advised to many times by kindly folk who thought they were suggesting a good thing for hard times. I had always managed without, but now I could see my things going, for I could not work with a young baby even as I had done before he was born. However, it was not so bad as I had anticipated, for a man who lived in the same house told my husband to go after a job at St. Pancras Station. He said it would be less money but it was better than nothing. . . .

My baby grew into a strong, sturdy little fellow, full of mischief. It was a great treat to look after him and help to earn the living. At the same time it meant taking him out in the daytime and working after my husband had gone to work at night. Many times till 4 o'clock in the morning in bitter cold weather I have been washing, and have just been able to get two hours' sleep before the child woke up, which he did about 6 o'clock. My second child, a boy, was born three years later. By that time my husband's wages had risen to £1 1s. a week, and he worked nearer home which was a little better for me.

# Middle-Class Domesticity

*Isabella Beeton (1836–1865) first published her advice manual for English housewives in 1861. Mrs. Beeton addressed her words to the "commanders" of the domestic sphere, in an attempt to raise the standards of their competence and thus improve family life. The book reflects the prevailing middle-class ideology of the day: the home was woman's sphere.*

## From Mrs. Beeton's *Book of Household Management*

I must frankly own, that if I had known beforehand that this book would cost me the labour which it has, I should never have been courageous enough to commence it. What moved me, in the first instance, to attempt a work like this, was the discomfort and suffering which I had seen brought upon men and women by household mismanagement. I have always thought that there is no more fruitful source of family discontent than a housewife's badly-cooked dinners and untidy ways. Men are now so well served out of doors,—at their clubs, well-ordered taverns, and dining-houses, that, in order to compete with the attractions of these places a mistress must be thoroughly acquainted with the theory and practice of cookery, as well as be perfectly conversant with all the other arts of making and keeping a comfortable home. . . .

As with the commander of an army, or the leader of an enterprise, so is it with the mistress of a house. Her spirit will be seen through the whole establishment; and just in proportion as she performs her duties intelligently and thoroughly, so will her domestics follow in her path. Of all those acquirements, which more particularly belong to the feminine character, there are none which take a higher rank, in our estimation, than such as enter into a knowledge of household duties; for on these are perpetually dependent the happiness, comfort, and well-being of a family. . . .

Early rising is one of the most essential qualities which enter into good Household Management, as it is not only the parent of health, but of innumerable other advantages. Indeed, when a mistress is an early riser, it is almost certain that her house will be orderly and well-managed. On the contrary, if she remain in bed till a late hour, then the domestics, who, as we have observed, invariably partake somewhat of their mistress's character, will surely become sluggards. . . .

Cleanliness is indispensable to health, and must be studied both in regard to the person and the house, and all that it contains. Cold or tepid baths should be employed every morning, unless, on account of illness or other circumstances, they should be deemed objectionable. . . .

Frugality and economy are home virtues, without which no household can prosper. . . . The necessity of practising economy should be evident to every one, whether in the possession of an income no more than sufficient for a family's requirements, or of a large fortune which puts financial adversity out of the question. . . .

In marketing, that the best articles are the cheapest, may be laid down as a rule; and it is desirable, unless an experienced and confidential housekeeper be kept, that the mistress should herself purchase

From Mrs. Beeton's *Book of Household Management* (London, 1880), pp. iii, 1–9.

all provisions and stores needed for the house. If the mistress be a young wife, and not accustomed to order "things for the house," a little practice and experience will soon teach her who are the best trades-people to deal with, and what are the best provisions to buy. Under each particular head of Fish, Meat, Poultry, Game, &c., will be de-scribed the proper means of ascertaining the quality of these comestibles.

A housekeeping account-book should invariably be kept, and kept punctually and precisely. The plan for keeping household accounts, which we should recommend, would be to enter, that is, write down in a daily diary every amount paid on each particular day, be it ever so small; then, at the end of a week or month, let these various payments be ranged under their specific heads of Butcher, Baker, &c.; and thus will be seen the proportions paid to each tradesman, and any week's or month's expenses may be contrasted with another. The housekeeping accounts should be balanced not less than once a month—once a week is better; and it should be seen that the money in hand tallies with the account. Judge Haliburton never wrote truer words than when he said—"No man is rich whose expenditure exceeds his means, and no one is poor whose incomings exceed his outgoings." Once a month it is advisable that the mistress overlook her store of glass and china, marking any breakages on the inventory of these articles.

When, in a large establishment, a housekeeper is kept, it will be ad-visable to examine her accounts regularly. Then, any increase of ex-penditure which may be apparent can easily be explained, and the housekeeper will have the satisfaction of knowing whether her efforts to manage her department well and economically have been successful. . . .

Engaging domestics is one of those duties in which the judgment of the mistress must be keenly exercised. One of the commonest modes of procuring servants is to answer advertisements inserted in the news-papers by those who want places; or to insert an advertisement, setting forth the kind of servant that is required. In these advertisements it is well to state whether the house is in town or country, and indicate pretty closely the amount of wages that the mistress proposes to give. There are some respectable registry-offices, where good servants may sometimes be hired. Another plan, and one to be recommended under certain conditions, is for the mistress to make inquiry amongst her cir-cle of friends and acquaintances, and her tradespeople. Shopkeepers generally know those in their neighbourhood who are wanting situa-tions, and will communicate with them, when a personal interview with some of them will enable the mistress to form some idea of the char-acters of the applicants, and to suit herself accordingly. . . .

The treatment of servants is of the highest possible moment, as well to the mistress as to the domestics themselves. On the head of the house the latter will naturally fix their attention; and if they perceive that the mistress' conduct is regulated by high and correct principles, they will not fail to respect her. If, also, a benevolent desire is shown to promote their comfort, at the same time that a steady performance of their duty is exacted, then their respect will not be unmingled with affection, and well-principled servants will be still more solicitous to continue to deserve her favour. . .

Having risen early, as we have already advised . . . and having given due attention to the bath, and made a careful toilet, it will be well at once to see that the children, where the house is blest with these, have received their proper ablutions, and are in every way clean, comfortable, and being well attended to. The first meal of the day, breakfast, will then be served, at which all the family should be punctually present, unless illness, or other circumstances, prevent.

After breakfast is over, it will be well for the mistress to make a round of the kitchen and other offices, to see that all are in order, and that the morning's work has been properly performed by the various domestics. The orders for the day should then be given; and any questions which the domestics desire to ask, respecting their several departments, should be answered, and any special articles they may require handed to them from the store-closet. . . .

After this general superintendence of her servants, the mistress, if the mother of a young family, may devote herself to the instruction of some of its younger members, or to the examination of the state of their wardrobe, leaving the latter portion of the morning for reading, or for some amusing recreation. . . .

# THE CHALLENGE OF LABOR

## English Chartism

*English working-class protest centered in the 1840s on achieving the six points of the People's Charter, drawn up in 1837. The loosely organized Chartist movement stressed the importance of political participation, especially universal manhood suffrage, as a way to ending the economic and social grievances of working people.*

### The People's Petition of 1838

#### National Petition

*Unto the Honourable the Commons of the United Kingdom of Great Britain and Ireland in Parliament assembled, the Petition of the undersigned, their suffering countrymen.*

HUMBLY SHEWETH,

That we, your petitioners, dwell in a land whose merchants are noted for enterprise, whose manufacturers are very skilful, and whose workmen are proverbial for their industry.

The land itself is goodly, the soil rich, and the temperature wholesome; it is abundantly furnished with the materials of commerce and trade; it has numerous and convenient harbours; in facility of internal communication it exceeds all others.

For three-and-twenty years we have enjoyed a profound peace.

Yet, with all these elements of national prosperity, and with every disposition and capacity to take advantage of them, we find ourselves overwhelmed with public and private suffering.

We are bowed down under a load of taxes; which, notwithstanding, fall greatly short of the wants of our rulers; our traders are trembling on the verge of bankruptcy; our workmen are starving; capital brings no profit, and labour no remuneration; the home of the artificer is desolate, and the warehouse of the pawnbroker is full; the workhouse is crowded, and the manufactory is deserted.

From *The Life and Struggles of William Lovett* (New York: Knopf, 1920), pp. 478–482.

We have looked on every side, we have searched diligently in order to find out the causes of a distress so sore and so long continued.

We can discover none in nature, or in Providence.

Heaven has dealt graciously by the people; but the foolishness of our rulers has made the goodness of God of none effect.

The energies of a mighty kingdom have been wasted in building up the power of selfish and ignorant men, and its resources squandered for their aggrandisement.

The good of a party has been advanced to the sacrifice of the good of the nation; the few have governed for the interest of the few, while the interest of the many has been neglected, or insolently and tyrannously trampled upon.

It was the fond expectation of the people that a remedy for the greater part, if not for the whole, of their grievances, would be found in the Reform Act of 1832.

They were taught to regard that Act as a wise means to a worthy end; as the machinery of an improved legislation, when the will of the masses would be at length potential.

They have been bitterly and basely deceived.

The fruit which looked so fair to the eye has turned to dust and ashes when gathered.

The Reform Act has effected a transfer of power from one domineering faction to another, and left the people as helpless as before.

Our slavery has been exchanged for an apprenticeship to liberty, which has aggravated the painful feeling of our social degradation, by adding to it the sickening of still deferred hope.

We come before your Honourable House to tell you, with all humility, that this state of things must not be permitted to continue; that it cannot long continue without very seriously endangering the stability of the throne and the peace of the kingdom; and that if by God's help and all lawful and constitutional appliances, an end can be put to it, we are fully resolved that it shall speedily come to an end.

We tell your Honourable House that the capital of the master must no longer be deprived of its due reward; that the laws which make food dear, and those which by making money scarce, make labour cheap, must be abolished; that taxation must be made to fall on property, not on industry; that the good of the many, as it is the only legitimate end, so must it be the sole study of the Government.

As a preliminary essential to these and other requisite changes; as means by which alone the interests of the people can be effectually vindicated and secured, we demand that those interests be confided to the keeping of the people.

When the State calls for defenders, when it calls for money, no consideration of poverty or ignorance can be pleaded in refusal or delay of the call.

Required as we are, universally, to support and obey the laws, nature and reason entitle us to demand, that in the making of the laws, the universal voice shall be implicitly listened to.

We perform the duties of freemen; we must have the privileges of freemen.

### We demand Universal Suffrage.

The suffrage to be exempt from the corruption of the wealthy, and the violence of the powerful, must be secret.

The assertion of our right necessarily involves the power of its uncontrolled exercise.

### We demand the Ballot.

The connection between the representatives and the people, to be beneficial must be intimate.

The legislative and constituent powers, for correction and for instruction, ought to be brought into frequent contact.

Errors, which are comparatively light when susceptible of a speedy popular remedy, may produce the most disastrous effects when permitted to grow inveterate through years of compulsory endurance.

To public safety as well as public confidence, frequent elections are essential.

### We demand Annual Parliaments.

With power to choose, and freedom in choosing, the range of our choice must be unrestricted.

We are compelled, by the existing laws, to take for our representatives, men who are incapable of appreciating our difficulties, or who have little sympathy with them; merchants who have retired from trade, and no longer feel its harassings; proprietors of land who are alike ignorant of its evils and their cure; lawyers, by whom the honours of the senate are sought after only as means of obtaining notice in the courts.

The labours of a representative, who is sedulous in the discharge of his duty, are numerous and burdensome.

It is neither just, nor reasonable, nor safe, that they should continue to be gratuitously rendered.

We demand that in the future election of members of your Honourable House, the approbation of the constituency shall be the sole qualification; and that to every representative so chosen shall be assigned, out of the public taxes, a fair and adequate remuneration for the time which he is called upon to devote to the public service.

Finally, we would most earnestly impress on your Honourable House, that this petition has not been dictated by any idle love of change; that it springs out of no inconsiderate attachment to fanciful theories; but that it is the result of much and long deliberation, and of convictions, which the events of each succeeding year tend more and more to strengthen.

The management of this mighty kingdom has hitherto been a subject for contending factions to try their selfish experiments upon.

We have felt the consequences in our sorrowful experience—short glimmerings of uncertain enjoyment swallowed up by long and dark seasons of suffering.

If the self-government of the people should not remove their distresses, it will at least remove their repinings.

Universal suffrage will, and it alone can, bring true and lasting peace to the nation; we firmly believe that it will also bring prosperity.

May it therefore please your Honourable House to take this our petition into your most serious consideration; and to use your utmost endeavours, by all constitutional means, to have a law passed, granting to every male of lawful age, sane mind, and unconvicted of crime, the right of voting for members of Parliament; and directing all future elections of members of Parliament to be in the way of secret ballot; and ordaining that the duration of Parliaments so chosen shall in no case exceed one year; and abolishing all property qualifications in the members; and providing for their due remuneration while in attendance on their Parliamentary duties.

# French Utopian Socialism

*Louis Blanc (1811–1882) argued that an end to workers' economic distress would come only with a reorganization of the economy. He urged the creation of state-financed producers' associations to end competition and ensure cooperation within French society. During the Revolution of 1848, Blanc was made director of a commission on labor, but he was unable to put his plans into effect.*

## From Louis Blanc. *The Organization of Labor (1840)*

The question should be put thus: Is competition a means of ASSURING work to the poor? To put a question of this kind, means to solve it. What does competition mean to workingmen? It is the distribution of work to the highest bidder. A contractor needs a laborer: three apply. "How much do you ask for your work?" "Three francs, I have a wife and children." "Good, and you?" "Two and a half francs, I have no children, but a wife." "So much the better, and you?" "Two francs will do for me; I am single." "You shall have the work." With this the affair is settled, the bargain is closed. What will become now of the other two proletarians? They will starve, it is to be hoped. But what if

From Louis T. Moore, J. M. Burnam, and H. G. Hartmann, eds., *University of Cincinnati Studies* (Cincinnati, 1911), Series II, Vol. 7, pp. 15–16, 51–56.

they become thieves? Never mind, why have we our police? Or murderers? Well, for them we have the gallows. And the fortunate one of the three; even his victory is only temporary. Let a fourth laborer appear, strong enough to fast one out of every two days; the desire to cut down the wages will be exerted to its fullest extent. A new pariah, perhaps a new recruit for the galleys. . . .

Who would be blind enough not to see that under the reign of free competition the continuous decline of wages necessarily becomes a general law with no exception whatsoever? Has population limits which it may never overstep? Are we allowed to say to industry, which is subjected to the daily whims of individual egotism, to industry, which is an ocean full of wreckage: "Thus far shalt thou go and no farther." The population increases steadily; command the mothers of the poor to be sterile and blaspheme God who made them fruitful; for if you do not command it, the space will be too small for all strugglers. A machine is invented; demand it to be broken and fling an anathema against science! Because if you do not do it, one thousand workmen, whom the new machine displaces in the workshops, will knock at the door of the next one and will force down the wages of their fellow-workers. A systematic lowering of wages resulting in the elimination of a certain number of laborers is the inevitable effect of free competition. . . .

The government ought to be considered as the supreme regulator of production and endowed for this duty with great power.

This task would consist of fighting competition and of finally overcoming it.

The government ought to float a loan with the proceeds of which it should erect *social workshops* in the most important branches of national industry.

As these establishments would demand considerable investments, the number of these workshops at the start ought to be carefully limited, still they would possess, by virtue of their organization—as we shall see later—an unlimited expansion.

The government, considered as the only founder of the workshops, must determine the statutes regulating them. This code, deliberated and voted for by the representatives of the people ought to have the power and force of a law.

All workmen who can give guarantee of morality shall be called to work in these social workshops up to the limit of the original capital gathered together for the purchase of tools. . . .

For the first years after the workshops are established, the government ought to regulate the scale of employment. After the first year it is no longer necessary, the laborers would then have time enough to truly estimate their respective work, and, all being equally interested as we will soon see, the success of the association would eventually depend on the elective principle. . . .

Every member of the social workshops would have the right to use, according to his discretion, the profits of his labor; but it would not be long before the evident economy and the incontestable excellence of this communal life would call forth other voluntary associations among the workmen according to their needs and pleasure.

Capitalists can also be taken into the association and would draw interest on their invested money, which would be guaranteed by the budget; but in the profits they would participate only if they were laborers at the same time.

If the social workshops were once established according to these principles, you could easily understand what the results would be. In every great industry, in machinery, for example, or the silk or cotton industry, or in printing establishments, the social workshops would be in competition with private industries. Would the fight be a long one? No, for the social workshops would have advantages over the others, the results of the cheaper communal life and through the organization by which all laborers, without exception, are interested in producing good and quick work. Would the fight be subversive? No, for the government would always endeavor to prevent the prices of the products of the social workshops from dropping to too low a level. If today an extremely rich man were to enter into a contest with another less wealthy, this unequal fight would be only disastrous, for the private man looks only to his personal interest, if he can sell twice as cheap as his competitors, he will do so, in order to ruin them and be master of the situation. But when the power itself steps into the place of a private individual, the question develops a different phase. . . .

From the common interest of all the laborers in the same workshop we infer the common interest of all workshops in the same industry. In order to complete the system, we must establish the solidarity of the various industries. Therefore, from the profit yielded by each industry, we must set aside a sum by means of which the State could give aid to every industry, which has suffered through extraordinary and unforeseen circumstances. Besides, in the system which we propose, crises would become rare. What causes them most frequently to-day? The veritable murderous contest between the interests, a contest from which no victor can come forth without leaving conquered ones on the field of battle; a combat, that like all wars, chains slaves to the chariot of the victor. In destroying competition we strangle at the same time the evils which it brings forth. No more victories and no more defeats! . . .

Is it necessary that I should continue to enumerate the advantages which the new system brings about? In the industrial world in which we live, all the discoveries of science are a calamity, first because the machines supplant the laborers who need work to live, and then, because they are also murderous weapons, furnished to industry which has the right and faculty to use them against all those who have not this right and power. What does *"new machines"* mean in the system of competition? It means monopoly; we have proven it. However, in the new system of association and solidarity there are no patents for inventors, no individual exploitation. The inventor will be recompensed by the State and his discovery is then placed at the service of all. What is to-day a means of extermination, becomes an instrument of universal progress; what to-day reduces the laborer to hunger, to despair and drives him to revolt, will serve only to render his task lighter and to produce a sufficient leisure to live a life of intelligence and happiness, in one word, that which has tolerated tyranny will aid in the triumph of fraternity.

# THE TRIUMPH OF THE BOURGEOISIE

## Middle-Class Values

*In* Self-Help *(1859), Samuel Smiles (1812–1904) offered a series of biographies of men who had risen from obscurity to fame and wealth. The book embodied Victorian notions of individual responsibility for one's fate.*

### From Samuel Smiles. *Self-Help*

The object of the book briefly is, to re-inculcate these old-fashioned but wholesome lessons—which perhaps cannot be too often urged,—that youth must work in order to enjoy,—that nothing creditable can be accomplished without application and diligence,—that the student must not be daunted by difficulties, but conquer them by patience and perseverance,—and that, above all, he must seek elevation of character, without which capacity is worthless and worldly success is naught. If the author has not succeeded in illustrating these lessons, he can only say that he has failed in his object.

"Heaven helps those who help themselves" is a well-tried maxim, embodying in a small compass the results of vast human experience. The spirit of self-help is the root of all genuine growth in the individual; and, exhibited in the lives of many, it constitutes the true source of national vigour and strength. Help from without is often enfeebling in its effects, but help from within invariably invigorates. Whatever is done *for* men or classes, to a certain extent takes away the stimulus and necessity of doing for themselves; and where men are subjected to over-guidance and over-government, the inevitable tendency is to render them comparatively helpless.

Even the best institutions can give a man no active help. Perhaps the most they can do is, to leave him free to develop himself and improve his individual condition. But in all times men have been prone to believe that their happiness and well-being were to be secured by means of institutions rather than by their own conduct. Hence the value of legislation as an agent in human advancement has usually been much over-estimated. To constitute the millionth part of a Legislature, by

From Samuel Smiles, *Self-Help* (London: John Murray, 1882), pp. v, 1–3, 5–7.

voting for one or two men once in three or five years, however conscientiously this duty may be performed, can exercise but little active influence upon any man's life and character. Moreover, it is every day becoming more clearly understood, that the function of Government is negative and restrictive, rather than positive and active; being resolvable principally into protection—protection of life, liberty, and property. Laws, wisely administered, will secure men in the enjoyment of the fruits of their labour, whether of mind or body, at a comparatively small personal sacrifice; but no laws, however stringent, can make the idle industrious, the thriftless provident, or the drunken sober. Such reforms can only be effected by means of individual action, economy, and self-denial; by better habits, rather than by greater rights.

The Government of a nation itself is usually found to be but the reflex of the individuals composing it. The Government that is ahead of the people will inevitably be dragged down to their level, as the Government that is behind them will in the long run be dragged up. In the order of nature, the collective character of a nation will as surely find its befitting results in its law and government, as water finds its own level. The noble people will be nobly ruled, and the ignorant and corrupt ignobly. Indeed all experience serves to prove that the worth and strength of a State depend far less upon the form of its institutions than upon the character of its men. For the nation is only an aggregate of individual conditions, and civilization itself is but a question of the personal improvement of the men, women, and children of whom society is composed.

National progress is the sum of individual industry, energy, and uprightness, as national decay is of individual idleness, selfishness, and vice. What we are accustomed to decry as great social evils, will, for the most part, be found to be but the outgrowth of man's own perverted life; and though we may endeavour to cut them down and extirpate them by means of Law, they will only spring up again with fresh luxuriance in some other form, unless the conditions of personal life and character are radically improved. If this view be correct, then it follows that the highest patriotism and philanthropy consist, not so much in altering laws and modifying institutions, as in helping and stimulating men to elevate and improve themselves by their own free and independent individual action. . . .

All nations have been made what they are by the thinking and the working of many generations of men. Patient and persevering labourers in all ranks and conditions of life, cultivators of the soil and explorers of the mine, inventors and discoverers, manufacturers, mechanics and artisans, poets, philosophers, and politicians, all have contributed towards the grand result, one generation building upon another's labours, and carrying them forward to still higher stages. This constant succession of noble workers—the artisans of civilisation—has served to create order out of chaos in industry, science, and art;

and the living race has thus, in the course of nature, become the inheritor of the rich estate provided by the skill and industry of our forefathers, which is placed in our hands to cultivate, and to hand down, not only unimpaired but improved, to our successors.

The spirit of self-help, as exhibited in the energetic action of individuals, has in all times been a marked feature in the English character, and furnishes the true measure of our power as a nation. Rising above the heads of the mass, there were always to be found a series of individuals distinguished beyond others, who commanded the public homage. But our progress has also been owing to multitudes of smaller and less known men. Though only the generals' names may be remembered in the history of any great campaign, it has been in a great measure through the individual valour and heroism of the privates that victories have been won. And life, too, is "a soldiers' battle,"—men in the ranks having in all times been amongst the greatest of workers. Many are the lives of men unwritten, which have nevertheless as powerfully influenced civilisation and progress as the more fortunate Great whose names are recorded in biography. Even the humblest person, who sets before his fellows an example of industry, sobriety, and upright honesty of purpose in life, has a present as well as a future influence upon the well-being of his country; for his life and character pass unconsciously into the lives of others, and propagate good example for all time to come.

Daily experience shows that it is energetic individualism which produces the most powerful effects upon the life and action of others, and really constitutes the best practical education. Schools, academies, and colleges, give but the merest beginnings of culture in comparison with it. Far more influential is the life-education daily given in our homes, in the streets, behind counters, in workshops, at the loom and the plough, in counting-houses and manufactories, and in the busy haunts of men. This is that finishing instruction as members of society, which Schiller designated "the education of the human race," consisting in action, conduct, self-culture, self-control,—all that tends to discipline a man truly, and fit him for the proper performance of the duties and business of life,—a kind of education not to be learnt from books, or acquired by any amount of mere literary training. With his usual weight of words Bacon observes, that "Studies teach not their own use; but that is a wisdom without them, and above them, won by observation;" a remark that holds true of actual life, as well as of the cultivation of the intellect itself. For all experience serves to illustrate and enforce the lesson, that a man perfects himself by work more than by reading,—that it is life rather than literature, action rather than study, and character rather than biography, which tend perpetually to renovate mankind.

Biographies of great, but especially of good men, are nevertheless most instructive and useful, as helps, guides, and incentives to others.

Some of the best are almost equivalent to gospels—teaching high living, high thinking, and energetic action for their own and the world's good. The valuable examples which they furnish of the power of self-help, of patient purpose, resolute working, and steadfast integrity, issuing in the formation of truly noble and manly character, exhibit in language not to be misunderstood, what it is in the power of each to accomplish for himself; and eloquently illustrate the efficacy of self-respect and self-reliance in enabling men of even the humblest rank to work out for themselves an honourable competency and a solid reputation.

# English Social Structure

*Thomas Escott (1844–1924) was the editor of the* Fortnightly Review. *His book stresses the lasting importance of aristocratic tastes and values, but it also indicates the incorporation into the highest levels of English society of middle-class professions, occupations, and standards.*

## From Thomas Escott. *England: Her People, Polity, and Pursuits*

The era of the enlargement of English society dates from the Reform Bill of 1832, and if it has brought with it some contradictions, anomalies, and inconveniences, it has also been instrumental in the accomplishment of great and undoubted good. It has substituted, in a very large degree, the prestige of achievement for the prestige of position. The mere men of fashion, the fops, dandies, and exquisites, the glory of whose life was indolence, and who looked upon any thing in the way of occupation as a disgrace, have gone out of date never to return. . . .

Before the eventful year 1832, there existed a society in England very like the old exclusive society of Vienna. The chief and indeed almost only road to it lay through politics, and politics were for the most part a rigidly aristocratic profession. Occasionally men of the people made their way out of the crowd, and became personages in and out of the House of Commons; but most of the places under Government were in the hands of the great families, as also were the close boroughs, and the tendency was to fill each from among the young men of birth and fashion. The Reform Bill admitted an entirely new element into political life, and threw open the whole of the political area. A host of applicants for Parliamentary position at once came forward, and as a consequence the social citadel was carried by persons who had

From T. H. S. Escott, *England: Her People, Polity and Pursuits* (New York: Henry Holt & Co., 1885), pp. 317–322.

nothing to do with the purely aristocratic section which had hitherto been paramount. The patrician occupants of the captured stronghold, if they were somewhat taken aback by the blow which had been dealt them, accepted the situation and decided upon their future tactics with equal wisdom and promptitude. If the new-comers were to be successfully competed with, they saw that they must compete with them on the new ground, and must assert their power as the scions of no *fainéant* aristocracy. The impulse given to the whole mass of the patriciate was immense, and the sum of the new-born or newly-displayed energies as surprising as it was satisfactory. The man of pleasure ceased to be the type to which it was expected, as a matter of course, that all those born in purple should conform.

The activity thus communicated directed itself into an infinite number of channels, and it has continued operative ever since. Our aristocrats of to-day are at least fired by a robust ambition. Many of them take up statesmanship as the business of their lives, and work at its routine duties as if it were necessary to the support of existence. Those whose tastes do not incline them in the direction of the senate, write books, paint pictures, or carve statues. Perhaps, even probably, they are of a theatrical turn, and subsidize a theater, or even manage a company. They go into business, or they dedicate their existence to agricultural enterprise. At least they do something. Society, in fact, has bidden adieu to its ideal of gilded and inglorious ease, and in strict conformity with the spirit of its new departure, selects its *protégés* and favorites upon a new principle. The question asked about any new aspirant to its freedom is not only, who is he? or how much has he a year? but, in addition, what has he done? and what can he do? The heroes and lions of society are not handsome young men, who can do nothing more than dress well, or dance well. They are seldom even those whose fame is limited to the hunting-field or the battue. They are men who have striven to solve the secret of the ice-bound pole, who have tramped right across the arid sands of a strange continent, who have scaled heights previously deemed inaccessible, who have written clever books, painted great pictures, done great deeds, in one shape or other. It is surely a considerable social advance to have substituted for the exquisites of a bygone period, as ideals of life for the rising generation, men who have followed in the track of Xenophon, or who have been the pioneers of civilization on a continent. . . .

The degrees of esteem allotted to the different English professions are exactly what might be expected in a society organized upon such a basis and conscious of such aims. Roughly it may be said professions in England are valued according to their stability, their remunerativeness, their influence and their recognition by the State. These conditions may partially explain the difference which English society draws between the callings of the merchant and the stock-broker. Stock-brokers make immense fortunes; but there attaches to them a suspicion of precariousness infinitely in excess of that which, in some degree or other, necessarily attaches to all fortunes accumulated in commerce or trade. The merchant represents an interest which is almost deserving of a place among the estates of the realm, and with the development of which the prosperity and prestige of England are bound up. His house of business is practically a public institution, and the speculative element—the fluctuation of prices and the uncertainty of markets—enters as little as possible into it. Merchants have from time immemorial been the friends and supporters of monarchs—have taken their place in the popular chamber of the legislature, have been elevated to distinguished stations among the titular aristocracy of the land. We have had not only our merchant-princes, but our merchant-peers and merchant-statesmen. The calling has been recognized in our social hierarchy for centuries, and if not exactly a liberal, is an eminently respectable and dignified profession. Nor is the merchant, as a rule, so much absorbed in the affairs of his own business as to be unable to devote as much time as is necessary to the pursuits of society and the affairs of the country. His operations run in a comparatively equal and tranquil channel, and to hint that he lives in an atmosphere of feverish excitement is equivalent to insinuating a doubt of his solvency. It is different with the stock-broker, whose social position is so sudden that it cannot yet be looked upon as assured—whose wealth, though great, has the garish hue of luck, and the glories associated with which may dissolve themselves at any moment into thin air, like Aladdin's palace, and who himself is popularly supposed to be more or less on the tenter-hooks of expectation and anxiety from morning to night. The merchant drives to his place of business in a family brougham or barouche; the stock-broker drives to the station, where he takes the morning express to the City, in a smart dog-cart, with a high-stepping horse between the shafts, and a very knowing-looking groom at his side.

Such, at least, is the conception formed by the public of the two men of business, and it indicates not incorrectly the corresponding view of English society. The British merchant, as has been said, is very probably a member of Parliament; the instances in which stock-brokers are members of Parliament at the present day might be counted as something less than the fingers of one hand. The life of the ideal stock-broker is one of display; that of the ideal merchant, one of dignified grandeur or opulent comfort. Possessed of a certain amount of education, often acquired at a public school, sometimes both at Eton and Oxford, the stock-broker of the period has decided social aspirations. He makes his money easily, and he spends it lightly in procuring all the luxuries of existence. He marries a handsome wife, sets up a showy establishment, lays in a stock of choice wines, hires a French cook; he has carriages and horses, a box at the opera, stalls at theaters and concerts innumerable. He belongs to one or two good though not always first-rate clubs. He has acquaintances in the highest circles, and congratulates himself on being in society.

# THE REVOLUTIONS OF 1848

*Beginning in France in February, revolutions swept the major European capitals in 1848. The initial demands of the revolutionaries were for political reforms: a republic in France, democratic constitutions in Germany and Hungary. Social and economic issues, however, came quickly to the fore. Workers in urban centers sought measures to alleviate the long-term effects of industrialization and the more immediate problems of the economic recession of the late 1840s. The two accounts that follow are by participants in the revolutions. Alphonse de Lamartine (1790–1869), a Romantic poet, was a member of the provisional government of France in February 1848. Carl Schurz (1829–1906), a German journalist, supported the republican position. When the revolutionaries were defeated, he was forced to flee, first to France and eventually to the United States.*

## France

### From Alphonse de Lamartine. *History of the Revolution of 1848*

The 12th arrondissement of Paris had arranged a banquet. The opposition had promised to verify the right by its presence, and the banquet was to take place on the 20th of February. The ministry did not oppose it by force. They merely proposed to certify the offence by a commissary of police, and to try the question by the courts of law. The opposition was unanimous for accepting the judicial debate on this ground. Everything was prepared for this peaceable demonstration.

On the eve of it, the ministry, disturbed by a summons addressed to the National Guards, without arms, by the impatient republicans, declared at the tribune that they retracted their concessions, and would disperse the manifestation by force.

M. Barrot summoned the constitutional opposition to his house to deliberate.

It was proposed to keep aloof from the extreme resolution of the government, and M. Barrot and his friends yielded to this counsel.

On the next day a second deliberation took place at a restorator's in the Place de la Madeleine, and M. de Lamartine, M. Berryer, and M. de Laroche-jacquelein were invited to attend. They went thither.

From Alphonse de Lamartine, *History of the Revolution of 1848* (Boston: Phillips, Sampson & Co., 1849), pp. 28–29, 36–38, 46–49, 51.

About two hundred deputies of all complexions of moderate opposition were present. The course to be pursued was discussed. The discussion was long, varied and embarrassing, and no firm or worthy decision was reached in any quarter. If the opposition receded, it would destroy itself, dishonor its name, and lose its moral influence over the nation. It would pass under the Caudine yoke of the ministry. If it persisted, it would incur the risk of conquering too much, and giving victory to the party which desired—what it feared—a revolution. But revolution for revolution, the risk of an advanced revolution seemed more acceptable to certain minds than a backward revolution. . . .

Night came without blood having been shed. It was silent as the day, disquieted as on the eve of a great event. However, the news of a probable change of ministry, which relaxed the danger, reassured the citizens. The troops bivouacked in the squares and streets. Some benches and chairs on the Champs-Elysées, set on fire by the children, lighted up the horizon with an irregular illumination. The government was everywhere master of Paris, except in that kind of citadel fortified by the nature of the construction and the narrow winding of the streets, near the convent Saint Méry, in the centre of Paris. There some indefatigable and intrepid republicans, who observed everything and despaired of nothing, were concentrated, either by a concerted plan of tactics, or by the same spontaneous revolutionary instincts. Even their chiefs disapproved their obstinacy and rashness. They were estimated at four or five hundred in number, more or less. Another detachment of republicans, without chiefs, disarmed during the night the National Guards of the Batignolles, burned the station of the barrier, and fortified themselves in a neighboring timberyard to await the event. They did not attempt to dislodge them.

At dawn the routes which led to the gates of Paris were covered with columns of cavalry, infantry and artillery, which the commands of government had collected. These troops were imposing, obedient, well-disciplined, but sad and silent. The sadness of civil war clouded their brows. They took successively their position on the principal streets branching off from the quarters which pour forth the population of Paris. The multitude did not fight en masse upon any point. Dispersed and floating bands disarmed only isolated stations, broke open the armorers' shops, and fired invisible shots upon the troops. The barricades, starting from the centre of the church Saint Méry, were raised, branching out and gradually multiplying almost under the feet of the army. Hardly were they reared when they were abandoned. The troops had only stones to contend with,—it was a silent battle, whose progress was felt without hearing the noise.

The National Guard, assembled by a tardy call, collected legion by legion. It remained neutral, and confined itself to interposing between the troops and the people, and demanding with loud voice the dismissal of the ministers, and reform. It thus served as a shield to the revolution. . . .

Such was the state of Paris on the morning of the twenty-fourth of February. The troops, fatigued from seeing no enemy, yet feeling hostility on all sides, stood faithful but sad at their different posts. The generals and officers discussed with low voices the inexplicable indecision of events. Groups of cavalry were seen at the ends of the principal streets, enveloped in their gray cloaks, with drawn swords in their hands, immovably stationed for thirty-six hours in the same place, allowing their horses to sleep under them, trembling with cold and hunger. The officers of ordnance gallop by every moment, carrying from one part of Paris to another orders and counterorders. There was heard in the distance, on the side of the Hotel de Ville, and the deep and winding labyrinths of the adjacent streets, some firing from groups of people, which appeared to subside and become silent as the day advanced. The people were not numerous in the streets; they seemed to allow the invisible spirit of revolution to fight for them, and that small band of obstinate combatants who were dying for them in the heart of Paris. It is said there was a watch-word between the masses of the people and that group of republicans—a silent signal of intelligence, which said to some, "Resist a few hours longer," and to others, "You have no need of mingling in the contest, and shedding French blood. The genius of the revolution fights for all; the monarchy is falling; it is only necessary to push it; before the sun sets the republic will have triumphed." . . .

The fate of the day was at the disposal of the National Guard. The government thus far had not wished to sound its equivocal disposition, by asking it to take an active part in the affair, and fire on the citizens of Paris. . . .

The National Guards, called, in fact, on the morning of the 24th, to interpose between the people and the troops of the line, answered slowly and weakly to the appeal. They recognized, in the prolonged movement of the people, an anti-ministerial demonstration, an armed petition in favor of electoral reform, which they were far from disapproving. They smiled upon it in secret. They felt an antipathy to the name of M. Guizot. His irritating and prolonged authority oppressed them. They loved his principles of government, perhaps; they did not love the man. They saw in him at one time a complaisance, at another an imprudent vexation, of England. They reproached him for a peace too dearly purchased by political servility in Portugal; they reproached him for the war too rashly risked, for the aggrandizement of the Orleans family, at Madrid. They rejoiced at the downfall and humiliation of this minister, equally unpopular in peace and war.

They were not too much alarmed by seeing the people vote with musket-shots against the system pursued by the king. . . .

A small number of combatants, concentrated in that quarter of Paris which forms, by the crookedness and narrowness of its streets, the natural citadel of insurrections, preserved alone a hostile attitude and an inaccessible position. These men were nearly all veterans of the republic, formed by the voluntary discipline of sects in the secret societies of the two monarchies; trained to the struggle, and even to martyrdom, in all the battles which had made Paris bleed, and contested the establishment of the monarchy. Their invisible chief had no name nor rank. It was the invisible breath of revolution; the spirit of sect, the soul of the people, suffering from the present, aspiring to bring light from the future; the cool and disinterested enthusiasm which rejoices in death, if by its death posterity can find a germ of amelioration and life.

To these men were joined two other kinds of combatants, who always throw themselves into the tumultuous movements of seditions; the ferocious spirits whom blood allures and death delights, and the light natures whom the whirlwind attracts and draws in, the children of Paris. But this germ did not increase. It watched in silence, musket in hand. It contented itself with thus giving time for the general insurrection.

This insurrection was nowhere manifested. It needed a war-cry to excite it, a cry of horror to sow fury and vengeance in that mass of floating population, equally ready to retire to their homes, or to go forth to overthrow the government. Some silent groups collected here and there at the extremity of the faubourgs of the Temple and of St. Antoine. Other groups, few in number, appeared at the entrance of the streets which open from the Chaussée d'Antin upon the boulevards.

These two kinds of groups were different in costume and attitude. The one was composed of young men belonging to the rich and elegant classes of the bourgeoisie, to the schools, to commerce, to the National Guard, to literature, and above all to journalism. These harangued the people, roused their anger against the king, the ministry, the Chambers, spoke of the humiliation of France to the foreigner, of the diplomatic treasons of the court, of the corruption and insolent servility of the deputies sold to the discretion of Louis Philippe. They discussed aloud the names of the popular ministers whom the insurrection must impose upon the Tuileries. The numerous loiterers and persons passing by, eager for news, stopped near the orators, and applauded their proposals.

The other groups were composed of men of the people, come from their workshops two days since at the sound of musketry; their working-clothes upon their shoulders, their blue shirts open at the breast, their hands yet black with the smoke of charcoal. These descended in silence, by small companies, grazing the walls of the streets which lead to Clichy, la Villette, and the Canal de l'Ourcq. One or two workmen, better clothed than the others, in cloth vests, or in surtouts with long skirts, marched before them, spoke to them in low tones, and appeared to give them the word of command. These were the chiefs of the sections of the Rights of Man, or of the Families.

The society of the Rights of Man, and of the Families, was a kind of democratic masonry, instituted, since 1830, by some active republicans. These societies preserved, under different names, since the destruction of the first republic by Bonaparte, the rancor of betrayed liberty, as well as some traditions of jacobinism, transmitted from Babeuf to Buonarotti, and from Buonarotti to the young republicans of this school. The members of these purely political societies were recruited almost entirely from among the chiefs of the mechanic workshops, locksmiths, cabinet-makers, printers, joiners, and carpenters of Paris.

Parallel to these permanent conspiracies against royalty, the keystone of the arch of privilege, philosophical societies were organized, composed of almost the same elements,—some under the auspices of St. Simon, others under those of Fourier,—the former comprising the followers of Cabet, the latter those of Raspail, of Pierre Leroux and of Louis Blanc. These conspiracies in open day were alone spread by means of eloquence, association and journalism. Sects so far pacific, these societies discussed their opinions, and caused them to be discussed freely.

The difference between these two kinds of revolutionists is, that the first were inspired by the hatred of royalty, the second by the progress of humanity. The republic and equality was the aim of the one; social renovation and fraternity the aim of the other. They had nothing in common but impatience against that which existed, and hope for that which they saw dawning in an approaching revolution.

Towards ten o'clock in the evening, a small column of republicans of the young *bourgeoisie* passed through the rue Lepelletier; it formed a group in silence around the gate of the journal *Le National,* as if a rendezvous had been appointed. In all our revolutions, counsel is held, the word of command is given, the impulse comes, from the journal office. It is the *comitia* of public union, the ambulatory tribune of the people. We hear a long conference between the republicans within and the republicans without. Short and feverish words were exchanged through the low, closed window of the porter's lodge. The column, inspired with the enthusiasm which had just been communicated to it, advanced with cries of *Vive la réforme! à bas les ministres!* towards the boulevards.

Hardly had it quitted the office of *Le National,* when another column of workmen and men of the people presented itself, and halted there, at the command of its chief. It seemed to have been expected. It was applauded by the clapping of hands from within the house. . . .

A red flag floated amidst the smoke of torches over the foremost ranks of this multitude. Its numbers thickened as it continued to advance. A sinister curiosity became intent upon this cloud of men, which seemed to bear the mystery of the day.

In front of the Hotel of Foreign Affairs, a battalion of the line, drawn up in battle array, with loaded arms, its commander at the head, barred the boulevard. The column suddenly halts before this hedge of bayonets. The floating of the flag and the gleaming of torches frighten the horse of the commander. Rearing and whirling on its hind legs, the horse throws itself back towards the battalion, which opens to surround its leader. A discharge of fire-arms resounds in the confusion of this movement. Did it proceed, as has been said, from a concealed and perverse hand, fired upon the people by an agitator of the people, in order to revive by the sight of blood the cooling ardor of the struggle? Did it come from the hand of one of the insurgents upon the troop? In fine, what is more likely, did it come accidentally from the movement of some loaded weapon, or from the hand of some soldier who believed his commander was wounded when he saw the fright of his horse? No one knows. Crime or chance, that discharge of fire-arms rekindled a revolution.

# Germany

## From Carl Schurz. *Reminiscences*

The political horizon which after the revolution in March looked so glorious soon began to darken. In South Germany, where the opinion had gained ground that the revolution should not have "stood still before the thrones," a republican uprising took place under the leadership of the brilliant and impetuous Hecker, which, however, was speedily suppressed by force of arms. In the country at large such attempts found at first little sympathy. The bulk of the liberal element did not desire anything beyond the establishment of national unity and a constitutional monarchy "on a broad democratic basis." But the republican sentiment gradually spread and was intensified as the "reaction" assumed a more and more threatening shape.

The national parliament at Frankfurt elected in the spring, which represented the sovereignty of the German people in the large sense and was to give to the united German nation a national government, counted among its members a great many men illustrious in the fields, not of politics, but of science and literature. It soon showed a dangerous tendency of squandering in brilliant, but more or less fruitless, debates much of the time which was sorely needed for prompt and decisive action to secure the legitimate results of the revolution against hostile forces.

But our eyes were turned still more anxiously upon Berlin. Prussia was by far the strongest of the purely German states. The Austrian empire was a conglomeration of different nationalities—German, Magyar,

From *The Reminiscences of Carl Schurz* (New York: The McClure Company, 1907), Vol. 1, pp. 134–135, 140–141, 161–163.

Slavic and Italian. The German element, to which the dynasty and the political capital belonged, had so far been the predominant one. It was most advanced in civilization and wealth, although inferior in numbers. But the Slavs, the Magyars and the Italians, stimulated by the revolutionary movements of 1848, were striving for national autonomy, and although Austria had held the foremost place in the later periods of the ancient German empire and then after the Napoleonic wars in the German Confederacy, it seemed problematic whether her large non-German interests would permit her to play a leading part now in the political unification of Germany under a constitutional government. In fact, it turned out subsequently that the mutual jealousies of the different races enabled the Austrian central government to subjugate to despotic rule one by the other, in spite of the hopeful beginnings of the revolution, and that the non-German interests of Austria and those of the dynasty were predominant in her policy. But Prussia, excepting a comparatively small Polish district, was a purely German country, and by far the strongest among the German states in point of numbers, of general education, of economic activity and especially of military power. It was, therefore, generally felt that the attitude of Prussia would be decisive in determining the fate of the revolution. . . .

On the whole the summer of 1848 was to me a time of work and worry. The newspaper for which I had to write articles, the agitation in clubs and popular meetings, and besides my studies, imposed upon me a very heavy burden of labor, in which—I must confess—my studies fell into a somewhat subordinate place. What troubled me most was the visibly and constantly growing power of the reactionary forces and the frittering away of the opportunities to create something real and durable, by the national parliament in Frankfurt and by the assembly in Berlin. . . .

Of the larger parliamentary bodies that had issued from the revolution of March, only the national parliament in Frankfurt was still in existence. That existence it had owed to the longing of the German people, or rather the German peoples, for national unity, and it was its natural and universally understood mission to weld the German peoples under a common constitution of national government into one great nation. Immediately after the revolution of March, 1848, the different German governments, and with them also Austria, because of her German possessions, had recognized this object as a legitimate one, and it was with their co-operation that in May the elections for the national parliament had taken place. The large majority of that body, in fact, the German people in general, regarded the Frankfurt parliament as the specific representative of the sovereignty of the German nation. It was to be expected that the princes and those of their adherents, who may be designated as court-parties, would submit to this conception of the powers of the parliament only so long, and only so far, as they found themselves forced to do so. But few of the princes, if any, were sufficiently liberal to accept a limitation of their princely prerogatives with equanimity. Every gain of the people in the matter of political power they felt to be their own loss. Of course they were also opposed to the institution of a strong national government for the reason that this would be conditioned upon the surrender to the national authority of many of the sovereignty-rights of the different states. It was not only a national republic that the individual German sovereigns feared, but they also dreaded a national Kaiser who would be apt to reduce them to the condition of mere vassals. The German princes, with the exception of the one who could hope himself to occupy the imperial throne, were therefore the natural adversaries of German unity, embodied in a strong national government. There may have been some men of national sentiment among them capable of overcoming this reluctance, but certainly there were very few. Austria desired a united Germany in some form, only if it could hope to occupy in it the position of the leading power.

Face to face with the princes and their parties stood the national parliament in Frankfurt, that child of the revolution, which might then have almost been called the orphan of the revolution. It had at its immediate disposal no administrative machinery, no army, no treasury, only its moral authority; all the other things were in the hands of the different German state governments. The only power of the national parliament consisted in the will of the people. And this power was sufficient for the fulfillment of its mission so long as the will of the people proved itself strong enough, even through revolutionary action in case of necessity, to counteract the adverse interests of the princes. The parliament would have been sure of success in creating a constitutional German empire, if it had performed that task quickly and elected and put into office its Kaiser while the revolutionary prestige of the people was still unbroken—that is to say, in the first two or three months after the revolution of March. No German prince would then have declined the imperial crown with a constitution ever so democratic, and not one of them would have dared to refuse the sacrifice of any of his sovereignty-rights to the national power.

But that parliament was laboring under an overabundance of learning and virtue and under a want of that political experience and sagacity which recognizes that the better is often the enemy of the good, and that the true statesman will be careful not to imperil that which is essential by excessive insistence upon things which are of comparatively little consequence. The world has probably never seen a political assembly that contained a larger number of noble, learned, conscientious and patriotic men, and it will be difficult to find a book of the same character richer in profound knowledge and in models of lofty eloquence than its stenographic reports. But it did not possess the genius that promptly discerns opportunity and with quick resolution takes fortune by the forelock; it was not mindful of the fact that in times of great commotion the history of the world does not wait for the theoretical thinker. And thus it failed.

# IX

---

# THEORIES OF SOCIETY—ECONOMICS, EVOLUTION, AND HISTORY

*THE TWO REVOLUTIONS of the end of the eighteenth century, the industrial and French revolutions, confronted contemporaries with evidence of unprecedented change in many areas of life. As they sought to explain the changes and to predict their direction, philosophers and scientists developed new theories.*

*English economists described industrial capitalism in terms of natural laws of supply and demand. Economists in other countries adapted and modified the English theories in the contexts of their own national interests. In biology, Charles Darwin explained the origin of the human species in terms of its evolution from lower animal forms. A new kind of inquiry into the origins and constitution of human societies (social science) developed, much of it based on Darwin's biological ideas.*

*Most of the theories assumed that the direction of human development was progressive, toward greater and greater improvement. Some writers insisted that progress required equality not only among men but also between women and men. Others insisted that differences between the sexes were rooted in biology and thus not susceptible to political interference.*

*If the direction of history was assumed to be toward increasing progress, theorists differed nonetheless about what created social change. Utilitarians like Jeremy Bentham asserted that the pursuit of happiness led to greater and greater improvements in all areas of social life. John Stuart Mill wrote of the need for liberty, especially liberty of thought, in the evolution of human civilization. Karl Marx, in contrast, believed that conflict based on economic differences between social classes was the "motor" of history.*

# THE NATURAL LAWS OF POLITICAL ECONOMY

## Supply and Demand

*Adam Smith's (1723–1790)* Wealth of Nations *set forth the doctrine of economic liberalism, arguing that there were natural laws that regulated the marketplace. Smith's book is the founding text of the classical school of political economy.*

### From Adam Smith. *The Wealth of Nations*

There is in every society or neighbourhood an ordinary or average rate both of wages and profit in every different employment of labour and stock. This rate is naturally regulated, as I shall show hereafter, partly by the general circumstances of the society, their riches or poverty, their advancing, stationary, or declining condition; and partly by the particular nature of each employment.

There is likewise in every society or neighbourhood an ordinary or average rate of rent, which is regulated too, as I shall show hereafter, partly by the general circumstances of the society or neighbourhood in which the land is situated, and partly by the natural or improved fertility of the land.

These ordinary or average rates may be called the natural rates of wages, profit, and rent, at the time and place in which they commonly prevail.

When the price of any commodity is neither more nor less than what is sufficient to pay the rent of the land, the wages of the labour, and the profits of the stock employed in raising, preparing, and bringing it to market, according to their natural rates, the commodity is then sold for what may be called its natural price.

The commodity is then sold precisely for what it is worth, or for what it really costs the person who brings it to market; for though in common language what is called the prime cost of any commodity does not comprehend the profit of the person who is to sell it again, yet if he sells it at a price which does not allow him the ordinary rate of

From Adam Smith, *The Wealth of Nations* (New York: Random House, 1937), pp. 55–62.

profit in his neighbourhood, he is evidently a loser by the trade; since by employing his stock in some other way he might have made that profit. His profit, besides, is his revenue, the proper fund of his subsistence. As, while he is preparing and bringing the goods to market, he advances to his workmen their wages, or their subsistence; so he advances to himself, in the same manner, his own subsistence, which is generally suitable to the profit which he may reasonably expect from the sale of his goods. Unless they yield him this profit, therefore, they do not repay him what they may very properly be said to have really cost him.

Though the price, therefore, which leaves him this profit, is not always the lowest at which a dealer may sometimes sell his goods, it is the lowest at which he is likely to sell them for any considerable time; at least where there is perfect liberty, or where he may change his trade as often as he pleases.

The actual price at which any commodity is commonly sold is called its market price. It may either be above, or below, or exactly the same with its natural price.

The market price of every particular commodity is regulated by the proportion between the quantity which is actually brought to market, and the demand of those who are willing to pay the natural price of the commodity, or the whole value of the rent, labour, and profit, which must be paid in order to bring it thither. Such people may be called the effectual demanders, and their demand the effectual demand; since it may be sufficient to effectuate the bringing of the commodity to market. It is different from the absolute demand. A very poor man may be said in some sense to have a demand for a coach and six; he might like to have it; but his demand is not an effectual demand, as the commodity can never be brought to market in order to satisfy it.

When the quantity of any commodity which is brought to market falls short of the effectual demand, all those who are willing to pay the whole value of the rent, wages, and profit, which must be paid in order to bring it thither, cannot be supplied with the quantity which they want. Rather than want it altogether, some of them will be willing to give more. A competition will immediately begin among them, and the market price will rise more or less above the natural price, according as either the greatness of the deficiency, or the wealth and wanton luxury of the competitors, happen to animate more or less the eagerness of the competition. Among competitors of equal wealth and luxury the same deficiency will generally occasion a more or less eager competition, according as the acquisition of the commodity happens to be of more or less importance to them. Hence the exorbitant price of the necessaries of life during the blockade of a town or in a famine.

When the quantity brought to market exceeds the effectual demand, it cannot be all sold to those who are willing to pay the whole value of the rent, wages and profit, which must be paid in order to bring it thither. Some part must be sold to those who are willing to pay less, and the low price which they give for it must reduce the price of the whole. The market price will sink more or less below the natural price, according as the greatness of the excess increases more or less the competition of the sellers, or according as it happens to be more or less important to them to get immediately rid of the commodity. The same excess in the importation of perishable, will occasion a much greater competition than in that of durable commodities; in the importation of oranges, for example, than in that of old iron.

When the quantity brought to market is just sufficient to supply the effectual demand and no more, the market price naturally comes to be either exactly, or as nearly as can be judged of, the same with the natural price. The whole quantity upon hand can be disposed of for this price, and cannot be disposed of for more. The competition of the different dealers obliges them all to accept of this price, but does not oblige them to accept of less.

The quantity of every commodity brought to market naturally suits itself to the effectual demand. It is the interest of all those who employ their land, labour, or stock, in bringing any commodity to market, that the quantity never should exceed the effectual demand; and it is the interest of all other people that it never should fall short of that demand.

If at any time it exceeds the effectual demand, some of the component parts of its price must be paid below their natural rate. If it is rent, the interest of the landlords will immediately prompt them to withdraw a part of their land; and if it is wages or profit, the interest of the labourers in the one case, and of their employers in the other, will prompt them to withdraw a part of their labour or stock from this employment. The quantity brought to market will soon be no more than sufficient to supply the effectual demand. All the different parts of its price will rise to their natural rate, and the whole price to its natural price.

If, on the contrary, the quantity brought to market should at any time fall short of the effectual demand, some of the component parts of its price must rise above their natural rate. If it is rent, the interest of all other landlords will naturally prompt them to prepare more land for the raising of this commodity; if it is wages or profit, the interest of all other labourers and dealers will soon prompt them to employ more labour and stock in preparing and bringing it to market. The quantity brought thither will soon be sufficient to supply the effectual demand. All the different parts of its price will soon sink to their natural rate, and the whole price to its natural price.

The natural price, therefore, is, as it were, the central price, to which the prices of all commodities are continually gravitating. Different accidents may sometimes keep them suspended a good deal above it, and sometimes force them down even somewhat below it. But whatever may be the obstacles which hinder them from settling in this center of repose and continuance, they are constantly tending towards it. . . .

But though the market price of every particular commodity is in this manner continually gravitating, if one may say so, towards the natural price, yet sometimes particular accidents, sometimes natural causes, and sometimes particular regulations of police, may, in many commodities, keep up the market price, for a long time together, a good deal above the natural price. . . .

The market price of any particular commodity, though it may continue long above, can seldom continue long below, its natural price. Whatever part of it was paid below the natural rate, the persons whose interest it affected would immediately feel the loss, and would immediately withdraw either so much land, or so much labour, or so much stock, from being employed about it, that the quantity brought to market would soon be no more than sufficient to supply the effectual demand. Its market price, therefore, would soon rise to the natural price. This at least would be the case where there was perfect liberty.

# The "Iron Law" of Wages

*The English banker David Ricardo (1772–1823) reasoned in a manner similar to Adam Smith. He maintained that wages naturally sought a minimum level corresponding to basic subsistence needs of the workers.*

## From David Ricardo. *On Wages*

Money, from its being a commodity obtained from a foreign country, from its being the general medium of exchange between all civilized countries, and from its being also distributed among those countries in proportions which are ever changing with every improvement in commerce and machinery, and with every increasing difficulty of obtaining food and necessaries for an increasing population, is subject to incessant variations. In stating the principles which regulate exchangeable value and price, we should carefully distinguish between those variations which belong to the commodity itself, and those which are occasioned by a variation in the medium in which value is estimated, or price expressed.

A rise in wages, from an alteration in the value of money, produces a general effect on price, and for that reason it produces no real effect

From *The Works of David Ricardo*, J. R. McCulloch, ed. (London: John Murray, 1881), pp. 31, 50–58.

whatever on profits. On the contrary, a rise of wages, from the circumstance of the labourer being more liberally rewarded, or from a difficulty of procuring the necessaries on which wages are expended, does not, except in some instances, produce the effect of raising price, but has a great effect in lowering profits. In the one case, no greater proportion of the annual labour of the country is devoted to the support of the labourers; in the other case, a larger portion is so devoted.

Labour, like all other things which are purchased and sold, and which may be increased or diminished in quantity, has its natural and its market price. The natural price of labour is that price which is necessary to enable the labourers, one with another, to subsist and to perpetuate their race, without either increase or diminution.

The power of the labourer to support himself, and the family which may be necessary to keep up the number of labourers, does not depend on the quantity of money which he may receive for wages, but on the quantity of food, necessaries, and conveniences become essential to him from habit, which that money will purchase. The natural price of labour, therefore, depends on the price of the food, necessaries, and conveniences required for the support of the labourer and his family. With a rise in the price of food and necessaries, the natural price of labour will rise; with the fall in their price, the natural price of labour will fall.

With the progress of society the natural price of labour has always a tendency to rise, because one of the principal commodities by which its natural price is regulated, has a tendency to become dearer, from the greater difficulty of producing it. As, however, the improvements in agriculture, the discovery of new markets, whence provisions may be imported, may for a time counteract the tendency to a rise in the price of necessaries, and may even occasion their natural price to fall, so will the same causes produce the correspondent effects on the natural price of labour.

The natural price of all commodities, excepting raw produce and labour, has a tendency to fall, in the progress of wealth and population; for though, on one hand, they are enhanced in real value, from the rise in the natural price of the raw material of which they are made, this is more than counterbalanced by the improvements in machinery, by the better division and distribution of labour, and by the increasing skill, both in science and art, of the producers.

The market price of labour is the price which is really paid for it, from the natural operation of the proportion of the supply to the demand; labour is dear when it is scarce, and cheap when it is plentiful. However much the market price of labour may deviate from its natural price, it has, like commodities, a tendency to conform to it.

It is when the market price of labour exceeds its natural price, that the condition of the labourer is flourishing and happy, that he has it in his power to command a greater proportion of the necessaries and enjoyments of life, and therefore to rear a healthy and numerous family. When, however, by the encouragement which high wages give to the increase of population, the number of labourers is increased, wages again fall to their natural price, and indeed from a reaction sometimes fall below it.

When the market price of labour is below its natural price, the condition of the labourers is most wretched: then poverty deprives them of those comforts which custom renders absolute necessaries. It is only after their privations have reduced their number, or the demand for labour has increased, that the market price of labour will rise to its natural price, and that the labourer will have the moderate comforts which the natural rate of wages will afford.

Notwithstanding the tendency of wages to conform to their natural rate, their market rate may, in an improving society, for an indefinite period, be constantly above it; for no sooner may the impulse, which an increased capital gives to a new demand for labour, be obeyed, than another increase of capital may produce the same effect; and thus, if the increase of capital be gradual and constant, the demand for labour may give a continued stimulus to an increase of people. . . .

Thus, then, with every improvement of society, with every increase in its capital, the market wages of labour will rise; but the permanence of their rise will depend on the question, whether the natural price of labour has also risen; and this again will depend on the rise in the natural price of those necessaries on which the wages of labour are expended. . . .

As population increases, these necessaries will be constantly rising in price, because more labour will be necessary to produce them. If, then, the money wages of labour should fall, whilst every commodity on which the wages of labour were expended rose, the labourer would be doubly affected, and would be soon totally deprived of subsistence. Instead, therefore, of the money wages of labour falling, they would rise; but they would not rise sufficiently to enable the labourer to purchase as many comforts and necessaries as he did before the rise in the price of those commodities. . . .

These, then, are the laws by which wages are regulated, and by which the happiness of far the greatest part of every community is governed. Like all other contracts, wages should be left to the fair and free competition of the market, and should never be controlled by the interference of the legislature.

The clear and direct tendency of the poor laws is in direct opposition to these obvious principles: it is not, as the legislature benevolently intended, to amend the condition of the poor, but to deteriorate the condition of both poor and rich; instead of making the poor rich, they are calculated to make the rich poor; and whilst the present laws are in force, it is quite in the natural order of things that the fund for the maintenance of the poor should progressively increase till it has absorbed all the net revenue of the country, or at least so much of it as the state shall leave to us, after satisfying its own never-failing demands for the public expenditure.

This pernicious tendency of these laws is no longer a mystery, since it has been fully developed by the able hand of Mr. Malthus; and every friend to the poor must ardently wish for their abolition.

# A German View

*George Friedrich List (1789–1846) dissented from the English political economists' view. He argued that economic policy had to be adapted to the needs of specific nations. Free trade was not practical in Germany, he insisted, until the country had attained a greater degree of industrial growth.*

## From George Friedrich List. *National System of Political Economy*

Political economy, in matters of international commerce, must draw its lessons from experience; the measures it advises must be appropriate to the wants of our times, to the special condition of each people; it must not, however, disavow the exigencies of the future nor the higher interests of the whole human race. Political economy must rest consequently upon Philosophy, Policy, and History.

For the interests of the future and the welfare of men, philosophy requires a more intimate union and communion of nations, a renunciation of war so far as possible, the establishment and development of international law, transition of the *jus gentium* to a federal law, freedom of communication among nations, as well in moral as in material concerns; lastly, the union of all nations under some rule of law, or in some aspects of the subject, a universal association.

In the case of any particular people, a wise administration, with extended views, pursues special objects, seeking guarantees for independence and for duration, measures calculated to hasten progress in civilization, well-being, and power, and to improve social condition so that the body politic shall be completely and harmoniously developed in all its parts, perfect in itself, and politically independent.

History, for its part, assists in no equivocal manner in providing for the exigencies of the future, by teaching how, in every epoch, progress, material and intellectual, has kept pace with the extent of political association and commercial relations. But it justifies at the same time the exigencies of government and nationality, showing how nations have

From George Friedrich List, *National System of Political Economy* (Philadelphia: Lippincott, 1856), pp. 63–64, 69–70, 73, 77–81.

perished for not having sufficiently watched over the interests of their culture and power; how a commerce entirely free with nations more advanced has been of advantage to those still in the first phases of their development; also how those which had made some progress have been able by proper regulations in their foreign trade, to make still greater progress and to overtake those which had preceded them. History thus shows the way of reconciling the respective exigencies of philosophy and government.

But practice and theory, such as actually exhibited, take their sides, the former exclusively for the particular exigencies of nationality, the latter for the absolute requirements of cosmopolitism. . . .

The practical importance of the great question of free trade between nations is generally felt in our day, as also the necessity of investigating, with impartiality, once for all, how far theory and practice have erred on this subject, and how far any reconciliation between them is possible. It is at least needful to discuss seriously the problem of such a reconciliation.

It is not indeed with any assumed modesty, it is with the feeling of a profound mistrust of his power, that the author ventures upon this attempt; it is after resisting many years his inclination, after having hundreds of times questioned the correctness of opinions and again and again verifying them; after having frequently examined opposing opinions, and ascertained, beyond a doubt, their inaccuracy, that he determined to enter upon the solution of this problem. He believes himself free from the empty ambition of contradicting old authorities and propounding new theories. If the author had been an Englishman, he would probably never have entertained doubts of the fundamental principle of Adam Smith's theory. It was the condition of his own country which begot in him, more than twenty years since, the first doubts of the infallibility of that theory; it was the condition of his country which, since that time, determined him to develop, first in anonymous articles, then in more elaborate treatises, not anonymous, contrary opinions. At this moment, the interests of Germany alone give him the courage to publish the present work; he will however not dissemble, that a personal motive is connected with those interests; that is, the necessity in which he is placed of showing by a treatise of some extent, that he is not quite incompetent to treat of political economy. . . .

The civilization, political education and power of nations, depend chiefly on their economical condition and reciprocally; the more advanced their economy, the more civilized and powerful will be the nation, the more rapidly will its civilization and power increase, and the more will its economical culture be developed. . . .

The anterior progress of certain nations, foreign commercial legislation and war have compelled inferior countries to look for special means of effecting their transition from the agricultural to the manufacturing stage of industry, and as far as practicable, by a system of duties, to restrain their trade with more advanced nations aiming at manufacturing monopoly.

The system of import duties is consequently not, as has been said, an invention of speculative minds; it is a natural consequence of the tendency of nations to seek for guarantees of their existence and prosperity, and to establish and increase their weight in the scale of national influence. . . .

In the economical development of nations by means of external trade, four periods must be distinguished. In the first, agriculture is encouraged by the importation of manufactured articles, and by the exportation of its own products; in the second, manufacturers begin to increase at home, whilst the importation of foreign manufactures to some extent continues; in the third, home manufactures mainly supply domestic consumption and the internal markets; finally, in the fourth, we see the exportation upon a large scale of manufactured products, and the importation of raw materials and agricultural products.

The system of import duties being considered as a mode of assisting the economical development of a nation, by regulating its external trade, must constantly take as a rule the principle of the industrial education of the country.

To encourage agriculture by the aid of protective duties is vicious policy; for agriculture can be encouraged only by promoting manufacturing industry; and the exclusion of raw material and agricultural products from abroad, has no other result than to impede the rise of national manufactures.

The economical education of a country of inferior intelligence and culture, or one thinly populated, relatively to the extent and the fertility of its territory, is effected most certainly by free trade, with more advanced, richer, and more industrious nations. Every commercial restriction in such a country aiming at the increase of manufactures, is premature, and will prove detrimental, not only to civilization in general, but the progress of the nation in particular. If its intellectual, political, and economical education, under the operation of free trade, has advanced so far, that the importation of foreign manufactures, and the want of markets for its own products has become an obstacle to its ulterior development, then only can protective measures be justified. . . .

Internal and external trade flourish alike under the protective system; these have no importance but among nations supplying their own wants by their own manufacturing industry, consuming their own agricultural products, and purchasing foreign raw materials and commodities with the surplus of their manufactured articles. Home and foreign trade are both insignificant in the merely agricultural countries of temperate climes, and their external commerce is usually in the hands of the manufacturing and trading nations in communication with them.

A good system of protection does not imply any monopoly in the manufacturers of a country; it only furnishes a guarantee against losses to those who devote their capital, their talents, and their exertions to new branches of industry.

There is no monopoly, because internal competition comes in the place of foreign competition, and every individual has the privilege of taking his share in the advantages offered by the country to its citizens; it is only an advantage to citizens as against foreigners, who enjoy in their own country a similar advantage.

# SCIENCE AND SOCIETY

## Evolution

*Charles Darwin (1809–1882), a naturalist, traveled widely and gathered evidence from his own and others' research. In 1859 he published* On the Origin of Species, *which set forth his theory that animals evolved through variation and natural selection of those most fit to survive in particular environments. In* The Descent of Man *(1871) he applied his theory directly to the question of human evolution.*

## From Charles Darwin. *The Descent of Man*

The main conclusion here arrived at, and now held by many naturalists who are well competent to form a sound judgment, is that man is descended from some less highly organised form. The grounds upon which this conclusion rests will never be shaken, for the close similarity between man and the lower animals in embryonic development, as well as in innumerable points of structure and constitution, both of high and of the most trifling importance,—the rudiments which he retains, and the abnormal revisions to which he is occasionally liable,—are facts which cannot be disputed. They have long been known, but until recently they told us nothing with respect to the origin of man. Now when viewed by the light of our knowledge of the whole organic world, their meaning is unmistakable. The great principle of evolution stands up clear and firm, when these groups of facts are considered in connection with others, such as the mutual affinities of the members of the same group, their geographical distribution in past and present times, and their geological succession. It is incredible that all these facts should speak falsely. He who is not content to look, like a savage, at the phenomena of nature as disconnected, cannot any longer believe that man is the work of a separate act of creation. He will be forced to admit that the close resemblance of the embryo of man to that, for instance, of a dog—the construction of his skull, limbs and whole frame on the same plan with that of other mammals, independently of the uses to which the parts may be put—the occasional re-appearance of

From Charles Darwin, *The Descent of Man and Selection in Relation to Sex* (New York: Appleton and Co., 1883), pp. 7, 609, 612–614, 618–619.

various structures, for instance of several muscles, which man does not normally possess, but which are common to the Quadrumana—and a crowd of analogous facts—all point in the plainest manner to the conclusion that man is the co-descendant with other mammals of a common progenitor.

We have seen that man incessantly presents individual differences in all parts of his body and in his mental faculties. These differences or variations seem to be induced by the same general causes, and to obey the same laws as with the lower animals. In both cases similar laws of inheritance prevail. Man tends to increase at a greater rate than his means of subsistence; consequently he is occasionally subjected to a severe struggle for existence, and natural selection will have effected whatever lies within its scope. A succession of strongly-marked variations of a similar nature is by no means requisite; slight fluctuating differences in the individual suffice for the work of natural selection; not that we have any reason to suppose that in the same species, all parts of the organisation tend to vary to the same degree.

By considering the embryological structure of man,—the homologies which he presents with the lower animals,—the rudiments which he retains,—and the reversions to which he is liable, we can partly recall in imagination the former condition of our early progenitors; and can approximately place them in their proper place in the zoological series. We thus learn that man is descended from a hairy, tailed quadruped, probably arboreal in its habits, and an inhabitant of the Old World. This creature, if its whole structure had been examined by a naturalist, would have been classed amongst the Quadrumana, as surely as the still more ancient progenitor of the Old and New World monkeys. The Quadrumana and all the higher mammals are probably derived from an ancient marsupial animal, and this through a long line of diversified forms, from some amphibian-like creature, and this again from some fish-like animal. In the dim obscurity of the past we can see that the early progenitor of all the Vertebrata must have been an aquatic animal, provided with branchiæ, with the two sexes united in the same individual, and with the most important organs of the body (such as the brain and heart) imperfectly or not at all developed. This animal seems to have been more like the larvæ of the existing marine Ascidians than any other known form.

The high standard of our intellectual powers and moral disposition is the greatest difficulty which presents itself, after we have been driven to this conclusion on the origin of man. But every one who admits the principle of evolution, must see that the mental powers of the higher animals, which are the same in kind with those of man, though so different in degree, are capable of advancement. . . .

The moral nature of man has reached its present standard, partly through the advancement of his reasoning powers and consequently of a just public opinion, but especially from his sympathies having been rendered more tender and widely diffused through the effects of habit, example, instruction, and reflection. It is not improbable that after long practice virtuous tendencies may be inherited. With the more civilised races, the conviction of the existence of an all-seeing Deity has had a potent influence on the advance of morality. Ultimately man does not accept the praise or blame of his fellows as his sole guide, though few escape this influence, but his habitual convictions, controlled by reason, afford him the safest rule. His conscience then becomes the supreme judge and monitor. Nevertheless the first foundation or origin of the moral sense lies in the social instincts, including sympathy; and these instincts no doubt were primarily gained, as in the case of the lower animals, through natural selection.

The belief in God has often been advanced as not only the greatest, but the most complete of all the distinctions between man and the lower animals. It is however impossible, as we have seen, to maintain that this belief is innate or instinctive in man. On the other hand a belief in all-pervading spiritual agencies seems to be universal; and apparently follows from a considerable advance in man's reason, and from a still greater advance in his faculties of imagination, curiosity and wonder. I am aware that the assumed instinctive belief in God has been used by many persons as an argument for His existence. But this is a rash argument, as we should thus be compelled to believe in the existence of many cruel and malignant spirits, only a little more powerful than man; for the belief in them is far more general than in a beneficent Deity. The idea of a universal and beneficent Creator does not seem to arise in the mind of man, until he has been elevated by long-continued culture. . . .

I am aware that the conclusions arrived at in this work will be denounced by some as highly irreligious; but he who denounces them is bound to shew why it is more irreligious to explain the origin of man as a distinct species by descent from some lower form, through the laws of variation and natural selection, than to explain the birth of the individual through the laws of ordinary reproduction. The birth both of the species and of the individual are equally parts of that grand sequence of events, which our minds refuse to accept as the result of blind chance. The understanding revolts at such a conclusion, whether or not we are able to believe that every slight variation of structure,— the union of each pair in marriage,—the dissemination of each seed,— and other such events, have all been ordained for some special purpose.

Sexual selection has been treated at great length in this work; for, as I have attempted to shew, it has played an important part in the history of the organic world. I am aware that much remains doubtful, but I have endeavoured to give a fair view of the whole case. In the lower divisions of the animal kingdom, sexual selection seems to have done nothing: such animals are often affixed for life to the same spot, or have the sexes combined in the same individual, or what is still more important, their perceptive and intellectual faculties are not sufficiently advanced to allow of the feelings of love and jealousy, or of the exertion of choice. When, however, we come to the Arthropoda and Vertebrata, even to the lowest classes in these two great Sub-Kingdoms, sexual selection has effected much. . . .

Sexual selection depends on the success of certain individuals over others of the same sex, in relation to the propagation of the species; whilst natural selection depends on the success of both sexes, at all ages, in relation to the general conditions of life. The sexual struggle is of two kinds; in the one it is between the individuals of the same sex, generally the males, in order to drive away or kill their rivals, the females remaining passive; whilst in the other, the struggle is likewise between the individuals of the same sex, in order to excite or charm those of the opposite sex, generally the females, which no longer remain passive, but select the more agreeable partners. . . .

The main conclusion arrived at in this work, namely that man is descended from some lowly organised form, will, I regret to think, be highly distasteful to many. But there can hardly be a doubt that we are descended from barbarians. The astonishment which I felt on first seeing a party of Fuegians on a wild and broken shore will never be forgotten by me, for the reflection at once rushed into my mind—such were our ancestors. These men were absolutely naked and bedaubed with paint, their long hair was tangled, their mouths frothed with excitement, and their expression was wild, startled, and distrustful. They possessed hardly any arts, and like wild animals lived on what they could catch; they had no government, and were merciless to every one not of their own small tribe. He who has seen a savage in his native land will not feel much shame, if forced to acknowledge that the blood of some more humble creature flows in his veins. For my own part I would as soon be descended from that heroic little monkey, who braved his dreaded enemy in order to save the life of his keeper, or from that old baboon, who descending from the mountains, carried away in triumph his young comrade from a crowd of astonished dogs—as from a savage who delights to torture his enemies, offers up bloody sacrifices, practises infanticide without remorse, treats his wives like slaves, knows no decency, and is haunted by the grossest superstitions.

Man may be excused for feeling some pride at having risen, though not through his own exertions, to the very summit of the organic scale; and the fact of his having thus risen, instead of having been aboriginally placed there, may give him hope for a still higher destiny in the distant future. But we are not here concerned with hopes or fears, only with the truth as far as our reason permits us to discover it; and I have given the evidence to the best of my ability. We must, however, acknowledge, as it seems to me, that man with all his noble qualities, with sympathy which feels for the most debased, with benevolence which extends not only to other men but to the humblest living creature, with his god-like intellect which has penetrated into the movements and constitution of the solar system—with all these exalted powers—Man still bears in his bodily frame the indelible stamp of his lowly origin.

# Social Evolution

*Herbert Spencer (1820–1903) popularized Darwinian ideas as they applied to the evolution of society. Spencer believed that society was evolving toward increasing freedom for individuals; as in the economic sphere, government intervention, he believed, ought to be minimal in social and political life.*

## From Herbert Spencer. *Progress: Its Law and Cause*

The current conception of Progress is somewhat shifting and indefinite. Sometimes it comprehends little more than simple growth—as of a nation in the number of its members and the extent of territory over which it has spread. Sometimes it has reference to quantity of material products—as when the advance of agriculture and manufactures is the topic. Sometimes the superior quality of these products is contemplated; and sometimes the new or improved appliances by which they are produced. When, again, we speak of moral or intellectual progress, we refer to the state of the individual or people exhibiting it; whilst, when the progress of Knowledge, of Science, of Art, is commented upon, we have in view certain abstract results of human thought and action. Not only, however, is the current conception of Progress more or less vague, but it is in great measure erroneous. It takes in not so much the reality of Progress as its accompaniments—not so much the substance as the shadow. That progress in intelligence which takes place during the evolution of the child into the man, or the savage into the philosopher, is commonly regarded as consisting in the greater number of facts known and laws understood: whereas the actual progress consists in those internal modifications of which this increased knowledge is the expression. Social progress is supposed to consist in the produce of a greater quantity and variety of the articles required for the satisfaction of men's wants; in the increasing security of person and property; in the widening freedom of action enjoyed: whereas, rightly understood, social progress consists in those changes of structure in the social organism which have entailed these consequences. The current conception is a teleological one. The phenomena are con-

From Herbert Spencer, "Progress: Its Law and Cause," *Westminister Review*, Vol. 67 (April 1857), pp. 445–447, 451, 454–456, 464–465.

templated solely as bearing on human happiness. Only those changes are held to constitute progress which directly or indirectly tend to heighten human happiness. And they are thought to constitute progress simply *because* they tend to heighten human happiness. But rightly to understand Progress, we must inquire what is the nature of these changes, considered apart from our interests. Ceasing, for example, to regard the successive geological modifications that have taken place in the Earth, as modifications that have gradually fitted it for the habitation of Man, and as therefore a geological progress, we must seek to determine the character common to these modifications—the law to which they all conform. And similarly in every other case. Leaving out of sight concomitants and beneficial consequences, let us ask what Progress is in itself.

In respect to that progress which individual organisms display in the course of their evolution, this question has been answered by the Germans. The investigations of Wolff, Goethe, and Van Baer have established the truth that the series of changes gone through during the development of a seed into a tree, or an ovum into an animal, constitute an advance from homogeneity of structure to heterogeneity of structure. In its primary stage, every germ consists of a substance that is uniform throughout, both in texture and chemical composition. The first step in its development is the appearance of a difference between two parts of this substance; or, as the phenomenon is described in physiological language—a differentiation. Each of these differentiated divisions presently begins itself to exhibit some contrast of parts; and by these secondary differentiations become as definite as the original one. This progress is continuously repeated—is simultaneously going on in all parts of the growing embryo; and by endless multiplication of these differentiations there is ultimately produced that complex combination of tissues and organs constituting the adult animal or plant. This is the course of evolution followed by all organisms whatever. It is settled beyond dispute that organic progress consists in a change from the homogeneous to the heterogeneous.

Now, we propose in the first place to show, that this law of organic progress is the law of all progress. Whether it be in the development of the Earth, in the development of Life upon its surface, the development of Society, of Government, of Manufactures, of Commerce, of Language, Literature, Science, Art, this same evolution of the simple into the complex, through a process of continuous differentiation, holds throughout. From the earliest traceable cosmical changes down to the latest results of civilization, we shall find that the transformation of the homogeneous into the heterogeneous, is that in which Progress essentially consists. . . .

Whether an advance from the homogeneous to the heterogeneous is or is not displayed in the biological history of the globe, it is clearly enough displayed in the progress of the latest and most heterogeneous creature—Man. It is alike true that, during the period in which the Earth has been peopled, the human organism has become more heterogeneous among the civilized divisions of the species; and that the species, as a whole, has been growing more heterogeneous in virtue of the multiplication of races and the differentiation of these races from each other. . . .

. . . . In the course of ages, there arises, as among ourselves, a highly complex political organization of monarch, ministers, lords and commons, with their subordinate administrative departments, courts of justice, revenue offices, &c., supplemented in the provinces by municipal governments, county governments, parish or union governments—all of them more or less elaborated. By its side there grows up a highly complex religious organization, with its various grades of officials, from archbishops down to sextons, its colleges, convocations, ecclesiastical courts, &c.; to all which must be added the ever-multiplying independent sects, each with its general and local authorities. And at the same time there is developed a highly complex aggregation of customs, manners, and temporary fashions, enforced by society at large, and serving to control those minor transactions between man and man which are not regulated by civil and religious law. Moreover it is to be observed that this ever-increasing heterogeneity in the governmental appliances of each nation, has been accompanied by an increasing heterogeneity in the governmental appliances of different nations: all of which are more or less unlike in their political systems and legislation, in their creeds and religious institutions, in their customs and ceremonial usages.

Simultaneously there has been going on a second differentiation of a still more familiar kind; that, namely, by which the mass of the community has become segregated into distinct classes and orders of workers. While the governing part has been undergoing the complex development above described, the governed part has been undergoing an equally complex development, which has resulted in that minute division of labour characterizing advanced nations. It is needless to trace out this progress from its first stages, up through the caste divisions of the East and the incorporated guilds of Europe, to the elaborate producing and distributing organization existing among ourselves. Political economists have made familiar to all, the evolution which, beginning with a tribe whose members severally perform the same actions each for himself, ends with a civilized community whose members severally perform different actions for each other; and they have further explained the evolution through which the solitary producer of any one commodity, is transformed into a combination of producers who, united under a master, take separate parts in the manufacture of such commodity. But there are yet other and higher phases of this advance from the homogeneous to the heterogeneous in the industrial structure of the social organism. Long after considerable progress has been made in the division of labour among different classes of workers, there is still little or no division of labour among the widely separated parts of the community: the nation continues comparatively homogeneous in the respect that in each district the same occupations are pursued. But when roads and other means of transit become numerous and good, the different districts begin to assume different functions, and to become mutually dependent. The calico manufacture locates itself in this county, the woollen-cloth manufacture in that; silks are produced here, lace there; stockings in one place, shoes in another; pottery, hardware, cutlery, come to have their special towns; and ultimately every locality becomes more or less distinguished from the rest by the leading occupation carried on in it. Nay, more, this subdivision of functions shows itself not only among the different parts of the same nation, but among different nations. That exchange of commodities which free-trade promises so greatly to increase, will ultimately have the effect of specializing, in a greater or less degree, the industry of each people. So that beginning with a barbarous tribe, almost if not quite homogeneous in the functions of its members, the progress has been, and still is, towards an economic aggregation of the whole human race, growing ever more heterogeneous in respect of the separate functions assumed by separate nations, the separate functions assumed by the local sections of each nation, the separate functions assumed by the many kinds of makers and traders in each town, and the separate functions assumed by the workers united in producing each commodity.

Not only is the law thus clearly exemplified in the evolution of the social organism, but it is exemplified with equal clearness in the evolution of all products of human thought and action; whether concrete or abstract, real or ideal. . . .

We might trace out the evolution of Science; beginning with the era in which it was not yet differentiated from Art, and was, in union with Art, the handmaid of Religion; passing through the era in which the sciences were so few and rudimentary, as to be simultaneously cultivated by the same philosophers; and ending with the era in which the genera and species are so numerous that few can enumerate them, and no one can adequately grasp even one genus. Or we might do the like with Architecture, with the Drama, with Dress. But doubtless the reader is already weary of illustrations; and our promise has been amply fulfilled. We believe we have shown beyond question, that that which the German physiologists have found to be the law of organic development, is the law of all development. The advance from the simple to the complex, through a process of successive differentiations, is seen alike in the earliest changes of the Universe to which we can reason our way back, and in the earliest changes which we can inductively establish; it is seen in the geologic and climatic evolution of the Earth, and of every single organism on its surface; it is seen in the evolution of Humanity, whether contemplated in the civilized individual, or in the aggregation of races; it is seen in the evolution of Society in respect both of its political and economical organization; and it is seen in the evolution of all those endless concrete and abstract products of human activity which constitute the environment of our daily life. From the remotest past which Science can fathom, down to the novelties of yesterday, that in which Progress essentially consists, is the transformation of the homogeneous into the heterogeneous.

# A Science of Society

*Auguste Comte (1798–1857) served as secretary to the French utopian socialist Henri de Saint-Simon. After Saint-Simon's death he developed his own philosophy, the science of positivism. He offered it as a systematic way to study the organization and laws of society*

## From Auguste Comte. *A General View of Positivism*

Positivism consists essentially of a Philosophy and a Polity. These can never be dissevered; the former being the basis, and the latter the end of one comprehensive system, in which our intellectual faculties and our social sympathies are brought into close correlation with each other. For, in the first place, the science of Society, besides being more important than any other, supplies the only logical and scientific link by which all our varied observations of phenomena can be brought into one consistent whole. Of this science it is even more true than of any of the preceding sciences, that its real character cannot be understood without explaining its exact relation in all general features with the art corresponding to it. Now here we find a coincidence which is assuredly not fortuitous. At the very time when the theory of society is being laid down, an immense sphere is opened for the application of that theory; the direction, namely, of the social regeneration of Western Europe. For, if we take another point of view, and look at the great crisis of modern history, as its character is displayed in the natural course of events, it becomes every day more evident how hopeless is the task of reconstructing political institutions without the previous remodelling of opinion and of life. To form then a satisfactory synthesis of all human conceptions is the most urgent of our social wants: and it is needed equally for the sake of Order and of Progress. During the gradual accomplishment of this great philosophical work, a new moral

From Auguste Comte, *A General View of Positivism* (London: Routledge and Sons, 1907), pp. 1–7.

power will arise spontaneously throughout the West, which, as its influence increases, will lay down a definite basis for the reorganization of society. It will offer a general system of education for the adoption of all civilized nations, and by this means will supply in every department of public and private life fixed principles of judgment and of conduct. Thus the intellectual movement and the social crisis will be brought continually into close connexion with each other. Both will combine to prepare the advanced portion of humanity for the acceptance of a true spiritual power, a power more coherent, as well as more progressive, than the noble but premature attempt of mediaeval Catholicism. . . .

The regenerating doctrine cannot do its work without adherents; in what quarter should we hope to find them? Now, with individual exceptions of great value, we cannot expect the adhesion of any of the upper classes in society. They are all more or less under the influence of baseless metaphysical theories, and of aristocratic self-seeking. They are absorbed in blind political agitation and in disputes for the possession of the useless remnants of the old theological and military system. Their action only tends to prolong the revolutionary state indefinitely, and can never result in true social renovation.

Whether we regard its intellectual character or its social objects, it is certain that Positivism must look elsewhere for support. It will find a welcome in those classes only whose good sense has been left unimpaired by our vicious system of education, and whose generous sympathies are allowed to develop themselves freely. It is among women, therefore, and among the working classes that the heartiest supporters of the new doctrine will be found. It is intended, indeed, ultimately for all classes of society. But it will never gain much real influence over the higher ranks till it is forced upon their notice by these powerful patrons. When the work of spiritual reorganization is completed, it is on them that its maintenance will principally depend; and so too, their combined aid is necessary for its commencement. Having but little influence in political government, they are the more likely to appreciate the need of a moral government, the special object of which it will be to protect them against the oppressive action of the temporal power.

. . . It is from the feminine aspect only that human life, whether individually or collectively considered, can really be comprehended as a whole. For the only basis on which a system really embracing all the requirements of life can be formed, is the subordination of intellect to social feeling: a subordination which we find directly represented in the womanly type of character, whether regarded in its personal or social relations. . . .

. . . The great object which Positivism sets before us individually and socially, is the endeavour to become more perfect. The highest importance is attached therefore to the imaginative faculties, because in every sphere with which they deal they stimulate the sense of perfection. Limited as my explanations in this work must be, I shall be able to show that Positivism, while opening out a new and wide field for art, supplies in the same spontaneous way new means of expression.

I shall thus have sketched with some detail the true character of the regenerating doctrine. All its principal aspects will have been considered. Beginning with its philosophical basis, I pass by natural transitions to its political purpose; thence to its action upon the people, its influence with women, and lastly, to its esthetic power. In concluding this work, which is but the introduction to a larger treatise, I have only to speak of the conception which unites all these various aspects. As summed up in the positivist motto, *Love, Order, Progress,* they lead us to the conception of Humanity, which implicitly involves and gives new force to each of them. Rightly interpreting this conception, we view Positivism at last as a complete and consistent whole. The subject will naturally lead us to speak in general terms of the future progress of social regeneration, as far as the history of the past enables us to foresee it. The movement originates in France, and is limited at first to the great family of Western nations. I shall show that it will afterwards extend, in accordance with definite laws, to the rest of the white race, and finally to the other two great races of man.

# THE EVOLUTION OF SEXUAL DIFFERENCE

## The Argument for Equality

*In his speech before Parliament arguing for the franchise for women, John Stuart Mill (1806–1873) rejected the idea that women are innately inferior to men. For Mill the issue was one of education and legal rights, which women had been unfairly denied.*

### From John Stuart Mill. *The Subjection of Women*

The social subordination of women thus stands out an isolated fact in modern social institutions; a solitary breach of what has become their fundamental law; a single relic of an old world of thought and practice exploded in everything else, but retained in the one thing of most universal interest. . . .

The least that can be demanded is, that the question should not be considered as prejudged by existing fact and existing opinion, but open to discussion on its merits, as a question of justice and expediency; the decision on this, as on any of the other social arrangements of mankind, depending on what an enlightened estimate of tendencies and consequences may show to be most advantageous to humanity in general, without distinction of sex.

Neither does it avail anything to say that the *nature* of the two sexes adapts them to their present functions and position, and renders these appropriate to them. Standing on the ground of common sense and the constitution of the human mind, I deny that anyone knows, or can know, the nature of the two sexes, as long as they have only been seen in their present relation to one another. If men had ever been found in society without women, or women without men, or if there had been a society of men and women in which the women were not under the control of the men, something might have been positively known about the mental and moral differences which may be inherent in the nature of each. What is now called the nature of women is an eminently artificial thing—the result of forced repression in some directions, unnat-

From John Stuart Mill, *The Subjection of Women* (New York: F. Stokes Co., 1911), pp. 42–51, 54.

ural stimulation in others. It may be asserted without scruple, that no other class of dependents have had their character so entirely distorted from its natural proportions by their relation with their masters; for, if conquered and slave races have been, in some respects, more forcibly repressed, whatever in them has not been crushed down by an iron heel has generally been let alone, and if left with any liberty of development it has developed itself according to its own laws; but in the case of women, a hot-house and stove cultivation has always been carried on of some of the capabilities of their nature, for the benefit and pleasure of their masters. Then, because certain products of the general vital force sprout luxuriantly and reach a great development in this heated atmosphere and under this active nurture and watering, while other shoots from the same root, which are left outside in the wintry air, with ice purposely heaped all round them, have a stunted growth, and some are burnt off with fire and disappear; men, with that inability to recognize their own work which distinguishes the unanalytic mind, indolently believe that the tree grows of itself in the way they have made it grow, and that it would die if one-half of it were not kept in a vapor-bath and the other half in the snow.

Of all difficulties which impede the progress of thought, and the formation of well-grounded opinions on life and social arrangements, the greatest is now the unspeakable ignorance and inattention of mankind in respect to the influences which form human character. Whatever any portion of the human species now are, or seem to be, such, it is supposed, they have a natural tendency to be: even when the most elementary knowledge of the circumstances in which they have been placed, clearly points out the causes that made them what they are.

. . . Because women, as is often said, care nothing about politics except their personalities, it is supposed that the general good is naturally less interesting to women than to men. History, which is now so much better understood than formerly, teaches another lesson: if only by showing the extraordinary susceptibility of human nature to external influences, and the extreme variableness of those of its manifestations which are supposed to be most universal and uniform. But in history, as in traveling, men usually see only what they already had in their own minds; and few learn much from history, who do not bring much with them to its study.

Hence, in regard to that most difficult question, what are the natural differences between the two sexes—a subject on which it is impossible in the present state of society to obtain complete and correct knowledge—while almost everybody dogmatizes upon it, almost all neglect and make light of the only means by which any partial insight can be obtained into it. This is, an analytic study of the most important department of psychology, the laws of the influence of circumstances on character. For, however great and apparently ineradicable the moral and intellectual differences between men and women might be, the evidence of there being natural differences could only be negative. Those only could be inferred to be natural which could not possibly be artificial—the residuum, after deducting every characteristic of either sex which can admit of being explained from education or external circumstances. The profoundest knowledge of the laws of the formation of character is indispensable to entitle anyone to affirm even that there is any difference, much more what the difference is, between the two sexes considered as moral and rational beings; and since no one, as yet, has that knowledge (for there is hardly any subject which, in proportion to its importance, has been so little studied), no one is thus far entitled to any positive opinion on the subject. . . .

Even the preliminary knowledge, what the differences between the sexes now are, apart from all question as to how they are made what they are, is still in the crudest and most incomplete state. Medical practitioners and physiologists have ascertained, to some extent, the differences in bodily constitution; and this is an important element to the psychologist; but hardly any medical practitioner is a psychologist. Respecting the mental characteristics of women, their observations are of no more worth than those of common men. It is a subject on which nothing final can be known, so long as those who alone can really know it, women themselves, have given but little testimony, and that little, mostly suborned. . . .

. . . We may safely assert that the knowledge which men can acquire of women, even as they have been and are, without reference to what they might be, is wretchedly imperfect and superficial, and always will be so, until women themselves have told all that they have to tell.

# The Argument for Inequality

*In 1889, the biologists Patrick Geddes and J. Arthur Thompson applied evolutionary theory to explain the psychological and social differences between men and women. These differences, they insisted, were rooted in biological necessity.*

## From Patrick Geddes and J. Arthur Thompson. *The Evolution of Sex*

Without multiplying instances, a review of the animal kingdom, or a perusal of Darwin's pages, will amply confirm the conclusion that on

From Patrick Geddes and J. Arthur Thompson, *The Evolution of Sex* (London: Walter Scott, Ltd., 1895), pp. 17–19, 25–27, 267–271.

an average the females incline to passivity, the males to activity. In higher animals, it is true that the contrast shows rather in many little ways than in any one striking difference of habit, but even in the human species the contrast is recognised. Every one will admit that strenuous spasmodic bursts of activity characterise men, especially in youth, and among the less civilised races; while patient continuance, with less violent expenditure of energy, is as generally associated with the work of women. . . .

To the above contrast of general habit, two other items may be added, on which accurate observation is still unfortunately very restricted. In some cases the body temperature, which is an index to the pitch of the life, is distinctly lower in the females, as has been noted in cases so widely separate as the human species, insects, and plants. In many cases, furthermore, the longevity of the females is much greater. Such a fact as that women pay lower insurance premiums than do men, is often popularly accounted for by their greater immunity from accident; but the greater normal longevity on which the actuary calculates, has, as we begin to see, a far deeper and constitutional explanation. . . .

We are now in a better position to criticise Mr. Darwin's theory. On his view, males are stronger, handsomer, or more emotional, because ancestral forms happened to become so in a slight degree. In other words, the reward of breeding success gradually perpetuated and perfected a casual advantage. According to the present view, males are stronger, handsomer, or more emotional, simply because they are males,—i.e., of more active physiological habit than their mates. In phraseology which will presently become more intelligible and concrete, the males live at a loss, are more *katabolic*,—disruptive changes tending to preponderate in the sum of changes in their living matter or protoplasm. The females, on the other hand, live at a profit, are more *anabolic*,—constructive processes predominating in their life, whence indeed the capacity of bearing offspring.

No one can dispute that the nutritive, vegetative, or self-regarding processes within the plant or animal are opposed to the reproductive, multiplying, or species-regarding processes, as income to expenditure, or as building up to breaking down. But within the ordinary nutritive or vegetative functions of the body, there is necessarily a continuous antithesis between two sets of processes,—constructive and destructive metabolism. The contrast between these two processes is seen throughout nature, whether in the alternating phases of cell life, or of activity and repose, or in the great antithesis between growth and reproduction; and it is this same contrast which we recognise as the fundamental difference between male and female. The proof of this will run through the work, but our fundamental thesis may at once be roughly enuciated in a diagrammatic expression:

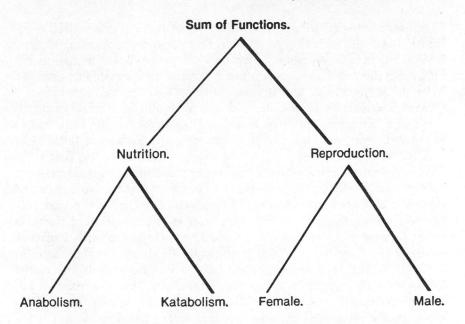

**Sum of Functions.**

Nutrition.

Reproduction.

Anabolism.

Katabolism.

Female.

Male.

Here the sum-total of the functions are divided into nutritive and reproductive, the former into anabolic and katabolic processes, the latter into male and female activities,—so far with all physiologists, without exception or dispute. Our special theory lies, however, in suggesting the parallelism of the two sets of processes,—the male reproduction is associated with preponderating katabolism, and the female with relative anabolism. In terms of this thesis, therefore, both primary and secondary sexual characters express the fundamental physiological bias characteristic of either sex. . . .

We have seen that a deep difference in constitution expresses itself in the distinctions between male and female, whether these be physical or mental. The differences may be exaggerated or lessened, but to obliterate them it would be necessary to have all the evolution over again on a new basis. What was decided among the prehistoric Protozoa cannot be annulled by Act of Parliament. In this mere outline we cannot of course do more than indicate the relation of the biological differences between the sexes to the resulting psychological and social differentiations; . . . We must insist upon the biological considerations underlying the relation of the sexes, which have been too much discussed by contemporary writers of all schools, as if the known facts of sex did not exist at all. . . .

The old view of the subjection of women was not, in fact, so much of tyranny as it seemed, but roughly tended to express the average division of labour; of course hardships were frequent, but these have been exaggerated. The absolute ratification of this by law and religion was merely of a piece with the whole order of belief and practice, in which men crushed themselves still more than their mates. Being absolute, however, such theories had to be overthrown, and the application of the idea of equality, which had done such good service in demolishing the established castes, was a natural and serviceable one. We have above traced the development of this, however, and it is now full time to re-emphasise, this time of course with all scientific relativity instead of a dogmatic authority, the biological factors of the case, and to suggest their possible service in destroying the economic fallacies at present so prevalent, and still more towards reconstituting that complex and sympathetic co-operation between the differentiated sexes in and around which all progress past or future must depend. Instead of men and women merely labouring to produce things as the past economic theories insisted, or competing over the distribution of them, as we at present think so important, a further swing of economic theory will lead us round upon a higher spiral to the direct organic facts. So it is not for the sake of production or distribution, of self-interest or mechanism, or any other idol of the economists, that the male organism organises the climax of his life's struggle and labour, but for his mate; as she, and then he, also for their little ones. Production is for consumption; the species is its own highest, its sole essential product. The social order will clear itself, as it comes more in touch with biology. . . .

That men should have greater cerebral variability and therefore more originality, while women have greater stability and therefore more "common sense," are facts both consistent with the general theory of sex and verifiable in common experience. The woman, conserving the effects of past variations, has what may be called the greater integrating intelligence; the man, introducing new variations, is stronger in differentiation. The feminine passivity is expressed in greater patience, more open-mindedness, greater appreciation of subtle details, and consequently what we call more rapid intuition. The masculine activity lends a greater power of maximum effort, of scientific insight, or cerebral experiment with impressions, and is associated with an unobservant or impatient disregard of minute details, but with a stronger grasp of generalities. Man thinks more, women feels more. He discovers more, but remembers less; she is more receptive, and less forgetful.

# THE MOTOR OF HISTORY

## The Pursuit of Happiness and Liberty of Thought

*John Stuart Mill explains the principles of utilitarianism and of liberalism in the following excerpts.*

## From John Stuart Mill. *Utilitarianism (1861)*

The creed which accepts as the foundation of morals, Utility, or the Greatest Happiness Principle, holds that actions are right in proportion as they tend to promote happiness, wrong as they tend to produce the reverse of happiness. By happiness is intended pleasure, and the absence of pain; by unhappiness, pain, and the privation of pleasure. To give a clear view of the moral standard set up by the theory, much more requires to be said; in particular, what things it includes in the ideas of pain and pleasure; and to what extent this is left an open question. But these supplementary explanations do not affect the theory of life on which this theory of morality is grounded—namely, that pleasure, and freedom from pain, are the only things desirable as ends; and that all desirable things (which are as numerous in the utilitarian as in any other scheme) are desirable either for the pleasure inherent in themselves, or as means to the promotion of pleasure and the prevention of pain.

According to the Greatest Happiness Principle, as above explained, the ultimate end, with reference to and for the sake of which all other things are desirable (whether we are considering our own good or that of other people), is an existence exempt as far as possible from pain, and as rich as possible in enjoyments, both in point of quantity and quality; the test of quality, and the rule for measuring it against quantity, being the preference felt by those who in their opportunities of experience, to which must be added their habits of self-consciousness

From John Stuart Mill, *Utilitarianism, Liberty and Representative Government* (New York: E. P. Dutton, 1951), pp. 8, 14–17.

and self-observation, are best furnished with the means of comparison. This, being, according to the utilitarian opinion, the end of human action, is necessarily also the standard of morality; which may accordingly be defined, the rules and precepts for human conduct, by the observance of which an existence such as has been described might be, to the greatest extent possible, secured to all mankind; and not to them only, but, so far as the nature of things admits, to the whole sentient creation. . . .

. . . If by happiness be meant a continuity of highly pleasurable excitement, it is evident enough that this is impossible. A state of exalted pleasure lasts only moments, or in some cases, and with some intermission, hours or days, and is the occasional brilliant flash of enjoyment, not its permanent and steady flame. Of this the philosophers who have taught that happiness is the end of life were as fully aware as those who taunt them. The happiness which they meant was not a life of rapture; but moments of such, in an existence made up of few and transitory pains, many and various pleasures, with a decided predominance of the active over the passive, and having as the foundation of the whole, not to expect more from life than it is capable of bestowing. A life thus composed, to those who have been fortunate enough to obtain it, has always appeared worthy of the name of happiness. And such an existence is even now the lot of many, during some considerable portion of their lives. The present wretched education, and wretched social arrangements, are the only real hindrance to its being attainable by almost all. . . .

. . . When people who are tolerably fortunate in their outward lot do not find in life sufficient enjoyment to make it valuable to them, the cause generally is, caring for nobody but themselves. To those who have neither public nor private affections, the excitements of life are much curtailed, and in any case dwindle in value as the time approaches when all selfish interests must be terminated by death: while those who leave after them objects of personal affection, and especially those who have also cultivated a fellow-feeling with the collective interests of mankind, retain as lively an interest in life on the eve of death as in the vigour of youth and health. Next to selfishness, the principal cause which makes life unsatisfactory is want of mental cultivation. A cultivated mind—I do not mean that of a philosopher, but any mind to which the fountains of knowledge have been opened, and which has been taught, in any tolerable degree, to exercise its faculties—finds sources of inexhaustible interest in all that surrounds it; in the objects of nature, the achievements of art, the imaginations of poetry, the incidents of history, the ways of mankind, past and present, and their prospects in the future. It is possible, indeed, to become indifferent to all this, and that too without having exhausted a thousandth part of it; but only when one has had from the beginning no moral or human interest in these things, and has sought in them only the gratification of curiosity.

## From John Stuart Mill. *On Liberty (1859)*

When we consider either the history of opinion, or the ordinary conduct of human life, to what is it to be ascribed that the one and the other are no worse than they are? Not certainly to the inherent force of the human understanding; for, on any matter not self-evident, there are ninety-nine persons totally incapable of judging of it for one who is capable; and the capacity of the hundredth person is only comparative; for the majority of the eminent men of every past generation held many opinions now known to be erroneous, and did or approved numerous things which no one will now justify. Why is it, then, that there is on the whole a preponderance among mankind of rational opinions and rational conduct? If there really is this preponderance—which there must be unless human affairs are, and have always been, in an almost desperate state—it is owing to a quality of the human mind, the source of everything respectable in man either as an intellectual or as a moral being, namely, that his errors are corrigible. He is capable of rectifying his mistakes, by discussion and experience. Not by experience alone. There must be discussion, to show how experience is to be interpreted. Wrong opinions and practices gradually yield to fact and argument; but facts and arguments, to produce any effect on the mind, must be brought before it. Very few facts are able to tell their own story, without comments to bring out their meaning. The whole strength and value, then, of human judgment, depending on the one property, that it can be set right when it is wrong, reliance can be placed on it only when the means of setting it right are kept constantly at hand. . . .

. . . It is the opinions men entertain, and the feelings they cherish, respecting those who disown the beliefs they deem important, which makes this country not a place of mental freedom. For a long time past, the chief mischief of the legal penalties is that they strengthen the social stigma. It is the stigma which is really effective, and so effective is it, that the profession of opinions which are under the ban of society is much less common in England than is, in many other countries, the avowal of those which incur risk of judicial punishment. In respect to all persons but those whose pecuniary circumstances make them independent of the good will of other people, opinion, on this subject, is as efficacious as law; men might as well be imprisoned, as excluded from the means of earning their bread. Those whose bread is already se-

From John Stuart Mill, *Utilitarianism, Liberty and Representative Government* (New York: E. P. Dutton, 1951), pp. 107–108, 122–126.

cured, and who desire no favours from men in power, or from bodies of men, or from the public, have nothing to fear from the open avowal of any opinions, but to be ill-thought of and ill-spoken of, and this it ought not to require a very heroic mould to enable them to bear. . . . But though we do not now inflict so much evil on those who think differently from us as it was formerly our custom to do, it may be that we do ourselves as much evil as ever by our treatment of them. Socrates was put to death, but the Socratic philosophy rose like the sun in heaven, and spread its illumination over the whole intellectual firmament. Christians were cast to the lions, but the Christian church grew up a stately and spreading tree, overtopping the older and less vigorous growths, and stifling them by its shade. Our merely social intolerance kills no one, roots out no opinions, but induces men to disguise them, or to abstain from any active effort for their diffusion. With us, heretical opinions do not perceptibly gain, or even lose, ground in each decade or generation; they never blaze out far and wide, but continue to smoulder in the narrow circles of thinking and studious persons among whom they originate, without ever lighting up the general affairs of mankind with either a true or a deceptive light. And thus is kept up a state of things very satisfactory to some minds, because, without the unpleasant process of fining or imprisoning anybody, it maintains all prevailing opinions outwardly undisturbed, while it does not absolutely interdict the exercise of reason by dissentients afflicted with the malady of thought. A convenient plan for having peace in the intellectual world, and keeping all things going on therein very much as they do already. But the price paid for this sort of intellectual pacification is the sacrifice of the entire moral courage of the human mind. A state of things in which a large portion of the most active and inquiring intellects find it advisable to keep the general principles and grounds of their convictions within their own breasts, and attempt, in what they address to the public, to fit as much as they can of their own conclusions to premises which they have internally renounced, cannot send forth the open, fearless characters, and logical, consistent intellects who once adorned the thinking world. . . .

# Class Struggle

*For the German philosophers Karl Marx (1818–1883) and Friedrich Engels (1820–1895), the motor of history was not simple evolution, but conflict between social classes. Written in 1848, as revolutions swept Europe, the* Communist Manifesto *set forth the view of history of the First International and of socialist movements in the second half of the nineteenth century.*

# From Karl Marx and Friedrich Engels. *The Communist Manifesto (1848)*

The history of all hitherto existing society is the history of class struggles.

Freeman and slave, patrician and plebeian, lord and serf, guild-master and journeyman, in a word, oppressor and oppressed, stood in constant opposition to one another, carried on an uninterrupted, now hidden, now open fight, a fight that each time ended, either in a revolutionary reconstitution of society at large, or in the common ruin of the contending classes.

In the earlier epochs of history, we find almost everywhere a complicated arrangement of society into various orders, a manifold gradation of social rank. In ancient Rome we have patricians, knights, plebeians, slaves; in the Middle Ages, feudal lords, vassals, guild-masters, journeymen, apprentices, serfs; in almost all of these classes, again, subordinate gradations.

The modern bourgeois society that has sprouted from the ruins of feudal society has not done away with class antagonisms. It has but established new classes, new conditions of oppression, new forms of struggle in place of the old ones.

Our epoch, the epoch of the bourgeoisie, possesses, however, this distinctive feature: it has simplified the class antagonisms. Society as a whole is more and more splitting up into two great hostile camps, into two great classes directly facing each other—bourgeoisie and proletariat.

The bourgeoisie, historically, has played a most revolutionary part.

The bourgeoisie, wherever it has got the upper hand, has put an end to all feudal, patriarchal, idyllic relations. It has pitilessly torn asunder the motley feudal ties that bound man to his "natural superiors," and has left no other nexus between man and man than naked self-interest, than callous "cash payment." It has drowned the most heavenly ecstasies of religious fervour, of chivalrous enthusiasm, of philistine sentimentalism, in the icy water of egotistical calculation. It has resolved personal worth into exchange value, and in place of the numberless indefeasible chartered freedoms, has set up that single, unconscionable freedom—Free Trade. In one word, for exploitation, veiled by religious and political illusions, it has substituted naked, shameless, direct, brutal exploitation. . . .

In proportion as the bourgeoisie, i.e., capital, is developed, in the same proportion is the proletariat, the modern working class, developed—a class of labourers, who live only so long as they find work, and who find work only so long as their labour increases capital. These la-

From E. Burns, ed., *A Handbook of Marxism*, (New York: International Publishers Co., 1935), pp. 22–23, 25, 30, 32–36. Reprinted by permission of the publisher.

bourers, who must sell themselves piecemeal, are a commodity, like every other article of commerce, and are consequently exposed to all the vicissitudes of competition, to all the fluctuations of the market. . . .

But with the development of industry the proletariat not only increases in number; it becomes concentrated in greater masses, its strength grows, and it feels that strength more. The various interests and conditions of life within the ranks of the proletariat are more and more equalised, in proportion as machinery obliterates all distinctions of labour, and nearly everywhere reduces wages to the same low level. The growing competition among the bourgeois, and the resulting commercial crises, make the wages of the workers ever more fluctuating. The unceasing improvement of machinery, ever more rapidly developing, makes their livelihood more and more precarious; the collisions between individual workmen and individual bourgeois take more and more the character of collisions between two classes. Thereupon the workers begin to form combinations (trades' unions) against the bourgeois; they club together in order to keep up the rate of wages; they found permanent associations in order to make provision beforehand for these occasional revolts. Here and there the contest breaks into riots.

Now and then the workers are victorious, but only for a time. The real fruit of their battles lies, not in the immediate result, but in the ever expanding union of the workers. This union is helped on by the improved means of communication that are created by modern industry, and that place the workers of different localities in contact with one another. It was just this contact that was needed to centralise the numerous local struggles, all of the same character, into one national struggle between classes. . . .

Of all the classes that stand face to face with the bourgeoisie to-day, the proletariat alone is a really revolutionary class. The other classes decay and finally disappear in the face of modern industry; the proletariat is its special and essential product. . . .

All previous historical movements were movements of minorities, or in the interest of minorities. The proletarian movement is the self-conscious, independent movement of the immense majority, in the interest of the immense majority. The proletariat, the lowest stratum of our present society, cannot stir, cannot raise itself up, without the whole superincumbent strata of official society being sprung into the air.

Though not in substance, yet in form, the struggle of the proletariat with the bourgeoisie is at first a national struggle. The proletariat of each country must, of course, first of all settle matters with its own bourgeoisie. . . .

The essential condition for the existence and for the sway of the bourgeois class is the formation and augmentation of capital; the condition for capital is wage-labour. Wage-labour rests exclusively on competition between the labourers. The advance of industry, whose involuntary promoter is the bourgeoisie, replaces the isolation of the labourers, due to competition, by their revolutionary combination, due to association. The development of modern industry, therefore, cuts from under its feet the very foundation on which the bourgeoisie produces and appropriates products. What the bourgeoisie therefore produces, above all, are its own grave-diggers. Its fall and the victory of the proletariat are equally inevitable.

# X

# STATE BUILDING AND IMPERIALIST EXPANSION

*DURING THE 1860s and '70s small states and territories consolidated into larger nation-states. Different ideas of nationhood spurred on these political movements. Some nationalists insisted that a common cultural heritage or language or history provided the foundation for political union. Others cited common beliefs or simply geography as the prerequisite for nationhood. Whatever the differences in ideas, the process of nation building was the same. As the examples of Italy, Austria-Hungary, and Germany show, the process involved skillful diplomatic negotiations and the use of force in war.*

*Once united, the new nation-states and the older powers, such as France and Britain, competed for territory in Africa, Asia, and the Pacific Islands. By 1900, the Western nations had divided most of the world among themselves. Colonies were either conquered, acquired as protectorates, or developed from trading concessions. Westerners attempted to impose their religious and political practices, as well as their technology and economic beliefs on the peoples they ruled.*

*Imperialism had its defenders throughout the Western world, those who argued that "civilization" was being brought to "savages." Increasingly, too, it had its critics, those who deemed imperialist expansion an unjust exploitation of the colonial countries, their resources, culture, and people, and who saw in competition among imperial powers the danger of world-wide war.*

# VARIETIES OF NATIONALISM

## Cultural Nationalism

*In his book, Nikolai Danilevsky (1822–1885) argued that Slav civilization was unified by common religious and historical traditions and was superior to other Western nations. Danilevsky offered his cultural arguments as the basis for a program of political struggle and eventual nationhood for the Slav peoples, under Russian leadership.*

### From Nikolai Danilevsky. *Russia and Europe: An Inquiry into the Cultural and Political Relations of the Slav World and of the Germano-Latin World (1869)*

Only a false concept of the general development of the relationship of the national to the pan-human, a concept incompatible with the real principles of the systematization of scientific-natural phenomena, as well as with so-called progress, could lead to the confusion of European or Germano-Roman civilization with universal civilization. Only such a concept could produce the pernicious delusion of Westernism, which fails to admit the close affinity between Russia and the Slav world, or the historical meaning of the latter, and assigns to us and our brothers the pitiful, insignificant role of imitators of the West. Such a delusion deprives us of the hope for any cultural significance, i.e., for a great historical future.

I attempted to develop this theoretical approach and to supplement it with indicators about the main differences between the Slavs and the Germano-Roman cultural-historical types, and about the fatal predicament to which this Westernization or Europeanization has led us, and the extent to which it is the cause of the disease from which Russia's social body suffers, a disease which is the source of all our social ills. Only historical events can remedy this disease and raise the spirit of our society, suffering from spiritual decay and abasement. The cure is possible and probable, because so far the disease has luckily penetrated

From Hans Kohn, ed., *The Mind of Modern Russia: Historical and Political Thought of Russia's Great Age* (New Brunswick, N.J.: Rutgers University Press, 1955), pp. 195–196, 200–203, 208–211. Copyright © 1955 by The Trustees of Rutgers College in New Jersey. Reprinted by permission of the publisher.

only the surface of the social structure. We can see such an event, or rather a whole series of events, endowed with a healthy dynamism, in the latest phase of the struggle known as the [Middle] Eastern question, whose origins are rooted in the general course of universal historical development. This struggle must shortly stamp its imprint upon an entire historical period  The importance of this inevitably approaching struggle forces us to try to understand the objections raised against the only decision useful to the Slav world—the full political liberation of all the Slav peoples and the formation of a Pan-Slav union under the hegemony of Russia. The Pan-Slav union will guarantee our success in this struggle. . . .

And now let us turn to the Slav world, and chiefly to Russia, its only independent representative, in order to examine the results and the promises of this world, a world still only at the beginning of its cultural-historical life. We must examine it from the viewpoint of the above four foci of reference: religion, culture, politics, and socio-economic structure, in order to elucidate what we rightfully expect as well as hope from the Slav cultural-historical type.

Religion constituted the most essential element of ancient Russian life, and at the present time, the overwhelming spiritual interest of the ordinary Russian is also involved in it; in truth, one cannot but wonder at the ignorance and the impertinence of these people who could insist (to gratify their fantasies) on the religious indifference of the Russian people.

From an objective, factual viewpoint, the Russian and the majority of Slav peoples became, with the Greeks, the chief guardians of the living tradition of religious truth. Orthodoxy, and in this way they continued the high calling, which was the destiny of Israel and Byzantium: to be the chosen people. . . .

We have already pointed to the special character of the acceptance of Christianity by Russia, not through subjection to a culturally higher Christian nation, nor through political supremacy over a nation, nor by way of an active religious propaganda—but out of an inner discontent, a dissatisfaction with paganism, and out of the unfettered search for truth. . . . The religious aspect of the cultural activity belongs to the Slav cultural type and to Russia in particular; it is its inalienable achievement, founded on the psychology of its people and on its guardianship of religious truth.

If we turn to the political aspect and to the extent to which the Slav peoples have manifested their ability to set up their body politic, we find the situation at first sight discouraging, because all the Slav peoples, with the exception of Russia, either did not succeed in establishing independent states, or were incapable of preserving their independence. The Slavophobes conclude from this that the Slav peoples are politically incapable. Such a conclusion cannot stand up if we face the facts as they are. These facts tell us that the vast majority of the

Slav tribes (at least two-thirds of them, if not more) have built a huge, continuous state, which has already had an existence of a thousand years and is all the time growing in strength and power in spite of the storms which it has had to weather during its long historical life. This one fact of the first magnitude demonstrates the political sense of the Slavs or at least of a significant majority of them. . . .

Whatever the future may bring we are entitled, on the evidence of the past alone, to consider the Slavs among the most gifted families of the human race in political ability. Here we may turn our attention to the special character of this political ability and show how it manifested itself during the growth of the Russian state. The Russians do not send out colonists to create new political societies, as the Greeks did in antiquity or the English in modern times. Russia does not have colonial possessions, like Rome or like England. The Russian state from early Muscovite times on has been Russia herself, gradually, irresistibly spreading on all sides, settling neighboring nonsettled territories, and assimilating into herself and into her national boundaries foreign populations. . . .

*[After examining Russian political history, Danilevsky goes on to look at culture.]*

Scientific and artistic activity can thrive only under conditions of leisure, of an overflow of forces that remain free from daily toil. Could much leisure be left over among Russians and Slavs? . . . All these considerations fully answer, it seems to me, the question why until now Russia and the other Slav countries could not occupy a respected position in purely cultural activities. . . . But indications of these aptitudes, of these spiritual forces, which are necessary for brilliant achievements in the fields of science and art are now indisputably present among the Slav peoples in spite of all the unfavorable conditions of their life; and, consequently, we are justified in expecting that with a change in these conditions, these peoples will bring forth remarkable creations. . . .

The Slav cultural type has already produced enough examples of artistic and, to a lesser degree, scientific achievements to allow us to conclude that it has attained a significant degree of development in these fields. The relative youth of the race and the concentration of all its forces upon other, more urgent types of activity have not, until now, given the Slavs the opportunity of acquiring cultural significance, in the exact meaning of the phrase. This should not embarrass us; rather, it points to the right path in our development. As long as there is no strong foundation, we cannot and we must not think of the erection of a durable edifice; we can only set up temporary buildings, which cannot be expected to display the talents of the builder in every respect. The political independence of the race is the indispensable foundation of culture, and consequently all the Slav forces must be directed towards this goal. Independence is indispensable in two respects: without the consciousness of Slav racial unity, as distinct from other races, an independent culture is impossible; and without fruitful interaction between the Slav peoples, liberated from foreign powers and from their national divisions, diversity and richness of culture are impossible. . . .

Thus, on the basis of our analysis of the preceding cultural-historical types and of the peculiarities of the Slav world, we can maintain the fundamental hope that the Slav cultural-historical type will, for the first time in history, accomplish a synthesis of all aspects of cultural activity—aspects which were elaborated by its precursors on the historical scene, either in isolation or in incomplete union. We may hope that the Slav type will be the first to embody all four basic cultural activities, the religious, the political, the esthetic-scientific, and the socio-economic. . . .

Two sources on the banks of the ancient Nile begin the main flow of universal history. One, heavenly and divine, has reached Kiev and Moscow with unsullied purity by way of Palestine and Tsargrad [Constantinople]; the other, earthly and human, divided itself into two main streams, that of esthetic-scientific culture and that of politics, which flowed through Athens, Alexandria, and Rome into Europe, drying up temporarily, then enriching themselves with new and ever more abundant waters. On Russian soil a new fountainhead, a fourth river, originates, providing the popular masses with a just socio-economic structure. These four streams will unite on the wide plains of Slavdom into a mighty sea.

## Liberal Nationalism

*The French historian Ernest Renan (1823–1892) offered his definition of a nation in a lecture given at the Sorbonne in 1882. Renan's piece embodies the doctrine of liberal nationalism.*

### From Ernest Renan. *What Is a Nation?*

I intend to analyze with you an idea which seems simple and clear but which lends itself to the most dangerous misunderstandings. . . . In our day one commits a serious error: one confounds nation and race, and one attributes to ethnographical or rather linguistic groups a sovereignty analogous to that of real peoples. Let us try for some precision in these difficult questions where the slightest confusion about the

From Hans Kohn, *Nationalism: Its Meaning and History* (Princeton, N.J.: Van Nostrand, 1965), pp. 136–140. Reprinted by permission of the Estate of Hans Kohn.

meaning of words, which are at the basis of our reasoning, can produce the most disastrous errors. . . .

Since the end of the Roman Empire, or rather since the dissolution of the empire of Charlemagne, Western Europe seems to be divided into nations. At certain times some of them have sought to exercise a hegemony over the others, without being able to arrive there in an enduring fashion. What Charles V, Louis XIV, Napoleon I could not achieve, nobody, probably, will be able to do in the future. The establishment of a new Roman Empire or a new empire of Charlemagne has become impossible. The division of Europe is too great for an attempt at universal domination not to provoke with speed a coalition which puts the ambitious nation back within its natural limits. . . .

Nations in this sense are something new in history. . . . What characterizes these various nations is the fusion of the populations which compose them. Nothing similar exists in Turkey, where the Turk, the Slav, the Greek, the Armenian, the Arab, the Syrian, the Kurd, are today as distinct as they were on the day of the conquest. . . . Even by the tenth century all the inhabitants of France are French. The idea of a difference of races in the population of France has completely disappeared with the French writers and poets after Hugues Capet. The distinction between the noble and the serf is highly emphasized, but this distinction is in no way an ethnic distinction. . . .

These great laws of the history of Western Europe become obvious if we contrast them with the events in Eastern Europe. Under the crown of St. Stephan, the Magyars and the Slavs have remained as distinct today as they were 800 years ago. In Bohemia, the Czech and the German elements are superimposed as water and oil in a glass. The Turkish policy of separating nationalities according to religion has had the most serious consequences: it caused the ruin of the Middle East. For, the essential element of a nation is that all its individuals must have many things in common, but must also have forgotten many things. Every French citizen must have forgotten the night of St. Bartholemew and the massacres in the thirteenth century in the South. There are not ten families in France who could prove their Frankish origin, and such a proof would be deficient because thousands of unknown mixed breedings could derange all genealogical systems. . . .

According to certain political theorists, the nation is above all the work of a dynasty representing an ancient conquest which was first accepted and later forgotten by the mass of the people. . . . Has such a law absolute validity? Certainly not. Switzerland and the United States, which arose as agglomerations of successive additions, have no dynastic basis. . . . One must therefore admit that a nation can exist without the dynastic principle, and even that nations which were formed by dynasties can separate themselves from them without losing their identity thereby. Against dynastic rights, the right of nationality has emerged. On what tangible fact could it be based?

I. Some people say that it could be based upon race. The artificial divisions created by the feudal past, by princely marriages and diplomatic congresses, have lapsed. What remains firm and permanent is the race of the people. It constitutes a legitimate right. According to this theory the Germans have the right to take back the scattered members of the Germanic family, even if these members do not seek annexation. Thus one creates a primordial right analogous to that of the divine right of kings. This is a very great fallacy whose dominance would ruin European civilization. . . .

To base one's policy on an ethnographical analysis means to establish it on a chimera. The noblest countries—England, France, Italy,—are those where the blood is most mixed. Germany is no exception. . . . Race as we historians understand it is something which is formed by history and undone by history. The study of race is of great importance for the study of the history of mankind, but it has no place in politics. . . . Will the Germans, who have raised the banner of ethnography so high, not see one day the Slavs analyze the names of the villages of Saxony and of Lusatia, seek the traces of populations long dead, and ask for an account of the massacres and the mass enslavement to which the Germans under their Ottonian emperors subjected their ancestors? It is good for all of us to know how to forget.

II. What we have said of race is as true of language. Language may invite us to unite, but it does not compel us to do so. . . . Languages are historical formations, which tell us very little about the race of those who speak them. In any event, they should not fetter human freedom when it concerns the fate of the group with whom we wish to unite for life or death. . . .

One abandons the great air which one breathes in the large camp of humanity in order to shut oneself up in conventicles of compatriots. Nothing could be worse for the mind; nothing could be more troublesome for civilization. Let us not abandon the fundamental principle that man is a rational and moral being before he is penned up in this or that language, before he is a member of this or that race, before he adheres to this or that culture. Above the French, German, or Italian culture, there is a human culture. Look at the great men of the Renaissance. They were neither French, Italian or German. By their intimacy with the spirit of antiquity, they had found the secret of the true education of the human mind, and they devoted themselves to it with all their heart. How well they acted!

III. Nor could religion offer a sufficient foundation for the establishment of a modern nation. . . . One can be a Frenchman, an Englishman or a German, by being a Catholic, a Protestant, a Jew or an agnostic. Religion has become something individual; it concerns the conscience of each person. . . .

IV. The community of interests is certainly a strong tie among men. But are interests sufficient to create a nation? I do not believe it. The community of interests creates commercial treaties. Nationality is something sentimental too; it is body and soul at the same time; a custom-union is not a fatherland.

V. Geography, or as one says, the natural frontiers, certainly plays a considerable part in the division of nations. . . . Can we say, however, as certain people believe, that the frontiers of a nation are marked on the map, and such a nation has the right to adjudicate to itself what it regards as necessary to round off its contours, to reach some mountain or some river, to which one credits a kind of a priori quality? I do not know of any doctrine which would be more arbitrarily disastrous. With it one can justify all violence. One speaks of strategic reasons. Nothing is absolute; clearly, certain concessions must be made to necessity. But these concessions should not go too far. Otherwise everybody would demand what is strategically convenient to him, and a war without end would ensue. . . .

A nation is a soul, a spiritual principle . . . A nation is a great solidarity, created by the sentiment of the sacrifices which have been made and of those which one is disposed to make in the future. It presupposes a past; but it resumes itself in the present by a tangible fact: the consent, the clearly expressed desire to continue life in common. The existence of a nation is a plebiscite of every day, as the existence of the individual is a perpetual affirmation of life. I well know that this is less metaphysical than the divine right and less brutal than the alleged historical right . . . We have driven the metaphysical and theological abstractions from politics. What remains? Man remains, his desires and his wants. You will object to me that the secession and eventual crumbling of nations are the consequences of a system which praises the old organic entities at the mercy of the will of frequently unenlightened peoples. Clearly, in matters like these, no principles should be carried to excess. Principles of this kind can be applied only in a very general way. Human will changes, but what does not change here on earth? Nations are nothing eternal. They had a beginning, they will have an end. The European confederation will probably replace them. But this is not the law of the century in which we live. At present, the existence of nations is good and even necessary. Their existence is a guarantee of liberty which would be lost if the world had only one law and one master. . . .

## Political Nationalism

*The German historian Heinrich von Treitschke (1834–1896) saw the state, created and maintained by force, as the way to protect and embody the nation.*

From Heinrich von Treitschke, *Politics,* Blanche Dugdale and Torben de Bille, trans. (London and Basingstoke: Macmillan, 1916), Vol. 1, pp. 3, 13, 22–26, 28–30. Reprinted by permission of the publisher.

# From Heinrich von Treitschke. *Politics*

The State is the people, legally united as an independent entity. By the word "people" we understand briefly a number of families permanently living side by side. This definition implies that the State is primordial and necessary, that it is as enduring as history, and no less essential to mankind than speech. . . . We . . . must deal here with man as an historical being, and we can only say that creative political genius is inherent in him, and that the State, like him, subsists from the beginning. The attempt to present it as something artificial, following upon a natural condition, has fallen completely into discredit. We lack all historical knowledge of a nation without a constitution. Wherever Europeans have penetrated they have found some form of State organization, rude though it may have been. . . .

When we assert the evolution of the State to be something inherently necessary, we do not thereby deny the power of genius or of creative Will in history. For it is of the essence of political genius to be national. There has never been an example of the contrary. . . .

Further, if we examine our definition of the State as "the people legally united as an independent entity," we find that it can be more briefly put thus: "The State is the public force for Offence and Defence." It is, above all, Power which makes its will to prevail, it is not the totality of the people as Hegel assumes in his deification of it. The nation is not entirely comprised in the State, but the State protects and embraces the people's life, regulating its external aspects on every side. It does not ask primarily for opinion, but demands obedience, and its laws must be obeyed, whether willingly or no. . . .

The State is not an Academy of Arts. If it neglects its strength in order to promote the idealistic aspirations of man, it repudiates its own nature and perishes. This is in truth for the State equivalent to the sin against the Holy Ghost, for it is indeed a mortal error in the State to subordinate itself for sentimental reasons to a foreign Power, as we Germans have often done to England.

Therefore the power of ideas in the life of the State is only limited. It is undoubtedly very great, but ideas by themselves do not move political forces. If they are to influence public life effectively they must find support in the vital economic interests of the people. . . .

We have described the State as an independent force. This pregnant theory of independence implies firstly so absolute a moral supremacy that the State cannot legitimately tolerate any power above its own, and secondly a temporal freedom entailing a variety of material resources adequate to its protection against hostile influences. Legal sovereignty, the State's complete independence of any other earthly power, is so rooted in its nature that it may be said to be its very standard and criterion.

The State is born in a community whenever a group or an individual has achieved sovereignty by imposing its will upon the whole body. . . .

For the notion of sovereignty must not be rigid, but flexible and relative, like all political conceptions. Every State, in treaty making, will limit its power in certain directions for its own sake. States which conclude treaties with each other thereby curtail their absolute authority to some extent. But the rule still stands, for every treaty is a voluntary curb upon the power of each, and all international agreements are prefaced by the clause "Rebus sic stantibus." No State can pledge its future to another. It knows no arbiter, and draws up all its treaties with this implied reservation. This is supported by the axiom that so long as international law exists all treaties lose their force at the very moment when war is declared between the contracting parties; moreover, every sovereign State has the undoubted right to declare war at its pleasure, and is consequently entitled to repudiate its treaties. Upon this constantly recurring alteration of treaties the progress of history depends; every State must take care that its treaties do not survive their effective value, lest another Power should denounce them by a declaration of war; for antiquated treaties must necessarily be denounced and replaced by others more consonant with circumstances.

It is clear that the international agreements which limit the power of a State are not absolute, but voluntary self-restrictions. Hence, it follows that the establishment of a permanent international Arbitration Court is incompatible with the nature of the State, which could at all events only accept the decision of such a tribunal in cases of second- or third-rate importance. When a nation's existence is at stake there is no outside Power whose impartiality can be trusted. Were we to commit the folly of treating the Alsace-Lorraine problem as an open question, by submitting it to arbitration, who would seriously believe that the award could be impartial? It is, moreover, a point of honour for a State to solve such difficulties for itself. International treaties may indeed become more frequent, but a finally decisive tribunal of the nations is an impossibility. The appeal to arms will be valid until the end of history, and therein lies the sacredness of war.

However flexible the conception of Sovereignty may be we are not to infer from that any self-contradiction, but rather a necessity to establish in what its pith and kernel consists. Legally it lies in the competence to define the limits of its own authority, and politically in the appeal to arms. An unarmed State, incapable of drawing the sword when it sees fit, is subject to one which wields the power of declaring war. To speak of a military suzerainty in time of peace obviously implies a *contradictio in adjecto*. A defenceless State may still be termed a Kingdom for conventional or courtly reasons, but science, whose first duty is accuracy, must boldly declare that in point of fact such a country no longer takes rank as a State.

This, then, is the only real criterion. The right of arms distinguishes the State from all other forms of corporate life, and those who cannot take up arms for themselves may not be regarded as States, but only as members of a federated constellation of States.

# THE UNIFICATION OF ITALY

*The next three documents illustrate aspects of Italian unification. Count Camillo Benso di Cavour (1810–1861), premier of Piedmont, sought the French emperor Napoleon III's aid in unifying the Italian states. His letter to Victor Emmanuel, king of Sardinia, after a secret meeting with Napoleon (July 24, 1858) shows the importance of diplomatic skills. Military conquest also helped unify the Italian nation. General Giuseppe Garibaldi (1807–1882) led his Red Shirts into Sicily and Naples. After they were conquered, the two states voted to join the northern federation. In March 1861, the Kingdom of Italy was proclaimed. In his address to parliament ten years later, Victor Emmanuel detailed the problems faced by the new nation.*

## Diplomacy

### From *Cavour's Letter to Victor Emmanuel (July 24, 1858)*

The ciphered letter which I sent Your Majesty from Plombières could give only a very incomplete idea of the long conversations I had with the Emperor. I believe you will be impatient to receive an exact and detailed narration. That is what I hasten to do having just left France, and I send it in a letter via M. Tosi, attaché at our legation in Berne.

As soon as I entered the Emperor's study, he raised the question which was the purpose of my journey. He began by saying that he had decided to support Piedmont with all his power in a war against Austria, provided that the war was undertaken for a nonrevolutionary end which could be justified in the eyes of diplomatic circles—and still more in the eyes of French and European public opinion.

Since the search for a plausible excuse presented our main problem before we could agree, I felt obliged to treat that question before any others. First I suggested that we could use the grievances occasioned by Austria's bad faith in not carrying out her commercial treaty. To this the Emperor answered that a petty commercial question could not be made the occasion for a great war designed to change the map of Europe. Then I proposed to revive the objections we had made at the Congress of Paris against the illegitimate extension of Austrian power in Italy: for instance, the treaty of 1847 between Austria and the Dukes of Parma and Modena; the prolonged Austrian occupation of the Romagna and the Legations; the new fortifications at Piacenza.

The Emperor did not like these pretexts. He observed that the

From Denis Mack Smith, ed. and trans., *The Making of Italy, 1796–1870* (New York: Walker and Co., 1968), pp. 238–242. Reprinted by permission of Denis Mack Smith.

grievances we put forward in 1856 had not been sufficient to make France and England intervene in our favor, and they would still not appear to justify an appeal to arms. "Besides," he added, "inasmuch as French troops are in Rome, I can hardly demand that Austria withdraw hers from Ancona and Bologna." This was a reasonable objection, and I therefore had to give up my second proposition; this was a pity, for it had a frankness and boldness which went perfectly with the noble and generous character of Your Majesty and the people you govern.

My position now became embarrassing because I had no other precise proposal to make. The Emperor came to my aid, and together we set ourselves to discussing each state in Italy, seeking grounds for war. It was very hard to find any. After we had gone over the whole peninsula without success, we arrived at Massa and Carrara, and there we discovered what we had been so ardently seeking. After I had given the Emperor a description of that unhappy country, of which he already had a clear enough idea anyway, we agreed on instigating the inhabitants to petition Your Majesty, asking protection and even demanding the annexation of the Duchies to Piedmont. This Your Majesty would decline, but you would take note of the Duke of Modena's oppressive policy and would address him a haughty and menacing note. The Duke, confident of Austrian support, would reply impertinently. Thereupon Your Majesty would occupy Massa, and the war could begin.

As it would be the Duke of Modena who would look responsible, the Emperor believes the war would be popular not only in France, but in England and the rest of Europe, because the Duke is considered, rightly or wrongly, the scapegoat of despotism. Besides, since he has not recognized any sovereign who has ruled in France since 1830, the Emperor need have less regard toward him than any other ruler.

Once we had settled this first question, the Emperor said: "Before going further we must consider two grave difficulties in Italy: the Pope and the King of Naples. I must treat both of them with some circumspection: the first, so as not to stir up French Catholics against me, the second so as to keep the sympathies of Russia, who makes it a point of honor to protect King Ferdinand."

I answered that, as for the Pope, it would be easy to keep him in possession of Rome by means of the French garrison there, while letting the provinces of the Romagna revolt. Since the Pope had been unwilling to follow advice over the Romagna, he could not complain if these provinces took the first occasion to free themselves from a detestable form of government which the Pope had stubbornly refused to reform. As for the King of Naples, there was no need to worry about him unless he took up the cause of Austria; but his subjects would be free to get rid of his paternal rule if the occasion offered.

This reply satisfied the Emperor, and we went on to the main question: what would be the objective of the war?

The Emperor readily agreed that it was necessary to drive the Austrians out of Italy once and for all, and to leave them without an inch of territory south of the Alps or west of the Isonzo. But how was Italy to be organized after that? After a long discussion, which I spare Your Majesty, we agreed more or less to the following principles, recognizing that they were subject to modification as the course of the war might determine. The valley of the Po, the Romagna, and the Legations would form a kingdom of Upper Italy under the House of Savoy. Rome and its immediate surroundings would be left to the Pope. The rest of the Papal States, together with Tuscany, would form a kingdom of central Italy. The Neapolitan frontier would be left unchanged. These four Italian states would form a confederation on the pattern of the German Bund, the presidency of which would be given to the Pope to console him for losing the best part of his estates.

This arrangement seemed to me fully acceptable. Your Majesty would be legal sovereign of the richest and most powerful half of Italy, and hence would in practice dominate the whole peninsula. . . .

After we had settled the fate of Italy, the Emperor asked me what France would get, and whether Your Majesty would cede Savoy and the County of Nice. I answered that Your Majesty believed in the principle of nationalities and realized accordingly that Savoy ought to be reunited with France; and that consequently you were ready to make this sacrifice, even though it would be extremely painful to renounce the country which had been the cradle of your family and whose people had given your ancestors so many proofs of affection and devotion. The question of Nice was different, because the people of Nice, by origin, language, and customs, were closer to Piedmont than France, and consequently their incorporation into the Empire would be contrary to that very principle for which we were taking up arms. The Emperor stroked his mustache several times, and merely remarked that these were for him quite secondary questions which we could discuss later.

Then we proceeded to examine how the war could be won, and the Emperor observed that we would have to isolate Austria so that she would be our sole opponent. That was why he deemed it so important that the grounds for war be such as would not alarm the other continental powers. Better still if they were also popular in England. He seemed convinced that what we had decided would fulfill this double purpose. The Emperor counts positively on England's neutrality; he advised me to make every effort to influence opinion in that country to compel the government (which is a slave to public opinion) not to side with Austria. He counts, too, on the antipathy of the Prince of Prussia toward the Austrians to keep Prussia from deciding against us. As for Russia, Alexander has repeatedly promised not to oppose Napoleon's Italian projects. Unless the Emperor is deluding himself, which I am not inclined to believe after all he told me, it would simply be a matter of a war between France and ourselves on one side and Austria on the other.

The Emperor nevertheless believes that, even reduced to these proportions, there remain formidable difficulties. There is no denying
that Austria is very strong. The wars of the first Empire were proof of
that. Napoleon Bonaparte had to fight her for fifteen years in Italy and
Germany; he had to destroy many of her armies, take away provinces
and subject her to crushing indemnities. But always he found her back
on the battlefield ready to take up the fight. And one is bound to recognize that, in the last of the wars of the Empire, at the terrible battle
of Leipzig, it was the Austrian battalions which contributed most to the
defeat of the French army. It will therefore take more than two or
three victorious battles in the valleys of the Po or Tagliamento before
Austria will evacuate Italy. We will have to penetrate to the heart of
the Empire and threaten Vienna itself before Austria will make peace
on our terms.

Success will thus require very considerable forces. The Emperor's
estimate is at least 300,000 men, and I think he is right. With 100,000
men we could surround the fortified places on the Mincio and Adige
and close the Tyrolean passes; 200,000 more will be needed to march
on Vienna by way of Carinthia and Styria. France would provide
200,000 men, Piedmont and the other Italian provinces 100,000. The
Italian contingent may seem little, but you must remember that
100,000 effective front-line soldiers will mean 150,000 under arms.

The Emperor seemed to me to have well-considered ideas on how to
make war, and on the role of each country. . . .

Once agreed on military matters, we equally agreed on the financial
question, and I must inform Your Majesty that this is what chiefly
preoccupies the Emperor. Nevertheless he is ready to provide us with
whatever munitions we need, and to help us negotiate a loan in Paris.
As for contributions from other Italian provinces in money and material, the Emperor believes we should insist on something, but use great
caution. All these questions which I here relate to you as briefly as possible were discussed with the Emperor from eleven o'clock in the
morning to three o'clock in the afternoon. At three the Emperor dismissed me but gave me another appointment at four o'clock to take a
drive with him.

# Conquest

## From Garibaldi's Report on the Conquest of Naples

Having reached the strait, it became necessary to cross it. To have rein-
stated Sicily in the great Italian family was certainly a glorious achievement. But what then? Were we, in compliance with diplomacy, to leave

From Christine Walsh, ed., Prologue: A Documentary History of Europe: 1846–
1960 (Australia: Cassell, 1968), pp. 96–97.

our country incomplete and maimed? What of the two Calabrias, and Naples, awaiting us with open arms? And the rest of Italy still enslaved by the foreigner and the priest? We were clearly bound to pass the strait, despite the utmost vigilance of the Bourbons and their adherents. . . .

Our entry into the great capital sounds more imposing than it was in reality. Accompanied by a small staff, I passed through the midst of the Bourbon troops still in occupation, who presented arms far more obsequiously than they did at that time to their own generals.

September 7th, 1860!—which of the sons of Parthenope will not remember that glorious day? On September 7th fell the abhorred dynasty which a great English statesman had called 'The curse of God', and on its ruins rose the sovereignty of the people, which, by some unhappy fatality, never lasts long.

. . . Though the Bourbon army was still in possession of the forts and the principal points of the city, whence they could easily have destroyed it, yet the applause and the impressive conduct of this great populace sufficed to ensure their harmlessness on September 7th, 1860.

I entered Naples with the whole of the southern army as yet a long way off in the direction of the Straits of Messina, the King of Naples having, on the previous day, quitted his palace to retire to Capua.

The royal nest, still warm, was occupied by the emancipators of the people, and the rich carpets of the royal palace were trodden by the heavy boots of the plebeian.

At Naples, as in all places we had passed through since crossing the strait, the populace were sublime in their enthusiastic patriotism, and the resolute tone assumed by them certainly had no small share in the brilliant results obtained.

Another circumstance very favourable to the national cause was the tacit consent of the Bourbon navy, which, had it been entirely hostile, could have greatly retarded our progress towards the capital. In fact, our steamers transported the divisions of the southern army along the whole Neapolitan coast without let or hindrance, which could not have been done in the face of any decided opposition on the part of the navy.

# Unification

## From *Victor Emmanuel's Address to Parliament (Rome, 1871)*

Senators and Deputies, gentlemen!

The work to which we consecrated our life is accomplished. After long trials of expiation Italy is restored to herself and to Rome. Here,

From Christine Walsh, ed., *Prologue: A Documentary History of Europe: 1846–1960* (Australia: Cassell, 1968), pp. 103–104.

where our people, after centuries of separation, find themselves for the first time solemnly reunited in the person of their representatives: here where we recognize the fatherland of our dreams, everything speaks to us of greatness; but at the same time it all reminds us of our duties. The joy that we experience must not let us forget them. . . .

We have proclaimed the separation of Church and State. Having recognized the absolute independence of the spiritual authority, we are convinced that Rome, the capital of Italy, will continue to be the peaceful and respected seat of the Pontificate. . . .

Economic and financial affairs, moreover, claim our most careful attention. Now that Italy is established, it is necessary to make it prosperous by putting in order its finances; we shall succeed in this only by persevering in the virtues which have been the source of our national regeneration. Good finances will be the means of re-enforcing our military organization. Our most ardent desire is for peace, and nothing can make us believe that it can be troubled. But the organization of the army and the navy, the supply of arms, the works for the defense of the national territory, demand long and profound study. . . .

Senators and deputies, a vast range of activity opens before you; the national unity which is today attained will have, I hope, the effect of rendering less bitter the struggles of parties, the rivalry of which will have henceforth no other end than the development of the productive forces of the nation.

I rejoice to see that our population already gives unequivocal proofs of its love of work. The economic awakening is closely associated with the political awakening. The banks multiply, as do the commercial institutions, the expositions of the products of art and industry, and the congresses of the learned. We ought, you and I, to favor this productive movement while giving to professional and scientific education more attention and efficiency, and opening to commerce new avenues of communication and new outlets.

The tunnel of Mont Cenis is completed; we are on the point of undertaking that of the St. Gotthard. The commercial route, which, crossing Italy, terminates at Brindisi and brings Europe near to India, will thus have three ways open to railway traffic across the Alps. The rapidity of the journeys, the facility of exchanges, will increase the amicable relations which already unite us to other nations, and will make more productive than ever the legitimate competition of labor and the national rivalry in advancing civilization.

A brilliant future opens before us. It remains for us to respond to the blessings of Providence by showing ourselves worthy of bearing among the nations the glorious names of Italy and Rome.

# THE HAPSBURG EMPIRE

## The Dual Monarchy

*After Austria was defeated in war by Prussia, it sought to strengthen its empire by securing Hungarian loyalty. Count von Beust negotiated the Compromise of 1867, which united the Austrian empire and the Kingdom of Hungary into a dual monarchy, ruled by the same Hapsburg monarch.*

### From *Memoirs of Count von Beust*

The dangers which Austria has to face are of a twofold nature. The first is presented by the tendency of her liberal-minded German population to gravitate towards that larger portion of the German-speaking people now represented by Prussia, Saxony, what was Hanover, Würtemberg, and Bavaria; the second is the diversity of language and race in the empire. Of Austria's large Slav population, the Poles have a natural craving for independence after having enjoyed and heroically fought for it for centuries; while the other nationalities are likely at a moment of dangerous crisis to develop pro-Russian tendencies. Everyone who has studied the German problem—which assumed an acute form in 1866, when I was Minister in Saxony—must feel that, setting aside the question of rivalry with France, which sooner or later will be decided at the point of the sword, it resolves itself simply into the question of political supremacy. The Germans, that is the majority of them, have been and are still anxious not to perpetuate the state of things typified by the German empire as constituted by Charles the Fifth. Bismarck's object is, so far as I know it, to consolidate Germany under one head, probably that of King William as Emperor. Germany has changed immensely in sentiment and policy since I was at Frankfort as Saxon Minister to the German Bund. The condition of affairs which then existed can never recur; and the action of Prussia in the Schleswig-Holstein question was the first practical demonstration of the underlying principle of Bismarck's policy, which means Germany for the Germans. . . .

 . . . The second danger I have . . . mentioned . . . presents a far

From *Memoirs of Friedrich Ferdinand Count von Beust* (London: Remington and Co., 1887), pp. xix–xxv.

more difficult problem. So long as Austria was a purely despotic State, and the Emperor ruled over it as an absolute monarch—Emperor in Vienna, King in Hungary and Bohemia, Ducal Prince in the other provinces of his vast empire—the local councils had a merely nominal existence, and the governors were there but to register the sovereign's Imperial will and to enforce it by arms if the necessity should arise. The revolutionary wave of 1848 swept over his territories as it did over those of other potentates; laws and decrees which the ignorance and apathy of his people had tolerated, if not approved, in the days of Maria Theresa and the monarchs who succeeded her, raised for the first time among the masses of the population objections and antipathies which generated the firm resolve in their minds to sweep the whole system away. The German element, then as now, took the initiative; but the feeble constitutional measures which were the outcome of popular strife and much bloodshed dwindled down year by year until but a semblance of constitutionalism remained. The comfortable and good-natured Austrian . . . soon forgot what had happened, and occupied himself more with his creature comforts and his dramatic performances than with the development of his constitutional liberties. And—which will show the difficulty of the position—the various nationalities of the empire preferred their servile condition to a state of things which on the very principle of Constitutional government would place all the component parts of the monarchy on an equality, and cause their representatives to meet in a common parliament on an equal footing. Now my object is to carry out a bloodless revolution . . . to show the various elements of this great empire that it is to the benefit of each of them to act in harmony with its neighbour, and that no Constitution can permanently exist unless every portion of the State is represented by it. But to this I have made one exception. Hungary is an ancient monarchy, more ancient as such than Austria proper. The kingdom of St. Stephen has a pedigree of centuries; and its constitutional principle was asserted in the earliest times. Its race and language are entirely different from those of the other peoples which constitute the monarchy; its territorial area is larger than theirs; its population, though less by six millions than that of the remainder of the empire, is much larger than that of any of the nationalities composing it. Its people are powerful, brave, united—and, notwithstanding 1848, loyal; for we must not forget that the terrible events of that year in Hungary were to a great extent caused by a system of military despotism, carried out by Windischgrätz and Haynau, which aroused the just indignation of men of such widely different views and position as Batthyany and Kossuth, and united them in an effort perhaps less directed against the Hapsburg dynasty than against the generals who, under a boy Emperor, were usurping and abusing the functions of Government. In the scheme which I have developed I have endeavoured to give Hungary not a new position with regard to the Austrian empire, but to secure her in the one which she has occupied. The Emperor of Austria is King of Hungary; my idea was that he should revive in his person the Constitution of which he and his ancestors have been the heads. The leading principles of my plan are, not the creation of a new kingdom and a new Constitution, but the resuscitation of an old monarchy and an old Constitution; not the separation of one part of the empire from the other, but the drawing together of the two component parts by the recognition of their joint positions, the maintenance of their mutual obligations, their community in questions affecting the entire empire, and their proportional pecuniary responsibility for the liabilities of the whole State. It is no plan of separation that I have carried out; on the contrary, it is one of closer union, not by the creation of a new power, but by the recognition of an old one. This cannot be too often repeated, for I know that there are many people who maintain that I have divided the empire.

# BISMARCK'S GERMANY

*In 1862 King William I of Prussia appointed as prime minister Otto von Bismarck (1815–1898). By 1871 Bismarck had unified the German states into an empire. His policy was one of realpolitik, and he pursued his goals through war and diplomacy. His 1862 speech was made to convince the Reichstag to grant new taxes; the one in 1888 outlined Germany's policy of military preparedness.*

## Iron and Blood

From Otto von Bismarck. *Speech to the Reichstag (September 30, 1862)*

... It is true that we can hardly escape complications in Germany, although we do not seek them. Germany does not look to Prussia's liberalism, but to her power. The south German States—Bavaria, Württemberg, and Baden—would like to indulge in liberalism, and because of that no one will assign Prussia's role to them! Prussia must collect her forces and hold them in reserve for an opportune moment, which has already come and gone several times. Since the Treaty of Vienna, our frontiers have not been favorably designed for a healthy body politic. Not by speeches and majorities will the great questions of the day be decided—that was the mistake of 1848 and 1849—but by iron and blood.

From Louis L. Snyder, ed., *Documents of German History* (New Brunswick, N.J.: Rutgers University Press, 1958). Copyright © 1958 by Rutgers, The State University. Reprinted by permission of the publisher.

## Empire

*The Imperial Proclamation (January 18, 1871)*

Whereas, the German Princes and the Free Cities have called unanimously upon us to revive and assume, with the restoration of the Ger-

From Louis L. Snyder, *Fifty Major Documents of the Nineteenth Century* (Princeton, N.J.: Van Nostrand, 1955), p. 147.

man Empire, the German imperial office, which has not been occupied for more than sixty years, and

Whereas, adequate arrangements have been made for this purpose in the Constitution of the German Confederation;

Therefore, we, William, by the grace of God, King of Prussia, do hereby proclaim that we have considered it to be a duty to our common Fatherland to respond to the summons of the unified German Princes and cities and to accept the German imperial title. As a result, we and those who succeed us on the throne of Prussia, henceforth, shall bear the imperial title in all our relations and in all the activities of the German Empire, and we trust to God that the German nation will be granted the ability to construct a propitious future for the Fatherland under the symbol of its ancient glory.

We assume the imperial title, aware of the duty of protecting, with German loyalty, the rights of the Empire and of its members, of maintaining the peace, and of protecting the independent rulers of Germany, which, in turn, is dependent upon the united power of the people.

We assume the title in the hope that the German people will be granted the ability to enjoy the fruits of its zealous and self-sacrificing wars in eternal peace, inside boundaries that give the Fatherland a security against renewed French aggression which has been lost for centuries. May God grant that we and our successors on the imperial throne may at all times enhance the wealth of the German Empire, not through military conquests, but by the blessings and the gifts of peace, within the realm of national prosperity, freedom, and morality.

Issued at General Headquarters, Versailles, January 18, 1871.

WILLIAM

# Military Preparedness

## From Otto von Bismarck. *Speech to the Reichstag (February 6, 1888)*

Great complications and all kinds of coalitions, which no one can foresee, are constantly possible, and we must be prepared for them. We must be so strong, irrespective of momentary conditions, that we can face any coalition with the assurance of a great nation which is strong enough under circumstances to take her fate into her own hands. We must be able to face our fate placidly with that self reliance and confidence in God which are ours when we are strong and our cause is just.

From T. S. Hameron, ed., *The Age of Bismark: Documents and Interpretations* (New York: Harper & Row, 1973), pp. 290–293.

And the government will see to it that the German cause will be just always.

We must, to put it briefly, be as strong in these times as we possibly can be, and we can be stronger than any other nation of equal numbers in the world. I shall revert to this later—but it would be criminal if we were not to make use of our opportunity. If we do not need our full armed strength, we need not summon it. The only problem is the not very weighty one of money—not very weighty I say in passing, because I have no wish to enter upon a discussion of the financial and military figures, and of the fact that France has spent three milliards for the improvement of her armaments these last years, while we have spent scarcely one and one half milliards, including what we are asking of you at this time. But I leave the elucidation of this to the minister of war and the representatives of the treasury department.

When I say that it is our duty to endeavor to be ready at all times and for all emergencies, I imply that we must make greater exertions than other people for the same purpose, because of our geographical position. We are situated in the heart of Europe, and have at least three fronts open to an attack. France has only her eastern, and Russia only her western frontier where they may be attacked. We are also more exposed to the dangers of a coalition than any other nation, as is proved by the whole development of history, by our geographical position, and the lesser degree of cohesiveness, which until now has characterized the German nation in comparison with others. God has placed us where we are prevented, thanks to our neighbors, from growing lazy and dull. He has placed by our side the most warlike and restless of all nations, the French, and He has permitted warlike inclinations to grow strong in Russia, where formerly they existed to a lesser degree. Thus we are given the spur, so to speak, from both sides, and are compelled to exertions which we should perhaps not be making otherwise. The pikes in the European carp-pond are keeping us from being carps by making us feel their teeth on both sides. They also are forcing us to an exertion which without them we might not make, and to a union among us Germans, which is abhorrent to us at heart. By nature we are rather tending away, the one from the other. But the Franco-Russian press within which we are squeezed compels us to hold together, and by pressure our cohesive force is greatly increased. This will bring us to that state of being inseparable which all other nations possess, while we do not yet enjoy it. But we must respond to the intentions of Providence by making ourselves so strong that the pikes can do nothing but encourage us. . . .

If we Germans wish to wage a war with the full effect of our national strength, it must be a war which satisfies all who take part in it, all who sacrifice anything for it, in short the whole nation. It must be a national war, a war carried on with the enthusiasm of 1870, when we were foully attacked. I still remember the earsplitting, joyful shouts in the

station at Köln. It was the same all the way from Berlin to Köln, in
Berlin itself. The waves of popular approval bore us into the war,
whether or no we wished it. That is the way it must be, if a popular
force like ours is to show what it can do. It will, however, be very difficult to prove to the provinces and the imperial states and their inhabitants that the war is unavoidable, and has to be. People will ask: "Are
you so sure? Who can tell?" In short, when we make an attack, the
whole weight of all imponderables, which weigh far heavier than material weights, will be on the side of our opponents whom we have attacked. France will be bristling with arms way down to the Pyrenees.
The same will take place everywhere. A war into which we are not
borne by the will of the people will be waged, to be sure, if it has been
declared by the constituted authorities who deemed it necessary; it will
even be waged pluckily, and possibly victoriously, after we have once
smelled fire and tasted blood, but it will lack from the beginning the
nerve and enthusiasm of a war in which we are attacked. In such a one
the whole of Germany from Memel to the Alpine Lakes will flare up
like a powder mine; it will be bristling with guns, and no enemy will
dare to engage this *furor teutonicus* which develops when we are attacked. We cannot afford to lose this factor of preeminence even if
many military men—not only ours but others as well—believe that today we are superior to our future opponents. Our own officers believe
this to a man, naturally. Every soldier believes this. He would almost
cease to be a useful soldier if he did not wish for war, and did not believe that we would be victorious in it. If our opponents by any chance
are thinking that we are pacific because we are afraid of how the war
may end, they are mightily mistaken. We believe as firmly in our victory in a just cause as any foreign lieutenant in his garrison, after his
third glass of champagne, can believe in his, and we probably do so
with greater certainty. It is not fear, therefore, which makes us pacific,
but the consciousness of our strength. We are strong enough to protect
ourselves, even if we should be attacked at a less favorable moment,
and we are in a position to let divine providence determine whether a
war in the meanwhile may not become unnecessary after all.

I am, therefore, not in favor of any kind of an aggressive war, and
if war could result only from our attack—somebody must kindle a fire,
we shall not kindle it. Neither the consciousness of our strength, which
I have described, nor our confidence in our treaties, will prevent us
from continuing our former endeavors to preserve peace. In this we
do not permit ourselves to be influenced by annoyances or dislikes.
The threats and insults, and the challenges, which have been made
have, no doubt, excited also with us a feeling of irritation, which does
not easily happen with Germans, for they are less prone to national
hatred than any other nation. We are, however, trying to calm our
countrymen, and we shall work for peace with our neighbors, especially with Russia, in the future as well as in the past. . . .

To sum up: I do not believe in an immediate interruption of peace, and I ask you to discuss this bill independently of such a thought or apprehension, looking upon it as a means of making the great strength which God has placed in the German nation fully available. If we do not need all the troops, it is not necessary to summon them. We are trying to avoid the contingency when we shall need them.

This attempt is as yet made rather difficult for us by the threatening newspaper articles in the foreign press, and I should like to admonish these foreign editors to discontinue such threats. They do not lead anywhere. The threats which we see made—not by the governments, but by the press—are really incredibly stupid, when we stop to reflect that the people making them imagine they could frighten the proud and powerful German empire by certain intimidating figures made by printer's ink and shallow words. People should not do this. It would then be easier for us to be more obliging to our two neighbors. Every country after all is sooner or later responsible for the windows which its press has smashed. The bill will be rendered some day, and will consist of the ill-feeling of the other country. We are easily influenced—perhaps too easily—by love and kindness, but quite surely never by threats! We Germans fear God, and naught else in the world! It is this fear of God which makes us love and cherish peace. If in spite of this anybody breaks the peace, he will discover that the ardent patriotism of 1813, which called to the standards the entire population of Prussia—weak, small, and drained to the marrow as it then was—has today become the common property of the whole German nation. Attack the German nation anywhere, and you will find it armed to a man, and every man with the firm belief in his heart: God will be with us.

# IMPERIALISM

## French Colonial Policy

*Jules Ferry (1832–1893) was premier of France twice in the years 1880–1885. During this period France added Tunisia to its empire. In 1890, in the preface to a book on Tonkin, Ferry explained his theory of colonialism.*

### From Jules Ferry. *Preface to Tonkin (1890)*

Colonial policy is the child of the industrial revolution. For wealthy countries where capital abounds and accumulates fast, where industry is expanding steadily, where even agriculture must become mechanized in order to survive, exports are essential for public prosperity. Both demand for labor and scope for capital investment depend on the foreign market. Had it been possible to establish, among the leading industrial countries, some kind of rational division of production, based on special aptitudes and natural resources, so that certain of them engaged in, say, cotton and metallurgical manufacture, while others concentrated on the alcohol and sugar-refining industries, Europe might not have had to seek markets for its products in other parts of the world. . . . But today every country wants to do its own spinning and weaving, forging and distilling. So Europe produces, for example, a surplus of sugar and must try to export it. With the arrival of the latest industrial giants, the United States and Germany; of Italy, newly resurrected; of Spain, enriched by the investment of French capital; of enterprising little Switzerland, not to mention Russia waiting in the wings, Europe has embarked on a competitive course from which she will be unable to turn back.

All over the world, beyond the Vosges, and across the Atlantic, the raising of high tariffs has resulted in an increasing volume of manufactured goods, the disappearance of traditional markets, and the appearance of fierce competition. Countries react by raising their own

From Jules Ferry, "Preface," to *Tonkin et la Mère-Patrie,* reprinted by Jules Ferry, *Discours et opinions* (Paris, 1897), Vol. 5, pp. 557–564. Translated by Harvey Goldberg, in *French Colonialism* (New York: Rinehart and Company, 1959), pp. 3–4. Reprinted by permission of Holt, Rinehart and Winston, CBS College Publishing.

tariff barriers, but that is not enough. . . . The protectionist system, unless accompanied by a serious colonial policy, is like a steam engine without a safety valve. An excess of capital invested in industry not only reduces profits on capital but also arrests the rise of wages. This phenomenon cuts to the very core of society, engendering passions and countermoves. Social stability in this industrial age clearly depends on outlets for industrial goods. The beginning of the economic crisis, with its prolonged, frequent strikes—a crisis which has weighed so heavily on Europe since 1877—coincided in France, Germany, and England with a marked and persistent drop in exports. Europe is like a commercial firm whose business turnover has been shrinking for a number of years. The European consumer-goods market is saturated; unless we declare modern society bankrupt and prepare, at the dawn of the twentieth century, for its liquidation by revolution (the consequences of which we can scarcely foresee), new consumer markets will have to be created in other parts of the world. . . . Colonial policy is an international manifestation of the eternal laws of competition.

Without either compromising the security of the country or sacrificing any of its past traditions and future aspirations, the Republicans have, in less than ten years, given France four kingdoms in Asia and Africa. Three of them are linked to us by tradition and treaty. The fourth represents our contribution to peaceful conquest, the bringing of civilization into the heart of equatorial Africa. Suppose the Republic had declared, with the doctrinaires of the Radical school, that the French nation ends at Marseilles. To whom would Tunisia, Indochina, Madagascar, and the Congo belong today?

# The White Man's Burden

*The English poet Rudyard Kipling (1865–1936) set forth the justification for imperialism in verse.*

## From Rudyard Kipling. *The White Man's Burden*

Take up the White Man's burden—
Send forth the best ye breed—
Go bind your sons to exile
To serve your captives' need;
To wait in heavy harness,
On fluttered folk and wild—

From Rudyard Kipling, *Verse,* Inclusive Edition (New York: Doubleday and Page, 1920), pp. 371–372. Reprinted by permission of The National Trust.

Your new-caught, sullen peoples,
Half-devil and half-child.

Take up the White Man's burden—
In patience to abide,
To veil the threat of terror
And check the show of pride;
By open speech and simple,
An hundred times made plain
To seek another's profit,
And work another's gain.

Take up the White Man's burden—
The savage wars of peace—
Fill full the mouth of Famine
And bid the sickness cease;
And when your goal is nearest
The end for others sought,
Watch sloth and heathen Folly
Bring all your hopes to nought.

Take up the White Man's burden—
No tawdry rule of kings,
But toil of serf and sweeper—
The tale of common things.
The ports ye shall not enter,
The roads ye shall not tread,
Go mark them with your living,
And mark them with your dead.

Take up the White Man's burden—
And reap his old reward:
The blame of those ye better,
The hate of those ye guard—
The cry of hosts ye humour
(Ah, slowly!) toward the light:—
'Why brought he us from bondage,
Our loved Egyptian night?'

Take up the White Man's burden—
Ye dare not stoop to less—
Nor call too loud on Freedom
To cloke your weariness;
By all ye cry or whisper,
By all ye leave or do,
The silent, sullen peoples
Shall weigh your gods and you.

Take up the White Man's burden—
Have done with childish days—
The lightly proferred laurel,
The easy, ungrudged praise.
Comes now, to search your manhood
Through all the thankless years,
Cold, edged with dear-bought wisdom,
The judgment of your peers!


# The Black Man's Oppression

*Edward Morel, a British journalist in the Congo, drew attention to the abuses of imperialism in 1903.*


## From Edward Morel. *The Black Man's Burden*

It is [the Africans] who carry the 'Black man's burden'. They have not withered away before the white man's occupation. Indeed . . . Africa has ultimately absorbed within itself every Caucasian and, for that matter, every Semitic invader, too. In hewing out for himself a fixed abode in Africa, the white man has massacred the African in heaps. The African has survived, and it is well for the white settlers that he has. . . .

What the partial occupation of his soil by the white man has failed to do; what the mapping out of European political 'spheres of influence' has failed to do; what the Maxim and the rifle, the slave gang, labour in the bowels of the earth and the lash, have failed to do; what imported measles, smallpox and syphilis have failed to do; whatever the overseas slave trade failed to do, the power of modern capitalistic exploitation, assisted by modern engines of destruction, may yet succeed in accomplishing.

For from the evils of the latter, scientifically applied and enforced, there is no escape for the African. Its destructive effects are not spasmodic: they are permanent. In its permanence resides its fatal consequences. It kills not the body merely, but the soul. It breaks the spirit. It attacks the African at every turn, from every point of vantage. It wrecks his polity, uproots him from the land, invades his family life, destroys his natural pursuits and occupations, claims his whole time, enslaves him in his own home. . . .

From E. D. Morel, *The Black Man's Burden*, in Louis L. Snyder, *The Imperialism Reader* (Princeton, N.J.: Van Nostrand, 1962), pp. 163–164. First published in 1920 in Great Britain. Reprinted in 1969 by Monthly Review Press. Reprinted by permission of Monthly Review Press.

. . . In Africa, especially in tropical Africa, which a capitalistic imperialism threatens and has, in part, already devastated, man is incapable of reacting against unnatural conditions. In those regions man is engaged in a perpetual struggle against disease and an exhausting climate, which tells heavily upon child-bearing; and there is no scientific machinery for salving the weaker members of the community. The African of the tropics is capable of tremendous physical labours. But he cannot accommodate himself to the European system of monotonous, uninterrupted labour, with its long and regular hours, involving, moreover, as it frequently does, severance from natural surroundings and nostalgia, the condition of melancholy resulting from separation from home, a malady to which the African is specially prone. Climatic conditions forbid it. When the system is forced upon him, the tropical African droops and dies.

Nor is violent physical opposition to abuse and injustice henceforth possible for the African in any part of Africa. His chances of effective resistance have been steadily dwindling with the increasing perfectibility in the killing power of modern armament. . . .

Thus the African is really helpless against the material gods of the white man, as embodied in the trinity of imperialism, capitalistic exploitation, and militarism. . . .

To reduce all the varied and picturesque and stimulating episodes in savage life to a dull routine of endless toil for uncomprehended ends, to dislocate social ties and disrupt social institutions; to stifle nascent desires and crush mental development; to graft upon primitive passions the annihilating evils of scientific slavery, and the bestial imaginings of civilized man, unrestrained by convention or law; in fine, to kill the soul in a people—this is a crime which transcends physical murder.

# The Economic Bases of Imperialism

*The English economist John A. Hobson (1858–1940) wrote his critique of the economic bases of imperialism in 1902.*

## From John A. Hobson. *Imperialism*

Amid the welter of vague political abstractions to lay one's finger accurately upon any "ism" so as to pin it down and mark it out by definition seems impossible. Where meanings shift so quickly and so subtly, not only following changes of thought, but often manipulated

From John A. Hobson, *Imperialism* (London: Allen and Unwin, 1948), pp. 3–5, 71–72, 77–78, 80–81, 92–93. Reprinted by permission of the publisher.

artificially by political practitioners so as to obscure, expand, or distort, it is idle to demand the same rigour as is expected in the exact sciences. A certain broad consistency in its relations to other kindred terms is the nearest approach to definition which such a term as Imperialism admits. Nationalism, internationalism, colonialism, its three closest congeners, are equally elusive, equally shifty, and the changeful overlapping of all four demands the closest vigilance of students of modern politics.

During the nineteenth century the struggle towards nationalism, or establishment of political union on a basis of nationality, was a dominant factor alike in dynastic movements and as an inner motive in the life of masses of population. That struggle, in external politics, sometimes took a disruptive form, as in the case of Greece, Servia, Roumania, and Bulgaria breaking from Ottoman rule, and the detachment of North Italy from her unnatural alliance with the Austrian Empire. In other cases it was a unifying or a centralising force, enlarging the area of nationality, as in the case of Italy and the Pan-Slavist movement in Russia. Sometimes nationality was taken as a basis of federation of States, as in United Germany and in North America.

It is true that the forces making for political union sometimes went further, making for federal union of diverse nationalities, as in the cases of Austria-Hungary, Norway and Sweden, and the Swiss Federation. But the general tendency was towards welding into large strong national unities the loosely related States and provinces with shifting attachments and alliances which covered large areas of Europe since the break-up of the Empire. This was the most definite achievement of the nineteenth century. The force of nationality, operating in this work, is quite as visible in the failures to achieve political freedom as in the successes; and the struggles of Irish, Poles, Finns, Hungarians, and Czechs to resist the forcible subjection to or alliance with stronger neighbours brought out in its full vigour the powerful sentiment of nationality.

The middle of the century was especially distinguished by a series of definitely "nationalist" revivals, some of which found important interpretation in dynastic changes, while others were crushed or collapsed. Holland, Poland, Belgium, Norway, the Balkans, formed a vast arena for these struggles of national forces.

The close of the third quarter of the century saw Europe fairly settled into large national States or federations of States, though in the nature of the case there can be no finality, and Italy continued to look to Trieste, as Germany still looks to Austria, for the fulfilment of her manifest destiny.

This passion and the dynastic forms it helped to mould and animate are largely attributable to the fierce prolonged resistance which peoples, both great and small, were called on to maintain against the imperial designs of Napoleon. The national spirit of England was roused by the tenseness of the struggle to a self-consciousness it had never experienced since "the spacious days of great Elizabeth." Jena made Prussia into a great nation; the Moscow campaign brought Russia into the field of European nationalities as a factor in politics, opening her for the first time to the full tide of Western ideas and influences.

Turning from this territorial and dynastic nationalism to the spirit of racial, linguistic, and economic solidarity which has been the underlying motive, we find a still more remarkable movement. Local particularism on the one hand, vague cosmopolitanism upon the other, yielded to a ferment of nationalist sentiment, manifesting itself among the weaker peoples not merely in a sturdy and heroic resistance against political absorption or territorial nationalism, but in a passionate revival of decaying customs, language, literature and art; while it bred in more dominant peoples strange ambitions of national "destiny" and an attendant spirit of Chauvinism.

No mere array of facts and figures adduced to illustrate the economic nature of the new Imperialism will suffice to dispel the popular delusion that the use of national force to secure new markets by annexing fresh tracts of territory is a sound and a necessary policy for an advanced industrial country like Great Britain. . . .

But these arguments are not conclusive. It is open to Imperialists to argue thus: "We must have markets for our growing manufactures, we must have new outlets for the investment of our surplus capital and for the energies of the adventurous surplus of our population: such expansion is a necessity of life to a nation with our great and growing powers of production. An ever larger share of our population is devoted to the manufactures and commerce of towns, and is thus dependent for life and work upon food and raw materials from foreign lands. In order to buy and pay for these things we must sell our goods abroad. During the first three-quarters of the nineteenth century we could do so without difficulty by a natural expansion of commerce with continental nations and our colonies, all of which were far behind us in the main arts of manufacture and the carrying trades. So long as England held a virtual monopoly of the world markets for certain important classes of manufactured goods, Imperialism was unnecessary. After 1870 this manufacturing and trading supremacy was greatly impaired: other nations, especially Germany, the United States, and Belgium, advanced with great rapidity, and while they have not crushed or even stayed the increase of our external trade, their competition made it more and more difficult to dispose of the full surplus of our manufactures at a profit. The encroachments made by these nations upon our old markets, even in our own possessions, made it most urgent that we should take energetic means to secure new markets. These new markets had to lie in hitherto undeveloped countries, chiefly in the tropics, where vast populations lived capable of growing economic needs which our manufacturers and merchants could sup-

ply. Our rivals were seizing and annexing territories for similar purposes, and when they had annexed them closed them to our trade.
The diplomacy and the arms of Great Britain had to be used in order
to compel the owners of the new markets to deal with us: and experience showed that the safest means of securing and developing such
markets is by establishing 'protectorates' or by annexation. . . .

It was this sudden demand for foreign markets for manufactures
and for investments which was avowedly responsible for the adoption
of Imperialism as a political policy. . . . They needed Imperialism because they desired to use the public resources of their country to find
profitable employment for their capital which otherwise would be superfluous. . . .

Every improvement of methods of production, every concentration
of ownership and control, seems to accentuate the tendency. As one
nation after another enters the machine economy and adopts advanced
industrial methods, it becomes more difficult for its manufacturers,
merchants, and financiers to dispose profitably of their economic resources, and they are tempted more and more to use their Governments in order to secure for their particular use some distant undeveloped country by annexation and protection.

The process, we may be told, is inevitable, and so it seems upon a
superficial inspection. Everywhere appear excessive powers of production, excessive capital in search of investment. It is admitted by all business men that the growth of the powers of production in their country
exceeds the growth in consumption, that more goods can be produced
than can be sold at a profit, and that more capital exists than can find
remunerative investment.

It is this economic condition of affairs that forms the taproot of Imperialism. If the consuming public in this country raised its standard
of consumption to keep pace with every rise of productive powers,
there could be no excess of goods or capital clamorous to use Imperialism in order to find markets: foreign trade would indeed exist. . . .

Everywhere the issue of quantitative versus qualitative growth comes
up. This is the entire issue of empire. A people limited in number and
energy and in the land they occupy have the choice of improving to
the utmost the political and economic management of their own land,
confining themselves to such accessions of territory as are justified by
the most economical disposition of a growing population; or they may
proceed, like the slovenly farmer, to spread their power and energy
over the whole earth, tempted by the speculative value or the quick
profits of some new market, or else by mere greed of territorial acquisition, and ignoring the political and economic wastes and risks involved by this imperial career. It must be clearly understood that this
is essentially a choice of alternatives; a full simultaneous application of
intensive and extensive cultivation is impossible. A nation may either,
following the example of Denmark or Switzerland, put brains into ag-

riculture, develop a finely varied system of public education, general and technical, apply the ripest science to its special manufacturing industries, and so support in progressive comfort and character a considerable population upon a strictly limited area; or it may, like Great Britain, neglect its agriculture, allowing its lands to go out of cultivation and its population to grow up in towns, fall behind other nations in its methods of education and in the capacity of adapting to its uses the latest scientific knowledge, in order that it may squander its pecuniary and military resources in forcing bad markets and finding speculative fields of investment in distant corners of the earth, adding millions of square miles and of unassimilable population to the area of the Empire.

The driving forces of class interest which stimulate and support this false economy we have explained. No remedy will serve which permits the future operation of these forces. It is idle to attack Imperialism or Militarism as political expedients or policies unless the axe is laid at the economic root of the tree, and the classes for whose interest Imperialism works are shorn of the surplus revenues which seek this outlet.

# XI

# ADVANCED INDUSTRIAL CAPITALISM

*DURING THE SECOND half of the nineteenth century, industrial growth continued. New technologies, the larger scale of production, and increased trade in an international market led some observers to call this period the "second industrial revolution." In agriculture as well as manufacturing large enterprises produced goods for a world market. Distribution as well as production became more complex; networks of wholesalers supplied goods to stores, and the department store replaced some of the small shops in large urban centers.*

*Although English and French manufacturing continued to grow, Germany experienced the most rapid industrial progress in the period after its unification. Its iron and steel production increased dramatically and it pioneered in new fields such as chemicals and electricity. Financed by modern banks, German manufacturers installed the latest machinery in their new plants. Cartels, which combined a number of enterprises into one huge monopoly, often controlled entire industries.*

*International trade required a common denominator for national currencies, and after the 1870s, the nations of Western Europe adopted the gold standard. The world economy shared periods of boom and bust; during the period from the 1870s through the 1890s, a depression lowered prices and profits, drove small producers out of business, and led some of those who survived the competition to demand protective tariffs for their goods.*

*The increased scale of industrial organization was matched by the appearance of national and international labor organizations. In France, Germany, and Britain, workers in different trades grouped their unions into national federations, coordinating resources and supporting one another's strikes. In this period, the strike became the typical way for workers to express grievances and attempt to negotiate with employers. Alongside labor unions, socialist parties claimed to represent working-class interests in politics. Throughout the 1880s and 1890s, socialists contested elections and won seats in parliaments. Although their goal was a revolutionary transformation of economy and society, the socialist parties of this period (organized in the Second International, which was founded in 1889) were committed to methods of gradual, political reform. On the eve of World War I, socialist parties were an important factor in European political life.*

# ORGANIZATION

## Networks of Factories

*The Englishman Harold Baron described the rapid growth of huge manufacturing plants in Germany. By the early 1900s, Germany led Britain and France in many fields, especially electrical equipment and chemicals.*

### From Harold Baron. *Chemical Industry on the Continent* (1909)

One of the most successful firms in Germany engaged in the manufacture of colours and pharmaceutical products, is the Farbenfabriken Friedr. Bayer & Co. of Elberfeld. This chemical works may be regarded as typical of a number of similar concerns engaged in the same branch of industry. The firm was originally founded by Friedrich Bayer in the year 1850 at Elberfeld on the banks of the Wupper. In 1881 it was registered as an Aktiengesellschaft[1] under the name Farbenfabriken vorm. Friedr. Bayer & Co. . . . It was found in 1891 to be impossible to obtain sufficient land in the immediate vicinity of the works to permit of the considerable extension which the progress of the company necessitated. A large site was, therefore, acquired at Leverkusen, which is about five miles north of Cologne on the right bank of the Rhine. The new works at Leverkusen has been planned on a huge scale. Ample provision has been made for the enlargement of the existing plant for many years to come. . . . Branch works exist at Schelphoh in Lüneberg, at Moscow, and at Flers, near Roubaix in France, and works are now being erected in England at Port Sunlight in order to conform with the provisions of the Patent and Designs Act of 1907.

The products manufactured by this firm still continue to be chiefly dyestuffs. . . .

A very important branch now being extensively developed is that of pharmaceutical products, such as Phenacetine, the well-known antipyretic, Sulphonal, and Trional, Iodothyrine, Salophen, Aspirine, etc.

A profitable branch has also been introduced in the manufacturing

[1]Joint-stock company.

From Sydney Pollard and Colin Holmes, eds., *Documents of European Economic History* (New York: St. Martin's Press, 1970), Vol. 2, pp. 85–87. Reprinted by permission of Sydney Pollard and Colin Holmes.

of invalid's and infant's food under the name Somatose. The output of this product is very large. The raw material for this is a bye-product obtained in the manufacture of meat extract consisting of the fibrous material of the meat. It comes in large quantities from Argentine.

Another branch consists in the manufacture of photographic chemicals, such as Edinol, which is a photographic developer, and Acetone-Sulphite.

Much research work is carried out in connection with dyeing and printing. Conferences are held daily at which new processes and inventions are brought before the staff and discussed with reference to their value to the firm. . . .

The works at Leverkusen cover an estate of about 448 acres, and there is a large open district in the neighbourhood allowing for a further extension and the creation of a garden city for the workmen and employees of the firm. Bayer's works at Leverkusen is certainly one of the best organized chemical establishments in the world. About 3,500 people are employed at Leverkusen alone, and the works are of such a gigantic nature that this number seems to be lost when a visitor is shown through the works. . . .

One of the research laboratories was visited. . . . The laboratories are arranged very much in the same manner as the University laboratories in this country. Benches and cupboards are provided, and to each bench is led a supply of electricity, compressed air, steam and hot and cold water. The research chemists are paid a salary of about £100 for the first year. If a chemist has shown himself to be useful in his first year, a contract is usually made for a term of years in accordance with his capabilities. The research chemist is also remunerated to some extent by receiving royalties on the output of products manufactured in accordance with processes invented by himself. . . . It is the policy of the large German colour works to keep the chemists strictly to their own department and not to allow them access to other departments. The object of this is to prevent employees becoming conversant with other than their own work, so that it is less easy for them to carry away secrets to competitors. The contracts under which the employees are engaged are also of a somewhat binding nature. If a chemist desires to leave before the expiration of his contract he cannot as a rule enter the service of a competing firm until the expiration of a prescribed term.

# German Banks

*A well-organized banking system financed the development of Germany's modern industrial economy and enabled it to outproduce other industrial nations by the beginning of the twentieth century.*

From Robert Franz, "The Statistical History of the German Banking System," *Miscellaneous Articles on German Banking*, U.S. Senate Document 508 (Washington, D.C.: Government Printing Office, 1910), pp. 29–33.

## From *Articles on German Banking*

Technical and economic reasons were the cause which in the first instance led to the amalgamation of coal and iron works, particularly during the last years, and these same factors tend more and more to bring about the establishment of great consolidated works combining the production of the raw material with that of the half-finished and manufactured articles. This development would not be possible at all, or would meet with great difficulties, without a corresponding organization of the money and credit markets, i.e., without strong banks which are in a position to carry through the necessary financial transactions.

Developments of industry and banking showed the same tendency and mutually influenced each other to a large extent. It can not be said that the banks created the industries, since the funds which are gathered by the banks in increasing volume are mainly the result of the increasing productivity of capital invested in industrial undertakings. It is true however that the creative power which in a comparatively short time placed German industry in its present commanding position took its origin with the men who put to practical use and in the interest of economic progress of the nation the achievements and inventions of the domain of science and technique.

It is the undisputed merit of the persons at the head of the banks that they appreciated those endeavors and supported them by advancing the requisite capital, oftentimes incurring great risks for the banks. The entire development was, moreover, vigorously furthered by a commercial and tariff policy favorable to industry, though it must be said that this policy was abandoned to a certain extent with the new customs tariff of 1902, the revision of the tariff and the renewal of our commercial treaties having been undertaken and carried out under the motto "Greater tariff protection for agriculture."

It is almost self-evident that the banks, which in carrying out their policy of furthering industry had often to assume considerable risks, have tried to secure, and in a large measure have succeeded in securing, a lasting and decisive control over industrial corporations.

This decisive influence of the banks on the industries reaches further than the mere possession of shares of industrial undertakings would warrant, as it is an easy matter for the banks to procure for stock-holders' meetings proxies of the shares which their customers have deposited with them. The result is that in many cases, the banks appear to wield a controlling power over the industrial corporations. The close relationship between the banks and industries finds expression also in the filling of places on the supervisory boards of directors.

As members of the boards of directors of industrial corporations the bank directors are at all times in a position to guard the interests of the banks, particularly by supervising the systematic and rational employment of the credit granted by the bank to the corporation.

On the other hand, in order to create and maintain friendly relations between the banks and industrial corporations, the directors of the latter are given places on the supervisory boards of the banks.

Such a condition of affairs may not reveal itself statistically to outsiders, but there can be no doubt that the bond between the bank and the industrial undertaking is thus made closer than by the mere stock control of the bank, which in most cases is not very large.

The progressive industrialization of Germany and the large increase of its population caused on the one hand increasing imports of industrial and auxiliary materials as well as of foodstuffs, and on the other steadily growing exports of industrial products. As a result Germany's share in the world's commerce shows a rapid growth.

Until the seventies of the last century the financial regulation of German foreign oversea trade had been almost exclusively in the hands of London banks. The establishment in 1870 of the Deutsche Bank at Berlin meant a turning point in this regard. The Bank in its charter adopted the following program: "It is the purpose of the corporation to do a general banking business, particularly to further and facilitate commercial relations between Germany, the other European countries, and oversea markets." The founders of the Deutsche Bank had recognized that there existed in the organization of the German banking and credit system a gap which had to be filled in order to render German foreign trade independent of the English intermediary, and to secure for German commerce a firm position in the international market. It was rather difficult to carry out this program during the early years, the more so, because Germany at that time had no gold standard and bills of exchange made out in various kinds of currency were neither known nor liked in the international market. The introduction of the gold standard in Germany in 1873 did away with these difficulties, and by establishing branches at the central points of German oversea trade (Bremen and Hamburg) and by opening an agency in London the Deutsche Bank succeeded in vigorously furthering its program. Very much later the other Berlin joint-stock banks, especially the Disconto Gesellschaft and the Dresdner Bank, followed the example of the Deutsche Bank, and during the last years particularly the Berlin joint-stock banks have shown great energy in extending the sphere of their interests abroad.

As regards the organization of the oversea business, the only foreign place where the banks have established agencies (apart from the branches in the German export cities, Bremen and Hamburg) is London. Agencies which the Deutsche Bank had established in Shanghai and Yokohama in the early seventies had soon to be liquidated by reason of considerable losses in exchange due to the depreciation of silver. For the express purpose of promoting foreign trade, the banks established subsidiary banks with the main offices in Germany (Berlin and Hamburg); these banks in their turn established agencies in oversea countries. The entire or almost the entire capital stock of these subsidiary banks is in the possession of the parent banks. The Berlin joint-stock banks, moreover, have become permanently interested in foreign banks and banking houses; they have also founded transportation, mining, and industrial enterprises whose sphere of activity is mostly abroad, and in which they acquired a permanent interest by taking over part of the capital stock.

The above account of the organization of the German credit-bank system, though somewhat sketchy in character, demonstrates, however, with sufficient clearness that the managers of the German credit banks, and particularly of the leading Berlin banks, have made constant and successful endeavors to place the banks in the service of German trade and industry and to accommodate the organization of the credit system to the variable and growing demands of national economic development. There can be no doubt that they have had a large share in raising German commerce and industry to its present world-wide commanding position.

# Retailing

*Pioneered by Parisians, the department store consolidated the distribution of many different kinds of goods, ushering in the age of mass consumption.*

## On Parisian Department Stores

It was in the reign of Louis-Philippe that department stores for fashion goods and dresses, extending to material and other clothing began to be distinguished. The type was already one of the notable developments of the Second Empire; it became one of the most important ones of the Third Republic. These stores have increased in number and several of them have become extremely large. Combining in their different departments all articles of clothing, toilet articles, furniture and many other ranges of goods, it is their special object so to combine all commodities as to attract and satisfy customers who will find conveniently together an assortment of a mass of articles corresponding to all their various needs. They attract customers by permanent display, by free entry into the shops, by periodic exhibitions, by special sales, by fixed prices, and by their ability to deliver the goods purchased to customers' homes, in Paris and to the provinces. Turning themselves into direct intermediaries between the producer and the consumer, even

From E. Lavasseur, *Questions ouvrières et industrielles en France sous la Troisième République* (Paris, 1907), in Sydney Pollard and Colin Holmes, eds., *Documents of European Economic History* (New York: St. Martin's Press, 1970), Vol. 2, pp. 95–96. Reprinted courtesy of the authors.

producing sometimes some of their articles in their own workshops, buying at lowest prices because of their large orders and because they are in a position to profit from bargains, working with large sums, and selling to most of their customers for cash only, they can transmit these benefits in lowered selling prices. They can even decide to sell at a loss, as an advertisement or to get rid of out-of-date fashions. Taking 5–6 per cent on 100 millions brings them in more than 20 per cent would bring to a firm doing a turnover of 50,000 francs.

The success of these department stores is only possible thanks to the volume of their business and this volume needs considerable capital and a very large turnover. Now capital, having become abundant, is freely combined nowadays in large enterprises, although French capital has the reputation of being more wary of the risks of industry than of State or railway securities. On the other hand, the large urban agglomerations, the ease with which goods can be transported by the railways, the diffusion of some comforts to strata below the middle classes, have all favoured these developments.

As example we may cite some figures relating to these stores, since they were brought to the notice of the public in the *Revue des Deux-Mondes*.

The *Belle-Jardinière*, starting as a modest shop set up by Mr. Parissot near the Petit-Pont, was moved to the Cité in 1856 near the Pont-Neuf on a plot of 3,400 metres: in 1893 it did business of 38 millions, realizing a net gain of 63 per cent. *Le Louvre*, dating to the time of the extension of the rue de Rivoli under the Second Empire, did in 1893 a business of 120 million at a profit of 6.4 per cent. *Le Bon-Marché*, which was a small shop when Mr. Boucicaut entered it in 1852, already did a business of 20 million at the end of the Empire. During the republic its new buildings were erected; Mme. Boucicaut turned it by her will into a kind of co-operative society, with shares and an ingenious organization; turnover reached 150 million in 1893, leaving a profit of 5 per cent. *La Samaritaine*, which had its most modest beginnings in 1869, today occupies the third rank among department stores of this kind by the number of its employees; it seeks its customers principally among the small consumers and makes great use of credit coupons.

It is worthy of note that the creators of these great department stores have arisen from the ranks of small shop assistants; they have succeeded because of their ability. The commercial organism shaped by them runs true to one type: strongly concentrated general authority, division of labour by departments and responsibility by each departmental head, individual effort of each employee in buying and selling stimulated by profit sharing or commission, etc.

According to the tax records of 1891, these stores in Paris, numbering 12, employed 1,708 persons and were rated on their site values at 2,159,000 francs; the largest had then 542 employees. These same stores had, in 1901, 9,784 employees; one of them over 2,000 and another over 1,600; their site value was doubled (4,089,000 francs).

# AN INTERNATIONAL MONETARY SYSTEM AND A WORLD MARKET

## The Gold Standard

*By making it possible to express the value of national currencies in gold, those countries which adopted the gold standard (in the 1870s in Western Europe) created an international monetary system. This document established the gold standard in Germany.*

### From *German Coinage Act, 9 July 1873*

1. In place of the local currencies circulating in Germany there shall be current the Reich gold currency. Its unit of account shall be the mark, as fixed in para. 2 of the Act of 4 December 1871 relating to the Minting of Reich Gold Coins.

The date on which the Imperial currency shall become operative in the whole territory of the Reich shall be fixed by order made by the Emperor with the consent of the Federal Council, to be promulgated at least three months before such date. The Land Governments are empowered to introduce the Reichsmark as unit of account before such date for their own territory. . . .

9. No one shall be obliged to take Reich silver coins in payment for sums greater than 20 marks, or nickel and copper coins in payment for sums greater than 1 mark. . . .

14. From the date of the Reich currency, the following regulations shall apply:

i. All payments due to be made hitherto in coinage of any land currency, or in foreign currency having been given equal validity by law with inland currency, are according to Sections 9, 15 and 16 to be made in Reich currency.

ii. The exchange rate of gold coins for which there is no legal ratio to silver coins, shall be according to the ratio of the legal fine

From Adolf Soetbeer, *Deutsche Münzverfassung* (n.d.), pp. 67, 86, 99–100, 115, in Sydney Pollard and Colin Holmes, eds., *Documents of European Economic History* (New York: St. Martin's Press, 1970), Vol. 2, pp. 237–239. Reprinted courtesy of the authors.

metal content of the coins in which payments were due, to the legal fine gold content of the Reich gold coins. . . .

iv. In all documents of courts of law or of notaries public which contain references to sums of money, as well as in all judicial decisions including sums of money, these sums shall be expressed in Reich currency if there is a legal fixed ratio to the Reich currency; but this shall not preclude the simultaneous expression in the denomination in which the liability was originally incurred. . . .

18. All bank notes expressed in denominations other than the Reich currency are to be withdrawn by 1 January 1876. After this date the only bank notes which may remain in circulation or be issued, are those expressed in Reich currency and worth at least 100 marks.

The same regulations apply to the notes issued hitherto by the Corporations.

Paper money issued by the Federal states must be withdrawn by 1 January 1876 at the latest, and be called in 6 months prior at the latest. However, an exception may be made in the case of Reich paper money, according to an Act to be passed in due course. This Act shall lay down the details of the issue and circulation of the Reich paper money, as well as the concessions to be granted to the individual federal states in the cancellation of their paper money.

# The World Economy

*The existence of a world economy meant that prosperity and depression were international developments. This description of the depression of 1873–1876 foreshadows the more disastrous occurrences during the depression of the 1890s and during the Great Depression of the 1930s.*

## From Robert Giffen. *On the Depression of 1873–1876*

What are the characteristic marks of the great depression of trade during the last three or four years? It is now ascertained that such depressions are periodical. They recur at tolerably regular intervals, following in the wake of equally regular periods of great prosperity in trade, when everybody makes profits or seems to make them. . . . The depressions, like the periods of prosperity coming before them, have also many features in common. Just as the prosperity is shown by the prevalence of good credit, an active money market, and a high range of

From Robert Giffen, "The Liquidations of 1873–1876," *The Fortnightly Review*, New Series, Vol. 22, No. 130 (October 1, 1877), pp. 510–525, in Shepard B. Clough and Carol G. Moodie, eds., *European Economic History: Documents and Readings* (Princeton, N.J.: Van Nostrand, 1965), pp. 108–113.

prices for both securities and commodities, so the depression is marked by a sluggish money market. But each depression has likewise its own special features and incidents. . . . An impression prevails that the present stagnation of trade is unprecedented in intensity and duration, and that it is likely to be permanent. A similar impression has often been found to prevail at such times, and it will be interesting to inquire whether it is now, for once, well founded, or whether in reality the depression is not much less than those to which trade has often been subject, and is not as likely as any other to terminate in a new period of prosperity.

Endeavouring to answer the question we have put, what we are first struck with, in a general survey of the last three or four years, is the universality of the depression. Almost every civilised country has been affected. The beginning was in 1873, with the great Vienna panic and crash in May of that year—a crash which was accompanied by immense agitation throughout Germany and in England, and the occurrence of incidents on almost every European Bourse which only stopped short of panic. Next came a great panic and crash in the autumn of 1873 in the United States, perhaps the greatest event of the kind to which that country, though it has had many great panics, has ever been subject. This was accompanied by a renewal of agitation in England, as well as generally on the Continent, as the rates of discount in November 1873 significantly prove. At that date the minimum bank rate of discount was in London no less than nine per cent, the maximum being two and three per cent higher; the minimum in Paris and Brussels was seven per cent; in Berlin and Frankfort, five per cent; Vienna, five per cent; and Amsterdam six and a half per cent. The following year was comparatively quiet, but it was marked by great monetary disturbances in South America, and by a great fall in prices both at home, on the Continent, and in the United States. In 1875 came renewed disturbances in South America, a renewal of agitation in the United States and Germany, and then the Im Thurn, Aberdare, Collie, Sanderson, and other failures, constituting the commercial crisis of that year in England. This was in turn succeeded by a great collapse in foreign loans, which had been heralded and partly rehearsed in 1873, on the occasion of the bankruptcy of Spain, and of which the conspicuous incident now was the non-payment of the Turkish debt interest. To all these events succeeded renewed depression and stagnation in trade at home, as well as on the Continent, the crisis in Russia in 1876 being very marked, and the whole continuing till it seemed to have a fresh cause in the apprehension and actual outbreak of the present war [*Russo-Turkish over Bulgaria, etc.*]. Thus the depression has been widespread and general, Italy, Spain, and France perhaps escaping with little hurt, but Austria, Germany, Russia, the United States, and the South American countries having all been in deep distress.

This universality, on a comparison with former periods of crisis, may be in fact apparent only, arising from the greatly increased facilities of observation at the present day. There never was a time, probably, since commerce was sufficiently advanced in more countries than one to admit of crises, in which the commercial misfortunes of one country did not react on countries with which it did business. At such periods as 1825, 1837–39, 1857–58, 1861–62, and 1866–68, it is undoubtedly the case that the crisis in England has been accompanied by more or less severe crises elsewhere—France, America, England, Holland, and the German towns on the Elbe, having shared each other's fortunes more or less during the whole period. Now the crisis is felt to be more extended, because we are immediately informed of the events in most distant places, because we see at once the association of failure at centres remote from each other, because we also see at once the effect in one place of the call upon it to render assistance at another disturbed centre of business. But it is also true that commercial relations are themselves far more extended than was the case before railways and telegraphs: that there are wide regions—in the United States, for instance—which could not have been the subject of crisis twenty or thirty years ago, because they were unpeopled; that such countries as Austria and Russia have lately shared more largely than before in industrial development; and that Germany has also advanced farther in the path which makes it possible for it to be the subject of a commercial crisis. There is consequently a real reason for the greater extension of the commercial depression of the last three years as compared with anything before witnessed, while it is equally true that steam and telegraphs, by facilitating communication, have destroyed the natural barriers between the different communities of the commercial world. The London money market appears to be the great equaliser of markets, because it receives the shock of every important business event throughout the world, and transmits the shock of what it feels to every other centre. But whatever the nature of the connection, it is certain that there is a connection between commercial crises in different parts of the world, and that the wider range of business increases the possible area of disaster when once disaster has set in.

# GOVERNMENTS AND INDUSTRY

## Protective Tariffs

*Jules Méline, who became prime minister of France in 1896, here defends the high protective tariff the French government leveled on both industrial and agricultural goods coming into the country.*

### Jules Méline. *Argument for Protection in France (1892)*

The causes which have brought about the agricultural crisis from which we have not yet emerged are today well-known, and nobody thinks of denying them.

There is first the considerable agricultural development among the nations of central and western Europe, such as Germany, Austria-Hungary, Russia and Rumania, whose agricultural products are increasingly flooding our markets, not to mention Italy and Spain, whose competition in wines has become so severe. But the principal cause is that the markets of Europe have now been entered by young nations, favored by nature and by the exceptional advantages of their financial situation, virgin land of very low value, unbelievably cheap labor, the absence of military burdens, and paltry taxes. In 1860 these peoples were lying dormant. That is the excuse made by the statesmen who neglected to take precautions for safeguarding the future of our agricultural production. But, suddenly, with the development of means of transport and communications, and the rapid drop in freight charges, within a few years the big markets have arrived on our doorstep, so that we have seen wheat from America and India reach Le Havre and Marseilles more cheaply than from our own principal centers of production. After wheat, it was cattle, even cattle on the hoof, which, thanks to ingenious improvements in the fitting out of the ships, is tending to replace French cattle; for slaughtered cattle the import facilities are even greater.

What we must protect by customs tariffs, therefore, is our manpower, bread and jobs for our workers. Our industrialists have made the greatest possible cuts in over-all costs; only the labor force can be

From David Thomson, ed., *France: Empire and Republic, 1850–1940* (New York: Harper & Row, 1968), 150–151.

reduced, and it would inevitably suffer if our new economic policy were inadequate.

Nobody can have the slightest inclination to reduce the wages of our workers, for in certain branches of production they are obviously insufficient. On the contrary, we ought to do our utmost to raise them and there is only one way: to maintain the price of our products at a profitable enough level, by preventing excessive cuts through foreign competition. That is how customs duties are linked to the social problem itself in its most acute form.

# Regulation of Working Conditions

*German prime minister Otto von Bismarck and French prime minister Georges Clemenceau (1841–1929) offered various policies for their governments to enact in relation to workers and working conditions. Both leaders defined their policies in explicit opposition to socialists within their countries.*

## From Otto von Bismarck. *On State Socialism (1884)*

I take this opportunity immediately to bring under discussion the question of competition of private insurance companies. . . . I want to express here in the name of the Imperial Government, the principle that we do not regard accidents and misfortunes in general suitable subjects for the extraction of higher interest or dividends, that we want to provide the worker with cheap insurance against these and other evils if that is at all possible, and that we regard it as our duty to hold down the cost of insurance so far as possible in the interest of the worker and of industry, of the employer as well as the employee. Now, I believe that there is no one who can establish such a low price as can be possible through the state. . . . I do not regard it as immoral for somebody to set up a private insurance company and I do regard it as human and entirely natural that in this business he strives for a return on his capital, if that can be, even a considerable surplus and the highest dividend possible. . . .

It is another question, however, whether the state has the right . . . to leave the performance of a public duty, namely that of protecting

From Otto von Bismarck, "Rede vom 15. März 1884," *Bismarck: Die gesammelten Werke* (Berlin, 1929), pp. 421–425, in Shepard Clough and Carol G. Moodie, eds., *European Economic History: Documents and Readings* (Princeton, N.J.: Van Nostrand, 1965), pp. 147–149.

the worker from accident and from need if he is injured or if he is old, to the chance that for the purpose private companies will be formed, which will charge workers and employers the highest rates they can. . . . As soon, however, as the state takes this matter in hand—and I believe this is its duty—it must seek the cheapest form and must make no profit from it, but rather concentrate on the welfare of the poor and the needy. Otherwise one could more justly relinquish certain state duties . . . such as education and defense to private companies, asking oneself who could do it most cheaply and efficiently. If provision for the needy on a level higher than the current law provides is a public duty then the state must assume it; the state cannot console itself that a private company will assume it. . . . The whole matter is rooted in the question: Has the state the duty of caring for its helpless fellow-citizens, or not? I maintain it has this duty. . . . It is folly for a community or local government to take up those tasks that individuals can perform. Those functions which the [*local*] community can fulfill with justice and advantage may be left to the community. But there are functions which only the state as a whole can perform. . . . To this last group belongs defense of the country. . . . Also to it belongs aid to the needy and prevention of such justified complaints as in fact offer really useful material for exploitation by the Social Democrats. This is the task of the state, and the state cannot long escape it.

If someone objects that this is socialism, I do not shrink from it in the least. The question is, where is the permissible limit of state socialism? Without it we cannot conduct our economy at all. Any poor law is socialism. There are indeed states which keep themselves so far from socialism that they have no poor laws at all—I remind you of France. These French conditions quite naturally explain the interpretation of the distinguished social thinker, Léon Say . . . ; there is expressed the French interpretation that every citizen has the right to starve, and that the state has no obligation to prevent the exercise of this right. . . .

The honorable Deputy [*who spoke previously*] characterizes it as something entirely new that we want to introduce a socialist element into the legislation. I have previously shown that the socialist element is nothing new and that the state cannot exist without a certain amount of socialism. . . . I believe that political parties—groups defined in terms of political ideals and programs—have outlived their day. They will gradually be forced, if they do not do it voluntarily, to take positions on economic questions and more than previously promote policies of [*social*] interest. This is called for by the spirit of the times. . . . In my opinion, a chief reason for the successes that the Social Democratic leaders have had . . . is that the state does not carry on enough state socialism; where it should be active it leaves a vacuum, and this is filled by others, by agitators who meddle with the state's business. The means of power in this field fall into other hands than the state's and we certainly cannot await with calm composure how they will be used. . .

# From Georges Clemenceau. *Speech on Strikes, Trade Unions, and Socialism (1906)*

I do not pretend to suppress vital competition with universal laws. I believe that vital competition is a phenomenon which should be regulated by social laws. I believe that as much as possible we should attempt to correct through law the fundamental evil in nature, but I believe at the same time that this is possible only if we establish our social organization on the only solid basis, the inalienable rights of all men.

The situation between the two competitors is not equal. It is inexact to say that both fight for the right to livelihood. The worker who demands work, who seeks it and finds it, fights for a living, to assure his own life and that of his family. But we cannot say that the worker who abandons his position for a higher wage fights for his life. . . .

I maintain that the worker who goes on strike is moved by the idea of bettering his situation, and this is legitimate.

But it often happens, as in the strikes in Paris, that the workers who go on strike to improve their situation are obliged by unforeseen circumstances to return to work under the conditions that they had disdained. It is thus inexact to say that they were fighting for a living. Moreover, one day in my office in Paris when I was talking with construction workers and excavators on strike, a great number of them told me in the presence of witnesses (the prefect of the Seine, the directors, and the president of the municipal council, who could support my testimony): "We do not fight for an increase in wages; we are fighting for a shorter work day."

That is legitimate; they are exercising a right. I am not their adversary. Insofar as I could, I helped them in this demand.

I have seen certain strikes at first hand in which my sentiments were on the side of the strikers; but I cannot hide the fact that I found myself terribly embarrassed when I heard a man who was reproached for presenting himself for hire answer: "You go on strike in order to gain a higher wage. We do not say that you are wrong. Only, we have wives and children and we have earned nothing for three months. Work is offered us. Will you nourish our little ones if we refuse?"

If you refuse the right of the employers to replace the workers on strike and the right of the free workers to present themselves for hire, what will you do with the women and children whom you will deprive of nourishment? . . .

Here now is my dispatch on the subject of strikes to all the prefects of France:

> I remind you that in case of a strike in your department, your double objective should be to safeguard equally the liberty to work and the liberty to strike.

From Eugene N. Anderson, S. J. Pincetl and D. J. Ziegler, eds., *Europe in the Nineteenth Century, 1815–1914* (Indianapolis: Bobbs-Merrill, 1961), pp. 288–289.

It is not at all my desire that troops of infantry or cavalry appear on the premises of the strike as a preventive measure when the strike is called, as used to be done.

You should bring these troops to the vicinity of the strike, concealing their presence as much as possible, and make advance arrangements for their prompt requisition.

If order is menaced, they should arrive during the night to occupy either the mine head or the workshops, workyards or factories, where they will remain concealed. Only if order is disturbed will they be put into action.

To insure order and carry out the patrols which appear necessary to you, you will first of all call up the total strength of the *gendarmerie* at your disposition, and if it is insufficient, detachments of cavalry. You should always tell me exactly what arrangements you have made, what effective strength you intend to employ, and how you will distribute it at the points to be protected, should the occasion arise.

# THE LABOR MOVEMENT

## Strikes

*Ben Turner (1863–1942) was an English weaver and a textile union organizer. His autobiography recounts his activities and includes vivid descriptions of strikes, some led by unionized workers, others leading to unionization.*

### From Ben Turner. *About Myself*

Early in the new year of 1883 there were rumblings and rumours about a new scale or rate of wages being prepared by the employers' association, and in February it came to a head. Some of the employers had got it into their heads that the weavers were earning too much money, so they tried the plan of a new proposal, which meant a change downwards. . . .

. . . In those days the bulk of the weavers were men, and the finest of fine cloths were manufactured in that area. . . . These men weavers felt angry at the new move, and the new scale, and rejected it. There were various attempts by well-meaning folks to get a settlement, but it was in vain, and in March the lock-out began and 90 per cent. of the looms and, therefore, the mills, closed down. It raged for eleven weeks. It was, generally speaking, a peaceful dispute. There were few blacklegs, for the employers, in place of running that costly risk, sent a quantity of their easier woven cloths to Bradford and Halifax. Generally, the sympathy of the workers in the town was with the locked out weavers, but the tradesmen and business men, as usual, backed the employers, and wanted the workpeople to settle—however they settled. There were demonstrations and processions, mass meetings and intrigues with intermediaries, but it dragged on its way and became a fight with hunger and despair, ranged against a wealthy plutocracy, and after eleven weeks it ended in a compromise, mostly in favour of the employers. . . .

The next big strike I had anything to do with was the strike at Leeds. It was of tailoresses at a big clothing factory. . . . I was called by Miss Isabella Leeds who became a noted Labour woman, a foundation

From Ben Turner, *About Myself* (London: H. Toulmin at the Cayme Press Ltd., 1930), pp. 75–90, 104–108, 110–112, 114–115.

member of the Independent Labour Party and a fighter for women's franchise. . . . We used to address the strikers in various halls and meeting places. It ended in a compromise, but it stirred Leeds up a bit, and from it came the Leeds Tailoresses' Union which is now merged in the Tailors and Garment Workers' Union. From it also came the old Clothiers' Operatives' Union, which is also merged in the national body. . . .

Another big dispute with which I was closely connected was the lockout or strike at Manningham Mills, Bradford. In December, 1890, Mr. S. Cunliffe-Lister, who later on became Lord Masham, decided that a big reduction should be made in the wages of his operatives. It ranged upwards of 25 per cent. These very fine mills employed towards 5,000 workpeople. All of them were not affected by the dispute, but the weavers, to the number of many hundreds, were faced with the proposal just on the eve of Christmas. At that time, when weavers were in trouble, they nearly always sent for our union. . . . We met them. A courteous note was sent to the firm, but it received no response. The reduction was placarded, and the workpeople, after a ballot vote, declined to accept it, and the strike, lock-out or dispute began. What a hectic time it was! It lasted nearly six months, and twice and sometimes three times a week we had processions of the workpeople marching from near the millgates by several routes to the centre of Bradford. . . .

The women strikers established a well-conducted soup kitchen, and the sympathy of the shopkeepers was very broad and the butchers gave their bones and greengrocers and grocers and bakers gave peas, lentils and loaves, and thus children were fed. Every Thursday 200 to 300 cigar boxes would be fastened up, handbills placed over them, holes cut in for coins to be placed in, and these brave women and a number of the men would set out on the Friday and Saturday to mills and workshops, mines and factories, for miles around. Each who went got a shilling and their fares, and when the boxes were brought in on the Saturday afternoon the totals were made up and a distribution followed to the most needy and extra supplies were provided for the soup kitchen.

The dispute went on until well into May, when a number of public men got Sam Lister to bend a little, and a settlement was arrived at. It was really a defeat, and many of the best men and women went overseas to make a new home in a new land.

# National Federations of Labor

*In France, the trade union movement organized independently of political parties. The General Confederation of Labor, organized in 1895, formulated the doctrine known as revolutionary syndicalism in 1906 at its congress at Amiens.*

## From *The French General Confederation of Labor, Charter of Amiens* (1906)

The Confederal Congress of Amiens confirms Article 2 of the Constitution of the *Confédération Générale du Travail:* "The C.G.T. unites, independently of all schools of politics, all workers conscious of the need to strive for abolition of employers and wage earners."

The Congress holds that this declaration is a recognition of the class war which, in economic life, rallies workers in revolt against all the forms of exploitation and oppression, material as well as moral, practiced by the capitalist class against the working class.

The Congress adds to this affirmation of general principle the following specific points:

In the process of making its everyday demands syndicalism seeks to coordinate the efforts of the workers, to better their conditions through achieving such immediate improvements as shorter working hours, wage increases, etc.

But this activity is only one side of the work of syndicalism. It is preparing that complete emancipation, which can be accomplished only when the capitalist is expropriated; it commends the general strike as a means of action, and it believes that the *syndicat,* which is now the nucleus of resistance, will in future become the nucleus for production and distribution, the foundation of social reorganization.

The Congress declares that this double task of everyday life and of the future is the outcome of the conditions of wage earners which is burdensome to all workers and makes it the duty of the wage-earning class, whatever their political or philosophical inclinations, to belong to that essential group, the *syndicat;*

Accordingly, so far as individuals are concerned, the Congress declares that all members have complete freedom to take part outside the corporate group in any form of struggle which their political or philosophical beliefs may require, and it confines itself to asking them, in return, not to introduce into the *syndicat* opinions which they profess outside; . . .

So far as organizations are concerned, the Congress decides that, for syndicalism to attain maximum effectiveness, economic action should be exercised directly against the employer class, and the Confederal Organizations must not, as syndicalist groups, pay heed to the parties and sects which, outside and by their side, are completely free to pursue their aims of social transformation.

From David Thomson, ed., *France: Empire and Republic, 1850–1940* (New York: Harper & Row, 1968), pp. 171–172.

# THE SOCIALIST MOVEMENT

## German Social Democracy

*The German Social Democratic Party was founded in 1875 and advocated a moderate program of social and economic reform. Outlawed by the government for many years, the party nonetheless grew in strength. In 1890, the new kaiser, William II, asked for Bismarck's resignation; the anti-socialist laws were then dropped. In 1891, at a congress at Erfurt, the Social Democrats set forth their program. Within the Social Democratic Party special efforts were devoted to organizing working women of the kind represented in the second document in this section by Anna Maier.*

## From *The Erfurt Program (1891)*

### Programme of the Social Democratic Party of Germany

The struggle of the working class against capitalistic exploitation is of necessity a political struggle. The working class cannot carry on its economic contests, and cannot develop its economic organisation, without political rights. It cannot bring about the transference of the means of production into the possession of the community, without having obtained political power.

To give to this fight of the working class a conscious and unified form, and to show it its necessary goal—that is the task of the Social Democratic Party.

The interests of the working classes are the same in all countries with a capitalistic mode of production. With the extension of the world's commerce, and of production for the world-market, the position of the worker in every country grows ever more dependent on the position of the worker in other countries. The liberation of the working class, accordingly, is a work in which the workmen of all civilised countries are equally involved. In recognition of this, the Social Democratic Party of Germany feels and declares itself to be *one* with the class-conscious workmen of all other countries.

From Bertrand Russell, *German Social Democracy* (London: Longmans, Green and Co., 1896), pp. 137–141.

398

The Social Democratic Party of Germany does not fight, accordingly, for new class-privileges and class-rights, but for the abolition of class-rule and of classes themselves, for equal rights and equal duties of all, without distinction of sex or descent. Starting from these views, it combats, within existing society, not only the exploitation and oppression of wage-earners, but every kind of exploitation and oppression, whether directed against a class, a party, a sex, or a race.

Proceeding from these principles, the Social Democratic Party of Germany demands, to begin with:

1. Universal, equal, and direct suffrage, with secret ballot, for all elections, of all citizens of the realm over twenty years of age, without distinction of sex. Proportional representation, and until this is introduced, legal redistribution of electoral districts after every census. Biennial legislative periods. Holding of the elections on a legal holiday. Compensation for the elected representatives. Abolition of every limitation of political rights, except in the case of legal incapacity.

2. Direct legislation through the people, by means of the rights of proposal and rejection Self-determination and self-government of the people in realm, state, province and parish. Election of magistrates by the people, with responsibility to the people. Annual voting of taxes.

3. Education of all to bear arms. Militia in the place of the standing army. Decision by the popular representatives on questions of war and peace. Settlement of all international disputes by arbitration.

4. Abolition of all laws which limit or suppress the right of meeting and coalition.

5. Abolition of all laws which place women, whether in a public or a private capacity, at a disadvantage as compared with men.

6. Declaration that religion is a private affair. Abolition of all expenditure of public funds upon ecclesiastical and religious objects. Ecclesiastical and religious bodies are to be regarded as private associations, which regulate their affairs entirely independently.

7. Secularisation of schools. Compulsory attendance at the public national schools. Free education, free supply of educational materials, and free maintenance in the public schools, as well as in the higher educational institutions, for those boys and girls who, on account of their capacities, are considered fit for further education.

8. Free administration of justice, and free legal assistance. Administration of the law through judges elected by the people. Appeal in criminal cases. Compensation of persons unjustly accused, imprisoned, or condemned. Abolition of capital punishment.

9. Free medical attendance, including midwifery, and free supply of medicines. Free burial.

10. Graduated income and property-tax for defraying all public expenses, so far as these are to be covered by taxation. Duty of self-assessment. Succession duties, graduated according to the amount of the inheritance and the degree of relationship. Abolition of all indirect

taxes, customs, and other economic measures, which sacrifice the interests of the community to those of a privileged minority.

For the protection of the working classes, the Social Democratic Party of Germany demands to begin with:

1. An effective national and international legislation for the protection of labour on the following principles:—

(a) Fixing of a normal working day, which shall not exceed eight hours.

(b) Prohibition of the employment of children under fourteen.

(c) Prohibition of night-work, except in those industries which, by their nature, require night-work, from technical reasons, or for the public welfare.

(d) An unbroken rest of at least thirty-six hours in every week for every worker.

(e) Prohibition of the truck-system.

2. Supervision of all industrial establishments, investigation and regulation of conditions of labour in town and country by a central labour department, district labour bureaus, and chambers of labour.

3. Legal equality of agricultural labourers and domestic servants with industrial workers; abolition of the laws concerning servants.

4. Confirmation of the right of coalition.

5. Taking over by the Imperial Government of the whole system of working people's insurance, though giving the working people a controlling share in the administration.

## From Anna Maier. *Autobiography (1912)*

When I am asked what brought me in touch with socialism, I must refer back to my childhood [to begin my answer]. My father was a weaver, my mother a spooler, and other than that, they worked at whatever they could find. I am the youngest of 12 children and I learned very early what work is all about. When other children were out playing in the street, I would watch them with envy from the window until my mother would slap me to remind me that I had to work. It is easier [for a mother] to discipline a child than for a child to understand why she is being disciplined. When one thinks that at six, a child has to give up all the pleasures of youth. That is a lot to ask! When I went to school my only desire was to learn. But that desire was an illusion because I had to get up at 5 o'clock, do some spooling and then run off to school poorly dressed. After school I had to run home in order to do some more spooling before lunch. Then after school in

From Eleanor Reimer and John Fout, eds., *European Women: A Documentary History 1789–1945* (New York: Shocken Books, 1980), pp. 93–95. Copyright © 1980 by Shocken Books, Inc. Reprinted by permission of the publisher.

the afternoons I had to spool again. I was able to accept that, but not being kept home from school to help with the work. But all the begging and crying in the world didn't help. I had to do what my mother said. When I was older and wiser, I often cursed all the splendours of nature because they had never meant anything to me.

When I turned thirteen my mother took me by the hand and we went to see the manager of a tobacco factory to get me a job. The manager refused to hire me but my mother begged him to change his mind, since she explained, my father had died. I was hired. When I was getting ready to go to work the next day, my mother told me that I was to keep quiet and do what I was told. That was easier said than done. The treatment you received in this factory was really brutal. Young girls were often abused or even beaten by the older women. I rebelled strongly against that. I tried anything that might help improve things for me. As a child I was very pious and used to listen enthusiastically to the priests telling stories from the Bible. So, when things were going badly for me [at work], I would go to church on Sundays where I prayed so intently that I saw or heard nothing going on around me. When I went back to work on Monday, things were not any better and sometimes they were worse. I asked myself: Can there be a higher power that rewards good and punishes evil? I said to myself, no, that cannot be.

Several years went by. The *Women Workers' Newspaper* [*Arbeiterinnen-Zeitung*] began to appear and a few issues were smuggled into the factory by one of the older women. The more I was warned to stay away from this woman, the more I went to her to ask her if she would lend me a copy of the newspaper since I didn't have enough money to buy my own. At that time work hours were very long and the pay was very low. When my friend lent me a copy of the newspaper, I had to keep it hidden and I couldn't even let my mother see it if I took it home. I came to understand many things, my circle of acquaintances grew and when a political organization was founded in Sternberg, the workers were urged to join—only the men, the women were left out. A party representative came to us since I was already married by then. When he came by for the third time I asked him if I wasn't mature enough to become a member of the organization. He was embarrassed but replied: "When do you want to?" So I joined and I am a member of the party to this day.

I attended all the meetings, took part in all the demonstrations and it was not long before I was punished by the manager of the factory. I was taken off a good job and put in a poorer one just because I had become a Social Democrat. Nothing stopped me though; I said to myself, if this official is against it, out of fear to be sure, then it can't be all bad. When the tobacco workers' union was founded in November 1899, I joined and we had some big battles before we were able to make progress. Through these two organizations I have matured into a class-conscious fighter and I am now trying to win over mothers to the cause so that future children of the proletariat will have a happier youth than I had.

# English Social Democracy

*William Morris (1834–1896), an artist and poet, joined the Social Demo-cratic Federation in 1883. He sought, with Henry Hyndman, the founder of the group, a society based on equality with public ownership of capital and land. In 1884, he quarreled with Hyndman and founded his own group, the Socialist League.*

## From William Morris. *How I Became a Socialist*

I am asked by the Editor to give some sort of a history of the above conversion, and I feel that it may be of some use to do so, if my read-ers will look upon me as a type of a certain group of people, but not so easy to do clearly, briefly and truly. Let me, however, try. But first, I will say what I mean by being a Socialist, since I am told that the word no longer expresses definitely and with certainty what it did ten years ago. Well, what I mean by Socialism is a condition of society in which there should be neither rich nor poor, neither master nor mas-ter's man, neither idle nor overworked, neither brain-sick brain work-ers, nor heart-sick hand workers, in a word, in which all men would be living in equality of condition, and would manage their affairs un-wastefully, and with the full consciousness that harm to one would mean harm to all—the realisation at last of the meaning of the word COMMONWEALTH.

Now this view of Socialism which I hold to-day, and hope to die holding, is what I began with; I had no transitional period, unless you may call such a brief period of political radicalism during which I saw my ideal clear enough, but had no hope of any realisation of it. That came to an end some months before I joined the (then) Democratic Federation, and the meaning of my joining that body was that I had conceived a hope of the realisation of my ideal. If you ask me how much of a hope, or what I thought we Socialists then living and work-ing would accomplish towards it, or when there would be effected any change in the face of society, I must say, I do not know. I can only say that I did not measure my hope, nor the joy that it brought me at the time. . . .

Before the uprising of *modern* Socialism almost all intelligent people

From William Morris, *How I Became a Socialist* (London: Twentieth Century Press Ltd., 1896), pp. 9, 11–13.

either were, or professed themselves to be, quite contented with the civilisation of this century. Again, almost all of these really were thus contented, and saw nothing to do but to perfect the said civilisation by getting rid of a few ridiculous survivals of the barbarous ages. To be short, this was the *Whig* frame of mind, natural to the modern prosperous middle-class men, who, in fact, as far as mechanical progress is concerned, have nothing to ask for, if only Socialism would leave them alone to enjoy their plentiful style.

But besides these contented ones there were others who were not really contented, but had a vague sentiment of repulsion to the triumph of civilisation, but were coerced into silence by the measureless power of Whiggery. Lastly there were a few who were in open rebellion against the said Whiggery—a few, say two, Carlyle and Ruskin. The latter, before my days of practical Socialism, was my master towards the ideal aforesaid, and, looking backward, I cannot help saying, by the way, how deadly dull the world would have been twenty years ago but for Ruskin! It was through him that I learned to give form to my discontent, which I must say was not by any means vague. Apart from the desire to produce beautiful things, the leading passion of my life has been and is hatred of modern civilisation. What shall I say of it now, when the words are put into my mouth, my hope of its destruction—what shall I say of its supplanting by Socialism?

What shall I say concerning its mastery of and its waste of mechanical power, its commonwealth so poor, its enemies of the commonwealth so rich, its stupendous organisation—for the misery of life! Its contempt of simple pleasures which everyone could enjoy but for its folly? Its eyeless vulgarity which has destroyed art, the one certain solace of labour? All this I felt then as now, but I did not know why it was so. The hope of the past times was gone, the struggles of mankind for many ages had produced nothing but this sordid, aimless, ugly confusion; the immediate future seemed to me likely to intensify all the present evils by sweeping away the last survivals of the days before the dull squalor of civilisation had settled down on the world. This was a bad look-out indeed, and, if I may mention myself as a personality and not as a mere type, especially so to a man of my disposition, careless of metaphysics and religion, as well as of scientific analysis, but with a deep love of the earth and the life on it, and a passion for the history of the past of mankind. Think of it! Was it all to end in a counting-house on the top of a cinder-heap, with Podsnap's drawing-room in the offing, and a Whig committee dealing out champagne to the rich and margarine to the poor in such convenient proportions as would make all men contented together, though the pleasure of the eyes was gone from the world, and the place of Homer was to be taken by Huxley? Yet believe me, in my heart, when I really forced myself to look towards the future, that is what I saw in it, and, as far as I could tell, scarce anyone seemed to think it worth while to struggle against such a consummation of civilisation. So there I was in for a fine pessimistic end of life, if it had not somehow dawned on me that amidst all this filth of civilisation the seeds of a great chance, what we others call Social Revolution, were beginning to germinate. The whole face of things was changed to me by that discovery, and all I had to do then in order to become a Socialist was to hook myself on to the practical movement, which, as before said, I have tried to do as well as I could.

# French Socialists Unite

*In 1905, the various French socialist parties united into a single group, the French Section of the Socialist International. Unification made possible cooperation among socialist deputies in parliament and contributed to steady gains for socialists at the polls. By May 1914, the socialists were the second largest group in the Chamber of Deputies, holding one-sixth of all seats.*

## From *Program of The Unified Socialist Party (1905)*

The delegates of the French organizations—the Revolutionary Socialist Workers' Party, the Socialist Party of France, the French Socialist Party, the Independent Federations, etc.—declare that the action of the Unified Socialist Party must be based on the principles which have been established by the international congresses, especially the most recent ones at Paris in 1900 and at Amsterdam in 1904.

They state that the divergences of views and different interpretations of tactics, which have so far been able to appear, are due above all to circumstances peculiar to France and to the absence of a general organization.

They affirm their common desire to found a party of the class war which, even while it takes advantage for the workers of minor conflicts among the rich, or is by chance able to concert its action with that of a political party for the defense of the rights or interests of the proletariat, remains always a party of fundamental and unyielding opposition to the whole of the bourgeois class and to the State which is its instrument.

Consequently, the delegates declare that their organizations are ready to collaborate forthwith in this work of unifying the socialist forces on the following bases:

1. The Socialist Party is a class party whose aim is to socialize the means of production and distribution, that is to transform capitalist society into a collectivist or communist society, and to adopt as its means

From David Thomson, ed., *France: Empire and Republic, 1850–1940* (New York: Harper & Row, 1968), pp. 283–284.

the economic or political organization of the proletariat. By its purpose, its ideal, by the means it adopts, the Socialist Party, while pursuing the achievement of the immediate reforms claimed by the working class, is not a party of reform but a party of class war and revolution.

2. Those whom it returns to Parliament form a single group as compared with all the bourgeois political sects. The Socialist group in Parliament must refuse the Government all the resources which ensure the power of the bourgeoisie and its domination, must refuse, therefore, military credits, credits for colonial conquests, secret funds and the whole of the budget.

Even in exceptional circumstances, those returned cannot commit the Party without its consent.

In Parliament the Socialist group must dedicate itself to the defense and the extension of the political liberties and rights of the workers, to the pursuit and realization of reforms such as will improve the conditions of life and advance the struggle of the working class.

Deputies, like all other selected members, must hold themselves at the disposition of the Party, to serve its action in the country, its general propaganda for organizing the proletariat, and the final ends of socialism. . . .

[Articles 3 to 7 assert the authority of the Party over all its elected representatives and over the Party press, exacting from deputies a portion of their parliamentary salaries and obedience to a *mandat impératif*—i.e., to prior instructions given to deputies by the Party organization. The statement also proposes a Congress of Unity to be held as soon as possible.]

# XII

# WORLD WAR I

MOUNTING TENSIONS AMONG the European powers broke forth into war in 1914. The murder of the Austrian Archduke Francis Ferdinand provoked conflict between Germany and Russia. As the Russians massed troops on German and Austrian borders, in defense of Serbia, the Germans declared war. France and England were quickly drawn into the fray on the Russian side. In 1917, angered by German submarine attacks on American ships, the United States entered the war on the side of the Allies.

The war took an appalling toll in every country in Europe. Whether bogged down in trenches on the western front or bombed by airplanes, which were used for the first time as weapons in this conflict, the fighting forces suffered tremendous casualties. World War I claimed the lives of more than 8 million people; it left thousands more wounded.

War production drew new workers, many of them women, into the industrial labor force. Governments took an increasingly large role in the planning and supervising of production and labor relations, in the interests of the war effort. The economic costs of war were enormous. Buildings, factories, roads, and bridges were destroyed wherever fighting took place.

When Germany finally surrendered in 1918, the Allies negotiated a harsh peace. Their goal was to prevent Germany from ever threatening Europe again, to force Germany to pay reparations for war damages, and to weaken its industrial capacity. Observers like the economist John Maynard Keynes argued that far from ending German aggressiveness, the Versailles Treaty might increase it in the future.

The war had many impacts: it destroyed the German and Austro-Hungarian empires; it changed the map of Europe; it weakened the Western economies and destroyed a future generation of leaders. In addition, it offered the spectacle of violence and cruelty to men and women who had been raised to believe in progress and human decency. With World War I the optimism born of nineteenth-century industrialization and its belief in progress turned to a bitter and disillusioned pessimism about the prospects for humanity's future.

# THE ROAD TO WAR

## National Rivalry

*In the context of heightening tensions between Germany and Great Britain, Kaiser William complained about British diplomacy and British ingratitude for German support in the Boer War. When it was published in the London* Daily Telegraph *in 1908, William's interview infuriated British officials, who vowed to prevent the German navy from surpassing the British.*

### From *An Interview with the German Kaiser (Daily Telegraph, 1908)*

... As I have said, his Majesty honoured me with a long conversation, and spoke with impulsive and unusual frankness. "You English," he said, "are mad, mad, mad as March hares. What has come over you that you are so completely given over to suspicions quite unworthy of a great nation? What more can I do than I have done? I declared with all the emphasis at my command, in my speech at Guildhall, that my heart is set upon peace, and that it is one of my dearest wishes to live on the best of terms with England. Have I ever been false to my word? Falsehood and prevarication are alien to my nature. My actions ought to speak for themselves, but you listen not to them but to those who misinterpret and distort them. That is a personal insult which I feel and resent. To be forever misjudged, to have my repeated offers of friendship weighed and scrutinized with jealous, mistrustful eyes, taxes my patience severely. I have said time after time that I am a friend of England, and your Press—or, at least, a considerable section of it—bids the people of England refuse my proffered hand, and insinuates that the other holds a dagger. How can I convince a nation against its will?

"I repeat," continued his Majesty, "that I am the friend of England, but you make things difficult for me. My task is not of the easiest. The prevailing sentiment among large sections of the middle and lower classes of my own people is not friendly to England. I am, therefore, so to speak, in a minority in my own land, but it is a minority of the

From Louis L. Snyder, ed., *Documents of German History* (New Brunswick, N.J.: Rutgers University Press, 1958), pp. 296–300. Copyright © 1958 by Rutgers, The State University. Reprinted by permission of the publisher.

best elements as it is in England with respect to Germany. That is another reason why I resent your refusal to accept my pledged word that I am the friend of England. I strive without ceasing to improve relations, and you retort that I am your arch-enemy. You make it hard for me. Why is it?"

Thereupon I ventured to remind his Majesty that not England alone, but the whole of Europe had viewed with disapproval the recent action of Germany in allowing the German consul to return from Tangier to Fez, and in anticipating the joint action of France and Spain by suggesting to the Powers that the time had come in Europe to recognize Muley Hafid as the new Sultan of Morocco.

His Majesty made a gesture of impatience. "Yes," he said, "that is an excellent example of the way in which German action is misrepresented. First, then, as regards to the journey of Dr. Vassel. The German Government, in sending Dr. Vassel back to his post at Fez, was only guided by the wish that he should look after the private interests of German subjects in that city, who cried for help and protection after the long absence of a Consular representative. And why not send him? Are those who charge Germany with having stolen a march on the other Powers aware that the French Consular representative had already been in Fez for several months before Dr. Vassel set out? Then, as to the recognition of Muley Hafid. The Press of Europe has complained with much acerbity that Germany ought not to have suggested his recognition until he had notified Europe of his full acceptance of the Act of Algeciras, as being binding upon him as Sultan of Morocco and successor of his brother. My answer is that Muley Hafid notified the Powers to that effect weeks ago, before the decisive battle was fought. He sent, as far back as the middle of last July, an intentional communication to the Governments of Germany, France, and Great Britain, containing an explicit acknowledgment that he was prepared to recognize all the obligations towards Europe which were incurred by Abdul Aziz during his Sultanate. The German Government interpreted that communication as a final and authoritative expression of Muley Hafid's intentions, and therefore they considered that there was no reason to wait until he had sent a second communication, before recognizing him as the de facto Sultan of Morocco, who had succeeded to his brother's throne by right of victory in the field. . . . There has been nothing in Germany's recent action with regard to Morocco which runs contrary to the explicit declaration of my love of peace, which I made both at Guildhall and in my latest speech at Strasbourg."

His Majesty then reverted to the subject uppermost in his mind—his proved friendship for England. "I have referred," he said, "to the speeches in which I have done all that a Sovereign can to proclaim my good will. But, as actions speak louder than words, let me also refer to my acts. It is commonly believed in England that throughout the South African War Germany was hostile to her. German opinion undoubtedly was hostile—bitterly hostile. But what of official Germany? Let my critics ask themselves what brought to a sudden stop, and, indeed, to absolute collapse, the European tour of the Boer delegates, who were striving to obtain European intervention? They were feted in Holland. France gave them a rapturous welcome. They wished to come to Berlin, where the German people would have crowned them with flowers But when they asked me to receive them—I refused. The agitation immediately died away, and the delegation returned empty-handed. Was that, I ask, the action of a secret enemy?

"Again, when the struggle was at its height, the German Government was invited by the Governments of France and Russia to join with them in calling upon England to put an end to the war. The moment had come, they said, not only to save the Boer Republics, but also to humiliate England to the dust. What was my reply? I said that so far from Germany joining in any concerted European action to put pressure upon England and bring about her downfall, Germany would always keep aloof from politics that could bring her into complications with a Sea Power like England. Posterity will one day read the exact terms of the telegram—now in the archives of Windsor Castle—in which I informed the Sovereign of England of the answer I had returned to the Powers which then sought to compass her fall. Englishmen who now insult me by doubting my word should know what were my actions in the hour of their adversity.

"Nor was that all. Just at the time of your Black Week, in the December of 1899, when disasters followed one another in rapid succession, I received a letter from Queen Victoria, my revered grandmother, written in sorrow and affliction, and bearing manifest traces of the anxieties which were preying upon her mind and health. I at once returned a sympathetic reply. Nay, I did more. I bade one of my officers procure for me as exact an account as he could obtain of the number of combatants in South Africa on both sides, and of the actual position of the opposing forces. With the figures before me, I worked out what I considered to be the best plan of campaign under the circumstances, and submitted it to my General Staff for their criticism. Then I dispatched it to England, and that document, likewise, is among the State papers at Windsor Castle, awaiting the severely impartial verdict of history. And, as a matter of curious coincidence, let me add that the plan which I formulated ran very much on the same lines as that which was actually adopted by Lord Roberts, and carried by him into successful operation. Was that, I repeat, the act of one who wished England ill? Let Englishmen be just and say!

"But, you will say, what of the German Navy? Surely, that is a menace to England! Against whom but England are my squadrons being prepared? If England is not in the minds of those Germans who are bent on creating a powerful fleet, why is Germany asked to consent to such new and heavy burdens of taxation? My answer is clear. Germany ıs a young and growing Empire. She has a world-wide commerce, which is rapidly expanding, and to which the legitimate ambition of patriotic Germans refuses to assign any bounds. Germany must have a powerful fleet to protect that commerce, and her manifold interests in even the most distant seas. She expects those interests to go on growing, and she must be able to champion them manfully in any quarter of the globe. Germany looks ahead. Her horizons stretch far away. She must be prepared for any eventualities in the Far East. Who can foresee what may take place in the Pacific in the days to come, days not so distant as some believe, but days, at any rate, for which all European Powers with Far Eastern interests ought steadily to prepare? Look at the accomplished rise of Japan; think of the possible national awakening of China; and then judge of the vast problems of the Pacific. Only those Powers which have great navies will be listened to with respect, when the future of the Pacific comes to be solved; and, if for that reason only, Germany must have a powerful fleet. It may even be that England herself will be glad that Germany has a fleet when they speak together on the same side in the great debates of the future." . . .

# Popular Propaganda

*The German "Chant of Hate" against England, published in 1914, is an example of how public sentiment was directed against England.*

## The German "Hasslied"

> French and Russian they matter not,
> A blow for a blow and a shot for a shot;
> We love them not, we hate them not,
> We hold the Weichsel and Vosges-gate,
> We have but one—and only hate,
> We love as one, we hate as one,
> We have one foe and one alone.
>
> He is known to you all, he is known to you all,
> He crouches behind the dark grey flood,
> Full of envy, of rage, of craft, of gall,
> Cut off by waves that are thicker than blood.
> Come, let us stand at the Judgment place,
> An oath to swear to, face to face,
> An oath of bronze no wind can shake,

From Ernst Lissaur, originally published in *Jugend* (1914). This translation by Barbara Henderson in *The New York Times*, October 15, 1914. Copyright © 1914 by The New York Times Company. Reprinted by permission.

An oath for our sons and their sons to take.
Come, hear the word, repeat the word,
Throughout the Fatherland make it heard.
We will never forego our hate,
We have all but a single hate,
We love as one, we hate as one,
We have one foe, and one alone—
        ENGLAND!

In the Captain's mess, in the banquet hall,
Sat feasting the officers, one and all,
Like a sabre-blow, like the swing of a sail,
One seized his glass held high to hail;
Sharp-snapped like the stroke of a rudder's play,
Spoke three words only: "To the Day!"
Whose glass this fate?
They had all but a single hate.
Who was thus known?
They had one foe, and one alone—
        ENGLAND!

Take you the folk of the Earth in pay,
With bars of gold your ramparts lay,
Bedeck the ocean with bow on bow,
Ye reckon well, but not well enough now.
French and Russian they matter not,
A blow for a blow, a shot for a shot,
We fight the battle with bronze and steel,
And the time that is coming Peace will seal.

You will hate with a lasting hate,
We will never forego our hate,
Hate by water and hate by land,
Hate of the head and hate of the hand,
Hate of the hammer and hate of the crown,
Hate of seventy millions, choking down.
We love as one, we hate as one,
We have one foe, and one alone—
        ENGLAND!

# War Declared

*When the heir to the Hapsburg empire, the Archduke Francis Ferdinand, was assassinated by Serbian nationalists at Sarajevo on June 28, 1914, the Austrians were determined to take action against Slavs in Serbia. The Austrians* consulted their German allies, who pledged support for whatever action Austria deemed necessary, in the famous "blank check" telegram of July 6, 1914. Several weeks later, Russia mobilized its forces on the German and Austrian borders in an effort to protect Serbia. In response, the Germans declared war on Russia on August 1 and on Russia's ally, France, on August 3.

## The "Blank Check" Telegram

### Telegram from the Imperial Chancellor, von Bethmann-Hollweg, to the German Ambassador at Vienna, Tschirschky, July 6, 1914

Berlin, July 6, 1914

*Confidential. For Your Excellency's
personal information and guidance*

The Austro-Hungarian Ambassador yesterday delivered to the Emperor a confidential personal letter from the Emperor Francis Joseph, which depicts the present situation from the Austro-Hungarian point of view, and describes the measures which Vienna has in view. A copy is now being forwarded to Your Excellency.

I replied to Count Szögyény today on behalf of His Majesty that His Majesty sends his thanks to the Emperor Francis Joseph for his letter and would soon answer it personally. In the meantime His Majesty desires to say that he is not blind to the danger which threatens Austria-Hungary and thus the Triple Alliance as a result of the Russian and Serbian Pan-Slavic agitation. Even though His Majesty is known to feel no unqualified confidence in Bulgaria and her ruler, and naturally inclines more toward our old ally Rumania and her Hohenzollern prince, yet he quite understands that the Emperor Francis Joseph, in view of the attitude of Rumania and of the danger of a new Balkan alliance aimed directly at the Danube Monarchy, is anxious to bring about an understanding between Bulgaria and the Triple Alliance. His Majesty will, therefore, direct his minister at Sofia to lend the Austro-Hungarian representative such support as he may desire in any action taken to this end. His Majesty will, furthermore, make an effort at Bucharest, according to the wishes of the Emperor Francis Joseph, to influence King Carol to the fulfillment of the duties of his alliance, to the renunciation of Serbia, and to the suppression of the Rumanian agitations directed against Austria-Hungary.

Finally, as far as concerns Serbia, His Majesty, of course, cannot interfere in the dispute now going on between Austria-Hungary and that country, as it is a matter not within his competence. The Emperor Francis Joseph may, however, rest assured that His Majesty will faithfully stand by Austria-Hungary, as is required by the obligations of his alliance and of his ancient friendship.

BETHMANN-HOLLWEG

*Until 1914, European socialists had vowed to prevent their governments from going to war. In his memoir, the German socialist Philipp Scheidemann (1865–1939) describes the failure of German Social Democrats and of international socialists to stem the tide of war.*

## From Philipp Scheidemann. *The Making of New Germany*

At express speed I had returned to Berlin. Everywhere where a word could be heard the conversation was of war and rumors of war. There was only one topic of conversation—war. The supporters of war seemed to be in a great majority. Were these pugnacious fellows, young and old, bereft of their senses? Were they so ignorant of the horrors of war? I only heard voices advocating peace in the circle of my own Party friends, apart from the few Social Democratic newspapers. Yet the vast majority of the people were opposed to war, without a doubt. Vast crowds of demonstrators paraded "Unter den Linden." Schoolboys and students were there in their thousands; their bearded seniors, with their Iron Crosses of 1870–71 on their breasts, were there too in huge numbers.

. . . Patriotic demonstrations had an intoxicating effect and excited the war-mongers to excess. "A call like the voice of thunder." Cheers! "In triumph we will smite France to the ground." "All hail to thee in victor's crown." Cheers! Hurrah!

The counterdemonstrations immediately organized by the Berlin Social Democrats were imposing, and certainly more disciplined than the Jingo processions, but could not outdo the shouts of the fire-eaters. "Good luck to him who cares for truth and right. Stand firmly round the flag." "Long live peace!" "Socialists, close up your ranks." The Socialist International cheer. The patriots were sometimes silenced by the Proletarians; then they came out on top again. This choral contest, "Unter den Linden," went on for days. . . .

From Philipp Scheidemann, *The Making of New Germany: The Memoirs of Philipp Scheidemann* (New York: D. Appleton and Co., 1929), Vol. 1, pp. 201–202, 212, 215–216. Copyright 1929 by D. Appleton and Company. Reprinted by permission of E. P. Dutton, Inc.

On 2d August the Executives of the Party and the Section of the Reichstag met together in the Party committee room. The Reichstag was to meet on 4th August to pass the War Credits—that had been told us officially. Haase and Ledebour advocated their rejection, all the others their adoption. Unanimity was impossible, abstention likewise, for a Party of our strength could not think of abstaining from voting in this critical hour for the Fatherland. . . .

[On 3d August] the Section met at once after dinner under my chairmanship. The discussion was extremely bitter, and in the course of it Müller arrived from Paris. Surprised by the declaration of War, he had had considerable trouble in recrossing the frontier. He reported as follows: he had been well and kindly received, as usual, by our French colleagues, but unfortunately no understanding had been reached. Pierre Renaudel had given the clearest statement of the attitude of our French colleagues at the meeting:

"The position of the French and German democrat is not the same. The French Socialists were fully informed of diplomatic proceedings by their Government in due course; in Germany this was not the case. If France, whose people and Government desired peace, were attacked by Germany, their French colleagues would be forced to vote for the War Budget, because measures for self-defence had to be taken by France, if attacked. Thus situated, the French democrat could not abstain from voting. The German democrat was in a different position, if Germany were the aggressor. They could perhaps vote against the War Credits."

After one of the French comrades had stated that Germany would be generally considered guilty for the outbreak of war, Müller replied:

"German Socialists are in the habit of speaking the truth in the most pointed way to their Government. We have latterly reproached our Government most bitterly in the public Press because they did not take sufficient care to inform the country before sending off the ultimatum to Serbia. But this is a thing that cannot be altered, and, as matters now stand, the greatest danger is threatened from Russia. . . . Yet it is the general opinion in all Party circles in Germany that Russia would be the guilty party if it now came to war, and that France is in a position to stop war if she will put the requisite pressure on St. Petersburg for preserving peace."

It was very soon clear to our friend Hermann Müller, in the course of his conversation with the French Socialists, that the French would vote for the War Credits. Identical declarations both in the Reichstag and the Chamber of Deputies were now out of the question. After Müller's report the Reichstag Section continued to discuss the War Credits, with the result that only fourteen members voted against passing the War Credits.

*The English poet Rupert Brooke (1887–1915) captures the feelings of a young soldier sent off to war.*

## From Rupert Brooke. *The Soldier*

If I should die, think only this of me:
　That there's some corner of a foreign field
That is for ever England. There shall be
　In that rich earth a richer dust concealed;
A dust whom England bore, shaped, made aware,
　Gave, once, her flowers to love, her ways to roam,
A body of England's, breathing English air,
　Washed by the rivers, blest by suns of home.

And think, this heart, all evil shed away,
　A pulse in the eternal mind, no less
　　Gives somewhere back the thoughts by England given;
Her sights and sounds; dreams happy as her day;
　And laughter, learnt of friends; and gentleness,
　　In hearts at peace, under an English heaven.

# STRATEGIES AND BATTLES

## The Western Front

*The French commander in chief, Joseph Joffre (1852–1931), describes French strategy for the Battle of the Marne (September 5–12, 1914), which forced a German retreat.*

## From Field Marshal Joffre. *Personal Memoirs*

### The Battle of the Marne

At the moment when the battle on which the fate of the country depended was about to open, the military situation had taken on an aspect infinitely more favourable than anything I could have dared to hope for a few days before.

The French Third, Fourth, Ninth and Fifth Armies, with their right resting on the entrenched camp of Verdun, were deployed along a front of about 125 miles, roughly marked by Sermaize, Vitry-le-François, Sommesous, the Saint-Gond Marshes, Esternay and Courtacon. Thrown forward on their left in an advanced echelon were the British Army and the French Sixth Army; the first south-west of Coulommiers, the second north-west of Meaux, covered on its left by Sordet's Cavalry Corps. The line, in its general aspect, presented the form of a vast pocket, into which five German armies seemed bent upon engulfing themselves. For all the information gathered during the day of September 5th went to show that the enemy was vigorously pursuing his march to the south. . . .

But however advantageous the general situation appeared—above all, now that I could count upon the co-operation of the British—it can well be conceived that I was none the less beset by grave preoccupa-

From *The Personal Memoirs of Joffre*, Colonel T. Bentley Mott, D. S. M., trans. (New York and London: Harper & Row, 1932), pp. 256–257, 259–261, 279–281. Copyright 1932, 1960 by Harper & Row, Publishers, Inc. Reprinted by permission of the publisher.

tions. For in spite of the assurances which Generals Foch and Franchet d'Esperey had given me, I could not blind myself to the fact that this offensive, suddenly undertaken with armies worn out by an exhausting retreat, presented a problem bristling with uncertainties. . . .

I was confident that our men understood me thoroughly when I told them that the fate of our country now hung in the balance, and I felt altogether sure that I could count upon their steadiness; on the other hand, I was no less certain that the enemy's spirits must be at the highest pitch. And yet, in weighing the matter carefully, I was convinced that this very fact presented a greater danger for him than for us; for we could count upon the effect of the surprise which was certain to be produced by a sudden attack coming at the moment when the Germans were convinced that all they now had to do was to sweep up the remnants of our routed armies. . . .

The Battle of the Marne . . . began as soon as we had succeeded in concentrating around the German right a mass sufficiently heavy to give us on this part of the strategic field the double advantage of position and numerical superiority. In spite of this situation, if we had tried to apply inflexibly a formula of envelopment at any price—which, moreover, was never my intention—we would have been playing into the enemy's hands. But our forces were sufficiently strong and our system sufficiently flexible to prevent the inevitable reaction of the enemy from catching us unawares. Von Kluck could only ward off the menace which threatened his right by creating between his army and that of von Bülow a breach which continued to widen progressively. In this way, beginning with the second day, the battle of the Marne took on the characteristics of a rupture of the enemy's line, a rupture which the German Commander-in-Chief had neither the time nor the means to avoid.

This conception of how a battle should be conducted, when it is fought under the conditions presented by the wide extension of modern fronts, presupposes not only the existence of a complete unity of doctrine between the commander-in-chief and his subordinates, but also implies that sure and rapid communication between them can be effected through the telegraph and telephone and by means of staff officers, who are, properly speaking, exponents of the very brain and will of the commander-in-chief. The task which fell to these liaison officers was extremely delicate, and they have sometimes been accused of assuming to themselves an authority out of all proportion to their rank. It is possible that errors were committed by these men; it is also likely that they at times became victims of the enmity aroused by pitiless decapitations which the interest of the country had induced me to make.

[*Joffre now describes the encounters between French and German troops and the eventual French victory.*]

Although the Battle of the Marne did not bring as much as I expected of it, I nevertheless think I am justified in briefly pointing out the main results obtained.

The month of August had given the first game of the rubber to the Germans; with the Belgians thrown back upon Antwerp, the British and French towards the Seine. Our left wing threatened with envelopment and Paris with capture; there can be small doubt that at this moment the Germans were looking forward to another Sedan repeated on an enormous scale. Our adversaries' plan had as its foundation a rapid victory in the West. The need of winning the war before the resources of Russia could be brought into play was now all the more imperative, since the British Empire had thrown itself into the conflict on our side. As I have said several times in the preceding pages, it would have been playing into the enemy's hands if I had risked the destinies of our country at a moment when the essential thing for us was above all to hold out and avoid destruction. It was this consideration which justified me in waiting for an always possible turn of fortune. I paid for this delay by sacrificing—temporarily, as I hoped—a considerable part of our territory. Although a total defeat of the Germans was not accomplished, nevertheless the occasion we had so patiently waited for did enable us to drive them back along the whole line, and our victory forced them to bury themselves in trenches. What a disappointment for men in a hurry! . . .

. . . For many people, the Marne came to be considered as a sort of miracle; for others, as a happy and unexpected piece of luck. For those persons who received their inspiration from the enemy press, the battle reduced itself to a manœuvre undertaken by the German Supreme Command, which, in the absence of the strategic results it had failed to achieve, from now on invariably pointed to the "war map" as being the argument most easy to comprehend.

Fortunately, the essential fact remained that the enemy had been driven back to a line fifty miles north of Paris and it could be said that he was definitely halted. People breathed once more, and confidence revived.

# Trench Warfare

*The British poet Siegfried Sassoon (1886–1967) portrays the horror of a war conducted from trenches. After the Battle of the Marne, warfare on the western front was carried on from trenches for four miserable years.*

## Siegfried Sassoon. *Attack*

At dawn the ridge emerges massed and dun
In the wild purple of the glow'ring sun,
Smouldering through spouts of drifting smoke that shroud
The menacing scarred slope; and, one by one,
Tanks creep and topple forward to the wire.
The barrage roars and lifts. Then, clumsily bowed
With bombs and guns and shovels and battle-gear,
Men jostle and climb to meet the bristling fire.
Lines of grey, muttering faces, masked with fear,
They leave their trenches, going over the top,
While time ticks blank and busy on their wrists,
And hope, with furtive eyes and grappling fists,
Flounders in mud. O Jesus, make it stop!

From Siegfried Sassoon, *Collected Poems* (New York: E. P. Dutton, 1918). Copyright 1918 by E. P. Dutton. Copyright 1946 by Siegfried Sassoon. Reprinted by permission of G. T. Sassoon and Viking Penguin, Inc.

# New Weaponry

*Airplanes were a new kind of weapon during World War I. Germany had the largest number of planes at the outbreak of the war; but France and Great Britain rapidly built up their air forces. Captain Manfred Freiherr von Richthofen (1892–1918) was a German pilot reputed to have destroyed eighty enemy planes. He was known as the Red Baron and deemed "the greatest aviator of the war."*

## From Captain Von Richthofen. *The Red Battle Flyer*

In Russia our battle squadron did a great deal of bomb throwing. Our occupation consisted of annoying the Russians. We dropped our eggs on their finest railway establishments. One day our whole squadron went out to bomb a very important railway station. The place was

From Captain Von Richthofen, *The Red Battle Flyer* (New York: McBride Co., 1918), pp. 99–102, 131–133.

called Manjewicze and was situated about twenty miles behind the Front. That was not very far. The Russians had planned an attack and the station was absolutely crammed with colossal trains. Trains stood close to one another. Miles of rails were covered with them. One could easily see that from above. There was an object for bombing that was worth while.

One can become enthusiastic over anything. For a time I was delighted with bomb throwing. It gave me a tremendous pleasure to bomb those fellows from above. Frequently I took part in two expeditions on a single day.

On the day mentioned our object was Manjewicze. Everything was ready. The aeroplanes were ready to start. Every pilot tried his motor, for it is a painful thing to be forced to land against one's will on the wrong side of the Front line, especially in Russia. The Russians hated the flyers. If they caught a flying man they would certainly kill him. That is the only risk one ran in Russia for the Russians had no aviators, or practically none. If a Russian flying man turned up he was sure to have bad luck and would be shot down. The anti-aircraft guns used by Russia were sometimes quite good, but they were too few in number. Compared with flying in the West, flying in the East is absolutely a holiday.

The aeroplanes rolled heavily to the starting point. They carried bombs to the very limit of their capacity. Sometimes I dragged three hundred pounds of bombs with a normal C-machine. Besides, I had with me a very heavy observer who apparently had not suffered in any way from the food scarcity. I had also with me a couple of machine guns. I was never able to make proper use of them in Russia. It is a pity that my collection of trophies contains not a single Russian.

Flying with a heavy machine which is carrying a great dead weight is no fun, especially during the mid-day summer heat in Russia. The barges sway in a very disagreeable manner. Of course, heavily laden though they are, they do not fall down. The 150 h. p. motors prevent it. At the same time it is no pleasant sensation to carry such a large quantity of explosives and benzine.

At last we get into a quiet atmosphere. Now comes the enjoyment of bombing. It is splendid to be able to fly in a straight line and to have a definite object and definite orders. After having thrown one's bombs one has the feeling that he has achieved something, while frequently, after searching for an enemy to give battle to, one comes home with a sense of failure at not having brought a hostile machine to the ground. Then a man is apt to say to himself, "You have acted stupidly." . . .

The great thing in air fighting is that the decisive factor does not lie in trick flying but solely in the personal ability and energy of the aviator. A flying man may be able to loop and do all the stunts imaginable and yet he may not succeed in shooting down a single enemy. In my opinion the aggressive spirit is everything and that spirit is very strong in us Germans. Hence we shall always retain the domination of the air.

The French have a different character. They like to put traps and to attack their opponents unawares. That cannot easily be done in the air. Only a beginner can be caught and one cannot set traps because an aeroplane cannot hide itself. The invisible aeroplane has not yet been discovered. Sometimes, however, the Gaelic blood asserts itself. The Frenchmen will then attack. But the French attacking spirit is like bottled lemonade. It lacks tenacity.

The Englishmen, on the other hand, one notices that they are of Germanic blood. Sportsmen easily take to flying, and Englishmen see in flying nothing but a sport. They take a perfect delight in looping the loop, flying on their back, and indulging in other stunts for the benefit of our soldiers in the trenches. All these tricks may impress people who attend a Sports Meeting, but the public at the battle-front is not as appreciative of these things. It demands higher qualifications than trick flying. Therefore, the blood of English pilots will have to flow in streams.

# America Enters the War

*Provoked by German submarine attacks on American ships, the United States declared war on April 6, 1917. President Woodrow Wilson defined the war as one "to make the world safe for democracy." Congressman Joe Henry Eagle of Texas supported the Allied effort in his speech of April 15.*

## From *Speech of Congressman Joe Henry Eagle (April 15, 1917)*

Mr. Chairman, without any mental reservation whatsoever, I give my voice and my vote to this resolution. It states the truth in plain, simple words. The Imperial German Government, without formally declaring, has nevertheless made and still is making, war upon the United States. While professing to obey international law, her submarines have sunk American ships upon the high seas without search or warning, and while professing friendship for our people and Nation, she has thus murdered our men, women, and children. While herself professing to desire a free sea and "a place in the sun" she has without authority of international law announced to us that from February 1, 1917, one American ship will each week be allowed by her to enter and one to leave a port of her enemies, provided we paint that ship such color as she may prescribe and carry such cargo as she may designate

From Jere C. King, *The First World War* (New York: Walker and Company, 1972), pp. 279–283. Reprinted by permission of Walker and Company, Inc.

and enter such port as she may permit, and that otherwise, without any warning, search, or seizure, her submarines will sink American ships and send American citizens to instant death. And she has made good her decree to this time. Thus she has as completely blockaded our ports and shores as if her fleet rode triumphant in our waters.

At every American port great steamships, laden with the cotton of the South, the corn and wheat and cattle of the West, the multiplied products of the North, and the manufactures of the East, lie at anchor afraid to move toward their destination because the German submarine lurks beneath the sea to sink ship and cargo and murder every soul on board without warning. And at each American port each warehouse is filled with American merchandise of both the raw and finished product which can not be discharged because the steamships thus lie at anchor, although a ready foreign market awaits such legitimate products of American farms, fields, mines, and factories, and although under unbroken international law for centuries it is lawful for such commerce to move. As a result tens of thousands of freight cars are similarly loaded and at the various ports of the country, ready to discharge, but used only as warehouses, thus entailing congestion and the paralysis of the Nation's transportation business. If this situation is not relieved, the normal and proper processes of the domestic peace and prosperity of the United States must shortly cease, and endless loss, confusion, and distress must ensue. As a result factories must close down, throwing hundreds of thousands of men out of employment; strikes and riots will prevail; the prices of wheat, cattle, corn, cotton, and all other raw products must fall, to the injury, if not the ruin, of the farmers; and an indescribable list of calamities must befall our people. And hence it is true that Germany has in effect blockaded our ports and shores.

It is more distressing that a great nation should, in violation of the accepted principles of international law, for which she has herself always heretofore stood, dictate to the neutral nations of the world where their ships, cargoes, and citizens may or may not go.

But more appalling still is the fact that Germany should, in the conduct of her submarine operations, lose all regard both for neutral rights under international law and for human life itself; for, notwithstanding her note to the United States less than a year ago that she would no longer sink merchant ships of neutrals without conforming to that provision of international law requiring first warning and search and the safety of passengers and crews, she has broken that solemn promise by her decree of January 31, 1917, and since then has sunk American ships at will without warning and has thus murdered American citizens. Thus the Imperial German Government has made and is making war upon the United States. The situation is intolerable. Any other but a calm, friendly, and peace-loving nation would promptly have declared war on Germany when, by order of her Government, her merciless submarine sank the *Lusitania,* carrying over a thousand human beings to instant death, of whom more than 100 were American citizens. But, in friendship, we employed diplomacy to induce Germany to forego such barbarity, and she gave her solemn word thereafter to conform to international law. When, by her decree of January 31, she broke her plighted faith with us, ignoring our rights and the dictates of humanity, and trampled under foot our most sacred sovereign rights, there is no alternate left to us but abject debasement or resort to armed force. As for me, there is no room left for argument. They have broken faith and friendship and denied our rights, without which our national sovereignty itself would be dishonored. To me the issue appears as plain as the light of day. The cave man has once again broken loose upon the world. He is mad and crazy. He knows not the impulses of humanity; he respects neither his own treaties and agreements nor the rights of others; he feels not the sentiments of truth or sympathy or justice; he is bent on the unwavering course of brute force, pillage, and murder. That cave man is the crazy German Emperor, and the heartless Prussian military caste and oligarchy of autocratic power which surrounds, urges, and supports him. . . .

The issue thus forced upon the United States is whether we shall abjectly crawl before organized hostile power or whether this Nation shall preserve its interests, its self-respect, its honor, its national existence. If the allies who are fighting the battle of the free democracies of the world shall fall before the mailed fist of Prussian militarism, the United States must be the next victim. . . . In final analysis, it is a war unto death between autocracy and democracy, and autocracy has brought the challenge to our doors. . . .

Now that the American people must take their firm and final stand for their acknowledged rights, let timidity and diplomacy and foreign sentiment and cowardly pacifism be engulfed at once in the mighty tide of American patriotic enthusiasm to defend our national rights, to uphold international law, to preserve civilization against autocratic brute force, to overthrow the last vestige of absolutism on earth, and to maintain our national sovereignty as the last and best hope of mankind.

# THE HOME FRONT

## England Mourns Her Dead

*The English poet Laurence Binyon (1869–1943) mourns the nation's casualties. The death toll for all parties to the war was extremely high: Britain (and her colonies) lost 1 million men; France, 1½ million; Russia, close to 1¾ million; and Germany, 2 million.*

### From Laurence Binyon. *For the Fallen (September 1914)*

> With proud thanksgiving, a mother for her children,
> England mourns for her dead across the sea.
> Flesh of her flesh they were, spirit of her spirit,
> Fallen in the cause of the free.
>
> Solemn the drums thrill: Death august and royal
> Sings sorrow up into immortal spheres.
> There is music in the midst of desolation
> And a glory that shines upon our tears.
>
> They went with songs to the battle, they were young,
> Straight of limb, true of eye, steady and aglow.
> They were staunch to the end against odds uncounted,
> They fell with their faces to the foe.
>
> They shall grow not old, as we that are left grow old:
> Age shall not weary them, nor the years condemn.
> At the going down of the sun and in the morning
> We will remember them. . . .

## Women's War Service

*As men were mobilized for war, women were recruited into industries to fill their places. Especially in munitions plants, women workers were in great demand. E. Sylvia Pankhurst (1882–1960), the suffragist leader, details the ac-*

From Laurence Binyon, *Collected Poems and the Burning of Leaves*. Reprinted by permission of Mrs. Nicolete Gray and The Society of Authors on behalf of the Laurence Binyon Estate.

*tivities of working women on the home front. Strikes were not uncommon during the war, especially in 1916–17, and they took place among male and female workers, in France, as well as England.*

## From E. Sylvia Pankhurst. *The Home Front*

Out of 27,241 women who had by this time registered for War service, only 2,332 had been given work. Propaganda was insistent to get women into the munition factories, and every sort of work ordinarily performed by men. The sections clamouring for the military conscription of men saw in the industrial service of women a means to their end. Feminists who were advocates of Conscription for men believed themselves adding to the importance of women by demanding that women also should be conscripts. . . .

[*Organizations of women, led by suffragists, demanded equal conditions for women in war work.*]

From all over the country we cited authentic wages scales: Waring & Gillow paying 3½d. an hour to women, 9d. to men for military tent making; the Hendon aeroplane works paying women 3d. per hour, at work for which men got 10d. per hour; women booking clerks at Victoria Station getting 15s. a week, though the men they replaced got 35s.; and so on, in district after district, trade after trade. The majority of the women war workers on time rates were getting from 6s. to 18s. per week, a relatively small number on piece rates making from 6s. to 7s. a week to £1 or £1 5s. 0d. Firms like Bryant and May's, the match makers, were now making munitions. Accustomed to employ large numbers of women and girls at ill-paid work, they knew by long experience that piece rates would secure them a higher production than could be induced by a bonus. Without a care for pre-war standards, in a trade new to their factory, they had fixed for munition work, often perilous and heavy, similar sweated piece rates to those paid for matches.

I told Dr. Addison that when I had published, under the heading, "Records of Disgraceful Sweating," the fact that Maconochies in their East End works were employing women at 13s. 9d. for a 55 hour week, pushing trucks weighing 50 to 75 lbs., the firm had protested that 13s. 9d. was "the recognised Government rate of pay for a 55 hour week." A copy of that letter I left for Lloyd George to study for himself.

Mrs. Cressall said that her husband had worked in a white lead works for seventeen years—a dangerous trade in which the workers ran the risk of a serious form of industrial poisoning. His wage was 26s. for a 60 hour week; a starvation wage. This firm was now gradu-

From E. Sylvia Pankhurst, *The Home Front* (London: Hutchinson & Co., 1932), pp. 198, 203–208.

ally discharging men and replacing them by boys at 17s. a week. Other such firms were employing women at a still lower wage.

We left reminders that women and girls were still working both by night and day on 12 hour shifts, and that many girls fell asleep on the night shift. Mrs. Leigh Rothwell of the National Federation of Women Workers, who was with us, cited instances of women at that time working from 7.30 a.m. to 11 p.m. and of women standing at work all day on floors covered with water, for lack of the little care which would have provided a grating to raise them above the wet.

We complained of the injurious working of the Munitions Tribunals. Men employed under the Trade Union rate of pay were appealing to the tribunals for leave to go where they would get the standard rate of wages and were meeting with refusals, workers were appealing in vain for leaving certificates, though the firms for which they were nominally working had nothing for them to do.

Dr. Addison told us that the Munitions Department had all the problems we had mentioned "acutely in mind"; and as soon as it had time to do so, it would set up excellent conditions for the workers. His promise carried no conviction; we knew that the war machine would grind on without heed, and that only by strenuous agitation would the smallest ameliorations be secured for the poor drudges who served it.

The Munitions Act was being rigorously applied. A fitter was fined £3 and costs at Wood Green Police Court for leaving his employment. In Glasgow, where industrial rebels were supposed to be plentiful as gooseberries, the Central Munitions Tribunal fined 17 workmen, who dared to strike, £10 each with the alternative of 30 days' imprisonment. An apprentice plater failed to obtain from the Munitions Tribunal permission to transfer to new employment, though his previous employers, James Fullerton & Co., of Paisley, had refused to restart him. He had left them and obtained work elsewhere because they were paying him less than the standard rate, but they had followed him up and procured his dismissal by another firm because he had left them without permission. Though Fullerton's would not take him back, the Munitions Act enabled them to punish the apprentice by keeping him unemployed for six weeks. It was all for the War, of course; but the interests of the employing class were by no means forgotten! At Armstrong Whitworth's in Manchester 151 men were discharged from the armour plate department, whilst the leaving certificates enabling them to accept work offered to them elsewhere were withheld. They appealed to the Munitions Tribunal for certificates permitting them to work elsewhere, but their case was shelved, lest the employer might possibly require them later.

At Cammell Laird's in Liverpool excessively long hours were being worked. It was common for a man to begin at 6 or 8 a.m. on Saturday, work through the day and after a couple of hours off go on night duty. Then after another short rest he would be expected to go on day duty till 8 p.m. on Sunday. If these exhausted workers were late on Monday morning, they were "docked a quarter," and reported for loss of time. The firm complained to the Munitions Tribunal that their 10,000 men had lost 1,500,000 hours in twenty weeks. The offenders were permitted not a word in their defence, but fined from 5s. to 60s. each. They cried out in their indignation that there would be a revolution in the country, and were ordered to leave the court; they went with defiant cheers.

The Munitions Act was being used to prevent workers from changing their employment in order to secure higher wages, or positions of greater responsibility, or to obtain work nearer home, or in another district in view of family responsibilities. Leaving certificates were refused when the work was proving prejudicial to the health of the worker and where the character of the work had been changed and the worker found the new machinery unmanageable or injurious. . . .

In the cotton trade the employers had refused the workers a 5 per cent increase in wages, to aid them in meeting the enhanced cost of living. Yet Lloyd George was appealing to the cotton operatives to agree to come under the compulsion of the Munitions Act on account of the huge quantities of cotton goods the Government was requiring for the War. The great majority of the operatives had always been women; the withdrawal of men for the Army thus affected the cotton industry less than others. To secure more cheap labour, the employers were demanding that children should begin work as half-timers at eleven years, instead of at twelve; and as full-timers at twelve years, instead of at thirteen. . . .

As the War progressed trade after trade was put under the Munitions Act. Employers were eager to seize the powers it gave them.

# THE DECLINE OF THE WEST?

## German Surrender

*In September 1918, the Germans decided to capitulate. In November an armistice was signed, followed by revolt in Berlin and the abdication of the kaiser. The Allies negotiated a treaty with the German government in 1919 at Versailles, France.*

### From *The Versailles Treaty*

*Article 42.* Germany is forbidden to maintain or construct any fortifications either on the left bank of the Rhine or on the right bank to the west of a line drawn 50 kilometres to the East of the Rhine.

*Article 45.* As compensation for the destruction of the coal-mines in the north of France and as part-payment towards the total reparation due from Germany for the damage resulting from the war, Germany cedes to France in full and absolute possession, with exclusive rights of exploitation, unencumbered and free from all debts and charges of any kind, the coal-mines situated in the Saar Basin. . . .

*Article 49.* Germany renounces in favour of the League of Nations, in the capacity of trustee, the government of the territory defined above.

*Article 51.* The territories which were ceded to Germany in accordance with the Preliminaries of Peace signed at Versailles on February 26, 1871, and the Treaty of Frankfurt of May 10, 1871, are restored to French sovereignty as from the date of the Armistice of November 11 1918.

The provisions of the Treaties establishing the delimitation of the frontiers before 1871 shall be restored.

*Article 80.* Germany acknowledges and will respect strictly the independence of Austria, within the frontiers which may be fixed in a Treaty between that State and the principal Allied and Associated Powers; she agrees that this independence shall be inalienable, except with the consent of the Council of the League of Nations.

From Louis L. Snyder, *Documents of German History* (New Brunswick, N.J.: Rutgers University Press, 1958), pp. 378–380.

*Article 81.* Germany, in conformity with the action already taken by the Allied and Associated Powers, recognizes the complete independence of the Czecho-Slovak State which will include the autonomous territory of the Ruthenians to the south of the Carpathians. Germany hereby recognizes the frontiers of this State as determined by the principal Allied and Associated Powers and the other interested States.

*Article 87.* Germany, in conformity with the action already taken by the Allied and Associated Powers, recognizes the complete independence of Poland, and renounces in her favour all rights and title on the territory [of Poland].

The boundaries of Poland not laid down in the present Treaty will be subsequently determined by the principal Allied and Associated Powers. . . .

*Article 88.* In the portion of Upper Silesia included within the boundaries described below, the inhabitants will be called upon to indicate by a vote whether they wish to be attached to Germany or to Poland. . . .

*Article 102.* The principal Allied and Associated Powers undertake to establish the town of Danzig, together with the rest of the territory described in Article 100, as a Free City. It will be placed under the protection of the League of Nations.

*Article 119.* Germany renounces in favour of the principal Allied and Associated Powers all her rights and titles over her overseas possessions.

*Article 159.* The German military forces shall be demobilized and reduced as prescribed hereinafter.

*Article 160.* By a date which must not be later than March 31, 1920 the German Army must not comprise more than seven divisions of infantry and three divisions of cavalry. . . .

*Article 168.* The manufacture of arms, munitions, or any war material, shall only be carried out in factories or works the location of which shall be communicated to and approved by the Governments of the Principal Allied and Associated Powers, and the number of which they retain the right to restrict.

*Article 170.* Importation into Germany of arms, munitions and war material of every kind shall be strictly prohibited.

The same applies to the manufacture for, and export to, foreign countries of arms, munitions and war material of every kind.

*Article 171.* The use of asphyxiating, poisonous or other gases and all analogous liquids, materials or devices being prohibited, their manufacture and importation are strictly forbidden in Germany.

The same applies to materials specially intended for the manufacture, storage and use of the said products or devices.

The manufacture and the importation into Germany of armoured cars, tanks and all similar constructions suitable for use in war are also prohibited. . . .

*Article 181.* After the expiration of a period of two months from the coming into force of the present Treaty the German naval forces in commission must not exceed:

6 battleships of the *Deutschland* or *Lothringen* type,
6 light cruisers,
12 destroyers,
12 torpedo boats,

or an equal number of ships constructed to replace them. . . .

No submarines are to be included.

All other warships, except where there is provision to the contrary in the present Treaty, must be placed in reserve or devoted to commercial purposes. . . .

*Article 183.* After the expiration of a period of two months from the coming into force of the present Treaty the total personnel of the German Navy, including the manning of the fleet, coast defences, signal stations, administration and other land services, must not exceed fifteen thousand, including officers and men of all grades and corps.

The total strength of officers and warrant officers must not exceed fifteen hundred.

*Article 198.* The armed forces of Germany must not include any military or naval air forces.

*Article 231.* The Allied and Associated Governments affirm and Germany accepts the responsibility of Germany and her allies for causing all the loss and damage to which the Allied and Associated Governments and their nationals have been subjected as a consequence of the war imposed upon them by the aggression of Germany and her allies.

*Article 232.* . . . The Allied and Associated Governments require, and Germany undertakes, that she will make compensation for all damage done to the civilian population of the Allied and Associated Powers and to their property during the period of the belligerency of each as an Allied or Associated Power against Germany by such aggression by land, by sea and from the air, and in general all damage as defined in Annex I hereto.

*Article 233.* The amount of the above damage for which compensation is to be made by Germany shall be determined by an Inter-Allied Commission, to be called the Reparation Commission. . . .

*Article 245.* Within six months after the coming into force of the present Treaty the German Government must restore to the French Government the trophies, archives, historical souvenirs or works of art carried away from France by the German authorities in the course of the war of 1870–1871 and during this last war, in accordance with a list which will be communicated to it by the French Government; particularly the French flags taken in the course of the war of 1870–1871 and all the political papers taken by the German authorities on October 10, 1870, at the chateau of Cercay, near Brunoy (Seine-et-Oise) belonging at the time to Mr. Rouher, formerly Minister of State.

*Article 428.* As a guarantee for the execution of the present Treaty by Germany, the German territory situated to the west of the Rhine, together with the bridgeheads, will be occupied by Allied and Associated troops for a period of fifteen years from the coming into force of the present Treaty.

# Disillusionment

*The war shattered the optimism of previous generations. The economist John Maynard Keynes (1883–1946) considered the terms of the peace disastrous for German rehabilitation. The psychologist Sigmund Freud (1856–1939) commented on the deeper impact of the war on human consciousness and on what it revealed of the state of human civilization.*

## From John Maynard Keynes. *The Economic Consequences of the Peace*

This chapter must be one of pessimism. The Treaty includes no provisions for the economic rehabilitation of Europe,—nothing to make the defeated Central Empires into good neighbors, nothing to stabilize the new States of Europe, nothing to reclaim Russia; nor does it promote in any way a compact of economic solidarity amongst the Allies themselves; no arrangement was reached at Paris for restoring the disordered finances of France and Italy, or to adjust the systems of the Old World and the New.

The Council of Four paid no attention to these issues, being preoccupied with others,—Clemenceau to crush the economic life of his enemy, Lloyd George to do a deal and bring home something which would pass muster for a week, the President to do nothing that was not just and right. It is an extraordinary fact that the fundamental economic problems of a Europe starving and disintegrating before their eyes, was the one question in which it was impossible to arouse the interest of the Four. Reparation was their main excursion into the economic field, and they settled it as a problem of theology, of politics, of electoral chicane, from every point of view except that of the economic future of the States whose destiny they were handling. . . .

The essential facts of the situation, as I see them, are expressed simply. Europe consists of the densest aggregation of population in the history of the world. This population is accustomed to a relatively high

From John Maynard Keynes, *The Economic Consequences of the Peace* (New York: Harcourt Brace Jovanovich, 1920), pp. 211–216. Copyright 1920 by Harcourt Brace Jovanovich, Inc.; renewed 1948 by Lydia Lopokova Keynes. Reprinted by permission of the publisher and by permission of The Royal Economic Society and Macmillan, London and Basingstoke.

standard of life, in which, even now, some sections of it anticipate improvement rather than deterioration. In relation to other continents Europe is not self-sufficient; in particular it cannot feed itself. Internally the population is not evenly distributed, but much of it is crowded into a relatively small number of dense industrial centers. This population secured for itself a livelihood before the war, without much margin of surplus, by means of a delicate and immensely complicated organization, of which the foundations were supported by coal, iron, transport, and an unbroken supply of imported food and raw materials from other continents. By the destruction of this organization and the interruption of the stream of supplies, a part of this population is deprived of its means of livelihood. Emigration is not open to the redundant surplus. For it would take years to transport them overseas, even, which is not the case, if countries could be found which were ready to receive them. The danger confronting us, therefore, is the rapid depression of the standard of life of the European populations to a point which will mean actual starvation for some (a point already reached in Russia and approximately reached in Austria). Men will not always die quietly. For starvation, which brings to some lethargy and a helpless despair, drives other temperaments to the nervous instability of hysteria and to a mad despair. And these in their distress may overturn the remnants of organization, and submerge civilization itself in their attempts to satisfy desperately the overwhelming needs of the individual. This is the danger against which all our resources and courage and idealism must now co-operate.

On the 13th May, 1919, Count Brockdorff-Rantzau addressed to the Peace Conference of the Allied and Associated Powers the Report of the German Economic Commission charged with the study of the effect of the conditions of Peace on the situation of the German population. "In the course of the last two generations," they reported, "Germany has become transformed from an agricultural State to an industrial State. So long as she was an agricultural State, Germany could feed forty million inhabitants. As an industrial State she could insure the means of subsistence for a population of sixty-seven millions; and in 1913 the importation of foodstuffs amounted, in round figures, to twelve million tons. Before the war a total of fifteen million persons in Germany provided for their existence by foreign trade, navigation, and the use, directly or indirectly, of foreign raw material." After rehearsing the main relevant provisions of the Peace Treaty the report continues: "After this diminution of her products, after the economic depression resulting from the loss of her colonies, her merchant fleet and her foreign investments, Germany will not be in a position to import from abroad an adequate quantity of raw material. An enormous part of German industry will, therefore, be condemned inevitably to destruction. The need of importing foodstuffs will increase considerably at the same time that the possibility of satisfying this demand is as greatly diminished. In a very short time, therefore, Germany will not be in a position to give bread and work to her numerous millions of inhabitants, who are prevented from earning their livelihood by navigation and trade. These persons should emigrate, but this is a material impossibility, all the more because many countries and the most important ones will oppose any German immigration. To put the Peace conditions into execution would logically involve, therefore, the loss of several millions of persons in Germany. This catastrophe would not be long in coming about, seeing that the health of the population has been broken down during the War by the Blockade, and during the Armistice by the aggravation of the Blockade of famine. No help, however great, or over however long a period it were continued, could prevent these deaths *en masse*." "We do not know, and indeed we doubt," the report concludes, "whether the Delegates of the Allied and Associated Powers realize the inevitable consequences which will take place if Germany, an industrial State, very thickly populated, closely bound up with the economic system of the world, and under the necessity of importing enormous quantities of raw material and foodstuffs, suddenly finds herself pushed back to the phase of her development, which corresponds to her economic condition and the numbers of her population as they were half a century ago. Those who sign this Treaty will sign the death sentence of many millions of German men, women and children."

I know of no adequate answer to these words. The indictment is at least as true of the Austrian, as of the German, settlement. This is the fundamental problem in front of us, before which questions of territorial adjustment and the balance of European power are insignificant. Some of the catastrophes of past history, which have thrown back human progress for centuries, have been due to the reactions following on the sudden termination, whether in the course of nature or by the act of man, of temporarily favorable conditions which have permitted the growth of population beyond what could be provided for when the favorable conditions were at an end

# From Sigmund Freud. *Thoughts for the Times on War and Death*

## I. The Disillusionment of the War

In the confusion of wartime in which we are caught up, relying as we must on one-sided information, standing too close to the great

From *Standard Edition of the Complete Works of Sigmund Freud*, Vol. 14, James Strachey, trans. and ed. (London: The Hogarth Press Ltd., 1957), pp. 275, 278–279, 280–281. Reprinted by permission of Sigmund Freud Copyrights, The Institute of Psycho-Analysis, and The Hogarth Press Ltd.

changes that have already taken place or are beginning to, and without a glimmering of the future that is being shaped, we ourselves are at a loss as to the significance of the impressions which press in upon us and as to the value of the judgements which we form. We cannot but feel that no event has ever destroyed so much that is precious in the common possessions of humanity, confused so many of the clearest intelligences, or so thoroughly debased what is highest. Science herself has lost her passionless impartiality; her deeply embittered servants seek for weapons from her with which to contribute towards the struggle with the enemy. Anthropologists feel driven to declare him inferior and degenerate, psychiatrists issue a diagnosis of his disease of mind or spirit. Probably, however, our sense of these immediate evils is disproportionately strong, and we are not entitled to compare them with the evils of other times which we have not experienced.

The individual who is not himself a combatant—and so a cog in the gigantic machine of war—feels bewildered in his orientation, and inhibited in his powers and activities. I believe that he will welcome any indication, however slight, which will make it easier for him to find his bearings within himself at least. I propose to pick out two among the factors which are responsible for the mental distress felt by non-combatants, against which it is such a heavy task to struggle, and to treat of them here: the disillusionment which this war has evoked, and the altered attitude towards death which this—like every other war—forces upon us. . . .

The enjoyment of this common civilization was disturbed from time to time by warning voices, which declared that old traditional differences made wars inevitable, even among the members of a community such as this. We refused to believe it; but if such a war were to happen, how did we picture it? We saw it as an opportunity for demonstrating the progress of comity among men since the era when the Greek Amphictyonic Council proclaimed that no city of the league might be destroyed, nor its olive-groves cut down, nor its water-supply stopped; we pictured it as a chivalrous passage of arms, which would limit itself to establishing the superiority of one side in the struggle, while as far as possible avoiding acute suffering that could contribute nothing to the decision, and granting complete immunity for the wounded who had to withdraw from the contest, as well as for the doctors and nurses who devoted themselves to their recovery. There would, of course, be the utmost consideration for the non-combatant classes of the population—for women who take no part in war-work, and for the children who, when they are grown up, should become on both sides one another's friends and helpers. And again, all the international undertakings and institutions in which the common civilization of peace-time had been embodied would be maintained.

Even a war like this would have produced enough horror and suffering; but it would not have interrupted the development of ethical relations between the collective individuals of mankind—the peoples and states.

Then the war in which we had refused to believe broke out, and it brought—disillusionment. Not only is it more bloody and more destructive than any war of other days, because of the enormously increased perfection of weapons of attack and defence; it is at least as cruel, as embittered, as implacable as any that has preceded it. It disregards all the restrictions known as International Law, which in peace-time the states had bound themselves to observe; it ignores the prerogatives of the wounded and the medical service, the distinction between civil and military sections of the population, the claims of private property. It tramples in blind fury on all that comes in its way, as though there were to be no future and no peace among men after it is over. It cuts all the common bonds between the contending peoples, and threatens to leave a legacy of embitterment that will make any renewal of those bonds impossible for a long time to come.

Two things in this war have aroused our sense of disillusionment: the low morality shown externally by states which in their internal relations pose as the guardians of moral standards, and the brutality shown by individuals whom, as participants in the highest human civilization, one would not have thought capable of such behaviour.

Let us begin with the second point and try to formulate, in a few brief words, the point of view that we wish to criticize. How, in point of fact, do we imagine the process by which an individual rises to a comparatively high plane of morality? The first answer will no doubt simply be that he is virtuous and noble from birth—from the very start. We shall not consider this view any further here. A second answer will suggest that we are concerned with a developmental process, and will probably assume that the development consists in eradicating his evil human tendencies and, under the influence of education and a civilized environment, replacing them by good ones. If so, it is nevertheless surprising that evil should re-emerge with such force in anyone who has been brought up in this way.

But this answer also contains the thesis which we propose to contradict. In reality, there is no such things as 'eradicating' evil. . . .

Civilized society, which demands good conduct and does not trouble itself about the instinctual basis of this conduct, has . . . won over to obedience a great many people who are not in this following their own natures. Encouraged by this success, society has allowed itself to be misled into tightening the moral standard to the greatest possible degree, and it has thus forced its members into a yet greater estrangement from their instinctual disposition. . . . Anyone thus compelled to act continually in accordance with precepts which are not the expression of his instinctual inclinations, is living, psychologically speaking, beyond his means, and may objectively be described as a hypocrite, whether he is clearly aware of the incongruity or not. It is undeniable

that our contemporary civilization favours the production of this form
of hypocrisy to an extraordinary extent. One might venture to say that
it is built up on such hypocrisy, and that it would have to submit to far-
reaching modifications if people were to undertake to live in accordance with psychological truth. Thus there are very many more cultural
hypocrites than truly civilized men—indeed, it is a debatable point
whether a certain degree of cultural hypocrisy is not indispensable for
the maintenance of civilization, because the susceptibility to culture
which has hitherto been organized in the minds of present-day men
would perhaps not prove sufficient for the task. On the other hand,
the maintenance of civilization even on so dubious a basis offers the
prospect of paving the way in each new generation for a more far-
reaching transformation of instinct which shall be the vehicle of a better civilization.

We may already derive one consolation from this discussion: our
mortification and our painful disillusionment on account of the unciv-
ilized behaviour of our fellow-citizens of the world during this war
were unjustified. They were based on an illusion to which we had given
way. In reality our fellow-citizens have not sunk so low as we feared,
because they had never risen so high as we believed. The fact that the
collective individuals of mankind, the peoples and states, mutually ab-
rogated their moral restraints naturally prompted these individual citizens to withdraw for a while from the constant pressure of civilization
and to grant a temporary satisfaction to the instincts which they had
been holding in check. This probably involved no breach in their relative morality within their own nations. . . .

## II. Our Attitude Towards Death

The second factor to which I attribute our present sense of estrangement in this once lovely and congenial world is the disturbance that has
taken place in the attitude which we have hitherto adopted towards
death.

That attitude was far from straightforward. To anyone who listened
to us we were of course prepared to maintain that death was the necessary outcome of life, that everyone owes nature a death and must expect to pay the debt—in short, that death was natural, undeniable and
unavoidable. In reality, however, we were accustomed to behave as if
it were otherwise. We showed an unmistakable tendency to put death
on one side, to eliminate it from life. We tried to hush it up; indeed
we even have a saying [in German]: 'to think of something as though
it were death'. That is, as though it were our own death, of course. It
is indeed impossible to imagine our own death; and whenever we attempt to do so we can perceive that we are in fact still present as spectators. Hence the psycho-analytic school could venture on the assertion
that at bottom no one believes in his own death, or, to put the same

thing in another way, that in the unconscious every one of us is convinced of his own immortality. . . .

It is evident that war is bound to sweep away this conventional treatment of death. Death will no longer be denied; we are forced to believe in it. People really die; and no longer one by one, but many, often tens of thousands, in a single day. And death is no longer a chance event. To be sure, it still seems a matter of chance whether a bullet hits this man or that; but a second bullet may well hit the survivor; and the accumulation of deaths puts an end to the impression of chance. Life has, indeed, become interesting again; it has recovered its full content. . . .

To sum up: our unconscious is just as inaccessible to the idea of our own death, just as murderously inclined towards strangers, just as divided (that is, ambivalent) towards those we love, as was primaeval man. But how far we have moved from this primal state in our conventional and cultural attitude towards death!

It is easy to see how war impinges on this dichotomy. It strips us of the later accretions of civilization, and lays bare the primal man in each of us. It compels us once more to be heroes who cannot believe in their own death; it stamps strangers as enemies, whose death is to be brought about or desired; it tells us to disregard the death of those we love. But war cannot be abolished; so long as the conditions of existence among nations are so different and their mutual repulsion so violent, there are bound to be wars. The question then arises: Is it not we who should give in, who should adapt ourselves to war? Should we not confess that in our civilized attitude towards death we are once again living psychologically beyond our means, and should we not rather turn back and recognize the truth? Would it not be better to give death the place in reality and in our thoughts which is its due, and to give a little more prominence to the unconscious attitude towards death which we have hitherto so carefully suppressed? This hardly seems as advance to higher achievement, but rather in some respects a backward step—a regression; but it has the advantage of taking the truth more into account, and of making life more tolerable for us once again. To tolerate life remains, after all, the first duty of all living beings. Illusion becomes valueless if it makes this harder for us.

We recall the old saying: *Si vis pacem, para bellum.* If you want to preserve peace, arm for war.

It would be in keeping with the times to alter it: *Si vis vitam, para mortem.* If you want to endure life, prepare yourself for death.

# XIII

440

# THE RUSSIAN REVOLUTION—FROM LENIN TO STALIN

*IN 1917, AS the European powers fought the Great War, revolution transformed the Russian state. Groups dissatisfied with the tsar's policies had long agitated for reform. Indeed, in 1905, liberals had won the right to elect members of a legislature, in the wake of protest movements by workers and others in St. Petersburg. In exile in London or Paris, socialists developed more far-reaching revolutionary strategies and waited for the occasion to return home and put them into practice.*

*The war created hardship in Russia and the tsar was unwilling and unable to meet the needs of his country for food supplies, military production, and constitutional reform. In March 1917 food riots and strikes in Petrograd (formerly St. Petersburg) led troops to mutiny. Revolutionary elements organized a soviet of workers' and soldiers' deputies and demanded a say in running the country. In response, legislators in the Duma (the parliament that ruled with the tsar) determined to control the situation and created first an executive committee and then a provisional government. The tsar abdicated, leaving Russia a republic.*

*By November 1917, the provisional government was divided among various liberal and socialist factions. Vladimir Lenin and the Bolsheviks offered a program of "peace, land, and bread" to war-weary Russians. The Bolsheviks gained support from the soviets and, on November 6–7, they seized power and disbanded the provisional government. The Bolsheviks implemented many of their policies: they negotiated the treaty of Brest-Litovsk with Germany and so withdrew from the war; they requisitioned grain from large farmers and redistributed it; and they began a redistribution of land as well. Their economic and political policies were opposed by many people, some of whom took up arms against the new government in 1918.*

*Despite the civil war, the early years of the Russian Revolution generated great enthusiasm among many writers and artists, socialists and feminists who saw it as the beginning of a new social order. Visitors from all over the world came to observe and to participate in the new experiment.*

*Lenin died in 1924. There then ensued a major power struggle between Leon Trotsky and Joseph Stalin over the direction of the revolution and its internal and external policies. In 1927, Stalin emerged as the new leader of the Communist Party (the name taken by the Bolsheviks after the revolution). He was determined to modernize the Russian state by developing its industry and to implement socialism in agriculture as well as manufacturing. Stalin consolidated state power during this period and, increasingly, he used force to do it. In the 1930s, he also enlarged his own power and destroyed his enemies—real and imagined—by executing them, purging them from government positions, or sending them to forced labor camps.*

*When Stalin died in 1953, Nikita Khrushchev came to power. He sought to dissociate the accomplishments of Soviet society from the dictatorial rule of Stalin.*

*The international impact of the Russian Revolution was far-reaching and has lasted to the present. The Soviet Union became for many political groups the representative of an economic alternative to capitalism and of political resistance to Western forms of imperialism. The Russian Revolution of 1917 changed European political alignments as well as the internal political and economic structure of the Russian state*

# THE ROAD TO REVOLUTION

## Lenin's Strategy

*Vladimir I. Lenin (1870–1924) led the Bolshevik (majority) faction of Russian Social Democrats at their party congress in London in 1903. A brilliant strategist, Lenin insisted on the importance of party organization and leadership in bringing about the socialist revolution Marx had envisioned.*

## From V. I. Lenin. *What Is to Be Done?*

The political struggle of Social-Democracy is far more extensive and complex than the economic struggle of the workers against the employers and the government. Similarly (indeed for that reason), the organisation of the revolutionary Social-Democratic Party must inevitably be of *a kind different* from the organisation of the workers designed for

From Vladimir I. Lenin, *Selected Works* (New York: International Publishers, 1967), vol. 1, pp. 189–191, 193, 195–196, 199–202. Reprinted by permission of the publisher.

this struggle. The workers' organisation must in the first place be a trade union organisation; secondly, it must be as broad as possible; and thirdly, it must be as public as conditions will allow (here, and further on, of course, I refer only to absolutist Russia). On the other hand, the organisation of the revolutionaries must consist first and foremost of people who make revolutionary activity their profession (for which reason I speak of the organisation of *revolutionaries*, meaning revolutionary Social-Democrats). In view of this common characteristic of the members of such an organisation, *all distinctions as between workers and intellectuals*, not to speak of distinctions of trade and profession, in both categories, *must be effaced*. Such an organisation must perforce not be very extensive and must be as secret as possible. Let us examine this threefold distinction.

In countries where political liberty exists the distinction between a trade union and a political organisation is clear enough, as is the distinction between trade unions and Social-Democracy. The relations between the latter and the former will naturally vary in each country according to historical, legal, and other conditions; they may be more or less close, complex, etc. (in our opinion they should be as close and as little complicated as possible); but there can be no question in free countries of the organisation of trade unions coinciding with the organisation of the Social-Democratic Party. In Russia, however, the yoke of the autocracy appears at first glance to obliterate all distinctions between the Social-Democratic organisation and the workers' associations, since *all* workers' associations and *all* study circles are prohibited, and since the principal manifestation and weapon of the workers' economic struggle—the strike—is regarded as a criminal (and sometimes even as a political!) offence. Conditions in our country, therefore, on the one hand, strongly "impel" the workers engaged in economic struggle to concern themselves with political questions, and, on the other, they "impel" Social-Democrats to confound trade-unionism with Social-Democracy. . . .

The workers' organisations for the economic struggle should be trade union organisations. Every Social-Democratic worker should as far as possible assist and actively work in these organisations. But, while this is true, it is certainly not in our interest to demand that only Social-Democrats should be eligible for membership in the "trade" unions, since that would only narrow the scope of our influence upon the masses. Let every worker who understands the need to unite for the struggle against the employers and the government join the trade unions. The very aim of the trade unions would be impossible of achievement, if they did not unite all who have attained at least this elementary degree of understanding, if they were not very *broad* organisations. The broader these organisations, the broader will be our influence over them—an influence due, not only to the "spontaneous" development of the economic struggle, but to the direct and conscious effort of the socialist trade union members to influence their comrades. But a broad organisation cannot apply methods of strict secrecy (since this demands far greater training than is required for the economic struggle). . . .

. . . A small, compact core of the most reliable, experienced, and hardened workers, with responsible representatives in the principal districts and connected by all the rules of strict secrecy with the organisation of revolutionaries, can, with the widest support of the masses and without any formal organisation, perform *all* the functions of a trade union organisation, in a manner, moreover, desirable to Social-Democracy. Only in this way can we secure the *consolidation* and development of a *Social-Democratic* trade union movement, despite all the gendarmes.

It may be objected that an organisation which is so *lose* that it is not even definitely formed, and which has not even an enrolled and registered membership, cannot be called an organisation at all. Perhaps so. Not the name is important. What is important is that this "organisation without members" shall do everything that is required, and from the very outset ensure a solid connection between our future trade unions and socialism. Only an incorrigible utopian would have a *broad* organisation of workers, with elections, reports, universal suffrage, etc., under the autocracy. . . .

. . . Centralisation of the most secret functions in an organisation of revolutionaries will not diminish, but rather increase the extent and enhance the quality of the activity of a large number of other organisations, that are intended for a broad public and are therefore as loose and as non-secret as possible, such as workers' trade unions; workers' self-education circles and circles for reading illegal literature; and socialist, as well as democratic, circles among *all* other sections of the population; etc., etc. We must have such circles, trade unions, and organisations everywhere in *as large a number as possible* and with the widest variety of functions; but it would be absurd and harmful *to confound* them with the organisation of *revolutionaries,* to efface the border-line between them, to make still more hazy the all too faint recognition of the fact that in order to "serve" the mass movement we must have people who will devote themselves exclusively to Social-Democratic activities, and that such people must *train* themselves patiently and steadfastly to be professional revolutionaries. . . .

# The Revolution of 1905

*A movement for political reform turned into a revolt in January 1905. A group of workers in St. Petersburg presenting a petition to the tsar was fired upon by troops. Strikes and protests followed and the tsar was eventually forced to create a parliament (Duma), an elected, representative legislative body. The Revolution of 1905 is usually seen as the prelude to the Revolution of 1917.*

## From *The Petition of January 9, 1905*

### A Most Humble and Loyal Address

of the Workers of St. Petersburg Intended for Presentation to HIS MAJESTY on Sunday at two o'clock on the Winter Palace Square

SIRE:

We, the workers *and inhabitants* of St. Petersburg, *of various estates,* our wives, our children, and our aged, helpless parents, come to Thee, O SIRE, to seek justice and protection. We are impoverished; we are oppressed, overburdened with excessive toil, contemptuously treated. We are not even recognized as human beings, but are treated like slaves who must suffer their bitter fate in silence and without complaint. And we have suffered, but even so we are being further (and further) pushed into the slough of poverty, arbitrariness, and ignorance.[1] We are suffocating in despotism and lawlessness. O SIRE, we have no strength left, and our endurance is at an end. We have reached that frightful moment when death is better than the prolongation of our unbearable sufferings. . . .

. . . Consider our demands attentively and without anger, for they are uttered not in malice but for the good, ours as well as Thine, O SIRE. We speak not in insolence, but from the realization of the necessity to find a way out of a situation intolerable to us all. Russia is too vast, and her needs are too great and manifold to be dealt with exclusively by the bureaucrats. *Popular representation is essential;* it is essential that the people help themselves *and govern themselves.* Truly, only they know their *real* needs. Refuse not their help, accept it (!) and command representatives of the Russian land, of all her classes, of all her estates, *as well as representatives of the workers,* to gather without delay. Let these include a capitalist, worker, official, priest, doctor, teacher—let everyone, whoever he may be, elect his representative. Let everyone be free and equal in his choice, and for this purpose let the elections to the constituent assembly be conducted under conditions of universal (direct), secret, and equal suffrage. . . .

---

[1][Words in italics were added and words in parentheses deleted during the last few days before the presentation of the petition.]

From Walter Sablinsky, *The Road to Bloody Sunday: The Role of Father Gapon and the Assembly in the St. Petersburg Massacre of 1905* (Princeton, N.J.: Princeton University Press, 1976), pp. 344–349. Copyright © 1976 by Princeton University Press. Published for the Russian Institute of Columbia University. Reprinted by permission of the publisher.

... We have come to Thee, SIRE, openly and directly as to the father, to tell Thee, *in the name of the entire toiling class of Russia,* that the following are essential:

I. Measures to eliminate the ignorance of and arbitrariness toward the Russian people.

    1. The immediate release and return of those who suffered for their political and religious convictions, for strikes and peasant disorders.

    2. *An immediate* proclamation of freedom and inviolability of the person, freedom of speech, press, association, and worship.

    3. Free universal and compulsory public education, financed by the State.

    4. Responsibility of the ministers before the people and guarantees that the government will act according to law.

    5. Equality of all before the law without any exceptions.

    6. *Separation of the church from the state.*

II. Measures to eliminate the poverty of the people.

    1. Abolition of indirect taxation and the introduction of a progressive income tax.

    2. Abolition of the land redemption payments, cheap credit, and the gradual transfer of the land to the people.

    3. *Contracts for orders of the war and naval departments are to be made in Russia and not abroad.*

    4. *Termination of the war in accordance with the will of the people.*

III. Measures to eliminate the oppression of labor by capital.

    1. *Abolition of the system of factory inspectors.*

    2. *Establishment in factories and plants of permanent elected worker committees, which are to participate with management in the consideration of worker grievances. Workers must not to be discharged without the consent of these committees.*

    3. Freedom of cooperative associations and professional worker unions *is to be allowed without delay.*

    4. An eight-hour workday and strict regulation of overtime work.

    5. Freedom of the struggle for labor against capital *is to be allowed without delay.*

    6. *Immediate* establishment of normal wage rates.

    7. Participation of representatives of the (workers) *working classes* in the drafting of a bill for state insurance of workers is *indispensable, and is to be put into effect without delay.*

There are two paths before us: one to freedom and happiness, the other into the grave. . . . (SIRE, show us either of them and we will follow it without a word, even if it leads us to death.) Let our lives be a sacrifice for suffering Russia. We do not regret this sacrifice, but offer it gladly. (!)

# REVOLUTION, WAR COMMUNISM, AND CIVIL WAR

## The Fall of the Tsar

*In March 1917, dissatisfaction with the tsarist regime culminated in revolution. Members of the Duma refused the tsar's orders to disband and instead set up an executive committee to govern the country. Workers in St. Petersburg, protesting food shortages and wartime scarcity, rioted and called for a new government. They established a Soviet of Workers' and Soldiers' Deputies. The Soviet and the Duma executive committee agreed to establish a provisional government on March 14, 1917. Three days later, Tsar Nicholas II abdicated and Russia was declared a republic.*

### First Statement of the Provisional Government, March 1917

Citizens of the Russian State,

An important event has taken place. By the powerful impulse of the Russian people, the old order has been overthrown. A new free Russia has been born. The overthrow crowns many years of struggle.

By the act of October 17, 1905, under pressure of the uprisen population, Russia saw itself promised Constitutional liberties. These promises were not kept. The Duma—the mouthpiece of the hopes of the populace—was dissolved. The second Duma suffered the same fate. Unable to break the popular will, the Government decided, by the Act of June 3, 1907, to withdraw from the people a part of its rights to participate in legislation, which had previously been granted. In the course of nine long years the people were deprived, one by one, of the rights which it had acquired. Once more the country was plunged into the void of arbitrary absolutism. All attempts to reason with the Government were fruitless and the Great World Conflict into which Mother Russia was dragged by the enemy found her in a state of moral bankruptcy, indifferent to the future, a stranger to her people, and drowned in corruption.

Neither the heroic efforts of the Army, crushed under the weight of

From Marc Ferro, *The Russian Revolution of February, 1917,* J. L. Richards, trans. (London: Routledge & Kegan Paul, 1972), pp. 346–348. Reprinted by permission of Georges Borchardt, Inc.

the internal chaos, nor the appeals of the representatives of the people, who united in face of the peril which threatened the nation, were able to lead the ex-Emperor or his Government on the way to an agreement with the people. And when Russia, because of the illegal and fatal action of its leaders, found itself faced with the gravest dangers, the nation has been forced to take power into its own hands. In its unanimity, the Revolutionary enthusiasm of the people, fully conscious of the gravity of the moment, and the determination of the Duma together have created the Provisional Government. The Provisional Government holds sacred its duty and responsibility to satisfy the hopes of the population and to lead the country on the bright road to a free and civil Regime.

The Government believes that the spirit of profound patriotism shown during the fight against the Old Order will inspire our valiant soldiers on the battlefield. For its part, it will do all that is possible to furnish the Army with the necessities for victory in war. The Government will consider the ties to its allies sacred and will observe to the letter its agreements with our allies.

While taking all measures for the defense of the country against its external enemy, the Government will consider it its main duty to permit the expression of the will of the people in what concerns the choice of a political regime and will convoke the Constituent Assembly as soon as possible on the basis of universal, direct, equal, and secret suffrage, guaranteeing equal participation in the elections to the valiant defenders of the land of our forefathers who are now shedding their blood on the battlefield. The Constituent Assembly will promulgate the fundamental laws which guarantee the country its inalienable rights to justice, freedom, and equality.

Understanding the gravity of this absence of rights which oppresses the Nation and constitutes an obstacle to the creative drive of the people at a time of national upheaval, the Provisional Government deems it necessary to furnish the country immediately, even before the convocation of the Constituent Assembly, with laws which will ensure civil rights and equality, which will allow all citizens to contribute freely to a creative undertaking for the benefit of all. The Government will also undertake the promulgation of laws which will ensure that everyone will partake equally in the elections of bodies for self-government on the basis of universal suffrage.

In the moment of national liberation, the whole country will recall with gratitude those who, while defending their religious and political convictions, fell victim to the Old Regime. And the Provisional Government considers it a pleasant duty to recall from exile and prison, with all honors, those who suffered for the good of the country.

In fulfilling these tasks, the Provisional Government is actuated by the conviction that it is thus carrying out the will of the people, and that the whole country will support it in its loyal efforts to ensure the well-being of Russia. This conviction gives it courage. The Provisional Government considers that only the warm support of the whole population will guarantee the triumph of the new order.

# The Bolsheviks Come to Power

*The provisional government had difficulty maintaining order, both in the countryside and the cities. The armies were demoralized and the Petrograd (St. Petersburg) Soviet was demanding far-reaching economic reform. A socialist, Alexander Kerensky, was made head of the provisional government in an effort to win popular support. By November 1917, however, the Bolsheviks, led by Lenin, had rallied the Petrograd and other soviets to their program, which promised peace, a redistribution of land to the peasants, and a reorganization of the economy with factories run by committees of workers. A government of soviets would replace the provisional government. On the night of November 6–7 the Bolsheviks, with the support of government troops and workers in Petrograd, took over the government of the Russian state. The following day the new government issued the Peace and Land Decrees.*

## Account of the Overthrow of the Provisional Government (November 8, 1917)

[November 7]

Kerenski remained at the office of the Staff from 2 until 7 A.M.... At 7 he set out for the front.... He is expected back any minute.... At 8:30 P.M., the Provisional Government at the Winter Palace received an ultimatum signed by the Petrograd Soviet. Members of the government were given 20 minutes in which to surrender, and in case of refusal they were threatened with having the guns of the Peter and Paul Fortress and the cruiser Aurora turned on the Winter Palace. The Government refused to discuss matters and to accept the ultimatum....

News reached us at 2 A.M. that the Winter Palace was taken, that the members of the Government were arrested ... and locked up at the Peter and Paul Fortress....

### Meeting of the Petrograd Soviet

The meeting opened at 2:35 P.M. with Trotski in the chair. He said: "In the name of the War-Revolutionary Committee, I announce that the Provisional Government no longer exists. (Applause.) Some of the

From Frank Alfred Golder, *Documents of Russian History: 1914–1917* (New York: The Century Company, 1927), pp. 617–619.

Ministers are already under arrest. (Bravo.) Others soon will be. (Applause.) The revolutionary garrison, under the control of the War-Revolutionary Committee, has dismissed the Assembly of the Pre-Parliament [Council of the Republic]. (Loud applause. "Long live the War-Revolutionary Committee") . . . The railway stations, post and telegraph offices, the Petrograd Telegraph Agency, and State Bank are occupied.". . .

Trotski continued by saying: "In our midst is Vladimir Ilich Lenin, who, by force of circumstances, had not been able to be with us all this time. . . . Hail the return of Lenin!" The audience gave him a noisy ovation. . . .

## Lenin's Speech

Comrades, the workmen's and peasants' revolution, the need of which the Bolsheviks have emphasized many times, has come to pass.

What is the significance of this revolution? Its significance is, in the first place, that we shall have a soviet government, without the participation of bourgeoisie of any kind. The oppressed masses will of themselves form a government. The old state machinery will be smashed into bits and in its place will be created a new machinery of government by the soviet organizations. From now on there is a new page in the history of Russia, and the present, third Russian revolution shall in its final result lead to the victory of Socialism.

One of our immediate tasks is to put an end to the war at once. But in order to end the war, which is closely bound up with the present capitalistic system, it is necessary to overthrow capitalism itself. In this work we shall have the aid of the world labor movement, which has already begun to develop in Italy, England, and Germany.

A just and immediate offer of peace by us to the international democracy will find everywhere a warm response among the international proletariat masses. In order to secure the confidence of the proletariat, it is necessary to publish at once all secret treaties.

In the interior of Russia a very large part of the peasantry has said: Enough playing with the capitalists; we will go with the workers. We shall secure the confidence of the peasants by one decree, which will wipe out the private property of the landowners. The peasants will understand that their only salvation is in union with the workers.

We will establish a real labor control on production.

We have now learned to work together in a friendly manner, as is evident from this revolution. We have the force of mass organization which has conquered all and which will lead the proletariat to world revolution.

We should now occupy ourselves in Russia in building up a proletarian socialist state.

Long live the world-wide socialistic revolution.

## The Peace and Land Decrees

### The Peace Decree

The Workers' and Peasants' Government, created by the revolution of November 6–7, and drawing its strength from the Soviets of Workers', Soldiers', and Peasants' Deputies, proposes to all warring people and their governments that negotiations leading to a just peace begin at once.

The just and democratic peace for which the great majority of war-exhausted, tormented toilers and laboring classes of all belligerent countries are thirsting; the peace for which the Russian workers and peasants are so insistently and loudly clamoring since the overthrow of the tsarist régime is, in the opinion of the Government, an immediate peace without annexation (*i. e.,* with the seizure of foreign lands and the forcible taking over of other nationalities) and without indemnity.

The Russian Government proposes that this kind of peace be concluded immediately between all the warring nations. It offers to take decisive steps at once, without the least delay, without waiting for a final confirmation of all the terms of such a peace by conferences of popular representatives of all countries and all nations. . . .

To prolong this war because the rich and strong nations cannot agree how to divide the small and weak nationalities which they have seized is, in the opinion of the Government, a most criminal act against humanity, and it [government] solemnly announces its decision to sign at once terms of peace bringing this war to an end on the indicated conditions, which are equally just to all nationalities without exception.

Moreover, the Government declares that it does not regard the above mentioned terms of peace in the light of an ultimatum. It will agree to examine all other terms. It will insist only that whatever belligerent nation has anything to propose, it should do so quickly, in the clearest terms, leaving out all double meanings and all secrets in making the proposal. The Government does away with all secret diplomacy and is determined to carry on all negotiations quite openly in the view of all people. It will proceed at once to publish all secret treaties, ratified or concluded by the government of landowners and capitalists, from March until November 7, 1917.

The Government annuls, immediately and unconditionally, the secret treaties, in so far as they have for their object, which was true in a majority of cases, to give benefits and privileges to the Russian landowners and capitalists, to maintain or to increase annexation by the Great Russians.

In proposing to the Governments and peoples of all countries to be-

From Frank Alfred Golder, *Documents of Russian History: 1914–17,* (New York: The Century Company, 1927), pp. 620–625.

gin open peace negotiations at once, the Government, on its part, expresses its readiness to carry on these negotiations in writing, by telegraph, by discussions between representatives of different countries, or at a conference of such representatives. . . .

. . . In making these peace proposals to the governments and peoples of all warring countries, the Provisional Government of Workers and Peasants of Russia appeals in particular to the intelligent workers of the three foremost nations of mankind, and the leading participators in this war, England, France, and Germany. The toilers of these countries have rendered the greatest service to the cause of progress and Socialism by their great examples, such as the Chartist movement in England, the series of revolutions of historical and world importance brought on by the French proletariat, and, finally, the heroic struggle against the Exemption Laws in Germany, and the example for the workers of all the world given by the German toilers in their stubborn, prolonged, and disciplined efforts to organize the proletarian masses. All these examples of proletarian heroism and historical development lead us to believe that the workers of the named countries will understand the task before them to free humanity from the horrors of war and its consequences. By decisive, energetic, and self-sacrificing efforts in various directions, these workers will help us not only to bring the peace negotiations to a successful end, but to free the toiling and exploited masses from all forms of slavery and all exploitation.

## The Land Decree

The final settlement of the land question belongs to the national Constituent Assembly.

The most equitable settlement is as follows:

1. The right of private ownership of land is abolished forever. Land cannot be sold, bought, leased, mortgaged, or alienated in any manner whatsoever. All lands—state, appanage, cabinet, monastery, church, entail, private, communal, peasant, and any other lands—pass to the nation without indemnification and are turned over for the use of those who till them.

Persons who have suffered from the loss of property will be entitled to public aid only during the time necessary for their readjustment to the changed conditions of existence.

2. All the underground resources, such as ores, petroleum, coal, salt, etc., as well as forests and waters which have national importance, are transferred for the exclusive use of the State. All small streams, lakes, forests, etc., are transferred for the use of the land communities, on condition that they be administered by the organs of local self-government.

3. Holdings under intensive agriculture—orchards, gardens, plantations, nurseries, etc., are not to be divided, but turned into model farms and handed over to the State or the community, depending upon size and importance.

Small private estates, city and village land in fruit or truck gardens, are to be left in possession of their present owners, but the size of these holdings and the amount of tax to be paid on them shall be determined by law.

4. Stud farms, State and private farms for breeding thoroughbred stock, poultry, etc., shall be confiscated, nationalized, and turned over either for the exclusive use of the State, or the land community, depending upon their size and importance. The question of indemnification is to be settled by the Constituent Assembly.

5. The entire livestock, tools, etc., of confiscated lands shall be turned over for the exclusive use of the State or land community, depending upon size and importance, without indemnification, but this does not apply to the small landholding peasants.

6. All Russian citizens (male and female) who are willing to till the land, either by themselves or with the assistance of their families or in collective groups, are entitled to the use of the land, as long as they are able to cultivate it. Hired labor is not permitted. In case a member of a rural community is incapacitated for a period of two years, it becomes the duty of the community to help him until he recovers, by collectively tilling his land. Farmers who are too old or physically unable to till the soil, lose the right to it, but receive instead a State pension.

7. The land is to be divided equally among the toilers, according to needs or labor capacity, depending on local conditions. Each community is to decide for itself how its land is to be apportioned, whether it is to be held collectively or as homesteads.

8. All the alienated land goes into one national fund. Its distribution among the toilers is carried out by local and central self-governing bodies, beginning with the democratic organization in villages and cities and ending with the central regional institutions. . . .

All that has been stated in this mandate is an expression of the strong wish of an overwhelming majority of politically conscious peasants and is proclaimed as a provisional law to be put into force before the meeting of the Constituent Assembly. Some portions of it are to go into effect as soon as possible, and other portions gradually, as may seem best to the . . . Soviets of Peasants' Deputies.

The lands of peasants and Cossacks of average means shall not be confiscated.

*President of the Council of Peoples' Commissars*
VLADIMIR ULIANOV LENIN

*November 8, 1917*

# War Communism

*The Bolsheviks introduced a number of emergency measures to deal with shortages of supplies and food as a result of war and revolution. This is an example of the measures taken to regulate supplies and prices of grain.*

## Decree on Grain (May 9, 1918)

On Assigning The People's Commissar of Food Emergency Powers In the Struggle Against The Rural Bourgeoisie Concealing Grain Reserves and Engaging In Grain Speculation.

The disastrous process of disorganization affecting the country's food supplies, the grave heritage of four years of war, continues to become increasingly widespread and increasingly acute. While the food-consuming gubernias[1] are starving, in the food-producing gubernias there are right now, as before, large reserves of grain, not yet even threshed, from the 1916 and 1917 harvests. This grain is in the hands of the village kulaks[2] and profiteers, in the hands of the rural bourgeoisie. Well fed and well provided for, having put aside huge sums of money obtained during the war years, the rural bourgeoisie remains stubbornly deaf and indifferent to the wailings of starving workers and the peasant poor. They do not bring their grain to the collecting points, reckoning on compelling the State to raise grain prices again and again while they themselves sell grain in the localities at fabulous prices to speculators. . . .

An end must be put to this obstinacy of the greedy village kulaks and profiteers. The practice of previous years for food has shown that the breaking of fixed prices for grain and the rejection of a grain monopoly would make it easier for our small band of capitalists to feast, but would make bread completely inaccessible to the many millions of toilers, subjecting them to inevitable death from starvation.

The answer to the violence of the grain owners towards the starving poor must be violence towards the bourgeoisie.

Not a single pood[3] should be left in the hands of those holding

[1]gubernias—Russian administrative provinces
[2]kulaks—rich peasants, employing others
[3]poods—a Russian weight equivalent to 36.1 lbs.

From Sydney Pollard and Colin Holmes, eds., *Documents of European Economic History: Vol. III, The End of Old Europe* (New York: St. Martin's Press, 1972), pp. 104–106. Reprinted by permission of Sydney Pollard and Colin Holmes.

grain except for the amount needed for sowing their fields and for feeding their families until the new harvest.

This policy must be implemented immediately, especially since the German occupation of the Ukraine compels us to get along with grain resources which are barely sufficient for sowing and reduced rations.

Having considered the situation created, and having taken into account that only through the strictest stock-taking and even distribution of grain reserves will Russia get out of the food crisis, the All-Russian Central Executive Committee of Soviets has resolved:

1. To reassert the firmness of the grain monopoly and fixed prices, and also the necessity of a ruthless struggle against grain speculators and bagmen; to compel each grain owner to declare the surplus above the quantity needed for sowing the fields and personal use, according to the established norms, until the new harvest, and to surrender the same within a week of the publication of this decree in each volost. The procedure for these declarations is to be determined by the People's Commissariat of Food through the local food organs.

2. To call upon all workers and poor peasants to unite at once for a merciless struggle against the kulaks.

3. To declare all those having surplus grain and not bringing it to the collection points, and also all those squandering grain reserves on illegal distilleries, enemies of the people; to turn them over to the Revolutionary Court with a view to sending the culprits to prison for a term of not less than 10 years; to expel them from the farm community for ever, all their property being subject to confiscation; to sentence illegal distillers, moreover, to socially-useful hard labour.

4. That in the event of discovering that someone has not declared his surplus grain for surrender in compliance with point 1, the grain shall be taken away from him without payment; after the actual receipt of the undeclared surpluses at the collection point, half their value, calculated at fixed prices, is to be paid to the person who pointed out the concealed surpluses, and the other half to the village commune. Declarations concerning concealed surpluses are to be made to local food organizations.

Further, taking into consideration that the fight against the food crisis demands the application of quick and decisive measures, that the most fruitful execution of these measures demands in its turn the centralization of all orders dealing with the food problem in a single body, and that such a body is the People's Commissariat of Food, the All-Russian Central Executive Committee of Soviets resolves to grant the People's Commissar of Food the following powers for a more successful fight against the food crisis:

1. To publish compulsory regulations, exceeding the usual limits of competence of the People's Commissar of Food, regarding the food situation.

2. To countermand regulations of local food organs and other organizations and bodies which contravene the plans and actions of the People's Commissar of Food.

3. To demand from institutions and organizations of all departments the unconditional and immediate execution of directives of the People's Commissar of Food in connection with the food situation.

4. To use armed force in the event of opposition being rendered to the removal of grain or other food products.

5. To disband or reorganize food organs in local areas in the event of their opposition to the directives of the People's Commissar of Food.

6. To dismiss, transfer, turn over to the Revolutionary Court, or subject to arrest officials and employees of all departments and public organizations in the event of their disorganizing interference with the directives of the People's Commissar of Food.

7. To transfer the present powers (except the right to subject to arrest, point 6) to other persons and bodies in the localities with the approval of the Council of People's Commissars.

8. All enactments of the People's Commissar of Food which are associated by their nature with departments of the People's Commissariat of the Means of Communication and the Supreme Council of the National Economy are to be carried out upon consultation with the corresponding departments.

9. Regulations and directives of the People's Commissar of Food issued under the present powers are to be verified by the College of the People's Commissariat of Food, which has the right, without suspending their execution, to appeal against them to the Council of People's Commissars.

The present decree takes force from the day of its signing and is to be put into operation by telegraph.

# Civil War

*In 1918, the Bolsheviks (who had taken the name Communists) negotiated a separate peace with Germany in the Treaty of Brest-Litovsk. They also instituted a number of social reforms, including the nationalization of factories and the requisitioning of food from large farmers. Opponents of these policies began to rally followers in 1918. They organized armed forces in some areas, with the assistance of the Allied governments, who hoped that a defeat of the Communists would bring Russia back into the war against Germany. Dubbed the "whites" (in contrast to the communist Red Army), the opponents of the Bolsheviks carried on a civil war until 1922.*

# From *Proclamation of the "Whites" (July 8, 1918)*

*To the Workers and Peasants:*

Citizens! The events of the last few days compel all those who love their country and the Russian people, all true defenders of freedom, to take up arms against the Soviet Government and defeat the usurpers who are disguising their nefarious acts by using the name of the people.

The Soviet of People's Commissars has brought ruin to Russia. . . . Instead of bread and peace it has brought famine and war. The Soviet of People's Commissars has made of mighty Russia a bit of earth dripping with the blood of peaceful citizens doomed to the pangs of hunger. In the name of the people the self-styled commissars have given the most fertile land to the enemies of Russia—the Austrians and Germans. There have been wrested from us the Ukraine, the Baltic and Vistula regions, the Kuban, the Don, and the Caucasus, which fed and supplied us with bread. That bread now goes to Germany. With that bread they are feeding those who, step by step, are conquering us and with the help of the Bolsheviks are placing us in the power of the German Kaiser. With that bread they are feeding the German army, which is slaughtering our people in cities and villages of the Ukraine, on the banks of the Don, in the mountains of the Caucasus, and in the fields of Great Russia.

The Soviet of People's Commissars is a plaything in the hands of the German Ambassador, Count Mirbach.

The Soviet of People's Commissars dictates decrees in the name of the people but Kaiser Wilhelm writes those decrees. Spurning agreement with the best citizens of the country, the Soviet of People's Commissars is not only in complete accord with the German imperialists but is carrying out unhesitatingly all their orders and demands.

By its treacherous policy of executing the orders of Count Mirbach the Soviet of People's Commissars forced the rising of the Czechoslovak army, which was marching to the Western front to fight the Germans. . . .

The Czechoslovaks are true republicans and serve the same sublime cause that we do. They are making war on the usurpers and will not permit the strangling of liberty. The People's Commissars, having long since betrayed the cause of the working class and knowing that the wrath of the people is terrible, now depend upon the bayonets of the Germans and the duped Letts to save their own lives and to keep in power.

The People's Commissars have brought about a terrible fratricidal war, sending detachments of Red Guards and Letts against the peas-

From James Bunyon, *Intervention, Civil War and Communism in Russia, April–December 1918* (New York: Octagon Books, 1976), pp. 194–196.

ants to take their grain. The People's Commissars are arresting and shooting workers who do not agree with their policies, are manipulating the elections, and are strangling all civil liberties. . . .

To arms all! Down with the Soviet of People's Commissars! Only by overthrowing it shall we have bread, peace, and freedom! Long live unity and order in Russia! When we put an end to the Soviet power we shall at the same time end civil war and return once more to our former strength and power.

And then the enemies of our country will not be terrifying to us. Down with the hirelings—the People's Commissars and their tools! Long live the coming Constituent Assembly!

Love live the free mighty fatherland!

# CULTURE AND SOCIETY IN THE 1920s

## Literature

*The Russian Revolution generated enormous excitement among intellectuals and artists in the 1920s. Vladimir Mayakovsky (1894–1930) conveys this sense of élan and the expectation that revolution would sweep the world in this poem addressed to Paris. Mayakovsky's initial enthusiasm turned to bitter disillusionment; in 1930 he committed suicide in the face of sharp criticism of his objections to the doctrine of socialist realism in art and literature.*

### From Vladimir Mayakovsky. *Paris*

PARIS
*(A little chat with the Eiffel Tower)*

By thousands of tyres outworn.
By millions of feet out-trod.
I furrow Paris—
so terribly alone,
it's terrible—not a soul,
terrible—nobody.
Around me—
autos fantastise a dance,
around me—
whistling water, fountain-poured
from beastfish snouts—
still left from Louis Quinze.
I enter
La Place de la Concorde.
I wait,
till
upraising its fretted peak,
tired from the trailing houses eyeing,
coming to meet me—
a Bolshevik—

From *Mayakovsky*, Herbert Marshall, trans. and ed. (New York: Hill and Wang, 1965), pp. 232–235. Reprinted by permission of Dobson Books Ltd.

Eiffel rears from the clouds defiant.
"S-s-s-sh . .
tower,
stalk quietly!
or they'll hear!
That moon's a guillotine leer."
(I lowered to a whisper)
"Listen to me"
(and murmured
buzzzzz
in her
radio-ear.)
"I've agitated all things made and built.
We only want to know—
if you are agreed,
tower—
do you want to head a revolt?
Tower—
if so
we elect you to lead!
It's not for you—
model genius of machines—
here
to pine away from Apollinairic verse.
No place for you—
this place of degradations.
This Paris of prostitutes,
poets,
Bourse.
The Metro's agreed,
the Metro's with us—
they'll spit out
from riveted tunnels
the crowd—
and wipe and scour
from their walls
with blood
placards-de-luxe of perfumes and powders.
They're convinced—
why should they stream and clatter
with first-class cars for the rich.
They're not rabble!
They're convinced:
our adverts
suit them better,

simple posters
and placards of struggle.
Tower—
don't fear the streets!
Or else
if the streets won't release the Metro—
the road-beds
are welded by rails,
I'll raise up the rails to revolt.
You're afraid?
Bistros in flocks will defend you.
Still afraid?
To our aid will come Rive-Gauche.
Don't be afraid!
I'll persuade the bridges too.
The river's
not so easy
to swim
across!
The bridges,
maddened by the traffic hell,
will rise from the river banks of Paris.
At the very first call
all bridges will rebel—
and dash passers-by on their buttressed piers!
Every thing uprears.
Things are beyond endurance.
In fifteen
maybe twenty years,
strength dissolves,
steel flabbies,
and one of these nights
things
will go
to Montmartre
and sell themselves.
Come, tower!
To us;
You—
there,
are much more
needed!
Steel-shining,
smoke-piercing,
we'll meet you.

Come to us!
You'll be more tenderly greeted
than our first love of loves.
Come to Moscow!
Moscow
is so
spacious.
You,
everyone
will have in their street!
Everyone
will cherish you.
A hundred times a day or so
we'll clean your steel and copper
like the sun.
Let
that city of yours,
Paris of dandies and dudes,
Paris of yap-yawning boulevards,
let it end the same, in old Boulogne woods,
and museums, an all-in cemetery Louvre.
March forward
those four mighty paws, endowed
and clamped by the blue-prints of Eiffel,
In our broad sky let your tall brow be radioed.
that even our red stars will get an eyeful!
Decide, tower—
all around you, revolts are
shattering from head to foot old Paris!
Come to us!
To US,
to the USSR!
Come on. Let's go—
I'll
get you a visa!

# The Family

*Soon after they assumed power, the Bolsheviks introduced laws "modernizing" family relationships; women were given legal status, divorce was permitted, and equality of property rights between husband and wife was introduced. In addition, feminists like Alexandra Kollantai (1872–1952) urged the collectivization of childrearing and housekeeping as a way of achieving equality between women and men.*

# From Alexandra Kollantai. *Communism and the Family*

## The Dawn of Collective Housekeeping

... The individual household has passed its zenith. It is being replaced more and more by collective housekeeping. The working woman will sooner or later need to take care of her own dwelling no longer; in the communist society of to-morrow this work will be carried on by a special category of working women who will do nothing else. The wives of the rich have long been freed from these annoying and tiring duties. Why should the working woman continue to carry out these painful tasks? In Soviet Russia, the life of the working woman should be surrounded with the same ease, with the same brightness, with the same hygiene, with the same beauty, which has thus far surrounded only the women of the richer classes. In a communist society the working women will no longer have to spend their few, alas too few, hours of leisure in cooking, since *there will be in a communist society public restaurants and central kitchens* to which everybody may come to take his meals.

These establishments have already been on the increase in all countries, even under the capitalist régime. In fact, for half a century the number of restaurants and cafés in all the great cities of Europe has increased day by day; they have sprung up like mushrooms after autumn rain. But while under the capitalist system only people with well-lined purses could afford to take their meals in a restaurant, in the communist city anyone who likes may come to eat in the central kitchens and restaurants. The case will be the same with washing and other work: the working woman will no longer be obliged to sink in an ocean of filth or to ruin her eyes in darning her stockings or mending her linen; she will simply carry these things to the *central laundries* each week, and take them out again each week already washed and ironed. The working woman will have one care less to face. Also, special clothes-mending shops will give the working women the opportunity to devote their evenings to instructive reading, to healthy recreation, instead of spending them as at present in exhausting labour. Therefore, the four last duties still remaining to burden our women, as we have seen above, will soon also disappear under the triumphant communist regime. And the working women will surely have no cause to regret this. Communist society will only have broken the domestic yoke of woman in order to render her life richer, happier, freer and more complete.

From Rudolph Schlesinger, *The Family in the USSR: Documents and Readings* (London: Routledge & Kegan Paul, 1949), pp. 62, 65, 69–71. Reprinted by permission of the publisher.

## The Child's Upbringing under Capitalism

But what will remain of the family after all these labours of individual housekeeping have disappeared? We still have *the children* to deal with. But here also the State of the working comrades will come to the rescue of the family by creating a substitute for the family. Society will gradually take charge of all that formerly devolved on parents. . . .

. . . In Soviet Russia, owing to the care of the Commissariats of Public Education and of Social Welfare, great advances are being made, and already many things have been done in order to facilitate for the family the task of bringing up and supporting the children. There are homes for the very small babies; day nurseries, kindergartens, children's colonies and homes, infirmaries, and health resorts for sick children, restaurants, free lunches at school, free distribution of textbooks, of warm clothing, of shoes to the pupils of the educational establishments—does not all this sufficiently show that the child is passing out of the confines of the family and being removed from the shoulders of the parents on to those of the community?

. . . Contrary to the practice of capitalist society, which has not been able to transform the education of youth into a truly social function, a State task, communist society will consider the social education of the rising generation as the very basis of its laws and customs, as the corner-stone of the new edifice. Not the family of the past, petty and narrow, with its quarrels between the parents, with its exclusive interest in its own offspring, will mould for us the man of the society of to-morrow. Our new man, in our new society, is to be moulded by socialist organizations, such as playgrounds, gardens, homes, and many other such institutions, in which the child will pass the greater part of the day and where intelligent educators will make of him a communist who is conscious of the greatness of this sacred motto: solidarity, comradeship, mutual aid, devotion to the collective life. . . .

## Social Equality of Men and Women

The Workers' State has need of a new form of relation between the sexes. The narrow and exclusive affection of the mother for her own children must expand until it embraces all the children of the great proletarian family. In place of the indissoluble marriage based on the servitude of woman, we shall see rise the free union, fortified by the love and the mutual respect of the two members of the Workers' State, equal in their rights and in their obligations. In place of the individual and egotistic family, there will arise a great universal family of workers, in which all the workers, men and women, will be, above all, workers, comrades. Such will be the relation between men and women in the communist society of to-morrow. This new relation will assure to humanity all the joys of so-called free love ennobled by a true social equality of the mates, joys which were unknown to the commercial society of the capitalist regime.

Make way for healthy blossoming children: make way for a vigorous youth that clings to life and to its joys, which is free in its sentiments and in its affections. Such is the watchword of the communist society. In the name of equality, of liberty, and of love, we call upon the working women and the working men, peasant women and peasants, courageously and with faith to take up the work of the reconstruction of human society with the object of rendering it more perfect, more just, and more capable of assuring to the individual the happiness which he deserves. The red flag of the social revolution which will shelter, after Russia, other countries of the world also, already proclaims to us the approach of the heaven on earth to which humanity has been aspiring for centuries.

# STALIN AND THE CONSOLIDATION OF THE MODERN SOVIET STATE

## Economic Planning

*Joseph Stalin (1879–1953) emerged as the head of the Communist Party in 1927, having defeated his rival, Leon Trotsky. Under Stalin's leadership, Russia embarked on a program of economic development that sought to promote rapid industrial growth and the collectivization of agriculture. The program was put forth in a series of Five-Year Plans. In the first document, Stalin reports on the achievements of the First Five-Year Plan (1928–1932). In the second, Max Belov describes the way the peasants were organized into collective farms (kolkhozes).*

### From Joseph Stalin. *The Results of the First Five-Year Plan*

The fundamental task of the Five-Year Plan was to transfer our country, with its backward, and in part medieval, technique, to the lines of new, modern technique.

The fundamental task of the Five-Year Plan was to convert the U.S.S.R. from an agrarian and weak country, dependent upon the caprices of the capitalist countries, into an industrial and powerful country, fully self-reliant and independent of the caprices of world capitalism.

The fundamental task of the Five-Year Plan was, in converting the U.S.S.R. into an industrial country, fully to eliminate the capitalist elements, to widen the front of socialist forms of economy, and to create the economic base for the abolition of classes in the U.S.S.R., for the construction of socialist society.

The fundamental task of the Five-Year Plan was to create such an industry in our country as would be able to re-equip and reorganize, not only the whole of industry, but also transport and agriculture—on the basis of socialism.

From Joseph Stalin, *Selected Writings* (New York: International Publishers, 1942), pp. 242, 246–247, 253–254, 260–262. Reprinted by permission of International Publishers Company.

The fundamental task of the Five-Year Plan was to transfer small and scattered agriculture to the lines of large-scale collective farming, so as to ensure the economic base for socialism in the rural districts and thus to eliminate the possibility of the restoration of capitalism in the U.S.S.R.

Finally, the task of the Five-Year Plan was to create in the country all the necessary technical and economic prerequisites for increasing to the utmost the defensive capacity of the country, to enable it to organize determined resistance to any and every attempt at military intervention from outside, to any and every attempt at military attack from without.

What dictated this fundamental task of the Five-Year Plan; what were the grounds for it?

The necessity of putting an end to the technical and economic backwardness of the Soviet Union, which doomed it to an unenviable existence; the necessity of creating in the country such prerequisites as would enable it not only to overtake but in time to outstrip, economically and technically, the advanced capitalist countries. . . .

What are the results of the Five-Year Plan in four years in the sphere of *industry*?

Have we achieved victory in this sphere?

Yes, we have. . . .

We did not have an iron and steel industry, the foundation for the industrialization of the country. Now we have this industry.

We did not have a tractor industry. Now we have one.

We did not have an automobile industry. Now we have one.

We did not have a machine-tool industry. Now we have one.

We did not have a big and up-to-date chemical industry. Now we have one.

We did not have a real and big industry for the production of modern agricultural machinery. Now we have one.

We did not have an aircraft industry. Now we have one.

In output of electric power we were last on the list. Now we rank among the first.

In output of oil products and coal we were last on the list. Now we rank among the first.

We had only one coal and metallurgical base—in the Ukraine—which we barely managed to keep going. We have not only succeeded in improving this base, but have created a new coal and metallurgical base—in the East—which is the pride of our country.

We had only one center of the textile industry—in the North of our country. As a result of our efforts we will have in the very near future two new centers of the textile industry—in Central Asia and Western Siberia.

And we have not only created these new great industries, but have created them on a scale and in dimensions that eclipse the scale and dimensions of European industry.

And as a result of all this the capitalist elements have been completely and irrevocably eliminated from industry, and socialist industry has become the sole form of industry in the U.S.S.R.

And as a result of all this our country has been converted from an agrarian into an industrial country; for the proportion of industrial output, as compared with agricultural output, has risen from 48 per cent of the total in the beginning of the Five-Year Plan period (1928) to 70 per cent at the end of the fourth year of the Five-Year Plan period (1932). . . .

. . . The object of the Five-Year Plan in the sphere of agriculture was to unite the scattered and small individual peasant farms, which lacked the opportunity of utilizing tractors and modern agricultural machinery, into large collective farms, equipped with all the modern implements of highly developed agriculture, and to cover unoccupied land with model state farms.

The object of the Five-Year Plan in the sphere of agriculture was to convert the U.S.S.R. from a small-peasant and backward country into a large-scale agriculture organized on the basis of collective labor and providing the maximum output for the market.

What has the party achieved in carrying out the program of the Five-Year Plan in four years in the sphere of agriculture? Has it fulfilled this program, or has it failed?

The party has succeeded, in a matter of three years, in organizing more than 200,000 collective farms and about 5,000 state farms specializing mainly in grain growing and livestock raising, and at the same time it has succeeded, in the course of four years, in enlarging the crop area by 21,000,000 hectares.

The party has succeeded in getting more than 60 per cent of the peasant farms, which account for more than 70 per cent of the land cultivated by peasants, to unite into collective farms, which means that we have *fulfilled* the Five-Year Plan *threefold*.

The party has succeeded in creating the possibility of obtaining, not 500,000,000 to 600,000,000 poods[1] of marketable grain, which was the amount purchased in the period when individual peasant farming predominated, but 1,200,000,000 to 1,400,000,000 poods of grain annually.

The party has succeeded in routing the kulaks as a class, although they have not yet been dealt the final blow; the laboring peasants have been emancipated from kulak bondage and exploitation, and a firm economic basis for the Soviet government, the basis of collective farming, has been established in the countryside.

The party has succeeded in converting the U.S.S.R. from a land of

[1]pood—a unit of weight equivalent to 36.1 lbs.

small peasant farming into a land where agriculture is run on the largest scale in the world.

Such, in general terms, are the results of the Five-Year Plan in four years in the sphere of agriculture.

## From Max Belov. *The History of a Soviet Collective Farm*

General collectivization in our village was brought about in the following manner: Two representatives of the Party arrived in the village. All the inhabitants were summoned by the ringing of the church bell to a meeting at which the policy of general collectivization was announced. At the meeting, however, someone distributed leaflets entitled "This Is How It Will Be on a Collective Farm." The leaflet showed a picture of a mother and child, the mother bent under the burden of overwork. The upshot was that although the meeting lasted two days, from the viewpoint of the Party representatives nothing was accomplished.

After this setback the Party representatives divided the village into two sections and worked each one separately. Two more officials were sent to reinforce the first two. A meeting of our section of the village was held in a stable which had previously belonged to a kulak. The meeting dragged on until dark. Suddenly someone threw a brick at the lamp, and in the dark the peasants began to beat the Party representatives who jumped out the window and escaped from the village barely alive. The following day seven people were arrested. The militia was called in and stayed in the village until the peasants, realizing their helplessness, calmed down.

It was difficult, however, for the Party and government to break down the old principles and traditions. The peasants stubbornly clung to their possessions. But "there are no fortresses which Bolsheviks cannot storm." . . .

By the end of 1930 there were two kolkhozes in our village. Though at first these collectives embraced at most only 70 per cent of the peasant households, in the months that followed they gradually absorbed more and more of them.

In these kolkhozes the great bulk of the land was held and worked communally, but each peasant household owned a house of some sort, a small plot of ground and perhaps some livestock. All the members of the kolkhoz were required to work on the kolkhoz a certain number of days each month; the rest of the time they were allowed to work on their own holdings. They derived their income partly from what they grew on their garden strips and partly from their work in the kolkhoz.

From Sidney Harcave, *Readings in Russian History* (New York: Thomas and Crowell Co., 1962), pp. 208–214.

When the harvest was over, and after the farm had met its obligations to the state and to various special funds (for insurance, seed, forage, etc.) and had sold on the market whatever undesignated produce was left, the remaining produce and the farm's monetary income were divided among the kolkhoz members according to the number of "labor days" each one had contributed to the farm's work. One day's actual work might be worth anywhere from one half to two or more labor days, depending on the difficulty of the task involved and the degree of skill required.

Our kolkhoz was built on the site of the former commune, the acreage of which had been increased at the expense of households which had been evicted to other parts of the village. The farm and administrative buildings of the collective were constructed from sheds which had formerly belonged to kulaks, the farm buildings of collectivized peasants, and other miscellaneous sources. Tombstones and stone crosses from the cemetery were used for the foundations of the building; for the roofs, the sheet-iron was ripped off the former kulak dwelling on the kolkhoz land. Willow and linden wood, of which the village had an ample supply, was also used in the farm's construction. By the summer of 1931, the kolkhoz had its own stud farm with space for 120 horses, a large barn for grain and a steam-operated flour mill. It included in its membership 85 per cent of all the peasant households of our section of the village, and had 90 horses, 24 oxen, 80 sheep, 160 swarms of bees, and several cows and pigs.

It was in 1930 that the kolkhoz members first received their portions out of the "communal kettle." After they had received their earnings, at the rate of 1 kilogram of grain and 55 kopecks per labor day, one of them remarked, "You will live, but you will be very, very thin."

In the spring of 1931 a tractor worked the fields of the kolkhoz for the first time. The tractor was "capable of plowing every kind of hard soil and virgin sod," as Party representatives told us at the meeting in celebration of its arrival. The peasants did not then know that these "steel horses" would carry away a good part of the harvest in return for their work and would devalue still further the "collective yardstick," the labor day.

By late 1932 more than 80 per cent of the peasant households in the raion had been collectivized. In the twenty-four villages of the raion there were fifty-two kolkhozes and three state farms (sovkhozes). That year the peasants harvested a good crop and had hopes that the calculations would work out to their advantage and would help strengthen them economically. These hopes were in vain. The kolkhoz workers received only 200 grams of flour per labor day for the first half of the year; the remaining grain, including the seed fund, was taken by the government. The peasants were told that industrialization of the country, then in full swing, demanded grain and sacrifices from them

That autumn the "red broom" passed over the kolkhozes and the individual plots, sweeping the "surplus" for the state out of the barns and corn-cribs. In the search for "surpluses," everything was collected. The farms were cleaned out even more thoroughly than the kulaks had been. As a result, famine, which was to become intense by the spring of 1933, already began to be felt in the fall of 1932.

The famine of 1932–1933 was the most terrible and destructive that the Ukrainian people have ever experienced. The peasants ate dogs, horses, rotten potatoes, the bark of trees, grass—anything they could find. Incidents of cannibalism were not uncommon. The people were like wild beasts, ready to devour one another. And no matter what they did, they went on dying, dying, dying. . . .

There was no one to gather the bumper crop of 1933, since the people who remained alive were too weak and exhausted. More than a hundred persons—office and factory workers from Leningrad—were sent to assist on the kolkhoz; two representatives of the Party arrived to help organize the harvesting. Out of the first threshing, the kolkhoz members were given 500 grams of flour per labor day for the first six months of the year; food was also prepared for them daily at their place of work.

During this period the peasants had to bear another burden: the forced loans to the government. Although the loans were relatively small that year, they were particularly burdensome, coming as they did on top of the famine and general impoverishment.

That summer (1933) the entire administration of the kolkhoz—the bookkeeper, the warehouseman, the manager of the flour mill, and even the chairman himself—were put on trial on charges of plundering the kolkhoz property and produce. All the accused were sentenced to terms of seven to ten years, and a new administration was elected. . . .

After 1934 a gradual improvement began in the economic life of the kolkhoz and its members. The economic conditions of a kolkhoz depend to a large degree on its acreage distribution, that is, on the amount of land which can be sown to the most profitable crops, and on the character of its organization and management. The peasants naturally took a great interest in the election of the chairman and the board of managers of the kolkhoz. . . .

In general, from the mid-1930's until 1941, the majority of kolkhoz members in the Ukraine lived relatively well. They were never in need of bread and other foodstuffs. If the market provided insufficient clothes and shoes, the shortage was made good by items made locally. In 1939 and 1940, however, the state demanded more grain from the kolkhozes than they had contributed before. The alliance with Germany, to which the grain was sent, stirred up dissatisfaction and disapproval among the peasants. The sharp changes in the amount delivered to the state and the fluctuating remuneration for the labor day constantly aroused a fear of tomorrow's fate among the kolkhoz members and drove them to steal grain and conceal it.

On the eve of war, our kolkhoz presented the following picture: its collective livestock consisted of 180 horses, 44 cows, 90 oxen, about 300 calves, more than 400 pigs, about 100 sheep, and more than 60 chickens. It had three automobiles, a flour mill, a sawmill, a creamery, machine and wood-working shops and other buildings. It was considered a "leading" kolkhoz in the raion and had participated in the all-Union agricultural exhibitions from 1935 to 1939; its chairman had attended several republic and oblast conferences of agricultural leaders.

# Family Organization

*In the 1930s the Russian government retreated from its initial liberal stance toward women and family structure. It reimposed more traditional moral standards and began to emphasize the importance of motherhood in Soviet life. Opportunities for women in work and politics were restricted, and Stalin directed some of his purges at high-ranking women activists.*

### From *Law on the Abolition of Legal Abortion (May 1936)*

The published draft of the law prohibiting abortion and providing material assistance to mothers has provoked a lively reaction throughout the country. It is being heatedly discussed by tens of millions of people and there is no doubt that it will serve as a further strengthening of the Soviet family. Parents' responsibility for the education of their children will be increased and a blow will be dealt at the lighthearted, negligent attitude towards marriage.

When we speak of strengthening the Soviet family, we are speaking precisely of the struggle against the survivals of a bourgeois attitude towards marriage, women and children. So-called "free love" and all disorderly sex life are bourgeois through and through, and have nothing to do with either socialist principles or the ethics and standards of conduct of the Soviet citizen. Socialist doctrine shows this, and it is proved by life itself.

The elite of our country, the best of the Soviet youth, are as a rule

From Rudolph Schlesinger, *The Family in the USSR: Documents and Readings* (London: Routledge & Kegan Paul, 1949), pp. 251–254. Reprinted by permission of the publisher.

also excellent family men who dearly love their children. And vice versa: the man who does not take marriage seriously, and abandons his children to the whims of fate, is usually also a bad worker and a poor member of society.

Fatherhood and motherhood have long been virtues in this country. This can be seen at the first glance, without searching enquiry. Go through the parks and streets of Moscow or of any other town in the Soviet Union on a holiday, and you will see not a few young men walking with pink-cheeked, well-fed babies in their arms. . . .

The great Utopians, More, Saint-Simon, Fourier, Cabet, who dreamed of a happy new society invariably devoted much space in their utopias to the children. Observing the crimes and sordidness of capitalism which was strangling the working women and depriving the children of their childhood and the adults of the joy of parenthood, the Utopians opposed this poor and gloomy reality with a beautiful dream of a life in which the children were treated with the utmost love and the grown-ups regained the delight of being parents. This love of children and this joy of parenthood have been given to men by the Soviet reality. Not on an imaginary isle of Utopia, but in this real and great country of ours the working people have found the bliss of being free and living a full life. . . .

It is impossible even to compare the present state of the family with that which obtained before the Soviet régime—so great has been the improvement towards greater stability and, above all, greater humanity and goodness. The single fact that millions of women have become economically independent and are no longer at the mercy of men's whims, speaks volumes. Compare, for instance, the modern woman collective farmer who sometimes earns more than her husband, with the pre-revolutionary peasant woman who completely depended on her husband and was a slave in the household. Has not this fundamentally altered family relations, has it not rationalized and strengthened the family? The very motives for setting up a family, for getting married, have changed for the better, have been cleansed of atavistic and barbaric elements. Marriage has ceased to be a matter of sell-and-buy. Nowadays a girl from a collective farm is not given away (or should we say "sold away"?) by her father, for she is now her own mistress, and no one can give her away. She will marry the man she loves. . . . There is no doubt that the free woman of our time values and loves her family differently. The collective farm system, by making peasant women independent, has strengthened the family in the rural areas in every way. The same can be seen in the towns, where the raising of the cultural level and of the workers' standard of living inevitably leads to a stabilization and regularization of family relations. . . .

The toilers of our land have paid with their blood for the right to a life of joy, and a life of joy implies the right to have one's own family and healthy, happy children. Millions of workers beyond the frontiers of our land are still deprived of this joy, for there unemployment, hunger and helpless poverty are rampant. Old maids and elderly bachelors, a rare thing in our country, are frequent in the West, and that is no accident.

We alone have all the conditions under which a working woman can fulfil her duties as a citizen and as a mother responsible for the birth and early upbringing of her children.

A woman without children merits our pity, for she does not know the full joy of life. Our Soviet women, full-blooded citizens of the freest country in the world, have been given the bliss of motherhood. We must safeguard our family and raise and rear healthy Soviet heroes!

# Destruction of the Opposition

*In 1936, Stalin began a series of purges aimed at destroying the vestiges of political opposition to him. He had these "enemies of socialism" imprisoned or executed and justified his actions in the following official account.*

*After Stalin's death in 1953, Nikita Khrushchev (1896–1971) became the head of the Russian Communist Party. In 1956, Khrushchev delivered a speech to the Twentieth Party Congress that repudiated many of Stalin's policies and particularly the "cult of personality" that he had fostered. (See Chapter XV, p. 539.)*

## Purges: The Official Explanation

The achievements of Socialism in our country were a cause of rejoicing not only to the Party, and not only to the workers and collective farmers, but also to our Soviet intelligentsia, and to all honest citizens of the Soviet Union.

But they were no cause of rejoicing to the remnants of the defeated exploiting classes; on the contrary, they only enraged them the more as time went on.

They infuriated the lickspittles of the defeated classes—the puny remnants of the following of Bukharin and Trotsky.

These gentry were guided in their evaluation of the achievements of

From *History of the Communist Party of the Soviet Union (Bolsheviks): Short Course* (Moscow, 1948), pp. 324–327, 329.

the workers and collective farmers not by the interests of the people, who applauded every such achievement, but by the interests of their own wretched and putrid faction, which had lost all contact with the realities of life. Since the achievements of Socialism in our country meant the victory of the policy of the Party and the utter bankruptcy of their own policy, these gentry, instead of admitting the obvious facts and joining the common cause, began to revenge themselves on the Party and the people for their own failure, for their own bankruptcy; they began to resort to foul play and sabotage against the cause of the workers and collective farmers, to blow up pits, set fire to factories, and commit acts of wrecking in collective and state farms, with the object of undoing the achievements of the workers and collective farmers and evoking popular discontent against the Soviet Government. And in order, while doing so, to shield their puny group from exposure and destruction, they simulated loyalty to the Party, fawned upon it, eulogized it, cringed before it more and more, while in reality continuing their underhand, subversive activities against the workers and peasants.

At the Seventeenth Party Congress, Bukharin, Rykov and Tomsky made repentant speeches, praising the Party and extolling its achievements to the skies. But the congress detected a ring of insincerity and duplicity in their speeches; for what the Party expects from its members is not eulogies and rhapsodies over its achievements, but conscientious work on the Socialist front. And this was what the Bukharinites had showed no signs of for a long time. The Party saw that the hollow speeches of these gentry were in reality meant for their supporters outside the congress, to serve as a lesson to them in duplicity, and a call to them not to lay down their arms.

Speeches were also made at the Seventeenth Congress by the Trotskyites, Zinoviev and Kamenev, who lashed themselves extravagantly for their mistakes, and eulogized the Party no less extravagantly for its achievements. But the congress could not help seeing that both their nauseating self-castigation and their fulsome praise of the party were only meant to hide an uneasy and unclean conscience. However, the Party did not yet know or suspect that while these gentry were making their cloying speeches at the congress they were hatching a villainous plot against the life of S. M. Kirov.

On December 1, 1934, S. M. Kirov was foully murdered in the Smolny, in Leningrad, by a shot from a revolver.

The assassin was caught red-handed and turned out to be a member of a secret counter-revolutionary group made up of members of an anti-Soviet group of Zinovievites in Leningrad.

S. M. Kirov was loved by the Party and the working class, and his murder stirred the people profoundly, sending a wave of wrath and deep sorrow through the country.

The investigation established that in 1933 and 1934 an underground counter-revolutionary terrorist group had been formed in Leningrad consisting of former members of the Zinoviev opposition and headed by a so-called "Leningrad Centre." The purpose of this group was to murder leaders of the Communist Party. S. M. Kirov was chosen as the first victim. The testimony of the members of this counter-revolutionary group showed that they were connected with representatives of foreign capitalist states and were receiving funds from them.

The exposed members of this organization were sentenced by the Military Collegium of the Supreme Soviet of the U.S.S.R. to the supreme penalty—to be shot.

Soon afterwards the existence of an underground counter-revolutionary organization called the "Moscow Centre" was discovered. The preliminary investigation and the trial revealed the villainous part played by Zinoviev, Kamenev, Yevdokimo and other leaders of this organization in cultivating the terrorist mentality among their followers, and in plotting the murder of members of the Party Central Committee and of the Soviet Government.

To such depths of duplicity and villainy had these people sunk that Zinoviev, who was one of the organizers and instigators of the assassination of S. M. Kirov, and who had urged the murderer to hasten the crime, wrote an obituary of Kirov speaking of him in terms of eulogy, and demanded that it be published.

The Zinovievites simulated remorse in court; but they persisted in their duplicity even in the dock. They concealed their connection with Trotsky. They concealed the fact that together with the Trotskyites they had sold themselves to fascist espionage services. They concealed their spying and wrecking activities. They concealed from the court their connections with the Bukharinites, and the existence of a united Trotsky-Bukharin gang of fascist hirelings.

As it later transpired, the murder of Comrade Kirov was the work of this united Trotsky-Bukharin gang. . . .

The chief instigator and ringleader of this gang of assassins and spies was Judas Trotsky. Trotsky's assistants and agents in carrying out his counter-revolutionary instructions were Zinoviev, Kamenev and their Trotskyite underlings. They were preparing to bring about the defeat of the U.S.S.R. in the event of attack by imperialist countries; they had become defeatists with regard to the workers' and peasants' state; they had become despicable tools and agents of the German and Japanese fascists.

The main lesson which the Party organizations had to draw from the trials of the persons implicated in the foul murder of S. M. Kirov was that they must put an end to their own political blindness and political heedlessness, and must increase their vigilance and the vigilance of all Party members. . . .

Purging and consolidating its ranks, destroying the enemies of the Party and relentlessly combating distortions of the Party line, the Bolshevik Party rallied closer than ever around its Central Committee, under whose leadership the Party and the Soviet land now passed to a new stage—the completion of the construction of a classless, Socialist society.

# XIV

# EUROPE—THE 1920'S TO WORLD WAR II

*T*HE END OF *World War I brought only temporary peace to Europe.
Economic depression and social unrest characterized domestic and
international politics. Strikes and political conflict led to the temporary
victories of the Labour Party in England in 1924 and 1929 and to the
triumph of a Conservative-dominated coalition known as the National
government in 1931. In France, a left-oriented coalition known as the
Popular Front emerged in 1936. In both countries social welfare measures were introduced in an attempt to alleviate the worst aspects of the
economic crisis.*

*In Germany and Italy, democratic governments were replaced by au-
thoritarian regimes, whose leaders endorsed fascist programs for economic
and political organization. Benito Mussolini in Italy and Adolf Hitler in
Germany used terrorist gangs (the Brown Shirts in Germany and the
Black Shirts in Italy) and repressive measures of other kinds to implement their rule. In Spain, a contest for power between coalitions of left-
wing and right-wing groups dragged on in a civil war from 1936 to
1939 and ended with the triumph of the right and its leader, Francisco
Franco.*

*War broke out in 1939 when Germany invaded Czechoslovakia and
then Poland, proving the futility of the policy of appeasement that Britain and France had followed in the preceding years. In 1940, France
abandoned the war and negotiated a treaty with Germany. The Allies
fought on, and war broadened to the Pacific in 1941, after the Japanese
attack on American bases in Hawaii. In 1944, the Allies recaptured
France and forced the surrender of Germany. American bombing of Japanese cities with a new weapon, the atomic bomb, ended the war in the
Pacific.*

*The human costs of the war are recorded in the economic losses, the
destruction of cities, and the statistics of dead and wounded. They are
also documented by the memories of survivors, those who fought in battles, languished in concentration camps, and witnessed the blinding flash
and the fallout that ushered in the age of nuclear weapons.*

# ECONOMIC DEPRESSION AND SOCIAL UNREST

## England

*During the 1920s and 1930s Britain experienced economic depression. There was widespread unemployment, the extent and effect of which were described in the report to the Pilgrim Trust.*

### From *Men Without Work: A Report Made to the Pilgrim Trust,* 1938

One of the main differences between the "working" classes and the "middle" classes is the difference of security. This is probably a more important distinction than income level. If working men and women seem to be unduly anxious to make their sons and daughters into clerks, the anxiety behind it is not for more money but for greater security. Rightly or wrongly, they feel that the black-coated worker has a more assured position. The semi-skilled man is at the mercy of rationalisation.

A week's notice may end half a lifetime's service, with no prospects, if he is elderly, but the dole, followed by a still further reduction in his means of livelihood when the old age pension comes. We take as an example a shoe laster from Leicester, who had worked thirty-seven years with one firm. "When I heard the new manager going through and saying: 'The whole of this side of this room, this room, and this room is to be stopped,' I knew it would be uphill work to get something." He went on to describe to us how he had not been able to bring himself to tell his wife the bad news when he got home, how she had noticed that something was wrong, how confident she had been that he would get work elsewhere, but how he had known that the chances were heavily against him. For months and indeed often for years such men go on looking for work, and the same is true of many casual la-

From *Men Without Work: A Report Made to the Pilgrim Trust, 1938*, pp. 144–149.

bourers. There were in the sample old men who have not a remote chance of working again but yet make it a practice to stand every morning at six o'clock at the works gates in the hope that perhaps they may catch the foreman's eye. There were young men who said that they could never settle to anything, but must be out all day, every day, looking for work. We had instances of men who had bicycled all over Lancashire and Yorkshire from Liverpool in the hopes of finding something. A young married man (aged 29) in Leicester, who was for some reason strongly criticized by the authorities for not looking for work, had tramped about for nearly a year in the hopes of getting some permanent, or at least temporary employment (his wife had gone back into service to make it possible for him to do so), but the only substantial work he had done during the whole period was pea picking. Another man, a shoehand, 38 years old, had come down on his own initiative from Lancashire, where the factory in which he worked had closed down, to Leicester. He was a neat, rather reserved type of man and had not perhaps the necessary push to squeeze himself into work, but he wanted it desperately. He tried to join the army and was refused for it, apparently on account of his age, and it was clear that as time went on he was getting a more and more defeatist attitude to work. He might go on trying, but his efforts were vitiated more and more by the knowledge that he was not going to succeed. The sample brought out scores of similar instances, but these two of comparatively young men in a city which by ordinary standards is exceedingly prosperous must stand for all of them. When a man is thrown out of employment the first thing that he wants is work, and very few of those who have a good employment history can settle down to accept the fact of unemployment till they have been out of work for months.

But when a man who has had perhaps ten years' steady employment is thrown on the streets, to look for work effectively is not always easy. A large number of the sample cases had lost good jobs at the time of the slump, when there was nothing else to be had. They had gone round from one works to another with hundreds of others all desperately anxious to secure employment, and failure after failure had gradually "got them down." The restlessness of which many wives spoke to us tells its own tale: "Now he's out of work he don't seem to be able to settle down to anything." When a man is out of work, anxiety is part of a vicious circle, and the more he worries, the more he unfits himself for work.

There were other symptoms of this nerviness. The high proportions of instances in which married men were living apart from their wives is certainly in some degree to be explained by it. Among many of the families visited, tension between man and wife was apparent. Thus we saw a man of 25 in Liverpool, who had had previously to 1935 a certain amount of work as a builder's labourer. At the time of the visit his wife was 19; they had been married when she was 16. The first child had died the day after it was born and the mother had suffered from anaemia and kidney trouble at the time. There was another baby a few months old, which was taken to hospital with pneumonia the night before the visit occurred. The man gave the impression of one who had been not unhappy for a time lounging, but was not getting to the end of his tether. Speaking of his wife, he said: "She's always crying. But crying don't make things no better": and the early marriage, poverty, illness, and finally the quarrel seemed to summarise in a single instance several of the worst features of the situation of the long unemployed. Friction may come out in other ways, also. The children may get on a man's nerves if he is at home all day. "When he was out of work we were always having rows over the children. He will never let them do anything. It's much better now he is at work." In several cases where the wife was earning but the husband unemployed, there was evidently unhappiness as a result. A striking example occurred among the Liverpool visits, the case of a printer, 42 years old, who had lost his chance of re-employment at his old trade, through a dispute with the union. A few weeks before our visit occurred, he had left Liverpool in the hopes of finding work in the Midlands, and the wife showed one of us a touching letter in which he told her that he had got work at 25s. a week and enclosed 10s. for her. While he was out of work she had been working regularly, with the result that he only drew 5s. Unemployment Assistance. She described how she used to lie awake at nights and hear him "tramping up and down the garden path, or up and down in the parlour, and it made her nearly mad; and it made her nearly mad to feel that she was keeping him by her earnings and they gaining nothing by her work." There was a somewhat similar case in Leicester, where the woman had left her work because she could not bear to be the breadwinner while her husband, young and fit, did nothing; another in Blackburn where a young married woman, working, with an unemployed husband, said that "it made him wild" to be about with no money in his pocket. It is in the light of such cases that we should read the figures showing the numbers of men in the sample who were living apart from their wives.

Similar questions are raised by the case of the man whose allowance takes into account the fact that his children are earning sums which permit of their contributing to his support and the general upkeep of the household. There were in the sample instances of men over 55 years of age who were either not in receipt of any income from the Unemployment Assistance Board, or in receipt of small amounts, 5s. or 7s. 6d., from the Board, because it was held that the household resources were otherwise sufficient. This view would be justified if the household were taken as a unit. The fact remains, however, that some men in this position feel the loss of an independent income, such as they enjoyed while on Unemployment Benefit very acutely, and in many such cases the home appears to represent two standards, the earning children being often smartly dressed and happy, while the fathers were shabby and suffering from a sense of their dependence. Such men gave the impression that they purposely avoided making any effort to keep up appearances in case the children might think that they were drawing an undue share of the family income. While among the sample as a whole, bitterness against the Unemployment Assistance Board is the exception rather than the rule, in cases of this kind it was the rule rather than the exception. The question has two sides, and we came across several instances in which children were behaving most unreasonably in refusing to contribute towards the household expenses the sum, not large, which the regulations expect of them. Nevertheless, there may be a case, even here, for making some larger payment from State funds.

The depression and apathy which finally settles down in many of the homes of these long-unemployed men lies at the root of most of the problems which are connected with unemployment. It is one of the reasons why they fail to get back to work. It is one of the reasons why the majority of them "have not the heart" for clubs or activities of other kinds, and it is one of the reasons why their homes seem so poverty-stricken. "I don't know how it is," said a young married woman in Blackburn, "but these last few years since I've been out of the mills I don't seem able to take trouble, somehow; I've got no spirit for anything. But I didn't use to be like that." One of us who saw her had little doubt "how it was." The woman looked thin and ill, and it was clear that what food there was was going to the children. Such a simultaneous onset of physical and psychological hardship can hardly help having serious results.

# France

*In France, economic depression intensified the activities of fascist leagues, threatening not only the reigning Radical Socialist Party but the very existence of the republic. A government scandal in 1934 (the Stavisky Affair) was followed by riots in which mobs threatened to invade the Chamber of Deputies. Soon afterward, Radical Socialists, Socialists, and Communists formed a coalition that was dubbed the Popular Front. The Popular Front won the elections of 1936 and Leon Blum (1872–1950), leader of the Socialists, became prime minister.*

# From *Program of the Popular Front (January 10, 1936)*

## I. Defense of Liberty

1. General amnesty for political prisoners
2. Against the fascist leagues:

   *(a)* Disarmament and effective dissolution of all quasi-military organizations, in conformance with the law.
   *(b)* Enforcement of laws against the provocation of rioting or against attacks upon the security of the State. . . .

3. The press:

   *(a)* Abrogation of decree-laws restricting freedom of opinion.
   *(b)* Reform of the press by the adoption of legislation:
      (1) effectively suppressing journalistic blackmailing; and
      (2) assuring to journalists decent means of existence, obliging them to make public the sources of their income, putting an end to private monopolies of commercial advertising and the scandals of financial publicity, and, finally, preventing the formation of newspaper "trusts."
   *(c)* Organization of goverment radio broadcasting with a view to insuring accuracy of information and equality to all political and social groups using the radio.

4. Trade-union liberties:

   *(a)* Application of and respect for the labor rights of all.
   *(b)* Respect for the right of women to work.

5. Education and liberty of conscience:

   *(a)* Strengthening of the public schools not only by adequate appropriations, but by such reforms as the raising of the compulsory school age to 14 years and, in secondary schools, the imposition of more rigorous standards of admission.
   *(b)* Guarantees, to pupils and teachers alike, of full liberty of conscience, particularly by respecting academic "neutrality," "secularization" and the civil rights of teachers.

## II. Defense of Peace

1. To appeal for popular support, especially from labor, for the maintenance and organization of peace.
2. To coöperate internationally, within the *cadre* of the League of

From William Rappard, Walter R. Sharp, et al., *Source Book on European Governments* (New York: Van Nostrand, 1937), Vol. 2, pp. 31–33.

Nations, for collective security, by defining aggression and by applying sanctions automatically and concertedly in case of aggression.

3. To strive incessantly to change from an "armed" to a "disarmed" peace, by agreements first to limit and then to reduce and control armaments generally and simultaneously.

4. To nationalize war industries and suppress the private traffic in arms. . . .

## III. Economic Demands

1. Restoration of consumer purchasing power destroyed or reduced by the economic depression:

   *(a)* by measures against unemployment and the industrial crisis—
   1. institution of a national unemployment fund,
   2. reduction of the working week without lowering the weekly wage,
   3. provision of more work for youth by establishing adequate retirement pensions for industrial workers, and
   4. rapid execution of a program of useful public works by the joint efforts of central and local governments and private capital.

   *(b)* by measures dealing with the agricultural and commercial crisis—
   1. revalorization of agricultural products, combined with an attack upon speculation and the high cost of living, in such a way as to reduce the spread between wholesale and retail prices;
   2. in order to eliminate the "tithe" now levied by speculators upon producers and consumers, the creation of a national cereal administration;
   3. support to agricultural coöperatives, the sale of fertilizer at low cost by national agencies; the development of agricultural credit, and the reduction of agricultural rents; and
   4. suspension of foreclosures and the alleviation of mortgages on property. . . .

2. Stoppage of the plunder of savings and a better organization of credit by:

   *(a)* regulation of the banking profession,
   *(b)* regulation of the balance-sheets of banks and private corporations,
   *(c)* stricter regulation of the powers of officers of private corporations,

*(d)* denial to retired civil servants of the right to sit on corporate boards of directors, and

*(e)* in order to free credit and savings from being dominated by an economic oligarchy, transformation of the Bank of France from a private into a public institution. . . .

3. A financial housecleaning by:

*(a)* regulation of war contracts along with the nationalization of munitions industries;

*(b)* elimination of waste in civil as well as military administration;

*(c)* institution of a war pensions fund;

*(d)* a democratic reform of the tax system with a view to stimulating economic recovery, . . .

*(e)* suppression of fraud in handling securities by rigorously putting into use the fiscal identification certificate recently voted by Parliament; and

*(f)* checks on the flight of capital by confiscating funds held in concealment abroad or their equivalent in France.

# THE RISE OF FASCISM

## Italy

*Benito Mussolini (1883–1945) was the leader of Italian Fascism. In October 1922, after the march on Rome by Mussolini's followers (the Black Shirts), Mussolini was named premier. By 1924, he had established a dictatorship.*

### From Benito Mussolini. *The Political and Social Doctrine of Fascism*

The foundation of Fascism is the conception of the State, its character, its duty, and its aim. Fascism conceives of the State as an absolute, in comparison with which all individuals or groups are relative, only to be conceived of in their relation to the State. The conception of the Liberal State is not that of a directing force, guiding the play and development, both material and spiritual, of a collective body, but merely a force limited to the function of recording results: on the other hand, the Fascist State is itself conscious, and has itself a will and a personality—thus it may be called the "ethic" State. In 1929, at the first five-yearly assembly of the Fascist régime, I said:

"For us Fascists, the State is not merely a guardian, preoccupied solely with the duty of assuring the personal safety of the citizens; nor is it an organization with purely material aims, such as to guarantee a certain level of well-being and peaceful conditions of life; for a mere council of administration would be sufficient to realize such objects. Nor is it a purely political creation, divorced from all contact with the complex material reality which makes up the life of the individual and the life of the people as a whole. The State, as conceived of and as created by Fascism, is a spiritual and moral fact in itself, since its political, juridical, and economic organization of the nation is a concrete thing: and such an organization must be in its origins and development a manifestation of the spirit. The State is the guarantor of security both internal and external, but it is also the custodian and transmitter of the spirit of the people, as it has grown up through the centuries in language, in customs, and in faith. And the State is not only a living real-

From Carnegie Endowment for International Peace, *International Conciliation*, No. 306 (January, 1935) *(Documents of the Year 1935)*, pp. 13–14, 16–17.

ity of the present, it is also linked with the past and above all with the future, and thus transcending the brief limits of individual life, it represents the immanent spirit of the nation. The forms in which States express themselves may change, but the necessity for such forms is eternal. It is the State which educates its citizens in civic virtue, gives them a consciousness of their mission and welds them into unity; harmonizing their various interests through justice, and transmitting to future generations the mental conquests of science, of art, of law and the solidarity of humanity. It leads men from primitive tribal life to that highest expression of human power which is Empire: it links up through the centuries the names of those of its members who have died for its existence and in obedience to its laws, it holds up the memory of the leaders who have increased its territory and the geniuses who have illumined it with glory as an example to be followed by future generations. When the conception of the State declines, and disunifying and centrifugal tendencies prevail, whether of individuals or of particular groups, the nations where such phenomena appear are in their decline."

The Fascist State is an embodied will to power and government: the Roman tradition is here an ideal of force in action. According to Fascism, government is not so much a thing to be expressed in territorial or military terms as in terms of morality and the spirit. It must be thought of as an empire—that is to say, a nation which directly or indirectly rules other nations, without the need for conquering a single square yard of territory. For Fascism, the growth of empire, that is to say the expansion of the nation, is an essential manifestation of vitality, and its opposite a sign of decadence. Peoples which are rising, or rising again after a period of decadence, are always imperialist; any renunciation is a sign of decay and of death. Fascism is the doctrine best adapted to represent the tendencies and the aspirations of a people, like the people of Italy, who are rising again after many centuries of abasement and foreign servitude. But empire demands discipline, the coordination of all forces and a deeply felt sense of duty and sacrifice: this fact explains many aspects of the practical working of the régime, the character of many forces in the State, and the necessarily severe measures which must be taken against those who would oppose this spontaneous and inevitable movement of Italy in the twentieth century, and would oppose it by recalling the outworn ideology of the nineteenth century—repudiated wheresoever there has been the courage to undertake great experiments of social and political transformation; for never before has the nation stood more in need of authority, of direction, and of order. If every age has its own characteristic doctrine, there are a thousand signs which point to Fascism as the characteristic doctrine of our time. For if a doctrine must be a living thing, this is proved by the fact that Fascism has created a living faith; and that this faith is very powerful in the minds of men, is demonstrated by those who have suffered and died for it.

Fascism has henceforth in the world the universality of all those doctrines which, in realizing themselves, have represented a state in the history of the human spirit.

# Germany

*Adolf Hitler's (1889–1945) Nazi Party attracted a number of disaffected Germans after Germany's defeat in World War I. Its nationalist and anti-Semitic appeal seems to have politicized former soldiers, like the one who speaks in the following document. In January 1933, Hitler came to power and soon declared the beginning of the Third Reich.*

## From *The Autobiography of an Anti-Semite*

The fifth son of a gardener, I was born on August 17, 1890, at Dittersbach, Kreis Lüben, in Lower Silesia. As the youngest in the family—my brothers and sisters had died before my birth—I was brought up mainly by my grandmother, who lived with my parents. My mother as well as my father had to work on the land from early in morning until late at night. Although both of them worked very hard, we had just enough for the most necessary things. Nevertheless a small, very modest part of their earnings was laid aside weekly for their old age. From my sixth year I attended the public school, which had only two teachers for all the classes. At the age of eight, like all children of that age whose parents worked the fields, I had to work in the afternoons. In addition, during school time the more gifted children were called upon by the teacher for his own agricultural work. Because of circumstances beyond their control, my parents often changed their place of work and thus also their residence. As a result, I attended five different public schools. My parents as well as I were intent on quick learning. For that reason I did not learn a trade nor become a teacher, as my parents had been advised; that would have required a longer attendance at school.

I would probably have remained on the estate as a worker if the pay had been better. In the city, which was only five miles away, I could earn three times as much as a piece-worker. Consequently I became a laborer in a paper factory. There, with my otherwise modest demands,

From Theodore Abel, *The Nazi Movement* (New York: Atherton Press, 1966), pp. 218–220, 225–226, 240. Copyright 1938. Reprinted by permission of Prentice-Hall, Inc., Englewood Cliffs, N. J.

I had enough money left to gratify my passion for books. As I had no advisers, I bought several Indian, robber, and detective books. My love of adventure was aroused, and in the first three and one-half years I changed my position about sixteen or eighteen times; to be sure in this way I became acquainted with many different people and cities. Even then, it struck me that in spite of good earnings there was seldom a satisfied person to be found in the city. At the age of seventeen and a half I learned to be a servant, because after a brief apprenticeship one was supposed to be able to earn much money. In this way my wish to learn to know the world was partially fulfilled. The view of laborers that rich people were happy was not confirmed by my experience. Probably then for the first time I put the question to myself, "What meaning does life have anyhow?" In almost all the people with whom I became acquainted the impulse to earn as much money as possible was present. In the so-called higher classes of society that I learned to know as a servant, the urge for still more possessions was strongly in evidence. One of my employers, a member of an old noble family, put his extensive library at my disposal. After two years I had with its aid formed my own opinion of life. Unconsciously I had become a revolutionist. Why did the higher classes of society have so many privileges? Why was the workman or subordinate treated so condescendingly? Why was one ashamed to sit down at a table with laborers? Why did the rich man say to his children, "You must not play with the children of workmen. They are too dirty and naughty?" Why did the master converse in a comradely tone when alone with the servant and why, when another "gentleman" was present, did he make the difference of rank so grossly evident? Up to this time I had seldom read any newspaper, the political part not at all. "Politics spoil the character," they said in bourgeois circles, and I wanted someday to become a member of the middle class, so as not to be despised as heretofore. Nevertheless I now read the newspaper of my master, the *Deutsche Tageszeitung.* Through this, class differences were brought more and more to my consciousness. Occasionally, I bought myself a labor newspaper in the city. The things printed there were facts that I daily witnessed myself and that gradually made me the enemy of the higher class of society. Naturally I dared not let my opinion be noticed; a servant must be a "nationalist." But why must a servant be a "nationalist?" Wherein did the expression of the national feeling of the higher classes consist? I could not answer this question. Nor did I find anyone who might have given me an answer.

It was a matter of course for me that I must some day become a soldier, and so after the second inspection I enlisted in the cavalry. It was with great pride that I went on leave at Christmas, 1911, in my beautiful uniform. My parents were just as proud of their son. My father who before had always voted for the National German party, had in recent time become an adherent of social democracy. He believed that his interests were better fostered there, and I supported this opinion. As a soldier, I did not bother with politics, and like all my other comrades I was happy when mobilization was announced. The enthusiasm was apparently shared by all classes of the population. . . .

[*He returns from the war disillusioned at the defeat of Germany, has difficulty finding work, goes to Berlin, and becomes involved in politics.*]

I had still not bothered with politics. One day I went to Köslin to shop with my brother-in-law from Berlin, who had returned from captivity and was visiting me. It was during the time when government officials also claimed the right to strike. There was talk of an intended strike of the railroad men. And then in the evening the strike had come and we could not return. We remained in the hope of getting away the next day by some sort of conveyance. To kill time, we went that evening to a meeting called by the *Schutz- und Trutzbund*,[1] of which we had read on posters. The hall was overcrowded; we could find seats only in the front row by the stage. We perceived from conversation that some were indignant, that people dared to hold a meeting directed against the Jews. A retired Captain Schmidt of Stettin made the speech, which lasted one and a half hours. During the first quarter of an hour he was often interrupted. Then he succeeded in fixing everyone's attention. It seemed to me as though scales had fallen from my eyes. There was no more interruptions; at last even those who had come with the purpose of breaking up the meeting seemed to be enthusiastic Representatives of nine parties had applied for discussion. The first eight said things that were of no account. The last to speak with a rabbi who was received with laughter. At first he was not taken seriously at all; after a quarter of an hour he had the audience on his side. I too was once more tormented by doubts. Yet there was something in me that struggled against the Jew despite his convincingly uttered remarks. At last not a soul in the hall seemed to have a different opinion from the Jew. The applause grew louder and louder. Fortunately, probably inspired by the applause, he became impudent, and inveighed against Hindenburg, Ludendorff, and our two million dead. Now the ban was broken. Everyone cried: "Out with the Jew!" More quickly than he had come he was outside again. A final talk by the main speaker restored my inner balance. That evening had shown to me the danger of the Jewish intelligence. When one considered now that public opinion was created almost exclusively by Jews, one was filled with horror. Every honest German artisan was of the firm conviction that everything printed in a newspaper is true. If it were not true, the state would have to take a hand. From this evening on I oc-

---

[1]An anti-Semitic organization.

cupied myself with the Jewish problem, and the more I understood it, the greater opponent of the Jews did I become. In this connection I also began to occupy myself with politics. . . .

Unfortunately I fell ill in February and had to go to the hospital for five weeks. There I had the opportunity to study Adolf Hitler's *Mein Kampf* properly. Even at that time I was confirmed in the opinion that the book must be the Bible of all National Socialists. The more I became absorbed in it, the more was I gripped by the greatness of the thoughts expounded therein. I felt that I was eternally bound to this man. Only one thing oppressed me, the thought that I could not repeat these ideas with the same passion and fanatical conviction with which they must have been written. After my illness I was soon offered the office of local group leader, which I accepted with great pride. I fully realized the importance of this office. Every fellow German who enters the Party must first be made thoroughly familiar with the philosophy of Adolf Hitler. The group leader has this responsible task. The more deeply he himself has penetrated into the idea, the more quickly will the party comrades entrusted to him be prepared for voluntary coöperation. He must be the soul physician of every individual.

# The Spanish Civil War

*In 1936, a Popular Front government, consisting of republicans, socialists, communists, and anarchists, won Spain's elections. Francisco Franco, an army general, led an uprising of right-wing groups against the new government. The Spanish Civil War raged until March 1939, when Franco triumphed and imposed fascist rule on his country. The Civil War quickly became an international event; soldiers and ammunition were sent to both sides by governments and political groups of Europe. The clash between republicanism and fascism represented what historians have called a "rehearsal" for World War II.*

## From George Orwell. *Looking Back on the Spanish War*

. . . I never think of the Spanish war without two memories coming into my mind. One is of the hospital ward at Lerida and the rather sad

From "Looking Back on the Spanish War" in *Such, Such Were the Joys* by George Orwell, pp. 211–215. Copyright 1953 by Sonia Brownell Orwell; renewed 1981 by Mrs. George K. Perutz, Mrs. Miriam Gross, Dr. Michael Dickson, Executors of the Estate of Sonia Brownell Orwell. Reprinted by permission of Harcourt Brace Jovanovich, Inc., and by permission of the Estate of the late Sonia Brownell Orwell and Martin Secker & Warburg Ltd.

voices of the wounded militiamen singing some song with a refrain that ended—

> *Una resolucion,*
> *Luchar hast' al fin!*

Well, they fought to the end all right. For the last eighteen months of the war the Republican armies must have been fighting almost without cigarettes, and with precious little food. Even when I left Spain in the middle of 1937, meat and bread were scarce, tobacco a rarity, coffee and sugar almost unobtainable.

The other memory is of the Italian militiaman who shook my hand in the guardroom, the day I joined the militia. I wrote about this man at the beginning of my book on the Spanish war, and do not want to repeat what I said there. When I remember—oh, how vividly!—his shabby uniform and fierce, pathetic, innocent face, the complex side-issues of the war seem to fade away and I see clearly that there was at any rate no doubt as to who was in the right. In spite of power politics and journalistic lying, the central issue of the war was the attempt of people like this to win the decent life which they knew to be their birthright. It is difficult to think of this particular man's probable end without several kinds of bitterness. Since I met him in the Lenin Barracks he was probably a Trotskyist or an Anarchist, and in the peculiar conditions of our time, when people of that sort are not killed by the Gestapo they are usually killed by the GPU. But that does not affect the long-term issues. This man's face, which I saw only for a minute or two, remains with me as a sort of visual reminder of what the war was really about. He symbolises for me the flower of the European working class, harried by the police of all countries, the people who fill the mass graves of the Spanish battlefields and are now, to the tune of several millions, rotting in forced-labour camps.

When one thinks of all the people who support or have supported fascism, one stands amazed at their diversity. What a crew! Think of a programme which at any rate for a while could bring Hitler, Petain, Montague Norman, Pavelitch, William Randolph Hearst, Streicher, Buchman, Ezra Pound, Juan March, Cocteau, Thyssen, Father Coughlin, The Mufti of Jerusalem, Arnold Lunn, Antonescu, Spengler, Beverley Nichols, Lady Houston, and Marinetti all into the same boat! But the clue is really very simple. They are all people with something to lose, or people who long for a hierarchical society and dread the prospect of a world of free and equal human beings. Behind all the ballyhoo that is talked about "godless" Russia, and the "materialism" of the working class lies the simple intention of those with money or privileges to cling to them. Ditto, though it contains a partial truth, with all the talk about the worthlessness of social reconstruction not accompanied by a "change of heart." The pious ones, from the Pope to the yogis of California, are great on the "change of heart," much more reassuring from their point of view than a change in the economic system. Petain attributes the fall of France to the common people's "love of pleasure." One sees this in its right perspective if one stops to wonder how much pleasure the ordinary French peasant's or workingman's life would contain compared with Petain's own. The damned impertinence of these politicians, priests, literary men, and what-not who lecture the working-class socialist for his "materialism"! All that the working man demands is what these others would consider the indispensable minimum without which human life cannot be lived at all. Enough to eat, freedom from the haunting terror of unemployment, the knowledge that your children will get a fair chance, a bath once a day, clean linen reasonably often, a roof that doesn't leak, and short enough working hours to leave you with a little energy when the day is done. Not one of those who preach against "materialism" would consider life livable without these things. And how easily that minimum could be attained if we chose to set our minds to it for only twenty years! To raise the standard of living of the whole world to that of Britain would not be a greater undertaking than the war we have just fought. I don't claim, and I don't know who does, that that would solve anything in itself. It is merely that privation and brute labour have to be abolished before the real problems of humanity can be tackled. The major problem of our time is the decay of the belief in personal immortality, and it cannot be dealt with while the average human being is either drudging like an ox or shivering in fear of the secret police. How right the working classes are in their "materialism"! How right they are to realise that the belly comes before the soul, not in the scale of values but in point of time! Understand that, and the long horror that we are enduring becomes at least intelligible. All the considerations that are likely to make one falter—the siren voices of a Petain or of a Gandhi, the inescapable fact that in order to fight one has to degrade oneself, the equivocal moral position of Britain, with its democratic phrases and its coolie empire, the sinister development of Soviet Russia, the squalid farce of left-wing politics—all this fades away and one sees only the struggle of the gradually awakening common people against the lords of property and their hired liars and bumsuckers. The question is very simple. Shall people like that Italian soldier be allowed to live the decent, fully human life which is now technically achievable, or shan't they? Shall the common man be pushed back into the mud, or shall he not? I myself believe, perhaps on insufficient grounds, that the common man will win his fight sooner or later, but I want it to be sooner and not later—some time within the next hundred years, say, and not some time within the next ten thousand years. That was the real issue of the Spanish war, and of the last war, and perhaps of other wars yet to come.

I never saw the Italian militiaman again, nor did I ever learn his name. It can be taken as quite certain that he is dead. Nearly two years later, when the war was visibly lost, I wrote these verses in his memory:

> *The Italian soldier shook my hand*
> *Beside the guard-room table;*
> *The strong hand and the subtle hand*
> *Whose palms are only able*
>
> *To meet within the sound of guns,*
> *But oh! what peace I knew then*
> *In gazing on his battered face*
> *Purer than any woman's!*
>
> *For the flyblown words that make me spew*
> *Still in his ears were holy,*
> *And he was born knowing what I had learned*
> *Out of books and slowly.*
>
> *The treacherous guns had told their tale*
> *And we both had bought it,*
> *But my gold brick was made of gold—*
> *Oh! who ever would have thought it?*
>
> *Good luck go with you, Italian soldier!*
> *But luck is not for the brave;*
> *What would the world give back to you?*
> *Always less than you gave.*
>
> *Between the shadow and the ghost,*
> *Between the white and the red,*
> *Between the bullet and the lie,*
> *Where would you hide your head?*
>
> *For where is Manuel Gonzalez,*
> *And where is Pedro Aguilar,*
> *And where is Ramon Fenellosa?*
> *The earthworms know where they are.*
>
> *Your name and your deeds were forgotten*
> *Before your bones were dry,*
> *And the lie that slew you is buried*
> *Under a deeper lie;*
>
> *But the thing that I saw in your face*
> *No power can disinherit:*
> *No bomb that ever burst*
> *Shatters the crystal spirit.*

# WORLD WAR II

## The Outbreak of War

*In September 1938, the British and French prime ministers, Neville Chamberlain and Edouard Daladier, met with Hitler at Munich to discuss German claims to Czechoslovakia. The policy of appeasement advocated by Chamberlain led to the granting of Hitler's demands in the interests of avoiding larger conflict. Less than a year after Munich, the Germans occupied all of Czechoslovakia; in September they invaded Poland. In response, the British and French declared war on Germany. What began as a European war developed a year later into a world-wide conflict.*

### From *Chamberlain's Statement to the Press (September 1938)*

There has been a growing feeling of anxiety in the country at the evident approach of a critical situation out of which war might possibly arise.

War in these days is something different from what it has been in the past. Even in 1914 war was an affair, to begin with at any rate, of military and naval forces, but now it is something which might in the very first few hours affect the civilian population. Thereby it becomes an even more dreadful and horrible thing than it was before.

The Government's policy and the Government's efforts are directed all the time to the avoidance of any such catastrophe as that.

We have recognised from the first that in this Czechoslovakian question there lay the possibilities of the most serious consequences.

We have felt, however, that difficult as the situation was, it ought not to be one impossible of solution by peaceful discussion and negotiation. . . .

A question which is constantly canvassed not only in this country but elsewhere is whether there is a full appreciation in Germany of the possible consequences of a forcible intervention in Czechoslovakia.

On repeated occasions the British Government has expressed as clearly as possible its view that if aggression were resorted to, that

From E. L. Woodward et al., *Documents on British Foreign Policy*, Third Series, Vol. 2, 1938 (London: His Majesty's Stationery Office, 1949), pp. 680–682.

might well cause the involving of France in the conflict, since France is bound by treaty obligations to come to the assistance of Czechoslovakia in the event of an unprovoked aggression.

On March 24 in the House of Commons I said in unmistakable terms that it was impossible to set a limit to the scope of the conflict if those events took place or to say what Governments might not ultimately be involved.

It was quite clear from that statement that we contemplated the possibility that this country could not stand aside if a general conflict were to take place in which the security of France might be menaced. . . .

Undoubtedly it is of the first importance that the German Government should be under no illusions in this matter and that they should not, as it has been suggested they might, count upon it that a brief and successful campaign against Czechoslovakia could be safely embarked upon without the danger of the subsequent intervention first of France and later of this country.

But although in view of what has been said already it hardly seems possible to us that in any responsible quarters in Germany there could be any doubt on that subject, nevertheless there have been opportunities for the British Ambassador during his stay at Nuremberg to meet all the principal leaders of Germany with the exception of Herr Hitler himself, and from the full reports which he has given us of his conversations we have every reason to feel confident that our views have been conveyed fully to the proper quarters. . . .

We shall all await the statement which Herr Hitler is going to make tomorrow night with a certain anxiety, realising how much may turn upon the nature of his speech.

But, after all, Herr Hitler has repeatedly expressed his own desire for peace and it would be a mistake to assume that those declarations were insincere. . . .

If out of all this there should come another great conflict in Europe it would indeed be a tragic disaster.

In our view it is an avoidable disaster and the British Government intend to leave no effort untried that will serve to avert it.


## From *Hitler's Speech to the Reichstag (September 1, 1939)*

Members of the German Reichstag:

For months we have been tormented by a problem once wished upon us by the dictated Treaty of Versailles and which has now assumed such a character as to become utterly intolerable. Danzig was

From *Documents on the Events Preceding the Outbreak of the War*, compiled and published by the German Foreign Office (Berlin, 1939; New York, 1940), pp. 498–504.

and is a German city. The Corridor was and is German. All these districts owe their cultural development exclusively to the German people, without whom absolute barbarism would prevail in these eastern tracts of country. Danzig was separated from us. The Corridor was annexed by Poland. The German minorities living there were ill-treated in the most appalling manner. More than a million persons with German blood in their veins were compelled to leave their homes as early as 1919/1920. Here, as always, I have attempted to change this intolerable state of affairs by means of peaceful proposals for a revision. It is a lie when the world alleges that we always used pressure in attempting to carry out any revision. There was ample opportunity for fifteen years before National Socialism assumed power to carry through revisions by means of a peaceful understanding. This was not done. I myself then took the initiative in every single case, not only once, but many times, to bring forward proposals for the revision of absolutely intolerable conditions.

As you know, all these proposals were rejected. I need not enumerate them in detail: proposals for a limitation of armaments, if necessary even for the abolition of armaments, proposals for restrictions on methods of warfare, proposals for eliminating methods of modern warfare, which, in my opinion, are scarcely compatible with international law. You know the proposals which I made as to the necessity of restoring German sovereign rights in certain territories of the Reich, those countless attempts I made to bring about a peaceful solution of the Austrian problem and, later on, of the Sudetenland, Bohemia and Moravia. It was all in vain. One thing, however, is impossible: to demand that a peaceful revision should be made of an intolerable state of affairs—and then obstinately refuse such a peaceful revision. It is equally impossible to assert that in such a situation to act on one's own initiative in making a revision is to violate a law. For us Germans the dictated Treaty of Versailles is not a law. It will not do to blackmail a person at the point of a pistol with the threat of starvation for millions of people into signing a document and afterwards proclaim that this document with its forced signature was a solemn law.

In the case of Danzig and the Corridor I have again tried to solve the problems by proposing peaceful discussions. One thing was obvious: they had to be solved. That the date of the solution may perhaps be of little interest to the Western Powers is conceivable. But this date is not a matter of indifference to us. First and foremost, however, it was not and could not be a matter of indifference to the suffering victims. In conversations with Polish statesmen, I have discussed the ideas which you have heard me express here in my last speech to the Reichstag. No one can maintain that this was an unjust procedure or even unreasonable pressure.

I then had the German proposals clearly formulated and I feel bound to repeat once more that nothing could be fairer or more modest than those proposals submitted by me. And I now wish to declare to the whole world that I, and I alone, was in a position to make such proposals. For I know quite definitely that I was thereby acting contrary to the opinion of millions of Germans.

Those proposals were rejected. But more than that, they were replied to by mobilization, by increased terrorism, by intensified pressure on the German minorities in those areas, and by a gradual economic and political strangulation of the Free City of Danzig, which during the past few weeks found its expression in military measures and traffic restrictions. Poland virtually began a war against the Free City of Danzig. Furthermore she was not prepared to settle the problem of the Corridor in a fair manner satisfying the interests of both parties. And lastly, Poland has never thought of fulfilling her obligations with regard to the minorities. In this connection I feel it necessary to state that Germany has fulfilled her obligations in this respect. Minorities domiciled in Germany are not subject to persecution. Let any Frenchman get up and declare that French citizens living in the Saar territory are oppressed, ill-treated or deprived of their rights. No one can make such an assertion. . . .

In spite of all I have made one last attempt. Although possessed of the innermost conviction that the Polish Government—perhaps also owing to their dependence on a now unrestrained wild soldiery—are not in earnest as regards a real understanding, I nevertheless accepted a proposal of mediation submitted by the British Government. The latter proposed not to carry on any negotiations themselves, but assured me of their establishing a direct connection between Poland and Germany for the purpose of thus facilitating direct discussions once more.

I must here state the following: I accepted that proposal. For these discussions I had drawn up the fundamentals which are known to you. And then I and my Government sat expectantly for two whole days in order to find out whether the Polish Government saw fit finally to dispatch an authorized representative or not. Up to last night the Polish Government did not dispatch an authorized representative, but informed us by their Ambassador that at present they were considering the question whether and to what extent they might be able to accept the British proposals; they would inform Britain of the result.

Members of the Reichstag, if such treatment could be meted out to the German Reich and its Head, and if the German Reich and its Head were to submit to such treatment, the German nation would not deserve a better fate than to vanish from the political arena. My love of peace and my endless patience must not be mistaken for weakness, much less for cowardice. Last night I informed the British Government that things being as they are, I have found it impossible to detect any inclination on the part of the Polish Government to enter into a really serious discussion with us.

These proposals of mediation are thus wrecked, for in the meantime the answer to these offers of mediation had been, first, the order for Polish general mobilization, and, secondly, serious additional outrages. Repetitions of the latter incidents occurred last night. Only recently during one single night 21 frontier incidents occurred, last night there were 14, three of them of a most serious character.

For that reason, I have now decided to address Poland in exactly the same language as Poland has been using toward us for months. . . .

Our aims: I am determined to solve:
firstly, the Danzig question;
secondly, the Corridor question;
thirdly, to see to it that a change takes place in Germany's relations to Poland, which will ensure a peaceful co-existence of the two States.

I am determined to fight either until the present Polish Government are disposed to effect this change or until another Polish Government are prepared to do so.

I am determined to eliminate from the German frontiers the element of insecurity, the atmosphere which permanently resembles that of civil war. I shall see to it that on the eastern frontier the same peaceful conditions prevail as on our other frontiers.

All actions in fulfillment of this aim will be carried out in such a way as not to contradict the proposals which I made known to you here, Members of the Reichstag, as my proposals to the rest of the world.

That is, I will not wage war against women and children! I have instructed my Air Force to limit their attacks to military objectives. But should the enemy think this gives him *carte blanche* to fight in the opposite way, then he will get an answer which will drive him out of his senses!

In the night Polish soldiers of the Regular Army fired the first shots in our own territory. Since 5.45 a. m. we have been returning their fire. And from now onwards every bomb will be answered by another bomb. Whoever fights with poison gas will be fought with poison gas. Whoever disregards the rules of human warfare can but expect us to do the same.

I will carry on this fight, no matter against whom, until such time as the safety of the Reich and its rights are secured!

For more than six years now I have been engaged in building up the German armed forces. During this period more than 90 billion Reichsmarks have been expended in creating our armed forces. Today, they are the best equipped in the world and are far superior to those of 1914. My confidence in them can never be shaken.

In calling up these forces, and in expecting the German people to make sacrifices, if necessary unlimited sacrifices, I have done only what I have a right to do; for I myself am just as ready today as I was in the past to make every personal sacrifice. There is nothing I demand of any German which I myself was not prepared to do at any moment for more than four years. There shall not be any deprivations for Germans in which I myself shall not immediately share. From this moment my whole life shall belong more than ever to my people. I now want to be nothing but the first soldier of the German Reich.

Therefore, I have once again put on that uniform which was always so sacred and dear to me. I shall not lay it aside until after the victory—or I shall not live to see the end.

Should anything happen to me in this war, my first successor shall be Party Member Göring. Should anything happen to Party Member Göring, his successor shall be Party Member Hess. To these men as your leaders you would then owe that same absolute loyalty and obedience that you owe me. In the event that something fatal should happen to Party Member Hess, I am about to make legal provisions for the convocation of a Senate appointed by me, who shall then elect the worthiest, that is to say the most valiant among themselves.

As a National Socialist and a German soldier I enter upon this fight with a stout heart! My whole life has been but one continuous struggle for my people, for the rebirth of Germany, and that whole struggle has been inspired by one single conviction: Faith in my people!

One word I have never known: Capitulation. If, however, there should be any one who thinks that we are on the verge of hard times, I would urge him to consider the fact that at one time a Prussian king ruling over a ridiculously small state confronted one of the greatest coalitions ever known and came forth victorious after three campaigns, simply because he was possessed of that undaunted spirit and firm faith which are required of us in these times.

As for the rest of the world, I can only assure them that November, 1918, shall never occur again in German history.

I ask of every German what I myself am prepared to do at any moment: to be ready to lay down his life for his people and for his country. . . .

I also expect every German woman to take her place with unflinching discipline in this great fighting community.

German Youth, needless to say, will do, with heart and soul, what is expected and demanded of it by the nation and by the National-Socialist State.

If we form this community, fused together, ready for everything, determined never to capitulate, our firm resolve will master every emergency.

I conclude with the words with which I once started my fight for power in the Reich. At that time, I said: "If our will is so strong that no emergency can break it, then our will and our good German sword will master and subjugate even need and distress."

Germany—Sieg Heil!

## From *Chamberlain's Announcement of War with Germany* *(September 3, 1939)*

When I spoke last night to the House I could not but be aware that in some parts of the House there were doubts and some bewilderment as to whether there had been any weakening, hesitation or vacillation on the part of His Majesty's Government. In the circumstances, I make no reproach, for if I had been in the same position as hon. Members not sitting on this Bench and not in possession of all the information which we have, I should very likely have felt the same. The statement which I have to make this morning will show that there were no grounds for doubt. We were in consultation all day yesterday with the French Government and we felt that the intensified action which the Germans were taking against Poland allowed no delay in making our own position clear. Accordingly, we decided to send to our Ambassador in Berlin instructions which he was to hand at nine o'clock this morning to the German Foreign Secretary and which read as follows:

> Sir,
>
> In the communication which I had the honour to make to you on 1st September, I informed you, on the instructions of His Majesty's Principal Secretary of State for Foreign Affairs, that unless the German Government were prepared to give His Majesty's Government in the United Kingdom satisfactory assurances that the German Government had suspended all aggressive action against Poland and were prepared promptly to withdraw their forces from Polish territory, His Majesty's Government in the United Kingdom would, without hesitation, fulfil their obligations to Poland.
>
> Although this communication was made more than 24 hours ago, no reply has been received, but German attacks upon Poland have been continued and intensified. I have, accordingly, the honour to inform you that unless not later than 11 a.m., British Summer Time, to-day, September 3rd, satisfactory assurances to the above effect have been given by the German Government and have reached His Majesty's Government in London, a state of war will exist between the two countries as from that hour.

From *Parliamentary Debates*, Fifth Series, Vol. 352; House of Commons Official Report, Eleventh Vol. of Session 1938–1939 (351 H.C. Deb. 5) (London, 1939), pp. 291–292.

That was the final Note. No such undertaking was received by the time stipulated, and, consequently, this country is at war with Germany. I am in a position to inform the House that, according to arrangements made between the British and French Governments, the French Ambassador in Berlin is at this moment making a similar démarche, accompanied also by a definite time limit. The House has already been made aware of our plans. As I said the other day, we are ready.

This is a sad day for all of us, and to none is it sadder than to me. Everything that I have worked for, everything that I have hoped for, everything that I have believed in during my public life, has crashed into ruins. There is only one thing left for me to do; that is, to devote what strength and powers I have to forwarding the victory of the cause for which we have to sacrifice so much. I cannot tell what part I may be allowed to play myself; I trust I may live to see the day when Hitlerism has been destroyed and a liberated Europe has been reestablished.

## W  H. Auden. *September 1, 1939*

I sit in one of the dives
On Fifty-second Street
Uncertain and afraid
As the clever hopes expire
Of a low dishonest decade:
Waves of anger and fear
Circulate over the bright
And darkened lands of the earth,
Obsessing our private lives;
The unmentionable odour of death
Offends the September night.

Accurate scholarship can
Unearth the whole offence
From Luther until now
That has driven a culture mad,
Find what occurred at Linz,
What huge imago made
A psychopathic god:
I and the public know
What all schoolchildren learn,

From W. H. Auden, *The English Auden: Poems, Essays and Dramatic Writings, 1927–1939*, Edward Mendelson, ed., pp. 57–59. Copyright 1940 by W. H. Auden. Reprinted by permission of Random House, Inc., and Faber and Faber Ltd.

Those to whom evil is done
Do evil in return.

Exiled Thucydides knew
All that a speech can say
About Democracy,
And what dictators do,
The elderly rubbish they talk
To an apathetic grave;
Analysed all in his book,
The enlightenment driven away,
The habit-forming pain,
Mismanagement and grief:
We must suffer them all again.

Into this neutral air
Where blind skyscrapers use
Their full height to proclaim
The strength of Collective Man,
Each language pours its vain
Competitive excuse:
But who can live for long
In an euphoric dream;
Out of the mirror they stare,
Imperialism's face
And the international wrong.

Faces along the bar
Cling to their average day:
The lights must never go out,
The music must always play,
All the conventions conspire
To make this fort assume
The furniture of home;
Lest we should see where we are,
Lost in a haunted wood,
Children afraid of the night
Who have never been happy or good.

The windiest militant trash
Important Persons shout
Is not so crude as our wish:
What mad Nijinsky wrote
About Diaghilev
Is true of the normal heart;
For the error bred in the bone
Of each woman and each man

Craves what it cannot have,
Not universal love
But to be loved alone.

From the conservative dark
Into the ethical life
The dense commuters come,
Repeating their morning vow;
"I *will* be true to the wife,
I'll concentrate more on my work,"
And helpless governors wake
To resume their compulsory game:
Who can release them now,
Who can reach the deaf,
Who can speak for the dumb?

Defenceless under the night
Our world in stupor lies;
Yet, dotted everywhere,
Ironic points of light
Flash out wherever the Just
Exchange their messages:
May I, composed like them
Of Eros and of dust,
Beleaguered by the same
Negation and despair,
Show an affirming flame.

# The Fall of France

*In June 1940, as German troops marched into France, the French government signed an armistice with Germany. The French journalist Alexander Werth explores the reasons for the defection of one of the major allies in the war against Germany in the following account.*

## From Alexander Werth. *The Last Days of Paris*

The decision not to defend Paris has often been criticized. I have no opinion on the question whether a successful defence of Paris was militarily possible; what evidence there is suggests that it was not. But

From Alexander Werth, *The Last Days of Paris* (London: Hamish Hamilton, 1940), pp. 263–266. Reprinted by permission of Hamish Hamilton Ltd.

there was the same psychological element in the decision not to defend Paris as in the formula *"avares du sang français."* Even a conquered France was better than a physically annihilated France; France might, in time, emancipate herself if her people were allowed to live on and rear children; and Paris might still be Paris provided it was not razed to the ground. To put it a little crudely: the old slogan of the Jacobins: *"Liberté ou la mort"* had been abandoned for *"Esclavage—plus ou moins provisoire—plutôt que la mort,"* on the ground that what was most important to save, if anything could yet be saved, were the seeds of national, or rather, racial survival. In all this, there was a vague conception of "regeneration through suffering" and there was the strangely Chinese-like belief that "France could not be destroyed." There was also a tendency to take a very long, and very philosophical view of the whole thing: the French, as men of a higher civilization, would eventually absorb and convert the German conquerors; and pleasant parallels from history—how the Franks were civilized by the Gallo-Romans and how in the fourteenth century the Kingdom of France was reduced to a tiny bit of country round Paris—appealed to many minds in these moments of distress. Already for a few years—particularly after Munich—writers like M. Detoeuf had liked to play about with such ideas of the inevitable regeneration of France through conquest and humiliation. Others, like Marcel Déat, went a lot further, and were, in effect, prepared to make the best of a bad situation by accepting wholeheartedly the New Order of Hitler and Mussolini, and by begging the supermen for a little place—oh, quite a little place—in the new scheme of things.

The motives that prompted the Bordeaux Government to surrender to Germany are, in fact, numerous and very mixed. The motif of expiation and renovation through suffering was present in some minds— and this perhaps was the most respectable of the motives. Others were prompted, either by cowardice or by what they believed to be their self-interest to bow to the German demands, in the hope that the Germans would allow these people to become, as it were, the ruling caste in France—a caste which could now wreak vengeance on its political opponents. On the soil of defeat and disaster the seeds of Vichy had rapidly developed into a great monstrous flower. Here was something of all the things that one had already seen sprouting, especially since 1934. The 6th of February spirit; the anti-liberal and anti-parliamentary spirit, which was not merely critical of the abuses of the French parliamentary system, but absolutely hostile to the parliamentary, democratic idea; the cultivation of the peasantry—that good French peasantry which had already supported Napoleon III through thick and thin—as against the turbulent industrial proletariat; the shouts of *La France aux Français* which had in the heyday of the Croix de Feu and Jeunesses Patriotes and Solidarité Française resounded up and down the Champs Elysées; the Nazi-inspired anti-semitism of *Gringoire* and

*Je Suis Partout*; and the more authentically French anti-semitism of the *Action Française*; the anti-Freemasonry of the old Stavisky days; and, above all, the anti-British explosions of *Gringoire* and the anti-British sentiments of many of the ordinary people, and also of the Lavals, the Bonnets, the Déats, the Paul Faures.

It was all there; the feeling that the British were selfish imperialists, who were ready to fight to the last French soldier; that the British had ruined Franco-Italian friendship; that the British had not sent enough troops and had let the French down. And even as late as the 16th and 17th of June, the men of Bordeaux were still full of pernicious illusions about Italy and Spain; even though Italy had declared war on France, and General Franco had converted his neutrality into non-belligerency. The Latin *bloc*—the *bloc* of the Latin Nations, which would, in the long run, offset and cancel out Germany's hegemony on the Continent—this Latin *bloc* was still a favourite idea with Laval and Baudouin, and the aged Marshal Pétain. Daladier had sent him to Spain as French Ambassador in March, 1939; he had allowed himself to be flattered and blackmailed by the Spaniards, and was ultimately persuaded by them that Hitler would offer him, the "hero of Verdun," an honourable soldier's peace.

# War in the Pacific

*On December 7, 1941, the Japanese, who had allied themselves with Germany and Italy the preceding year, attacked an American naval base at Pearl Harbor (Hawaii). The Americans responded by declaring war on Japan.*

## Japan's Declaration of War on the United States and Great Britain (December 8, 1941)

Imperial Rescript.

We, by grace of heaven, Emperor of Japan, seated on the Throne of the line unbroken for ages eternal, enjoin upon ye, Our loyal and brave subjects.

We hereby declare war on the United States of America and the British Empire. The men and officers of Our Army and Navy shall do their utmost in prosecuting the war, Our public servants of various departments shall perform faithfully and diligently their appointed tasks, and all other subjects of Ours shall pursue their respective duties; the

From H. A. Jacobsen and A. Smith, *World War II: Policy and Strategy* (Santa Barbara, Calif., and Oxford: Clio Press, 1979), pp. 182–183.

entire nation with a united will shall mobilize their total strength so that nothing will miscarry in the attainment of our war aims.

To insure the stability of East Asia and to contribute to world peace is the far-sighted policy which was formulated by Our Great Illustrious Imperial Grandsire and Our Great Imperial Sire succeeding Him, and which We have constantly to heart. To cultivate friendship among nations and to employ prosperity in common with all nations has always been the guiding principle of Our Empire's foreign policy. It has been truly unavoidable and far from Our wishes that Our Empire has now been brought to cross swords with America and Britain. More than four years have passed since the government of the Chinese Republic, failing to comprehend the true intentions of Our Empire, and recklessly courting trouble, disturbed the peace of East Asia and compelled Our Empire to take up arms. Although there has been re-established the National Government of China, with which Japan has effected neighbourly intercourse and co-operation, the regime which has survived at Chungking, relying upon American and British protection, still continues its fratricidal opposition. Eager for the realization of their inordinate ambition to dominate the Orient, both America and Britain, giving support to the remaining [T. N. Chungking] regime, have, under the false name of peace, aggravated the disturbances in East Asia. Moreover, these two Powers, inducing other countries to follow suit, increased military preparations on all sides of Our Empire to challenge us. They have obstructed by every means our peaceful commerce, and finally resorted to a direct severance of economic relations, menacing gravely the existence of Our Empire.

Patiently have We waited and long have We endured, in the hope that Our Government might retrieve the situation in peace. But our adversaries, showing not the least spirit of conciliation, have unduly delayed a settlement; and in the meantime, they have intensified the economic and military pressure to compel thereby Our Empire to submission. This trend of affairs would, if left unchecked, not only nullify Our Empire's efforts of many years for the sake of the stabilization of East Asia, but also endanger the very existence of Our nation. The situation being such as it is, Our Empire for its existence and self-defence has no other recourse but to appeal to arms and to crush every obstacle in its path.

The hallowed spirits of Our Imperial Ancestors guarding Us from above, We rely upon the loyalty and courage of Our subjects in Our confident expectation that the task bequeathed by Our Forefathers will be carried forward, and that the sources of evil will be speedily eradicated and an enduring peace immutably established in East Asia, preserving thereby the glory of Our Empire.

The 8th day of the 12th month of the 16th year of Showa.

HIROHITO

## Roosevelt's Request for Declaration of War on Japan (December 8, 1941)

To The Congress of the United States:

Yesterday, December 7, 1941—a date which will live in infamy—the United States of America was suddenly and deliberately attacked by naval and air forces of the Empire of Japan.

The United States was at peace with that Nation and, at the solicitation of Japan, was still in conversation with its Government and its Emperor looking toward the maintenance of peace in the Pacific. Indeed, one hour after Japanese air squadrons had commenced bombing in Oahu, the Japanese Ambassador to the United States and his colleague delivered to the Secretary of State a formal reply to a recent American message. While this reply stated that it seemed useless to continue the existing diplomatic negotiations, it contained no threat or hint of war or armed attack.

It will be recorded that the distance of Hawaii from Japan makes it obvious that the attack was deliberately planned many days or even weeks ago. During the intervening time the Japanese Government has deliberately sought to deceive the United States by false statements and expressions of hope for continued peace.

The attack yesterday on the Hawaiian Islands has caused severe damage to American naval and military forces. Very many American lives have been lost. In addition American ships have been reported torpedoed on the high seas between San Francisco and Honolulu.

Yesterday the Japanese Government also launched an attack against Malaya.

Last night Japanese forces attacked Hong Kong.

Last night Japanese forces attacked Guam.

Last night Japanese forces attacked the Philippine Islands.

Last night the Japanese attacked Wake Island.

This morning the Japanese attacked Midway Island.

Japan has, therefore, undertaken a surprise offensive extending throughout the Pacific area. The facts of yesterday speak for themselves. The people of the United States have already formed their opinions and well understand the implications to the very life and safety of our Nation.

As Commander-in Chief of the Army and Navy I have directed that all measures be taken for our defense.

Always will we remember the character of the onslaught against us.

No matter how long it may take us to overcome this premeditated invasion, the American people in their righteous might will win through to absolute victory.

From H. A. Jacobsen and A. Smith, *World War II: Policy and Strategy* (Santa Barbara, Calif., and Oxford: Clio Press, 1979), pp. 183–185.

I believe I interpret the will of the Congress and of the people when I assert that we will not only defend ourselves to the uttermost but will make very certain that this form of treachery shall never endanger us again.

Hostilities exist. There is no blinking at the fact that our people, our territory, and our interests are in grave danger.

With confidence in our armed forces—with the unbounded determination of our people—we will gain the inevitable triumph—so help us God.

I ask that the Congress declare that since the unprovoked and dastardly attack by Japan on Sunday, December seventh, a state of war has existed between the United States and the Japanese Empire.

FRANKLIN D. ROOSEVELT

# THE WAR ENDS

## D-Day, June 6, 1944

*Allied forces landed on beaches in Normandy, France, on June 6, 1944, in what was the beginning of the final assault against Germany and the liberation of France.*

### Churchill's Announcement to House of Commons (June 6, 1944)

I have also to announce to the House that during the night and the early hours of this morning the first of the series of landings in force upon the European continent has taken place. In this case the liberating assault fell upon the coast of France. An immense armada of upwards of 4000 ships, together with several thousand smaller craft, crossed the Channel. Massed airborne landings have been successfully effected behind the enemy lines, and landings on the beaches are proceeding at various points at the present time. The fire of the shore batteries has been largely quelled. The obstacles that were constructed in the sea have not proved so difficult as was apprehended. The Anglo-American Allies are sustained by about 11,000 first-line aircraft, which can be drawn upon as may be needed for the purposes of the battle. I cannot of course commit myself to any particular details. Reports are coming in in rapid succession. So far the commanders who are engaged report that everything is proceeding according to plan. And what a plan! This vast operation is undoubtedly the most complicated and difficult that has ever taken place. It involves tides, winds, waves, visibility, both from the air and the sea standpoint, and the combined employment of land, air, and sea forces in the highest degree of intimacy and in contact with conditions which could not and cannot be fully foreseen.

There are already hopes that actual tactical surprise has been attained, and we hope to furnish the enemy with a succession of surprises during the course of the fighting. The battle that has now begun will grow constantly in scale and in intensity for many weeks to come, and I shall not attempt to speculate upon its course. This I may say

From H. A. Jacobsen and A. Smith, *World War II: Policy and Strategy* (Santa Barbara, Calif., and Oxford: Clio Press, 1979), pp. 309–310.

however. Complete unity prevails throughout the Allied Armies. There is a brotherhood in arms between us and our friends of the United States. There is complete confidence in the Supreme Commander, General Eisenhower, and his lieutenants, and also in the commander of the Expeditionary Force, General Montgomery. The ardour and spirit of the troops, as I saw myself, embarking in these last few days was splendid to witness. Nothing that equipment, science, or forethought could do has been neglected, and the whole process of opening this great new front will be pursued with the utmost resolution both by the commanders and by the United States and British Governments whom they serve.

# The Bombing of Hiroshima

*On August 6, 1945, the United States dropped an atomic bomb on the Japanese city of Hiroshima. Several days later the city of Nagasaki was bombed. The single explosions destroyed the cities and tens of thousands of people. Several weeks later the Japanese surrendered and the war in the Pacific ended.*

## Truman Announces Use of A-Bomb at Hiroshima (August 6, 1945)

Sixteen hours ago an American airplane dropped one bomb on Hiroshima, an important Japanese Army base. That bomb had more power than 20,000 tons of T.N.T. It had more than two thousand times the blast power of the British "Grand Slam" which is the largest bomb ever yet used in the history of warfare.

The Japanese began the war from the air at Pearl Harbor. They have been repaid many fold. And the end is not yet. With this bomb we have now added a new and revolutionary increase in destruction to supplement the growing power of our armed forces. In their present form these bombs are now in production and even more powerful forms are in development.

It is an atomic bomb. It is a harnessing of the basic power of the universe. The force from which the sun draws its power has been loosed against those who brought war to the Far East.

Before 1939, it was the accepted belief of scientists that it was theoretically possible to release atomic energy. But no one knew any practical method of doing it. By 1942, however, we knew that the Germans were working feverishly to find a way to add atomic energy to the other engines of war with which they hoped to enslave the world. But they failed. We may be grateful to Providence that the Germans got

From H. A. Jacobsen and A. Smith, *World War II: Policy and Strategy* (Santa Barbara, Calif., and Oxford: Clio Press, 1979), pp. 346–348.

the V-1's and V-2's late and in limited quantities and even more grateful that they did not get the atomic bomb at all.

The battle of the laboratories held fateful risks for us as well as the battles of the air, land and sea, and we have now won the battle of the laboratories as we have won the other battles.

Beginning in 1940, before Pearl Harbor, scientific knowledge useful in war was pooled between the United States and Great Britain, and many priceless helps to our victories have come from that arrangement. Under that general policy the research on the atomic bomb was begun. With American and British scientists working together we entered the race of discovery against the Germans.

The United States had available the large number of scientists of distinction in the many needed areas of knowledge. It had the tremendous industrial and financial resources necessary for the project and they could be devoted to it without undue impairment of other vital war work. In the United States the laboratory work and the production plants, on which a substantial start had already been made, would be out of reach of enemy bombing, while at that time Britain was exposed to constant air attack and was still threatened with the possibility of invasion. For these reasons Prime Minister Churchill and President Roosevelt agreed that it was wise to carry on the project here. We now have two great plants and many lesser works devoted to the production of atomic power. Employment during peak construction numbered 125,000 and over 65,000 individuals are even now engaged in operating the plants. Many have worked there for two and a half years. Few know what they have been producing. They see great quantities of material going in and they see nothing coming out of these plants, for the physical size of the explosive charge is exceedingly small. We have spent two billion dollars on the greatest scientific gamble in history—and won.

But the greatest marvel is not the size of the enterprise, its secrecy, nor its cost, but the achievement of scientific brains in putting together infinitely complex pieces of knowledge held by many men in different fields of science into a workable plan. And hardly less marvelous has been the capacity of industry to design, and of labor to operate, the machines and methods to do things never done before so that the brain child of many minds came forth in physical shape and performed as it was supposed to do. Both science and industry worked under the direction of the United States Army, which achieved a unique success in managing so diverse a problem in the advancement of knowledge in an amazingly short time. It is doubtful if such another combination could be got together in the world. What has been done is the greatest achievement of organized science in history. It was done under high pressure and without failure.

We are now prepared to obliterate more rapidly and completely every productive enterprise the Japanese have above ground in any city. We shall destroy their docks, their factories, and their communications. Let there be no mistake; we shall completely destroy Japan's power to make war.

It was to spare the Japanese people from utter destruction that the ultimatum of July 26 was issued at Potsdam. Their leaders promptly rejected that ultimatum. If they do not now accept our terms they may expect a rain of ruin from the air, the like of which has never been seen on this earth. Behind this air attack will follow sea and land forces in such numbers and power as they have not yet seen and with the fighting skill of which they are already well aware.

The Secretary of War, who has kept in personal touch with all phases of the project, will immediately make public a statement giving further details.

His statement will give facts concerning the sites at Oak Ridge near Knoxville, Tennessee, and at Richland near Pasco, Washington, and an installation near Santa Fe, New Mexico. Although the workers at the sites have been making materials to be used in producing the greatest destructive force in history they have not themselves been in danger beyond that of many other occupations, for the utmost care has been taken of their safety.

The fact that we can release atomic energy ushers in a new era in man's understanding of nature's forces. Atomic energy may in the future supplement the power that now comes from coal, oil, and falling water, but at present it cannot be produced on a basis to compete with them commercially. Before that comes there must be a long period of intensive research.

It has never been the habit of the scientists of this country or the policy of this Government to withhold from the world scientific knowledge. Normally, therefore, everything about the work with atomic energy would be made public.

But under present circumstances it is not intended to divulge the technical processes of production or all the military applications, pending further examination of possible methods of protecting us and the rest of the world from the danger of sudden destruction.

I shall recommend that the Congress of the United States consider promptly the establishment of an appropriate commission to control the production and use of atomic power within the United States. I shall give further consideration and make further recommendations to the Congress as to how atomic power can become a powerful and forceful influence towards the maintenance of world peace.

# The Human Costs

*Long after the war, those who experienced it recounted their stories. Those who managed to survive Hitler's plan to exterminate Jews have told of the horrors of the holocaust. Those who survived Hiroshima have described the impact of the first use of nuclear weapons in war.*

## From *Deposition by Mrs. Liuba Daniel on the Stutthof Concentration Camp*

We were loaded standing up in small open railway freight cars, and rode to Stutthof. The trip has remained a sharp memory, because that was the first time I began to feel a helpless, suffocating hate. We passed through the peaceful landscape, towns, villages, fields, and woods, and somehow it seemed unnatural to me that the sun was shining and that men went about their normal business. . . .

The sight of Stutthof, surrounded by high double fences of barbed wire with watchtowers, hundreds of SS men and trained dogs, was shattering. The unloading was even more cruel than at Tiegenhof station. Inside the camp, one's first view was fixed on a mountain of children's shoes. To tell the truth I did not understand what that meant. Then we noticed hundreds of shadowy female figures. They were Hungarian women with shaved heads, barefoot, in gray prison uniforms. I should like to stress that these Hungarian Jews had left their homes only four months before.

We were driven into huge barracks where we were assigned with shouts to our beds of wooden planks. Next morning we went to the delousing station.

Today when so many ask why all of the Jews in the diverse concentration camps did not simply hurl themselves with bare hands at the Germans, I want to say only one thing: There is no better method depriving people of their last measure of human dignity than to undress them completely. . . .

We stood trembling, but not because we were cold and not even because of shame, between SS men who strolled back and forth trying their whips on their polished boots. Various uniformed women and women in civilian clothes (who later turned out to be inmates) shoved us in various directions. Mouths, hair and other places were examined for valuables. (Our luggage had already been taken from us.) Then we came to the doctor and he too looked for jewels. Thereafter we were subjected to an ice cold dripping shower with soap as hard as stone (of questionable origin), and given striped rags. We were now full-fledged inmates of a German concentration camp.

We stayed for three weeks in the barracks where some members of my group were not even able to find wooden planks for sleep. Everything was so full that we slept on the floor in the so-called dining area of the barracks. We saw very few uniformed Germans in the camp. They of course sat in their watchtowers, and every approach to the electrified barbed wire—which did not even lead to freedom, but only to another part of the camp area—was greeted with wild laughter and a salvo of bullets. Corpses were hanging on the fences like drying laundry.

From Raul Hilberg, ed., *Documents of Destruction* (Chicago: Quadrangle Books, 1971), pp. 225–227. Reprinted by permission of Raul Hilberg.

Our true bosses were ethnic German [women] who—we learned later—were all criminals and were doing time here for robbery, murder, or theft. They wore civilian clothes, the most wonderful suits from the huge storehouse which grew daily with some of the best belongings of Europe's Jewry. . . .

[Winter] The prison garb, which we were given for our civilian clothes, had been washed, but all the same it harbored eggs of lice. Everyone had diarrhea at best and often it was dysentery. No one dreamt of the end of the war anymore—only of a piece of wet bread or another potato and a day without beatings. For the capos beat us without mercy, when we were lined up for food or during the count. . . .

The corpses in front of the blocks accumulated daily. We passed them with indifference. Even the glimpse of a familiar face that had belonged to a person with whom one had conversed only a few days before produced no reaction. It wasn't even hunger the way normal people feel it, but an indescribable emptiness.

It came to the point that a woman was discovered trying to open the belly of a corpse with a rusted knife. When we heard the sudden commotion and loud crying in front of our barracks, curiosity conquered our physical weakness and we shuffled to the scene just as the inmate block elders were about to drag away the woman whom they had almost beaten to death. When she was brought to the Germans and asked why she had opened a corpse, she replied that she had been *so* hungry and that she wanted to eat only the liver. Apparently that was too much for the German masters; the woman was dismissed without a word and then came instructions that she should be given a second portion of soup.

On April 24 [1945] an order was issued for the evacuation of Stutthof. Apparently the front line was already close, for the Germans were panicky. Everybody was rushed to his feet. Those who could not get up any more were routed from their wooden planks with giant dogs. Everyone received a loaf of bread—which we had not seen in three months—and we marched, stumbling and limping for a whole day, to the shore. There we were loaded like cattle during the night into a completely closed-off hold of a freighter. This was the most terrible night of my life. We were so crowded that one could not move an arm. Since no air came in, some began to lose consciousness, but they were unconscious standing up. Besides, most of us had stomach ills. Even if there had been a toilet somewhere, we were unable to take a single step. People howled, cried, pleaded, beat about wildly—all in vain.

*The Japanese poet Hara Tamiki (1905–1951) was in Hiroshima when the atomic bomb was dropped. In 1951, he committed suicide when he learned he had "atom disease."*

## Hara Tamiki. *Glittering Fragments*

Glittering fragments
Ashen embers
Like a rippling panorama,
Burning red then dulled.
Strange rhythm of human corpses.
All existence, all that could exist
Laid bare in a flash. The rest of the world
The swelling of a horse's corpse
At the side of an upturned train,
The smell of smouldering electric wires.

From Hara Tamaki, in *The Penguin Book of Japanese Verse*, trans. and intro. by Geoffry Bownas and Anthony Thwaite (New York: Penguin Books, 1964), p. 221. Copyright © 1964 by Geoffry Bownas and Anthony Thwaite. Reprinted by permission of Penguin Books Ltd.

# XV

# POSTWAR POLITICS—COLD WAR AND THIRD WORLD

*THE UNITED STATES and the Soviet Union fought World War II as allies; but when peace came each saw the other as a dangerous adversary. The ensuing "cold war" between the two superpowers has dominated international politics in the second half of the twentieth century.*

*The conflict involved ideological issues as well as old-fashioned power politics. Soviet leaders held that the inner logic of capitalism would necessarily lead to new wars against the Soviet Union. Western leaders held that Russian communism necessarily aimed at stirring up revolutions that would eventually subject the whole world to Soviet power. The Soviets claimed a right to establish friendly governments in bordering states; the West saw this as the spread of a tyrannical empire.*

*The creation and use of the atom bomb at the end of World War II gave a new dimension to the conflict. For the first time in the history of international relations each side in a dispute was capable of annihilating the other and, perhaps, of annihilating all established civilization in the process.*

*The cold war can be seen most simply as a polarization of the world between two great powers, each supported by a cluster of ancillary nations. But this simplified view ignores some of the complications of world politics. In fact, each side has had difficulties in maintaining the unity of its alliance. The Russians have had to contend with major rebellions against Soviet power in the satellite countries of eastern Europe. The Americans have had to reckon with the susceptibilities of European allies. And, elsewhere, American governments have often been embarrassed by the repressive internal policies of regimes that they sought to defend against communism. In the Near East, the creation of the state of Israel gave rise to a new set of tensions. Finally, the dissolution of the old Western colonial empires produced a host of new nations that have often sought to adopt a position of "nonalignment" in the East-West conflict.*

# UNIVERSALIST IDEALS

## The United Nations

From *Charter of the United Nations*

### Chapter 1. Purposes and Principles

Article 1

The Purposes of the United Nations are:

1. To maintain international peace and security, and to that end: to take effective collective measures for the prevention and removal of threats to the peace, and for the suppression of acts of aggression or other breaches of the peace, and to bring about by peaceful means, and in conformity with the principles of justice and international law, adjustment or settlement of international disputes or situations which might lead to a breach of the peace;

2. To develop friendly relations among nations based on respect for the principle of equal rights and self-determination of peoples, and to take other appropriate measures to strengthen universal peace;

3. To achieve international cooperation in solving international problems of an economic, social, cultural, or humanitarian character, and in promoting and encouraging respect for human rights and for fundamental freedoms for all without distinction as to race, sex, language, or religion; and

4. To be a center for harmonizing the actions of nations in the attainment of these common ends.

### Chapter III. Organs

*Article 7* 1. There are established as the principal organs of the United Nations: a General Assembly, a Security Council, an Economic and Social Council, a Trusteeship Council, an International Court of Justice, and a Secretariat.

From Department of State, *The United Nations Conference on International Organization* (Washington, D.C.: Government Printing Office, 1946), pp. 943–954.

2. Such subsidiary organs as may be found necessary may be established in accordance with the present Charter.

*Article 8* The United Nations shall place no restrictions on the eligibility of men and women to participate in any capacity and under conditions of equality in its principal and subsidiary organs.

## Chapter IV. The General Assembly

### Composition

*Article 9* 1. The General Assembly shall consist of all the Members of the United Nations.

### Functions and Powers

*Article 11* 1. The General Assembly may consider the general principles of cooperation in the maintenance of international peace and security, including the principles governing disarmament and the regulation of armaments, and may make recommendations with regard to such principles to the Members or to the Security Council or to both.

2. The General Assembly may discuss any questions relating to the maintenance of international peace and security brought before it by any Member of the United Nations, or by the Security Council.

3. The General Assembly may call the attention of the Security Council to situations which are likely to endanger international peace and security.

### Voting

*Article 18* 1. Each member of the General Assembly shall have one vote.

## Chapter V. The Security Council

### Composition

*Article 23* 1. The Security Council shall consist of eleven Members of the United Nations. The Republic of China, France, the Union of Soviet Socialist Republics, the United Kingdom of Great Britain and Northern Ireland, and the United States of America shall be permanent members of the Security Council. The General Assembly shall elect six other Members of the United Nations to be non-permanent members of the Security Council, due regard being specially paid, in the first instance to the contribution of Members of the United Nations to the maintenance of international peace and security and to the other purposes of the Organization, and also to equitable geographical distribution.

## Functions and Powers

*Article 24* 1. In order to ensure prompt and effective action by the United Nations, its Members confer on the Security Council primary responsibility for the maintenance of international peace and security, and agree that in carrying out its duties under this responsibility the Security Council acts on their behalf.

2. In discharging these duties the Security Council shall act in accordance with the Purposes and Principles of the United Nations.. .[1]

## Voting

*Article 27* 1. Each member of the Security Council shall have one vote.

2. Decisions of the Security Council on procedural matters shall be made by an affirmative vote of seven members

3. Decisions of the Security Council on all other matters shall be made by an affirmative vote of seven members including the concurring votes of the permanent members. . . .

*Article 39* The Security Council shall determine the existence of any threat to the peace, breach of the peace, or act of aggression and shall make recommendations, or decide what measures shall be taken in accordance with Articles 41 and 42, to maintain or restore international peace and security.

*Article 41* The Security Council may decide what measures not involving the use of armed force are to be employed to give effect to its decisions, and it may call upon the Members of the United Nations to apply such measures. These may include complete or partial interruption of economic relations and of rail, sea, air, postal, telegraphic, radio, and other means of communication, and the severance of diplomatic relations.

*Article 42* Should the Security Council consider that measures provided for in Article 41 would be inadequate or have proved to be inadequate, it may take such action by air, sea, or land forces as may be necessary to maintain or restore international peace and security. Such

---

[1]This provision gave a veto to each of the permanent members. The veto power was especially important to the Soviet Union since the United States seemed to have a permanent majority in the General Assembly and Security Council. [Ed.]

action may include demonstration, blockade, and other operations by air, sea, or land forces of Members of the United Nations.

*Article 43* 1. All Members of the United Nations, in order to contribute to the maintenance of international peace and security, undertake to make available to the Security Council, on its call and in accordance with a special agreement or agreements, armed forces, assistance, and facilities, including rights of passage, necessary for the purpose of maintaining international peace and security.

*Article 51* Nothing in the present Charter shall impair the inherent right of individual or collective self-defense if an armed attack occurs against a Member of the United Nations, until the Security Council has taken measures necessary to maintain international peace and security. Measures taken by Members in the exercise of this right of self-defense shall be immediately reported to the Security Council and shall not in any way affect the authority and responsibility of the Security Council under the present Charter to take at any time such action as it deems necessary in order to maintain or restore international peace and security.

## Chapter VIII. Regional Arrangements

*Article 52* 1. Nothing in the present Charter precludes the existence of regional arrangements or agencies for dealing with such matters relating to the maintenance of international peace and security as are appropriate for regional action, provided that such arrangements or agencies and their activities are consistent with the Purposes and Principles of the United Nations.

# Control of Atomic Energy

*Bernard Baruch proposed the following plan on behalf of the United States on June 14, 1946.*

## From *Speech of Bernard Baruch*

We are here to make a choice between the quick and the dead.

That is our business.

Behind the black portent of the new atomic age lies a hope which, seized upon with faith, can work our salvation. If we fail, then we have damned every man to be the slave of Fear. Let us not deceive ourselves: We must elect World Peace or World Destruction.

From *Department of State Bulletin*, June 23, 1946, pp. 1057–1062.

Science has torn from nature a secret so vast in its potentialities that our minds cower from the terror it creates. Yet terror is not enough to inhibit the use of the atomic bomb. The terror created by weapons has never stopped man from employing them. For each new weapon a defense has been produced, in time. But now we face a condition in which adequate defense does not exist. . . .

The United States proposes the creation of an International Atomic Development Authority, to which should be entrusted all phases of the development and use of atomic energy, starting with the raw material and including—

1. Managerial control or ownership of all atomic-energy activities potentially dangerous to world security.

2. Power to control, inspect, and license all other atomic activities.

3. The duty of fostering the beneficial uses of atomic energy.

4. Research and development responsibilities of an affirmative character intended to put the Authority in the forefront of atomic knowledge and thus to enable it to comprehend, and therefor to detect, misuse of atomic energy. To be effective, the Authority must itself be the world's leader in the field of atomic knowledge and development and thus supplement its legal authority with the great power inherent in possession of leadership in knowledge.

I offer this as a basis for beginning our discussion. . . .

We of this nation, desirous of helping to bring peace to the world and realizing the heavy obligations upon us arising from our possession of the means of producing the bomb and from the fact that it is part of our armament, are prepared to make our full contribution toward effective control of atomic energy.

When an adequate system for control of atomic energy, including the renunciation of the bomb as a weapon, has been agreed upon and put into effective operation and condign punishments set up for violations of the rules of control which are to be stigmatized as international crimes, we propose that—

1. Manufacture of atomic bombs shall stop;

2. Existing bombs shall be disposed of pursuant to the terms of the treaty; and

3. The Authority shall be in possession of full information as to the know-how for production of atomic energy. . . .

Let me repeat, so as to avoid misunderstanding: My country is ready to make its full contribution toward the end we seek, subject of course to our constitutional processes and to an adequate system of control becoming fully effective, as we finally work it out.

Now as to violations: In the agreement, penalties of as serious a nature as the nations may wish and as immediate and certain in their execution as possible should be fixed for—

1. Illegal possession or use of an atomic bomb;

2. Illegal possession, or separation, of atomic material suitable for use in an atomic bomb;

3. Seizure of any plant or other property belonging to or licensed by the Authority;

4. Wilful interference with the activities of the Authority;

5. Creation or operation of dangerous projects in a manner contrary to, or in the absence of, a license granted by the international control body.

It would be a deception, to which I am unwilling to lend myself, were I not to say to you and to our peoples that the matter of punishment lies at the very heart of our present security system. It might as well be admitted, here and now, that the subject goes straight to the veto power contained in the Charter of the United Nations so far as it relates to the field of atomic energy. The Charter permits penalization only by concurrence of each of the five great powers—the Union of Soviet Socialist Republics, the United Kingdom, China, France, and the United States.

I want to make very plain that I am concerned here with the veto power only as it affects this particular problem. There must be no veto to protect those who violate their solemn agreements not to develop or use atomic energy for destructive purposes.

The bomb does not wait upon debate. To delay may be to die. The time between violation and preventive action or punishment would be all too short for extended discussion as to the course to be followed.


## Freedom of Access

Adequate ingress and egress for all qualified representatives of the Authority must be assured. Many of the inspection activities of the Authority should grow out of, and be incidental to, its other functions. Important measures of inspection will be associated with the tight control of raw materials, for this is a keystone of the plan. The continuing activities of prospecting, survey, and research in relation to raw materials will be designed not only to serve the affirmative development functions of the Authority but also to assure that no surreptitious operations are conducted in the raw-materials field by nations or their citizens.

*This plan proved unacceptable to the Soviet Union. Russia objected to the undermining of the veto power, the "free access" provision, and America's retention of a monopoly over the atom bomb while the proposed treaty was being discussed.*

# THE COLD WAR BEGINS

*Relations between the United States and the Soviet Union had begun to deteriorate before Baruch's speech. Differences over the postwar settlement of eastern Europe appeared at the Yalta Conference, held in February 1945. The case of Poland was particularly difficult because two rival governments existed—a government-in-exile established in London and a Soviet-sponsored government at Lublin.*

## Yalta and the Aftermath

From *Minutes of the Yalta Conference*

### February 8, 1945

The Prime Minister said that we were now at the crucial point of this great conference. He said we would be found wanting by the world should we separate recognizing different Polish governments. This would be accepted by the world as evidence of a breach between Great Britain and the United States on one hand and the Soviet Union on the other hand, with lamentable consequences in the future. It was stamping this conference with a seal of failure, and nothing else we did here would overcome it. He admitted, on the other hand, that we take different views of the same basic facts. According to the information of the British Government, the Lublin, or Warsaw, government does not commend itself to the overwhelming masses of the Polish people, and it is certainly not accepted abroad as representative of the people. If the British Government brushed aside the London government and went over to the Lublin government there would be an angry outcry in

From Department of State, *Foreign Relations of the United States: The Conferences at Malta and Yalta* (Washington, D.C.: Government Printing Office, 1955), pp. 778–781, 853–854, 980.

Great Britain. . . . Great Britain would be charged with forsaking the cause of Poland and he was bound to say that the debates in Parliament would be most painful and he might add most dangerous to Allied unity. . . . His Majesty's Government would have to be convinced that a new government, representative of the Polish people, had been created, pledged to an election on the basis of universal suffrage by secret ballot with the participation of all democratic parties and the right to put up their candidates. When such elections were held in Poland, he said Great Britain would salute the government which emerges without regard for the Polish government in London.

## February 9, 1945

Prime Minister: In Parliament I must be able to say that the elections will be held in a fair way. I do not care much about Poles myself.

Stalin: There are some very good people among the Poles. They are good fighters. Of course, they fight among themselves too. . . .

President: I want this election in Poland to be the first one beyond question. It should be like Caesar's wife. I did not know her but they said she was pure.

Stalin: They said that about her but in fact she had her sins. . . .

## February 11, 1945

The following Declaration on Poland was agreed by the Conference:

A new situation has been created in Poland as a result of her complete liberation by the Red Army. This calls for the establishment of a Polish Provisional Government which can be more broadly based than was possible before the recent liberation of the Western part of Poland. The Provisional Government which is now functioning in Poland should therefore be reorganised on a broader democratic basis with the inclusion of democratic leaders from Poland itself and from Poles abroad. This new Government should then be called the Polish Provisional Government of National Unity.

M. Molotov, Mr. Harriman and Sir A. Clark Kerr are authorised as a commission to consult in the first instance in Moscow with members of the present Provisional Government and with other Polish democratic leaders from within Poland and from abroad, with a view to the reorganisation of the present Government along the above lines. This Polish Provisional Government of National Unity shall be pledged to the holding of free and unfettered elections as soon as possible on the basis of universal suffrage and secret ballot. In these elections all democratic and anti-Nazi parties shall have the right to take part and to put forward candidates. . . .

## From *Letter of President Roosevelt to Premier Stalin (April 1, 1945)*

. . . The part of our agreements at Yalta which has aroused the greatest popular interest and is the most urgent relates to the Polish question. You are aware of course that the Commission which we set up has made no progress. I feel this is due to the interpretation which your Government is placing upon the Crimean decisions. In order that there shall be no misunderstanding I set forth below my interpretation of the points of the agreement which are pertinent to the difficulties encountered by the Commission in Moscow.

In the discussions that have taken place so far your Government appears to take the position that the new Polish Provisional Government of National Unity which we agreed should be formed should be little more than a continuation of the present Warsaw Government. I cannot reconcile this either with our agreement or our discussions. While it is true that the Lublin Government is to be reorganized and its members play a prominent role it is to be done in such a fashion as to bring into being a new Government. This point is clearly brought out in several places in the text of the agreement. I must make it quite plain to you that any such solution which would result in a thinly disguised continuance of the present Warsaw regime would be unacceptable and would cause the people of the United States to regard the Yalta agreement as having failed.

From Department of State, *Foreign Relations of the United States, 1945,* Vol. 5 (Washington, D.C.: Government Printing Office, 1967), pp. 194–195.

*President Roosevelt died on April 12, 1945. The American ambassador to Moscow reported to President Truman at the White House on April 20.*

## From *Minutes of White House Conference*

Ambassador Harriman said that in effect what we were faced with was a "barbarian invasion of Europe", that Soviet control over any foreign country did not mean merely influence on their foreign relations but the extension of the Soviet system with secret police, extinction of freedom of speech, etc., and that we had to decide what should be our attitude in the face of these unpleasant facts. He added that he was not pessimistic and felt that we could arrive at a workable basis with the Russians but that this would require a reconsideration of our policy and the abandonment of the illusion that for the immediate future the Soviet Government was going to act in accordance with the principles which the rest of the world held to in international affairs. He said that obviously certain concessions in the give and take of negotiation would have to be made. The President said that he thoroughly understood

From Department of State, *Foreign Relations of the United States, 1945,* Vol. 5 (Washington, D.C.: Government Printing Office, 1967), pp. 232–233.

this and said that we could not, of course, expect to get 100 percent of what we wanted but that on important matters he felt that we should be able to get 85 percent.

The Ambassador then outlined briefly the issues involved in the Polish question explaining his belief that Stalin had discovered from the Lublin Poles that an honest execution of the Crimean decision would mean the end of Soviet-backed Lublin control over Poland since any real democratic leader such as Mikolajczyk would serve as a rallying point for 80 or 90 percent of the Polish people against the Lublin Communists. He said it was important for us to consider what we should do in the event that Stalin rejected the proposals contained in the joint message from the President and the Prime Minister and if Molotov proved adamant in the negotiations here in Washington.

He said he would like to inquire in this connection of the President how important he felt the Polish question was in relation to the San Francisco Conference and American participation in the world organization. The President replied immediately and decisively that in his considered opinion unless settlement of the Polish question was achieved along the lines of the Crimean decision that the treaty of American adherence to a world organization would not get through the Senate. He added that he intended to tell Molotov just this in words of one syllable.

## From *Letter of Premier Stalin to President Truman (April 24, 1945)*

I have received your joint with Prime Minister Churchill message of April 18, and have also received on April 24 the message transmitted to me through V. M. Molotov.

From these messages it is clear that you continue to consider the Provisional Polish Government not as a kernel for the future government of national unity, but just like one of the groups equal to any other group of Poles.

Such an understanding of the position of the Polish Government and such an attitude towards it is very difficult to reconcile with the decisions of the Crimea Conference on Poland. . . .

It is also necessary to take into account the fact that Poland borders with the Soviet Union, what cannot be said of Great Britain and the United States. . . .

You, apparently, do not agree that the Soviet Union has a right to make efforts that there should exist in Poland a government friendly toward the Soviet Union, and that the Soviet government cannot agree to existence in Poland of a government hostile toward it. Besides everything else, this is demanded by the blood of the Soviet people abun-

From Department of State, *Foreign Relations of the United States, 1945*, Vol. 5 (Washington, D.C.: Government Printing Office, 1967), pp. 263–264.

dantly shed on the field of Poland in the name of liberation of Poland. I do not know whether there has been established in Greece a really representative government, and whether the government in Belgium is really democratic. The Soviet Union was not consulted when these governments were being established there. The Soviet Government did not lay claim to interference in these affairs as it understands the whole importance of Belgium and Greece for the security of Great Britain.

It is not clear why, while the question on Poland is discussed it is not wanted to take into consideration the interests of the Soviet Union from the point of view of its security. . . .

I am ready to fulfill your request and do everything possible to reach a harmonious solution, but you demand too much of me. In other words, you demand that I renounce the interests of security of the Soviet Union, but I cannot turn against my country.

*Subsequently Stalin established a pro-Communist government at Warsaw. The "free election" was never held.*

# The Iron Curtain

## From *Winston Churchill's Speech at Fulton, Missouri (March 5, 1946)*

From Stettin in the Baltic to Trieste in the Adriatic, an iron curtain has descended across the continent. Behind that line lie all the capitals of the ancient states of central and eastern Europe. Warsaw, Berlin, Prague, Vienna, Budapest, Belgrade, Bucharest, and Sofia, all these famous cities and the populations around them lie in the Soviet sphere and all are subject, in one form or another, not only to Soviet influence but to a very high and increasing measure of control from Moscow. Athens alone, with its immortal glories, is free to decide its future at an election under British, American, and French observation.

The Russian-dominated Polish Government has been encouraged to make enormous and wrongful inroads upon Germany, and mass expulsions of millions of Germans on a scale grievous and undreamed of are now taking place. The Communist parties, which were very small in all these eastern states of Europe, have been raised to preeminence and power far beyond their numbers and are seeking everywhere to obtain totalitarian control. Police governments are prevailing in nearly every case, and so far, except in Czechoslovakia, there is no true democracy.

From *Congressional Record*, 79th Congress, 2d Session, A, pp. 1145–1147.

Turkey and Persia are both profoundly alarmed and disturbed at the claims which are made upon them and at the pressure being exerted by the Moscow government. An attempt is being made by the Russians in Berlin to build up a quasi-Communist party in their zone of occupied Germany by showing special favors to groups of left-wing German leaders. At the end of the fighting last June, the American and British Armies withdrew westward, in accordance with an earlier agreement, to a depth at some points of 150 miles on a front of nearly 400 miles, to allow the Russians to occupy this vast expanse of territory which the western democracies had conquered.

If now the Soviet Government tries, by separate action, to build up a pro-Communist Germany in their areas, this will cause new serious difficulties in the British and American zones, and will give the defeated Germans the power of putting themselves up to auction between the Soviets and the western democracies. Whatever conclusions may be drawn from these facts—and facts they are—this is certainly not the liberated Europe we found to build up. Nor is it one which contains the essentials of permanent peace. . . .

Last time I saw it all coming, and cried aloud to my own fellow countrymen and to the world, but no one paid any attention. Up till the year 1933 or even 1935, Germany might have been saved from the awful fate which has overtaken her and we might all have been spared the miseries Hitler let loose upon mankind.

There never was a war in all history easier to prevent by timely action than the one which has just desolated such great areas of the globe. It could have been prevented without the firing of a single shot, and Germany might be powerful, prosperous, and honored today, but no one would listen and one by one we were all sucked into the awful whirlpool.

We surely must not let that happen again. This can only be achieved by reaching now, in 1946, a good understanding on all points with Russia under the general authority of the United Nations and by the maintenance of that good understanding through many peaceful years, by the world instrument, supported by the whole strength of the English-speaking world and all its connections.

Let no man underrate the abiding power of the British Empire and Commonwealth. Because you see the 46,000,000 in our island harassed about their food supply, of which they only grow one-half, even in wartime, or because we have difficulty in restarting our industries and export trade after 6 years of passionate war effort, do not suppose that we shall not come through these dark years of privations as we have come through the glorious years of agony, or that half a century from now, you will not see seventy or eighty millions of Britons spread about the world and united in defense of our traditions, our way of life, and of the world causes we and you espouse. If the population of the English-speaking Commonwealth be added to that of the United States, with all that such cooperation implies in the air, on the sea, and in science and industry, there will be no quivering, precarious balance of power to offer its temptation to ambition or adventure. On the contrary there will be an overwhelming assurance of security. If we adhere faithfully to the Charter of the United Nations and walk forward in sedate and sober strength, seeking no one's land or treasure, or seeking to lay no arbitrary control on the thoughts of men, if all British moral and material forces and convictions are joined with your own in fraternal association, the high roads of the future will be clear, not only for us but for all, not only for our time but for a century to come.

## From *Stalin's Reply to Churchill*

. . . In substance, Mr. Churchill now stands in the position of a firebrand of war. And Mr. Churchill is not alone here. He has friends not only in England but also in the United States of America.

In this respect, one is reminded remarkably of Hitler and his friends. Hitler began to set war loose by announcing his racial theory, declaring that only people speaking the German language represent a fully valuable nation. Mr. Churchill begins to set war loose, also by a racial theory, maintaining that only nations speaking the English language are fully valuable nations, called upon to decide the destinies of the entire world.

The German racial theory brought Hitler and his friends to the conclusion that the Germans, as the only fully valuable nation, must rule over other nations. The English racial theory brings Mr. Churchill and his friends to the conclusion that nations speaking the English language, being the only fully valuable nations, should rule over the remaining nations of the world. . . .

As a result of the German invasion, the Soviet Union has irrevocably lost in battles with the Germans, and also during the German occupation and through the expulsion of Soviet citizens to German slave labor camps, about 7,000,000 people. In other words, the Soviet Union has lost in men several times more than Britain and the United States together.

It may be that some quarters are trying to push into oblivion these sacrifices of the Soviet people which insured the liberation of Europe from the Hitlerite yoke.

But the Soviet Union cannot forget them. One can ask therefore, what can be surprising in the fact that the Soviet Union, in a desire to ensure its security for the future, tries to achieve that these countries should have governments whose relations to the Soviet Union are

From "Stalin's Reply to Churchill," March 14, 1946 (interview with Pravda), *The New York Times*, p. 4. Reprinted by permission.

loyal? How can one, without having lost one's reason, qualify these peaceful aspirations of the Soviet Union as "expansionist tendencies" of our Government? . . .

Mr. Churchill wanders around the truth when he speaks of the growth of the influence of the Communist parties in Eastern Europe. . . . The growth of the influence of communism cannot be considered accidental. It is a normal function. The influence of the Communists grew because during the hard years of the mastery of fascism in Europe, Communists showed themselves to be reliable, daring and self-sacrificing fighters against fascist regimes for the liberty of peoples.

Mr. Churchill sometimes recalls in his speeches the common people from small houses, patting them on the shoulder in a lordly manner and pretending to be their friend. But these people are not so simple-minded as it might appear at first sight. Common people, too, have their opinions and their own politics. And they know how to stand up for themselves.

It is they, millions of these common people, who voted Mr. Churchill and his party out in England, giving their votes to the Labor party. It is they, millions of these common people, who isolated reactionaries in Europe, collaborators with fascism, and gave preference to Left democratic parties.

*On March 12, 1947, President Harry S. Truman addressed a joint session of Congress. While appealing specifically for economic and military aid to Greece and Turkey, he gave a general explanation of American policy that became known as the Truman Doctrine.*

## From *Speech of President Truman*

At the present moment in world history nearly every nation must choose between alternative ways of life. The choice is too often not a free one.

One way of life is based upon the will of the majority, and is distinguished by free institutions, representative government, free elections, guarantees of individual liberty, freedom of speech and religion, and freedom from political oppression.

The second way of life is based upon the will of a minority forcibly imposed upon the majority. It relies upon terror and oppression, a controlled press and radio, fixed elections, and the suppression of personal freedoms.

I believe that it must be the policy of the United States to support free peoples who are resisting attempted subjugation by armed minorities or by outside pressures.

From *Public Papers of the Presidents: Harry S Truman, 1947* (Washington, D.C.: Government Printing Office, 1963), pp. 178–180.

I believe that we must assist free peoples to work out their own destinies in their own way.

I believe that our help should be primarily through economic and financial aid which is essential to economic stability and orderly political processes.

The world is not static, and the status quo is not sacred. But we cannot allow changes in the status quo in violation of the Charter of the United Nations by such methods as coercion, or by such subterfuges as political infiltration. In helping free and independent nations to maintain their freedom, the United States will be giving effect to the principles of the Charter of the United Nations.

*In testimony before the United States Senate, Secretary of State-designate John Foster Dulles described some basic assumptions of United States policy in the 1950s.*

## From *Testimony of John Foster Dulles*

The threat of Soviet communism, in my opinion, is not only the gravest threat that ever faced the United States, but the gravest threat that has ever faced what we call western civilization, or, indeed, any civilization which was dominated by a spiritual faith.

Soviet communism is atheistic in its philosophy and materialistic. It believes that human beings are nothing more than somewhat superior animals, that they have no soul, no spirit, no right to personal dignity, and that the best kind of a world is that world which is organized as a well-managed farm is organized, where certain animals are taken out to pasture, and they are fed and brought back and milked, and they are given a barn as shelter over their heads, and that is a form of society which is most conducive to the material welfare of mankind, that is their opinion. That can be made into a persuasive doctrine if one does not believe in the spiritual nature of man.

If you do believe in the spiritual nature of man, it is a doctrine which is utterly unacceptable and wholly irreconcilable.

I do not see how, as long as Soviet communism holds those views, and holds also the belief that its destiny is to spread those views throughout the world, and to organize the whole world on that basis, there can be any permanent reconciliation.

That does not exclude the possibility of coming to working agreements of a limited character, but basically, between the doctrine of Soviet communism, and the doctrine of a Christian or Jewish or, indeed, any religion, this is an irreconcilable conflict.

From U.S. Senate, Committee on Foreign Relations, 83rd Congress, First Session, *Nomination of John Foster Dulles, Secretary of State—Designate* (Washington, D.C.: Government Printing Office, 1953), pp. 10–11.

# Atlantic Alliance

*A speech by General George C. Marshall on June 5, 1947, led to establishment of the European Recovery Program. The expenditure of some 12 billion dollars in support of the European economy stimulated a major economic recovery in the 1950s.*

## From *General George C. Marshall's Speech (June 5, 1947)*

In considering the requirements for the rehabilitation of Europe the physical loss of life, the visible destruction of cities, factories, mines and railroads was correctly estimated, but it has become obvious during recent months that this visible destruction was probably less serious than the dislocation of the entire fabric of European economy. For the past ten years conditions have been highly abnormal. . . .

The truth of the matter is that Europe's requirements for the next three or four years of foreign food and other essential products—principally from America—are so much greater than her present ability to pay that she must have substantial additional help, or face economic, social and political deterioration of a very grave character.

The remedy lies in breaking the vicious circle and restoring the confidence of the European people in the economic future of their own countries and of Europe as a whole. The manufacturer and the farmer throughout wide areas must be able and willing to exchange their products for currencies, the continuing value of which is not open to question.

Aside from the demoralizing effect on the world at large and the possibilities of disturbances arising as a result of the desperation of the people concerned, the consequences to the economy of the United States should be apparent to all. It is logical that the United States should do whatever it is able to do to assist in the return of normal economic health to the world, without which there can be no political stability and no assured peace.

Our policy is directed not against any country or doctrine but against hunger, poverty, desperation and chaos. Its purpose should be the revival of a working economy in the world so as to permit the emergence of political and social conditions in which free institutions can exist. Such assistance, I am convinced, must not be on a piecemeal basis as various crises develop. Any assistance that this government may develop in the future should provide a cure rather than a mere palliative.

From *Department of State Bulletin*, June 15, 1947, pp. 1159–1160.

*The Department of State called the North Atlantic Treaty (April 4, 1949) a "necessary complement" to the European Recovery Program.*

## From *The North Atlantic Treaty*

PREAMBLE. The parties to this treaty reaffirm their faith in the purposes and principles of the Charter of the United Nations and their desire to live in peace with all peoples and all governments.

They are determined to safeguard the freedom, common heritage and civilization of their peoples, founded on the principles of democracy, individual liberty and the rule of law.

They seek to promote stability and well-being in the North Atlantic area.

They are resolved to unite their efforts for collective defense and for the preservation of peace and security.

They therefore agree to this North Atlantic Treaty:

Article 1. The parties undertake, as set forth in the Charter of the United Nations, to settle any international disputes in which they may be involved by peaceful means in such a manner that international peace and security, and justice, are not endangered, and to refrain in their international relations from the threat or use of force in any manner inconsistent with the purposes of the United Nations.

Article 2. The parties will contribute toward the further development of peaceful and friendly international relations by strengthening their free institutions, by bringing about a better understanding of the principles upon which these institutions are founded, and by promoting conditions of stability and well-being. They will seek to eliminate conflict in their international economic policies and will encourage economic collaboration between any or all of them.

Article 3. In order more effectively to achieve the objectives of this treaty, the parties, separately and jointly, by means of continuous and effective self-help and mutual aid, will maintain and develop their individual and collective capacity to resist armed attack.

Article 4. The parties will consult together whenever, in the opinion of any of them, the territorial integrity, political independence or security of any of the parties is threatened.

Article 5. The parties agree that an armed attack against one or more of them in Europe or North America shall be considered an attack against them all; and consequently they agree that, if such an armed attack occurs, each of them, in exercise of the right of individual or collective self-defense recognized by Article 51 of the Charter of the United Nations, will assist the party or parties so attacked by taking forthwith, individually and in concert with the other parties, such action as it deems necessary, including the use of armed force, to restore and maintain the security of the North Atlantic area. . . .

From *Congressional Record*, 81st Congress, 1st Session, p. 9380.

# CONCILIATION AND CONFLICT

## Peaceful Coexistence

*In February 1956, Nikita Khrushchev startled the Twentieth Congress of the Communist Party of the Soviet Union with a lengthy address that announced a new program of "peaceful coexistence" with the West and inveighed against the terrorist policies of Stalin. (The latter part of the speech was at first kept secret.)*

### From *Khrushchev's Public Speech*

Comrades! I should like to dwell on some fundamental questions concerning present-day international development which determine not only the present course of events but also future prospects.

These are the questions of peaceful coexistence of the two systems, the possibility of preventing wars in the present era. and the forms of transition to socialism in different countries.

Let us examine these questions briefly.

The peaceful coexistence of the two systems. The Leninist principle of peaceful coexistence of states with different social systems has always been and remains the general line of our country's foreign policy.

It has been alleged that the Soviet Union advances the principle of peaceful coexistence merely out of tactical considerations, considerations of expediency. Yet it is common knowledge that we have always, from the very first years of Soviet power, stood with equal firmness for peaceful coexistence. Hence it is not a tactical move, but a fundamental principle of Soviet foreign policy.

This means that, if there is indeed a threat to the peaceful coexistence of countries with differing social-political systems it by no means comes from the Soviet Union or the socialist camp. Is there a single reason why a socialist state should want to unleash aggressive war? Do we have classes and groups that are interested in war as a means of enrichment? We do not; we liquidated them long ago. Or perhaps do we not have enough territory or natural resources, do we lack sources of raw materials or markets for our goods? No, we have enough of all those, and to spare. Why then should we want war? We do not want it.

From *Current Soviet Policies*, Vol. 2 (New York: Frederick A. Praeger, 1957), pp. 36–37, 172, 174, 179.

As a matter of principle we renounce any policy that might lead to millions of people being plunged into war for the sake of the selfish interests of a handful of billionaires. Do those who shout about the "aggressive intentions" of the U. S. S. R. know all this? Of course they do. Why then do they keep up the monotonous, old refrain about an imaginary "Communist aggression"? Only to muddy the waters, to conceal their own plans for world domination, for a "crusade" against peace, democracy and socialism.

To this day, the enemies of peace allege that the Soviet Union is out to overthrow capitalism in other countries by "exporting" revolution. It goes without saying that among us Communists there are no supporters of capitalism. But this does not at all mean that we have interfered or plan to interfere in the internal affairs of countries where the capitalist order exists. Romain Rolland was right when he said: "Freedom is not brought in from abroad in baggage trains, like Bourbons." It is ridiculous to think that revolutions are made to order. One often hears representatives of bourgeois countries reasoning thus: "The Soviet leaders claim that they are for peaceful coexistence between the two systems. At the same time, they declare that they are fighting for communism and say that communism is bound to win in all countries. How can there be any peaceful coexistence with the Soviet Union if it is fighting for communism?" This interpretation is formed under the influence of bourgeois propaganda. The ideologists of the bourgeoisie, distorting the facts, deliberately confuse questions of ideological struggle with questions of relations between states in order to make the Communists of the Soviet Union seem aggressive people.

When we say that the socialist system will win in the competition between the two systems—the capitalist and the socialist—this by no means signifies that its victory will be achieved through armed interference by the socialist countries in the internal affairs of capitalist countries. Our certainty of the victory of communism is based on the fact that the socialist mode of production possesses decisive superiority over the capitalist mode of production. Precisely because of this, the ideas of Marxism-Leninism are more and more capturing the minds of the broad masses of the working people in the capitalist countries, just as they have captured the minds of millions of men and women in our country and the people's democracies. We believe that all the working people on earth, once they have become convinced of the advantages communism brings, will sooner or later take the road of struggle for the construction of a socialist society. Building communism in our country, we are resolutely against war. We have always held and continue to hold that the establishment of a new social system in one or another country is the internal affair of the peoples of the countries concerned. This is our position, based on the great Marxist-Leninist teaching. The principle of peaceful coexistence is gaining ever wider international recognition. This principle has become one of the cornerstones of the foreign policy of the Chinese People's Republic and the other people's democracies. It is being actively implemented by the Republic of India, the Union of Burma, and a number of other countries. And this is natural, for there is no other way in present-day conditions. Indeed, there are only two ways: either peaceful coexistence or the most destructive war in history. There is no third way.

## From *Khrushchev's Secret Speech*

Comrades, in the report of the Central Committee of the Party at the 20th Congress, in a number of speeches by delegates to the Congress, as also formerly during the plenary CC/CPSU sessions, quite a lot has been said about the cult of the individual and about its harmful consequences.

After Stalin's death the Central Committee of the Party began to implement a policy of explaining concisely and consistently that it is impermissible and foreign to the spirit of Marxism-Leninism to elevate one person, to transform him into a superman possessing supernatural characteristics akin to those of a god. Such a man supposedly knows everything, sees everything, thinks for everyone, can do anything, is infallible in his behavior.

Such a belief about a man, and specifically about Stalin, was cultivated among us for many years. . . .

It was precisely during this period (1935–1937–1938) that the practice of mass repression through the government apparatus was born, first against the enemies of Leninism—Trotskyites, Zinovievites, Bukharinites, long since politically defeated by the Party, and subsequently also against many honest Communists, against those Party cadres who had borne the heavy load of the Civil War and the first and most difficult years of industrialization and collectivization, who actively fought against the Trotskyites and the rightists for the Leninist Party line.

Stalin originated the concept "enemy of the people." This term automatically rendered it unnecessary that the ideological errors of a man or men engaged in a controversy be proven; this term made possible the usage of the most cruel repression, violating all norms of revolutionary legality, against anyone who in any way disagreed with Stalin, against those who were only suspected of hostile intent, against those who had bad reputations. This concept, "enemy of the people," actually eliminated the possibility of any kind of ideological fight or the making of one's views known on this or that issue, even those of a practical character. In the main, and in actuality, the only proof of guilt used, against all norms of current legal science, was the "confession" of

From *Congressional Record*, 84th Congress, 2d Session, Vol. 102, Part 7, pp. 9389–9402 (June 4, 1956).

the accused himself; and, as subsequent probing proved, "confessions" were acquired through physical pressures against the accused.

This led to glaring violations of revolutionary legality, and to the fact that many entirely innocent persons, who in the past had defended the Party line, became victims.

We must assert that in regard to those persons who in their time had opposed the Party line, there were often no sufficient serious reasons for their physical annihilation. The formula, "enemy of the people" was specifically introduced for the purpose of physically annihilating such individuals. . . .

Thus, Stalin had sanctioned in the name of the Central Committee of the All-Union Communist Party (Bolsheviks) the most brutal violation of Socialist legality, torture and oppression, which led as we have seen to the slandering and self-accusation of innocent people.

# Hungary

*There were strict limits to Khrushchev's tolerance. A few months after the speech to the Party Congress he sent Soviet troops to crush a rebellion in Hungary. (A rebellion in Czechoslovakia was suppressed in the same way in 1968.)*

## From *Statement of the Soviet Government (October 30, 1956)*

The Soviet Government regards it as indispensable to make a statement in connection with the events in Hungary.

The course of the events has shown that the working people of Hungary, who have achieved great progress on the basis of their people's democratic order, correctly raise the question of the necessity of eliminating serious shortcomings in the field of economic building, the further raising of the material well-being of the population, and the struggle against bureaucratic excesses in the state apparatus.

However, this just and progressive movement of the working people was soon joined by forces of black reaction and counterrevolution, which are trying to take advantage of the discontent of part of the working people to undermine the foundations of the people's democratic order in Hungary and to restore the old landlord and capitalist order.

The Soviet Government and all the Soviet people deeply regret that the development of events in Hungary has led to bloodshed. On the request of the Hungarian People's Government the Soviet Government

From *Department of State Bulletin,* Nov. 12, 1956, pp. 746–747.

consented to the entry into Budapest of the Soviet Army units to assist the Hungarian People's Army and the Hungarian authorities to establish order in the town. Believing that the further presence of Soviet Army units in Hungary can serve as a cause for even greater deterioration of the situation, the Soviet Government has given instructions to its military command to withdraw the Soviet Army units from Budapest as soon as this is recognized as necessary by the Hungarian Government.

At the same time, the Soviet Government is ready to enter into relevant negotiations with the Government of the Hungarian People's Republic and other participants of the Warsaw Treaty on the question of the presence of Soviet troops on the territory of Hungary.

### From *Imry Nage's Last Message* (November 4, 1956)

This fight is the fight for freedom by the Hungarian people against the Russian intervention, and it is possible that I shall only be able to stay at my post for one or two hours. The whole world will see how the Russian armed forces, contrary to all treaties and conventions, are crushing the resistance of the Hungarian people. They will also see how they are kidnapping the Prime Minister of a country which is a Member of the United Nations, taking him from the capital, and therefore it cannot be doubted at all that this is the most brutal form of intervention. I should like in these last moments to ask the leaders of the revolution, if they can, to leave the country. I ask that all that I have said in my broadcast, and what we have agreed on with the revolutionary leaders during meetings in Parliament, should be put in a memorandum, and the leaders should turn to all the peoples of the world for help and explain that today it is Hungary and tomorrow, or the day after tomorrow, it will be the turn of other countries because the imperialism of Moscow does not know borders, and is only trying to play for time.

## Vietnam

*In spite of Khrushchev's announced policy of peaceful coexistence, friction with the West continued. President Kennedy emerged successfully from a confrontation over the placement of Soviet missiles in Cuba (1962). But then America became involved in a long-drawn-out war against Communist forces in Vietnam.*

From "United Nations Report of the Special Committee on the Problem of Hungary," *General Assembly Official Records,* 11th Session Supplement No. 18A/3592.

## From *President Lyndon B. Johnson's News Conference (July 28, 1965)*

Why must young Americans, born into a land exultant with hope and with golden promise, toil and suffer and sometimes die in such a remote and distant place?

The answer, like the war itself, is not an easy one, but it echoes clearly from the painful lessons of half a century. Three times in my lifetime in two world wars and in Korea Americans have gone to far lands to fight for freedom. We have learned at a terrible and a brutal cost that retreat does not bring safety and weakness does not bring peace.

It is this lesson that has brought us to Viet-Nam. This is a different kind of war. There are no marching armies or solemn declarations. Some citizens of South Viet-Nam at times with understandable grievances have joined in the attack on their own government.

But we must not let this mask the central fact that this is really war. It is guided by North Viet-Nam and it is spurred by Communist China. Its goal is to conquer the South, to defeat American power, and to extend the Asiatic dominion of communism.

There are great stakes in the balance.

Most of the non-Communist nations of Asia cannot, by themselves and alone, resist the growing might and the grasping ambition of Asian communism.

Our power, therefore, is a very vital shield. If we are driven from the field in Viet-Nam, then no nation can ever again have the same confidence in American promise, or in American protection.

In each land the forces of independence would be considerably weakened and an Asia so threatened by Communist domination would certainly imperil the security of the United States itself.

We did not choose to be the guardians at the gate, but there is no one else. . . .

From *Weekly Compilation of Presidential Documents*, Vol. 1, No. 1, August 2, 1965, p. 15.

## From *Senator J. William Fulbright's Speech (April 2, 1970)*

How have we come to inflate so colossally the importance of Indochina to our own security? The answer lies in that hoariest, hardiest, most indestructible myth of them all: the myth of the international Communist conspiracy. . . .

The myth distorts our perceptions. It has made it difficult for us to

From *Congressional Record*, 91st Congress, 2d Session, pp. 10150–10151, 10157.

see the Soviet Union for what it has become—a traditional, cautious, and rather unimaginative great power, jealously clinging to its sphere of domination in Eastern Europe but limited to methods of pressure and persuasion in its dealings with other Communist movements, especially in Asia. China has engendered a myth all its own: If there is not a world Communist conspiracy—so we are told—then there is surely an Asian one, and the unshakeable faith in it of some of our recent leaders has permitted them to brush aside the fact that China, after all, has kept its combat soldiers within its own borders.

The obsession with the ideological aspects of the struggle which began about 21 years ago have overwhelmed our commonsense in this respect. The Chinese have been extremely cautious in engaging people abroad. The only case of any significance was when we went up to the border in Korea, and they had warned us that they would intervene. I expect that we would react the same way if the Chinese were to approach our borders from Mexico. It is a normal reaction. . . .

We are fighting a double shadow in Indochina—the shadow of the international Communist conspiracy and the shadow of the old, obsolete, mindless game of power politics. Armed with weapons that have given war a new dimension of horror, and adorned with the sham morality of ideological conflict, the struggle for power and influence has taken on a deadly, new intensity at exactly the time when it has lost much of the meaning it once had. All the old power politics bromides—about "stability," "order," and "spheres of influence"—are largely without meaning to a global superpower armed with nuclear weapons. The world balance of power on which our security depends is a nuclear balance involving Russia, China, Western Europe, and the United States. The preservation of a non-Communist—as against a Communist—dictatorship in South Vietnam is not going to protect us, or anybody else, from Soviet or Chinese missiles. It simply does not matter very much for the United States, in cold, unadorned strategic terms, who rules the states of Indochina. . . .

We have one great liability and one great asset for negotiating a political settlement. The liability is our peculiar devotion to the Saigon dictators. Since they survive at our sufferance, the handicap could be removed by the simple expedient of putting Mr. Thieu and Mr. Ky on notice that they either join us in negotiating a compromise peace or make some arrangement of their own. Of all the options open to the Thieu government, the only one we can and should remove is their present veto on American policy.

I have always been puzzled—I might mention parenthetically—by our gratuitous tender-heartedness toward right-wing dictators who need us far more than we need them. It is one thing to tolerate such regimes, because it is not our business to be overthrowing foreign governments anyway. But in the case of such unsavory military dictatorships as those in Greece and South Vietnam, we have been much more than tolerant; we have aided and supported these regimes against their own internal enemies. I do not think this is done out of softheartedness—although our Embassy in Saigon has seemed extravagantly solicitous to Mr. Thieu, even to the extent that Ambassador Bunker has staunchly refused to intercede on behalf of Tran Ngoc Chau, the South Vietnamese deputy who was sentenced by a kangaroo court to 10 years at hard labor for maintaining contacts with his brother, a North Vietnamese agent—despite the fact that Chau reported these contacts to the CIA and the U.S. Embassy.

It takes more than Realpolitik to explain such gratuitous friendliness toward rightwing dictators. Here again I suspect that the explanation lies in that attitude of crusading anticommunism which has colored so much of American foreign policy over the years. The charm of the rightwing dictators has been their staunch anticommunism, and that appears to have been enough to compensate for such trivial defects as their despotism and corruption. I recall a member of the Senate, not so long ago, going so far as to defend the Greek colonels as democratic on the ground that they were resisting communism.

This is not the hardheaded de factoism favored by the old school diplomats. It is ideological obsession on the part of old school cold warriors. I am not against tolerating these rightwing dictators any more than I am against tolerating Communist regimes. But our attitude over the last 25 years has not been one of toleration; it has been one of intolerance of Communist regimes giving rise to excessive friendliness toward rightwing regimes. The inspiration for such an outlook comes not from the practical Metternich but from John Calvin, or from the religious crusades.

To return to my theme: if devotion to Thieu and Ky are the obstacle to a compromise political settlement, the asset we have is our remaining force of over 400,000 men in Vietnam—and our freedom to take them out. The Communists want them out, and it is supremely in our interests to get them out. That would seem a promising basis for doing business. . . .

Our country very much needs a political settlement in Indochina. For reasons mostly traceable to the war things are already coming unstuck in America: young people are losing confidence in the country's institutions and resorting to dangerous and disorderly forms of protest. Encouraged by high officials, a nasty vigilantism against dissent has arisen in reaction on the right. . . . A disaster of great proportions to American foreign policy in Asia would induce a wave of recrimination at home, which in turn could set off a chain of events culminating in a disaster to American democracy. What a price to pay for the myth that Vietnam ever really mattered to the security of the United States. . . .

# The Sino-Soviet Rift

*Khrushchev's speech to the Twentieth Party Congress in 1956 led to a dispute with China. The following statement gives the Chinese point of view.*

## From *Statement of the Chinese Communist Party (1963)*

There is a saying, "It takes more than one cold day for the river to freeze three feet deep." The present differences in the international communist movement did not, of course, begin just today.

The open letter of the Central Committee of the CPSU spreads the notion that the differences in the international communist movement were started by the three articles which we published in April 1960 under the title of *Long Live Leninism!* This is a big lie.

What is the truth?

The truth is that the whole series of differences of principle in the international communist movement began more than seven years ago.

To be specific, it began with the 20th Congress of the CPSU in 1956.

From the very outset we held that a number of views advanced at the 20th Congress concerning the contemporary international struggle and the international Communist movement were wrong, were violations of Marxism-Leninism. In particular, the complete negation of Stalin on the pretext of "combating the personality cult" and the thesis of peaceful transition to Socialism by "the parliamentary road" are gross errors of principle. . . .

In completely negating Stalin at the 20th Congress of the CPSU, Khrushchev in effect negated the dictatorship of the proletariat and the fundamental theories of Marxism-Leninism which Stalin defended and developed. It was at that congress that Khrushchev, in his summary report, began the repudiation of Marxism-Leninism on a number of questions of principle.

In his report to the 20th Congress, under the pretext that "radical changes" had taken place in the world situation, Khrushchev put forward the thesis of "peaceful transition." He said that the road of the October Revolution was "the only correct road in those historical conditions," but that as the situation had changed, it had become possible to effect the transition from capitalism to Socialism "through the parliamentary road." In essence, this erroneous thesis is a clear revision of the Marxist-Leninist teachings on the state and revolution and a clear denial of the universal significance of the road of the October Revolution.

In his report, under the same pretext that "radical changes" had

From William E. Griffith, *The Sino-Soviet Rift* (Cambridge, Mass.: MIT Press, 1972), pp. 389–392, 394–395, 399, 402–403.

taken place in the world situation, Khrushchev also questioned the continued validity of Lenin's teachings on imperialism and on war and peace, and in fact tampered with Lenin's teachings.

Khrushchev pictured the U.S. Government and its head as people resisting the forces of war, and not as representatives of the imperialist forces of war. He said, ". . . the advocates of settling outstanding issues by means of war still hold strong positions there [in the United States]," and ". . . they continue to exert big pressure on the President and the Administration." He went on to say that the imperialists were beginning to admit that the positions-of-strength policy had failed and that "symptoms of a certain sobering up are appearing" among them. It was as much as saying that it was possible for the U.S. Government and its head not to represent the interests of U.S. monopoly capital and for them to abandon their policies of war and aggression and that they had become forces defending peace.

Khrushchev declared: "We want to be friends with the United States and to co-operate with it for peace and international security and also in the economic and cultural spheres." This wrong view later developed into the line of "Soviet-U.S. co-operation for the settlement of world problems." . . .

The errors of the 20th Congress brought great ideological confusion in the international Communist movement and caused it to be deluged with revisionist ideas. Along with the imperialists, the reactionaries and the Tito clique, renegades from Communism in many countries attacked Marxism-Leninism and the international Communist movement. . . .

In 1958 the leadership of the CPSU put forward unreasonable demands designed to bring China under Soviet military control. These unreasonable demands were rightly and firmly rejected by the Chinese Government. Not long afterwards, in June 1959, the Soviet Government unilaterally tore up the agreement on new technology for national defence concluded between China and the Soviet Union in October 1957, and refused to provide China with a sample of an atomic bomb and technical data concerning its manufacture. . . .

In July [1960] the Soviet Government suddenly unilaterally decided to recall all the Soviet experts in China within one month, thereby tearing up hundreds of agreements and contracts. The Soviet side unilaterally scrapped the agreement on the publication of the magazine *Druzhba* (Friendship) by China in the Soviet Union and of *Su Chung You Hao* (Soviet-Chinese Friendship) by the Soviet Union in China and their distribution on reciprocal terms; it took the unwarranted step of demanding the recall by the Chinese Government of a staff member of the Chinese Embassy in the Soviet Union; and it provoked troubles on the Sino-Soviet border.

Apparently the leaders of the CPSU imagined that once they waved their baton, gathered a group of hatchetmen to make a converging assault, and applied immense political and economic pressures, they could force the Chinese Communist Party to abandon its Marxist-Leninist and proletarian internationalist stand and submit to their revisionist and great-power chauvinist behests. But the tempered and long-tested Chinese Communist Party and Chinese people could be neither vanquished nor subdued. Those who tried to subjugate us by engineering a converging assault and applying pressures completely miscalculated.

*One thing that the Chinese and American governments had in common was antagonism to the Soviet Union. This made possible a rapprochement between the two powers, announced by President Nixon in an address to a joint session of Congress in 1972.*

## From *Speech of President Richard M. Nixon* (February 28, 1972)

When I announced this trip last July, I described it as a journey for peace. In the last 30 years, Americans have in three different wars gone off by the hundreds of thousands to fight, and some to die, in Asia and in the Pacific. One of the central motives behind my journey to China was to prevent that from happening a fourth time to another generation of Americans.

As I have often said, peace means more than the mere absence of war. In a technical sense, we were at peace with the Peoples Republic of China before this trip, but the gulf of almost 12,000 miles and 22 years of non-communication and hostility separated the United States of America from the 750 million people who live in the Peoples Republic of China, and that is one-fourth of all of the people in the world.

As a result of this trip, we have started the long process of building a bridge across that gulf, and even now we have something better than the mere absence of war. Not only have we completed a week of intensive talks at the highest levels; we have set up a procedure whereby we can continue to have discussions in the future. We have demonstrated that nations with very big and fundamental differences can learn to discuss those differences calmly, rationally, and frankly, without compromising their principles. This is the basis of a structure for peace, where we can talk about differences, rather than fight about them.

The primary goal of this trip was to reestablish communication with the Peoples Republic of China after a generation of hostility. We achieved that goal. Let me turn now to our joint communique.

We did not bring back any written or unwritten agreements that will guarantee peace in our time. We did not bring home any magic for-

From *Congressional Record*, 92d Congress, 2d Session, p. 7592.

mula which will make unnecessary the efforts of the American people
to continue to maintain the strength so that we can continue to be free.

We made some necessary and important beginnings, however, in
several areas. We entered into agreements to expand cultural, educational and journalistic contacts between the Chinese and American
people. We agreed to work to begin and broaden trade between our
two countries. We have agreed that the communications that have now
been established between our governments will be strengthened and
expanded.

Most important, we have agreed on some rules of international conduct which will reduce the risk of confrontation and war, in Asia and
in the Pacific.

We agreed that we are opposed to domination of the Pacific area by
any one power. We agreed that international disputes should be settled
without the use of the threat of force and we agreed that we are prepared to apply this principle to our mutual relations.

With respect to Taiwan, we stated our established policy that our
forces overseas will be reduced gradually as tensions ease, and that our
ultimate objective is to withdraw our forces as a peaceful settlement is
achieved.

We have agreed that we will not negotiate the fate of other nations
behind their backs, and we did not do so in Peking. There were no
secret deals of any kind. We have done all this without giving up any
United States commitments to any other country.

In our talks, talks that I had with the leaders of the Peoples Republic
and the Secretary of State had with the office of the Government of
the Peoples Republic in the foreign affairs area, we both realized that
a bridge of understanding that spans almost 12,000 miles and 22 years
of hostility, can't be built in one week of discussions. But we have
agreed to begin to build that bridge, recognizing that our work will require years of patient effort. We made no attempt to pretend that major differences did not exist between our two governments, because
they do exist.

This communique was unique in honestly setting forth differences
rather than trying to cover them up with diplomatic double talk.

One of the gifts that we left behind in Hangchow was a planted sap-
ling of the American redwood tree. As all Californians know, and as
most Americans know, redwoods grow from saplings into the giants of
the forest. But the process is not one of days or even years; it is a process of centuries.

Just as we hope that those saplings, those tiny saplings that we left
in China, will grow one day into mighty redwoods, so we hope, too,
that the seeds planted on this journey for peace will grow and prosper
into a more enduring structure for peace and security in the Western
Pacific.

# ISRAEL AND THE ARABS

*The establishment of the state of Israel in 1947 created new tensions in the Near East.*

## The Zionist Case

### From *Statement of the World Zionist Conference (1945)*

1. The Conference notes with deep regret and resentment that the White Paper of 1939[1] is, even after the termination of the war, still in force. The White Paper constituted a repudiation of the international pledge undertaken towards the Jewish people; it ignored the recognition granted in public law to the historic connection between the Jewish people and Palestine; it violated the natural and historic right of the Jews, acknowledged in the Mandate, to return to their homeland; it barred the access of Jews to the soil of Palestine, and confined their freedom of settlement within a small fraction of the country's territory, thereby subjecting them to a measure of racial discrimination which today, after the repeal of the Nuremberg laws, is the only survival of its kind in the civilised world; it condemned the Jews to remain in Palestine, as in all countries of their dispersion, a permanent minority; it denied to the Jews the right enjoyed by every nation to be free and independent in its own country.

2. The Policy of the White Paper is responsible for the loss of tens of thousands, perhaps hundreds of thousands, of Jewish lives. But for the White Paper, these Jews, who perished in Europe, could have been saved in time by being admitted to Palestine. . . . Even now, tens of thousands of Jews are languishing in the camps of Central Europe, and suffering acute distress, merely because the contamination of the White Paper policy makes their rehabilitation impossible.

3. The White Paper was issued without the approval of the League of Nations, and without consultation with the Government of the U.S.A. . . .

[1]The British White Paper of 1939 severely restricted Jewish immigration into Israel. [Ed.]

From *Book of Documents Submitted to the General Assembly of the United Nations Relating to the Establishment of a National Home for the Jewish People* (New York: Jewish Agency Publication Office, 1947), pp. 239–242.

4. The White Paper signified at the time a concession to Arab terrorism which raged in Palestine from 1936 onwards, with the support of Hitler and Mussolini. It was part of the appeasement policy pursued by the Chamberlain Government, with special application to the then Mufti of Jerusalem, and his henchmen. Its purpose was to gain Arab support in the event of a war with the Axis. But the White Paper failed to achieve even that practical objective. . . .

5. The Jews of Palestine were the only national entity in the Middle East which mobilised its whole potential for the support of Great Britain and her Allies. . . .

6. Only some 60,000 Jews managed to escape from Europe to Palestine during the war. A hundred times as many—some six million men, women and children—were put to death by the Nazis and their satellites. What happened to our people in Europe did not and could not happen to any people in the world which has a country and a State of its own. The remnants of European Jewry cannot and will not continue their existence among the graveyards of the millions of their slaughtered brethren. Their only salvation lies in their speediest settlement in Palestine. Hundreds of thousands of Jews in some countries of the Orient live under precarious conditions amidst hatred and religious intolerance. Their eyes are turned to Zion. The vast majority of the Jewish people throughout the world feel that they have no chance of "freedom from fear" unless the status of the Jews, as individuals and as a nation, has been made equal to that of all normal peoples, and the Jewish State in Palestine has been established.

7. The return of Jews to Palestine and their settlement in it has not proceeded and will not proceed at the expense of others. The Arabs and other inhabitants of Palestine will continue to benefit, not less than in the past, from the increasing economic opportunities. In addition to full equality of rights, they will enjoy every freedom in organising autonomously their religious, cultural, and social affairs. Jewish immigration and settlement will continue to be based, as hitherto, on the development of resources untapped by others. Jewish and non-Jewish experts have already worked out irrigation, power and development schemes which will enable both new large-scale colonisation, and the raising of the standard of life of all inhabitants, Jews and Arabs alike. Jewish Palestine will also act as a lever of progress and prosperity for the whole Middle East. The Arab States, with their under-populated and under-developed territories, will find in the Jewish State a faithful ally: it will contribute to the best of its ability to the progress of its neighbours.

8. The Conference endorses the declaration of the Jewish Agency for Palestine, communicated at the time to H.M. Government, that the White Paper is devoid of any moral and legal validity. Now that the war has ended, the Jews cannot possibly acquiesce in the continuance of the White Paper under any circumstances whatsoever, whether in its

present or in any modified form. There can be no solution to the inseparable twin problems of the Jewish people and Palestine except by constituting Palestine, undivided and undiminished, as a Jewish State, in accordance with the purpose of the Balfour Declaration.

9. Any delay in the solution of the problem, any attempt at half-measures, any decision which, however favourable, remains on paper, and is not faithfully and speedily implemented, would not meet the tragedy of the hour, and might only increase suffering amongst the Jewish people and tension in Palestine.

ii) The Conference proclaims its full endorsement of the following requests submitted by the Jewish Agency to H.M. Government on the 22nd May, 1945:

*a)* That an immediate decision be announced to establish Palestine as a Jewish State;

*b)* That the Jewish Agency be vested with all necessary authority to bring to Palestine as many Jews as it may find necessary and possible to settle, and to develop, fully and speedily, all the resources of the country—especially land and power resources;

*c)* That an international loan and other help be given for the transfer of the first million Jews to Palestine, and for the economic development of the country;

*d)* That reparations in kind from Germany be granted to the Jewish people for the upbuilding of Palestine, and—as a first instalment—that all German property in Palestine be used for the re-settlement of Jews from Europe;

*e)* That international facilities be provided for the exit and transit of all Jews who wish to settle in Palestine.

The Conference begs to address an urgent appeal to H.M. Government to implement these requests without delay. It appeals to the principal Allies of H.M. Government, and to all the United Nations, to give H.M. Government their full moral and material support in the adoption and implementation of this policy.

## Appeal to Arabs

The World Zionist Conference addresses to the Arabs and other peoples of the Middle East a brotherly appeal to realise the tragedy of the Jewish people. It is our dire need and firm resolve to rebuild our national life in Palestine, the cradle of our history and traditions, the land of our ancestors and of the Book.

The Conference earnestly hopes that the peoples of the Middle East will appreciate that the Zionist work is undertaken in the spirit of national liberation and reconstruction which in no way injures others. What has been achieved by the Jews in Palestine was created by their own toil on land formerly derelict. Jewish Palestine will be happy to co-operate with the Arabs of Palestine and the neighbouring Arab peoples in a common effort to bring greater prosperity to the whole Middle East.

*In 1947 the United Nations General Assembly recommended a partition of Palestine and the creation of a Jewish state.*

# The Arab Case

## From *Statement of the Arab Higher Committee (1948)*

### The Facts of the Palestine Case

Palestine is an Arab country and has been so for the last thirteen centuries. It is an integral part of the Arab world. . . . The population of Palestine in 1919 was composed of 93 per cent Arabs and 7 per cent Jews.

In 1920, Great Britain was appointed as the mandatory power over Palestine in order to lead the country to complete independence.

In 1922, the draft of the Palestine Mandate was prepared by Anglo-Zionist authorities in a way inconsistent with the aforesaid principle of mandates. They inserted in it the Balfour Declaration, whereby Great Britain announced that its government viewed with favor the establishment of a national home for the Jews in Palestine without prejudice to the civil and religious rights of the inhabitants of that country.

For thirty years, Britain administered Palestine as a Crown colony, deprived of any trace of self-government. Instead of leading Palestine to independence, Great Britain put the country under political, administrative and economic conditions favorable to the creation of a Jewish national home. Consequently the Jewish population in Palestine increased from 52,000 in 1917 to 700,000 in 1947.

Britain suppressed the Arab national movement, exiled Arab leaders, put in concentration camps thousands of Arabs, enacted coercive laws and adopted severe measures to crush Arab resistance to Jewish immigration and to the Zionist policy adopted in Palestine.

While keeping the Arabs in Palestine defenseless and unarmed, Great Britain armed the Jews and acquiesced in their smuggling and acquiring of arms and ammunition. With Great Britain's tacit knowledge, Jews put up military fortifications in their towns and villages. While banning any form of Arab military training, Great Britain al-

From *Memorandum of the Arab Higher Committee Delegation for Palestine to the United Nations, 1947,* in I. L. Gendzier, *A Middle East Reader* (New York: Pegasus, 1969), pp. 335–337, 340–342.

lowed Hagana units to be formed and shut its eyes to the vast military training and preparations made by Jews.

Since 1945, the Jews openly challenged the authority of the Mandatory Power by invading Palestine with thousands of illegal immigrants. When Great Britain started to exercise control over the flow of Jewish immigration, Jews revolted against the Mandatory. Jewish gangs, financed by funds raised in the United States and aided by the whole Jewish community in Palestine, committed the most outrageous crimes against both the Arabs and the British.

In 1947, Britain threw the question of Palestine into the lap of the United Nations for a final peaceful settlement.

On November 29, 1947, the General Assembly under very strong pressure by the United States, recommended in a resolution the partition of Palestine into an Arab state and a Jewish state, with economic union.

The said resolution was not a decision of the United Nations; it was a recommendation under Article 10 of the Charter. It was addressed to the Mandatory Power, to the Security Council, and to the people of Palestine.

On November 30 (one day after adoption of the partition resolution), the Arabs of Palestine rose in self-defense against partition which deprived them of the greater and better part of their country. The Jews, on the other hand, committed the most atrocious crimes. They bombed and destroyed Arab dwellings, murdered innocent and defenseless old men, women and children, as in Deir Yasin, committed acts of sacrilege against churches and mosques, as attested to by all Christian religious authorities. These perpetrations caused 300,000 Arabs to leave their homes and belongings and take refuge in adjacent Arab countries.

The overwhelming majority of the people of Palestine—namely the 1,300,000 Arabs—refused to accept the recommendation to partition Palestine. . . .

Basis of the Jewish Claim:   On the other hand, an armed Jewish minority, aided by international Jewry, carried out an armed insurrection, unilaterally declaring independence in an area where the native Arabs are the overwhelming majority.

What was called a declaration of independence was issued by the Jewish Agency and the General Zionist Council  Their claim was alleged to be based on the natural and historical right of the Jewish people and the recommendation of the General Assembly of the United Nations.

Against this alleged natural and historical right, there exists the natural right of the Arabs established by actual continuous occupation and possession of all of Palestine for more than 1,300 years. In all of Palestine now there are only 258,000 Palestinian Jews against 1,300,000 Palestinian Arabs. The rest of the Jews who are residing in Palestine still retain their foreign nationalities. Neither they, the international Jewish Agency, nor the General World Zionist Council, have natural or legal rights in Palestine. The Jewish minority at present existing in Palestine is an immigrant minority mainly from Eastern Europe, who have come to Palestine during the last thirty years. . . . Furthermore, the plan of partition as recommended by the General Assembly is conditioned by the acceptance of the people of Palestine, because it envisages the establishment of two independent states with economic union. No such regime could be established by a unilateral declaration of an armed minority supported by international Jewish bodies as long as the 1,300,000 Arabs, whose land it is, do not agree.

# THE THIRD WORLD

*Many "undeveloped" countries sought to avoid direct involvement in the East-West conflict and to find their own paths to economic and political progress.*

## India

*A major contribution of the "third world" to Western political movements was the doctrine of nonviolent resistance formulated by Mohandas Gandhi (1869–1948).*

### From Mohandas Gandhi. *Satyagraha*

Carried out to its utmost limit, Satyagraha (nonviolent resistance) is independent of pecuniary or other material assistance; certainly, even in its elementary form, of physical force or violence. Indeed, violence is the negation of this great spiritual force, which can only be cultivated or wielded by those who will entirely eschew violence. It is a force that may be used by individuals as well as by communities. It may be used as well in political as in domestic affairs. Its universal applicability is a demonstration of its permanence and invincibility. It can be used alike by men, women and children. It is totally untrue to say that it is a force to be used only by the weak so long as they are not capable of meeting violence by violence. This superstition arises from the incompleteness of the English expression, *passive resistance*. It is impossible for those who consider themselves to be weak to apply this force. Only those who realize that there is something in man which is superior to the brute nature in him and that the latter always yields to it, can effectively be Satyagrahis. This force is to violence, and therefore, to all tyranny, all injustice, what light is to darkness. In politics, its use is based upon the immutable maxim, that government of the people is possible only so long as they consent either consciously or unconsciously to be governed. . . .

. . . All Satyagrahis do not understand the full value of the force, nor have we men who always from conviction refrain from violence. The use of this force requires the adoption of poverty, in the sense that we must be indifferent whether we have the wherewithal to feed or clothe ourselves. During the past struggle, all Satyagrahis, if any at all, were

From Mohandas K. Gandhi, *Satyagraha* (Non-Violent Resistence) (Ahmadabad, India: Navajivan Publishing House, 1951), pp. 34–36.

not prepared to go that length. Some again were only Satyagrahis so called. They came without any conviction, often with mixed motives, less often with impure motives. Some even, whilst engaged in the struggle, would gladly have resorted to violence but for most vigilant supervision. Thus it was that the struggle became prolonged; for the exercise of the purest soul-force, in its perfect form, brings about instantaneous relief. For this exercise, prolonged training of the individual soul is an absolute necessity, so that a perfect Satyagrahi has to be almost, if not entirely, a perfect man. We cannot all suddenly become such men, but if my proposition is correct—as I know it to be correct— the greater the spirit of Satyagraha in us, the better men we will become. Its use, therefore, is, I think, indisputable, and it is a force which, if it became universal, would revolutionize social ideals and do away with despotisms and the ever-growing militarism under which the nations of the West are groaning and are being almost crushed to death, and which fairly promises to overwhelm even the nations of the East. If the past struggle has produced even a few Indians who would dedicate themselves to the task of becoming Satyagrahis as nearly perfect as possible, they would not only have served themselves in the truest sense of the term, they would also have served humanity at large. Thus viewed, Satyagraha is the noblest and best education. It should come, not after the ordinary education in letters, of children, but it should precede it. It will not be denied, that a child, before it begins to write its alphabet and to gain worldly knowledge, should know what the soul is, what truth is, what love is, what powers are latent in the soul. It should be an essential of real education that a child should learn, that in the struggle of life, it can easily conquer hate by love, untruth by truth, violence by self-suffering.

# Africa

*Kwame Nkrumah (1909–1972) of Ghana was for a time one of the most eloquent and successful leaders among the newly independent nations of black Africa. (He was deposed by a coup d'état in 1963.)*

## From Kwame Nkrumah. *I Speak of Freedom* (1961)

For centuries, Europeans dominated the African continent. The white man arrogated to himself the right to rule and to be obeyed by the non-white; his mission, he claimed, was to "civilise" Africa. Under this

From Kwame Nkrumah, *I Speak of Freedom: A Statement of African Ideology* (London: William Heinemann Ltd., 1961), pp. xi–xiv.

cloak, the Europeans robbed the continent of vast riches and inflicted unimaginable suffering on the African people.

All this makes a sad story, but now we must be prepared to bury the past with its unpleasant memories and look to the future. All we ask of the former colonial powers is their goodwill and co-operation to remedy past mistakes and injustices and to grant independence to the colonies in Africa. . . .

It is clear that we must find an African solution to our problems, and that this can only be found in African unity. Divided we are weak; united, Africa could become one of the greatest forces for good in the world.

Although most Africans are poor, our continent is potentially extremely rich. Our mineral resources, which are being exploited with foreign capital only to enrich foreign investors, range from gold and diamonds to uranium and petroleum. Our forests contain some of the finest woods to be grown anywhere. Our cash crops include cocoa, coffee, rubber, tobacco and cotton. As for power, which is an important factor in any economic development, Africa contains over 40% of the potential water power of the world, as compared with about 10% in Europe and 13% in North America. Yet so far, less than 1% has been developed. This is one of the reasons why we have in Africa the paradox of poverty in the midst of plenty, and scarcity in the midst of abundance.

Never before have a people had within their grasp so great an opportunity for developing a continent endowed with so much wealth. Individually, the independent states of Africa, some of them potentially rich, others poor, can do little for their people. Together, by mutual help, they can achieve much. But the economic development of the continent must be planned and pursued as a whole. A loose confederation designed only for economic co-operation would not provide the necessary unity of purpose. Only a strong political union can bring about full and effective development of our natural resources for the benefit of our people.

The political situation in Africa today is heartening and at the same time disturbing. It is heartening to see so many new flags hoisted in place of the old; it is disturbing to see so many countries of varying sizes and at different levels of development, weak and, in some cases, almost helpless If this terrible state of fragmentation is allowed to continue it may well be disastrous for us all.

There are at present some 28 states in Africa, excluding the Union of South Africa, and those countries not yet free. No less than nine of these states have a population of less than three million. Can we seriously believe that the colonial powers meant these countries to be independent, viable states? The example of South America, which has as much wealth, if not more than North America, and yet remains weak and dependent on outside interests, is one which every African would do well to study.

Critics of African unity often refer to the wide differences in culture, language and ideas in various parts of Africa. This is true, but the essential fact remains that we are all Africans, and have a common interest in the independence of Africa. The difficulties presented by questions of language, culture and different political systems are not insuperable.

The greatest contribution that Africa can make to the peace of the world is to avoid all the dangers inherent in disunity, by creating a political union which will also by its success, stand as an example to a divided world. A Union of African states will project more effectively the African personality. It will command respect from a world that has regard only for size and influence. The scant attention paid to African opposition to the French atomic tests in the Sahara, and the ignominious spectacle of the U.N. in the Congo quibbling about constitutional niceties while the Republic was tottering into anarchy, are evidence of the callous disregard of African Independence by the Great Powers.

We have to prove that greatness is not to be measured in stockpiles of atom bombs. I believe strongly and sincerely that with the deeprooted wisdom and dignity, the innate respect for human lives, the intense humanity that is our heritage, the African race, united under one federal government, will emerge not as just another world bloc to flaunt its wealth and strength, but as a Great Power whose greatness is indestructible because it is built not on fear, envy and suspicion, nor won at the expense of others, but founded on hope, trust, friendship and directed to the good of all mankind. The emergence of such a mighty stabilising force in this strife-worn world should be regarded not as the shadowy dream of a visionary, but as a practical proposition, which the peoples of Africa can, and should, translate into reality. There is a tide in the affairs of every people when the moment strikes for political action. Such was the moment in the history of the United States of America when the Founding Fathers saw beyond the petty wranglings of the separate states and created a Union. This is our chance. We must act now. Tomorrow may be too late and the opportunity will have passed, and with it the hope of free Africa's survival.

# Latin America

*Different kinds of revolutionary movements grew up in Argentina and Cuba. Juan Perón's nationalist, populist dictatorship was described admiringly by his wife, Eva Perón, who became a major political figure in her own right.*

# From Eva Perón. *History of Peronismo*

The working forces have triumphed, thanks to the humble, good men and the workers who saw in Peron not only the social reformer, but also the patriot, the man who brought security to the nation, the man who would fight so that when he retired the country would be bigger, happier, and more prosperous than when he found it. These men made the triumph of Peron possible. This is why we Argentines may enjoy our social justice, and our economic independence which grows greater every day, thanks to the patriotic effort and extraordinary vision of General Peron. We Argentines are proud of our sovereignty, and, as I said on the 1st of May: "When our flag parades along the roads of humanity, the men of the world remember their hope, like a lost sweetheart dressed in white and blue to show them the way to happiness."

This is why we, the *peronistas*, may never forget the people; our heart must always be with the humble, the comrades, the poor, the dispossessed, for this is how to carry out best the doctrine of General Peron; and so that the poor, the humble, the working forces, and we ourselves, do not forget, we have pledged to be missionaries of Peron; to do this is to expand his doctrine, not only within our own country, but to offer it to the world as well, as a hope of the rewards always wished for by the working classes. . . .

General Peron has defeated both capitalism and communism. He has defeated capitalism by supressing oligarchy, by fighting the economic forces, the Bembergs and the trusts. *La Prensa,* that capitalistic cancer, was not suppressed by Peron, but by the paperboys and the working force. But could the paperboys, the most humble workers of the country, have confronted the powerful paper, through a strike against a business that had so much support, especially from the outside, if there had been no justice, no government which would let them discuss freely and on an equal basis with their bosses. Before, the poor paperboys would have been machine gunned, drowning their hopes forever.

Peron has also defeated internal capitalism, through social economy, putting capital at the service of the economy, and not vice versa, which only gave the workers the right to die of hunger. The law of the funnel, as it is called, the wide part for the capitalists and the narrow part for the people.

Peron suppressed imperialist action. Now we have economic independence. He knows well all the insults he will receive for committing

From Eva Perón, *Historia del Peronismo* (Buenos Aires: Presidencia de la Nación, 1951), translated in R. Cameron, *Civilization Since Waterloo* (Itasca, Ill.: F. E. Peacock Publishers, 1971), pp. 529–531. Reprinted by permission of Harlan Davidson Inc.

the "crime" of defending the country. Some Argentines allied themselves with foreigners in order to slander him, because General Peron was the first to make foreign powers respect Argentina, and treat it as an equal.

General Peron took communism away from the masses, for justice and greater well-being replacing it with syndicalism, about which I would like to say a few words.

Syndicalism supports justice and Peron, but this does not mean that syndicalism participates in political action. It is simply a doctrine of social justice, and its creator, Peron, is now above all politics, because the Argentine syndicates (trade unions), by forming syndicalism, that is, by placing themselves within the doctrine of justice, are authentically representing their members; that which before was discussed with guns is no longer discussed; conquests are defended, which is very different. Syndicalism and the Argentine syndicates, within the doctrine of social justice, support Peron politically; they do not support parties or party candidates, because there will never be another Peron, despite his imitators, whose works are always disastrous. The working classes, by supporting Peron, support the leader of the Argentine workers and not the leader of any political party. Peron is the nation, Peron is work, and Peron is well-being

## From *Fidel Castro Speaks*

To the accusation that Cuba wants to export its revolution, we reply: Revolutions are not exported, they are made by the people. . .

What Cuba can give to the people, and has already given, is its example.

And what does the Cuban Revolution teach? That revolution is possible, that the people can make it, that in the contemporary world there are no forces capable of halting the liberation movement of the peoples.

Our triumph would never have been feasible if the Revolution itself had not been inexorably destined to arise out of existing conditions in our socio-economic reality, a reality which exists to an even greater degree in a good number of Latin American countries.

It inevitably occurs that in the nations where the control of the Yankee monopolies is strongest, the exploitation of the oligarchy cruelest, and the situation of the laboring and peasant masses most unbearable, the political power appears most solid. The state of siege becomes habitual. Every manifestation of discontent by the masses is repressed by force. The democratic path is closed completely. The brutal character of dictatorship, the form of rule adopted by the ruling classes, reveals

From *Fidel Castro Speaks*, M. Kenner and J. Petras, eds. (New York: Grove Press, 1969), pp. 112–113. Reprinted by permission of Grove Press, Inc.

itself more clearly than ever. It is then that the revolutionary explosion of the peoples becomes inevitable.

Although it is true that in those underdeveloped countries of America the working class is generally relatively small, there is a social class which, because of the subhuman conditions in which it lives, constitutes a potential force that, led by the workers and the revolutionary intellectuals, has a decisive importance in the struggle for national liberation—the peasants. . . .

In our countries are two conditions: an underdeveloped industry and an agrarian regime of feudal character. That is why, with all the hardships of the conditions of life of the urban workers, the rural population lives in even more horrible conditions of oppression and exploitation; but it is also, with exceptions, the absolute majority sector, at times exceeding seventy per cent of the Latin American population.

Discounting the landlords, who often reside in the cities, the rest of that great mass gains its livelihood working as peons on the *haciendas* for the most miserable wages, or work the land under conditions of exploitation which in no manner puts the Middle Ages to shame. These circumstances determine that in Latin America the poor rural population constitutes a tremendous potential revolutionary force.

The armies, built and equipped for conventional war, which are the force on which the power of the exploiting classes rests, become absolutely impotent when they have to confront the irregular struggle of the peasants on their own terrain. They lose ten men for each revolutionary fighter who falls. Demoralization spreads rapidly among them from having to face an invisible and invincible enemy who does not offer them the opportunity of showing off their academy tactics and their braggadocio which they use so much in military displays to curb the city workers and the students.

The initial struggle by small combat units is incessantly fed by new forces, the mass movement begins to loosen its bonds, the old order little by little begins to break into a thousand pieces, and that is the moment when the working class and the urban masses decide tne battle.

What is it that from the beginning of the struggle of those first nuclei makes them invincible, regardless of the numbers, power, the resources of their enemies? It is the aid of the people, and they will be able to count on that help of the people on an ever-growing scale.

# XVI

# THE MODERN WORLD—HOPES AND ANXIETIES

*SINCE WORLD WAR II the Western world has enjoyed higher living standards than those of any other society in history. Western technology and ideas—either liberal or Marxist—have spread throughout the world. Humans for the first time have ventured beyond the earth into space. Yet this has not been a period of tranquil achievement; on the contrary, our time is often called an "age of anxiety."*

*The very successes of scientific civilization seem to create new problems. Technology gives us, not only new means of prolonging life, but also thermonuclear bombs, which threaten mass death. And the prolongation of life—especially the reduction of infant mortality—can create problems of overpopulation that threaten to exhaust or pollute the limited resources of our planet. For many contemporary observers, belief in inevitable progress is giving way to a sense of necessary limits.*

*In past centuries people debated the role of women in society, but recently the debate has taken a new form. Besides calling for the political, economic, educational, and legal rights of women (as Olympe de Gouges or John Stuart Mill had), many in the women's movement have called for a reassessment of women's sexual and family roles.*

*The postwar revelations of atrocities in Hitler's Germany and Stalin's Russia produced widespread revulsion in the West. But, to many activists, there still seemed a need for radical change in society and for radical action against its abuses. This has taken many forms, from acts of terrorism to mass protests against perceived injustices.*

*Finally, underlying all the other tensions of the modern world is the problem of finding a basis for morality in a universe of matter and energy that seems indifferent to the concerns of mankind. The problem is not a new one, but it has acquired a new urgency mainly because of recent advances in the biological sciences. In the eighteenth century the philosopher Holbach suggested that human life might be just "the result of a fortuitous meeting of atoms." Nowadays many biologists would regard the proposition as scientifically valid. But in that case, "Who shall decide what is good and what is evil?" (Jacques Monod). And how can we live together without giving meaning to such concepts?*

*In the following chapter we have presented some of these problems of contemporary humanity and some of the suggested solutions.*

# THE THREAT OF NUCLEAR WAR

## Three Approaches

*During the 1950s movements of protest against the use of nuclear weapons grew up in England and other Western countries.*

### From Philip Toynbee. *The Fearful Choice (1959)*

There is a simple test for deciding whether or not we have truly contemplated the reality of nuclear warfare. Have we decided how we are to kill the other members of our household in the event of our being less injured than they are? This will sound morbid and melodramatic to most English ears, but in reality we ought already to be making sober plans for killing off our injured before disposing of ourselves. If nuclear war begins, a great many rockets are likely to fall on this country simultaneously. Those who are fortunate enough to live in the "safest" areas—London, East Anglia—can reasonably expect to be killed outright. But over most of the country there will probably be a chaos of people dying in isolation from each other, and in great agony. In most areas there will probably be no organised rescue work and no prospect of any organised rescue work. Much needless anguish can be avoided if we are at least prepared with our methods of euthanasia.

At the moment of writing we know that many bomb-bearing rockets are aimed at this country from Russian territory. We know that these rockets are effective and accurate. We can assume that the rocket-batteries are manned throughout the twenty-four hours.

We also know that American bombers are constantly in the air above England carrying Hydrogen bombs which can be made active within a few minutes. We know that the Americans wish to establish their own perpetually-manned rocket batteries in this country and in other countries of Western Europe. In fact, we know that we have now reached the in some ways familiar situation of two hostile but adjacent countries with tension running high between them. There are many points of resemblance between the present diplomatic and military relations of

From Philip Toynbee, *The Fearful Choice* (Detroit: Wayne State University Press, 1959), pp. 10–14, 17–20. Reprinted by permission of Victor Gollancz Ltd.

America and Russia and the relations between, for example, Israel and Jordan today or Bulgaria and Serbia before the 1914 war. We know that this older situation is one which leads to constant frontier incidents. Shots are suddenly exchanged; a few soldiers or civilians are killed on either side of the frontier. These incidents are not necessarily due to bad-will even on the part of the soldier or junior officer who is responsible for causing them. They are often due to panic, or to mistaking an order. And when they occurred in the cases we have known before they never led to war unless the government of one or both countries desired a war.

It is here that the parallel breaks down. If an "incident" should happen on the present frontier between America and Russia it must lead not only to war but to the total destruction of this country and perhaps of the human race. If one Russian rocket commander mistakes an order; if one American bomber pilot suddenly finds the strain too much for his mind, it is inevitable that rockets and bombers will be massively launched from both sides. That is the meaning of the word "deterrent" which both sides use so freely. . . .

That is one choice.

The other choice involves, in the first place, the possibility of giving Russia a small immediate advantage over the West. It involves the further possibility that Russia will gradually dominate the world by political and economic means. It involves the extremely remote possibility that Russia will carry out a military occupation of the world. It is hard to see how anyone can believe that the worst of these possibilities is a more appalling prospect than the worst possible result of continuing the arms race. It is not a question of making a personal choice in favour of death rather than Russian domination; that choice is always available to the individual in any case. It is a question of allowing the human race to survive, possibly under the domination of a régime which most of us detest, or of allowing it to destroy itself in appalling and prolonged anguish.

We now believe that the thousand-year Reich is a myth; and the major lesson of the post-Stalin epoch is that even communist régimes are incapable of totally denaturalising human nature. An attempted communist domination of such fantastically indigestible morsels as Paris, London, Rome and New York would almost certainly result in a violent indigestion and a radical change in the nature of the dominating power. The Orwell nightmare of an everlasting tyranny seems to be truly a nightmare rather than a probable future for mankind.

It seems, then, that the worst, and least probable, result of adopting the choice of life rather than death would be a severe set-back to human freedom. In terms of history, as well as in terms of human misery, this would be a trivial reverse compared with the horrifying probabilities of nuclear war.

*The physicist Edward Teller played a major role in the design and construction of the hydrogen bomb.*

## From Edward Teller. *The Legacy of Hiroshima* (1962)

Owing to my experience in the field of atomic explosives, it is proper that I should particularly emphasize the influence that these powerful instruments have on all questions of war and peace. One fact seems inescapable to me: It will not be possible to preserve peace unless we are willing to think carefully and in detail about war.

My contention is not that our preparation for war is insufficient. My main point is that our preparation is misdirected. We have been frightened by the display of our own power at Hiroshima, and we have lost our sense of proportion. On the one hand, we think of an all-out war as a cataclysm that will wipe out mankind. On the other hand, we think of an abolition of nuclear weapons as a means to restore stability and to avoid a future war. These two patterns of ideas are driving us toward a tragedy which, when it comes, will be of our own making. . . .

Some of our people insist that nuclear disarmament is desirable at any price, and they advocate a simple approach to the problem: Unilateral disarmament. The magnificent example of Gandhi and the high moral principles of many of our most thoughtful people have inspired the idea that the United States should abstain from development and possession of deadly nuclear weapons no matter what other nations may do.

But at least one point cannot be forgotten: The story of Gandhi has two sides. Only one is told in a recounting of the sufferings, determination, and eventual success of this great man. The other side, in its way, is as admirable. This is the story of the British willingness to limit their own power and to permit Gandhi's movement enough freedom so that his ideas of peaceful resistance could take hold and achieve ultimate success. We know of no Gandhi in any Communist country. Many decades might have to pass before the high-minded advocates of unilateral disarmament can hope to find in the Soviet Union the liberalism and generosity which is necessary if passive resistance is to become practical.

Unilateral disarmament on the part of the United States would, indeed, prevent future war. It might even save us from attack. Disarmed, we would be unprepared, and we would have to submit and surrender to a mere threat of attack. A surprising number of our people profess a preference for crawling to Moscow in surrender rather than risking the dangers of a nuclear war. It is, of course, of paramount importance to avoid the great suffering of a third world war. That terrible conflict as well as an all-out nuclear attack on our nation can be avoided, I am convinced, if we are prepared. But if we are not prepared, if we were to disarm unilaterally, our only remaining alternative would be surrender or defeat. Disarmament is justified only if it decreases the probability of war without creating a situation in which surrender or defeat would be inevitable. . . .

The United States today is not properly defended. We literally invite attack because our potential enemies know that the United States today could not survive a big thermonuclear attack.

Two defeatist arguments have convinced the majority of Americans that civilian defense is futile. Even if some of our people managed to survive a sudden attack, according to one argument, the world after a nuclear war would not be fit for humans: The atmosphere would be poisoned for years; food could not be eaten safely; our factories would be destroyed; there would be no creature comforts; unlucky survivors of a nuclear attack would die of starvation, loneliness, or sorrow. Another argument, because of its simplicity and frequent and skillful repetition, has been accepted widely. This argument holds that survival simply is impossible, that rapid development of nuclear weapons will make today's civilian defense preparations inadequate for tomorrow, that our adversaries can and will devise bombs to destroy any civilian defense shelters we can build.

No prophecy about a future war can be completely reliable. But this much is certain: Properly defended, we can survive a nuclear attack; we can dig out of the ruins; we can recover from the catastrophe. The shelters we need for our defense, properly constructed, will not be made obsolete by the development of new weapons. The strength of nuclear weapons since Hiroshima has increased a thousandfold. The increase of shelter depth required to withstand a direct hit by these bigger weapons has been less than tenfold.

As a nation, we shall survive, and our democratic ideals and institutions will survive with us, if we make adequate preparations for survival now—and adequate preparations are within our reach and our capabilities.

Mere survival, however, is not the only compelling reason for civilian defense. There is another reason that is even more important: Peace. If we are adequately prepared, if we cannot be defeated even by the most sudden and savage attack, then the main motivation for a nuclear attack upon our nation will have vanished. . . .

Under no circumstances would we be justified in striking the first blow in an all-out war. If we had certain knowledge that the Russians would unleash the full fury of an atomic attack against us tomorrow, I still would say that in anticipation we should not strike the first blow today. My reason for saying this is not practical. I say it because I think this is right. But I believe that to abstain from striking the first blow also happens to be the only practical policy.

If we had the most excellent evidence that a Communist attack against us was imminent, we should send our people into shelters, put our strategic force into readiness—and then wait. Our preparedness would give our enemies the most excellent reason not to attack. If they still did attack, our country could and would react with unity and determination; in the end, we could win the hard struggle for the future of freedom.

If we saw signals on our radar screens and received information from our satellites that could mean only that Russian rockets were on their way, we still should not attack Russia. The possibility of error might still exist, and we must do everything humanly possible to avoid all-out war by mistake. Once Russian rockets were flying, we could not save our cities and prime target areas with a counterattack.

By following this policy of never striking first under any circumstance, we would have strength in the knowledge that all-out war was not our doing. But to follow this policy, to act in this way, and to have confidence in the future, we must be strong.

Our strategic retaliatory force must be able to survive any attack. It must be a true second-strike force. We are negligent today in building and securing such a second-strike force. . . .

Any defense can be outwitted. But a multiple defense is hardest to defeat. We should put our retaliatory force into airplanes, many of which should be in the air constantly; we should put bomb-carrying missiles in many small nuclear submarines, into many inconspicuous carriers such as trucks and railroad cars. Development of lightweight, mobile retaliatory missiles would improve our chances of defense because such targets could be maintained as moving targets. Additional retaliatory bombs should be located in many solidly built and well-defended bases. It may be impossible to shoot down all approaching missiles. But if a missile has to make a precise hit on a missile base to be effective, there is a real chance for an anti-missile defense protecting a sharply defined point. Much thought and work will have to go into this second-strike force, but better nuclear explosives are the beginning and the end of every improvement. Smaller explosives will make our missiles more mobile and easier to defend. Better explosives will make the hard task of point-defense against missiles somewhat easier.

The plan to launch our counterattack only after we have been bombed decreases the chances of accidental war. But a second-strike force requires many retaliatory missiles which must be kept in constant readiness. This may seem to increase the chances of a tragic mistake Actually, a great deal of thought has been given to devices which will eliminate the possibility that the human error or aberration of a single person in charge of a retaliatory missile could unleash a war. Using past accomplishments and future progress, we can make absolutely sure that our government has a restraining power and that as long as our government is functioning, only the most responsible persons to whom we have entrusted our fate can order a counterattack. Our strength would give these men the assurance that they never need act in haste.

*The encyclical letter* Pacem in Terris *(Peace on Earth) was written by Pope John XXIII (1958–1963).*

# From Pope John XXIII. *Pacem in Terris (1963)*

... It is with deep sorrow that We note the enormous stocks of armaments that have been and still are being made in more economically developed countries, with a vast outlay of intellectual and economic resources. And so it happens that, while the people of these countries are loaded with heavy burdens, other countries as a result are deprived of the collaboration they need in order to make economic and social progress.

The production of arms is allegedly justified on the grounds that in present-day conditions peace cannot be preserved without an equal balance of armaments. And so, if one country increases its armaments, others feel the need to do the same; and if one country is equipped with nuclear weapons, other countries must produce their own, equally destructive.

Consequently, people live in constant fear lest the storm that every moment threatens should break upon them with dreadful violence. And with good reason, for the arms of war are ready at hand. Even though it is difficult to believe that anyone would deliberately take the responsibility for the appalling destruction and sorrow that war would bring in its train, it cannot be denied that the conflagration may be set off by some unexpected and obscure event. And one must bear in mind that, even though the monstrous power of modern weapons acts as a deterrent, it is to be feared that the mere continuance of nuclear tests, undertaken with war in mind, will prove a serious hazard for life on earth.

Justice, then, right reason and humanity urgently demand that the arms race should cease; that the stockpiles which exist in various countries should be reduced equally and simultaneously by the parties concerned; that nuclear weapons should be banned; and that a general agreement should eventually be reached about progressive disarmament and an effective method of control. In the words of Pius XII, Our Predecessor of happy memory: *The calamity of a world war, with the economic and social ruin and the moral excesses and dissolution that accompany it, must not be permitted to envelop the human race for a third time.*

From Pope John XXIII, *Pacem in Terras* (New York: Paulist Press, 1963), pp. 38–40.

All must realize that there is no hope of putting an end to the building up of armaments, nor of reducing the present stocks, nor, still less, of abolishing them altogether, unless the process is complete and thorough and unless it proceeds from inner conviction: unless, that is, everyone sincerely co-operates to banish the fear and anxious expectation of war with which men are oppressed. If this is to come about, the fundamental principle on which our present peace depends must be replaced by another, which declares that the true and solid peace of nations consists not in equality of arms but in mutual trust alone. We believe that this can be brought to pass, and We consider that it is something which reason requires, that it is eminently desirable in itself and that it will prove to be the source of many benefits.

In the first place, it is an objective demanded by reason. There can be, or at least there should be, no doubt that relations between States, as between individuals, should be regulated not by the force of arms but by the light of reason, by the rule, that is, of truth, of justice and of active and sincere co-operation.

Secondly, We say that it is an objective earnestly to be desired in itself. Is there anyone who does not ardently yearn to see war banished, to see peace preserved and daily more firmly established?

And finally, it is an objective which will be a fruitful source of many benefits, for its advantages will be felt everywhere, by individuals, by families, by nations, by the whole human family. The warning of Pius XII still rings in our ears: *Nothing is lost by peace; everything may be lost by war.*

# POPULATION, ECOLOGY, NATURAL RESOURCES

## Population Pressures

*The following figures were presented in a background paper for a United Nations conference held in 1965.*

### From *World Health*

Tracing the history of man on earth has always been an inexact science, but most experts agree that he was a relatively rare creature some half million years ago, moving up from tens or hundreds of thousands to perhaps 200–300 million at the beginning of the Christian era. It then took, according to the generally accepted assumption, another 1600 years or so for that figure approximately to double to 500 million. The 1,000 million mark was reached some two centuries later—by 1850—and in the succeeding 110 years, the population reached the 3,000 million mark.

Thus, ages passed before the 250 million mark was reached two thousands year ago and sixteen centuries more before the population reached 500 million. Then it suddenly doubled in two and a half centuries and again in less than one century.

Now, world population is increasing at a rate (1.9 per cent annually) that will double the number in about 40 years. According to "plausible long-range" projections made recently by the United Nations, world population, approximately 3,000 million in 1960, will rise to the order of 5,300–6,800 million by the year 2000. A figure near 6,000 million seems a comparatively likely expectation, according to the projections.

As a result of rapidly declining death rates in most parts of the world, while birth rates in many areas remain high, we are now adding about 60,000,000 persons annually to a world population which, by mid-1964, was estimated to have reached 3,220,000,000. For purposes of comparison, this yearly increase is equal to the combined populations of Poland and Spain. During the past decade alone, the net population increase—some 480,000,000—was greater than the total number of persons presently living in all of Europe, excluding the USSR

From *World Health* 18, November 1965, pp. 4, 6, 8.

While on the average the world total is now increasing at a rate of 1.9 per cent there is considerable disparity between the rates of increase in developed and developing countries. The populations of Latin America, Africa and Asia are multiplying at a much faster rate than those of Europe and Northern America.

Despite the rapid population growth in developing regions and countries, Europe remains the most densely populated continent with an average of 89 people per square kilometre. Asia, though comprising enormous wastelands, is next with an average of 64 persons to the square kilometre, followed by Africa, Northern America and the USSR with 10 each. Oceania has a density of only 2 persons per square kilometre. . . .

. . . Public opinion is focused on the developing countries where the phenomenon is seen at its most dramatic: in some countries the annual growth rate exceeds 3 per cent, a rate which means that the population will double in less than 25 years, apparently setting at nought any hopes for a better life. A paradox, which many people find more and more difficult to account for, is that while mortality rates are shrinking because of the effects of modern science, birth rates continue to be governed mainly by traditional values. Mankind, however, is refusing to leave its destiny to chance. The planners—economists and others— are numerous in reminding us of the tremendous impact of population trends.

*The authors of the following study explored five "scenarios" dealing with the impact of demographic growth in South Asia. The first four scenarios, based on a continuation of existing trends or allowing for modest reforms, all led to massive human suffering. The fifth scenario required a radical reorientation of the world economic system.*

## From M. Mesarovic and E. Pestel. *Mankind at the Turning Point*

In the *fifth scenario*, investment aid is provided to South Asia in sufficient amount and at the time needed to close the food-supply gap and the export-import imbalance. The magnitude of such a program will require a concerted effort by the entire Developed World. The export potential of South Asia would be increased substantially, and the world economic system would have to be modified so that South Asia could pay from exports for most of its food imports. These exports would

From Mihajlo Mesarovic and Eduard Pestel, *Mankind at the Turning Point: The Second Report to the Club of Rome* (New York: Dutton, 1974), pp. 125, 127, 129. Copyright © 1974 by the authors. Reprinted by permission of the publisher, E. P. Dutton, Inc.

have to be industrial, since the regional food demands obviously will absorb the local agricultural output. But to make this scenario feasible, the Developed World must help South Asia to develop its own exportable and competitive industrial specialization.

Scenario five—the only way to avert unprecedented disaster in South Asia—requires the emergence of a new global economic order. Industrial diversification will have to be worldwide and carefully planned with special regard for regional specificity. The most effective use of labor and capital, and the availability of resources, will have to be assessed on a global, long-term basis. Such a system cannot be left to the mercy of narrow national interests, but must rely on long-range world economic arrangements.

*In summary, the only feasible solution to the world food situation requires:*

*1. A global approach to the problem.*

*2. Investment aid rather than commodity aid, except for food.*

*3. A balanced economic development for all regions.*

*4. An effective population policy.*

*5. Worldwide diversification of industry, leading to a truly global economic system.*

*Only a proper combination of these measures can lead to a solution. Omission of any one measure will surely lead to disaster. But the strains on the global food production capacity would be lessened if the eating habits in the affluent part of the world would change, becoming less wasteful.*

The situation is more than urgent. Even our "solution" requires drastic, unprecedented changes in the world system. These changes cannot be effected without compromise on the part of the other regions. Even if there is willingness to work toward a solution, such compromises require a lot of time. In this case there is no time. Our analysis shows that if the population policy is less stringent and the transition period is extended from fifteen to thirty-five years, the number of accumulated child deaths in the fifty-year period will increase by 80 percent. If we wait twenty years to implement a policy with a transition period of 15 years, there will be, between 1975 and 2025, an increase in child deaths of 300 percent!

The most thorough analyses of a large number of scenarios using our world system computer model lead to the inescapable conclusion that mankind's options for avoiding castrophe are decreasing, while delays in implementing the options are, quite literally, deadly.

# Natural Environment

*The British economist E. F. Schumacher discusses mankind's use (and abuse) of the earth's "natural capital."*

## From E. F. Schumacher. *Small Is Beautiful*

Fossil fuels are merely a part of the "natural capital" which we stead-fastly insist on treating as expendable, as if it were income, and by no means the most important part. If we squander our fossil fuels, we threaten civilisation; but if we squander the capital represented by living nature around us, we threaten life itself. People are waking up to this threat, and they demand that pollution must stop. They think of pollution as a rather nasty habit indulged in by careless or greedy people who, as it were, throw their rubbish over the fence into the neighbour's garden. A more civilised behaviour, they realise, would incur some extra cost, and therefore we need a faster rate of economic growth to be able to pay for it. From now on, they say, we should use at least some of the fruits of our ever-increasing productivity to improve "the quality of life" and not merely to increase the quantity of consumption. All this is fair enough, but it touches only the outer fringe of the problem.

To get to the crux of the matter, we do well to ask why it is that all these terms—pollution, environment, ecology, etc.—have *so suddenly* come into prominence. After all, we have had an industrial system for quite some time, yet only five or ten years ago these words were virtually unknown. Is this a sudden fad, a silly fashion, or perhaps a sudden failure of nerve?

The explanation is not difficult to find. As with fossil fuels, we have indeed been living on the capital of living nature for some time, but at a fairly modest rate. It is only since the end of World War II that we have succeeded in increasing this rate to alarming proportions. In comparison with what is going on now and what has been going on, progressively, during the last quarter of a century, all the industrial activities of mankind up to, and including, World War II are as nothing. The next four or five years are likely to see more industrial production, taking the world as a whole, than all of mankind accomplished up to 1945. In other words, quite recently—so recently that most of us have hardly yet become conscious of it—there has been a unique quantitative jump in industrial production.

Partly as a cause and also as an effect, there has also been a unique qualitative jump. Our scientists and technologists have learned to compound substances unknown to nature. Against many of them, nature is virtually defenceless. There are no natural agents to attack and break them down. It is as if aborigines were suddenly attacked with machine-gun fire: their bows and arrows are of no avail. These substances, unknown to nature, owe their almost magical effectiveness precisely to nature's defencelessness—and that accounts also for their dangerous ecological impact. It is only in the last twenty years or so that they have made their appearance *in bulk*. Because they have no natural enemies, they tend to accumulate, and the long-term consequences of this accumulation are in many cases known to be extremely dangerous, and in other cases totally unpredictable.

In other words, the changes of the last twenty-five years, both in the quantity and in the quality of man's industrial processes, have produced an entirely new situation—a situation resulting not from our failure but from what we thought were our greatest successes. And this has come so suddenly that we hardly noticed the fact that we were very rapidly using up a certain kind of irreplaceable capital asset, namely the *tolerance margins* which benign nature always provides.

Now let me return to the question of "income fuels" with which I had previously dealt in a somewhat cavalier manner. No one is suggesting that the world-wide industrial system which is being envisaged to operate in the year 2000, a generation ahead, would be sustained primarily by water or wind power. No, we are told that we are moving rapidly into the nuclear age. Of course, this has been the story for quite some time, for over twenty years, and yet, the contribution of nuclear energy to man's total fuel and energy requirements is still minute. In 1970, it amounted to 2.7 per cent in Britain; 0.6 per cent in the European Community; and 0.3 per cent in the United States, to mention only the countries that have gone the furthest. Perhaps we can assume that nature's tolerance margins will be able to cope with such small impositions, although there are many people even today who are deeply worried, and Dr. Edward D. David, President Nixon's Science Adviser, talking about the storage of radioactive wastes, says that "one has a queasy feeling about something that has to stay underground and be pretty well sealed off for 25,000 years before it is harmless."

However that may be, the point I am making is a very simple one: the proposition to replace thousands of millions of tons of fossil fuels, every year, by nuclear energy means to "solve" the fuel problem by creating an environmental and ecological problem of such a monstrous magnitude that Dr. David will not be the only one to have "a queasy feeling." It means solving one problem by shifting it to another sphere—there to create an infinitely bigger problem.

Having said this, I am sure that I shall be confronted with another, even more daring proposition: namely, that future scientists and technologists will be able to devise safety rules and precautions of such perfection that the using, transporting, processing and storing of radioactive materials in ever-increasing quantities will be made entirely safe; also that it will be the task of politicians and social scientists to create a world society in which wars or civil disturbances can never happen. Again, it is a proposition to solve one problem simply by shifting it to another sphere, the sphere of everyday human behaviour. And this takes us to the third category of "natural capital" which we are recklessly squandering because we treat it as if it were income: as if it were something we had made ourselves and could easily replace out of our much-vaunted and rapidly rising productivity.

Is it not evident that our current methods of production are already eating into the very substance of industrial man? To many people this is not at all evident. Now that we have solved the problem of production, they say, have we ever had it so good? Are we not better fed, better clothed, and better housed than ever before—and better educated? Of course we are: most, but by no means all, of us: in the rich countries. But this is not what I mean by "substance." The substance of man cannot be measured by Gross National Product. Perhaps it cannot be measured at all, except for certain symptoms of loss. However, this is not the place to go into the statistics of these symptoms, such as crime, drug addiction, vandalism, mental breakdown, rebellion, and so forth. Statistics never prove anything.

I started by saying that one of the most fateful errors of our age is the belief that the problem of production has been solved. This illusion, I suggested, is mainly due to our inability to recognise that the modern industrial system, with all its intellectual sophistication, consumes the very basis on which it has been erected. To use the language of the economist, it lives on irreplaceable capital which it cheerfully treats as income. I specified three categories of such capital: fossil fuels, the tolerance margins of nature, and the human substance. Even if some readers should refuse to accept all three parts of my argument, I suggest that any one of them suffices to make my case.

And what is my case? Simply that our most important task is to get off our present collision course. And who is there to tackle such a task? I think every one of us, whether old or young, powerful or powerless, rich or poor, influential or uninfluential. To talk about the future is useful only if it leads to action *now*. And what can we do *now*, while we are still in the position of "never having had it so good"? To say the least—which is already very much—we must thoroughly understand the problem and begin to see the possibility of evolving a new life-style, with new methods of production and new patterns of consumption: a life-style designed for permanence. To give only three preliminary examples: in agriculture and horticulture, we can interest ourselves in the perfection of production methods which are biologically sound, build up soil fertility, and produce health, beauty and permanence. Productivity will then look after itself. In industry, we can interest ourselves in the evolution of small-scale technology, relatively nonviolent technology, "technology with a human face," so that people have a chance to enjoy themselves while they are working, instead of working solely for their pay packet and hoping, usually forlornly, for enjoyment solely during their leisure time. In industry, again—and, surely, industry is the pace-setter of modern life—we can interest ourselves in new forms of partnership between management and men, even forms of common ownership.

We often hear it said that we are entering the era of "the Learning Society.' Let us hope this is true. We still have to learn how to live peacefully, not only with our fellow men but also with nature and, above all, with those Higher Powers which have made nature and have made us; for, assuredly, we have not come about by accident and certainly have not made ourselves.

*At the edge of fantasy, some writers have suggested that space exploration might solve the world's problems of overpopulation.*

## From *To Walk the Moon*

In a world long given to marking off its historical progress in periods—the Age of Faith, the Renaissance, the Age of Reason, the Industrial Revolution—language seems too impoverished to encompass so neatly the era that begins with man's first walk on the moon. As a term, the Space Age is grossly inadequate, failing completely to convey the nature of the change that this event portends. For the lunar landing of the astronauts is more than a step in history; it is a step in evolution.

The journey of Neil Armstrong and his companions cannot be viewed in the same perspective as the voyage of Columbus or of any other traveler in recorded time—and the difference is not at all in degrees of courage or individual skill. In truth, Columbus's feat may well have taken more courage than Armstrong's because it was preceded by no unmanned probes and took him to regions unknown to the science of his day, in contrast to the photographed, spectographed and charted terrain of the moon.

What gives the astronauts' expedition a different dimension entirely, what removes it indeed from any venture in the whole history of the human race, are two circumstances that stagger the mind: it is man's first step in adapting to an environment beyond this planet's and it is a *willed* step in the evolutionary process, one made deliberately and in the full consciousness of its import.

For the adaptation itself there are comparable precedents in nature, though for one as full of meaning for the future one might have to go back to the first fishy creature that emerged from the Devonian sea to make a feeble try at life on dry land.

For the conscious willing of an evolutionary act there is no precedent. Man has of course taught himself to ride over and under the waves and to fly through space, but what is contemplated now is no such passing accommodation but in time the transfer of human life to other sites in the universe—with ultimate consequences that almost surely must be evolutionary in nature.

It will take years, decades, perhaps centuries, for man to colonize even the moon, but that is the end inherent in Armstrong's first step on extraterrestrial soil. Serious and hard-headed scientists envision, even in the not remote future, lunar communities capable of growing into domed cities subsisting on hydroponically grown food, of developing the moon's resources, and eventually of acquiring a breathable atmosphere and a soil capable of being farmed. What with the dire threats of population explosion at best and nuclear explosion at worst, the human race, as Sir Bernard Lovell warns, may find itself sometime in the 21st century "having to consider how best to insure the survival of the species."

It is not possible to imagine that any such cosmic movement would leave the transported segment of mankind unchanged. Over the centuries and through countless transitions it would adapt biologically and psychologically, following Darwinian law, to existence in an environment differing as much from its earthly ancestors as that of the early mammals differed from the environment in the primeval seas.

Reflections on man's social shortcomings, speculation on what else he might have done instead of sending men to the moon—all this melts away in the moment of awe and wonder.

# FORMS OF GOVERNMENT, FORMS OF PROTEST

## Totalitarian Government

*Hannah Arendt found the ultimate symbol and expression of totalitarian government in the concentration camps of Nazi Germany and Soviet Russia.*

### From Hannah Arendt. *The Origins of Totalitarianism*

The concentration and extermination camps of totalitarian regimes serve as the laboratories in which the fundamental belief of totalitarianism that everything is possible is being verified. Compared with this, all other experiments are secondary in importance—including those in the field of medicine whose horrors are recorded in detail in the trials against the physicians of the Third Reich—although it is characteristic that these laboratories were used for experiments of every kind.

Total domination, which strives to organize the infinite plurality and differentiation of human beings as if all of humanity were just one individual, is possible only if each and every person can be reduced to a never-changing identity of reactions, so that each of these bundles of reactions can be exchanged at random for any other. The problem is to fabricate something that does not exist, namely, a kind of human species resembling other animal species whose only "freedom" would consist in "preserving the species." Totalitarian domination attempts to achieve this goal both through ideological indoctrination of the elite formations and through absolute terror in the camps; and the atrocities for which the elite formations are ruthlessly used become, as it were, the practical application of the ideological indoctrination—the testing ground in which the latter must prove itself—while the appalling spectacle of the camps themselves is supposed to furnish the "theoretical" verification of the ideology.

The camps are meant not only to exterminate people and degrade human beings, but also serve the ghastly experiment of eliminating, under scientifically controlled conditions, spontaneity itself as an expression of human behavior and of transforming the human person-

From Hannah rendt, *The Origins of Totalitarianism*, new edition (New York: Harcourt, Brace and World, 1966), pp. 437–438, 442.

ality into a mere thing, into something that even animals are not; for Pavlov's dog, which, as we know, was trained to eat not when it was hungry but when a bell rang, was a perverted animal.

Under normal circumstances this can never be accomplished, because spontaneity can never be entirely eliminated insofar as it is connected not only with human freedom but with life itself, in the sense of simply keeping alive. It is only in the concentration camps that such an experiment is at all possible, and therefore they are not only *"la société la plus totalitaire encore réalisée"*[1] (David Rousset) but the guiding social ideal of total domination in general. . . . Thus the fear of concentration camps and the resulting insight into the nature of total domination might serve to invalidate all obsolete political differentiations from right to left and to introduce beside and above them the politically most important yardstick for judging events in our time, namely: whether they serve totalitarian domination or not.

# Humanism and Rebellion

*Albert Camus defended rebelliousness while rejecting totalitarianism. (Camus was awarded the Nobel Prize for Literature in 1957.)*

## From Albert Camus. *The Rebel*

### The Kingdom of Ends

. . . Lenin spoke with a precision which left little doubt about the in definite continuation of the proletarian super-State. "With this machine, or rather this weapon [the State], we shall crush every form of exploitation, and when there are no longer any possibilities of exploitation left on earth, no more people owning land or factories, no more people gorging themselves under the eyes of others who are starving, when such things become impossible, then and only then shall we cast this machine aside. Then there will be neither State nor exploitation." Therefore as long as there exists on earth, and no longer in a specific society, one single oppressed person and one proprietor, so long the State will continue to exist. It also will be obliged to increase in strength during this period so as to vanquish one by one the injustices, the governments responsible for injustice, the obstinately bourgeois nations, and the people who are blind to their own interests. And when, on an earth that has finally been subdued and purged of enemies, the final

---

[1]The most totalitarian society yet realized.

From Alber Camus, *The Rebel*, Anthony Bower, trans. (New York: Alfred A. Knopf, 1956), pp. 232–233, 304–306. Copyright © 1956 by Alfred A. Knopf Inc. Reprinted by permission of the publisher.

iniquity shall have been drowned in the blood of the just and the unjust, then the State, which has reached the limit of all power, a monstrous idol covering the entire earth, will be discreetly absorbed into the silent city of Justice.

Under the easily predictable pressure of adverse imperialism, the imperialism of justice was born, in reality, with Lenin. But imperialism, even the imperialism of justice, has no other end but defeat or world empire. Until then it has no other means but injustice. From now on, the doctrine is definitively identified with the prophecy. For the sake of justice in the far-away future, it authorizes injustice throughout the entire course of history and becomes the type of mystification which Lenin detested more than anything else in the world. It contrives the acceptance of injustice, crime, and falsehood by the promise of a miracle Still greater production, still more power, uninterrupted labor, incessant suffering, permanent war, and then a moment will come when universal bondage in the totalitarian empire will be miraculously changed into its opposite: free leisure in a universal republic. Pseudo-revolutionary mystification has now acquired a formula: all freedom must be crushed in order to conquer the empire, and one day the empire will be the equivalent of freedom. And so the way to unity passes through totality.

## Beyond Nihilism

... Rebellion .. is love and fecundity or it is nothing at all. Revolution without honor, calculated revolution which, in preferring an abstract concept of man to a man of flesh and blood, denies existence as many times as is necessary, puts resentment in the place of love. Immediately rebellion, forgetful of its generous origins, allows itself to be contaminated by resentment; it denies life, dashes toward destruction, and raises up the grimacing cohorts of petty rebels, embryo slaves all of them, who end by offering themselves for sale, today, in all the marketplaces of Europe, to no matter what form of servitude. It is no longer either revolution or rebellion but rancor, malice, and tyranny. Then, when revolution in the name of power and of history becomes a murderous and immoderate mechanism, a new rebellion is consecrated in the name of moderation and of life. We are at that extremity now. At the end of this tunnel of darkness, however, there is inevitably a light, which we already divine and for which we only have to fight to ensure its coming. All of us, among the ruins, are preparing a renaissance beyond the limits of nihilism. But few of us know it.

Already in fact, rebellion, without claiming to solve everything, can at least confront its problems. From this moment high noon is borne away on the fast-moving stream of history. Around the devouring flames, shadows writhe in mortal combat for an instant of time and then as suddenly disappear, and the blind, fingering their eyelids, cry out that this is history. The men of Europe, abandoned to the shadows, have turned their backs upon the fixed and radiant point of the present. They forget the present for the future, the fate of humanity for the delusion of power, the misery of the slums for the mirage of the eternal city, ordinary justice for an empty promised land. They despair of personal freedom and dream of a strange freedom of the species; reject solitary death and give the name of immortality to a vast collective agony. They no longer believe in the things that exist in the world and in living man; the secret of Europe is that it no longer loves life. Its blind men entertain the puerile belief that to love one single day of life amounts to justifying whole centuries of oppression. That is why they wanted to efface joy from the world and to postpone it until a much later date. Impatience with limits, the rejection of their double life, despair at being a man, have finally driven them to inhuman ex cesses. Denying the real grandeur of life, they have had to stake all on their own excellence. For want of something better to do, they deified themselves and their misfortunes began; these gods have had their eyes put out. Kaliayev, and his brothers throughout the entire world, refuse, on the contrary, to be deified in that they refuse the unlimited power to inflict death. They choose, and give us as an example the only original rule of life today: to learn to live and to die, and, in order to be a man, to refuse to be a god.

At this meridian of thought, the rebel thus rejects divinity in order to share in the struggles and destiny of all men. We shall choose Ithaca, the faithful land, frugal and audacious thought, lucid action, and the generosity of the man who understands. In the light, the earth re mains our first and our last love. Our brothers are breathing under the same sky as we; justice is a living thing. Now is born that strange joy which helps one live and die, and which we shall never again postpone to a later time. On the sorrowing earth it is the unresting thorn, the bitter brew, the harsh wind off the sea, the old and the new dawn. With this joy, through long struggle, we shall remake the soul of our time, and a Europe which will exclude nothing. Not even that phantom Nietzsche, who for twelve years after his downfall was continually invoked by the West as the blasted image of its loftiest knowledge and its nihilism; nor the prophet of justice without mercy who lies, by mistake, in the unbelievers' plot at Highgate Cemetery; nor the deified mummy of the man of action in his glass coffin; nor any part of what the intelligence and energy of Europe have ceaselessly furnished to the pride of a contemptible period. All may indeed live again, side by side with the martyrs of 1905, but on condition that is understood that they correct one another, and that a limit, under the sun, shall curb them all. Each tells the other that he is not God; this is the end of romanticism. At this moment, when each of us must fit an arrow to his bow and enter the lists anew, to reconquer, within history and in spite of it, that which he owns already, the thin yield of his fields, the brief love of this earth, at this moment when at last a man is born, it is time to forsake our age and its adolescent furies. The bow bends; the wood complains.

At the moment of supreme tension, there will leap into flight an unswerving arrow, a shaft that is inflexible and free.

# Revolutionary Protest

*On March 22, 1968, a group of students occupied administration buildings at the University of Nanterre. The student revolt spread to Paris. Then in May millions of French workers went on strike. For a few days it seemed that the government might fall. In fact the protest movements were suppressed and a general election held in June returned a strengthened Gaullist majority to the National Assembly.*

*In the following dialog a student leader, Daniel Cohn-Bendit, speaks as "March 22nd."*

## From *The French Student Revolt*

MARCH 22nd: ... The workers' crisis was unleashed by the student movement which was itself no more than a reflection of an acute crisis.

With de Gaulle, capitalism hoped to modernize itself, but it was the working class that was to pay the costs of the operation. Look at the 500,000 unemployed and the rise in the cost of living. Once the economy had reached a certain level of modernization, education had to be modernized, too; hence the Fouchet plan and the Fifth plan. At a particular moment, the petty and middle bourgeoisie had to pay the costs. Education was rationalized to train technocrats. Thus, the contradictions of capitalism re-emerged in education....

H.B.: So you want to destroy the capitalist system. How do you hope to succeed?

MARCH 22nd: We won't succeed on our own; we cannot make a revolution by ourselves.

H.B.: Well, then, how can you talk of a revolutionary situation?

MARCH 22nd: Such a situation is growing every day, and leads us to think that revolution is now possible. Hence we must fix on a date.... But concrete revolutionary perspectives are more total than when the movement began. For us, the first step in the establishment of a classless society must be workers' control. When the workers return to work, they will ask, how and for whom shall we return? Couldn't we run the factory without the bosses? Workers' control must be installed to destroy capitalism.

H.B.: Why this primacy of workers' control?

From Hervé Bourges, ed., *The French Student Revolt* (New York: Hill and Wang, 1968), pp. 49, 51, 58–60. Reprinted by permission of Georges Borchardt, Inc.

MARCH 22nd: Workers' control, self-management, the words aren't important. But we must prevent a rigid socialism succeeding capitalism. Seizure of responsibility by the workers leaves out centralism, organization, party. State power will not survive forever. ..

H.B.: Who, then, are your allies? The new revolutionary party that is being set up?

MARCH 22nd: More than one party is being formed at the moment. And those who are concocting these new parties are students and intellectuals, and it will lead to a new vanguard party controlling the workers' struggles.

As for us, we have never had any intention of creating a new party, but rather an objective situation that would make self-expression possible at all levels. Now that people are organizing themselves, we are not totally in agreement with what they are aiming at, but neither do we have to join the game: the movement has been launched and every current can express itself freely.

H.B.: So you don't want a movement that coalesces, you leave the doors open. But you do still have a minimum rule: the revolution must come from the base.

MARCH 22nd: Exactly. All groups can express themselves in the student milieu, there can be no question of excluding anyone that is basic. The climate in the factories is getting just as democratic. In the present situation trade-union and political propaganda at the factory gates have grown more flexible. This is, of course, a defeat for Stalinism, and it could reach a point of no return. The true revolution gives everyone the means to act. That is what we mean by workers' democracy. . . .

H.B.: In other words, you do not want to impose revolution, but to maintain its ardor. Raymond Aron has spoken of the student move ment as a "psycho-drama" or a "pseudo-revolution."

MARCH 22nd: I don't think anyone in the March 22nd Movement has said that students could make a revolution: if Aron claims the students wanted to do so alone, he is wrong. His social situation and his political opinions lead him to minimize everything that might constitute a revolutionary force.

H.B.: As a last question, does not the fidelity of the PCF,[1] the unions, the peasants, the petty bourgeoisie and the traditional left to parliamentary democracy prick your conscience? Haven't you overestimated the revolutionary capacity of the base? Won't you soon find yourselves isolated?

MARCH 22nd: The working class has proved its combativity. Not only had it to struggle with the bourgeoisie, but also to sustain the enor-

[1]Parti Communiste Français (French Communist Party)

mous weight of the Stalinist and trade-union bureaucracies. If it can still produce new types of struggle, it will hang onto this gain. The revolutionary nucleus has grown and tomorrow it will constitute a firm point of departure.

*The "Red Army Fraction" in West Germany, commonly known as the Baader-Meinhof Gang, supported acts of terrorism as a form of revolutionary protest.*

## From *The Urban Guerrilla Concept*

If we are correct in saying that American imperialism is a paper tige i.e., that it can ultimately be defeated, and if the Chinese Communists are correct in their thesis that victory over American imperialism has become possible because the struggle against it is now being waged in all four corners of the earth, with the result that the forces of imperialism are fragmented, a fragmentation which makes them possible to defeat—if this is correct, then there is no reason to exclude or disqualify any particular country or any particular region from taking part in the anti-imperialist struggle because the forces of revolution are especially weak there and the forces of reaction especially strong. .

The concept of the "urban guerrilla" originated in Latin America. Here, the urban guerrilla can only be what he is there: the only revolutionary method of intervention available to what are on the whole weak revolutionary forces.

The urban guerrilla starts by recognizing that there will be no Prussian order of march of the kind in which so many so-called revolutionaries would like to lead the people into battle. He starts by recognizing that by the time the moment for armed struggle arrives, it will already be too late to start preparing for it; that in a country whose potential for violence is as great and whose revolutionary traditions are as broken and feeble as the Federal Republic's, there will not—without revolutionary initiative—even be a revolutionary orientation when conditions for revolutionary struggle are better than they are at present—which will happen as an inevitable consequence of the development of late capitalism itself.

To this extent, the "urban guerrilla" is the logical consequence of the negation of parliamentary democracy long since perpetrated by its very own representatives; the only and inevitable response to emergency laws and the rule of the hand grenade; the readiness to fight with those same means the system has chosen to use in trying to eliminate its opponents. The "urban guerrilla" is based on a recognition of the facts instead of an apologia of the facts. . . .

From Rote Armee Fraktion (Red Army Fraction), *Das Konzept Stadtguerilla* (1971), translated in Walter Laqueur, *The Terrorist Reader* (New York: New American Library, 1978), pp. 176–179. Copyright © 1978 by Walter Laqueur. Published by arrangement with The New American Library.

The urban guerrilla can concretize verbal internationalism as the requisition of guns and money. He can blunt the state's weapon of a ban on communists by organizing an underground beyond the reach of the police. The urban guerrilla is a weapon in the class war.

The "urban guerrilla" signifies armed struggle, necessary to the extent that it is the police which make indiscriminate use of firearms, exonerating class justice from guilt and burying our comrades alive unless we prevent them. To be an "urban guerrilla" means not to let oneself be demoralized by the violence of the system.

The urban guerrilla's aim is to attack the state's apparatus of control at certain points and put them out of action, to destroy the myth of the system's omnipresence and invulnerability.

The "urban guerrilla" presupposes the organization of an illegal apparatus, in other words apartments, weapons, ammunition, cars, and papers. A detailed description of what is involved is to be found in Marighella's *Minimanual for the Urban Guerrilla.* As for what else is involved, we are ready at any time to inform anyone who needs to know because he intends to do it. We do not know a great deal yet, but we do know something.

What is important is that one should have had some political experience in legality before deciding to take up armed struggle. Those who have joined the revolutionary left just to be trendy had better be careful not to involve themselves in something from which there is no going back.

The Red Army Fraction and the "urban guerrilla" are that fraction and praxis which, because they draw a clear dividing line between themselves and the enemy, are combatted most intensively. This presupposes a political identity, presupposes that one or two lessons have already been learned.

In our original concept, we planned to combine urban guerrilla activity with grass-roots work. What we wanted was for each of us to work simultaneously within existing socialist groups at the work place and in local districts, helping to influence the discussion process, learning, gaining experience. It has become clear that this cannot be done. These groups are under such close surveillance by the political police, their meetings, timetables, and the content of their discussions so well monitored, that it is impossible to attend without being put under surveillance oneself. We have learned that individuals cannot combine legal and illegal activity.

Becoming an "urban guerrilla" presupposes that one is clear about one's own motivation, that one is sure of being immune to "Bild-Zeitung" methods, sure that the whole anti-Semite-criminal-subhuman-murderer-arsonist syndrome they use against revolutionaries, all that shit that they alone are able to abstract and articulate and that still influences some comrades' attitude to us, that none of this has any effect on us.

# WOMEN AND FAMILY

## Women's Roles

*Simone de Beauvoir's book* The Second Sex, *originally published in France in 1949, became one of the seminal works of the modern women's movement.*

### From Simone de Beauvoir. *The Second Sex*

. . . We must face the question: what is a woman?

To state the question is, to me, to suggest, at once, a preliminary answer. The fact that I ask it is in itself significant. A man would never get the notion of writing a book on the peculiar situation of the human male. But if I wish to define myself, I must first of all say: "I am a woman"; on this truth must be based all further discussion. A man never begins by presenting himself as an individual of a certain sex; it goes without saying that he is a man. The terms *masculine* and *feminine* are used symmetrically only as a matter of form, as on legal papers. In actuality the relation of the two sexes is not quite like that of two electrical poles, for man represents both the positive and the neutral, as is indicated by the common use of *man* to designate human beings in general; whereas woman represents only the negative, defined by limiting criteria, without reciprocity. In the midst of an abstract discussion it is vexing to hear a man say: "You think thus and so because you are a woman"; but I know that my only defense is to reply: "I think thus and so because it is true," thereby removing my subjective self from the argument. It would be out of the question to reply: "And you think the contrary because you are a man," for it is understood that the fact of being a man is no peculiarity. A man is in the right in being a man; it is the woman who is in the wrong. It amounts to this: just as for the ancients there was an absolute vertical with reference to which the oblique was defined, so there is an absolute human type, the masculine. Woman has ovaries, a uterus; these peculiarities imprison her in her subjectivity, circumscribe her within the limits of her own nature. It is often said that she thinks with her glands. Man superbly ignores the fact that his anatomy also includes glands, such as the testicles, and that they secrete hormones. He thinks of his body as a direct and normal connection with the world, which he believes he apprehends objectively, whereas he regards the body of woman as a hindrance, a prison, weighed down by everything peculiar to it. "The female is a female by virtue of a certain *lack* of qualities," said Aristotle; "we should regard the female nature as afflicted with a natural defectiveness." And St. Thomas for his part pronounced woman to be an "imperfect man," an "incidental" being. This is symbolized in Genesis where Eve is depicted as made from what Bossuet called "a supernumerary bone" of Adam.

Thus humanity is male and man defines woman not in herself but as relative to him; she is not regarded as an autonomous being. . . .

. . . The ideal of happiness has always taken material form in the house, whether cottage or castle; it stands for permanence and separation from the world. . . . In domestic work, with or without the aid of servants, woman makes her home her own, finds social justification, and provides herself with an occupation, an activity, that deals usefully and satisfyingly with material objects—shining stoves, fresh, clean clothes, bright copper, polished furniture—but provides no escape from immanence and little affirmation of individuality. Such work has a negative basis: cleaning is getting rid of dirt, tidying up is eliminating disorder. And under impoverished conditions no satisfaction is possible; the hovel remains a hovel in spite of woman's sweat and tears: "nothing in the world can make it pretty." Legions of women have only this endless struggle without victory over the dirt. And for even the most privileged the victory is never final.

Few tasks are more like the torture of Sisyphus than housework, with its endles repetition: the clean becomes soiled, the soiled is made clean, over and over, day after day. The housewife wears herself out marking time: she makes nothing, simply perpetuates the present. She never senses conquest of a positive Good, but rather indefinite struggle against negative Evil. A young pupil writes in her essay: "I shall never have house-cleaning day"; she thinks of the future as constant progress toward some unknown summit; but one day, as her mother washes the dishes, it comes over her that both of them will be bound to such rites until death. Eating, sleeping, cleaning—the years no longer rise up toward heaven, they lie spread out ahead, gray and identical. The battle against dust and dirt is never won. . . .

But it is a sad fate to be required without respite to repel an enemy instead of working toward positive ends, and very often the housekeeper submits to it in a kind of madness that may verge on perversion, a kind of sado-masochism. The maniac housekeeper wages her furious war against dirt, blaming life itself for the rubbish all living growth entails. When any living being enters her house, her eye gleams with a wicked light: "Wipe your feet, don't tear the place apart, leave that alone!" She wishes those of her household would hardly breathe; everything means more thankless work for her. Severe, preoccupied, always on the watch, she loses *joie de vivre*, she becomes overprudent and avaricious. She shuts out the sunlight, for along with that come insects, germs, and dust, and besides, the sun ruins silk hangings and fades upholstery; she scatters naphthalene, which scents the air. She becomes bitter and disagreeable and hostile to all that lives: the end is sometimes murder. . .

The preparation of food, getting meals, is work more positive in nature and often more agreeable than cleaning. First of all it means marketing, often the bright spot of the day. And gossip on doorsteps, while peeling vegetables, is a gay relief for solitude. . . . But as with other housework, repetition soon spoils these pleasures. The magic of the oven can hardly appeal to Mexican Indian women who spend half their lives preparing tortillas, identical from day to day, from century to century. And it is impossible to go on day after day making a treasure-hunt of the marketing or ecstatically viewing one's highly polished faucets. The male and female writers who lyrically exalt such triumphs are persons who are seldom or never engaged in actual housework. It is tiresome, empty, monotonous, as a career. If, however, the individual who does such work is also a producer, a creative worker, it is as naturally integrated in life as are the organic functions; for this reason housework done by men seems much less dismal; it represents for them merely a negative and inconsequential moment from which they quickly escape. What makes the lot of the wife-servant ungrateful is the division of labor which dooms her completely to the general and the inessential.

According to French law, obedience is no longer included among the duties of a wife, and each woman citizen has the right to vote; but these civil liberties remain theoretical as long as they are unaccompanied by economic freedom. A woman supported by a man—wife or courtesan—is not emancipated from the male because she has a ballot in her hand; if custom imposes less constraint upon her than formerly, the negative freedom implied has not profoundly modified her situation; she remains bound in her condition of vassalage. It is through gainful employment that woman has traversed most of the distance that separated her from the male; and nothing else can guarantee her liberty in practice. Once she ceases to be a parasite, the system based on her dependence crumbles; between her and the universe there is no longer any need for a masculine mediator.

The curse that is upon woman as vassal consists, as we have seen, in the fact that she is not permitted to do anything; so she persists in the vain pursuit of her true being through narcissism, love, or religion. When she is productive, active, she regains her transcendence; in her projects she concretely affirms her status as subject; in connection with the aims she pursues, with the money and the rights she takes possession of, she makes trial of and senses her responsibility. . . .

We must not lose sight of those facts which make the question of woman's labor a complex one. An important and thoughtful woman recently made a study of the women in the Renault factories; she states that they would prefer to stay in the home rather than work in the factory. There is no doubt that they get economic independence only as members of a class which is economically oppressed; and, on the other hand, their jobs at the factory do not relieve them of housekeeping burdens. If they had been asked to choose between forty hours of work a week in the factory and forty hours of work a week in the home, they would doubtless have furnished quite different answers. And perhaps they would cheerfully accept both jobs, if as factory workers they were to be integrated in a world that would be theirs, in the development of which they would joyfully and proudly share. At the present time, peasants apart, the majority of women do not escape from the traditional feminine world; they get from neither society nor their husbands the assistance they would need to become in concrete fact the equals of the men. . . .

There are, however, a fairly large number of privileged women who find in their professions a means of economic and social autonomy. These come to mind when one considers woman's possibilities and her future. This is the reason why·it is especially interesting to make a close study of their situation, even though they constitute as yet only a minority; they continue to be a subject of debate between feminists and antifeminists. The latter assert that the emancipated women of today succeed in doing nothing of importance in the world and that furthermore they have difficulty in achieving their own inner equilibrium. The former exaggerate the results obtained by professional women and are blind to their inner confusion. There is no good reason, as a matter of fact, to say they are on the wrong road; and still it is certain that they are not tranquilly installed in their new realm: as yet they are only halfway there. The woman who is economically emancipated from man is not for all that in a moral, social, and psychological situation identical with that of man. The way she carries on her profession and her devotion to it depend on the context supplied by the total pattern of her life. For when she begins her adult life she does not have behind her the same past as does a boy; she is not viewed by society in the same way; the universe presents itself to her in a different perspective. The fact of being a woman today poses peculiar problems for an independent human individual

# Feminist Protest

*These verses are from an American poet, writing in 1972.*

## Adrienne Rich. *Translations*

You show me the poems of some woman
my age, or younger
translated from your language

Certain words occur: *enemy, oven, sorrow*
enough to let me know
she's a woman of my time

obsessed

with Love, our subject:
we've trained it like ivy to our walls
baked it like bread in our ovens
worn it like lead on our ankles
watched it through binoculars as if
it were a helicopter
bringing food to our famine
or the satellite
of a hostile power

I begin to see that woman
doing things: stirring rice
ironing a skirt
typing a manuscript till dawn

trying to make a call
from a phonebooth

The phone rings unanswered
in a man's bedroom
she hears him telling someone else
*Never mind. She'll get tired.*
hears him telling her story to her sister

who becomes her enemy
and will in her own time
light her own way to sorrow

ignorant of the fact this way of grief
is shared, unnecessary
and political

From Adrienne Rich, *Poems, Selected and New, 1950–1974* (New York: Norton, 1973), pp. 40–41. Copyright © 1975, 1973, 1971, 1969, 1966 by W. W. Norton & Company, Inc. Reprinted by permission of W. W. Norton & Company, Inc.

# SCIENCE AND MORALITY

## Evolution and Matter

*Jacques Monod, who received a Nobel Prize for his work in molecular biology, thought that all life originated in chance assemblages of matter behaving in accordance with the permanent laws of chemistry and physics.*

### From Jacques Monod. *Chance and Necessity*

The riddle remains, and in so doing masks the answer to a question of profound interest. Life appeared on earth: what, *before the event*, were the chances that this would occur? The present structure of the biosphere far from excludes the possibility that the decisive event occurred *only once*. Which would mean that its *a priori* probability was virtually zero. . . .

Among all the occurrences possible in the universe the *a priori* probability of any particular one of them verges upon zero. Yet the universe exists; particular events must take place in it, the probability of which (before the event) was infinitesimal. At the present time we have no legitimate grounds for either asserting or denying that life got off to but a single start on earth, and that, as a consequence, before it appeared its chances of occurring were next to nil.

Not only for scientific reasons do biologists recoil at this idea. It runs counter to our very human tendency to believe that behind everything real in the world stands a necessity rooted in the very beginning of things. Against this notion, this powerful feeling of destiny, we must be constantly on guard. Immanence is alien to modern science. Destiny is written concurrently with the event, not prior to it. Our own was not written before the emergence of the human species, alone in all the biosphere to utilize a logical system of symbolic communication. Another unique event, which by itself should predispose us against any anthropocentrism. If it was unique, as may perhaps have been the appearance of life itself, then before it did appear its chances of doing so were infinitely slender. The universe was not pregnant with life nor the biosphere with man. Our number came up in the Monte Carlo game. Is it any wonder if, like the person who has just made a million at the casino, we feel strange and a little unreal?

If it is true that the need for a complete explanation is innate, that its absence begets a profound ache within; if the only form of explanation capable of putting the soul at ease is that of a total history which discloses the meaning of man by assigning him a necessary place in nature's scheme; if, to appear genuine, meaningful, soothing, the "explanation" must blend into the long animist[1] tradition, then we understand why it took so many thousands of years for the kingdom of ideas to be invaded by the one according to which objective knowledge is the *only* authentic source of truth.

Cold and austere, proposing no explanation but imposing an ascetic renunciation of all other spiritual fare, this idea was not of a kind to allay anxiety, but aggravated it instead. By a single stroke it claimed to sweep away the tradition of a hundred thousand years, which had become one with human nature itself. It wrote an end to the ancient animist covenant between man and nature, leaving nothing in place of that precious bond but an anxious quest in a frozen universe of solitude. With nothing to recommend it but a certain puritan arrogance, how could such an idea win acceptance? It did not; it still has not. It has however commanded recognition; but that is because, solely because, of its prodigious power of performance.

In the course of three centuries science, founded upon the postulate of objectivity, has conquered its place in society—in men's practice, but not in their hearts. Modern societies are built upon science. They owe it their wealth, their power, and the certitude that tomorrow far greater wealth and power still will be ours if we so wish. But there is this too: just as an initial "choice" in the biological evolution of a species can be binding upon its entire future, so the choice of scientific *practice,* an unconscious choice in the beginning, has launched the evolution of culture on a one-way path; onto a track which nineteenth-century scientism saw leading infallibly upward to an empyrean noon hour for mankind, whereas what we see opening before us today is an abyss of darkness.

Modern societies accepted the treasures and the power that science laid in their laps. But they have not accepted—they have scarcely even heard—its profounder message: the defining of a new and unique source of truth, and the demand for a thorough revision of ethical premises, for a total break with the animist tradition, the definitive abandonment of the "old covenant," the necessity of forging a new one. Armed with all the powers, enjoying all the riches they owe to science, our societies are still trying to live by and to teach systems of values already blasted at the root by science itself.

---

[1]By "animist" Monod means all traditional doctrines which discern some nonmaterial spirit or purpose at work in the universe.

No society before ours was ever rent by contradictions so agonizing In both primitive and classical cultures the animist tradition saw knowledge and values stemming from the same source. For the first time in history a civilization is trying to shape itself while clinging desperately to the animist tradition to justify its values, and at the same time abandoning it as the source of knowledge, of *truth*. For their moral bases the "liberal" societies of the West still teach—or pay lip-service to—a disgusting farrago of Judeo-Christian religiosity, scientistic progressism, belief in the "natural" rights of man, and utilitarian pragmatism. The Marxist societies still profess the materialist and dialectical religion of history; on the face of it a more solid moral framework than the liberal societies boast, but perhaps more vulnerable by virtue of the very rigidity that has made its strength up until now. However this may be, all these systems rooted in animism exist at odds with objective knowledge, face away from truth, and are strangers and fundamentally *hostile* to science, which they are pleased to make use of but for which they do not otherwise care. The divorce is so great, the lie so flagrant, that it afflicts and rends the conscience of anyone provided with some element of culture, a little intelligence, and spurred by that moral questioning which is the source of all creativity. It is an affliction, that is to say, for all those among mankind who bear or will come to bear the responsibility for the way in which society and culture shall evolve.

What ails the modern spirit is this lie gripping man's moral and social nature at the very core. It is this ailment, more or less confusedly diagnosed, that provokes the fear if not the hatred—in any case the estrangement—felt toward scientific culture by so many people today. Their aversion, when openly expressed, usually directs itself at the technological by-products of science: the bomb, the destruction of nature, the soaring population. The easy reply, of course, is that technology and science are not the same thing, and moreover that the use of atomic energy will soon be vital to mankind's survival; that the destruction of nature denotes a faulty technology rather than too much of it; and that the population soars because children by the millions are saved from death every year. Are we to go back to letting them die?

Confusing the symptoms of the disorder with its underlying cause, this is a superficial reply. Indeed, it merely begs the question. For behind the protest is the denial of the essential message of science. The fear is the fear of sacrilege: of outrage to values. A wholly justified fear. It is perfectly true that science outrages values. Not directly, since science is no judge of them and *must* ignore them; but it subverts every one of the mythical or philosophical ontogenies upon which the animist tradition, from the Australian aborigines to the dialectical materialists, has made all ethics rest: values, duties, rights, prohibitions.

If he accepts this message—accepts all it contains—then man must at last wake out of his millenary dream; and in doing so, wake to his total solitude, his fundamental isolation. Now does he at last realize that.

like a gypsy, he lives on the boundary of an alien world. A world that is deaf to his music, just as indifferent to his hopes as it is to his suffering or his crimes.

But henceforth who is to define crime? Who shall decide what is good and what is evil? All the traditional systems have placed ethics and values beyond man's reach. Values did not belong to him; he belonged to them. He now knows that they are his and his alone, and they no sooner come into his possession than lo! they seem to melt into the world's uncaring emptiness. It is then that modern man turns toward science, or rather against it, finally measuring its terrible capacity to destroy not only bodies but the soul itself.

Where is the remedy? Must one adopt the position once and for all that objective truth and the theory of values constitute eternally separate, mutually impenetrable domains? This is the attitude taken by a great number of modern thinkers, whether writers, or philosophers, or indeed scientists. For the vast majority of men, whose anxiety it can only perpetuate and worsen, this attitude I believe will not do; I also believe it is absolutely mistaken, and for two essential reasons.

First, and obviously, because values and knowledge are always and necessarily associated in action just as in discourse.

Second, and above all, because *the very definition of "true" knowledge reposes in the final analysis upon an ethical postulate.* . . .

Animism, we said earlier, neither wants nor for that matter is able to set up an absolute discrimination between value judgments and statements based upon knowledge; for having once assumed that there is an intention, however carefully disguised, present in the universe, what would be the sense of such a distinction? In an objective system the very opposite holds: any mingling of knowledge with values is unlawful, *forbidden*. But—and here is the crucial point, the logical link which at their core weds knowledge and values together—this prohibition, this "first commandment" which ensures the foundation of objective knowledge, is not itself objective. It cannot be objective: it is an ethical guideline, a rule for conduct. True knowledge is ignorant of values, but it cannot be grounded elsewhere than upon a value judgment, or rather upon an *aniomatic* value. It is obvious that the positing of the principle of objectivity as the condition of true knowledge *constitutes an ethical choice and not a judgment arrived at from knowledge, since, according to the postulate's own terms, there cannot have been any "true" knowledge prior to this arbitral choice.* In order to establish the *norm* for knowledge the objectivity principle defines a *value:* that value is objective knowledge itself. Thus, assenting to the principle of objectivity one announces one's adherence to the basic statement of an ethical system, one asserts *the ethic of knowledge*.

*Hence it is from the ethical choice of a primary value that knowledge starts.* The ethic of knowledge thereby differs radically from animist ethics, which all claim to be based upon the "knowledge" of immanent laws, religious or "natural," which are supposed to assert themselves over man. The ethic of knowledge does not obtrude itself upon man; *on the contrary, it is he who prescribes it to himself,* making of it the *axiomatic* condition of authenticity for all discourse and all action. The *Discours de la Méthode* proposes a normative epistemology, but it must also be read above all as a moral meditation, as a spiritual exercise.

Authentic discourse in its turn lays the foundation of science, and returns to the hands of man the immense powers that enrich and imperil him today. Modern societies, woven together by science, living from its products, have become as dependent upon it as an addict on his drug. They owe their material wherewithal to this fundamental ethic upon which knowledge is based, and their moral weakness to those value-systems, devastated by knowledge itself, to which they still try to refer. The contradiction is deadly. It is what is digging the pit we see opening under our feet. The ethic of knowledge that created the modern world is the only ethic compatible with it, the only one capable, once understood and accepted, of guiding its evolution.

# Evolution and Spirit

*Pierre Teilhard de Chardin, a Jesuit priest and distinguished paleontologist, found it possible to reconcile his religious and scientific convictions.*

## From Pierre Teilhard de Chardin *The Phenomenon of Man*

What makes and classifies a 'modern' man (and a whole host of our contemporaries is not yet 'modern' in this sense) is having become capable of seeing in terms not of space and time alone, but also of duration, or—and it comes to the same thing—of biological space-time; and above all having become incapable of seeing anything otherwise—anything—*not even himself.*

This last step brings us to the heart of the metamorphosis. Obviously man could not see evolution all around him without feeling to some extent carried along by it himself. Darwin has demonstrated this. Nevertheless, looking at the progress of transformist views in the last hundred years, we are surprised to see how naïvely naturalists and physicists were able at the early stages to imagine themselves to be standing outside the universal stream they had just discovered. Almost incurably subject and object tend to become separated from each other in the act of knowing. We are continually inclined to isolate ourselves from the things and events which surround us, as though we were looking at them from outside, from the shelter of an observatory into which they were unable to enter, as though we were spectators, not elements, in what goes on. That is why, when it was raised by the concatenations of life, the question of man's origins was for so long restricted to the purely somatic and bodily side. A long animal heredity might well have formed our limbs, but our mind was always above the play of the realities it enumerated. However materialistic they might be, it did not occur to the first evolutionists that their scientific intelligence had anything to do in itself with evolution.

At this stage they were only half-way to the truth that concerned them.

From the very first pages of this book, I have been relentlessly insisting on one thing: for invincible reasons of homogeneity and coherence, the fibres of cosmogenesis demand their prolongation in us in a way that goes far deeper than flesh and blood. . . . The very act by which the fine edge of our minds penetrates the absolute is a phenomenon, as it were, of *emergence*.

. . . So let us bow our heads with respect for the anxieties and joys of 'trying all and discovering all.' The passing wave that we can feel was not formed in ourselves. It comes to us from far away; it set out at the same time as the light from the first stars. It reaches us after creating everything on the way. The spirit of research and conquest is the permanent soul of evolution. And hence, throughout all time, *unity of movement*. 'The rise and expansion of consciousness.'

Man is not the centre of the universe as once we thought in our simplicity, but something much more wonderful—the arrow pointing the way to the final unification of the world in terms of life. Man alone constitutes the last-born, the freshest, the most complicated, the most subtle of all the successive layers of life.

This is nothing else than the fundamental vision and I shall leave it at that. . . .

We are accusomted to consider (and with what a refinement of analysis!) only the sentimental face of love, the joy and miseries it causes us. It is in its natural dynamism and its evolutionary significance that I shall be dealing with it here, with a view to determining the ultimate phases of the phenomenon of man.

Considered in its full biological reality, love—that is to say the affinity of being with being—is not peculiar to man. It is a general property of all life and as such it embraces, in its varieties and degrees, all the forms successively adopted by organised matter. In the mammals, so close to ourselves, it is easily recognised in its different modalities: sexual passion, parental instinct, social solidarity, etc. Farther off, that is to say lower down on the tree of life, analogies are more obscure until they become so faint as to be imperceptible. But this is the place to repeat what I said earlier when we were discussing the *'within* of things.' If there were no internal propensity to unite, even at a prodigiously rudimentary level—indeed in the molecule itself—it would be physically impossible for love to appear higher up, with us, in 'hominised' form. By rights, to be certain of its presence in ourselves, we should assume its presence, at least in an inchoate form, in everything that is. And in fact if we look around us at the confluent ascent of consciousness, we see it is not lacking anywhere.

It may be said that this is the precise point at which we are invoking the impossible. Man's capacity, it may seem, is confined to giving his affection to one human being or to very few. Beyond that radius the heart does not carry, and there is only room for cold justice and cold reason. To love all and everyone is a contradictory and false gesture which only leads in the end to loving no one.

To that I would answer that if, as you claim, a universal love is impossible, how can we account for that irresistible instinct in our hearts which leads us towards unity whenever and in whatever direction our passions are stirred? A sense of the universe, a sense of the *all*, the nostalgia which seizes us when confronted by nature, beauty, music—these seem to be an expectation and awareness of a Great Presence. The 'mystics' and their commentators apart, how has psychology been able so consistently to ignore this fundamental vibration whose ring can be heard by every practised ear at the basis, or rather at the summit, of every great emotion? Resonance to the All—the keynote of pure poetry and pure religion. Once again: what does this phenomenon, which is born with thought and grows with it, reveal if not a deep accord between two realities which seek each other; the severed particle which trembles at the approach of 'the rest'?

We are often inclined to think that we have exhausted the various natural forms of love with a man's love for his wife, his children, his friends and to a certain extent for his country. Yet precisely the most fundamental form of passion is missing from the list, the one which, under the pressure of an involuting universe, precipitates the elements one upon the other in the Whole—cosmic affinity and hence cosmic direction. A universal love is not only psychologically possible; it is the only complete and final way in which we are able to love.

But, with this point made, how are we to explain the appearance all around of us of mounting repulsion and hatred? If such a strong potentiality is besieging us from within and urging us to union, what is it waiting for tc pass from potentiality to action? Just this, no doubt: that we should overcome the 'anti-personalist' complex which paralyses us, and make up our minds to accept the possibility, indeed the reality, of some *source* of love and *object* of love at the summit of the world above our heads  So long as it absorbs or appears to absorb the person, the collectivity kills the love that is trying to come to birth. As such the collectivity is essentially unlovable. That is where philanthropic systems break down. Common sense is right. It is impossible to give oneself to anonymous number. But if the universe ahead of us assumes a face and a heart, and so to speak personifies itself, then in the atmosphere created by this focus the elemental attraction will immediately blossom. Then, no doubt, under the heightened pressure of an unfolding world, the formidable energies of attraction, still dormant between human molecules, will burst forth.

The discoveries of the last hundred years, with their unitary perspectives, have brought a new and decisive impetus to our sense of the world, to our sense of the earth, and to our human sense. Hence the rise of modern pantheism. But this impetus will only end by plunging us back into super-matter unless it leads us towards someone.

For the failure that threatens us to be turned into success, for the concurrence of human monads to come about, it is necessary and sufficient for us that we should extend our science to its farthest limits and recognise and accept (as being necessary to close and balance space-time) not only some vague future existence, but also, as I must now stress, the radiation *as a present reality* of that mysterious centre of our centres which I have called Omega.

# About the Editors

After serving in the Royal Air Force, Brian Tierney received his B.A. and Ph.D. from Cambridge University. He has taught at Catholic University, Washington, D.C., and at Cornell, where he is now Bryce and Edith M. Bowmar Professor in Humanistic Studies. He has been the recipient of Guggenheim Fellowships and of fellowships from the American Council of Learned Societies and the National Endowment for the Humanities. Professor Tierney has been awarded the honorary degrees of Doctor of Theology by Uppsala University, Sweden, and Doctor of Humane Letters by Catholic University. A specialist in medieval church history, he has published many articles and several books, among them *Foundations of the Conciliar Theory; Medieval Poor Law;* and *Origins of Papal Infallibility, 1150–1350.* He is coeditor with Donald Kagan and L. Pearce Williams of *Great Issues in Western Civilization.* His most recent work is *Religion, Law, and the Growth of Constitutional Thought, 1150–1650.*

Joan W. Scott received her Ph.D. in history from the University of Wisconsin. She has taught at the University of Illinois at Chicago Circle, Northwestern University, the University of North Carolina at Chapel Hill, and Brown University, where she is currently Nancy Duke Lewis University Professor and professor of history. She also is director of Brown's Pembroke Center for Teaching and Research on Women. Professor Scott has held fellowships from the Social Science Research Council, the National Endowment for the Humanities, and the American Council of Learned Societies. She has directed seminars for college teachers sponsored by the National Endowment for the Humanities and has served as a consultant for projects in labor history and women's history. Her fields of research are nineteenth-century French social history and European women's history. She has written numerous articles on both topics and was awarded a prize by the Berkshire Conference of Women Historians for "Women's Work and the Family in Nineteenth Century Europe," coauthored with Louise Tilly. She is author of *The Glassworkers of Carmaux: French Craftsmen and Political Action in a Nineteenth Century City,* which won the American Historical Association's Herbert Baxter Adams prize in 1974. She is coauthor, with Louise Tilly, of *Women, Work and Family.*

## A NOTE ON THE TYPE

The text of this book has been set on the Linotron 202 in a typeface called "Baskerville." The face is a facsimile reproduction of types cast from molds made for John Baskerville (1706–75) from his designs. John Baskerville's original face was one of the forerunners of the type-style known as "modern face" to printers—a "modern" of the period A.D. 1800.

Composed by P & M Typesetting, Waterbury, Connecticut. Printed and bound on Cameron press by Banta Company, Harrisonburg, Virginia.

Text design by Barbara Sturman. Cover design by Mary Chris Welch